Baedeker

Portugal

Hints for using the Guide

Following the tradition established by Karl Baedeker in 1844, buildings and works of art, places of natural beauty and sights of particular interest, are distinguished by one ★ or two ★★.

To make it easier to locate the various places listed in the "A to Z" section of the Guide, their co-ordinates are shown in red at the head of each entry: e.g., Lisbon A 6.

Coloured lines down the right-hand side of the page are an aid to finding the main heading in the Guide: blue stands for the Introduction (Nature, Culture, History, etc.), red for the "A to Z" section, and yellow indicates Practical Information.

Only a selection of hotels, restaurants and shops can be given; no reflection is implied therefore on establishments not included.

In a time of rapid change it is difficult to ensure that all the information given is entirely accurate and up-to-date, and the possibility of error can never be entirely eliminated.

Although the publishers can accept no responsibility for inaccuracies and omissions, they are constantly endeavouring to improve the quality of their Guides and are therefore always grateful for criticisms, corrections and suggestions for improvement.

Preface

This guide to Portugal is one of the new generation of Baedeker guides.

These guides, illustrated throughout in colour, are designed to meet the needs of the modern traveller. They are quick and easy to consult, with the principal places of interest described in alphabetical order, and the information is presented in a format that is both attractive and easy to follow.

The present guide covers the whole of mainland Portugal, the Atlantic Ocean islands of the Azores and the Madeira archipelago.

The guide is in three parts. The first part gives a general account of the country, its geography, climate, flora and fauna, population, education system, government and society, economy, communications, notable personalities, culture and art. After a small selection

*Coimbra –
a traditional
university town
at twilight*

of quotations there follows a number of suggested routes for visitors which provide a lead-in to the second part, in which the places and features of tourist interest – cities and towns, regions and provinces, and islands – are described. The third part contains a variety of practical information. Both the sights and the practical information are listed in alphabetical order.

The new Baedeker guides are noted for their concentration on essentials and their convenience of use. They contain numerous specially drawn plans and colour illustrations; and at the end of the book is a large map making it easy to locate the various places described in the "A to Z" section of the guide with the help of the co-ordinates given at the head of each entry.

Contents

Nature, Culture, History
Pages 10–87

Sights from A to Z
Pages 90–343

Practical Information from A to Z
Pages 346–424

Baedeker Specials

An Emerging

Fantastic beaches, idyllic rocky coves, picturesque fishing villages, endless sunshine, the tangy spray of the Atlantic and a cuisine rich in sea-food – Portugal can indeed provide all these ingredients for a refreshing seaside holiday.

But this holiday paradise has much, much more to offer. Anyone travelling through the extreme south-west point of Europe will discover that, far away from its wonderful beaches, there is a Portugal almost unknown to foreigners. Perhaps some may remember the press headlines describing the "Carnation Revolution" of 1974 and the devastating Lisbon fire of 1988, and may possibly be vaguely familiar with the soulful *fado* singing, but few will associate much else with this country which joined the European Union in 1986. It is perhaps hard to believe that in the most important epoch in its history, the "Golden Age" of the 15th and 16th centuries, Portugal played a predominant role in Europe. It was then that daring seafarers set out from its coasts in search of new continents and rich treasure. Ancient Lusitania basked in all its glory. Even today the buildings in Belém, Tomar, Batalha and Alcobaça, with their over extravagant stone decoration, tell of old seadogs and their adventures and of other facets of the country's cultural history. After this age of ascendancy, however, Portugal sank into obscurity for several centuries. For a long time the country contented itself

Azulejos
Elaborately decorated glazed tiles

Óbidos
This picturesque village has remained quiet and tranquil

Porto Moniz
On the "flower island" of Madeira

Algarve
This most beautiful coastline in the country offers 3200 hours of sunshine per year

Country

simply with basking in its past glories (and still does so quite often . . .). Time has tended to stand still in Portugal.

For some years now, however, things have been on the move in the south-west of the Iberian Peninsula; the country is fitting itself for Europe. An exciting time for a visit. Old Portugal can still be found everywhere – in the countryside, of course, in particular. Remote, picturesque villages, women dressed in black, donkey-carts, sometimes an almost archaic way of life linked to illiteracy and unimaginable poverty. And even the smaller towns have an appearance of yesteryear – the university town of Coimbra, steeped in tradition, the religious centres of Braga or Évora, the "pearl" of the Alentejo. It is in its capital, Lisbon, however, that the forward-looking Portugal is now coming to the fore – much that is mid-European, a dynamic everyday life, ultra-modern new buildings and the latest thing in fashions.

The ever-changing countryside displays a timeless beauty. High mountains in the north with typical granite villages, delightful undulating hilly regions in the south speckled with groves of cork and olive trees, cornfields and meadows filled with sweet-smelling flowers in spring. Mass tourism is found only in the south, in the Algarve; elsewhere the visitor will travel along little-used roads and byways and find a warm welcome among the proverbially friendly and hospitable Portuguese.

Torre de Belém
The symbol of Lisbon

Marvão
Like almost every other place in Portugal, Marvão has its own castle

Nature, Culture History

Facts and Figures

This relatively small country, which in earlier centuries was one of the European great powers and has lost its large overseas possessions only in quite recent times, offers a wide range of both scenic and cultural attractions which are still relatively little known.

The mainland has an 832km/520 mile Atlantic coastline, the finest parts of which are to be found at its climatically favoured southern end, in the Algarve, with its beautiful sandy beaches and rugged cliffs. The country's cosmopolitan capital, Lisbon, on the broad estuary of the Tagus, is one of the most strikingly situated cities in the world.

In the interior of the country, too, there are many culturally and historically interesting and attractive towns, villages and abbeys, as well as a wide range of varied and beautiful scenery – hills, valleys and plateaux – in every region of Portugal.

General

Geographical Situation

The Portuguese mainland lies in the extreme south-west of Europe between latitude 42°9' and 36°58'N, and 6°11' and 9°30'W. Portugal has a common frontier of some 1300km/800 miles – more than half its total length of frontier – with Spain, its only neighbouring state, with the other half formed by the Atlantic Ocean.

Also included within the territory of Portugal are the "Ilhas adjacentes", the two Atlantic archipelagos of Madeira and the Azores, and the former colony of Macao on the southern coast of China, which is administered by Portugal but enjoys self-government in internal affairs.

Area

The mainland of Portugal, with an area of 88,944sq.km/34,332 sq. miles, occupies roughly a sixth of the Iberian peninsula, and is broadly rectangular in shape, measuring some 550km/340 miles from north to south and averaging some 150km/95 miles from west to east (greatest width 200km/125 miles). The archipelagos of Madeira and the Azores have a total area of 3041sq.km/1173sq. miles.

National Territory

Mainland Portugal has preserved its frontiers unchanged for almost eight centuries – a circumstance which can be attributed mainly to its geographic situation. As a frontier territory of the Old World, rather than an area of passage, the kingdom of Portugal remained after its foundation in the 12th c. a region of only marginal significance in the conflicts between European states. The country's military efforts were directed solely towards the consolidation of its frontiers, at first against the Moors, then being driven back during the Reconquest, and later against Spanish claims to sovereignty.

Most of Portugal's common frontier with Spain follows the course of the three great Iberian rivers – the Minho (Spanish Miño) in the north, the Duoro (Spanish Duero) in the north-east, and the Guadiana in the south-east – or the rugged ranges of the hills in the north of the

◄ Castle of Lindoso on the Portuguese–Spanish border

country. These sections of the frontier which are easily accessible and without natural barriers are nevertheless readily identifiable as frontier areas, since the maintenance of the same frontier for so many centuries and the building of castles and other fortifications during those centuries have led to a movement of population away from these areas. As almost half of Portugal's frontier is formed by the Atlantic Ocean it is not surprising that throughout its history the whole country, including the inland as well as the coastal regions, should have shown a marked orientation towards the sea and should – thanks also to its traditional hankering for national independence – have differentiated itself so strikingly from its Spanish neighbour.

The large overseas provinces of the old Portuguese colonial empire have been given up only quite recently. Portuguese India was annexed by India in 1961; Portuguese Guinea became independent as Guinea-Bissau in 1974; and in 1975 Mozambique, the Cape Verde Islands (Cabo Verde), the islands of São Tomé and Príncipe, and finally Angola, one after the other, achieved independence. In 1975 Portuguese Timor was invaded by Indonesian troops, and in 1976 it was officially incorporated in Indonesia.

Former Overseas Provinces

Topography

Geologically Portugal is the south-western part of the Iberian land mass, a region of gneisses, granites, quartzites, greywackes, limestones and Palaeozoic schists subjected to ancient folding movements, making up the Iberian mesetas, averaging some 700m/2300ft in height. It slopes gradually down from the higher hills in the north and has been much reduced and levelled by erosion.

General

Many perennial rivers traverse this rump formation and they play a major part in determining the climatic pattern and plant life. In recent years they have acquired additional importance as sources of hydroelectric power. Only a few of the larger rivers, including the Minho, Douro, Tagus, Sado and Guadiana, are navigable in the lower parts of their courses, but there are no river ports of any size.

Two of Portugal's great rivers, the Douro and the Tagus, both with their source in Spain, effectively divide the country into three sections topographically.

Northern Portugal is the area between the Minho, which forms the northern frontier, and the Douro in the south. The rump formations in this part of the country are overlaid by a number of massifs of early volcanic origin, often of imposing size, rising to heights of almost 2000m/6560ft and forming part of the Spanish mountain system. The "Montanhas" hill and mountain scenery is particularly wild and rugged in the Serra do Soajo, Serra da Peneda and Serra do Gerês, making this a region of extraordinary natural beauty and tourist interest (Peneda-Gerês National Park).

Northern Portugal

The Douro valley is equally picturesque. On the terraced slopes of the valley, in this "Pais do Vinho" (land of wine), are grown the grapes used for making port, which is carried down to the "lodges" of Oporto and shipped from there to countries all over the world.

South of the Douro rises the mighty ridge of the Serra da Estrêla (Malhão da Estrêla; 1991m/6532ft), the western spur of the Castilian dividing range, much broken up by erosion and battered by violent storms from the west – the highest mountain in mainland Portugal and the country's only major winter sports area. The Serra da Estrêla is continued to the south-west in the uplands of Estremadura, a region of pleasant climate and great fertility; its westernmost spurs reach down to the coast and form promontories such as the Cabo da Roca, the most westerly point in Europe.

Central Portugal

Major rivers, lakes and mountains in Portugal

(mainland)

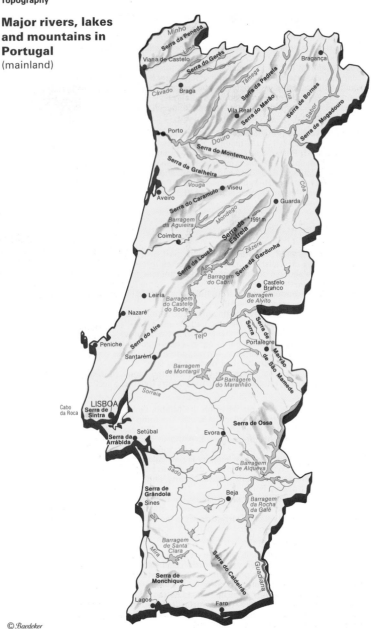

© Baedeker

Vineyards in north Portugal

Central Portugal is not all mountainous and here, as in the south, the Iberian rump formations are broken up by tectonic depressions. These are found particularly in the Ribatejo area and around the estuary of the Rio Sado, where the land is highly fertile as a result of the soil deposited by the river and the abundant water supply. These areas are still subject to earth tremors and contain numerous thermal springs.

Just before reaching the Atlantic the valley of the lower Tagus (Portuguese Tejo, Spanish Tajo) opens out into a kind of inland sea, forming a huge natural harbour for the country's capital, Lisbon (Lisboa).

To the south of the Tagus is Alentejo, a great expanse of rolling country and level plateaux with occasional small ranges of hills (Serra da Ossa, etc.) rising to 700m/2300ft. This vast and featureless tract of arable country interspersed with heathland extends south to the Serra de Monchique, a range rising to some 900m/2950ft, which forms a protective barrier against cold weather from the north and with its numerous streams provides an abundance of nourishment for the subtropical and tropical vegetation of the Algarve.

Southern Portugal

The rump formations of the Iberian land mass extend for some 15–20km/9–12 miles out to sea at a shallow depth and then plunge steeply down to 300m/1000ft. Along the whole coastline they are overlaid by a fringe of Mesozoic sedimentary rocks deposited by the sea, which then reached farther inland. In the course of geological time these rocks were thrust upwards, forming the famous and exceedingly picturesque cliffs and stacks which are seen at their finest in the "Rocky Algarve", interspersed with bays and coves containing broad sandy beaches which shelve gently into the sea. In the estuaries of the Douro and Tagus in northern Portugal and of the Guadiana in the "Sandy Algarve" the sedimentary rocks have been much eroded and ground down, forming a landscape of dunes and lagoons.

Coastal Topography

Climate

General

Its position on the western edge of the Iberian peninsula means that mainland Portugal, together with Madeira and the Azores, enjoys a maritime version of the Mediterranean climate, which as a general rule is wet and fairly warm in winter, and hot and dry in summer. This seasonal variation is because the weather is governed by the subtropical dry high pressure area in summer and, in winter, the western cyclone area from the temperate latitudes, which shift during the year according to the position of the sun. Portugal's climate is maritime insofar as there is little temperature variation between day and night, or between summer and winter, and there is also the heavy rainfall that can occur in the north and along the coast in particular, even in summer.

Climatic Variations

Within Portugal the climate varies according to the part of the country. In the west, on the coast, the climate is very much maritime, but towards the east continental influences become stronger, with a steadily greater range of variation between summer and winter, and day and night, temperatures, and increasingly less rainfall. Towards the south temperatures increase and rainfall decreases (annual average temperatures of Oporto 14.4°C/58°F, Coimbra 15.9°C/60.6°F, Lisbon 16.6°C/62°F, and Praia da Rocha 16.9°C/62.4°F). The number of dry summer months increases along the same lines. The greater the altitude the lower the temperature and the higher the rainfall. This correlation between altitude and precipitation means that rainfall is high on the mountain ridges near the coast facing the westerly winds and the sea, but gets less towards the east in the lee of the mountains.

Climate Tables

The climate tables show the features of the climate in particular regions in terms of temperature and rainfall from January (J) to December (D). The blue columns show the monthly rainfall in millimetres, and the orange curve shows the temperatures in centigrade, with the upper edge of the band representing average maximum daytime temperatures, and the lower edge average minimum nighttime temperatures. These tables can also be used to estimate what the climate will be like for the parts of the country between these particular measuring points – Oporto represents the northern coastal area, Bragança the northern interior, Lisbon the central coastal area, Campo Maior the southern interior and Praia da Rocha the Algarve.

Northern Coastal Area

Rainfall in the coastal area of northern Portugal (around Oporto) is quite heavy and even in the summer months there are more than five to seven days of rain. Winds in summer are predominantly north-westerly, averaging 5m/19.7ft per second. These "nortadas", blowing from the area of high pressure over the Azores, are accompanied by northerly currents in the sea, resulting in relatively cold water temperatures. In the height of summer these are only 17–18°C/62.5–64.5°F, some 6–7°C/42–45°F less than the Costa Brava on the Spanish east coast of the Iberian peninsula. Rainfall in Coimbra, 100km/62 miles south of Oporto and 40km/25 miles inland, is distinctly lower at 900mm/35in. Fogs along the coast in summer are relatively frequent.

Northern Interior

The Atlantic has little effect on the climate in the northern interior measured at Bragança. The temperature variations as between day and night and winter and summer are markedly greater than in the lowland on the coast, and this is reflected in the steeper curve and broader band for temperature in the climate table. Much of the rain coming from the Atlantic falls in the mountains west of the city, so that despite the altitude annual rainfall is lower than on the coast. The drop in rainfall in summer is indicative of the Mediterranean climate. This area is bordered in the south by the mighty mountain ridge of the Serra

Climate in Portugal

Typical regional climates on the mainland

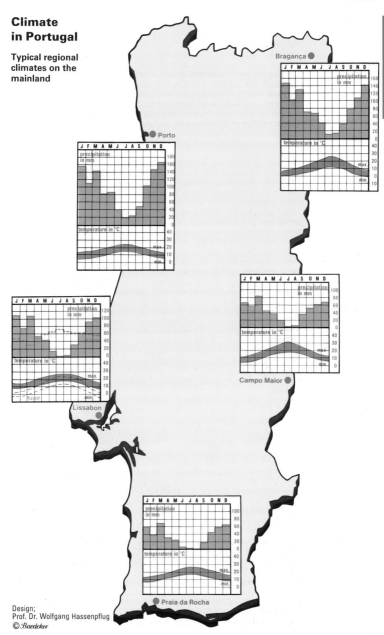

Design;
Prof. Dr. Wolfgang Hassenpflug
© Baedeker

15

da Estrêla, rising to almost 2000m/6560ft, and the annual rainfall at altitudes over 1400m/4595ft exceeds 2000mm/80in. a year, with snowfall in winter in excess of 300mm/11in. a month, and correspondingly low temperatures.

Central Coastal Area

Portugal's central coastal area, around Lisbon, is sheltered on the north by the south-western continuation of the Serra da Estrêla, which wards off the northerly and north-easterly winds and the rain they carry with them. Temperatures are therefore perceptibly higher than in the north, as can be seen from comparison with the table for Oporto, and the summer months are markedly dryer than in the north, with an annual rainfall of 708mm/28in. and only two days rain on average in July and August. Water temperatures, at around 18–19°C/64.5–66°F, are also several degrees higher than in the northern coastal area.

Southern Interior

This part of Portugal, around Campo Maior, has the most markedly continental climate in the country. The annual rainfall gets progressively less the further east you go until it can be under 500mm/19in.; the only exceptions being in the mountains with their greater precipitation.

The variations in temperature between day and night and summer and winter are much greater than in Lisbon. During the year the variations as between the hottest and the coldest months are between 11° and 17°C/51.8 and 64.5°F.

Algarve (south coast)

The southward facing Atlantic coast (measuring point Praia da Rocha) has Portugal's mildest winters, tempered by the Atlantic and in the shelter of the ridge of the Alto Algarve to the north. The smallest annual range in temperature in the whole of the Iberian Peninsula is recorded at Cape St Vincent in the west (6.2°C/43°F). Minimum temperatures drop only briefly in winter, and even then they go little below 10°C/50°F. In summer maximum temperatures stay well below 30°C/86°F but minimum temperatures also drop below 20°C/68°F so that it is often advisable to wear warmer clothing in the evening.

Summers are long and dry. There is likely to be less than a day's rainfall in July and August, and the hours of sunshine are correspondingly lengthy as well. With a total of 3162 hours a year, 387 of them in July, the Algarve gets more hours of sunshine than anywhere else in Portugal.

Madeira

The island of Madeira has a climate that is very maritime but warm as well, owing to its location in the lower latitudes. The weather is governed by low pressure areas from further north in the winter and north-easterly trade-winds in the summer. This makes for dramatic differences in climate between the windward side of the island in the north and the lee side in the south, where there are also distinct variations according to altitude. The northern side, where the trade-winds impact on the mountain slopes, gets heavy rainfall, mostly in winter (Santana: annual 1314mm/52in., July 27mm/1in., November 215mm/8½in.). Higher up the annual rainfall is over 2000mm/78in. (Encumeada pass at 950m/3115ft, 2675mm/105in.). On the southern side, where the annual rainfall stays under 600mm/23in., there are distinct zones: below 400m/1313ft a warm dry bottom zone that is hot and dry in summer, above that a more temperate, less dry zone, followed by a cloud zone, starting at 1000m/3282ft, below the condensation level, with rainfall all the year round, and, finally, from 1400–1500m/4595–4923ft, an upper dry zone above the cloud formed by the trade-winds, similar to the Canaries.

The Azores

The Azores high pressure area moves from north to south and back again with the sun, so that the islands lie on the frontier zone between polar and tropical air masses. Out in the Atlantic and constantly exposed to strong winds which in summer blow mainly from the north-east and in winter from the south-west, they have rainfall all the year round – at its sparsest in summer – and a more equable climate.

The variations in climate are considerable both during the year and as between one island and another, not to mention one side of an island and the other. The annual rainfall decreases from north-west (1447mm/57in.) to south-east (697mm/27½in.). In the mountains it can be as high as 3000mm/118in.

The Azores have distinctly fewer hours of sunshine than the Portuguese mainland. For Ponta Delgada these amount to 1626 hours per annum, with the most hours' sunshine in August (204, cf. Lisbon 357) and the least in January (80, cf. Lisbon 161).

Flora and Fauna

The natural vegetation of Portugal originally consisted of sparse forest, but the country's forests have been decimated by centuries of over-felling and neglect and the original natural forests are now only to be found in the less accessible mountain regions. Reforestation is urgently necessary if the land is to be prevented from degenerating into a steppe-like waste. Accordingly in recent years there has been planned replanting in the dune and mountain areas. The trees now found mainly in the north of the country are deciduous species, with coniferous woodlands in the higher altitudes. In the south evergreens predominate, and the dunes along the coast are fringed with pines.

Flora

General

The umbrella pine (*pinus pinea*), which owes its name to the shape of its crown, is an inescapable feature of the Portuguese landscape, and can be found growing singly, in groups or, very occasionally, in small stands. The seeds of the big round cones are edible and taste like hazelnuts.

Conifers

Whereas the umbrella pine requires a relatively fertile site the clustered pine (*pinus pinaster*) can actually grow in dry infertile soil. This species of pine, which characteristically retains its dead branches, is very fast-growing in its early years, and is mainly used as a source of resin, obtained by tapping through small incisions in the bark.

Cypresses are also among the typical trees of Portugal. These "cupressus sempervirens", to use their Latin title, were known as "everlasting" because they can be up to 2000 years old. Their pillar shape, which cuts down the area exposed to the glaring light, makes them particularly suited to the climate.

As in the rest of the Mediterranean region the olive tree (*olea europea*) is widespread throughout Portugal. It enjoys ideal conditions in Alentejo, but grows in the north of the country as well. For the olives to ripen the trees need a long dry summer and relatively low temperatures in winter. They form inconspicuous pale yellow flowers in May/June and the harvest starts in November, carrying on until March. Whether the olives are green or black depends on how ripe they are.

Deciduous trees

Since Portugal has become the world's biggest cork producer (see Economy), large stands of cork-oaks (*quercus suber*) are very much in evidence in the southern and central parts of the country. Cork-oaks form a layer of cork from dead cells to counteract temperature fluctuations and prevent waterloss. When this layer is stripped from the tree the sap-bearing layer of bark must be left undamaged for the tree to survive. The stripped surface of the trunk appears pinkish-yellow at first, turning later to reddish-brown.

The *quercus occidentalis*, which is mainly found in northern Portugal, is a species of cork-oak with very little cork on its bark.

The Peneda Gerês National Park, in particular, has big stands of holm-oaks (*quercus ilex*), an evergreen species of oak with dark-green leathery leaves that have whitish felty undersides.

Population

Another relatively common tree, especially in southern Portugal, is the eucalyptus (*eucalyptus globulus*). The leaves are round on the young trees but distinctly narrower on the older ones. To protect itself against too much light this tree species can position its leaves in a north/south direction so that the sunlight only hits the edges of the leaves. A noticeable feature of the eucalyptus is that it often casts long strips of its bark, revealing a smooth green gleaming trunk.

The vegetation of the north of the country, with its harsher climate, also includes plenty of sweet chestnut, lime, maple, poplar and beech trees.

Palms

Portugal's only native palm is the dwarf palm (*chamaerops humilis*), which occurs mostly in its trunkless, sprouting form.

Also, as throughout the Mediterranean, the Canary date-palm (*phoenix canariensis*) is a familiar sight in parks and gardens. Closely related to the north African-Arabic date palm, it has a stockier trunk and a more decorative, fuller crown with larger and lusher fronds. Its small fruits are woody and inedible.

Shrubs and herbs

In the undergrowth of the rainier regions of the north-west gorse and heather predominate; in the south and east large areas are covered by aromatic herbs and semi-shrubs, including broom, cistus, rosemary, thyme and lavender, with various colourful bulbous plants.

In spring and summer most parks and gardens are truly a magnificent display of blooms, awash in many places in a sea of oleander, camellia and hibiscus blossom.

Fauna

The wildlife of mainland Portugal is similar to that of Central Europe. In the wooded hills of northern Portugal are found not only species which occur north of the Alps, including roe-deer, chamois and foxes, but also wolves, lynx, wild horses, golden eagles and aurochs. In the Peneda Gerês National Park rare species enjoy full statutory protection. Nevertheless many of Portugal's animals are very much endangered species, and its population of wolves, for example, is thought to number only one to two hundred animals.

The coastal lagoons are the haunt of numerous waterfowl, including flamingo. Small game is abundant everywhere, and shooting is a popular sport. The many rivers, lakes, and reservoirs, are well stocked with trout, pike, salmon, carp and eel.

Population

Density

Portugal's population of about 9.8 million is very unevenly distributed over the country (see map page 19). The average density of 106 inhabitants per sq. kilometre/274 per sq. mile is below the figure for other European countries. Some 35% of the population is concentrated in the large urban regions around Lisbon and Oporto, which have the very high densities of 770 and 697 per sq.km/1995 and 1806 per sq.mile. At the other extreme is Alentejo, with the very low density of 18 per sq.km/47 per sq. mile in the Beja district and 24 per sq.km/62 per sq. mile and 23 per sq.km/60 per sq. mile in the districts of Évora and Portalegre. In addition the drift of population from the rural areas to the rising industrial areas is still continuing.

Trends

The birth rate (12 per 1000) is relatively high but falling. The expected population increase is moderated by the traditionally high rate of emigration to the United States, Canada, France and South America (Brazil, Venezuela). During the last decade, however, large numbers of people have returned to Portugal from the country's former overseas possessions, so that overall the population growth has been quite reasonable, averaging 0.7% in the first half of the eighties and about 0.4% thereafter.

Population in Portugal's mainland districts

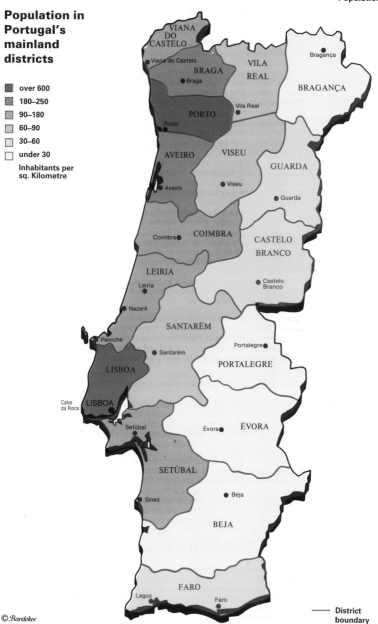

■ over 600
■ 180–250
■ 90–180
□ 60–90
□ 30–60
□ under 30

Inhabitants per sq. Kilometre

VIANA DO CASTELO
Viana do Castelo
BRAGA
Braga
VILA REAL
Vila Real
BRAGANÇA
Bragança
PORTO
Porto
AVEIRO
Aveiro
VISEU
Viseu
GUARDA
Guarda
COIMBRA
Coimbra
CASTELO BRANCO
Castelo Branco
LEIRIA
Leiria
Nazaré
Peniche
SANTARÉM
Santarém
PORTALEGRE
Portalegre
LISBOA
Lisboa
Cabo da Roca
Setúbal
ÉVORA
Évora
SETÚBAL
Sines
BEJA
Beja
FARO
Lagos
Faro

© Baedeker

—— District boundary

19

Population

Structure

The earliest inhabitants of Portugal were the Lusitanians, a Celtiberian people. The native population, particularly in the coastal region, received an admixture of blood at an early stage from visiting seamen and traders – Phoenicians, Carthaginians, Greeks, Jews. The 600 years of Roman rule not only left their mark on the ethnic composition of the population but gave Portugal its language. Evidence of the relatively brief stays of the Suevi and the Visigoths can still be seen in the north of the country, where tall, fair-skinned types are occasionally encountered. Particularly marked, and in the south of the country quite unmistakable, are the traces left by the Moorish period, which influenced both the physical type and the way of life of the population. During the Middle Ages the Inquisition drove large numbers of Jews out of Spain into Portugal, where – still persecuted and harried by pogroms – they became converts to Christianity and were absorbed into the Portuguese people.

Thus in the course of millennia this mingling between the native population and successive incomers, combined with the country's isolation from Spain and the rest of Europe, gave rise to a population structure which was homogeneous and distinctively Portuguese, both ethnically and culturally.

The Portuguese are predominantly dark-haired, of small to medium height and of sturdy, almost stocky, build. In contrast to the lively Spaniards they tend to be quiet, gentle, thoughtful, warm-hearted and friendly, strongly attached to their home and their family – a characteristic reflected in the return of so many emigrants. The relatively peaceful course of the 1974 "Carnation Revolution" can also be ascribed to these qualities.

The small African minorities in the population are either descendants of former slaves or have come to Portugal from the country's former African possessions.

Settlement

Outside the large urban regions the predominant form of settlement is the densely built-up village which sometimes reaches the status of a small town. In the fertile valley basins scattered settlements predominate. Villages built along one main street are rare, being found mainly in newly developed agricultural areas on the coast.

Religion

More than 95% of the population are Roman Catholic. Of the remainder an estimated 38,000 are Protestants, 15,000 Muslims and 6000 Jews.

Constitutionally there is no established church and since no tithes are levied clerics have to be funded locally, with fees charged for marriages, christenings and funerals. Administratively Portugal is divided up into three Catholic ecclesiastical provinces – Lisbon (plus Madeira and the Azores), Braga and Évora.

Language

Portuguese (*português*), a Romance language, is spoken in mainland Portugal, the Portuguese Atlantic islands (the Azores and Madeira) and the territory of Macao in southern China. It is also still used in the former Portuguese colonies in Africa, India and Indonesia. Portuguese, in a locally modified form, is also the official language of the 115 million inhabitants of Brazil, while Galician, spoken in north-west Spain, is a dialect of Portuguese.

Altogether between 125 and 135 million people in the world speak Portuguese, giving it seventh place (after Chinese, English, Spanish, Hindi, Russian and Arabic) among the world's most widely spoken languages.

Portuguese is the direct descendant of the Lusitanian form of Vulgar Latin (the ordinary spoken Latin language). Among the Romance languages it is most closely related to Spanish, though it tends to be of more archaic form than Spanish. The differences between the various dialects of Portuguese are less marked than dialectal differences in other western Romance languages.

The vocabulary of Portuguese is overwhelmingly Romance (i.e. Latin). There are only trifling Basque and Germanic elements, the latter mainly of Visigothic origin. Since Portugal was reconquered from the Moors considerably earlier than Spain there are fewer traces of Arabic influence in Portuguese than in Castilian. The Portuguese spoken in Brazil includes a significant vocabulary of words taken over from the indigenous Indian population or from Africa.

The Portuguese literary language and the received pronunciation – mainly influenced by the language of educated people in Lisbon and Coimbra – assimilated French, Italian and Spanish elements from an early stage.

State and Society

The 1933 Portuguese constitution was swept away by the almost bloodless "Carnation Revolution" of April 1974 and replaced by a new one, promulgated on April 25th 1976, making the Portuguese Republic (República Portuguesa) a parliamentary democracy. In November 1982 the original underlying socialism was watered down by amendment of the constitution.

Constitution and Government

The head of state is the President, who is elected for a five-year term. The current incumbent is Mário Soares, former Prime Minister and General Secretary of the Socialist Party (PS), who was voted into office at the Presidential Election in February 1986 by the left and right of centre electorate.

The Portuguese parliament, the Assembly of the Republic (Assembleia Nacional), is elected every four years and has 254 members, including four representatives of Portuguese citizens living abroad. Abiding by the verdict of the polls, the President appoints the Prime Minister, currently right wing businessman and former Chancellor of the Exchequer Anibal Cavaco Silva from the PSD – the Popular Democratic Party (Partido Popular Democratico), but also known as the Social Democratic Party (hence the acronym of its Portuguese initials).

The two largest parties are the Partido Social Democrático (PSD) founded in 1974 and the Partido Socialista (PS). In spite of its name the PSD follows a liberal-conservative policy. The PS, founded in 1973 by Mário Soares while in exile, is social-democratic. There are also the Partido Popular (PP), which developed from the Christian-democratic CDS, and the Partida Comunista Português (PCP), founded in 1921 following the Russian October Revolution and prohibited by Salazar. The Green Party (Os Verdes or Partido Verde) was founded in 1982. The Partido Popular Monárquico (PPM) also follows a green line, but would also like to see the monarchy restored.

Political Parties

Portugal has national conscription, although conscientious objection is possible. Service in the Army is for 16 months, in the Navy and Air Force 21–24 months. The total armed forces currently number 73,000, the Supreme Commander being the President.

Armed forces

Portugal is a member of the United Nations, NATO, OECD, the European Union, and CERN (European Nuclear Research Centre).

International Organisations

Portugal currently has about 4.6 million in work. Income per capita averages about £550 a month, 66% of the EU average. They have a 36 to 45-hour working week, usually with four weeks paid holiday. Unemployment has varied between 5 and 7% in recent years, although many jobs are only seasonal. Open-ended contracts of employment are the exception rather than the rule.

Employment

According to the statistics almost every second Portuguese family lives below a "relative poverty line", and about 25% of the population

Standard of Living

21

Portugal
República
Portuguesa
Administrative
districts (mainland)

P

VIANA
DO
CASTELO

Viana do Castelo

BRAGA
● Braga

VILA
REAL

Bragança ●

BRAGANÇA

PORTO

Vila Real ●

● Porto

AVEIRO

VISEU

GUARDA

● Aveiro

Viseu ●

Guarda ●

Coimbra ●

COIMBRA

CASTELO
BRANCO

LEIRIA

Leiria
●

Castelo
Branco ●

● Nazaré

Peniche ●

SANTARÉM

Portalegre ●

● Santarém

PORTALEGRE

LISBOA

Cabo
da Roca

LISBOA ●

Setúbal ●

Évora ● ÉVORA

SETÚBAL

● Sines

● Beja

BEJA

FARO

Lagos ●

Faro ●

© Baedeker

22

probably has to survive on minimum subsistence, due to the low earnings and minimal social security. There is no social assistance and very little unemployment benefit, with about 75% of all unemployed getting no help whatsoever, and this is made worse by the fact that many employers do not pay their workers for months on end, or do not let them have the full amount. Many put up with these awful conditions for fear of losing their jobs, so innumerable families are left with no alternative but to keep themselves going by begging.

Housing in Portugal is in dire straits, with a national shortage of about 400,000 dwellings. For the poorest of the poor (about 36,000) there are only the miserable corrugated-iron shanty-towns, the "*bairros da lata*", such as those in Lisbon and Porto. A change in the Rent Acts in 1985 led to a completely unbalanced situation in the housing market. Until 1985 rents could be increased only when there was a change of tenant, which resulted in dwellings staying in the same family for generations. Even today numerous families pay very low rents indeed. The object of the new law was to encourage landlords to invest in order to maintain the values of their properties, but as a result rents have increased very steeply indeed, putting them beyond the means of families on low incomes.

Housing Market

In Portugal, as elsewhere, few people choose to have a traditional large family these days, but in the countryside the extended family of several generations under one roof still tends to be the rule. In northern Portugal in particular there are still more families with a number of children than there are in Lisbon, Oporto or southern Portugal, where the one or two child family is predominant.

Family Life

The place of women in modern Portugal is distinctly historical by nature. Under the Salazar 1933 Constitution women were excluded from universal suffrage "because of their variable temperament and in the interests of the family". Women did not get the vote until 1968, and could not vote in local elections until 1974. Men and women are now equal under the 1976 constitution, although the traditional gender roles still tend to be commonplace. Generally speaking women are less well educated than men, and less professionally qualified, while in public life male dominance goes virtually unchallenged.

Education

Since 1987 compulsory schooling in Portugal has been for nine years compared with four years until the mid-Sixties and then six years. These nine years are made up of four years primary school, two years middle school and three years secondary school, with the option of continuing for another three years at upper school, the final year being orientated towards vocational or academic study. Schooling is free for the first nine years, but fees are charged for attendance thereafter.

Primary and Secondary Education

An astonishing number of youngsters – as many as 34.7% in the first year of secondary school in 1982/83 – fail to make enough progress to move up into the next class at the end of the school year. Even more disturbing is the fact that 20% of the children of school age do not attend school at all, or leave before they have been there six years; 45% leave before the end of their ninth year, and a further 22% go at the end of that year.

About 8–10% of school pupils go on to University. There is no general entrance qualification which means that they have to decide on what they want to study by the start of their final year in order to gain the relevant qualification.

Universities

There is also a "numerus clausus" for all subjects studied and every year each of Portugal's nine universities (in Lisbon, Porto, Coimbra,

Évora and Braga) and its many colleges of further education stipulate anew the minimum marks required of school-leavers for entry to each subject.

Economy

General

Since joining the European Community (as it then was) in 1986 Portugal's fortunes have taken a distinct turn for the better, and the country has completed the conversion from an agricultural to an industrial nation. In the period 1985 to 1995 its annual rate of economic growth averaged 3.17% (compared with 2.29% in the EU as a whole). Recently inflation has been 5%. The official unemployment rate fluctuates between 4 and 7%. Income per capita has also risen appreciably and is now almost 70% of the EU average.

Responsiblity for the "economic miracle" achieved in the late 1980s and 1990s lay with the liberal-conservative government under Anibal Cavacao Silva. His programme of "more growth, less state" was pursued with the help of financial aid from the EU. Foreign investment also played an important role; British, American, French, Spanish and German firms found Portugal a profitable base for their operations because of the low level of wages and ancillary costs.

Portugal has visibly changed in the last ten years as the result of new roads and improved infrastructure. Giant shopping centres have replaced small shops, and towns in general have a more modern look. However, it is still a land of contrasts, modernisation having passed by many regions in the interior.

Since 1994, however, a degree of disillusionment and the disadvantagese of growing integration in the European internal market have become apparent (some 75% of its imports and exports are with EU countries). Local industry is suffering as a result of slow economic growth in the larger European countries. Its export-dependent industries are under increasing pressure as a result of cheap competition from East European and Asian markets.

Farming, Forestry and Fisheries

Entry into Europe has to some extent had difficult and negative consequences for agriculture. Fruit and vegetables from Portugal do not meet the standard required by the EU. Agriculture also has to cope with infertile soil, antiquated methods of cultivation and uneconomic labour. The EU agricultural policy is in many instances limited to payments for "set aside" (non-use of land) and early retirement, the prerequisites for which many small farmers cannot meet. A further problem may not come to light until some years hence; only 8.6% of those engaged in agriculture are under 35 years of age, while 25% are over 65. This indicates that a shortage of workers could mean that future agricultural production is not guaranteed. In the last few years already the number of people employed in this field has reduced rapidly and is now only 11% of the total labour force.

About 40% of the land area of Portugal is arable and 21% of this (over 630,000ha/1,556,730 acres) is irrigated. The most important agricultural area is between the Douro and the Tagus, where the river valleys, warmed by the summer sun, provide the country with its major wine-producing areas, as well as citrus fruits, peaches, figs and almonds. The arable land, dotted everywhere with olive-trees, is in the uplands, interspersed with Portugal's famous cork-oak forests. Crops grown include cereals, potatoes and pulses. Wheat, rye, oats, barley and rice are the major cereals and grown mostly in the south, with the cultivation of maize and potatoes concentrated in the north.

Domestic Market/ Exports

Fruit is still grown very largely for the home market. Olive production, which is relatively small-scale, also goes mainly for domestic consumption. However, exports of oranges, cherries, almonds, olives, new potatoes and onions are on the increase. Tomato production has long since been aimed at the export market, with most of it going abroad as tomato pulp.

Wine is produced throughout Portugal, but the most important vine-growing areas are in the northern part of the country. The best known Portuguese wine is, of course, port. Madeira, the sweet dessert wine grown on the island of the same name, goes almost exclusively for export. With an average annual output of 10 million hectolitres/2.2 million gallons Portugal ranks seventh among the wine-producing countries.

Wine

Stock-farming is particularly a feature of northern Portugal, where cattle predominate. The areas south of the Tagus, away from the coast, are given over mainly to sheep and pigs, grazing in the extensive cork-oak forests. In terms of numbers Portugal has 1.1 million cattle, 737,000 of them dairy-cows, 3.5 million pigs and 5.1 million sheep.

Stock-farming

Dairy-farming is also chiefly centred on northern Portugal, together with the fodder production that goes with it. There are also many intensive dairy units around Lisbon, although as a general rule dairy cattle are kept in small numbers. Very often farms only have a single cow, and only 3% actually have more than five.

The yields from Portuguese agriculture tend to be relatively small. This is due to poor soil quality, old-fashioned farming methods, unsuitable crop rotation and insufficient fertilisation, together with a failure to get to grips with pest infestation. Livestock farming is also often prone to suffer because of the spread of disease.

Productivity

The agricultural sector nevertheless still feeds nearly a quarter of the population, even though, given the poor productivity, this is largely at subsistence level.

In terms of size of holdings small farms predominate, with at the last count 44% of the 784,000 holdings less than 1ha/2½ acres, 53% between 1 and 20ha/49 acres and only 3% greater than 20 ha. In northern Portugal in particular fragmentation of ownership has left holdings that would not generally be considered viable in European terms. In the south of the country, on the other hand, farms tend to be the traditional larger holdings, and more than 45% of the cultivable area is farmed by holdings of over 100ha/247 acres.

Farm Structure

The cultivation of eucalyptus trees is of great importance, the wood being used for the production of cellulose. Because of the comparatively low environmental regulations imposed, the ecologically problematical cellulose industry has increasingly established itself in Portugal – mainly on the Tagus. The paper industry and the cultivation of eucalyptus are both environmentally damaging. The rapidly-growing tree takes a lot of moisture out of the soil and dries it out.

Forestry/Cork Production

The growing of cork is playing an increasingly minor role. Even though Portugal is still the world's largest producer, the cork industry has suffered badly from the use of plastic as a substitute (see Baedeker Special, pp.100/101).

Traditionally of considerable importance, Portugal's fisheries net an annual sea-catch of between 260,000 and 280,000 tonnes. A third of all fish landed are sardines. While enough of the latter are caught to meet domestic demand, some other types of fish have to be imported. Portugal's fishing fleet is out of date and cannot compete with other European fleets, especially the Spanish. Because of inadequately equipped boats many fishermen can only fish in coastal waters.

Fisheries

The fish processing industry has been declining for many years in Portugal and few businesses are still operating profitably today

Salt

Salt-pans in the Vouga, Tagus and Sado estuaries and around Faro in the Algarve supply sea-salt for Portugal's canning industry.

Mining and Energy Supply

Its mining offers Portugal considerable opportunities to boost its economic development. It has, for example, become one of the world's most important producers of tungsten, and is already seventh in the world so far as uranium mining is concerned, with the second largest uranium deposits in Europe after France. It has substantial pyrites deposits in eastern Alentejo and its sources of iron ore in the north-east are the biggest on the Iberian peninsula. The mining of manganese, lead, copper, and tin is leading to the building of foundries and refineries.

Portugal's good quality marble and granite also make their particular sector ripe for development. Portugal's coal, petroleum and natural gas resources are, however, so far very meagre, and although off-shore exploration is well under way the prospects of finding oil and natural gas are rather slim.

Energy Supply

Its as yet comparative lack of industrialisation has meant that Portugal has the lowest energy consumption in the European Union: 2626KW hours per capita (EU average is 5289KW hours). Half its electricity supply comes from hydro-electric plants in the north and centre of the country.

Oil is the second most important source of energy for the electricity supply. Coal provides the fuel for thermal power stations near Oporto and Sines, and there are also plans for four nuclear power stations.

Industry

In recent years Portugal has completed its conversion from an agricultural to an industrial state. Industry now acounts for 39% of the gross domestic product and employs 33% of the work force.

A start was made in de-centralising industry during the Salazar period, with the result that, Oporto, Setúbal, Aveiro and Braga, in addition to Lisbon, are relatively important in this field. However, because of its port and the favourable road links Lisbon remains the leading industrial centre.

Industrial sites

Labour-intensive industries such as textiles, clothing and leather goods traditionally dominate in Portugal. In addition there are now other relatively strong industries closely allied to local raw materials. These produce such things as building materials (e.g., concrete goods, bricks, glass) or process wood and manufacture paper. Cork production still has a part to play, and the food and semi-luxury foods and tobacco industries are deserving of mention. Of relatively minor importance are the various branches of the metal industry. Machinery manufacture is concentrated on building, agricultural and textile equipment. In 1994 a factory opened at Palmela near Lisbon for the manufacture of large limousines; this was a group project by Ford and Volkswagen. The electrical industry produces mainly radios, T.V.s and electrical motors. Pharmacy and agricultural chemicals are the major products of the chemical industry.

Branches of industry

Tourism

One economic sector showing signs of development is tourism. After a decline in the early 1990s operators are again optomistic. Ignoring short-

Marble quarry near Borba

break visitors from Spain, more than 10 million tourists came to Portugal in 1997.

More than 50% of all visitors to Portugal spend their holiday in the Algarve, as opposed to 25% in Lisbon and its surroundings, the remainder going to the North Atlantic coast and the islands belonging to Portugal. The rest of Portugal does not experience the same degree of mass tourism that has developed in recent years on the Algarve coast, where it has grown by 15% annually in recent years. In 1983 the Algarve could provide accommodation for 75,000 hotel guests; today the figure is nearer 250,000.

Building in the Algarve has escalated in recent years to the extent that it has attracted considerable criticism. In future the emphasis must be on quality tourism, with the hope that this will bring about improvements in the landscape, fauna and flora and natural parks. In 1994 a six-year plan was laid down governing tourism throughout Portugal; it will be financed by the state, the EU and by private investors. A third of the money will be invested in the Algarve.

Communications

Road

Portugal's road network has been considerably extended in recent years. the industrial centres of the north and the coastal regions are easily accessible by wide expressways, some of which have four lanes. A motorway links Lisbon and Oporto, and a further motorway links the individual holiday resorts of the Algarve. Many of the towns in the north-east, however, are accessible only along narrow mountain roads.

The increase in the number of vehicle owners has resulted in traffic jams and bottlenecks in the larger towns, but steps are being taken to alleviate these. A noticeable relief in the Lisbon area was brought about by the completion in 1998 of the motorway bridge over the Tagus.

Rail

The Portuguese railway network totalling some 3400km/2110 miles is rather limited, and the only stretch that is fully two-way and electrified is the line between Lisbon and Oporto, which takes about half the country's rail traffic. The lack of a rail bridge over the Tagus at Lisbon means there is still no direct rail link between the capital and the south of the country. Although adaptation of the existing bridge to take rail traffic has been planned for years, passengers still have to change from their trains to a ferry, and freight has to make a 100km/62-mile detour.

Sea and River

Portugal has a long seafaring tradition and although the importance of its shipping has been declining for some time much of its foreign trade still goes by sea, and there are also regular services between the mainland and Madeira and the Azores. Because of the nature of parts of the Atlantic coastline there is not much shipping in those coastal waters. Lisbon is Portugal's major port, but there are also important seaports for trade and fisheries at Oporto (Leixões), Setúbal, Sines and Aveiro.

Inland shipping is confined to the lower reaches of a few rivers, particularly the Tagus, and the Douro is also being made more navigable.

Air

Recent years have seen a speedy growth in air traffic. The international airports on the mainland are at Lisbon, Faro and Oporto.

History

From Prehistory to Emergence of the Nation State

The coastal regions of present-day Portugal were already occupied by man in the Palaeolithic period. The nature of the indigenous population is not yet clearly established, but the Portuguese were probably a mixture of Ligurians in the south, Iberians in the middle of the country and Celts in the north. Only at a very late period, in the 12th c. A.D., were they able to establish their position as a separate country with a history of its own and to assert their independence of Spain.

Evidence of Mesolithic occupation in large cemeteries (in one of which more than 200 skeletons were found).	10,000–5000 B.C.
Megalithic culture – monumental cult structures erected in the Chalcolithic period (e.g the well-preserved Dolmen da Barrosa, north of Vila Praia de Ancora).	2000–1600
Iberians arrive in the peninsula, probably coming from North Africa.	From 2000
Phoenicians probably trading in amber and copper on the Portuguese coast.	From 1000
Celtic peoples settle in Portugal and in subsequent centuries mingle with the Iberians to become Celtiberians. Some 30 tribes of Lusitanians settle in southern Portugal (the larger part of the country), building strongly fortified hilltop settlements (castros, citânias), some of which – e.g. the Citânia de Briteiros and the Castro de Sabroso, near Braga – are still occupied in Roman times.	From 700
Trading posts founded by Carthaginians and Greeks at a few places on the coast.	From 500
During the Second Punic War the Romans fight mainly on Carthaginian territories in the Iberian peninsula and try to defend the frontiers against the Lusitanians in the west and the Celtiberians in the north.	218–206
After the bitterly contested Lusitanian War Lusitania is incorporated in the Roman province of Hispania Ulterior.	197–179
The Lusitanians rebel against the Romans under the leadership of Viriathus (later honoured in literature and art as a national hero). Their resistance collapses only after the murder of Viriathus near Viseu in 139.	147–139
During the Roman civil war the Lusitanians support Sertorius against Sulla.	80–72
After the death of Sertorius (72) Pompey quells the Lusitanian rising. Rapid Romanisation starts in the south and along the coastline.	71
Caesar finally subdues the province of Hispania Ulterior.	61–54
Under Augustus the peninsula is pacified (*pax romana*) and Roman authority consolidated by the extensive settlement of colonists. The province of Hispania Ulterior is divided into the two provinces of Baetica (Andalusia) and Lusitania. Lusitania, a province of only marginal importance within the Roman Empire, comprises the whole of	27–15 B.C.

History

Portugal south of the Douro, together with the Spanish region of Extramadura and province of Salamanca. The region north of the Douro falls within the Roman province of Gallaecia. Emerita Augusta (Spain's Mérida) becomes Lusitania's capital, and Bracara Augusta (Braga) is one of Gallaecia's main settlements. The Romans demolish the old Castros but encourage development of towns such as Bracara Augusta (Braga), Portus Cale (Oporto), Aeminium/Conimbriga (Coimbra), Felicitas Iulia/Olisipo (Lisbon), Pax Iulia (Beja) and Scallabis (Santarém).

From A.D. 200   The Christianisation of Lusitania is believed to have begun at a very early stage, and the establishment of the bishoprics of Braga and Évora are attested in the 3rd c.

From 410   During the Great Migrations of the Germanic peoples the Suevi press into northern Gallaecia, the Asdingian Vandals into southern Gallaecia and the Alans into Lusitania.

About 414–418   The Visigoths defeat the Alans and the Vandals, who withdraw to the south of Spain (and later to Africa).

585   The Suevic kingdom is conquered by the Visigoths under their king Leovigild (568–586), who unites it with the powerful Visigothic kingdom of Toledo.

589   King Reccared and the Visigoths adopt the Roman Catholic faith. Soon afterwards the persecution of the Jews begins.

711   After the victory of the Arabs (Moors) over the last Visigothic king, Roderick, they occupy the whole of the Iberian peninsula except the mountainous regions in the north (713–718). The territory of present-day Portugal becomes part of the Arab Emirate (later Caliphate) of Córdoba; although the only evidence of Moorish influence (e.g. in farming, buildings, words borrowed from Arabic, etc.) is in the southern part of the country (Algarve).

717   The Reconquista (the recovery of Arab-occupied territory) starts out from the Visigothic kingdom of Asturias.

From 722   Asturias recovers the territory between the Minho (Miño) and the Douro (Duero), with the stronghold of Portus Cale (Portucale, now Oporto).

1035–65   Under King Ferdinand I, the Great, of Castile and León the reconquest of the main part of Portugal begins. In 1064 he manages to recapture Coimbra.

1094   King Alfonso VI of León (from 1065) and Castile (from 1072), after repeatedly advancing to the Tagus, is thrown back by the Moors at Lisbon.

From the emergence of Portugal as an independent state to the end of the Portuguese empire in the 16th c.

After establishing its independence as a state Portugal achieves territorial unity at a very early stage – the first European state to do so. In the 15th c. Prince Henry the Navigator initiates the Portuguese voyages of discovery in the Atlantic and along the African coast, and thus lays the foundations of the later Portuguese empire.

1095   Alfonso VI of León and Castile establishes the County of Portucalia (named after the town of Portus Cale, now Oporto), between the rivers

Douro and Mondego, and grants it as a fief to his son-in-law Count Henry of Burgundy (1095–1112), a Capetian.

After the death of Alfonso VI, Henry of Burgundy frees Portugal for a time from its feudal dependence on León-Castile.

1109

Henry of Burgundy's widow Teresa, illegitimate daughter of Alfonso VI of Castile, acting as regent on behalf of her son Afonso Henriques (1112–85), takes advantage of the turbulent situation in Castile to gain greater independence for Portucalia.

From 1112

After a brilliant victory over the Moors at Ourique (Beja district) Afonso Henriques assumes the title of King as Afonso I and shakes off Castilian overlordship.

1139

Afonso I submits himself to the feudal superiority of the Pope. Alfonso VII of León-Castile recognises the independence of Portugal under the Burgundian dynasty.

1143

During the Second Crusade Afonso captures Lisbon from the Moors. His successors extend the kingdom by further conquests in the south.

1147

Pope Alexander III recognises Portugal as a kingdom.

1179

Rapid progress in the development of towns (Lisbon, Oporto, Braga, Coimbra, Lagos, etc.), craft industry and maritime trade (thanks to Portugal's favourable situation on the Atlantic coast).

From 1200

With the help of the knightly order of Santiago Afonso III (1245–79) conquers the province of Algarve in southern Portugal. The Portuguese Reconquista is thus complete, and the frontier with Castile established on the Guadiana.
    Portugal as the first European state reaches the limits of its territorial expansion which remain unchanged to the present day.

Circa 1250

The towns are represented in the Cortes (parliament).

From 1254

Lisbon becomes capital, displacing Coimbra.

1256

New taxes to be levied only with the agreement of the Cortes.

1261

King Dinis, the "Farmer", promotes agriculture, afforestation, mining, trade and navigation.

1279–1325

Dinis concludes a concordat with Pope Nicolas IV to settle the disputes with the Church.

1289

The first Portuguese university is founded in Lisbon (later transferred in 1307 to Coimbra).

1290

The frontier between Portugal and Castile is definitively established.

1297

Treaty of friendship with England.

1308

Afonso IV (1325–57) sides with the Castilians in the Battle of Salado against the Sultan of Morocco whose invasion is rebuffed.

1340

The murder of Inês de Castro to whom Pedro, the heir to the throne, is secretly betrothed, leads to a war between Afonso IV and his son, who becomes king as Pedro I ("the Cruel", 1357–67).

1355

In order to prevent Portugal reverting to Castile after the extinction of the male line, the Cortes elect Pedro's illegitimate son as Regent and

1383

later king. As João I (1383/85–1433) he becomes the founder of the House of Avis.

1385	João's decisive victory over Castile at Aljubarrota consolidates the independence of Portugal. His reign sees the beginnings of the colonial expansion in Africa and the voyages of discovery which prepare the way for Portugal's rise as the leading maritime and colonial power in western Europe. With the rapid expansion of the merchant shipping fleet Lisbon develops into a major commercial city.
1386	The alliance with England is renewed in the Windsor Treaty.
1415	Capture of the trading post of Ceuta in Morocco.
From 1418	João I's younger son Henry the Navigator (Henrique "O Navigador"; 1394–1460) promotes voyages of discovery along the West African coast and in the Atlantic. School of navigation founded at Sagres.
1419–57	Discovery and settlement of Madeira, the Azores and the Cape Verde Islands. Beginnings of the negro slave trade (abolished by law only in 1850).
Circa 1470	Occupation of the coast of Guinea.
1471	Afonso V, the "African" (1438–81), takes Tangier and other coastal settlements.
1476	Afonso V, who is betrothed to a natural daughter of Henry IV of Castile and therefore lays claim to the Castilian throne, is defeated by Ferdinand of Aragon at Toro.
1482	The Portuguese reach the mouth of the Congo.
1488	Bartolomeu Dias rounds the southern tip of Africa, the Cape of Good Hope.
1494	In the Treaty of Tordesillas Portugal and Spain agree on a demarcation line between their colonial spheres of interest in Latin America.
1495–1521	Manuel I, the Fortunate, establishes Portugal's commercial power, with the foundation of trading posts in the East Indies, Eastern Asia, South Africa and Brazil. Lisbon becomes a focal point of world trade.
1498	Vasco da Gama discovers the sea route to India.
1500	Pedro Alvares Cabral reaches Brazil.
From 1510	Franciso de Almeida and Afonso de Albuquerque, appointed viceroys in India, establish trading posts in India and south-east Asia (Goa 1510, Malacca 1511, Ormuz, Diu, etc., 1514) and for a time hold the monopoly of the world spice trade. Thanks to its worldwide trade Portugal enjoys an upsurge of prosperity during the reign of Manuel I. The crown, nobility and merchants enjoy fabulous riches, but the unusual colonial expansion places such a strain on the Portuguese people that population figures drop rapidly from two to one million. However, the contacts with foreign lands act as a powerful stimulus to art and literature. Portugal's greatest poet, Luis Vaz de Camões (1524–80), glorifies the great voyages and conquests in his "Lusiads", in which he describes Vasco da Gama's voyage to India.
1518	Capture of Ceylon.

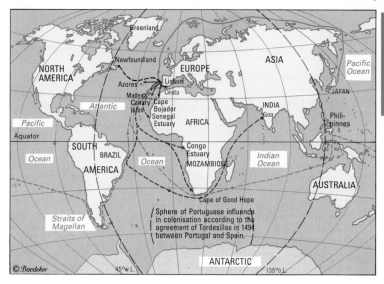

The Great voyages of discovery of the Portuguese

⟶ School of navigation founded at Sagres by Henry the Navigator (1394–1460); capture of Ceuta, 1415; Madeira, 1420; Azores, 1427; Gil Eanes at Cape Bojador, 1434.

- -⟶ Sea route to India:
Diogo Cão reaches the mouth of the Congo, 1482.
Bartolemeu Dias rounds the Cape of Good Hope, 1492.
(Columbus, sailing in the Spanish service, reaches the West Indies, 1492.)
Pedro Álvares Cabral reaches Brazil, 1500.
Vasco da Gama sails in 1497 from Belém, near Lisbon, rounds the Cape of Good Hope, calls in at Mozambique in SE Africa (1498) and reaches India. (The poet Luís de Camões describes the voyage in "The Lusiads".)

-⟶ Gaspar Corte Real reaches Newfoundland, 1501.

- -⟶ Fernão de Magalhães (Magellan) sails in the Spanish service from Sanlúcar de Barrameda, crosses the S Atlantic and continues through the Strait of Magellan, at the souther tip of S America, into the Pacific, and is killed in 1521 during a fight with natives on the island of Mactan in the Philippines. One of his ships returns to Europe in 1522 by way of the Indian Ocean and the S Atlantic, thus completing the first circumnavigation of the globe.

⟶ David Melgueiro sails from Japan in a Dutch ship which makes the passage along the N of Asia and Europe and so to Portugal.

Under João III the colonial empire in the Far East disintegrates and economic prosperity starts to wane.	1521–57
Treaty of Saragossa (Zaragoza), a further agreement between Portugal and Spain on the demarcation of their colonial spheres of interest. Taking of the Moluccas.	1529
The establishment of the Inquisition in Portugal and the foundation of a Jesuit university at Évora (closed 1759) promote the success of the Counter Reformation.	1536/58
The Portuguese establish a trading post at Macao, the first European settlement in China.	1557
King Sebastião I (1557–78) undertakes a crusade against Morocco but is killed, along with many Spanish nobles, in the battle of Alcácer-Kibir.	1578
Death of King (and Cardinal) Henrique II (1578–80), the last ruler of the House of Avis.	1580

Rulers of Portugal

House of Burgundy

Henrique
(Henry of Burgundy)
Count of Portucalia ... 1093–1112
    After Henry's death his widow
    Teresa acts as Regent during the
    minority of her son Afonso

Afonso Henriques, the Conqueror
King of Portugal ... 1139–85

Sancho I, the Populator ... 1185–1211

Afonso II, the Fat ... 1211–23

Sancho II ... 1223–45
(deposed 1245, d. 1248)

Afonso III, the Restorer ... 1245–79
(brother of Snacho II)

Dinis I, the Farmer ... 1279–1325

Afonso IV, the Brave ... 1325–57

Pedro I, the Cruel
or the Inexorable ... 1357–67

Fernando ... 1367–83

House of Avis

João I, Defender of the Kingdom
(illegitimate son of Pedro I;
Grand Master of the Order of Avis)
Regent ... 1383–85
King of Portugal ... 1385–1433

Duarte ... 1433–38
    His brothers are Pedro (Duke of
    Coimbra), Henrique (Henry the
    Navigator), Fernão (d. in Moorish
    captivity) and João (Grand Master
    of the Order of Santiago)

Afonso V, the African ... 1438–81

João II, the Perfect Prince ... 1481–95

Manuel I, the Fortunate ... 1495–1521

João III, the Pious ... 1521–57

Sebastião ... 1557–78
(grandson of João III)

Henrique II ... 1578–80
(brother of João III;
Cardinal Archbishop of Lisbon)

Spanish Kings of the House of Habsburg

Filipe I
(Philip II of Spain)
King of Portugal ... 1580–98

Filipe II ... 1598–1621
(Philip III of Spain)

Filipe III ... 1621–40
(Philip IV of Spain)

House of Bragança

João IV
(Duke of Bragança)
King of Portugal ... 1640–56

Afonso VI ... 1656–67

Pedro II ... Regent 1667–83
(brother of Afonso VI) ... King 1683–1706

João V, the Magnanimous ... 1706–50

José ... 1750–77

Maria I ... 1777–92
(wife of Pedro III, who d. 1786)

João VI ... Prince Regent 1792–1816
... King 1816–26

Pedro IV ... 1826–28
(Emperor Pedro I of Brazil)

Miguel ... 1828–34
(brother of Pedro IV)

Maria II ... 1834–53
(daughter of Pedro IV; m. Duke Ferdinand
of Saxe-Coburg-Koháry 1836)
Duke Ferdinand rules as Regent during
the minority of his son Pedro ... 1853–55

Pedro V ... 1855–61

Luís ... 1861–89

Carlos ... 1889–1908
(assassinated in Lisbon in 1908
together with his heir Luís Filipe)

Manuel II ... 1908–10
(second son of Carlos I; leaves
Portugal 1910, d. in exile 1932)

From Spanish rule to the fall of the monarchy

Although Portugal succeeds, with British help, in winning its independence from Spain, it falls increasingly under British influence, politically and economically. Despite the huge influx of money from its colonial possessions the country grows poorer since it fails to establish a productive economy of its own. Portugal remains a backward agrarian country, wracked in the 19th c. by civil war, political and constitutional conflicts, and financial and economic crises that finally lead to the fall of the monarchy.

Philip II of Spain, a grandson of Manuel I on his mother's side, occupies the whole of Portugal by force and expels the Portuguese claimant to the throne, António. | 1580

Portugal is united with Spain through rule from the Spanish throne. | 1580–1640

The Cortes recognise Philip II of Spain as King Filipe I of Portugal. The country is ruled by viceroys; the colonies have a separate administration of their own. | 1581

During the period of Spanish rule Portugal loses part of its colonial empire. The Dutch take the Moluccas (1607), Ceylon (1638), Malacca (1641) and north-eastern Brazil (1630 onwards; recovered 1654). | 1607–30

The heavy taxation imposed to finance Spanish wars, combined with much activity by French agents, leads to a successful rising in Lisbon. Its leader, the Duke of Bragança, descended from the old royal family through his grandmother, restores the independent kingdom of Portugal and is crowned king as João IV (1640–56). | 1640

1st Dec. Independence Day

A treaty of friendship and commercial co-operation with Britain (ratified in 1656) ensures Portugal's independence of Spain but also guarantees British predominance in Portugal. | 1654

Catherine of Braganza (Bragança), sister of King Afonso VI (1656–67), marries Charles II of England. | 1661

Treaty of Lisbon: Spain recognises Portugal's independence. | 1668

During the war of the Spanish Succession Pedro II (1683–1706) signs a treaty of alliance with France, but under British military pressure is forced to revoke it. | 1701

Under pressure from Britain, Austria and Holland, Portugal is compelled to join the anti-French coalition.
    The Methuen Treaty, a commercial treaty between Britain and Portugal, provides for the sale of Portuguese wine in exchange for British textiles. The Portuguese woollen industry is thus destroyed. | 1703

Under its spendthrift King João V, who sides with Austria in the War of Spanish Succession, Portugal becomes totally impoverished despite its vast holdings of Brazilian gold and diamond mines, and grows financially dependent on Great Britain. | 1706–50

The reign of King José I is the great age of enlightened absolutism. His chief minister, the Marquês de Pombal (1699–1782), carries through a series of reforms based on the principles of the Enlightenment and Mercantilism – the encouragement of manufacturing and trading companies, the reorganisation of the fiscal and financial systems and of the army, the promulgation of a new code of laws, the secularisation of education, etc. | 1750–77

After the devastating Lisbon earthquake (November 1st), in which more than 30,000 people are killed, Pombal directs the rebuilding of the shattered capital. | 1755

Historic Provinces of Portugal
(mainland)

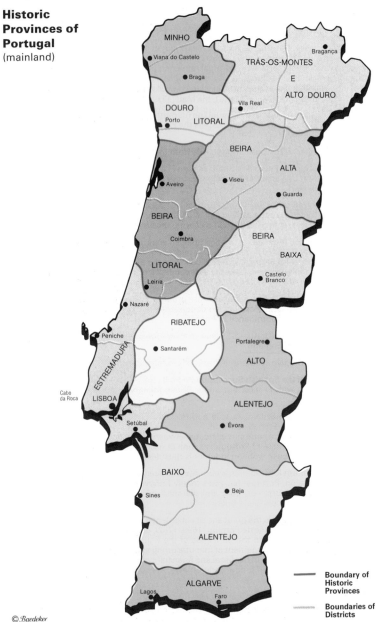

MINHO

Viana do Castelo

Braga

TRÁS-OS-MONTES

Bragança

E

ALTO DOURO

DOURO
LITORAL

Porto

Vila Real

BEIRA

ALTA

Aveiro

Viseu

Guarda

BEIRA

LITORAL

Coimbra

BEIRA

BAIXA

Leiria

Castelo
Branco

Nazaré

RIBATEJO

Peniche

ESTREMADURA

Santarém

Portalegre

ALTO

Cabo
da Roca

LISBOA

ALENTEJO

Setúbal

Évora

BAIXO

Sines

Beja

ALENTEJO

ALGARVE

Lagos

Faro

—— Boundary of
Historic
Provinces

········ Boundaries of
Districts

© Baedeker

Expulsion of the Jesuits from Portugal and the Portuguese colonies and confiscation of their property.	1759

Portugal repulses Spain's invasion attempt in the Seven Years' War.   1762

Refoundation of Coimbra University.   1772

After the death of José I the authoritarian Pombal is compelled to go into exile. During the reign of Maria I, the Mad (1777–92/1816), there is a clerical reaction and the Jesuits return. Most of Pombal's reforms are reversed, and the ideas of the Enlightenment are combated with the help of the Inquisition.   1777

João VI becomes Regent in place of his mentally disordered mother. During the French Revolution Portugal allies itself with Britain as a member of the anti-French coalition.   1792

João VI refuses to take part in the Continental System or to fight alongside the French against Britain.   1805

Under the Treaty of Fontainebleau (October) between France and Spain Napoleon gains the right to march his troops through Spain. The French General Junot is thus able to occupy the whole of Portugal. The royal family flees to Brazil under the protection of the British fleet (November).   1807

War of National Liberation against rule by the French: General Arthur Wellesley (later Duke of Wellington) lands in Portugal in August 1808 with a British force and defeats Junot's French army. Under the Convention of Cintra (Sintra) on August 30th the French withdraw from Portugal. Napoleon himself, with 300,000 soldiers, now seeks to reconquer Spain and Portugal.
  In 1810 Wellesley succeeds in repelling an attack on Lisbon by Marshal Masséna at Torres Vedras.   1808–10

After the complete liberation of Portugal, General William Carr Beresford remains in control of the country, the king being still in exile in Brazil.   1811

British forces quell a rising by Portuguese army officers.   1817

Liberal revolution, starting in Oporto.   1820

A new liberal constitution (modelled on the Spanish constitution of 1812) is proclaimed by the Cortes, confirming João as king on his return to Lisbon.   1821

With British help João VI defeats a conspiracy, directed against the new liberal measures, which is supported by his wife Carlotta (sister of Ferdinand VII of Spain) and their younger son Dom Miguel. Miguel is banished from Portugal.   1824

Since Pedro I of Brazil (Pedro IV of Portugal) is unable to unite his two kingdoms, he abdicates the Portuguese crown after his father's death in favour of his seven-year-old daughter Maria da Glória (Maria II), promulgating a moderate constitution and appointing Miguel as Regent.   1826

After a counter-revolution Miguel revokes the constitution and has himself elected king by the Cortes as Miguel I.   1828

Miguelist Wars. Pedro I of Brazil, having renounced the Brazilian throne in 1831 in favour of his son Pedro II, overthrows the reactionary regime of Miguel I, with British help. Miguel leaves Portugal.   1832–34

History

1833–34	Land belonging to the Church is secularised and sold to nobles and wealthy middle-class citizens.
1834	On her father's death Maria da Glória becomes queen as Maria II, but is unable to prevent the continuance (until 1847) of party strife between conservatives ("Chartists", after the constitutional charter of 1826) and liberals ("Septembrists", after the constitution of 1822).
1836	The Queen marries Duke Ferdinand of Saxe-Coburg-Koháry, who is accorded the title of King in 1837. After the September Revolution the 1822 constitution is reintroduced, but replaced only two years later by a more moderate constitution.
1839–46	Antonio Bernardo da Costa Cabral restores the 1826 constitution and rules as a dictator.
1846/47	A popular rising is suppressed with Spanish and British help.
1851	After a military revolt Septembrists and some Chartists found a new party of "Regeneration" (Regeneração). They introduce direct elections, municipal self-government and a lower qualification for the vote.
1853	Construction of the first Portuguese railway line.
1855–61	During the reign of Pedro V Portugal is ruled by a dictator, Saldanha (until 1857). Repeated efforts to put the country's finances on a proper footing are unsuccessful.
1855	Portugal's first telegraph lines.
1861–89	During the reign of Luis I the country is governed alternately by conservatives and liberals.
1867	The Civil Code enters into force.
1875	Foundation of the first Portuguese Socialist Party.
1876	Foundation of the Republican Party and the Progressist Party.
1889–1908	King Carlos I extends Portuguese colonial possessions in Africa but is unable to overcome the country's increasing financial difficulties.
1890	A British ultimatum compels Portugal to abandon a colonial expedition aimed at linking Angola and Mozambique.
1891	Unsuccessful Republican revolt.
1892	A declaration of national bankruptcy severely damages the prestige of the crown.
1899	In the secret Treaty of Windsor Britain guarantees the security of the Portuguese colonies and receives in return the right to send troops through Portuguese territories in Africa.
1901	Carlos I is compelled to allow British, French and German representatives to participate in the control of the national budget.
1902/1906	Military and naval risings, underlining the crisis of the monarchy.
1906–08	The king attempts to rule without Parliament, with his minister João Franco exercising dictatorial powers, in order to maintain the monarchy in face of the rising wave of republicanism.

Carlos is assassinated in Lisbon, along with the heir to the throne, Luis
Filipe (February 1st). 1908

Carlos's younger son Manuel II is unable to save the monarchy, in spite
of an amnesty and minor concessions. 1908–10

Revolution in Lisbon; Manuel is compelled to abdicate and flees to
Britain. 1910

From the foundation of the Republic to the present day

After the abolition of the monarchy continuing party strife prevents the
necessary radical reforms (particularly land reform) from being carried
through, and the new form of government is accordingly unable to
achieve stability. Although Salazar overcomes the financial crisis, his
authoritarian Fascist regime and colonial policy lead after the Second
World War to the isolation of Portugal in the United Nations and the
Western world. After the fall of the dictatorship the development of a
new pattern of government is hampered by political, economic and
social problems resulting from the country's colonial wars. Conflicts
between parties of the left and the right make it difficult to form a stable
government. Entry into the European Community confirms democratic Portugal's stated intent to help create a united Europe.

Proclamation of the Republic (October 5th). The interim President,
Joaquim Teófilo Fernandes Braga, forms an anti-clerical government. 1910

Separation of State and Church (April 20th). Republic constitution
comes into force (September 11th); Manuel d'Arriaga becomes President (1911–15). Reforms are carried through, but the urgently necessary land reform is not. Party strife among the Republicans, who are
divided among themselves, together with revolutionary unrest,
strikes, political corruption, the continuing financial crisis and other
problems, prevent the formation of a stable government (between
1911 and 1926, under 8 Presidents, there are no fewer than 44
governments). 1911

The use of troops to repress disturbances in Évora leads to a general
strike in Lisbon. 1912

During the First World War Portugal at first remains neutral then in
1915 is persuaded by Great Britain to come into the war on the side of
the Allies. 1914–18

Social conflicts become more acute (frequent strikes). 1919/20

Foundation of the Portuguese Communist Party. 1921

After a military rising (May 28th) under General Manuel de Oliveira
Gomes da Costa Parliament is dissolved and the constitution suspended. The Communist Party is banned. 1926

Gomes da Costa is displaced by General António Oscar de Fragosa
Carmona, who represses uprisings in Oporto and Lisbon aimed at
returning to a parliamentary regime. 1927

General Carmona is elected President (until 1951). He dissolves the
Cortes and puts down several revolts against the military dictatorship.
The economist António de Oliveira Salazar (1889–1970), finance minister in the new government, brings the national finances under control
within a year and becomes the dominant political figure in Portugal. 1928

History

| 1930 | Salazar founds the National Union (União Nacional), the Fascist party of a one-party state. |

1930   Salazar founds the National Union (União Nacional), the Fascist party of a one-party state.

1931   Suppression of riots on Madeira and in Lisbon.

1932   Salazar becomes prime minister.

1933   The new constitution is ratified by a national referendum (March 19th). The Estado Novo (New State) is an authoritarian corporative state on the Fascist model. Strikes are prohibited and the trade unions dissolved.

1936–38   During the Spanish Civil War Portugal is officially neutral but favours General Franco by indirect means.

1939   Iberian Pact, a treaty of friendship and non-aggression with Spain (continued for another ten years in 1948). Renewal of the alliance with Britain. Concordat with the Vatican.

1939–45   During the Second World War Portugal remains neutral. It breaks off diplomatic relations with Germany in May 1943, and gives Britain and the USA bases in the Azores in 1943 and 1944 respectively.

1948   Portugal receives Marshall Aid and joins the Organisation for European Economic Co-operation (OEEC).

1949   Portugal becomes one of the founder members of the North Atlantic Treaty Organisation (NATO).

1951   Agreement with the United States (later extended several times) allowing the Americans and other NATO countries to establish military bases in the Azores.
    Francisco Higino Craveiro Lopes becomes President on the death of President Carmona.
    The Portuguese colonies are declared to be part of Portugal (overseas provinces).

1955   Portugal becomes a member of the United Nations. Treaty with Brazil providing for mutual consultation.

1958   Admiral Américo de Deus Rodrigues Tomás is elected President.

1960   Portugal becomes a member of the Organisation for Economic Co-operation and Development (OECD) and the European Free Trade Area (EFTA).

1961   Seizure of the Portuguese liner "Santa Maria" in the Caribbean by opponents of Salazar (January).
    Annexation by India of the Portuguese enclaves of Goa, Damão and Diu (not recognised by Portugal until 1974). Increasing unrest in Angola and Mozambique. The United Nations repeatedly condemn Portuguese colonial policy.

1962   Officers fail in an attempt to overthrow the dictator in Beja.

1963   An agreement with West Germany allows German troops to be stationed at a NATO airbase in Beja.

1964   Portugal concludes an agreement with France allowing it a base in the Azores.

From 1967   Inflationary trend in Portugal as a result of the country's colonial wars and its entry to EFTA.

Salazar retires on health grounds and is succeeded by Marcelo José 1968
das Neves Alves Caetano, a lawyer who has long been associated with
him in the government. He tries briefly to take a more liberal line but is
frustrated by steadily increasing opposition, particularly in the army.

PIDE, the notorious secret police organisation, is renamed the Directo- 1969
rate General of Security (DGS).

The period of compulsory military service is extended from two to 1970
three (in case of emergency four) years (February 5th). The National
Union becomes the National People's Action (Acção Nacional Popular:
February 21st).
   Portugal fails to win its colonial war against Guinea.

Treaty between the European Community and EFTA states not willing 1972
to join the Community providing for the reduction of duties on industrial products (July 22nd)

Portuguese-Guinea declares its independence, recognised by Portugal 1973
in 1974. Earthquake in the Azores.

The dictatorship is overthrown (April 25th) in the "Carnation Revolu- 1974
tion", an almost bloodless coup d'état by the MFA (Movimento das
Forças Armadas, Armed Forces Movement). Tomás and Caetano are
removed from office, and General António Sebastião Ribeiro de Spínola (whose book "Portugal and its Future" prepared the ground for
the military putsch) becomes President. He is succeeded on September 30th by General Franciso da Costa Gomes.
   The head of the left-wing democratic government is Adelino da
Palma Carlos, a lawyer, who gives place on July 15th to Colonel Vasco
dos Santos Gonçalves. A Council of State is established as an instrument of government, and a variety of parties are permitted. The
government's domestic plans, which include the nationalisation of
banks, insurance corporations and large companies and the expropriation of large estates as the first stage in land reform, give rise to violent
political conflicts.
   The country's acute economic problems are aggravated by the influx
of refugees from the newly independent colonies. The overseas provinces are granted the right of self-determination (August).

Unsuccessful attempt at a putsch by right-wing elements under the 1975
leadership of General Spínola (March 11th); Spínola emigrates to
Brazil. The Council of State is superseded by a Council of the Revolution, composed of military leaders, which initiates the nationalisation
of the economy and land reform.
   The elections for a new legislative assembly show a strong body of
opinion in favour of a pluralist democracy (April 25th). When the
Council of the Revolution takes no account of this there are bitter
conflicts between the MFA and members of the socialist and communist parties. The MFA sets up a "Triumvirate" of three military men (F.
da Costa Gomes, V. dos Santos Gonçalves and Otelo Saraiva de Carvalho) as the highest political authority (end July). Vice-Admiral José
Baptista Pinheiro de Azevado becomes prime minister (end August).
Unsuccessful putsch by extreme left-wing paratroopers in which Carvalho plays an ambiguous role (end November); Carvalho is removed
from office.
   The former colonies of Mozambique, the Cape Verde Islands, the
islands of São Tomé and Príncipe, and Angola become independent
during 1975.

The effects of the worldwide energy crisis and economic recession Mid 1975 to mid
aggravate Portugal's internal difficulties: increased inflation (35%), 1976

41

April 25th 1974

On the evening of April 24th 1974 an army of 5000 men stood in readiness, but less than 1000 of them were aware that a revolution had been planned. Shortly after midnight the Catholic radio station "Renascença" broadcast the prohibited song "Grândola, Vila Morena", by the opposition singer José Afonso who – unwavering and undeterred by bans, arrests and torture – was a respected member of the opposition to the dictatorship. A commando unit of the Portuguese army had taken over the radio transmitter and at the appointed time had broadcast this song, which tells of the little farmworking town of Grândola in the Alentejo, the "dark town where the people rule". Only a few people heard the song on the radio, but those in the know knew what it meant. It was the signal to go. Troop detachments positioned near Lisbon moved off. Approach roads, government buildings, public squares, army barracks, radio transmitters and the airport were occupied by the revolutionary units almost without encountering any resistance. The rebels had prepared well; by three o'clock in the morning the centre of Lisbon was completely in their control. In other parts of Portugal, too, strategically important centres were seized by rebel units.

At first, however, large sections of the population did not know who the rebels actually were. Were they left-wing young officers aiming to over-throw the dictatorship or were they right-wing military opportunists in-tending to seize political power for themselves? The Portuguese writer José Cardoso Pires wrote later that he received a telephone call at 3am from an unknown person who briefly informed him that he should flee because the hunt for the democrats had begun.

The writer then wandered through the city accompanied by friends who knew as little about what was happening as he did. The streets were almost empty and there were hardly any passengers on the buses. The nearer they got to the city centre, however, the more troops and armoured cars were to be seen on the street corners. Then they witnesed something quite amazing – people running up to the soldiers and hugging them or clapping them on the back. The citizens hoped that the coup would free them from the hated dictatorship. Everywhere there were enthusiastic mass demonstrations; the streets were packed with people cheering the soldiers. On the Praça do Comércio, where the government ministries were housed, soldiers and civilians together besieged the official buildings and watched as the officials surrendered. In Chiado armoured cars fired on the headquarters of the Republican Guard, the members of which were renowned for their harsh repressive measures and who now, filled with rage and fear, had taken refuge behind locked doors.

The Carmo Barracks on the Largo do Carmo, where the government sat, found itself surrounded by the rebel army demanding their surrender and by a vast crowd of people. The inhabitants handed out food and cigarettes to their liberators, climbed on the armoured cars, sang and stuck red carna-tions in the soldiers' rifle barrels. They obtained the carnations from the flower-shops in the smart area of the city and from the popular markets on the left bank of the Tagus; as it happened, 1974 had been a particularly good year for carnations and they were comparatively cheap to buy, and so it was this flower that the people chose to symbolise the uprising and the start of a new era in Portugal.

It was an almost bloodless revolution. Many sections of the army not yet involved broke their oath of allegiance and went over to the rebels. Police and soldiers who had remained faithful to the regime found themselves surrounded and laid down their arms in the street. President Caetano, deserted by his people and his army, finally came to the telephone and surrendered unconditionally; he was taken to the airport in an armoured car and lived the rest of his life in Brazil, an embittered man. Only three young men died when agents of the hated secret police, the PIDE, shot aimlessly into the crowd from their headquarters in which they had barricaded themselves. Political prisoners were released, PIDE thugs imprisoned, and the former dictators sent into exile – but nobody instigated witch-hunts. Some agents of the secret police fled to Spain; many big industrialists and bankers tried to get their money out of the country – some trunks full of escudos were confiscated at the airport. Everything happened very noisily but peacefully. In Lisbon car-drivers produced a deafening concert on their horns, military police directed the traffic with carnations instead of batons, at night tin cans served as drums, and hundreds of political slogans appeared on the walls of houses – everybody painted or sprayed what he or she felt of the present or hoped from the future.

During the course of April 25th everybody realised who had been behind the uprising – the MFA (Movimento das Forças Armadas, Armed Forces Movement).

From the early 1970s, there had been signs of resistance among Portuguese military leaders to the wars in the African colonies of Angola, Guinea and Mozambique. They realised that, as a result of the hugely increased pressure from African freedom movements, these wars could not be won, that time was against Portugal and that political solutions must be sought instead. In February 1974 the acting Chief of Staff António Spinola, with the agreement of his superior Costa Gomes, published his book "Portugal and its Future", in which he called for political dialogue with the colonies. The book immediately caused an uproar and Spinola and Costa Gomes were removed from office. In addition, as early as 1973 left-wing officers had founded the MFA, a democratically orientated resistance movement which did not escape the attentions of the secret police, the PIDE; in March 1974 numerous MFA members were arrested. The MFA therefore had to act before it was too late. On 12.30am on April 25th 1974 the "Young Captains", as they were called, struck. They were aware of the general hatred the people felt for the dictatorial regime and were certain that would find support among the population; moreover, they had the silent agreement of Spinola and Costa Gomes.

The semi-bloodless "Carnation Revolution" brought an end to 48 years of continuous dictatorship. Under the transitional military government exiled opposition politicians returned to their homeland, individual political parties and trades unions were permitted, and the colonial wars came to an end. In the same year Guinea obtained its independence, followed by Angola and Mozambique in 1975. Exactly one year after the Carnation Revolution proper free elections were held to elect members of the constitutional assembly.

high unemployment (over 15%), a growing stream of refugees from the former colonies (nearly half a million), anti-communist riots in northern Portugal, occupation of large estates in the south by peasants, strikes and unrest in industry, flight of capital. Economic and financial collapse is averted only by financial help from the European Community and credits from Germany and other countries.

1976

The Constitutional Assembly promulgates (although the Social Democratic Centre Party votes against it) the new socialist constitution establishing a democratic parliamentary Republic (April 2nd). The Socialists are victorious in an election on April 25th, but without an absolute majority.

After a rising in Portuguese Timor the territory becomes part of Indonesia (June 24th).

General António Ramalho Eanes is elected President (June 26th) and appoints the Socialist Mário Soares as head of a minority government.

Portugal becomes a full member of the Council of Europe (September 22nd).

Resumption of relations with Angola (September 30th).

1977

Foundation of a new party of the right, the Independent Movement for National Reconstruction (MIRN). Devaluation of the escudo (February) – the first devaluation since 1931. Extension of Portuguese territorial waters to 200 miles from the coast (March 11th). The government officially applies for membership of the European Community (March 28th).

Second law on land reform, providing on the one hand for the return of illegally occupied land to the owner and on the other for further collectivisation of large estates (August 11th); it gives rise to protests and unrest in the south. Government control of exchange rates is abandoned (August–September). Political and economic problems lead to the fall of the minority Socialist government (December 8th).

1978

Coalition government of the Socialists and Social Democratic Centre Party led by Mário Soares (February 12th).

Portugal receives a large credit from the International Monetary Fund, with conditions as to restriction of imports and consumption; further devaluation of the escudo (May). Ten-year treaty of friendship and co-operation with Spain (May 5th). Fascist organisations banned (June 16th).

After the dissolution of the coalition government President Eanes appoints the former minister of industry, Alfredo Nobre da Costa, head of a government of technocrats (August 28th). After only 17 days Nobre da Costa's non-party government is defeated by the Socialists and Centre Democrats (September 14th). The return to private ownership of nationalised land in the Alentejo wheat belt, which gives rise to protests, mainly from the Communists, leads to violent incidents in the agricultural areas (October). Mass demonstrations in Lisbon against the interim government formed by Nobre da Costa (November).

Carlos Mota Pinto, a non-party man with Social Democratic leanings, forms another government of technocrats, which takes the oath on November 22nd. The Council of the Revolution rejects the electoral laws passed by Parliament as unconstitutional (December 14th). Wave of resignations by Socialists (December).

1979

Mota Pinto demands State aid for the private sector. Country-wide demonstrations and strikes against the amendment of the land reform laws. Foundation of the Socialist Trade Union in Oporto (January). The government's plans for putting the country's finances on to a proper footing meet violent opposition. Mass demonstrations by both the left and the right face the government with another crisis (March 17th).

Split in the Social Democratic Party over the premature demand for an election by the party leader, Francisco Sá Carneiro. New electoral law passed by Parliament (April).

After no-confidence motions by the Communists and Socialists the Mota Pinto government resigns (June 6th). The parties of the central right – Social Democratic Centre Party, Popular Monarchist Party, Social Democratic Party and breakaway Socialists – form a "Democratic Alliance" (July 5th).

President Eanes asks Maria de Lurdes Pintassilgo, Portuguese representative at UNESCO, to form an interim government (July 19th).

A special election on December 2nd (in which 87.5% of the electorate vote) gives the conservative Democratic Alliance a clear majority. A liberal Social Democrat, Francisco Sá Carneiro, becomes prime minister.

A severe earthquake in the Azores on New Year's Day takes a heavy toll in human lives and damage to property. **1980**

The Conservative "Democratic Alliance" wins the normal elections (October 5th). Sá Carneiro again forms the government. A little later he is killed in an air crash (December 4th).

General Ramalho Eanes is once more elected as President (December 12th). Portugal's caretaker government under the acting Prime Minister Amaral resigns (December 8th).

The Social Democrat Francisco Pinto Balsemão (PSD) becomes prime minister (January 5th). Mário Soares is confirmed as General Secretary of the Socialist Party of Portugal (May 10th). After disagreements within the PSD Pinto Balsemão resigns (August 11th). Three weeks later he again forms a government (September 1st). **1981**

On the occasion of a pilgrimage to Fatíma Pope John Paul II escapes an attempt on his life (May 13th). Changes in the cabinet (June 5th). **1982**

As a result of the early elections on April 25th the Socialists with 36.3% of all votes emerge as the strongest party. Together with the Social Democrats (PSD) they form a coalition of the left centre led by Prime Minister Mário Soares. **1983**

Parliament accepts the abortion bill put forward by the Socialists, the Conservatives voting against (January). **1984**

The ruling coalition breaks up and the Soares government resigns (October). The Social Democrats (PSD) emerge as the largest party from the early general elections but the new prime minister, Anibal Cavaco Silva, has to govern with a minority cabinet. **1985**

On January 1st Portugal (and Spain) become full members of the EEC. Former prime minister Mário Soares is elected President in the second round of presidential elections. **1986**

Anibal Cavaco Silva's minority government is toppled by an opposition vote of no confidence. President Mário Soares dissolves parliament and calls new elections for July 19th. Cavaco Silva's PSD scores a convincing victory and becomes the first party since the 1974 Revolution to achieve an absolute majority, winning 148 of the 250 parliamentary seats. As on-going prime minister Cavaco Silva's programme is uncompromisingly aimed at reducing state influence on the Portuguese economy and amending the constitution to water down or eliminate its basic Socialist principles. **1987**

The visit by US Secretary of Defence Frank Calucci in February occasions a Portuguese government statement that the Lajes base in the Azores will continue to be available to the American Air Force. **1988**

Cavaco Silva's measures meet with stubborn resistance from some of the population and March sees a wave of strikes protesting against planned new labour laws to facilitate dismissals and fixed-term working.

A fire on August 25th destroys much of Lisbon's inner city Chiado district.

1989 An American charter flight crashes on landing at Santa Maria in the Azores, killing all on board.

1991 In January Mário Soares is re-elected President with a large majority.

In October Cavaco Silva wins an absolute majority of parliamentary seats for the PSD.

1992 In June Lisbon is awarded the contract to stage Expo 98, a world exhibition on the theme "The Ocean, the Heritage of the Future" (see Baedeker Special, p. 213).

1994 Lisbon is nominated "European City of Culture" for one year.

1995 Following the parliamentary elections of October 1st António Guterres of the Socialist Party (PS) becomes Prime Minister. He takes over from the Liberal-Conservative Anibal Cavaco Silva.

1996 The election of the Socialist Jorge Sampaio (PS) as the new President of Portugal perpetuates the noticeable move to the left which has been evident in recent years.

1998 The Portuguese capital of Lisbon hosts Expo 98, under the title "The Ocean – the Heritage for the Future". The Ponte Vasco da Gama bridge over the Tagus is opened for traffic in time for Expo 98. With a length of 17km/10½ miles, it is the longest bridge in Europe.

Famous People

The following famous people were all connected in some way or other with Portugal, whether as the place of their birth or death, or because they lived or worked there.

Afonso I (1109/1110–85)

Afonso Henriques, later Afonso I, founded the Portuguese monarchy. Born in 1109 or 1110 (or even 1112, according to some sources), he was the son of Count Henry of Burgundy who had been invested with the fiefdom of Portugal by León-Castile but had succeeded in freeing it from its feudal dependence as early as 1109. When his father died in 1112 Afonso succeeded him, initially under the regency of his mother then, from 1128, in his own right.

His brilliant victory over the Moors at Ourique in 1139 brought him such prestige he was able to assume the title of King of Portugal. In 1143, by submitting himself to the feudal authority of the Pope, he forced León-Castile to recognise his independence. Further military successes, including capturing Lisbon from the Moors in 1143, enabled him to keep on extending the boundaries of his kingdom.

Afonso probably did not actively take part in all the campaigns, but he masterminded the plan of action and also ensured that the newly conquered territory was properly defended and administered.

Little is known of the life of Afonso I apart from the famous conquests. In 1145 or 1146 he married Matilda (d. 1158 and the daughter of Count Amadeus of Moriana) and they had several children. Afonso's heir – subsequently Sancho I – was born in 1154.

Afonso received a wound during an assault on Badajoz in 1168 which made it impossible for him ever to ride again. From 1170 onwards he lived in Coimbra where he died on December 6th 1185 after a short illness. In accordance with his wishes he was buried in the church of the monastery of Santa Cruz.

Mariana Alcoforado (1640–1723)

The Portuguese nun Mariana Alcoforado figures in European literature as the author of the love letters addressed to Noël Bouton de Chamilly, Count of Saint-Léger, which form the so-called "Letters of a Portuguese Nun" (Lettres Portugaises) of 1669. It may well be that she was not, however, the author of these letters which, as well as being very full of feeling, are extremely well-expressed. They are as likely to have come from the pen of the French author G.-J. de Guilleragues who purports to have translated them. The "Letters" were translated into English for the first time as early as 1678 by Sir Roger l'Estrange. At the time when the Letters were first published the name of the presumed authoress was not known; it was not until the nineteenth century that it was discovered, and efforts were made to cast light on the nun's biography. Modern critics generally treat the Letters as nothing other than a work of fiction.

Mariana Alcoforado was born in 1640, the daughter of Francisco Alcoforado, an army officer, and of Leonor Menezes, a lady of wealth. She was still very young when she entered the convent of Nossa Senhora da Conceição in Beja. It was through the bars of the window of her convent cell that in 1665 she is supposed to have first set eyes on a young Frenchman, Noël de Bouton de Chamilly, who was serving in the same regiment as her brother (at the time France was supporting Portugal in the Spanish–Portuguese War). They struck up a friendship and, despite the convent walls, fell in love. 1667 spelt the end of their happiness when the count had to return home. Mariana Alcoforado sent him letters which at first were full of passion and then, as she came to realise that she had been no more than a passing fancy for the count,

Famous People

Afonso I

Luís Vaz de Camões

Vasco da Gama

became expressions of her disappointment and her sense of distance. Her former lover is supposed to have felt nothing but amusement when he received her letters and to have enjoyed reading them out aloud to his friends.

In her last letter the nun hinted that she might put an end to her life, but she must have managed to overcome her grief, since she died in the convent at the ripe old age of 83. Her memorial, which survives to this day, records that for thirty years she subjected herself to the strictest penance.

Diogo de Boytaca (c. 1470–1520)

Although the exact dates of the life of the architect Diogo de Boytaca (or Boytac or Boitaca) are uncertain, it is known that he was active between about 1490 and 1520. His nationality is also unclear, and he may have been French, Italian or actually Portuguese – for which there are some grounds in that there is a village near Batalha with the similar-sounding name of Boutaca.

Boytaca is inseparably linked with the Manueline style of architecture. His buildings are almost without exception characterised by their exuberant decoration. His first major work was the Convent of Jesus in Setúbal, then after 1509 he headed the building of the abbey at Batalha and, after 1514, the Hieronymite convent in Belém. He also worked on the palace at Sintra, and in Galegã, Caldas da Rainha and Montemor-o-Velho, as well as being responsible for many fortifications in North Africa.

Luís Vaz de Camões (1524/1525–80)

Lisbon and Coimbra dispute the honour of being the birthplace of Luís Vaz de Camões, who is certainly Portugal's most important poet. There are doubts too about the date of his birth, which may be either 1524 or 1525. He came from a respected family, his father holding the King's command of one of his ships.

After studying in Coimbra, Camões went to Lisbon where he was received at court and commissioned to write plays and poems. He was, however, soon to be banished from court circles because of a love affair. In the hope of winning his way back into favour he volunteered to serve in North Africa where he lost his right eye in a skirmish. He had scarcely arrived back in Lisbon when he was imprisoned in 1552 for taking part in a duel. He was pardoned, but ordered to leave the kingdom. He was first sent to Goa, where he again fell out of favour, and had to go further afield, presumably to Macao. His post, which involved responsibility for those who were dead or missing in China, left him enough time for his poetry. There is a rocky cave which now bears his name in which he is supposed to have written his great epic "The Lusiads", (Os Lusíadeas, a reference to Lusus, the mythical ancestor of the Portuguese).

It was not until 1570 that Camões returned to Lisbon, where "The Lusiads" was first published two years later. Even then, however, fate was unkind to Camões, who nowadays is revered as the Portuguese national poet. He lived out his last years in abject poverty. In 1580, on June 10th – now celebrated as a national holiday – he died of the plague.

Besides "The Lusiads" Camões published numerous poems and several comedies.

Inês de Castro was born of a distinguished Castilian noble family and came to Portugal in the entourage of Constança, the wife of the Infante Dom Pedro. She and Pedro, the heir to the throne, soon fell passionately in love. This did not suit the reigning monarch, King Afonso IV, who had Inês sent back to Spain. Pedro had to accept his father's decision, but did not forget the woman he loved. When his wife died giving birth to a son, he had Inês brought back to Portugal. He lived with her quite openly and the couple had four children.

Inês de Castro
(c. 1320–55)

Their happiness was, however, short-lived. The king feared the de Castros would become too influential and got the Privy Council to order the death of Inês. She was murdered in Coimbra in the "Jardim das Lágrimas", the "Garden of Tears", as it henceforth was known, and her body was interred in the convent of Santa Clara in Coimbra. Pedro dreamt of revenge but was obliged at first to bow to his father's will. When, however, his father died in 1357 and he succeeded to the throne he ordered those who had taken part in the murder of his beloved to be most cruelly tortured and executed. Not satisfied with that, he ordered the exhumation of the corpse of Inês which was then crowned queen in a macabre ceremony in Coimbra Cathedral and thereafter reinterred in Alcobaça Abbey.

This love story has been treated in more than 200 literary works, the first being the third canto of Camões' "Lusiads".

The seafarer Vasco da Gama came from Sines, the port in southern Portugal. The actual year of his birth is not known, but it is put at somewhere between 1460 and 1469. It was King Manuel I who ordered da Gama to find the sea route to India, though precisely why he was chosen remains uncertain. What is known is that he had already won something of a name for himself when serving in the fleet under João II. Opinions differ as to his temperament. In contemporary sources he is described as valiant, tough and proud, but also irascible and hot-tempered.

Vasco da Gama
(1460?–1524)

Da Gama left the harbour of Restelo near Lisbon with four ships on July 8th 1497. The crews totalled 170 men (of whom a third would perish on the voyage), plus priests and some convicts who could escape execution by going on particularly dangerous enterprises. One week out the ships passed the Canaries, and on November 22nd they rounded the Cape of Good Hope to continue sailing up the east coast of Africa and finally, in May 1498, anchored off the west coast of India. Da Gama started the return voyage on October 8th 1498, arriving back in Lisbon on July 10th 1499. Although he had in fact returned almost empty-handed from his travels, he was envied and admired by the whole world of his day for the contacts he had forged with the spice lands. The King rewarded him richly, awarding him an annuity and granting him the title of "Dom".

In 1502/1503 da Gama set out on his second India voyage, this time at the head of an armada charged with setting up trading relations and compelling recognition of Portuguese dominion. On this voyage da Gama allowed his irascibility full rein "lapsing into near transports of cruelty". This time he returned to Portugal richly laden with treasure.

The seafarer embarked on his third and final voyage to India in 1524. The King had appointed him viceroy, and now it was a matter of assuming this office in India. Within four months of his arrival "ulcers were forming in his neck", and he died on December 24th 1524.

Vasco da Gama's deeds were glorified by Camões in "The Lusiads".

Calouste Sarkis
Gulbenkian
(1869–1955)

Virtually every visitor to Lisbon will come across the name Gulbenkian. The son of a well-to-do Armenian petroleum dealer, Calouste Sarkis Gulbenkian was born near Istanbul on March 1st 1869 and studied engineering in London. So great was his success that as early as 1891 he was appointed adviser to the Ottoman court on petroleum matters. In the years that followed he became one of the most important experts in this field, and in 1911 he founded the Iraq Petroleum Company, incorporating all the biggest oil companies of the day. Gulbenkian's 5% share of the profits won him the nickname "Mr Five Per Cent" and also a huge fortune: at times he was reckoned to be the richest man in the world.

For the most part Gulbenkian invested his wealth in Great Britain. He had in fact held British nationality since 1902, but at the start of the Second World War the British confiscated Gulbenkian's goods and chattels as "enemy property". His efforts to leave the country were not successful until he managed to get to neutral Portugal in 1942. He settled in Lisbon, living in a suite in the Aviz Hotel (on the site of the present Sheraton) and set about rebuilding his fortune.

Calouste Gulbenkians' great love, after the oil business, was art ("I'm head over heels in love with beauty and every form of artistic expression"). Before the war and during his stay in Lisbon he collected choice works of art, buying Egyptian statuary and French furniture, Chinese porcelain and Turkish faïence, as well as works by Rembrandt, Rubens, Van Dyck, Frans Hals, Degas and Monet. Over the years he purchased some 5000 works of art, making him owner of one of the most important private collections in the world.

Gulbenkian lived in Lisbon until his death in 1955, and bequeathed his whole estate said to be over 66 million dollars, and works of art worth at that time 15 million dollars, to the Fundação Calouste Gulbenkian.

This foundation built a large cultural centre with several theatres, concert halls and cinemas, a library and a museum that has become world-famous since its opening in 1969. A centre for modern art was added to the complex in 1984.

Henry the
Navigator
(1394–1460)

Henry (Henrique in Portuguese), born the third son of King Joãos I on March 4th 1394, has gone down in history as "Henry the Navigator" (o Navegador), though he himself never went on any long sea voyages.

The Prince distinguished himself at the conquest of Ceuta (1415), and as a result his fame soon spread throughout Europe. The King granted him the titles of Duke of Viseu and Lord of Covilhã, at the same time entrusting him with the defence and administration of Ceuta.

It was then, if not before, that the prince began to take an interest in seafaring, poring over charts and documents and seeking information from seafarers. Otherwise, according to Zurora, the court biographer, he lived a very secluded life, dressing extremely simply, a man of deep piety and asceticism.

Henry's appointment in 1418 as Grand Master of the Order of Christ (the successor to the the Order of Knights Templar in Portugal) brought him huge financial resources. This allowed him from then on to turn his seafaring dreams into reality. He is thought to have built a kind of science centre at Sagres where geographical and nautical knowledge was developed. In the shipyards at nearby Lagos a new type of vessel was built, the caravel, which was far superior to conventional sailing ships in terms of manoevrability and seaworthiness.

Since Sagres was not suitable as a port because it lacked a hinterland, the voyages of exploration that Henry financed and organised set out from nearby Lagos, first discovering (or rediscovering) the islands

Calouste Sarkis Gulbenkian

Henry the Navigator

Marquês de Pombal

of Madeira (colonised by 1423), then the Azores (1427). Later Henry the Navigator's ships pressed on further along the west coast of Africa, reaching Cape Verde, Gambia and finally Guinea. Henry's seafaring enterprises, which laid the foundation for Portugal's development as a colonial power, were motivated as much by the struggle against Islam as by the desire to set up trading networks, and the lure of gold, spices and slaves.

By the end of his life Henry had nearly exhausted the vast riches of the Order of Christ, since the expenditure on the voyages of discovery was offset by very little in the way of income.

Henry the Navigator died of fever in his palace at Sagres on November 13th 1460.

Manuel (or Emanuel) I is also known as Manuel "the Great" or "the Fortunate" because it was under him that Portugal experienced its golden age.

Manuel I (1469–1521)

He was born in 1469, the youngest son of the Infante Fernando. When the heir to the throne, the Infante Afonso, died unexpectedly after a riding accident, Manuel was proclaimed King in Alcácer do Sal on October 27th 1495.

Manuel I used his marriage policy to establish close links with the Spanish royal house. His first marriage, in 1497, was to Isabella of Castile, the widow of the Infante Afonso. After her death he married her sister, Maria of Castile, who was to provide him with his heir, João III. His third and last wife was Leonor of Spain, who had, in fact, been promised to his son.

Manuel I's rule was aimed at strengthening royal power against the nobility. Administration was centralised, taxation and customs duties were standardised, and the "Fortunate King" was able to keep his country out of any wars, but above all Manuel's reign is associated with the voyages of discovery which he encouraged, primarily out of trading policy considerations. It was on his orders that Vasco da Gama found the sea route to India and Pedro Alvares Cabral sailed to Brazil. These seafaring feats made Lisbon Europe's paramount trading port, and riches poured into the country, leading to a great flowering in the arts and sciences and, above all, architecture. In their magnificent buildings Belém, Batalha and Tomar still bear impressive witness to the Manueline Style named after the king.

Portugal's "Golden Age" was, however, only short-lived, and had already passed its peak when Manuel died of a fever in Lisbon in 1521.

During his lifetime **Fernando Pessoa** – Fernando António Nogueira Pessoa, to give him his full name – who is considered to be Portugal's

Fernando Pessoa (1888–1935)

greatest poet after Camões, published nothing but various articles in newspapers and journals and just the one book. Only after his death was the discovery made of two trunks full of manuscripts, primarily fragments.

Fernando Pessoa was born in Lisbon on June 13th 1888. His childhood was sadly clouded by the premature death of his father. On his mother's second marriage, to the Portuguese consul in Durban, the whole family moved to South Africa. Pessoa grew up to be bilingual, enjoyed a good education and composed his first poems in English; until his death he continued to write poetry and stories in both English and Portuguese. With the intention of studying at the University of Lisbon, Pessoa went back to Portugal when he was seventeen, but found it hard to settle down there. He soon abandoned his studies, and made poetic writing the most important thing in his life. He earned his living doing foreign language correspondence for various Lisbon firms, and, since this only afforded him a modest income, lived with relatives or in furnished rooms.

To stop himself being lonely Fernando Pessoa had already begun as a boy to create companions to talk to in his poetry, and as an adult he lived almost without any human ties, in total isolation. He got over the situation by using several different names as a poet, signing his work not only with his own name but also Albert Caeira, Alvaro de Campos and Ricardo Reis. For Pessoa each of these poets' names represented an independent poetic personality complete with his own biography, a particular style and a special choice of themes.

Pessoa's utter introspection meant that there is little of any note to report about his private life. Apart from his mother there was only one woman in his life, a colleague called Ophélia. It was, he himself records, out of consideration for his poetic work that he decided not to marry her.

Towards the end of his life Pessoa became increasingly addicted to alcohol, dying of liver failure on November 30th 1935.

Sebastião José de Carvalho e Mello Marquês de Pombal (1699–1782)

Marquês de Pombal made a decisive impact on the history of his country as the man who paved the way for enlightened despotism. Born into Lisbon's minor aristocracy, his first experiences of the diplomatic service were as envoy to London and Vienna, where he also dealt particularly with economic matters. José I appointed him Foreign Secretary in 1750 and Prime Minister in 1756.

Pombal proved skilful at carrying out the offices he held entirely to suit his own ideas, although he showed himself none too squeamish about the means he judged necessary to achieve his long-term ends. He saw his most important tasks as reorganising state finances, reforming education, promoting trade and industry so as to get free of Britain's economic hegemony, and the abolition of slavery.

The part he played in the reconstruction of Lisbon after the devastating earthquake of 1755 was outstanding. He fought passionately with the Jesuits and minor nobility whose inherited privilege stood in the way of his attempts at reform.

The Marquês lost favour after the death of José I and in 1781 the pressure from his many enemies brought about his banishment to Pombal where he died the following year.

Amália da Piedade Rodriques (b. 1920)

Amália Rodrigues ranks as the most famous fado singer of the 20th c. Amália, as she is usually known, was born in Lisbon in July 1920. She was raised by her grandparents in slum conditions in the harbour area of Alcântara. From an early age her extraordinary vocal talents attracted much attention. She very soon realised that she could make more money from singing than from selling fruit in the street, the means by which she and her sister Celeste had until then managed to pay for the basic necessities of life.

At the age of 18 she started out on a fairy-tale career which took her from "poor girl of the harbour area" to "lady of the world". At 19 she appeared for the first time on the stage of the Retiro de Severa, a very well-known Lisbon fado restaurant of the time. A year later she enjoyed her first success in the musical theatre. She was 23 when made her debut outside the country, in Madrid. Shortly afterwards she was singing in the Olympia in Paris, in Casablanca, Rio de Janeiro, Rome, Berlin and later in Sweden, Turkey, Japan, the USSR, Africa and South America. Thus she brought the fado on to the worldwide stage. Her greatest successes were and still are "uma casa portuguesa", "nem às paredes confesso" and "barco negro". In the 1940s Amália Rodrigues also appeared in some of the best-known Portuguese films in the part of the *fadista*, the interpreter of the fado.

Her great popularity was cemented in 1990 when, to mark her 70th birthday and 50 years on the stage, a large exhibition in honour of the legendary fadista was held in the Lisbon Theatrical Museum. A biography was also published and five new CDs of her major hits were issued.

Verdicts differ widely on the politician António de Oliveira Salazar. Some see him as a repressor *par excellence* while others view him as the man who helped his country to regain respect and a degree of prosperity.

António de Oliveira Salazar (1889–1970)

Salazar was born into a modest background on April 28th 1889 in a small village in the Dão valley, the son of an estate steward. He had a happy childhood imbued with the values of Catholicism. At eleven he entered the seminary at Viseu where he was to be educated by the Jesuits until he was twenty. In 1910 he went to Coimbra to study law and economics, earning his living by undertaking various teaching duties. His academic career progressed smoothly, and in 1916 he became professor of economics at Coimbra, quickly making a name for himself as a finance expert. In 1928 Carmona brought him into the government as Minister of Finance, and in 1932 he was promoted to Prime Minister, an office he held until 1968. The new constitution adopted in 1932 provided him with the basis for an elitist, authoritarian state (with only about 16% of the population permitted to vote), which he headed, backed by the União Nacional that he founded.

During his 40 years in government Salazar succeeded in reorganising the country's finances, improving the administration, taking a firmer stand on corruption and, last but not least, keeping Portugal out of the Second World War. However, Salazar implemented his policies using total censorship and a state security police (the PIDE) which did not hesitate to use terror and torture. The independence movements in Portugal's overseas territories were ruthlessly suppressed.

Privately Salazar lived extremely simply and in some seclusion, hating anything like a personality cult and was always reserved towards his friends, in so far as he could be said to have any. His closest confidante in his final years could be considered to have been his housekeeper, Dona Maria.

In September 1968 Salazar suffered a stroke, leaving him paralysed on his left side and unable to work. Marcello Caetano was appointed the new Prime Minister but Salazar still sometimes believed he was in charge right up until his death on July 27th 1970.

Art and Culture

General

Until the 12th c. Portugal to a great extent shared the destinies of its neighbour Spain. With the emergence of a Portuguese national consciousness in the reign of King Afonso Henriques (1139–85) there began also the country's independent artistic development – though political circumstances often involved a close relationship with Spain. Throughout its history Portuguese art reflects a great variety of influences: the old pre-Christian and pagan heritage, the Christian civilisation of Asturias, itself strongly influenced by France, Moorish culture, vigorous folk elements and later echoes of the cultures of Portuguese colonial territories in India, Africa and South America.

Phoenicians, Greeks, Carthaginians

Although this old-established area of settlement, occupied by the stocky and dark-skinned Iberians, and later by the mixed race of Celtiberians, lay on the outermost edge of Europe, remote from the rest of the Western world, it was already being visited in antiquity by seafaring Mediterranean peoples. At the mouth of the Tagus the Phoenicians established a staging point on the route to Britain which they called *Alis Ubbo*, later known as Olisipo and now as Lisbon. Thereafter Greeks and Carthaginians also settled at Alis Ubbo.

Romans

Under the Romans – who took almost 200 years (until A.D. 19) to subdue the Iberians – the Romanisation of the province of Lusitania proceeded relatively slowly (prehistoric and Roman antiquities in the Archaeological and Ethnological Museum at Belém, near Lisbon). In

There is countless evidence of a megalith culture to be found in the area around Évora: stone circle in Xeres

A huge aqueduct was erected in Elvas in the 16–17th century on the site of an old Roman plumbing system

Lisbon (*Felicitas Iulia*), which during the Roman period was apparently a place of no particular consequence compared with Mérida in Spain, few Roman remains have been preserved (Open-air Archaeological Museum in the church of the Carmo which was destroyed by the 1755 earthquake). On the highest point in the town of Évora, which seems to have been a flourishing place in Roman times (*Liberalitas Iulia*), are the impressive remains, with 14 Corinthian columns, of a temple of the 2nd or 3rd c. A.D., traditionally ascribed to Diana. The temple, of which the cella is missing, was converted into a fortress in the Middle Ages and restored only in 1870.

During the period of Roman rule numbers of *villae rusticae* – country houses – were built by Roman landowners, the forerunners of the *quintas* which are so characteristic of Portugal. Some of the finest of these are: the famous Quinta das Lágrimas ("House of Tears") near Coimbra (see A to Z), in the gardens of which Pedro I's tragic bride Inês de Castro was murdered in 1355; the Quinta da Penha Verde, near Sintra, built in the 16th c. by Dom João de Castro, fourth Viceroy of India, with a beautiful park (round chapel in Renaissance style, with 17th c. faïence, probably by Miguel de Arruda); and the Oriental-style Quinta de Monserrate, also near Sintra (see A to Z), built in 1856 for Sir Francis Cook, which likewise has beautiful gardens.

The site of Conimbriga (see A to Z Coimbra), a Roman town originally founded in the 2nd c. B.C. and destroyed by the Suevi in A.D. 468, has yielded remains of walls, an aqueduct, fountains and baths with magnificent mosaics (Museu Monográfic, near the excavations). In Coimbra, which took over the name of Conimbriga after its destruction, Roman remains can be seen in the Museu Machado de Castro, housed in the former Bishop's Palace in the Largo da Feira, a picturesque old building originally dating from the Romanesque period (restored 1529). There are also remains of Roman buildings at Beja (*Pax Iulia*;

walls and an arched gateway) and at Milreu in the Algarve (*Ossonoba*, discovered 1876).

Migration, Visigoths

The Great Migrations brought Germanic peoples into Portugal – the Vandals, the Suevi and the Visigoths, who originally settled in the Roman provinces as *foederati*. These were allies of Rome, who were granted land in return for the performance of certain services, but who established their own independent states after the fall of the Western Empire. Thus the Suevi established themselves in the north, with Braga as their capital and Oporto as their port, while the southern part of the country was incorporated in the Visigothic kingdom. Surviving buildings from the Visigoth period are the Byzantine-style chapel of São Frutuoso, near Braga, and the hall-church of São Pedro de Balsemão at Lamego.

Moors

After the battle of La Janda in 711 Portugal fell into the hands of the Moors, but was of relatively minor importance compared with the Spanish part of the Caliphate. Lisbon, now known as Al Oshbuna or Lashbuna, probably changed relatively little under Moorish rule; the castle, originally built by the Visigoths in the 5th c. (now the Castelo de São Jorge), became the Moorish king's residence. Moorish rule seems to have left a more obvious mark on the Algarve, and certain features (house types, chimneys) are often ascribed to Moorish influence – though it must be said that this has not been established beyond doubt. Buildings of the Moorish period – and indeed of the Migration period – are few and far between in Portugal, but the churches at Mértola and Lourosa (10th c.) are based on Moorish models.

Reconquista

The Reconquista, the recovery of Christian territory from the Moors, left a distinctive imprint on Portugal. Starting from Asturias in the middle of the 8th c., it moved south stage by stage and was concluded by the occupation of the Algarve in 1249.

Romanesque

The art and architecture of the Romanesque period in Portugal were influenced both by the magnificent cathedral of Santiago de Compostela in north-west Spain and by the architecture of France (particularly Auvergne and Normandy). Evidence of these influences can be seen in the cathedrals (originally designed as defensive structures) of Lisbon, Coimbra, Évora, Oporto and Braga.

Lisbon Cathedral (the Sé: Latin *sedes*, the "seat" of the bishop; see A to Z Lisbon), the oldest church in the city, is said to have been built by Afonso Henriques in 1147 on the site of an earlier mosque. Over the centuries it was much altered and rebuilt, and its Romanesque lantern tower and Gothic choir were destroyed by the 1755 earthquake; but the Romanesque nave, triforium and aisles still survive. The fortress-like west front dates from 1380. The cloister contains a fine Romanesque wrought-iron screen). Oporto Cathedral (see A to Z), also built in the 12th c. on the site of a Suevic castle, was originally Gothic but was completely rebuilt in the 17th and 18th c. There are remains of a late Romanesque cloister and its Gothic successor of 1385. The interior is notable for its richly decorated altars (silver Altar of the Sacrament, 1632–72). The Old Cathedral of Coimbra (see A to Z), built by Afonso Henriques in 1170, has a sumptuously decorated west doorway surmounted by a balcony and a window. The richly decorated north doorway (Porta Especiosa, *c.* 1530), like the severe 12th c. façade, betrays French influence. The high altar, in Flamboyant style, is of polychrome carved wood (by Oliver of Ghent and John of Ypres, 1503); the Manueline font is by John of Rouen. Braga Cathedral (see A to Z), begun in 1180 was much altered in later centuries, and the Romanesque cloister (1110) was demolished in the 18th c. Évora Cathedral (see A to Z), with its beautiful tower and imposing interior, dates mainly from the 13th c. The last of the great Romanesque cathedrals, it already shows the strong influence of French Gothic.

The order of Templars, which came to Portugal in 1126, began in 1160 to build a new stronghold at Tomar (see A to Z), which in the early 12th c. had stood on the frontier between Christendom and Islam. Little is left of this fortress but a commanding square watch-tower. After the suppressions of the Templars the castle was taken over by the order of the Knights of Christ, which rose to great magnificence, particularly under the Grand Master Henry the Navigator. The wealthiest order in Christendom during the reign of Manuel I (1495–1521), this knightly order became a monastic one in 1523 and was dissolved in 1910. The Convent-Castle of the Knights of Christ at Tomar is a large complex of buildings ranging in date from the 12th to the 17th c. and in style from Romanesque to Baroque. Following the model of the round church originally built by Constantine the Great over the Holy Sepulchre in Jerusalem, frequently destroyed and regularly rebuilt, the Templars built round Churches of the Holy Sepulchre all over Europe. The Templar church at Tomar is a sixteen-sided structure of Syro-Byzantine type on a centralised plan. It was begun in 1160 with a central octagon, which in the time of Manuel I became the high choir (*coro alto, capela-mór*) of the church of the Knights of Christ, the nave of which was enlarged in Manueline style by Diogo de Arruda after 1510. The magnificent south doorway was the work of João de Castilho (1510). The conventual buildings around the church have a number of interesting cloisters.

Templar Castle in Tomar

Little sculpture of the Romanesque period has been preserved in Portugal, and much, even of the monumental sculpture, has been lost. The only item calling for mention is the tomb of Egas Moniz (1144) in the Romanesque church of the Benedictine monastery at Paço de Sousa near Oporto.

Romanesque Sculpture

The Cistercians, who like the Templars were summoned to Portugal by Afonso Henriques, built a series of abbey churches which mark the final establishment of the Gothic style in Portugal. Gothic architecture was strongly influenced by France; but during the 13th and 14th c. different European countries evolved their own distinctive variants of the style.

Gothic

The cathedral at Évora, consecrated in 1204, already shows indications of the transition to a somewhat severe form of Gothic in Portugal. The Franciscan convent at Santarém (see A to Z), completed in 1240 and now unfortunately in a state of considerable dilapidation, has a fine cloister of the 13th–15th c. with pointed arches and charming twin columns.

The Cistercian abbey of Alcobaça (see A to Z), founded by Afonso Henriques in 1153, was a daughter house of Clairvaux in Burgundy and is built on the same plan as Clairvaux. The church was consecrated in 1253 but the building of the abbey continued into the 14th c. Much rebuilding was required to make good the devastation caused by the 1755 earthquake, flooding and Napoleon's troops. The church – an austere hall-church in early Gothic style with pointed vaulting – contains the tombs of Pedro I and his beloved Inês de Castro, with a profusion of figural decoration along the sides and recumbent figures of Pedro and Inês, lying with their feet towards one another so that they would see one another at once on the day of resurrection (14th c.). Other notable features in the church are a 17th c. terracotta group depicting the death of St Bernard and two fine Renaissance doors by João de Castilho.

On the north side of the church is the impressive two-storey Claustro do Silêncio (or Claustro de Dom Dinis), a jewel of Cistercian Gothic

Alcobaça Abbey

built in 1311 (upper storey 16th c.), with pointed vaulting and triple windows, separated by twin colonettes and surmounted by rosettes, opening into the central garden. The two-storey hexagonal fountain-house has 16th c. relief decoration.

Other Gothic
Buildings

The octagonal Dominican church (consecrated 1267) at Elvas (see A to Z), with an azulejo-faced dome supported on columns, is the first master-work of Gothic architecture in Portugal. With its wide aisles and five chapels it is a marvel of simplicity and restrained elegance of proportion. The steadily increasing refinement of Portuguese Gothic, originally somewhat severe, can be observed in the romantic remains of the convent of Santa Clare-a-Velha in Coimbra (1286; see A to Z), now partly silted up by the flooding of the River Mondego (west wall with fine rose window, Renaissance chapels). In addition to the beautiful Gothic cloisters already referred to, which rank among the finest achievements of Gothic architecture in Portugal, with their two tiers of galleries, their sturdy pillars and their graceful arches, mention should also be made of the cloister of Lisbon Cathedral.

During this period King Dinis (1279–1325) caused a series of mighty fortresses to be built along the frontiers of his kingdom – the Torre de Menagem at Bragança, the castle of Leiria (originally founded by Afonso Henriques in 1135 and enlarged by Dinis; the Gothic chapel attributed to Master Huguet of Batalha) and the castle at Beja (see entries A to Z).

Batalha Abbey

The finest example of 14th c. Gothic architecture in Portugal is the church of Batalha Abbey (1388–1402; see A to Z), built to commemorate the decisive Portuguese victory over Castile at Aljubarrota in 1385. One of the great achievements of Christian architecture, the church is now a Portuguese national shrine. The architects involved in building the Batalha church were Afonso Domingues (d. before 1402), Master Huguet, probably a Frenchman (attested until 1438), Martin Vásques (d. before 1448), Fernão d'Évora (d. 1477) and the famous João de Castilho (d. before 1553). The interior of the church, with fine stained glass (particularly in the choir) and massive piers, is of impressive effect. The square Founder's Chapel contains a number of notable tombs – the sarcophagus, supported on lions, of João I (d. 1433) and his English queen, Philippa of Lancaster, and the monuments of the Infante Fernardo (Caldéron's "Steadfast Prince") and Henry the Navigator (d. 1460). The west front of the church with its sculptural decoration and the richly articulated south side are seen to particular effect, due to the open location of the church. Adjoining the church are three cloisters – the Claustro de João III (destroyed in 1811), the 15th c. Claustro de Dom Afonso V with its simple lines and the Claustro Real, a truly royal cloister laid out around a garden-like court which is a masterpiece and a perfect exemplar of Portuguese Gothic, with arched galleries which range from the simplest forms to fantastic riots of Manueline ornament and offer charming glimpses of the fountain-house. On the east side of the cloister is the chapterhouse, with pointed vaulting. At the east end of the church are the Capelas Imperfeitas (Unfinished Chapels), with seven funerary chapels enclosing a central octagon; the tombs include those of King Duarte I and his wife Eleanor of Aragon.

Gothic Sculpture

Cistercian Gothic paid little attention to sculpture: only funerary sculpture flourished. Notable among tombs of the 14th c. are those of Archbishop Gonçalo Pereira (1336) in Braga Cathedral, and of Pedro I and Inês de Castro at Alcobaça which have already been referred to.

Manueline Style

The period of prosperity and cultural flowering in the reign of Manuel I (1495–1521) led to the emergence of a "Batalha school" and the development of a distinctively Portuguese version of late Gothic. This

*The Batalha monastery was built in memory of Portugal's decisive
independence battle against Spain in 1358*

Manueline style incorporates Early Renaissance features, elements
taken over from the Moorish Mudéjar style and Oriental and Indian
influences. It is notable for its delightful ornament, which – as in the
Plateresque style of Spain – often includes naturalistic details,
with a marked preference for the world of the sea and seafaring
(e.g. twisted ropes, knots, shells, coral, etc.), symbolising the
territories which Portugal had won under the leadership of Henry the
Navigator.

The most striking example of the Manueline style is the Hieronymite
convent at Belém (now a suburb of Lisbon; see A to Z), which mira-
culously survived the 17th c. earthquake unscathed. Designed by an
architect named Boytac (Boitac, Boytaca, Boutaca, etc.; see Famous
People), probably a Frenchman, it was begun in 1502. The south doorway of the church has a profusion of sculptural decoration expressing
the new power and wealth of Portugal. The west doorway, strongly
reminiscent of a doorway at Champmol, near Dijon (Burgundy), was
the work of Nicolas Chanterene. The interior of the church, of the type
known as *igrejas salões* (saloon churches), is notable for its width
and fine proportions and for the delicately carved decoration of the
piers. The church contains the sarcophagus of Vasco da Gama and
the cenotaph (empty tomb) of the poet Luís de Camões. Adjoining the
church is a magnificent two-storey cloister. Both the church and
the cloister were completed by João Castilho, the great master of the
Manueline style.

Hieronymite
Convent at Belém

Another splendid Manueline building is the Tower of Belém (Torre de
Belém; see A to Z Lisbon) commanding the Tagus estuary, built between 1515 and 1521 by Francisco Arruda, brother of the famous
architect Diogo de Arruda who worked at Tomar. With its flat domes,

Other Manueline
Buildings

elegant loggias, Arab-style twin windows and intricate stone tracery the Tower is of strikingly Arab and Moorish style.

Other fine examples of the Manueline style at Batalha and Tomar have already been mentioned. Also of interest is the famous Manueline window of the old chapterhouse at Tomar (by Diogo de Arruda) with its striking and very typical ornament, here carried to excess.

Sintra, once the summer residence of the Portuguese kings, has three castles – the Castelo dos Mouros, the old Moorish castle (7th–8th c., much altered in later periods), the Palácio da Pena (19th c.) and the Paço Real or Royal Palace (14th–15th/16th c.), on the foundations of an earlier Moorish castle; it is built in a Manueline style which shows clear Mudéjar influence.

Manueline
Sculpture

The Manueline style laid great stress on architectural sculpture, and Coimbra became the place of origin of two schools of sculpture, one of which, stimulated by influence from Rouen, played an important part in bringing the Renaissance to Portugal. Nicolas Chanterene was responsible for the north doorway of the abbey church at Belém and for the tombs of Afonso Henriques and his son Sancho I in the church of the Santa Cruz convent at Coimbra, while to John of Rouen (João de Ruão) is attributed the Porta Especiosa of the Old Cathedral, Coimbra. Other notable foreign sculptors working in Portugal were Loguin and Oliver of Ghent (polychrome wood sculpture in the dome of the Rotunda at Tomar). The other, more "national" school continued to work in the traditional style; a leading member of the school was Diogo Pires the Younger. Fine work was still produced in the field of funerary sculpture (tomb monuments), while the goldsmith's art which had long flourished in Portugal created some of its finest achievements.

Pelourinhos

Between the 12th and the 18th c. the stone columns known as *pelourinhos* or pillories were erected in towns and villages all over Portugal.

Pelourinho in Óbidos . . .   *. . . and in Elvas*

They were not, however, primarily designed for the punishment of thieves and other criminals but were emblems of municipal or feudal authority (*pelouro* = local authority). This function explains both the form of the pelourinhos, which are often elaborately decorated, and the choice of site, usually near areas of secular or ecclesiastical authority such as town halls and bishop's palaces. The pelourinhos erected in the 16th c. have the sumptuous decoration of the Manueline style. Columns of this type are particularly numerous, reflecting the large number of communities which were granted charters of privileges by Manuel I.

The shaft of the column, richly decorated, may be cylindrical, conical, prismatic or spiral in form; occasionally it may resemble an obelisk. The summit also has sculptural decoration, often including the sword of justice as a symbol of legal jurisdiction.

The Mudéjar style is the particular architectural and decorative style **Mudéjar Style**
practised by the Moors who were allowed to stay on after the Reconquest and by Christians imitating them. It is basically a late Gothic style incorporating Moorish elements, and often with Manueline features. Particular marks of Moorish influence are the beautiful dark-coloured coffered ceilings and above all the use of azulejos, one of the most characteristic features of Portuguese art (see Baedeker Special pp. 62/63).

Portugal's political and economic decline, beginning at the end of the **Renaissance**
heroic age after the disastrous Moroccan campaign of 1580, also had its effect on the country's artistic development.

The choir of the monastic church at Belém betrays the influence of the High Renaissance (marble choir-stalls; royal tombs supported on marble elephants). But on the whole the Renaissance – its influence postponed and weakened by the great flowering of the Manueline style – never really established itself in Portugal, in spite of the country's intensive cultural and economic contacts with Italy, but remained a phenomenon of merely marginal importance.

An example of Late Renaissance architecture, though much influenced **Foreign influences**
by the Manueline style, is the Claustro dos Filipes, the main cloister of the Convent-Castle of Tomar (see A to Z). This was begun by João de Castilho, but work was suspended after his death in 1551, and when it was resumed in 1562 the Neo-Classical Palladian style had come into fashion. The new architects were either trained in Italy, like Diogo de Torralva, or were themselves Italian, like Filippo Terzi. The latter built the church of São Roque in Lisbon (façade rebuilt after the 1755 earthquake; see A to Z), a fine example of the Jesuit style, with an impressive interior (trompe-l'oeil painting). The church contains a masterpiece of the most sumptuous Italian Baroque in the form of the Chapel of St John the Baptist, originally built in Rome in 1742, then dismantled and re-erected in São Roque in the reign of João V. The church of São Vicente de Fora in Lisbon (the tower of which collapsed in the 1755 earthquake) was also built by Terzi.

The influence of foreign artists remained considerable after the Portuguese revival (under the Portuguese kings of the House of Bragança from 1640): the native power of artistic creation appeared to be exhausted.

The development of Portuguese painting followed a roughly parallel **Painting from the**
course to that of Spain. The first individual artistic personality emerged **15th to the 18th c.**
in Nuno Gonçalves (active between 1450 and 1480), whose principal work is the famous altarpiece, the "Adoration of St Vincent", a polyptych with numerous figures which clearly shows the influence of Flemish models (Museu Nacional de Arte Antiga, Lisbon). There followed a flowering of late medieval painting which lasted until the middle of the 16th c., its finest achievements being in the field of portraiture.

Tiles, Tiles Everywhere

Historical pictures often contain some quaint and curious features – such as the one in the entrance hall to the Augustinian priory of São Vicente de Fora in Lisbon, where the observer is instructed about the taking of the town by Afonso Henriques in 1147: on the shield of the first king of Portugal can be seen the coat-of-arms with the seven castles, although the said arms were not in fact created until later; and in the painting of what was still a Moorish town can be seen the cathedral looking just as it did in the 18th century with its two Baroque towers (later removed). On closer examination still more anachronisms can be discovered. Above all, however, note the form of the "painting"; it consists of *azulejos*, painted and glazed ceramic tiles measuring 14cm×14cm/5½in.×5½in., and is one of the most beautiful tile-pictures in Portugal.

Everywhere in Portugal – on Madeira and in the Azores as well as on the mainland – azulejos can be found on the walls of of churches, chapels, monasteries, palaces and mansions, in ordinary houses, on park seats, fountains, staircases, floors, in town halls, post-offices, market halls, restaurants and railway stations. Sometimes the tiles are beautifully ornamented or decorated with exotic animals and flowers; sometimes they portray scenes from Portugal's history or episodes from Greek mythology or perhaps the fables of La Fontaine; they might depict hunting scenes, show the country's most ravishing sights, provide plans of towns or serve as street signs, name-plates or house numbers. Portugal without its azulejos is unthinkable! However, these ornamental glazed tiles are in fact not a Portuguese invention, as they came originally from Persia. The Moors brought azulejos to the Iberian Peninsula (the name is probably derived from the Arabic *az-zuleycha* for mosaic pieces, rather than from *azul*, which is Spanish/Portuguese for blue). The first tiles which were imported to Portugal in the 14th century portrayed – in accordance with Islamic law – no human figures, only geometric patterns or plant-like ornamentation. So that the different colours did not run into one another during the firing process they were separated either by greased cord (the cuerda-seca method) or by raised divisions (the cuenca technique), giving the azulejos a relief-like surface. When the Moorish kingdom of Granada came to an end the Portuguese initially obtained supplies from the Moorish tile-makers who remained. However, in the second half of the 16th century, when stocks of such tiles dwindled after the Moors were expelled from Spain and the majolica technique developed by Italian and Flemish craftsmen became more widespread in Europe, the first azulejo factories were established in Portugal, especially in Lisbon, Oporto and Coimbra. Thanks to the majolica technique tiles could now be made with a flat surface instead of in relief. They were given a white tin glaze on which the designs were painted in metallic pigments without the risk of the colours running into one another.

Gradually the Portuguese tile-painters weaned themselves off ornamental decoration à l'arabe and employed human and animal figures in their designs; everyday life became the focal point of decorative art. The predominant colours were blue, yellow, green and white. In the 17th century *azulejos de tapete* became fashionable. These were large, carpet-like tiles incorporating compositions in blue, white and yellow and embracing all conceivable subjects – Christian legends, historical and patriotic events, hunting and even amorous scenes. At the end of the 17th century Dutch merchants imported into Europe individual blue and white Ming dynasty tiles from China; the Portuguese welcomed the new fashionable colours with enthusiasm. Massive azulejo paintings in all shades of blue soon appeared. Later multi-coloured tiles – predominantly green, blue and yellow – came back into fashion. The introduction of Baroque art into Portugal about 1700 produced a boom in the production of azulejos; most of those which can today be admired in the country's churches, palaces, parks and staircases date from this period. The great earthquake of 1755, which affected Lisbon in particular, brought this boom to an end. A form of mass production became essential to facilitate the rebuilding of the damaged houses and city areas. For this purpose King José I founded the Royal Factory (Real Fábrico do Rato). Here, however, the tiles were painted with the aid of stencils and templates and thus the designs were inevitably of lesser quality.

In the early 19th century, when the court fled to Brazil and the country was convulsed by civil war, the production of azulejos ceased almost completely. By the middle of the century, however, they enjoyed a revival in popularity and benefited from the new industrial processes introduced from Great Britain. The tiles no longer needed to be painted by hand with a brush; the pattern was printed on, making the product much cheaper. Following the Brazilian model, tiles now began to be used for the decoration, both externally and internally, of ordinary middle-class houses and commercial, municipal and other public buildings throughout the country. Since then artists have been inspired when painting azulejos by the various building styles and art trends – from Art Nouveau via Art Déco to abstract art.

Even though at one time it seemed that tile-painting might disappear completely from Portuguese architecture, azulejos have again enjoyed a boom since the 1960s and now decorate the façades and interiors of hotels, banks, offices and underground stations, employing traditional as well as modern abstract scenes. These tiles are not only decorative, they also protect against damp, heat and noise, keep the fronts of buildings clean and protect the underlying brickwork.

Nowadays only two or three azulejos manufacturers in Oporto and Lisbon produce truly hand-made tiles; however, the bulk of their products are exported to wealthier customers abroad. Perhaps you too – like many before you – will treat yourself to some azulejos as a small, but rather expensive, memento of your holiday?

Azulejos in Fronteira Palace

In addition to Gonçalves, leading figures of this period included Jorge Afonso (d. after 1540) who had a studio in Lisbon, Guilherme de Belles, João Mestre (d. 1528), Luis de Velasco, António Taca and Vasco Fernandes (b. about 1542), known as Grão Vasco, who worked in Viseu (works in Museu Grão Vasco, Viseu).

During the reign of João III the Dutch "Romanist" school exerted still stronger influence on Portuguese painters including Gregório Lopes (d. 1550: "Salome", "St Augustine"), but particularly on Cristóvão de Figueiredo (attested between 1515 and 1540: retable on high altar of Santa Cruz church, Coimbra) and the Master of Santa Auta ("Martyrdom of the 11,000 Virgins", Museu Nacional de Arte Antiga, Lisbon).

The next generation of painters – represented, for example, by Cristóvão Lopes (1516–1606) – show Italian influence, now coming direct and no longer through Flemish intermediaries. The old tradition of portrait-painting, a notable practitioner of which was Cristóvão de Morais, declined in importance with the departure of A. Sanchez Coelho (1513–90) for the Spanish court.

During the Baroque period painting was of subordinate importance, being used mainly for the decoration of palaces and the vaulting of churches. Painters of this period include Francisco Vieira Lusitano (1699–1783), the fresco-painter Domingos António de Sequeira (1769–1837), Francisco Portuense (1765–1805) and Pedro Carvalho Alexandrino (1730–1810).

Baroque

In the field of Baroque architecture a leading place is occupied by the massive complex at Mafra (see A to Z), planned on the model of the Spanish Escorial to include a royal palace, a church and a monastery in a unified group and built between 1717 and 1770. This enormous building, designed by two German architects, Johann Friedrich Ludwig and his son Johann Peter Ludwig, broke away from the severity of Spanish Baroque with its profusion of decoration and its chinoiserie and influenced a whole architectural generation in the late Baroque and Rococo periods, which became steadily more luxuriant and fantastic. At the same time there was a great flowering of azulejos.

Taljas douradas

In the early Baroque period there first appears in Portugal an ornate form of decorative art which was to achieve its finest flowering here, though it was also practised in Spain and other countries. This was the wood sculpture covered with gold leaf known as talhas douradas, predominantly used in religious art. In many 18th c. churches in Portugal altars, walls, recesses, domes and ceilings were covered either in whole or in part with carving of this kind, foliage and arabesques combining with figures in rich decorative patterns.

Foreign Influences

Foreign architects also worked in Oporto, where an Italian, Nicoló Mazzoni, built the church of the Clérigos with its fine Capela-mór and famous tower (1732–48). The French architect J. B. Robillon completed the royal palace at Queluz, which had been begun in 1758 by Mateus Vicente (1747–86) on the model of Versailles – a likeness which is enhanced by the park, laid out in the style of Le Nôtre. The interior is of great magnificence, the Throne Room and the Hall of the Ambassadors being particularly fine.

Baroque Sculpture

The sculpture of the Baroque period – affected, like architecture and painting, by Portugal's cultural decline in the 17th c. – can claim few artists of any importance apart from Joaquim Machado de Castro (1736–1828), whose vigorous work can be seen on the sumptuous façade of the late Baroque Basilica da Estrêla in Lisbon, built in the Roman style at the end of the 18th c.

The great earthquake on All Saints' Day in 1755, which laid Lisbon in ruins and spread alarm throughout Europe, offered a unique opportunity for architects and town planners, which José I's chief minister the Marquês de Pombal, ruling in the spirit of enlightened absolutism, was quick to grasp. Rebuilt under the direction of Eugénio dos Santos, Lisbon became one of the finest capitals in Europe.

The new town thus created (though the wide Avenida da Liberdade and the Praça do Marquês de Pombal, with the huge monument to Pombal, were not completed until the end of the 19th c.) is laid out on spacious lines. Streets intersect at right angles and there are three superb squares: the Praça da Figueira, the even larger Praça de Dom Pedro IV (Rossio) and the Praça do Comércio (Terreiro do Paça), one of the most famous squares in the world, with an equestrian statue of José I (by Joaquim Machado de Castro, 1755). The uniform layout of the square and its three ranges of arcaded buildings with coloured façades contrast attractively with the surprising width of the fourth side, and with its marble steps leading down to the Tagus, is reminiscent of St Mark's Square in Venice.

Planned Redevelopment of Lisbon

After the catastrophe of the 1775 earthquake there was a general reaction against the decorative excesses of Baroque and Rococo, and a more sober Neo-Classicism came into vogue. In Lisbon work began in 1802 on the Palácio da Ajuda, which remained unfinished and has been completed only in recent years as a convention complex; the Teatro Nacional de Dona Maria II was built on the Rossio in 1846. In Oporto the church of the Third Order of St Francis was built, not to be confused with the adjoining church of São Francisco, originally Gothic, with a Renaissance doorway altered in the Baroque period.

Neo-Classicism

Although the Neo-Classical school of architecture long remained dominant, the school known as Historicism, with its romantic leanings towards the past, became established in Portugal, as elsewhere in Europe, in the second half of the 19th c. French influence can be detected but so, too, can influences from Britain and Germany, as in the Palácio da Pena at Sintra (1840–50; see A to Z), built for Ferdinand of Saxe-Coburg-Koháry by Baron Eschwege in the style of a medieval castle (borrowing some ideas from the extraordinary castles built for King Ludwig II of Bavaria). This fantastic mixture of styles – Arab, Gothic, Manueline, Renaissance, Baroque – has a curious charm. A striking and typical feature is the monstrous figure above the main entrance, a riot of fancy which is half man, half fish or tree. Other examples of Historicist architecture are the Moorish-style bullring in the Campo Pequeno in Lisbon (1892) and the Palace Hotel in the beautiful Buçaco Forest (now a national park, with many rare trees), a Neo-Manueline structure built at the end of the 19th c. as a royal summer residence.

Historicism

Portugal is especially rich in fine parks and gardens, illustrating the development of landscape architecture from the Moorish style by way of the formal gardens of the Baroque period to the more natural English style.

Parks and Gardens

Modern art and architecture were slow to establish themselves in Portugal. Gustave Eiffel, best known for the Eiffel Tower in Paris, built the Ponte de Dom Luís I in Oporto, the famous two-storey bridge which spans the Douro at an impressive height (1877–78), and was also responsible for the Elevador de Santa Justa, the lift which links the upper and lower towns of Lisbon. About 1940 the massive complex of the University City (Cidade Universitária) was built in Lisbon. The monumental style of an authoritarian regime found expression in the huge figure of Christ the King (1959) on the left bank of the Tagus near Lisbon and the 52m/170ft high Monument of the Discoveries (Padrão dos Descrombrimentos, 1960) on the banks of the Tagus at Belém. The Ponte do 25 de Abril (originally Ponte Salazar, 1966), a suspension

Modern

Lisbon: Monument of the Disoveries ...   *... and the bridge over the Tagus*

bridge 2227m/2436yd long which provides a rapid link between Lisbon and southern Portugal, is an impressive technological achievement. Worth mentioning is Alvaro Siza Viera (b. 1933 in Oporto). He devoted himself in the mid-70s to building single family houses, a priority of housing estates such as the São Victorin quarter in Oporto and the Barrio da Malagueria in Évora. Opinions are divided on the "post-modern" architecture of the Eighties. One of the country's best-known architects is currently Tomás Taveira whose Amoreiras Center in Lisbon is one of Portugal's largest and most elegant shopping malls.

19th and 20th c.
Painting

In painting, developments in the 19th c. followed the general European pattern. Notable figures during this period were the portrait-painter Miguel Lupi (1826–83), Tomás de Anunciação (1818–79) and the landscape artist António Carvalho da Silva (1850–93). The "Grupo de Leão", established in 1881, had close affinities with Impressionism. The portrait and fresco painter Columbano (1867–1929) remained within the romantic tradition. Other schools also had their adherents, including Fauvism, Cubism – a leading representative of which was Amadeu de Souza Cardoso (1887–1918) – and a rather strident revolutionary Naturalism. Between the two world wars the Futurist Almada Negreiros gained a considerable reputation with his tapestries and frescoes.

The Salazar regime discouraged artists with unduly progressive leanings, and only after the "Carnation Revolution" of 1974 did Portuguese art fall into line with the international movements of the day. A great reputation is enjoyed by the Franco-Portuguese woman painter Maria Helena Vieira da Silva (b. 1908). Lourdés Castro (b. 1930 in Funchalm, Madeira) is a sculptress whose figures are mounted on coloured plastic panels.

House Types in
Rural Portugal

Situated as it is on the western margin of Europe, exposed to influences from other countries only on the north and east, Portugal has

A farmstead in the south of Portugal (Algarve)

developed its own distinctive house types, particularly in rural areas. As in many southern countries, building is mostly in stone. The peasants' houses and farmhouses usually have no more than two storeys.

In Minho the two-storey house type is common, with stables and working areas on the lower floor and living accommodation on the upper storey, usually opening on to a balcony and reached by an external stair. Characteristic features of this northern region are the *espigueiros*, small granaries or storehouses built on piles and constructed either of granite or timber.

Farther south, where Moorish influence can be detected, the house fronts are mostly whitewashed, with the doors and window-frames painted in vivid colours. Depending on the local topography, single-storey farmhouses become more common. The doors and windows are smaller in order to keep out the heat of summer. Since the winters become more severe with increasing distance from the moderating influence of the Atlantic, open fires are more usual in the inland regions and the chimney becomes a prominent feature of the house.

In the deep south of the country, the Algarve, the single-storey house is predominant, frequently in the shape of a cube. Flat roofs are sometimes used to collect rainwater, which is then stored in a cistern. Particularly characteristic of the Algarve are the richly decorated chimneys with their lantern-like tops.

In no other country in Europe are there so many water mills and windmills still working as in Portugal. There are some thousands of water mills of different types (azenhas with vertical wheels, sesicas with horizontal wheels) on rivers, streams and reservoirs all over the country, used for grinding corn but more particularly, and increasingly, for irrigating fields and gardens.

Water Mills and Windmills

67

In parts of the country with little water or wind power winches or gins are used, worked either by animal power or by an engine. Visitors to Portugal are more likely, however, to be impressed by the characteristic old windmills (first referred to in the 13th c.) which are still to be seen in considerable numbers, adding a picturesque touch to the landscape. The mills are usually round, with a conical roof. The triangular sails are suspended between long wooden spokes which form a giant wheel. There are sometimes clay vessels attached to the ropes which make a whistling sound as the sails turn in the wind.

Literature

The development of literature in Portugal went in step with the formation of the Portuguese nation-state and the sense of national and linguistic identity in the Portuguese people. Throughout this period of development and down to modern times the characteristic features of Portuguese literature have been a rather melancholy sensibility, marked national feeling and a leaning towards criticism of the society of the day; and this Portuguese sensibility is underlined by the soft and gentle tonal colouring of the language.

Middle Ages

The earliest courtly lyric poetry, found in the neighbouring region of Galicia as well as in Portugal, had its leading practitioners in King Alfonso X of Castile (d. 1284) and Kings Sancho I (1185–1211) and Dinis I (1279–1325) of Portugal. This poetry consists exclusively of songs in Provençal style, some 2000 of which – love songs (cantigas de amor), women's songs (cantigas de amigo) and satirical songs (cantigas de maldizer) – are preserved in three collections, the "Cancioneiro da Ajuda", the "Cancioneiro da Vaticana" and the "Cancioneiro Colocci-Brancuti".

In the 14th c. this poetry rapidly declined in quality and the first cautious beginnings of prose writing appeared, at first taking the form of works written for a practical purpose: genealogical registers recording the lineage of noble families (livros de linhagem) and dry chronicles of modest literary pretension but great documentary value. During this period translations of religious and edifying works from Latin, French and Spanish were also produced. Then towards the end of the century lyric poetry enjoyed an astonishing renaissance under the influence of the Galician troubadour Macias o Enamorado ("Macias the Enamoured").

The beginning of the 15th c. brought a temporary decline in the literary use of Portuguese, and Castilian usage increasingly asserted itself in the written language. The work of the "palace poets" (poetas palacianos) who now came into fashion was collected by Garcia de Resenda in his "Cancioneiro geral".

Humanism

With the Renaissance and the great voyages of discovery by Portuguese navigators the ideas of humanism gained entry to the court, and literature, particularly prose writing, enjoyed generous royal patronage. Prominent in this respect were King Duarte I (1391–1438) and his brother Dom Pedro (1392–1449) the authors of treatises on moral philosophy of no great literary merit. Historical writing was institutionalised by the creation of the post of historiographer royal, and Fernão Lopes (c. 1384–c. 1460), Gomes Eanes de Zurura (c. 1410–73), Rui de Pina (c. 1440–c. 1522) and João de Barros (c. 1496–1570) wrote works showing a very modern objectivity. Unofficial chronicles of a more speculative and picturesque character were written by Damião de Gois (1502–74), Caspar Correia (c. 1495–c. 1565), Fernão Lopes de Castanheda (c. 1500–59) and Fernão Mendes Pinto (c. 1510–c. 1583).

Other genres which now established themselves were the bucolic poems of Bernardim Ribeiro (1482–1552; "Saudades") and Cristóvão

Falcão, whose existence in the first half of the 16th c. is still the subject of dispute, and the pastoral plays of Gil Vicente (*c.* 1465–*c.* 1540), who thus introduced the drama to the court and into Portuguese literature, always taking his subjects from popular life. During this period, too, Francisco Sá de Miranda (*c.* 1481–1558) introduced Italian stylistic features in his sonnets, cançones and comedies; and while these, like the sensitive lyric poetry of António Ferreira (1528–69) and Diogo Bernardes (1530–1600), enjoyed great success they did not displace the more popularly written works of other contemporaries such as Gonçalo Eanes Bandarra.

In the second half of the 16th c. Portuguese literature gained international status with the appearance of the country's greatest writer, Luís Vaz de Camões (see Famous People). After a life of adventure and many vicissitudes he glorified the achievements of the Portuguese people in the national epic "Os Lusiadas" ("The Lusiads", 1572; after Lusus, the legendary ancestor of the Portuguese), which exerted a powerful influence on the Portuguese literature of the day and later periods. Camões' wide-ranging and sensitive work, often reflecting his own experiences, attracted numerous imitators, who treated similar national themes with markedly inferior talent, setting the pattern for Portuguese literature until the beginning of the 17th c.

Luís Vaz de Camões

The period of decline during the Baroque age in the 17th c. brought a return to the old forms of bucolic poetry and religious and moralising prose. The personal union with Spain, seen by the Portuguese as the imposition of foreign rule, led to an increase in the cultural and linguistic influence of Castile and a decline in the writing of Portuguese. Only Franciso Rodrigues Lobo (1580–1622), with his idyllic pastoral poems, Francisco Manuel de Melo (1608–66), Manuel de Sousa Coutinho, known as Frei Luís de Sousa (*c.* 1555–1632), and the Jesuit preacher António de Vieira (1608–97) achieved reputations which outlasted their own day.

Baroque Poetry

At the turn of the 17th c. the Enlightenment, coming from France, began to make headway in Portugal, where it took on a curiously melancholy note. The 18th c. was the heyday of various literary societies committed to the renewal of literature, the most notable being the "Arcádia Lusitana" (1757–74) and the "Nova Arcádia" (1790–94), with such figures as Francisco Manuel do Nascimento (1734–1819), a committed opponent of rhyme in poetry, António Correia (1724–72), José Agostinho Macedo (1761–1831) and Manuel Maria Barbosa do Bocage (1765–1805). All these writers sought to renew Portuguese drama in the classical style.

Enlightenment

The prose writing of the later 18th c. consisted mainly of reports, letters and didactic works by such writers as the diplomat Francisco Xavier de Oliveira (1702–82), António da Costa (d. 1780), António Nunes (d. 1783) and Luís António Verney (1718–92), António José da Silva (1705–39) wrote librettos for puppet operas on popular themes.

After 1825 the Romantic movement, coming from Germany, France and Britain, began to make rapid headway in Portugal. Fostered and emotionally reinforced by the serious and sentimental cast of mind of the Portuguese, it soon led to a new flowering of the national literature. The first Portuguese Romantics and the most brilliant representatives of the movement were João Baptista de Silva Leitão de Almeida Garrett (1799–1854), author of romances, epics and lyrical dramas, and Alexandre Herculano de Carvalho e Araújo (1810–77), a historian who also wrote historical novels. Historical novels and novels of manners were written by Camilo Castelo Branco (Visconde de Correia Botelho, 1825–90), Augusto Rebelo da Silva, Pinheiro Chagas and others, novels of country life and love by Júlio Dinis (pseudonym of Joaquim Guilherme Gomes; 1839–71).

Romantic Movement

Music

The excesses of Romanticism were countered from 1865 onwards by the "Coimbra school", the leader of which was João de Deus Nogueira Ramos (1830–96). Towards the end of the century this developed into a Realist school, with such writers as Antero de Quental (1842–91), José Maria Eça de Queirós (1845–1900) and Teófilo Braga (1843–1924).

20th Century

The first decades of the 20th c. were notable for their lyric poetry. Symbolism, largely concerned with patriotic themes, was represented by António Nobre (1867–1900), Camilo Pessanha (1867–1926), Eugénio de Castro e Almeida (1869–1944) and Mário de Sá-Carneiro (1890–1916), who founded the review "Orpheu" in 1915. The "Saudosismo" of Texeira de Pascoaes (1877–1952) took on an almost messianic tone. The literary review "Aguia", published between 1910 and 1932, provided a forum for the writers of the period. One of the major lyric poets of recent times was Fernando António Nogueira Pessoa (1888–1935), who grew up in South Africa and wrote some of his work in English. Like his contemporaries he had a strong sense of mission, and with his linguistic virtuosity and profundity of content he exerted an influence which extended beyond the bounds of Portugal, impinging on both the English Romantics and the French Symbolists. Together with José Régio (pseudonym of José Maria dos Reis Pereira, 1901–69) Pessoa introduced the modern movement in Portuguese literature, which found a mouthpiece in the review "Presença" (1927–40). Other representatives of this trend are Vitorino Nemésio (Vitorino Nemésio Mendes Pinheiro da Silva, b. 1901), José Sobral Almada-Negreiros (b. 1893) and Miguel Torga (pseudonym of Adolfo Correia da Rocha, b. 1907).

In more recent times there has been a trend, in both poetry and prose, towards neo-realism and social criticism. Among notable lyric poets are José Gomes Ferreira (b. 1900), Eugénio de Andrade (b. 1923) and Alberto de Lacerda (b. 1928); among novelists and short story writers Raul Brandão (1867–1930), Aguilino Ribeiro (1885–1963), José Maria Ferreira de Castro (b. 1898), António Alves Redol (1901–69), Fernando Namora (b. 1919) and Carlos de Oliveira (b. 1921).

Since the revolution of 1974, which put an end to a long period of authoritarian government, liberal and more particularly socialist ideas have increasingly found expression in literature: thus Manuel Alegre (b. 1936), while actively engaged in politics, has also made a name for himself as a writer.

Luso-Brazilian Literature

Until the end of the 18th c. Luso-Brazilian literature was a mere offshoot of Portuguese literature and wholly under the influence of mainland Portugal. At the turn of the century there were signs of a distinctively Brazilian approach, particularly in religious writings, and with the separation of Brazil from Portugal in the mid 19th c. this trend was strengthened.

Music

Middle Ages

From the earliest days of Portugal's existence as an independent state there is evidence in both literature and art of a distinctive Galician/Portuguese musical culture.

Composed music (as distinct from folk music) went through the same phases of development in Portugal as in other European countries. Various song-books of the 12th–14th c. ("Cancioneiro da Ajuda", "Cancioneiro de Colocci-Brancuti", "Cancioneiro da Vaticana") have been preserved, but these give only the texts, not the music. During this period the art of the troubadours flourished at the courts, particularly in Lisbon, producing distinctively Portuguese genres in the *cantares de amigo* and *cantares de escarnio e maldizer*. The songs of the troubadours were accompanied on various instruments, including the fiddle, the psaltery, the harp, the rattle, the tambourine and the gittern (a seven-stringed plucked instrument with a cranked neck). During the 15th c. Portuguese music was exposed to increased influence from other countries (England, Burgundy, the Low Countries) as a result of the royal family's foreign alliances and the growth in trade. Singing to the accompaniment of a guitar or a keyboard instrument enjoyed a considerable vogue. Two song-books of this period, "De Palacio" and "Da Biblioteca Publia Hortênsia", contain part-songs with Galician/Portuguese texts. Music also played an important part in theatrical performances (singspiels).

At the court of Manuel I, Gil Vicente (c. 1465–1540) performed his famous autos (Corpus Christi plays) and tragi-comedies, in which both instrumental and vocal music figured prominently, using such musical forms as the *vilancico*, the *chacota*, the *folia* and the *entrada*, the forerunner of the early Baroque toccata.

Gil Vicente

In the 16th and 17th c. polyphonic instrumental and vocal music enjoyed a great flowering (motets, cantatas, masses, psalms), influenced by the Dutch music of the period. Notable names include Damião de Goes (1502–74), António Pinheiro (c. 1530–90), Vicente Lusitano (c. 1550–1610), Cosme Delgado (1540–1603), Manuel Mendes (c. 1547–1605), D. Lobo (1565–1646) and J. L. Rebello (1609–61).

16th and 17th c.

Fine music for keyboard instruments (organ, harpsichord) was written by António Carreira (1590–1650) and Duarte Lobo (c. 1570–1643), while Manuel Cardoso (1571–1650), Pedro Vaz (c. 1585–1640) and Alejandro de Aguiar (c. 1590–1645) wrote mainly for the guitar.

In 1620 Manuel Rodrigues Coelho (c. 1580–after 1633) published his "Flores de Música para o instrumento de Tecla e Harpa" – the first printed instrumental music in Portugal.

During the 18th c., in spite of increasing Italian influence, the instrumental music of José António Carlos de Seixas (1704–42), Frederico Jacinto (1700–55) and João de Sousa Carvalho (1720–98) shows a characteristically Portuguese lyrical sensibility.

18th c.

The main contribution to the music of the 18th c. was made by opera. In 1733 the poet António José da Silva (1705–39), known as "O Judeo" ("the Jew"), and the composer António Teixeiras founded a musical puppet theatre where they put on popular shows (satires, parodies) resembling singspiels. Da Silva wrote pieces such as "Os Encantos", "O Labirinto de Creta" and the puppet opera "Guerras do alecrim e da mangerona" ("Wars of Rosemary and Marjoram", first performed during the Carnival in 1737). Accused by the Inquisition of heresy, da Silva was burned at the stake in 1739 at the age of 34.

King João V (who married Maria Ana of Austria in 1708) was a great lover of Italian opera, and accordingly this came to dominate the musical scene in Portugal as it did in other countries. The king sent Portuguese composers to Italy to study and brought Italians to his court as teachers. Among them was Domenico Scarlatti, who was court harpsichordist at Lisbon from 1721 to 1725 and composed many of his famous sonatas there.

In 1732 the first Italian touring company came to Portugal. The leading representative of Portuguese opera in the Italian style was Franciso António de Almeida (d. about 1765; "Il Pentimento de Davide", "La Finta pazza"), whose opera buffa "La Pazienza di Socrate" was performed in the Teatro Paco da Ribeira in 1733, the first opera written by a Portuguese composer. Marcos da Fonseca Portugal (1762–1830; "La morte di Semiramide", "Le nozze di Figaro", "Zaira"), long-time director of the Teatro de São Carlos in Lisbon, also made a major contribution to the creation of opera in Portuguese.

The 1755 earthquake destroyed Lisbon's five opera-houses, and it was nearly 40 years before the new Teatro de São Carlos was built

Teatro de São Carlos

on the initiative of Diogo de Pina Manique. It was opened in 1793 with a performance of Domenico Cimarosa's work "La Ballerina amante", and is still Portugal's leading opera-house. Famous foreign singers and instrumentalists (including Franz List in 1845) performed there, and by 1910 more than 60 operas by Portuguese composers had been produced. The great majority of the operas were performed in Italian, but Gounod's "Faust" was sung in French in 1884 and Wagner's "Ring" in German in 1909.

19th c.

In the 19th c. Portuguese composers turned mainly to the romantic opera, reflecting both French and German (from 1850 Wagner) influence in their work. The foundation of the Philharmonic Academy (1838) and the Lisbon Conservatoire by João Alberto Rodrigues da Costa (1798–1870) and João Domingos Bomtempo (1775–1842) enriched the quality of Portuguese musical life in an enduring fashion.

Francisco Xavier Migone (1811–61) wrote two operas ("Sampiero", "Mocana") which were performed in the Teatro de São Carlos; Francisco Norberto dos Santos Pinto (1815–60) composed much music for the theatre and ballet as well as church music. Eugénio Ricardo Monteiro d'Almeda (1826–98) wrote operas and sacred music, including a "Libera me" which was highly praised by Rossini. Francisco de Freitas Gazul (1842–1925) composed one opera ("Fra Luigi di Sousa") and numerous operettas, symphonies, oratorios and overtures.

Domingos Ciriaco de Cardoso (1846–1900) ranks as the leading Portuguese operetta composer ("Girofle-Girofle").

Romantic School

Representatives of the Portuguese Romantic school were the composers Augusto Machado (1845–1924) and Alfredo Keil (1850–1907). Machado's main work was in the field of lyric opera, sometimes showing French influence ("Laureana", "Os Dorias"), and in operettas of considerable musical quality ("Ticão Negro", "O Rapto de Helena", "Venus"). Both in his piano music and his songs Keil shows strong national feeling. His song "A Portuguesa" was chosen as the national anthem on the proclamation of the republic in 1910. He also wrote operas ("Serrana", "Irene"), cantatas and symphonic poems ("Uma Caçada na Corte").

20th Century

At the beginning of the 20th c. Portuguese music was in a state of stagnation, having become unduly subject to the influence of Italian music. J. Vianna da Motta (1868–1948), a pupil of Liszt, turned away from Italianism and gave fresh vitality to instrumental music.

With Luís de Freitas Branco (1890–1955) the music of the modern age came to Portugal. In his extensive oeuvre ("Vathek 1914", "Artificial Paradises", symphonies and sonatas for violin and piano) he showed affinities with the atonality of the school of Schönberg and gave a major stimulus to the development of Impressionism in Portuguese music. Rui Coelho (b. 1892) also followed in the footsteps of Schönberg's twelve-tone music ("Camoniana"; "Inês de Castro", 1926), while Frederico de Freitas (b. 1902; "Wall of Contention", "Nazaré") adopted the linear polytonality of Milhaud and Honegger for the first time in his sonata for violin and piano.

Fernando Lopes Graça (b. 1905) represents a Portuguese classical style, devoting himself mainly to the Portuguese folk-song and developing a very personal technique of harmonisation, particularly in the treatment of a cappella voices ("Prayer for the Souls of the Departed", "Traditional Portuguese Christmas Music").

The leading figure among younger Portuguese composers is Jorge Peixinho (b. 1940), who studied in Venice with Luigi Nono and in Basle with Pierre Boulez with the aid of a scholarship from the Gulbenkian Foundation, and worked with Karlheinz Stockhausen in Darmstadt. In 1970 he founded the Contemporary Music Group in Lisbon.

The leading Portuguese orchestra, consisting exclusively of professional musicians, is the National Radio Symphony Orchestra (Emissora Nacional), established in 1934. The Lisbon Opera House, the Teatro São Carlos as well as the Gulbenkian Orchestra, the Gulbenkian Choir and the Gulbenkian Ballet also make their contribution to the musical life of Portugal.

Folklore

In Portugal, as in all Romance countries, folk festivals, dances and music play a central part in people's lives.

In contrast to Spain, the folk music of Portugal shows little Arab or Moorish influence except in the southerly region of Algarve. The folk dances performed at the numerous religious and secular festivals are usually accompanied by singing and a music accompaniment on traditional instruments such as the guitar (*guitarra, viola*), fiddle (*rabeca*), flute (*flauta*), bagpipe (*gaita*), drum (*tambor*) and *reque-reque*, a percussion instrument, probably of African origin, consisting of reed pipes which are struck with a wooden rod.

Folk Music

The folk dances show considerable regional variation. In the northern coastal regions between the Minho and the Douro the commonest dance is the *vira*, a lively round dance. The Galician *gota* is danced to an even faster tempo. In the *malhão* and *cana verde* the women wear beautiful traditional costumes. In the hill country of Trás-os-Montes, Beira Alta and Beira Baixa the most popular dance is the *chula*. The *dança dos pauliteiros* which is also danced in these regions is performed by men bearing staves, probably substitutes for sabres used in the old warlike dances. The vira performed at Nazaré on the coast of Estremadura is a graceful fisherfolk's dance. In the Ribatejo region men dance the solo *escovinho* and *fandango*.

Folk Dance

To the south of the Tagus, where the people are of a more serious cast of mind, the dances are stately, almost melancholy. The best known folk dances of Alentejo are the *saia* and the *balha*. In the Algarve on the other hand, the lively and vigorous *corridinho* is danced.

The old folk dances are mostly danced at the various popular festivals (*romarias, festas*) which are particularly numerous in spring and late summer. In country areas the harvest thanksgiving festival is an occasion for great celebration, based on a service giving thanks for a good harvest or on the blessing of the livestock and the fields.

In a profoundly Catholic country like Portugal the various religious festivals are naturally of prime importance. Paricularly in the conservative north there are numerous *romarias* in honour of a particular saint or in commemoration of some miracle or apparition. The more important of these may last several days, with secular celebrations as well as religious ceremonies.

Romarias

The romaria is basically a pilgrimage, with long processions of pilgrims, festively dressed, and splendidly decorated floats. Sometimes a romaria is dedicated to a particular craft (in a fishing town, for example, to the fishermen); but this does not prevent large numbers of spectators and visitors from joining in and playing their part in the celebrations.

The central feature of the religious ritual is a solemn procession accompanying some sacred symbol, which in some cases may be merely a large candle (*cirio*), to the place of pilgrimage, usually a church. On arriving at the church the procession usually walks round it several times, to the accompaniment of music and a great deal of noise, before setting up the cross or candle or other symbol by the high altar.

In order to obtain forgiveness for their sins the pilgrims perform a variety of ritual acts or offer ex-votos to the saint in gratitude for help

Easter procession at Graciosa in the Azores

received. The Portuguese, however, are not uncritical of their saints and if a pilgrim thinks a saint has let him down it is quite common for him to scold and denigrate that saint before placing any trust in him the following year.

The romarias are mainly financed by offerings from the community. A few days before the festival the organisers arrange for the collection of alms, accompanied by music to encourage cheerful giving.

Some of the larger romarias are widely famed, and offer an excellent opportunity of getting to know the way of life and customs of Portugal. Among the most notable are those of Viana do Castelo, Póvoa de Varzim, Amarante and Loulé.

Festas

Associated with the religious ceremonies there are usually *festas* – fairs offering a variety of attractions and entertainments, with dancing and singing, eating and drinking.

Costumes

The various festas and romarias give visitors an opportunity of seeing a great range of splendid traditional costumes (*trajes*). As in many other countries, the women's costumes are particularly fine. Those of the northern provinces of Minho and Douro are notable for their richness of colouring, the brightly coloured embroidered jackets and waistcoats being set off by white blouses and stockings, with headscarves, kerchiefs and jewellery to complete the effect.

Black costumes, with long gold-embroidered skirts fitting closely on the hips which are reminiscent of Provençal dress, are also found in northern Portugal, and black costumes are common in the Algarve, at the other end of the country. In Alentejo the costumes are adapted to the peasants' hard work in the fields, which is often done by women, wearing trouser-like nether garments, with a kerchief or a floppy hat on their heads. In Ribatejo the *campesinos* (cattle-herders) wear breeches, brightly coloured waistcoats and stockings, light-coloured shirts and the stocking caps which are found all over Portugal.

In the little fishing town of Nazaré and the surrounding area young women and girls wear simple coloured dresses with a flower pattern in black or white and a white or black woollen jersey or shawl over their shoulders to protect them from the rough Atlantic winds which often blow in this area.

There are great processions (*procissões*) in the pilgrimage centre of Fátima twice a year (on May 13th and October 13th), with smaller pilgrimages on the 12th and 13th of every month.

Processions

There are also processions in many towns and villages at Easter, carrying figures connected with the story of the Passion.

Particularly notable is the Festa dos Tabuleiros, celebrated at Tomar in alternate years. White-clad girls walk in procession through the town bearing on their heads the elaborate tower-like structures known as *tabuleiros*, each incorporating thirty loaves of bread and a decoration of ears of corn, flowers and foliage. The tabuleiros is usually as tall as the girl carrying it. The procession is supposed to commemorate a 14th c. ceremony during which the Order of the Holy Ghost distributed food to the poor.

Portuguese folklore includes many traditions of pagan origin, and numerous everyday habits and customs which to the outsider may appear exotic or even antiquated. Among these for example is the way in which the fishermen of Nazaré launch their boats into the heavy surf and haul them ashore on their return by their own muscle-power or with the help of oxen. Local colour is also provided by the women sitting outside their houses doing embroidery or pillow-lace work, the women selling shellfish in the street, the fisherfolk mending nets or setting out fish to dry in the sun on special racks, and the people grilling sardines on little charcoal stoves outside their houses, producing the penetrating aroma which pervades whole villages and will be one of every visitor's memories of Portugal. The heaviest of loads are carried on people's heads, the women balancing theirs with great poise and dignity.

Traditions

The bullfight (*tourada*) is very much part of Portuguese tradition. It is quite different from the Spanish "corrida" which to the Portuguese is almost a swear word. Unlike Spain and some towns in the South of France, in Portugal the bull is not killed – in the arena at any rate – and there are no picadores to soften the bull up.

Bullfighting

The central character in a Portuguese bullfight is the *cavaleiro*, a kind of mounted torero clad in an elegant costume of the time of Louis XV of France, a legacy from the days when all cavaleiros were noblemen. After some demonstrations of haute école horsemanship the bull is released into the arena and the cavaleiro begins his *faena* (the Portuguese borrow the Spanish word for the occasion), dexterously avoiding the bull's charge and planting *farpas*, or *bandarilhas* in its neck. In order to avoid injury to the horse the bull's horns are blunted by leather pads (*emboladas*).

Unmounted aides – *toureiros* or *capinhas* – sometimes enter the ring to allow the cavaleiro a short breathing-space. After the cavaleiro has planted all his farpas he withdraws from the contest and leaves the field to eight *forcados*, on foot and unarmed, who set about bringing the bull to a standstill in the phase of the fight known as the *pega*. When the bull has been defeated the *campinos* enter the arena with a small herd of oxen or young bulls, and after a brief period of hesitation the bewildered beast joins the herd and leaves the arena with them.

The bullfighting season in Portugal is from Easter to October. Bullfights are held not only in the special bullrings (*praças de touros*) in the larger towns but also in market squares and sports grounds in smaller places.

Mounted bullfighting is also practised in Spain and the South of France, where it is known as the *rejonea*. This is very similar to the Portuguese form, except that there are no forcados. In the rejonea the bull is often killed in the arena, usually by a torero on foot, rarely by the rider. In Spain, too, the bull's horns are usually not padded, increasing the hazard for both horse and rider. Portuguese cavaleiros occasionally appear in rejoneas outside Portugal.

Portugal in Quotations

After sunrise we saw that we really were close to land. Was it the cliffs of Cintra? On to Lisbon, then? Really there was no other choice.

Christopher Columbus (1451–1506)

At midday we were already close to the shore. I tried to put in at Cassaes, but the gale drove me away from the coast time and again. Perhaps it will be possible to sail up the Tagus.

I succeeded in anchoring off Rastello. We are saved. Saved? Whether we are or not will appear by and by. Immediately after coming ashore I sent a messenger to Juan II with a detailed letter informing him of my arrival and asking for help – and also for leave to continue on my way to Lisbon. I did not let the opportunity pass of remarking that I had not been to Guinea but to India. The best way of protecting yourself against an ox is to grasp it by the horns! Perhaps he will be so surprised that he will forget to gore me.

Christopher Columbus made these entries in his ship's log book on March 5th 1492.

Lisbon, before which we now lay at anchor, is said to be built on the same number of hills with old Rome; but these do not all appear to the water; on the contrary, one sees from thence one vast high hill and rock, with buildings arising above one another, and that in so steep and almost perpendicular a manner, that they all seem to have but one foundation.

Henry Fielding (1707–54)

As the houses, convents, churches, etc., are large, and all built with white stone, they look very beautiful at a distance; but as you approach nearer, and find them to want every kind of ornament, all idea of beauty vanishes at once. While I was surveying the prospect of this city, which bears so little resemblance to any other that I have ever seen, a reflection occurred to me, that if a man were suddenly to be removed from Palmyra hither, and should take a view of no other city, in how glorious a light would the ancient architecture appear to him! and what desolation of arts and sciences would he conclude had happened between the several eras of these cities! . . .

About seven in the evening I got into a chaise on shore, and was driven through the nastiest city in the world, though at the same time one of the most populous, to a kind of coffee-house, which is very pleasantly situated on the brow of a hill about a mile from the city and hath a very fine prospect of the river Tajo from Lisbon to the sea. Here we regaled ourselves with a good supper.

From Henry Fielding's "Journal of a Voyage to Lisbon", undertaken in 1754.

Two leagues to Coimbra over a rich and lovely country. The view opened from the last eminence upon the mountains, and one snowy summit of the Serra Estrella. Halfway down the heights were floating clouds, all silver in the sunshine. The nearer ground was hill and dale, olives, oranges, quinces blossoming in the hedgerows – and cypresses peering everywhere. At the last the Mondego appeared swol'n with the rains – a broad and ample stream, winding among olive wooded hills – and a long low bridge reaching to Coimbra, whose convents and colleges were on the opposite height, large and fine buildings, of that unsullied whiteness which stone preserves only in a climate like this. I never saw a scene more magnificent – a city more gloriously seated. The olives large and healthy shaded all the hills, in every garden the fine oranges were hung with fine fruit, and everywhere the cypress – thick as the poplars near London. There are

Robert Southey (1774–1843)

frequent openings on the bridge to let the current pass. We entered the city thro an ancient gate . . .

From Robert Southey, "Journals of a Residence in Portugal", March 13th 1801.

Duke of
Wellington, the
"Iron Duke"
(1769–1852)

PEOPLE OF PORTUGAL.

The time is arrived to rescue your country and restore the government of your lawful Prince.

His Britannic Majesty, our most gracious King and master, has, in compliance with the wishes and ardent supplications for succour from all parts of Portugal, sent to your aid a British army, directed to co-operate with his fleet, already on your coast.

The English soldiers, who land upon your shore, do so with every sentiment of friendship, faith and honour.

The glorious struggle upon which you are engaged is for all that is dear to man – the protection of your wives and children; the restoration of your lawful Prince; the protection, nay, the very existence of your Kingdom; and for the preservation of your holy religion. Objects like these can only be obtained by distinguished examples of fortitude and constancy.

The noble struggle against the tyranny and usurpation of France will be jointly maintained by Portugal, Spain and England; and in contributing to the success of a cause so just and glorious, the views of His Britannic Majesty are the same as those by which you are yourselves animated.

Proclamation issued by General Sir Arthur Wellesley (later the Duke of Wellington) when British troops landed in Portugal in August 1808.

Lord Byron
(1788–1824)

I am very happy here, because I loves oranges, and talk bad Latin to the Monks, who understand it as it is like their own. And I goes into society (with my pocket pistols) and I swims in the Tagus all across at once, and I have got a diarrhoea, and bites from the mosquitoes. But what of that? Comfort must not be expected by folks that go a pleasuring.

Lord Byron, letter to the Rev. F. Hodgson, July 16th 1809.

We sailed from Falmouth on July 2nd, reached Lisbon after a very favourable passage of four days and a half, and took up our abode in that city. It has been often described without being worthy of description; for, except for the view from the Tagus, which is beautiful, and some fine churches and convents, it contains little but filthy streets, and more filthy inhabitants. To make amends for this, the village of Cintra, about fifteen miles from the capital, is, perhaps in every respect, the most delightful in Europe; it contains beauties of every description, natural and artificial. Palaces and gardens rising in the midst of rocks, cataracts, and precipices; convents on stupendous heights – a distant view of the sea and the Tagus . . . It unites in itself all the wildness of the western highlands, with the verdure of France.

Lord Byron, letter to his mother, August 11th 1809.

Sir William
Wraxall
(1751–1831)

In the year 1772 the Court of Lisbon offered scarcely any sources of amusements to the foreigner. Neither levees nor drawing-rooms were ever held, except on birth-days, and on a few particular festivals. The King, Queen, his brother Don Pedro, his three daughters and the young Prince of Beyra, lived all under the same roof and inhabited a long wooden range of apartments at Belem, lower down the bank of the Tagus than Lisbon. The terrors and recollections of the earthquake of 1755 were so deeply impressed on their minds that they preferred residing in a wooden building, however mean or inconvenient, rather than encounter the perils annexed to a stone edifice. Joseph had never slept under a house, properly so denominated, during near sixteen years. Wherever he moved, either wooden barracks or tents were provided for his accommodation. I have seen tents pitched for his reception in the fields adjoining the palace of Maffra, while that immense and costly edifice was totally abandoned, neglected and unfurnished. These precautions, however singular and almost pusillanimous they may at first sight seem, were nevertheless necessary. Evidence had fully demonstrated that most solid, massy and well-constructed buildings of stone only exposed the inhabitant to greater and more inevitable destruction, in the event of an earthquake, because the resistance made by such materials to the undulation or shock produced their overthrow. On the contrary, any structure composed of wood, supported like the barracks inhabited by the Royal Family, on pillars of the same materials, yielding to the concussion of the earth, rocked and waved with the convulsion, thus escaping its worst effects.

From Sir N. William Wraxall's "Historical Memoirs of My Own Time", first published in 1815.

On the authority of British travellers, most of whom, like Byron, have approached by sea, Lisbon has been called the most beautiful city in Europe after Constantinople and Naples, and as an old saying asserts "quem não tem visto Lisboa, não tem visto cousa bona" (he who has not seen Lisbon does not know what beauty is). However this may be, everyone will willingly allow that nature and man have here co-operated to great advantage, and that the city, in spite of the absence of a mountain background or distinguished buildings, possesses a beauty of its own in the picturesque disposition of its terraces, its view of the wide expanses of the Tagus, and the luxuriant vegetation of its public gardens and parks.

Lisbon is now one of cleanest towns of Southern Europe, though at the beginning of the last century it was notorious for its dilapidation, insecurity and dirt.

From Karl Baedeker's Spain and Portugal: "Handbook for Travellers", third edition, 1908.

Baedeker's Spain and Portugal 1908 edition

Portuguese Melody – "April in Portugal". Music by Raul Ferrao

Suggested Routes

The following suggested itineraries are intended to help the motorist touring Portugal, without denying him freedom to make his own plans and choice of route. The routes have been chosen so that the principal places of interest in the country are visited. However, not all the places of interest in this guide can be covered without making detours. The proposed routes can be followed on the map at the back of this book which simplifies detailed planning.

Places and areas which are covered in the A to Z section under a main heading are printed in **bold**.

Most of the towns, villages, areas, rivers, etc. mentioned in the routes, as well as individual sights, whether they are under main headings or in the surroundings, can be found in the index at the end of the guide.

The figures in brackets after the headings are approximate distances and refer to the direct route; distances of detours or alternative roads on fairly long stretches are specially noted.

Tour of southern Portugal (820km/510 miles)

This tour of southern Portugal is aimed at anyone wanting to combine a relaxing holiday on the Algarve with some sightseeing. It can be done in three days – in which case it would be best to stop overnight in Lisbon and Évora – but to do justice to the sights and the scenery it should really take at least a week.

Algarve

Many visitors enter Portugal via the little town of **Vila Real de Santo António** on its south-eastern frontier. From here take the N 125 coast-road west as far as Portimão (this section of the route is described in detail under ★★**Algarve**). It is definitely worth planning stops at ★**Tavira**, a little town with as yet uncrowded beaches and a look still very much all its own, and ★**Faro**, chief resort of the Algarve. Past Faro the landscape gradually becomes the "Rocky Algarve", and the bizarre rock formations such as those near Carvoeiro (Algar Seco) are to be admired. Soon after that it is worth making a stop at the still unspoiled fishing village of ★Ferragudo, the neighbouring village to **Portimão**.

Detour to Cape St Vincent

The detour from Portimão to windswept ★Cape St Vincent (Cabo de São Vicente), via the pretty town of ★**Lagos** and ★**Sagres**, the centre of the Portuguese sightseeing routes, is a round-trip of about 100km/ 62 miles. This stretch presents quite a different picture of the Algarve. The vegetation is sparser, thanks to the much harsher climate, but this also ensures that the countryside is not overrun by tourists.

From Portimão to Alcácer do Sal

From Portimão the route runs north on the N 124 then the N 266 through the delightful ★★**Serra de Monchique**. The winding mountain road, from which there are lovely views, skirts the old-established spa of Caldas de Monchique then goes through the little hill town of Monchique. Following the N 266 then the N 123 the route picks up the N 120 at Odemira and speeds northward to Tanganheira where it forks right to avoid the industrial port of **Sines**. Twenty km/12 miles further on lies the attractive hill-top town of **Santiago do Cacém**. From here to Grândola it is worth leaving the main road and taking the narrow country road which runs through some pretty countryside via Cruz de João Mendes. Back on the N 120 it is a further 20km/12 miles to **Alcácer**

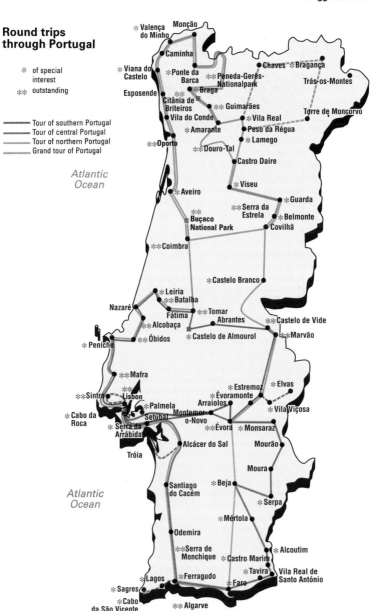

Round trips through Portugal

* of special interest
** outstanding

Tour of southern Portugal
Tour of central Portugal
Tour of northern Portugal
Grand tour of Portugal

Atlantic Ocean

Atlantic Ocean

©Baedeker

do Sal, where the best view of this ancient little town is from the bridge over the Rio Sado as you enter.

Detour to the Tróia peninsula

The tip of the Tróia peninsula, with its mile upon mile of shining sandy beaches, is about 45km/28 miles from Alcácer do Sal.

From Alcácer do Sal to Lisbon

The route follows the busy N 5 and then, forking left, the N 10 to **Setúbal**, which remains a pleasant place despite its industry.

Although there is a motorway from here to Lisbon the lovely scenery makes it definitely well worth taking the long way round along the coast road west out of Setúbal through the ★ Serra da Arrábida, with its wonderful views over the rocky bays and coves of the coastline. The fishing village of Portinho da Arrábida is a good place for a quick stop.

Passing through beautiful and as yet largely unspoilt scenery the road eventually arrives at Vila Nogueira de Azeitão, famous for its wineries. (**Sesimbra**, 13km/8 miles south-west, is a good place for anyone wanting to stay in this area overnight.) A few miles to the east it is possible to visit what is probably the earliest "azulejo" tile-picture in Portugal at Vila Fresca de Azeitão.

Back on the N 10 the route soon joins the motorway to ★★ **Lisbon**, Portugal's capital, which needs a visit of at least two days to do anything like justice to its many sights.

Detour along the Costa do Sol to Sintra

A day-trip worth taking from Lisbon is the drive along the **Costa do Sol** to ★★ **Sintra**. It's only 60km/37 miles but contains many sights of interest (more detailed description in tour of Central Portugal).

From Lisbon to Évora

The best way south out of Lisbon is the motorway straight to Setúbal, but it is also possible to go by car ferry from the city centre over to the south bank of the Tagus. With perhaps a brief stop in ★ **Palmela** the route then retraces the N 10 from Setúbal back 20km/12 miles east to the cross-roads just past Águas de Moura after which it turns north, still on the N 10, before soon taking the N 4 east towards Montemor-o-Novo, a small town overshadowed by its castle. **Arraiolos**, noted for its carpets, lies about 25km/16 miles east of here, and ★★ **Évora**, one of Portugal's finest cities, a further 22km/14 miles to the south.

From Évora via Moura to Beja

If enough time is available, it is a good idea not to take the direct route, but instead to follow the N 18 and then the N 256 in an easterly direction. Near Reguengos de Monsaraz a small road turns off to the extremely picturesque ★ Monsaraz, situated on a hill. Leaving the town in a southerly direction the road passes an impressive stone circle and then joins the N 256, 5km/3 miles along this road lies Mourão. Continue through unspoilt scenery along the N 386 to **Moura**. The route continues to the walled town of ★ Serpa and on to ★ **Beja** with its well-preserved old town.

From Beja via Mértola to Vila Real de Santo António

The N 122 leads south from Beja. After 15km/9½ miles keep to the left and continue for another 40km/25 miles to ★ **Mértola**. From the castle there is a fine view of the town centre and the parish church, formerly a mosque. There are few villages along the little-used N 122. 30km/19 miles beyond Mértola a road branches off to the left to ★ Alcoutim. From here there is a fine view of the Rio Guadiana, which forms the border. A new road leads south along the river bank. Near Foz de Odeleite the road again turns inland and finally comes to ★ Castro Marim with its great castle. From here it is only 6km/4 miles to Vila Real de Santo António.

Tour of central Portugal (730km/455 miles)

Anyone particularly wanting to visit Portugal's art treasures would be best advised to choose this tour of central Portugal and to allow about a week. It takes in two of the country's loveliest cities (Lisbon and Évora), the major abbeys and convents (Batalha, Tomar and Alcobaça), the most impressive castles (Sintra and Mafra), but also offers glimpses of smaller romantic places in unusually fine settings such as Castelo de Vide and Marvão.

Leaving ★★**Lisbon** by its western suburb of Belém, with its outstanding examples of Manueline architecture, the route runs along the part of the coast known as the **Costa do Sol**, the four-lane motorway ending just before the popular resorts of **Estoril** and **Cascais**. On the left just past Cascais is "Hell's Mouth", the Boca do Inferno – cliffs hollowed out by the sea into caves – and there are also impressive views over the rocky coastline from Cabo Raso and especially Cabo da Roca.

From Lisbon to Batalha via Sintra

At Colares the route leaves the coast road and heads inland to ★★**Sintra** which, with its two castles, many royal residences and extremely beautiful parks and gardens, requires almost a whole day in itself.

From there the route runs north on the N 9 to ★★**Mafra** and its enormous palace-monastery, and then turns north-west towards Ericeira, a further 10km/6 miles ahead on the coast. Continuing to hug the coastline (sightseeing in **Torres Vedras** can be given a miss) the next destination is ★**Peniche**, on its rocky peninsula projecting far out to sea, then, heading inland, 25km/16 miles further on, the picturesque walled town of ★★**Óbidos**, which, with its whitewashed houses and pretty shop-lined alleys, is now well on the tourist map, possibly making it difficult to get accommodation here at the height of the season. Keeping on the N 8, just 6km/4 miles to the north lies **Caldas da Rainha**, a centre for majolica ware, and 25km/16 miles up the road one of the great sights of Portugal, the magnificent abbey of ★★**Alcobaça**. From here it is possible either to make a detour to take in ★**Nazaré**, where the pilgrimage chapel high above the town commands some of Portugal's most impressive views of its Atlantic coast and then via Marinha Grande to ★**Leiria** with its well-preserved castle, or to keep on up the N 8 and go direct to ★★**Batalha**, which has an abbey that is one of the very best examples of Manueline architecture.

Whether it be for its religious aspects or not, a brief visit should be fitted in to **Fátima**, Portugal's place of pilgrimage, if only for the approach on the N 356 that connects it to Batalha. From Fátima via Vila Nova de Ourem it is a bare 35km/22 miles to ★★**Tomar** which has a massive convent, The route continues southward through very pretty countryside. About 6km/4 miles past Tomar it is possible to turn left off the main road and head for Castelo de Bode where there is a pousada in a delightful wooded lakeside setting. At Constância the country road joins the main road to **Abrantes**. Although there is nothing very special to see in Abrantes it is definitely worth making the short detour to ★Castelo de Almourol (turn right at Constância towards Tancos then left along a road leading to the castle which stands on an island in the Tagus).

From Batalha to Marvão via Tomar

Beyond Abrantes a 370m/1214ft bridge crosses the Tagus and a fine view of the town can be obtained by looking back from the village of Rossio on this side of the river. The route follows the river upstream for a time then leaves it at Gavião; rice, agave and figs gradually give way to what eventually become bleak hillsides. About 18km/11 miles beyond Gavião the N 118 forks right to ★★**Castelo de Vide** which, like ★★**Marvão** just a few miles to its south-east and also definitely worth a visit, is an extremely attractive little town that still retains its medieval character and atmosphere.

From Marvão to Estremoz via Elvas

From Marvão the route goes south to Portalegre through the lovely mountain landscapes of the Serra do São Mamede. There is no need to spend too long in **Portalegre**, which is the rather noisy and hectic district capital. Leaving on the N 18 the southward bound route speeds up over the 60km/37 miles to ⋆**Estremoz**, with its picturesque old upper town and busy newer lower town.

Detour to Elvas

This round trip to Elvas of about 90km/56 miles begins by taking the N 4 eastwards from Estremoz. In Borba, 11km/7 miles along the road, branch off to ⋆**Vila Viçosa**. After some large marble quarries the route passes the former royal residence with the vast Palace of the Dukes of Bragança. Returning to Borba and back on the N 4 again the route continues to ⋆**Elvas**. This old fortified frontier town still has many well-preserved fortifications, not to mention an amazing four-tier aqueduct, which are worth seeing.

From Estremoz to Lisbon via Évora

From Estremoz the route continues towards Évora along the N 18. After 17km/11 miles it is worth taking a brief detour along the little road to Évoramonte off to the right and following it for about half a mile to get right into the massive ruins of Évoramonte Castle. Back on the main road it is just 30km/19 miles to ⋆⋆**Évora** and the many sights it has to offer. The way back to Lisbon is via Montemor-o-Novo (it is possible to make a trip first to **Arraiolos**, where the famous rugs are made), Vendas Novas and **Setúbal**, then on through the ⋆Serra da Arrábida (described in detail in the tour of southern Portugal).

Tour of northern Portugal (850km/528 miles)

While the central Portugal tour is to be recommended for anyone chiefly interested in culture, the tour of northern Portugal will be the one that particularly appeals to lovers of nature, taking in some unique and still quite unspoilt scenery (especially in the north-east of the country) and two interesting but completely different national parks, not to mention several very attractive old towns and cities.

Because the bends in the road will make it necessary to travel slowly in many places, to enjoy the tour at least a week, or, if the detour to the north-east is included ten days, should be allowed.

From Oporto to Braga via Monção

The metropolis of northern Portugal, and clearly Lisbon's rival, is ⋆⋆**Oporto**, and no visit there is complete without visiting one of the port wine lodges in Vila Nova de Gaia. From Oporto the route goes north on the N 13 to **Vila do Conde** which almost merges with **Póvoa de Varzim** further up the coast. Although there is quite a lot of industry in and around the two towns they are both very popular seaside resorts. Esposende, further north, is rather quieter. Anyone considering a beach holiday on this part of the "green coast", the **Costa Verde**, should be prepared for relatively cool sea temperatures and some strong winds off the sea.

Continuing along the coast on the N 13 the route crosses the wide Rio Lima on an iron bridge 560m/1838ft long (under the railway), built in 1877 by Eiffel & Co in Paris, to get to ⋆**Viano do Castelo**, the district capital with a very attractive town centre. From here it carries on northwards, through countryside that is getting prettier all the time, to its next destination, **Caminha**. The road now turns north-west, running up the valley of the Minho – the Spanish–Portuguese frontier at this point – where vineyards alternate with heath and pine-woods. After the fortress town of ⋆**Valença do Minho** the route leaves the N 13 but continues along the pleasing Minho valley to the rather sleepy-seeming spa of **Monção**.

Bragança in the north of Portugal

Here the route turns south down the N 101, passing through quite well populated hilly country, dotted with many villages and home-steads. Past Barroças the road winds its way up to the Serra do Extremo (chapel with good view) then drops down again after Aboim das Chocas. Arcos de Valdevez and ⋆**Ponte da Barca** are both picturesque little towns worth a quick visit.

Just a few miles east of Ponte da Barca is the start of the ⋆⋆**Peneda Gerês National Park**. For anyone pressed for time and who only wants to take a short drive through this largely unspoilt area the best route is to go from Ponte da Barca to Lindoso then drive on out into Spain and get back into the park again through the entrance at Portelá do Homem. The route then goes through the little spa of Gerês and runs south past various reservoirs to pick up the N 103, taking it west to ⋆**Braga**, with its many churches.

From Braga follow the signs in an easterly direction to Bom Jesús do Monte, the pilgrimage church. A narrow road via Sobreposta leads from there to the Iron Age site ⋆**Citânia de Briteiros**. The road then snakes downhill to Caldelas where it joins the N 101, the main road to ⋆⋆**Guimarães**. This historic town is known as "the cradle of the nation" and still has many of its fine old buildings. Keeping on the N 101 the route continues to ⋆**Amarante**, where it crosses the Rio Tâmega – the new bridge affording a superb view of the heart of the old town. The main road from here eastward to ⋆**Vila Real** is still full of twists and turns, but a new one is projected.

From Braga to Vila Real

Only those who have plenty of time should take on this 310km/193 mile trip which heads north from Vila Real to **Chaves** and then east to ⋆**Bragança**, traversing the rugged mountain province of **Trás os Montes**, still a largely untouched and very poor region. From Bragança the route goes south on the N 15 then after 37km/23 miles forks left

Tour Extension to Bragança via Chaves

onto the N 102 and crosses the Serra de Bornes, providing lovely views almost all the way. It eventually crosses the Rio Sabor and enters the ancient town of **Torre de Moncorvo**. The next destination is Vila Nova de Foz Côa, which has a fine Manueline church, then just over a mile further on the route leaves the N 102 to go left onto the N 222 to Touça and then winds its way down to the ★**Douro Valley**. This region is known as "País do Vinho", the land of wine, because of the vineyards on the terraced slopes which provide the rather heavy wine used for making port. The route now carries on down the valley to rejoin the main route (described below) at Peso da Régua.

From Vila Real to Guarda

Leave Vila Real and travel south, crossing the Douro at Peso da Régua then heading for ★**Lamego**, with its pilgrimage church attractively located overlooking the town. Still moving south on the N 2 the route passes through Castro Daire to ★**Viseu** which besides its fine cathedral and churches also boasts handsome burghers' houses and palaces of the Renaissance and Baroque periods. The next stretch westward on the N 16 to Guarda can be quite a fast one and contains a section of new road, with work continuing on the rest of it. Its altitude of 1057m/3468ft makes ★**Guarda** Portugal's highest town.

From Guarda to Coimbra through the Serra da Estrela

From Guarda take the N 18 south then turn left off the main road after about 19km/12 miles to have a look at the Roman watch-tower at Centum Cellas. Back on the N 18 the turning to the charming little hill town of ★**Belmonte** is only a few hundred yards further on. The 20km/12 miles from Belmonte to **Covilhã** is a fast run before the tour enters the ★★**Serra da Estrela**, renowned for the beauty of its mountain scenery. From Covilhã take the road to Tortosendo and turn west along the N 230 which twists and turns until it eventually connects up with N 17 to ★**Coimbra**.

From Coimbra to Oporto

Although there is a motorway from Coimbra to Oporto it is worth doing at least the first part of the trip off the main road, leaving Coimbra on the N 110 heading eastward towards Penacova, passing through particularly pretty countryside on the north bank of the Rio Mondego. Just before Penacova there is a turning on the left to the convent of Lorvão a little way off the road. On narrow little roads follow the signs to ★★**Buçaco National Park** where the dense network of paths allows visitors to explore the beauties of the forest. After Luso, the little spa on the northern edge of the park, head back west to the motorway and stay on it until the turn-off to ★**Aveiro**. Although it is an exaggeration to compare this little fishing town with Amsterdam or Venice, its canals make it a pleasant place in which to finish off this tour by taking a stroll around the town before rejoining the motorway back to Oporto.

Grand Tour of Portugal (2000km/1243 miles)

The three tours of Portugal can easily be joined together to make one grand tour. Anyone who wanted to acquaint themselves with the best of Portugal's towns, sights and scenery would need to take at least four weeks.

The individual stops on the tour are only touched on in greater detail when this tour deviates from the other three. Since many visitors from abroad enter Portugal through Faro, the main town of the Algarve, that is where this tour begins.

Tour Stages

From ★**Faro** head west through the flourishing countryside of the ★★**Algarve** to the busy town of **Portimão**, then turn inland and traverse the charming ★★**Serra de Monchique**. The next destinations are Odemira (at this juncture Vila Nova de Milfontes is a good place to rest for a day), **Santiago do Cacém**, Grândola and **Alcácer do Sal**. From the port of **Setúbal** it is definitely worth making a detour to sample the charming scenery of the ★ Serra da Arrábida. From here it is not far to ★★**Lisbon**, Portugal's capital. No tour would be complete without ★★**Sintra** and ★★**Mafra** either. (If another rest day is needed nearby Ericeira has a good swimming beach.) Next it is northwards via ★★**Óbidos** to ★★**Alcobaça**, from where it is only 15km/9 miles to the pretty beach resort of ★**Nazaré**. Further on, at ★**Batalha**, the abbey is one of the great sights of Portuguese architecture. Turning inland the tour takes in **Fátima** and ★★**Tomar** before heading north to ★★**Coimbra**. The stretch from here via Penacova to the ★★**Buçaco National Park** is full of lovely views. Next on the route is ★**Aveiro** then ★★**Oporto**. The route follows the coastline north of the **Costa Verde** as far as ★**Viana do Castelo** (which also has some very good beaches). Here the route turns inland up the valley of the Rio Lima, via ★**Ponte da Barca**, to ★★**Peneda Gerês National Park**. Next on the programme comes ★**Braga**, city of churches, not forgetting a small detour to ★★**Citânia de Briteiros**. Subsequent destinations are ★★**Guimarães** and ★**Amarante**. Deviating from the earlier tour of central Portugal it would be possible to follow the Rio Tâmega downstream for a stretch, cross the Douro at Entre os Rios, then follow the Douro upstream as far as Cinfães so as eventually to get to Castro Daire through the Serra de Montemuro. ★**Viseu** is next on the sightseeing itinerary, followed by ★**Guarda**, Portugal's highest town, and eventually ★**Belmonte**. A detour from here into the ★★**Serra da Estrela** should not be missed. The tour heads south through Fundão and ★**Castelo Branco**, with its lovely gardens, to ★★**Castelo de Vide** and ★★**Marvão** which must be highlights of any tour of Portugal. After only a brief stop in **Portalegre** the route continues south to ★**Elvas** or direct to ★**Estremoz**. Further on lies Évoramonte with its fine views from a splendid setting, and from there it's not far to one of Portugal's major cities, ★★**Évora**. From here the route speeds across the uplands of **Alentejo** heading for ★**Beja** and ultimately, via **Castro Verde** and the Serra do Malhão, returns to the starting point at Faro.

**Sights
from A to Z**

Portugal A to Z

Abrantes
B 5

Historical province: Ribatejo. District: Santarèm
Altitude: 190m/623ft. Population: 20,000

Situation and Importance

An old-world little town of white houses and flower-bedecked streets perched high above the north bank of the Tagus, Abrantes occupies an exposed situation which made it a keypoint in the defence of the old Beira provinces. Until now the town has been able to retain its original character in spite of some ugly new buildings.

A local speciality is "Palha de Abrantes", a sweet egg floss.

Sights

Castelo

Above the town are the remains of the once mighty Castelo, built by King Dinis in 1301. It was destroyed by an earthquake in 1533 and finally demolished in 1807 by French troops under Marshal Junot, whom Napoleon created Duke of Abrantes. Within the castle precincts is the church of Santa Maria do Castelo (originally built in 1215; restored in the 15th c.), now housing the Museu Dom Lopo de Almeida, which contains, in addition to the fine late Gothic monuments of the Almeida family (15th–16th c.), valuable old tiles (16th c.), Gothic sculpture, a Gothic head of Christ and two Roman statues of the 1st c. A.D. A visit to the castle is worthwhile because of the magnificent view over Abrantes and the Tagus valley.

Old Town

Other features of interest in Abrantes, to be found in the picturesque alleyways of the old town below the Castelo, are the church of São João Baptista (founded 1300, rebuilt 1589), with a Renaissance coffered ceiling and rich woodcarving, and the church of the Misericórdia (16th c.) which has a Renaissance doorway and paintings of the 16th c. Portuguese school. Also worth seeing is the nearby Convento de São Domingos (originally 1472; much altered and rebuilt), with a beautiful two-storey cloister. The church of São Vicente, in the northern part of the old town, near the road to Sardoal, dates almost entirely from the late 16th c.

Surroundings

Constância

12km/7½ miles west on a beautiful road with splendid views Constância, the Roman Pugna Tagi, is situated at the junction of the Rio Zêzere and the Tagus. The Church of the Misericórdia, with tile decoration, and a parish church (1636; restored in the 19th c. with a ceiling painting from 1890) are both worth seeing.

★ Castelo de Almourol

5km/3 miles south-west of Constância, on a rocky islet in the Tagus, stands the Templar castle of Almourol. Built on Roman and Moorish foundations, with eleven towers, it is undoubtedly one of Portugal's finest 12th c. castles (restored in the 19th c. in the Romantic style).

There is a ferry over to the castle during the tourist season. From the massive keep there are fine views of the Tagus.

Tancos

Tancos, just 2km/½ mile west of the castle, has a pretty Renaissance-style parish church.

◀ *Torre de Belém*

Castelo de Almourol

Castelo do Bode (pousada), 10km/6 miles north of Constância, is particularly popular with the Portuguese for its water sports and leisure facilities. Its 115m/377ft high dam forms an enormous lake (Barragem do Castelo do Bode) and is the lowest of a series of dams on the Rio Zêzere creating a string of lakes stretching for more than 50km/31 miles. Boat trips to the dam from Castelo do Bode can be arranged on request.

Castelo do Bode

The most interesting feature of Sardoal, about 12km/7 miles north of Abrantes, is the altarpiece (polyptych) by an unknown 16th c. master in the parish church.

Sardoal

The little town of Belver (alt. 220m/720ft; pop. 2000) on the right bank of the Tagus 30km/19 miles east of Abrantes is dominated by a castle begun in 1194, in the reign of King Sancho I, completed in 1212 and restored in the 14th c. There is a beautiful carved 13th c. reredos in the castle chapel and "Sancho I's balcony" affords a splendid view of the Tagus valley.

Belver

Albufeira

B 7

Historical province: Algarve. District: Faro
Altitude: 0–35m/0–115ft. Population: 17,000

In a bay on Portugal's south coast and beautifully located, like an amphitheatre in the shelter of bizarrely shaped cliffs (Ponta da Baleeira), Albufeira has developed in recent years into one of the major seaside resorts of the Algarve.

It has lost much of its former character as the haunt of painters and would-be artists – in the sixties and seventies it was known as the "St Tropez of the Algarve" – but, offsetting this, provides a whole range of

Situation and Importance

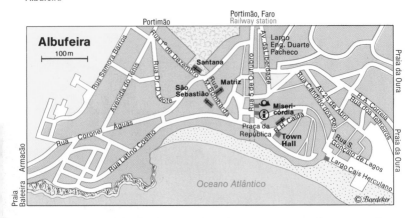

sport and recreation facilities (water-skiing, windsurfing, tennis riding, golf, etc.).

Townscape

Despite the dual carriageways and big new hotels, holiday complexes, etc. constantly springing up in its outskirts Albufeira has still managed to retain, in its old town, something of its original Moorish character as a picturesque little town of white houses and steep, narrow streets where visitors can enjoy a stroll among inviting cafés, shops and little boutiques.

There is plenty of nightlife and restaurants and bars abound, especially along the Rua Cândido dos Reis.

Albufeira on the Algarve coast

Sights

Before setting out on a tour of Albufeira a panoramic view of the bay and the Old Town can be enjoyed from the terrace east of the town.

★View

After the earthquake of 1755 the Igreja Matriz was rebuilt by the then Bishop of the Algarve, Francisco Gomes de Avelar. In 1993 the whole building was renovated, although this did not add much to its charm.

Igreja Matriz

The Igreja of Sant'Ana (church of St Anne) on the Largo Jacinto d'Ayete, on the corner of Rua 1° de Dezembro, on the other hand, is very pretty. This typical, whitewashed 18th c. Algarve church stands out as a rural feature in urban surroundings. Note the crossing cupola and Baroque gables.

Igreja of Sant'Ana

The newly laid-out Largo Engenheiro Duarte Pacheco is Albufeira's main square, a meeting point for both locals and tourists. It is lined with cafés, restaurants and snack bars, together with postcard kiosks and fashion jewellery shops. The fountain portrays the town's churches and a mosaic picture shows a view of old Albufeira.

Largo Engenheiro Duarte Pacheco

The Gruta do Xorino are where the revolutionaries sought refuge in 1833 when the town was besieged by monarchist Miguelists. They reached the caves by an underground tunnel and from there fled by boat to Faro. Fishermen offer boat trips to the Xorino Grottos from the centre of Albufeira; it is also possible to walk to them along a cliff path.

Gruta do Xorino

From Rua 5 de Outubro a tunnel leads to Albufeira's municipal beach, but it is usually crowded in summer. Above the beach is a short promenade, where the view can be enjoyed from one of the cafés.
   To the west of Albufeira there are several small beaches in pretty bays, as well as Praia da Galé stretching as far as Armação de Pêra. The Oura, Balaia and Maria Luisa beaches to the east of the town form part of the tourist suburbs of Montechoro and Areias de São João. Generally speaking, the restaurants and water sports facilities are good.

Beaches

Surroundings

At Guia, 6km/4 miles north-west of Albufeira, lies the well-known Zoomarine Park, with small lakes, gardens and restaurants, which attracts some 400,000 visitors annually. The many animals include talking parrots, dolphins and seals, while numerous species of fish swim in various pools and aquaria. There is a large swimming pool for children and adults. Four hours should be allowed to enjoy all the main attractions and animals (open: daily 10am–6pm, to 8pm in summer; closed Jan. and Feb.).

Zoomarine Park

For other places of interest in the surroundings of Albufeira see Algarve.

Other places to visit

Alcácer do Sal   B 6

Historical province: Alentejo. District: Setúbal
Altitude: 30m/100ft. Population: 16,000

The ancient little town of Alcácer do Sal ("castle of salt"), the Roman Salacia, lies above the right bank of the Rio Sado, which here opens out into a wide estuary. The banks of the river are lined with the salt-pans which have given the town its name.
   A number of fine old buildings bear witness to the town's earlier prosperity, achieved from medieval times onwards by its flourishing trade in salt and corn, and the growing of rice in the warm low lying marshland along the river, a crop that has increased in importance since recent decades have seen many of the salt-pans around the town abandoned.

Situation and Importance

Sights

Castelo	Above the town the ruins of the castle (today a Pousada), still ringed round by its walls, afford fine views of the town and river.
Igreja de Santa Maria	The Romanesque church of Santa Maria next to the castle dates from the 12th/13th c. and has a Renaissance doorway to the Chapel of the Sacrament and beautiful 17th c. tile decoration.
Santo António	To the north of the town centre is the former Convent of Santo António (16th c.), which also has an impressive Renaissance doorway, as well as lavish marble decoration in the Chapel of the 11,000 Virgins (16th c.).
Museu Municipal	Near the Town Hall, which stands on the riverbank and houses the tourist information centre, is the former church do Espírito Santo (Manueline window) containing the town museum, the Museu Municipal, with Stone Age and Roman material, relics of the Moorish period and coins.
Santuário do Senhor dos Mártires	The Romanesque and Gothic church do Senhor dos Mártires (13th/14th c.) on the western edge of town contains the stone sarcophagus of Diogo de Pereira (1427) who, as Grand Master of the Knights of São Tiago, played a crucial role in recapturing the city from the Moors (1217).

Surroundings

Torrão	Located on the banks of the Barragem de Vale de Gaio reservoir some 30km/19 miles south-east of Alcácer do Sal, Torrão is the birthplace of Bernardim Ribeiro (c. 1482–c. 1552), famous for his poem "Saudades", published in 1554, probably posthumously. The Manueline church contains 17th c. azulejo tiling.
Grândola	The little country town of Grândola (alt. 95m/312ft; pop. 5500) 23km/ 14 miles south of Alcácer do Sal is an important centre for the Portuguese cork industry. It is also the town that featured in the song that in April 1974 heralded the "Carnation Revolution" ("Grândola, vila morena" = "Grândola, brown town", see Baedeker Special, pp. 42/43).
Tróia	See Costa de Lisboa

Alcobaça   B 5

Historical province: Estremadura. District: Leiria
Altitude: 42m/138ft. Population: 11,000

Situation and Importance	Alcobaça, about 20km/12 miles south of Batalha and known by the Romans as Eburobriga, is charmingly set between two little rivers, the Alcoa and the Baça, below the ruins of a Moorish castle. Its principal attraction is its magnificent Cistercian abbey.
	Alcobaça is the cultural and economic heart of a large and fertile agricultural region (fruit canning), first brought under cultivation by St Bernard's monks in the 14th c.
	The town is noted for its blue painted pottery which, with other handicrafts, can be found on sale in the square fronting the abbey.

★★Real Abadia de Santa Maria de Alcobaça

History	The Cistercian abbey of Alçobaça – once one of the most prosperous and influential religious houses in Portugal – is now one of its outstanding

The Church of Alcobaça Abbey ▶

architectural monuments (open: daily 9am–5pm, in summer to 7pm). It was declared a building of world cultural interest by UNESCO in 1989.

In 1154 King Afonso (Henriques) I granted land in this area, recovered during the liberation of Santarém from the Moors (March 15th 1147), to Bernard of Clairvaux, who had supported him in the long-drawn-out negotiations for Papal recognition of the newly established kingdom of Portugal, for the foundation of a Cistercian abbey. The king had himself already laid the foundation stone of a first church in 1148, and 1154 saw the first monastic buildings. The influx of monks from Burgundy soon necessitated larger quarters and the building of a new abbey was begun in 1178 and largely completed by 1222. It was to be much altered in subsequent centuries, the new buildings combining with the old to form an ensemble of notable harmony.

In accordance with the rules of the order there were always 999 monks ("one less than a thousand"), who cultivated fruit and vines in the valleys of the Alcoa and the Baça, thus laying the foundations of what is still the largest area of orchards and vineyards in Portugal. Here, too, in the 13th c., the monks established the first public school in the kingdom, and this later played a part in securing the establishment of the first Portuguese university at Coimbra. The abbot of Alcobaça, who styled himself "Counsellor to His Majesty and Almoner of the Crown", had dominion over thirteen towns and villages, three ports and two castles; and between the 13th and the 18th c. the abbey was one of the country's leading intellectual and spiritual institutions, providing the Portuguese kings not only with a refuge in case of need but also with a place for retreat and meditation.

The 1775 earthquake severely damaged the abbey, and in 1811 it was occupied by French troops under Marshal Junot and plundered of many of its treasures. In 1834 the abbey was secularised and the buildings converted to various uses (barracks, stables, etc.). Finally, in 1930, the importance of this national monument was recognised and it was given statutory protection.

General layout

The abbey layout is modelled on that of the mother house at Cluny, and its excellent state of preservation makes it the finest example of Cistercian architecture in Europe. Basically Gothic in structure, the abbey is approximately square in plan. In addition to the mighty church and the usual offices it contains five cloisters, seven dorters (dormitories), accommodation for guests, a library and a huge kitchen. Some parts of the building are occupied by government offices and a school, and hence not open to the public.

Abbey church

The main front of the abbey, 221m/725ft long, is dominated by the Baroque façade (1725) of the church with its two low towers and its numerous statues. Of the original Gothic façade there survive only the doorway (also decorated with Baroque sculpture) and the large rose window.

The interior of the early Gothic hall-church is of Cistercian clarity, austerity and simplicity. The most spacious church interior in Portugal (106m/348ft long, 21.5m/71ft wide and 20m/65ft high), it is divided into three aisles of equal height, the lateral aisles being very narrow. Twenty-four massive piers, recessed on the inner side to take the choir-stalls (which were burned by the French), support twelve bays of Gothic vaulting. Around the choir are nine chapels and the high altar is surrounded by eight columns.

In the transepts are the sumptuous tombs of King Pedro I (south transept) and his beloved Inês de Castro (north transept), who was murdered at the behest of Pedro's father King Afonso IV. After his accession Pedro had her exhumed and crowned in due form at Coimbra as queen. The tragic story of the unhappy lovers and the bloody vengeance which Pedro exacted on the murderers after he became king, earning him the sobriquet of Pedro the Cruel, are celebrated by Camões in the third canto of his "Lusiads".

At Pedro's wish the tombs were so placed that when they arose on the Day of Judgment the two lovers would see each other at once. The

Alcobaça Abbey

Real Abadia de Santa Maria de Alcobaça

1 Tomb of Pedro I
2 Tomb of Inês de Castro
3 Choir
4 "Death of St Bernard" (terracotta)
5 Sala dos Túmulos
6 Chapel of the Sacrament
7 Manueline doorways
8 Sacristy
9 Chapterhouse
10 Dorter (upper floor) Store (lower floor)
11 Kitchen
12 Refectory
13 Fountain-house

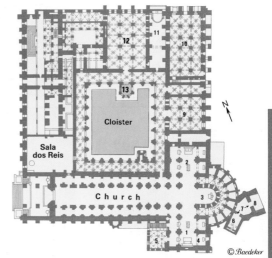

© Baedeker

sarcophaguses, hewn from soft Ançã sandstone, with rich figural decoration, are in the Flamboyant style of the second half of the 14th c. They were much damaged by Junot's troops in 1811.

On the sarcophagus of Inês de Castro, which is supported by crouching figures, is the recumbent figure of the dead woman, surrounded by six praying angels. Along the sides are scenes from the life of Christ, at the foot the Last Judgment, at the head Christ on Calvary. The stone sarcophagus of King Pedro, borne by six lions, has the recumbent figure of the king, also surrounded by praying angels. Along the sides are scenes from the life of St Bartholomew, and at the head is a wheel of fortune with 18 episodes from the life of the two lovers, including the murder of Inês.

In the transept chapels are painted terracotta figures of unnamed monks (17th c.) and a fine representation of the death of St Bernard. To the east of the ambulatory the two fine Manueline doorways (16th c.) are by João de Castilho. In the antechamber of the sacristy is the only example of reticulated vaulting in the abbey.

On the west side of the south transept is the Sala dos Túmulos, a funerary chapel containing a number of tombs.

On the north side of the church are the medieval monastic buildings. A doorway in the north aisle leads into the beautiful two-storey Claustro do Silêncio or Claustro de Rei Dinis. The lower cloister was built by Domingo and Diogo Domingues between 1308 and 1311; the upper gallery (by the Castilho brothers) was built for King Manuel in the 16th c.

Monastic buildings

On the north side of the cloister stands the Gothic fountain-house. Here, too, is the entrance to the refectory (fine reading-desk), one of the oldest parts of the abbey. Adjoining is the large kitchen, 18m/60ft high, with a huge open fireplace and a fish-tank supplied with water from the Alcoa which was once an important feature of the abbey, since the Cistercians were forbidden to eat meat.

On the south-east side of the cloister is the chapterhouse (Sala do Capítulo, 14th c.), at the south-west corner the Sala dos Reis (Hall of Kings), the walls of which are decorated with azulejos depicting scenes from the history of the abbey. Also on the walls are terracotta statues (probably by monks) of most of the Portuguese kings down to José I. On the upper floor are the dorters, the library, etc.

Claustro do Silêncio (cloister of silence) . . .   *. . . and well-house*

Surroundings

Museu Nacional do Vinho

Located on the road to Batalha leading eastward out of Alcobaça this "national wine museum" illustrates the regional winemaking methods and traditions.

Aljubarrota

Aljubarrota, 7km/4½ miles further along the same road, is the scene of a famous battle on August 15th 1385 in which a Portuguese army commanded by Nuno Alvares Pereira won a decisive victory over the Spaniards. In token of thanksgiving King João I founded Batalha Abbey (see entry). The town has a number of handsome 17th and 18th c. houses and the church of Nossa Senhora dos Prazeres (originally Romanesque; the 13th c. doorway still exists).

Termas da Piedade

Termas da Piedade is a little spa 2km/1¼ miles north of Alcobaça specialising in cures for diseases of the stomach and intestines.

Coz

5km/3 miles north the former monastery at Coz is open to visitors; the Manueline doorway is 17th c.

Alenquer   A 5

Historical province: Estremadura. District: Lisboa
Altitude: 160m/525ft. Population: 10,000

Situation and Importance

The seemingly rather sleepy little town of Alenquer is tucked away about 45km/28 miles north of Lisbon. Its population is mainly employed in the woollen and papermaking industries.
   It was the birthplace of the navigator and pilot Pero de Alenquer who was with Bartolomeu Dias when he discovered the Cape of Good Hope and with

Vasco da Gama on his expedition to discover the sea route to India. Pero, a man of humble origin, won a great reputation for his extraordinary achievements, earning himself the nickname "prince of pilots" and access to the court. His exploits were vividly described in the writings of the diplomat and chronicler of Manuel I, Daimão de Góis (1507–71), scion of a noble Alenquer family.

Alenquer's particular charm lies in its setting, with even the simplest of its houses clinging picturesquely to the slopes of the hillside on which it stands.

Townscape

The local museum is the Museu de Hipólito Cabaço containing archaeological (particularly Stone Age) material.

Above the town, and only partially accessible, is the Convent of São Francisco, the oldest Franciscan house in Portugal, founded in 1222 during the saint's lifetime.

Surroundings

Vila Franca de Xira, some 10km/3 miles south of Alenquer, is the centre of Portuguese bullfighting where most of the fighting bulls are bred and where the "Agrinxira" agricultural and livestock show is held annually in May and the lively "Festival of the Red Waistcoat" (Colete Encardo), with processions and bullfights, is celebrated every July.

Vila Franca de Xira

Alentejo   B/C 6/7

Historical province: Alentejo
Districts: Portalegre, Évora, Beja and Setúbal
Area: 28,747sq.km/11,096sq. miles
Population: 370,000. Chief town: Évora

The southern Portuguese province of Alentejo extends to the south-east of the Tagus ("além Tejo", beyond the Tagus) over a seemingly endless tableland as far as the Algarve, bounded on the east by the Spanish frontier and on the west by the Atlantic Ocean. It is divided into the Alto Alentejo (Upper Alentejo, to the north) and Baixo Alentejo (Lower Alentejo, to the south). The Alentejo is one of the most unspoiled regions in the whole Iberian Peninsula. Comparatively few tourists come here, in spite of the fact that it has much to offer – endless green meadows, olive groves and cork-oaks glittering in the sun, as well as some magical little medieval towns, such as Castel de Vide, Elvas, Estremoz, Beja and Marvão (see entries). Évora (see entry), the chief town of the whole province, should not be missed by any traveller to Portugal.

General Information

The lonely, barren and almost featureless landscape is reminiscent of more northerly latitudes, and a remarkable contrast to the hilly terrain and luxuriant vegetation of most of the Portuguese provinces.

Topography

Geologically Alentejo is a continuation of the Castilian Meseta, a residual expanse worn down and levelled by erosion, resting on Palaeozoic rocks of the Iberian basement. The land rises to average heights of between 150 and 350m/500 and 1150ft, reaching barely 400m/1300ft at its highest point in the south-west and with its only "real" mountains in the north-east, the Serra de São Mamede (1025m/3365ft).

The climate is Mediterranean, but with some continental features: a cold but snow-free winter, a short spring with little rain, a hot, dry summer and frequent showers of rain in the autumn. The rainfall is relatively low, an annual average of 600–700mm/24–28in.

Climate

Given this climatic pattern, the natural vegetation is confined to modest evergreen heaths and oaks and sclerophyllous evergreens (woody plants

Vegetation

Cork – more than just bottle stopper

In the 17th century the European "drink market" experienced a revolution. First of all it was enriched by chocolate from Central America, then by coffee from Arabia and subsequently by tea from China. Spirits were also imported after the Dutch had mastered the art of distillation; beer could be kept longer with the aid of hops, and at last clean water was available in the large towns and cities – thanks to pipe installations like those the Romans had used. The only problem not yet solved was how to keep wine for long periods! Since Roman times wine had been stored "in the wood", but this adversely affected its quality in two respects – storage in barrels for too long could detract from its bouquet, and it quickly lost its character once it was served. It therefore had to be consumed quickly – there was no question of enjoying a mature vintage wine. Glass bottles had been in use since the early 17th century, but they merely served to bring the wine from the cellar to the table – until some clever fellow thought of linking bottle, cork and corkscrew! It was soon realised that, kept in a sterile and airtight glass bottle, with a cork stopper, wine could mature gently and accordingly keep longer. However, the revolutionary bottle/cork method was still in its infancy. Bottles at that time were so bulbous that they could only be stored vertically, with the result that the corks dried out and allowed air to enter. By the end of the 18th century it was found that wine would mature just as well in a taller, slimmer bottle laid horizontally as it did in an old Roman amphora, for as soon as the wine comes into contact with the wine it renders the bottle airtight. The change in bottle shape can best be seen in the case of Portuguese port wine bottles – from the very bulbous *carafe* dating from 1708 via taller and slimmer bottles to those we know today (first made in 1812).

So far no better substitute for cork has been found. Connoisseurs and epicures alike value highly these stoppers made from the bark of the cork-oak (*quercus suber*), which protect the wine and at the same time provide it with the degree of acid necessary for the maturing process. The Portuguese also "love" this natural product for very understandable reasons – cork from Portugal accounts for 38% of the world production and 65% of that of Europe, putting it at the forefront of all cork-producing countries. Portugal's 70 million or so cork-oaks grow mainly in the Ribatejo, Alentejo and Algarve regions. The trees grow to a height of 6–10m/20–33ft and live for an average of 150 years. The first pieces of bark cannot be removed until the cork-oak, known to the Portuguese as the *sobreiro*, is at least twenty years old. The cork bark is peeled off in the hot summer months, for it is then that the metabolism of the tree is at its greatest and the bark comes off the most easily. With an axe, two notches are made around the trunk and joined by a further vertical one; then the cork crust, several centimetres thick, is gradually loosened until it can be removed. Of course, the whole bark must not be removed because then it would not re-form. It takes at least six years for the now bare and blood-red tree trunk to grow fresh cork that can be peeled off once again. A number is painted on the trunk to indicate when cork can next be harvested; the number is the last number of the calendar year, i.e., the figure "9" currently means that cork can be removed again in 1999. After the harvest the cork bark – some 150kg/330lb from each tree – is stacked and left to dry in the open for three

A forest of cork-oaks

months before being taken to the cork factories, most of which are in the north of Portugal. In order to free the cork of pests and to cleanse it of any mineral salts and tannic acid the material is first boiled. This produces strong and foul-smelling vapours. The boiling process also causes the cells of the cork to expand, giving it its elasticity and softness. Then the bark is pressed, dried and cut into slices. Now the cork can be sorted out, according to its intended purpose. As it is very light, elastic, gas and water proof and does not readily burn, conduct electricity or lose its beneficial properties, it can be put to a number of uses – as table-mats and coasters, buoys for fishing nets, life-jackets, shoe insoles, pin-boards, wall-cladding, insulation, sound-proofing, washers, etc. However, the cylindrical bottle corks bored from strips of cork and dispatched in sacks of up to 20,000 corks are the most important product. For over 200 years Portugal has been exporting these not exactly cheap corks (they can cost between 5 and 25 pence/8 and 40 US cents each depending on the quality) which are particularly suitable as stoppers for wine bottles because cork contains no poisonous materials and imparts no taste or smell of its own. Its marked ability to expand and the small suckers on the cork walls make it ideal for sealing bottles and for preventing the entry of putrefiers. And as cork does not essentially change its make-up it is ideal for storing wines.

Finally, here are two tips. As mentioned above, wine should never be stored upright. The cork must always be in contact with the liquid, otherwise it will dry out and then too much air will enter the wine and it will oxodise more quickly. Uncork the wine sometime before serving – wine needs oxygen to release its aroma.

Mértola in the Alentejo

with small leathery leaves). The few trees mostly grow in isolated clumps. The cork-oak is widely distributed, and makes an important contribution to the economy of the region.

Population

With only 370,000 inhabitants – barely 4% of Portugal's population – spread over at least a fifth of the country's area, Alentejo is very sparsely populated, with a density of 21 to the sq.km/54 to the sq. mile. There are concentrations of population in a few smallish towns and large villages, but for the rest the rural population is widely dispersed, living in and around large isolated farms (*montes*). These are often on low hills and consist of the farmhouse itself, the houses of the farm workers and the various farm buildings and are usually surrounded by great expanses of farmland. The buildings, with walls of beaten earth, are carefully white-washed, and with their flat roofs and intricately decorated openwork chimneys have preserved many Moorish features.

Farms of this kind, which with the addition of day labourers and seasonal workers can amount to settlements of considerable size, are characteristic of the old type of large estate which has long given rise to social tensions in Portugal. The expropriation measures introduced after the 1974 revolution have since been largely revoked. As a result many landworkers and day labourers have become redundant and can find no employment in the Alentejo – the unemployment rate here is 11% much higher than in the rest of the country.

Culture

Alentejo is a region of very ancient settlement, with numerous remains of Stone Age occupation (standing stones and megalithic chamber tombs, known as *antas*, being particularly common in Alto Alentejo) and of the Roman and Moorish periods.

The purely agricultural character of the region is reflected in the architecture: here the seafaring motifs common in the architectural ornament of the Manueline period give place to agricultural motifs (ears of corn, plants, farm implements).

Although Alentejo has a fifth of Portugal's total coastline the life and activities of the region revolve around the interior. The west coast is developing very gradually as far as tourism is concerned, for example, near Vila Nova de Milfontes. Less than 1% of the country's total catch of fish comes from here, and the endless stretches of broad beach are empty and scarcely known to tourists. The people of the Alentejo region live almost exclusively from agriculture. In spite of the sparse population and the extreme aridity, almost the whole area is carefully cultivated. In the west, on poor soils, extensive monoculture predominates (corn, grown by dry-farming methods); in addition grazing farming (with a third of the total Portuguese stock of cattle) is carried on throughout the year, together with the growing of cork-oaks (montados), pig-farming and charcoal-burning. The wet and fertile coastal areas and the land on the weather side of the hills in the north-east are the granary of Portugal, growing in addition to grain (wheat, rye, maize) large quantities of fruit and olives.

Alentejo is also the home of a celebrated breed of horses, the Alter Real, which has been reared here since the mid 18th c. and is particularly prized for dressage.

The problem of irrigation is of fundamental importance in this agricultural province. The rivers which flow through the region are almost dry in summer and are thus of little use for irrigation; but there is an ambitious plan to build a series of dams on the Tagus and Guadiana and the Guadiana's left-bank tributary, the Rio Chança, and pump the water throughout the region in a dense network of canals.

Economy

Algarve

B/C 7/8

Historical province: Algarve. District: Faro
Area: 4960sq.km/1915sq. miles
Population: 350,000. Chief town: Faro

The southern Portuguese province of the Algarve, lying in the extreme south-west corner of Europe, is a broad strip of land, some 155km/95 miles long and up to 50km/30 miles wide, on the southern Atlantic coast of Portugal, extending from Cabo de São Vincente (Cape St Vincent) in the west to the Rio Guadiana, the frontier with Spain, in the east. Sheltered on the north by a mountain range, which increases in height from east to west and isolates it from the rest of Portugal, the Algarve has preserved its own distinctive character and is very different in scenery, climate and culture from the more northerly parts of the country. It is also the province of Portugal where tourism has had the greatest impact on the landscape.

Although the Algarve is much poorer in art and architecture than other parts of the country, it has developed into the most popular tourist and holiday region in Portugal thanks to its equable climate, its luxuriant sub-tropical vegetation and its beautiful beaches of fine sand.

Recent decades have seen rapid growth in this tourism and although building excesses have not been on the scale that has marred the Spanish Mediterranean coast the Algarve, especially its "rocky" parts, also has its share of blots on the landscape from intrusive hotels and holiday complexes.

Nevertheless there has been a real attempt to preserve the natural beauty of the landscape, and to blend hotels into their surroundings. Most of the new developments are spaciously and attractively laid out, often in the Moorish style. Clearly there is a price to be paid for this luxury and comfort, and rates are considerably higher in the Algarve than elsewhere in Portugal, pricing this part of the coast beyond the reach of most Portuguese.

General

The name Algarve comes from the Arabic "Al-Gharb", "the West", referring to this region's location at the western edge of the Islamic empire (see History).

Name

Algarve

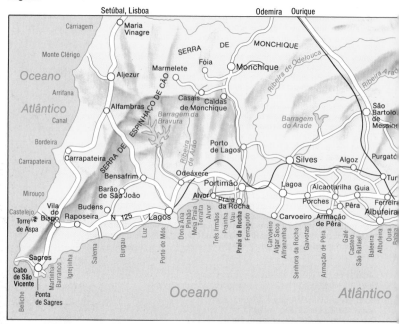

Praia da Rocha, etc. = Names of Algarve beaches

★★Topography	The sparsely populated northern part of the province, the Alto Algarve (Upper Algarve), is a hilly region of schists and sandstones, overlaid in the west by the intrusive rocks of the Serra de Monchique. Apart from one or two features there is little here to interest the holidaymaker.

The coastal strip, the Baixo Algarve (Lower Algarve), a Mesozoic table-land of limestone and sandstone, has two parts. The western half, from Cabo São Vicente to Vale do Lobo (just west of Faro), is the better known and scenically more striking Rocky Algarve, world-famous for its pictur-esque golden-yellow cliffs, slashed by crevices and caves, its sheltered beaches of fine sand, its emerald-green water and its deep blue sky.

To the east, from Faro to the Spanish frontier, is the Sandy Algarve, with endless expanses of sandy beach, dunes and pine-groves but without any outstanding scenic beauties. This area has seen less tourism development.

Climate	The Algarve has one of the most settled climates in the world, with 3000 hours of sunshine in the year. The climate on the coast is similar to that of North Africa. Sheltered on the north and north-west by the hills of the Alto Algarve and exposed to the moderating influence of the Atlantic, the Algarve escapes climatic extremes.

Winter temperatures rarely fall below 10°C/50°F; the summers are dry and hot, but there is always a light sea breeze to bring a pleasant coolness. Temperatures fall rapidly in the evening, and visitors are advised to take some warm clothing. Rainfall is low (an annual 350–600mm/14–24in.) and mostly concentrated in November; but there are abundant resources of groundwater which is used for irrigation, making it possible to get three or four crops a year off the land.

In choosing where to go for a holiday visitors should consider wind conditions. The farther west they go the less protection there is from the

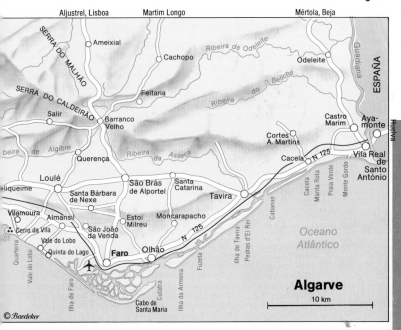

Aljustrel, Lisboa — Martim Longo — Mértola, Beja

SERRA DO MALHÃO
SERRA DO CALDEIRÃO
Ameixial
Cachopo
Ribeira de Odeleite
Odeleite
Guadiana
ESPAÑA
Feitaria
Ribeira do Beliche
Salir
Barranco Velho
Querença
beira de Algibre
Ribeira da Asseca
Castro Marim
Aya-monte
Huelva
Cortes A. Martins
Cacela
N 125
Vila Real de Santo António
Loulé
São Brás de Alportel
Santa Catarina
Tavira
Cacela
Manta Rota
Praia Verde
Monte Gordo
liqueime
Santa Bárbara de Nexe
Vilamoura
Almansil
Estoi Milreu
Moncarapacho
Cabanas
Oceano Atlântico
Cerro da Vila
São João da Venda
N 125
Ilha de Tavira
Pedras d'El Rei
Quarteira
Vale do Lobo
Vale do Lobo
Quinta do Lago
Faro
Olhão
Fuzeta
Ilha da Armona
Algarve
Ilha de Faro
Culatra
Cabo de Santa Maria
Ilha da Armona
10 km

© Baedeker

winds blowing off the Atlantic and the more bracing the climate. The bathing resorts in the most westerly quarter of the Algarve are for the hardy, or for diving enthusiasts and anglers, since in this area there is usually a brisk, cool wind and the sea tends to be rough.

The purplish-red soil of the Algarve supports flourishing plantations of almond-trees, olives, figs and carob-trees. The carob-tree grows to heights of 15–20m/50–65ft, with a short trunk and dense foliage; the carob beans are edible. In the irrigated valleys are orange-groves, cotton plantations and fields of rice and sugar-cane. Most of the gardens and orchards are enclosed by hedges of agaves. Camellias and oleanders make an attractive show, and the almond-trees, which flourish in the mild Mediterranean climate, come into blossom as early as January or February.

Vegetation

Shut off by a barrier of hills in the north, the Algarve developed on its own. The fertility of the soil and the pleasant climate attracted human settlement from an early period. It is known that the Phoenicians and later the Greeks established colonies here, though only scanty remains have survived. In the 6th and 5th c. B.C. Celts settled in this region, followed soon afterwards by Carthaginians: it is said that Portimão was founded by Hannibal. In Roman times the Algarve, then known as Cyneticum, was a prosperous and flourishing region, and evidence of the busy trade carried on here has been recovered by excavation.

History

After the Romans came the Visigoths, who controlled the region for almost 300 years. The Visigoths in turn gave way to the Moors, who remained for 500 years and left an enduring mark on the population and way of life of the Algarve. The physical type of the inhabitants – swarthy, short and stocky – bears witness to a Moorish ancestry, the local style of

105

building and the traditional costumes show clear Moorish features, and the language and place-names, not least the Algarve itself, include many elements of Arab origin.

The capture of Faro by King Afonso III of Portugal in 1249 marked the first stage in the recovery of the territory from the Moors. The Algarve then became the last element to be incorporated in Portugal, an independent kingdom subject to the Portuguese crown in a personal union.

In the 15th c. the Algarve attracted worldwide interest when Henry the Navigator founded his famous school of seamanship at Sagres and with his systematic technical research laid the foundations for the great voyages of discovery of the following century.

Economy

Tourism is now the major factor in the economy of the Algarve. 50% of all visitors to Portugal spend their holidays here; the rest of the country does not experience anything like the degree of mass tourism that has developed in the Algarve during recent years. In 1983 there were 75,000 hotel beds, today the figure is nearer 250,000. Until the late 1960s fishing and agriculture were the major sources of income in the Algarve, but their importance has since been drastically reduced, and its industry forms only a minor part of that of the country as a whole.

Along the Algarve coast

★Cabo de São Vicente

At the western tip of the coast is the windswept Cabo de São Vicente, a rocky headland rising 60m/200ft above the sea, familiar in British history as the scene of the naval victory of Cape St Vincent over a Spanish fleet in 1797. On the cape a lighthouse 24m/80ft high, with a light which is visible at a distance of 35km/22 miles. The fortifications all around date back to the early 16th c., when the Bishop of Silves built the first lighthouse here together with defensive walls and a monastery. Most of these buildings were destroyed in 1587 during an attack by Sir Francis Drake's fleet. The buildings we see today were commissioned by Queen Maria II in 1846.

Here in the 12th c. a ship bearing the body of St Vincent (martyred in 304) came ashore, accompanied by two ravens. The mortal remains of the patron saint of seafarers and vinegrowers were subsequently interred in Lisbon (see entry) in a silver shrine in Sé Patriarcal.

Fortaleza de Beliche

From Cape St Vincent the coast road runs north-east over a windy heath for 1km/¾ mile to Fort Beliche with its former sea fort housing a restaurant.

Sagres

From here it is 5km/3 miles to the port of Sagres (see entry) with its fort to the south of the town.

Vila do Bispo

The "Bishop's town" of Vila do Bispo (pop. 1400), 10km/6 miles north of Sagres, has a 17th c. parish church richly decorated with blue azulejos and gilded woodcarving.

Torre de Aspa

For those with time for a walk, 3.5km/2 miles to the west is the Torre de Aspa. It can also be reached by car going south from Vila do Bispo via Pisten. The Torre de Aspa is an obelisk marking the highest point (156m/512ft) on the southwest coast of the Algarve.

★Ermida de Nossa Senhora de Guadelupe

The 13th c. Romanesque and Gothic chapel of Nossa Senhora de Guadalupe 4km/2½ miles east of Vila do Bispo is where Henry the Navigator is supposed to have prayed for the successful outcome of his projected voyages of discovery.

Salema, Burgau, Luz

Further along the N 125 side roads lead to the coastal resorts of Salema, Burgau and Luz, all with good beaches. Some large hotels and apartment blocks have been built around Salema in recent years. Burgau has retained its character as a fishing village, but the Praia da Luz in Luz is now a sizeable tourist centre.

Rock formations on the Algarve coast ▶

Algarve

Lagos

Beyond Luz the main road continues through increasingly sheltered and fertile countryside to Lagos (see entry). Solitude has become a thing of the past with the advent of modern hotels and holiday complexes, but Lagos has nevertheless managed to retain much of its special charm.

Alvor

Alvor, or Portus Hannibalis, as it was known to the Romans and Albur as it was called by the Moors, lies just 20km/12 miles east of Lagos on the Rio Alvor estuary. Its people lived mostly from fishing until well into the 1970s but nowadays tourism is the main industry. Nevertheless, Alvor has been able to retain its original character as a fishing village. Small white fishermen's houses line the narrow streets of the town centre. There are some restaurants, cafés and souvenir shops, but all in all it is still a village in character. Particularly attractive is the harbour with its fish market and simple shops. To the east of Alvor, however, there are largish hotel blocks at Torralta and on the Praia dos Três.

Praia da Rocha

From Alvor a small road runs close to the coast to Praia da Rocha (see entry), famous for its magnificent beaches between picturesque cliffs.

Portimão

The port of Portimão (see entry), just north of Praia da Rocha, although not picturesque or boasting any particular sights, is a good shopping centre with some quite original bars and restaurants.

From here the road to Porto de Lagos leads up into the Serra de Monchique (see entry).

Ferrugado

Leaving Portimão by the suburb of Vila Nova de Portimão the coast road crosses the Rio Arade on a long viaduct, with the picturesque fishing village of Ferrugado (see Portimão) at the other end.

Lagoa

Lagoa (pop. 6500), 8km/5 miles east of Portimão, is a modest little country town with wine-making establishments. From here a road goes off left to Silves (see entry) and right to Carvoeiro.

The nearby Slide and Splash water pleasure park (see Practical Information, Water Pleasure Parks) has plenty of giant waterslides and other attractions to keep the children amused!

Carvoeiro

Carvoeiro is frequently cited as a particularly successful example of the new-style coastal resort but development of exclusive vacation homes, etc. on the rocky hills above the old town centre has reached such a pitch that the beautiful craggy coast and hinterland is almost completely smothered with Moorish style holiday villas. There are cafés and restaurants in abundance.

★★Algar Seco

At the eastern end of the resort is the picturesque rock arch the "Algar Seco", where the sea has scoured strange shapes and caves out of the white limestone. These are best explored on foot. There is a small café in the middle of this "limestone world".

Porches

There is another big water pleasure park, "the Big One", at Porches, on the N 125 (see Practical Information, Water Pleasure Parks).

Armação de Pêra

From Porches and Alcantarilha roads lead south from the N 125 to Armação de Pêra. The uniformity of its plain multi-storey buildings, and its limited, more simple accommodation than that offered by Carvoeiro is offset by its excellent and seemingly endless beach. It is popular with both Portuguese and foreign holidaymakers.

Just over 1km/¾ mile west, on a high crag, is the 13th c. chapel of Nossa Senhora da Rocha.

Barely 5km/2 miles east of Alcantarilha a road leads to the Algarve's biggest and best-known holiday resort, Albufeira (see entry).

Vilamoura

About 10km/6 miles east of Albufeira is a planning development straight off the drawing board. The little holiday villages dotted over the hilly country-

Coast near Lagos (aerial photo)

side offer every conceivable leisure activity – golf-courses, casinos, marinas, etc.

Building works near Vilamoura's marina revealed the remains of the original Roman settlement Cerro da Vila, and the "mosaic house" dating from the 3rd c. A.D. is particularly worth seeing.

Quarteira, 3km/2 miles south of Vilamoura, is less attractive with its serried ranks of hotels and apartment blocks.

Vale do Lobo (wolf valley) and Quinta do Lago (estate by the sea), a few kilometres south-east of Quarteira, revert to exclusive holiday complexes, with comfortable villas and hotels in a park landscape. This pleasant scenery was the setting for the 1989 session of the NATO assembly in Quinta do Lago.

Quarteira,
Vale do Lobo,
Quinta do Lago

Just before Almansil a road leaves the N 125 for Loulé (see entry) which is supposed to have the best decorated chimneys in the region.

Loulé

Just past Almansil, still on the N 125 to Faro, the Baroque church of São Lourenço de Matos (1730) on the left of the road contains splendid azulejos (1730) depicting the life of St Lawrence. A little way down from the church is the Centro Cultural São Lourenço (exhibitions and concerts).

São Lourenço

Faro (see entry), the chief town of Algarve province, lies about 10km/ 6 miles beyond São Lourenço.

Faro

The coast road runs east from Faro over the irrigated plain, which resembles one enormous fertile garden. From here to the Spanish frontier extends a long succession of broad sandy beaches. This part of the coast is not as popular with tourists as the rocky Algarve and the hotels and holiday settlements are fewer and further between so that, outside the high season, secluded beaches are still to be found.

View of Carvoeiro

Olhão	The next place of any size is Olhão (see entry), which cannot be appreciated from the road – it takes a stroll around this little fishing town to sense something of its Moorish atmosphere.
Tavira	No tour of the Algarve should overlook Tavira (see entry), 22km/14 miles east of Olhão.
Cabanas, Cacela	The little fishing villages of Cabanas and Cacela, just east of Tavira, are still relatively free of mass tourism, with only a limited amount of holiday accommodation among their small white square-stone houses. They are good places for getting away from the crowds, and anyone wanting to enjoy a quiet swim from the offshore spit can get there on foot at low tide or be ferried out by fishing boat.
Monte Gordo	20km/12½ miles beyond Tavira a road forks right to the resort of Monte Gordo, much favoured by British and Dutch visitors, with its casino and promenade, complete with gardens, running alongside the broad beach.
Vila Real de Santo António	Vila Real de Santo António (see entry), 3km/2 miles east of Monte Gordo, is on the Rio Guadiana, the frontier between Portugal and Spain.

Amarante   B 3

Historical province: Duoro Litoral. District: Porto (Oporto)
Altitude: 125m/410ft. Population: 11,000

Situation and Importance	The little town of Amarante, well known for its wine, lies picturesquely on both sides of the Rio Tâmega, on the north-west slopes of the Serra de Marão, about 70km/43 miles east of Oporto.

The annual festival of Romaria de São Gonçalo on the first Saturday in June is a very popular event. In honour of the town's patron saint, who is also patron of married couples and lovers, it may well be a survival of a pre-Christian fertility cult, phallic-shaped biscuits are traditionally exchanged during the festival.

Civic Festival

The old part of the town has a number of fine burghers' houses of the 16th–18th c., most of them roofed with shingles and surrounded by wooden balconies. The best view of this part of town and the beautiful 18th c. bridge over the Rio Tâmega, the Ponte de São Gonçalo, is from the new bridge or one of the café terraces on the south bank of the river.

★ Townscape

Sights

The Ponte de São Gonçalo is a fine three-arched granite bridge over to the old town and was built in 1790 to replace an earlier river crossing.

Ponte de São Gonçalo

The bridge brings the visitor into the 16th c. Convento de São Gonçalo, dominated by its tile-clad central dome. The convent, originally founded by King João III and his queen, Catherine of Castile, was enlarged in the reign of Filipe III in the "Philippine" style of the Renaissance period. The exterior, with arcades decorated with sculpture on the granite façade, is reminiscent of Italian Renaissance architecture. Inside the church and to the left of the high altar is the tomb of São Gonçalo (d. about 1260), in an over-decorated chapel. The organ has a fine carved case (17th c.). In the sacristy are paintings (damaged by Napoleon's troops) of scenes from life of the saint.

Convento de São Gonçalo

There are two adjoining cloisters. One contains the Museu Municipal Amadeo de Souza-Cardoso.

The Convento de São Gonçalo in Amarante

Arraiolos

Museu Municipal Amadeo de Souza-Cardoso

The Museu Municipal Amadeo de Souza-Cardoso on the upper floor of the cloister is a museum of Portuguese art from 1900 onwards, and includes works by the Cubist painter Amadeu de Souza-Cardoso, a native of the town. There is a special archaeological section as well.

São Pedro

The round church of São Pedro, above the convent church, is 17th c. apart from its façade which dates from 1725. The interior is richly decorated with talha dourada and azulejos.

Surroundings

Freixo de Baixo

Freixo do Baixo, 6km/4 miles north-west, has the fine Romanesque church of São Salvador (1210).

Travanca

In a valley about 25km/15 miles north-west of Amarante, Travanca is worth visiting for its fortified church belonging to the former Benedictine convent. The church (three-aisled), originally founded in 970, was rebuilt in Romanesque style in the 12th c. and has remained substantially unchanged since then apart from the apse added in the 16th c. It has preserved very fine 12th c. sculpture and the main portal abounds with mythical and animal carving.

★Serra do Marão

A very attractive excursion winds its way eastward over about 50km/ 30 miles through the wooded Serra do Marão (1415m/4643ft), reaching a height of 1020m/3347ft at the Alto do Espinho pass then descending past the Pousada de São Gonçalo (885m/2904ft), where there is a magnificent view, despite the ravages of forest fires and road-building.
There are fine views all along the rest of the route which carries on to Vila Real (see entry).

Arraiolos   C 6

Historical province: Alto Alentejo. District: Évora
Altitude: 275m/900ft. Population: 6000

Carpet

The ancient little town of Arraiolos about 20km/12 miles north of Évora, referred to by the Alexandrian geographer Ptolemy under the name of Arandia, is set in delightful surroundings on a low hill above the wide Alentejo plain, with magnificent views.
The town is noted for its brightly coloured woollen carpets which are made in a kind of cross-stitch.
This form of carpetmaking, presumably inherited from the Moors, has been practised here since the 17th c. The early designs were mainly Persian imitations, subsequently becoming geometric and more local. Arraiolos carpets, still mostly in strong colours, have been back in fashion since the mid 1970s, and are sold in other Alentejo towns, such as Évora, as well as in Arraiolos itself.

Sights

Castelo

Above the white houses of the town, with their coloured (mostly blue) window-frames, rise the massive ruins of the 14th c. castle, with two gates and six square towers and, within its walls, a 16th c. church.
From here there is a superb view over the town and the fertile Alentejo plain.

Town hall/Carpet exhibition

The late 19th c. town hall, next to the tourist office, houses a permanent exhibition of Arraiolos carpets (also on sale).

Igreja da Misericórdia

The church of the Misericórdia, just south of the town hall, dates from the 16th c. and contains beautiful azulejo decoration (18th c.) and some notable paintings.

View of Arraiolos

Outside the town, to the north, stands the old Convento (now Quinta) dos Lóios (16th c.), now used by a commercial estate. Its church has a Manueline doorway and is completely faced with azulejos (*c.* 1700); the size of the interior is apparently increased by trompe-l'oeil painting. In the two-storey cloister is a beautiful marble basin of 1575.

Quinta dos Lóios

Surroundings

The village church of Santana do Campo 6km/4 miles north-west of Arraiolos was built on the site of a Roman temple.

Santana do Campo

The little town of Montemor-o-Novo (alt. 291m/955ft) 23km/14 miles south-west has a Moorish appearance, with its white houses rising up the slopes of a hill. High above the town are the ruins of a medieval castle, occupying the site of a Roman fortress. In the archaeological museum in the former Convento de São Domingos (16th–18th c.) can be seen reproductions of drawings and finds from the Gruta do Escoural. This cave, 12km/8 miles south-east of Montemor-o-Novo (above the little town of Santiago do Escoural), came to light during blasting operations in 1963. Inside were found 12,000 year-old rock drawings and engravings.

Montemor-o-Novo

Aveiro   B 4

Historical province: Beira Litoral. District: Aveiro
Altitude: sea level. Population: 40,000

About halfway between Oporto and Coimbra, the old port and fishing town of Aveiro is attractively situated on the east side of the Ria de Aveiro, a

Situation and Importance

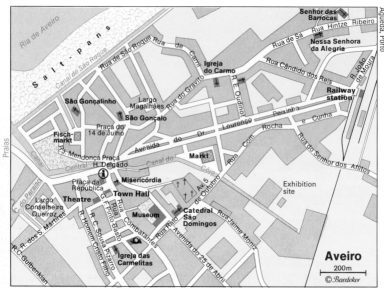

Figueira da Foz, Coimbra

lagoon 47km/29 miles long and up to 7km/4½ miles wide, well stocked with fish, with many branches and windings which earn it the local name of the *pólipo aquático* (sea polyp). Chief town of the district, Aveiro is the see of a bishop and one of Portugal's main west coast ports. The people of Aveiro and the surrounding area live chiefly from the production of salt, obtained from the salt-pans on the shores of the Ria de Aveiro, the gathering of seaweed for use as a fertiliser, and the manufacture of porcelain and ceramics, an industry established here in the early 19th c.

As well as being an attractive town, Aveiro has magnificent beaches in the vicinity and fine alluvial countryside along the Ria de Aveiro.

History

In Roman times the town, then known as Talabriga, lay directly on the sea. In the course of time, however, alluvium brought down by the Rio Vouga built up a spit of land off the coast, leaving only a narrow channel to the sea, the Barra. The town thus acquired one of the most sheltered harbours on the west coast of the peninsula, and enjoyed a period of high prosperity in the 15th and 16th c. as a result of the voyages of discovery which set out from here. The town still preserves many fine old buildings dating from this period.

In 1575 a violent storm devastated the town and closed its outlet to the sea. The harbour was now landlocked and useless, and all attempts to reopen the passage to the sea were unsuccessful; the fishermen, deprived of their livelihood, migrated in the 18th c. to the new port of Vila Real de Santo António at the mouth of the Guadiana, founded by Pombal. A further storm in 1808 opened up the old channel to the sea, and this is now protected from silting-up by dykes and weirs. Aveiro harbour now ranks once again among the finest harbours in Portugal.

Seaweed-fishers

An unusual harvest is gathered by the *moliceiros* of Aveiro, the seaweed-fishers with their characteristic boats, the *barcos moliceiros*; they fish up seaweed (*moliço*), used as a natural fertiliser, from the Ria de Aveiro.

The moliceiros sail their wooden boats, with naïve pictures painted in bright colours on the high prow and stern, through the many branches of

Aveiro: Barcos moliceiros are the characteristic craft

the estuary, gathering the seaweed with large rakes. When the shallow vessels have a full load the "crop" is landed or loaded into ox-carts in the shallows. The boats are up to 15m/50ft long and 2–2.2m/6½–7ft wide. If there is sufficient wind a trapezoid sail is hoisted; otherwise the boats are propelled by long poles or towed along narrow channels by long cables.

In recent times the number of boats has fallen from its original total of over a thousand to about thirty. The once busy and profitable trade of seaweed-gathering is now gradually dying out because of the increasing use of artificial fertilisers. As the demand for seaweed has fallen the moliceiros have begun to harvest wrack-grass (*junco*) which is dried and used as litter for livestock. The difficulty of making a living and the drift of young people to the towns, however, mean that few young men are now prepared to take up this ancient trade.

During the Festa da Ria, held annually in the second half of July, the last of the moliceiros take part in a regatta, with contests of skill and a competition for the finest paintings on the boats.

Aveiro is often compared with Amsterdam or Venice, despite having only three canals, but the many medieval features it has managed to preserve do make it very attractive. This is due in no small measure to the *barcos moliceiros* and a canal trip on one of these boats shows Aveiro at its most appealing. On such a trip visitors can see some magnificent Art Nouveau buildings and house fronts decorated with beautiful azulejos (particularly attractive are the tiles in the railway station).

★ Townscape

Sights

In the Praça da República, opposite the town hall, stands the church of the Misericórdia (16th–17th c.), with a fine Baroque doorway and beautiful 19th c. azulejo decoration on the façade.

Igreja da Misericórdia

Catedral de São Domingos	To the south-east is the Catedral de São Domingos, presented to the Dominicans by the Infante Dom Pedro and consecrated in 1464. It was much altered in the 18th c., and the Baroque porch on the granite façade dates from 1719. The Cathedral contains the tomb of Catarina de Atalíde (d. 1551), who was celebrated by Camões in his sonnets under the name of Natércia. The verses were so passionate that in 1546 the poet was forced to flee from Lisbon.

In front of the Cathedral is one of Portugal's finest calvaries, the Gothic Cruizeiro de São Domingos.

★ Museu de Aveiro	Opposite the Cathedral is the former Dominican convent, the Convento de Jesús, which houses the Museu de Aveiro. The daughter of King Afonso V, Infante Joana, entered this convent in 1472 against her father's wishes. She died here in 1490 at the age of only 38 and was buried in the convent church. Her readiness to endure privation and her renunciation of all privileges won her many admirers, and she is now much revered as the town's patron saint.

The Museu de Aveiro (open: Tues.–Sun. 10am–12.30pm and 2–5pm) was installed in the church, cloisters and other convent buildings in 1911. It provides an excellent and almost complete survey of Portuguese Baroque art, as well as showing pictures of the 15th to 18th c., sculpture and archaeological material. The most important exhibits include a portrait of St Joana (15th c.) which is attributed to Nuno Gonçalves. In the vestibule of the church, which is richly decorated with talha dourada and azulejos, is the Baroque tomb of St Joana (1699–1711, by João Antunes).

Capela do Senhor das Barrocas	In the north of the town is the octagonal chapel of Senhor das Barrocas (1730), also the work of João Antunes. As is usual with Baroque it has richly decorated portals.
Museu de Caça e Pesca	The Museum of Hunting and Fishing lies in the middle of charming parkland. On display are birds, mammals and fish which are denizens of the Aveiro region.

Surroundings of Aveiro

★ Costa Nova	Along the Atlantic coast west of Aveiro stretch the beautiful sandy beaches of the "Silver Coast", the Costa de Prata (see entry). These include São Jacinto, about 8km/5 miles west of Aveiro, and, further south, Barra and Costa Nova, one of the region's finest coastal villages. They offer not only good sea bathing but excellent water sports facilities in the lagoon (sailing, rowing, motorboats, water-skiing).
★ Ria de Aveiro	A boat-trip round the Ria de Aveiro lagoon is well worth undertaking (angling, wildfowling) as it provides an opportunity to see buildings on piles to cope with varying water levels, and the racks for drying the cod (stockfish) landed by the deep-sea fishermen. It also may be possible to get a glimpse of the remaining boats of the seaweed-gathering moliceiros in Bico harbour at Murtosa.
Avanca	25km/16 miles north-east of Aveiro, at Avanca, there is a little museum about Portugal's only Nobel prizewinner, António Egas Moniz, a doctor who won his Nobel Prize in 1949 for his contribution to medicine.
Ovar	At the north end of the Ria de Aveiro is Ovar (pop. 25,000, timber), famous for its Carnival with splendid processions through the streets of the town.

The Calvário, with six chapels, is a scheduled national monument. The interesting local museum contains modern painting, folk art and ethnographical material.

4km/2½ miles further north-west is the pretty little resort of Praia do Furadouro (good beach), where, as at Nazaré (see entry), the fishermen use oxen to haul in their full nets.

An attractive centre for tourists – Costa Nova with its picturesque fishing houses

Farther south, also on the spit of land between the estuary and the sea, are the village of Torreira and the Pousada da Ria.

About 12km/7½ miles north-east of Ovar, the little market town of Vila da Feira (or Santa Maria da Feira; pop. 5000) is dominated by the imposing ruins of a castle built in the 11th c. and later much altered and enlarged. There is a large Gothic hall on the first floor of the well-preserved keep.

Vila da Feira

It is worth making the 40km/25 mile trip eastwards from Vila de Feira to Arouca along narrow roads leading through lonely mountain countryside. The convent at Arouca was founded in the 10th c., but the present buildings are 17th and 18th c. In the convent church note particularly the choir-stalls (1725) and the Baroque organ (1739). The museum on the first floor of the old convent contains a valuable collection of Portuguese religious art (open: Tues.–Sun. 9am–noon and 2–5pm).

Arouca

In the old fishing port of Ilhavo (pop. 6500 and now completely silted up) about 7km/4½ miles south of Aveiro there is an interesting regional and maritime museum (Museu Marítimo e Regional) which also has exhibits of Vista Alegre procelain.

Ilhavo

The best way to see Vista Alegre porcelain is to visit the town itself, 2km/1¼ mile south of Ilhavo. Famous throughout Portugal, the local porcelain has been made here since 1824 and the factory has its own sales outlet and adjacent museum showing the long tradition of porcelain manufacture.
In the nearby little chapel of Nossa Senhora da Penha de França (17th c.) is the tomb of Bishop Manuel de Moura (1699) by the French sculptor Claude Laparde.

Vista Alegre

117

Azores (Ilhas dos Açores)

Autonomous Region of the Azores. (Região Autónoma dos Açores)
Area of islands: 2247sq.km/867sq. miles. Population: 252,000

Situation and General

The archipelago of the Azores (Ilhas dos Açores, "islands of the hawks"), still little involved in tourism, lies in the Atlantic 1400–1800km/870–1120 miles west of the Cabo da Roca on the mainland of Portugal and 1800–2500km/1120–1150 miles east of Newfoundland, between lat. 39°43' and 36°55' north and long. 24°46' and 31°16' west.

The nine largest islands lie in three widely separated groups. To the east are Santa Maria, with the little Formigas Islands, and São Miguel, the principal island of the whole archipelago; in the middle are the islands of Terceira, Graciosa, São Jorge, Faial and Pico, with Portugal's highest mountain (Pico, 2351m/7714ft); and to the north-west Flores and Corvo. Two broad arms of the sea, more than 2000m/6500ft deep and respectively 137km/85 miles and 222km/138 miles wide, separate the three groups, the farthest points of which are 635km/395 miles apart.

Topography

Like other groups of islands in the Atlantic, the Azores are of volcanic origin, consisting of basaltic lavas, mainly of Tertiary date, and trachytes overlying the Central Atlantic anticline. There are numbers of huge caldeiras, and some of these craters (particularly on São Miguel) contain lakes of considerable size. The general topography of the islands is strikingly impressive, with a variegated pattern of hills and uplands, deeply slashed gorges, steep coastal cliffs and numerous hot springs.

Some islands have frequent earthquakes (São Miguel was completely destroyed in 1522, and there were severe earthquakes on Terceira, São Jorge, Faial and Pico on New Year's Day 1980), while others (Santa Maria, Graciosa) are almost free from seismic activity. Sea-quakes are of frequent occurrence in the offshore waters.

Climate

Thanks to their oceanic location and the influence of the Gulf Stream, which flows past the islands to the north, the Azores have a very equable subtropical climate. The annual variation of temperature is scarcely greater than on the more southerly island of Madeira (see entry; January average at Ponta Delgada 14.1°C/57.4°F, August 21.9°C/71.4°F), but the rainfall is higher than on Madeira and the summers in particular are not so dry (average rainfall at Ponta Delgada 1083mm/43 in.; average duration of

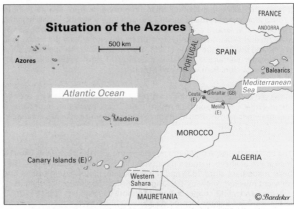

São Miguel, the "green island" in the Azores ▶

sunshine in the year 1580 hours). The islands are exposed throughout the year to strong winds, in summer blowing mainly from the north-east (trade winds), in winter often violent, mostly coming from the south-west.

The Azores are of great importance to weather forecasters, since very stable zones of high pressure frequently build up in the area, particularly to the south and west, from which they move north-east towards Europe, bringing a settled period of good weather.

Vegetation

The vegetation of the Azores, thanks to the high humidity content of the air, is of almost tropical abundance, though it falls short of the luxuriance and variety found on Madeira. The flora is mainly of either European or African origin.

In spite of excessive felling of trees since the colonisation of the islands the hillsides are still covered with fine coniferous forests. Plans are now under way for replanting the deforested areas. Laurels, chestnuts and eucalyptuses are frequently found, either in fair-sized stretches of woodland or in smaller groves. The undergrowth includes bamboos and ferns. Palms are rare, and olive-trees are found in large numbers only on Terceira.

Fauna

Apart from a few native species of birds and bats the animal life is of European origin. Curiously, the sparrow so ubiquitous elsewhere has never established itself in the Azores. Rabbits, mice and rats – common everywhere, and in some places so numerous as to have become pests – were brought in by ships.

Population

The population of the Azores is predominantly of Portuguese origin, with some admixture of Irish, Flemish and Breton blood and small numbers of negroes and mulattoes.

The overwhelming majority of the population is Roman Catholic. In the past an unduly high population density and the unequal distribution of the land, most of which has remained since the colonial period in the hands of a few large landowners, led to a high rate of emigration, particularly to North and South America.

History

The Azores were known to the Phoenicians in the 6th c. B.C., and many centuries later were visited by Norsemen. Thereafter they were forgotten for centuries, first reappearing on an Italian map of 1351. The islands were rediscovered in 1427 by Portuguese seafarers sent out by Henry the Navigator. In 1432 Gonçalo Velho Cabral landed on Santa Maria, in 1444 a Portuguese vessel put in at São Miguel, and by 1452 the other islands were also known. From 1439 the archipelago, until then uninhabited, began to be settled and colonised by the Portuguese. In 1466 Afonso V made the islands of Faial and Pico over to his aunt Duchess Isabella of Burgundy, and thereafter there was a considerable influx of Flemish settlers. As an important port of call on the voyages of exploration in the 15th and 16th c. the islands enjoyed a period of great prosperity. From 1580 to 1640 the Azores, like the rest of Portugal, were under Spanish rule. They played an important part in the constitutional conflicts in Portugal between 1829 and 1832.

During both world wars, in spite of Portugal's neutrality, the United States established important naval and air bases in these strategically situated islands, and these appear set to continue under relatively recent treaties between the two countries.

The political movements for independence from the Portuguese mainland (Frente de Libertação dos Açores, FLA, and other groups) lost their importance when the Azores acquired autonomous region status in 1976.

The islands are currently represented by five members of Parliament in Lisbon.

Economy

The economy, now as in the past, depends mainly on agriculture. All the islands are well cultivated, producing grain (wheat, maize), fruit (apricots, pomegranates, bananas, figs, citrus fruits; pineapples on São Miguel), tea and tobacco for export, chiefly to mainland Portugal. Wine is produced on all the islands. There is also a considerable amount of stock-farming (cattle, pigs, sheep, goats). There are productive fisheries off the coasts. Whaling, long based on Faial and Pico, is now very much in decline. A contribution is also made to the economy by the gathering of seaweed, which produces the agar-agar used in the manufacture of gelatine.

There is practically no industry in the Azores apart from a few recently established textile plants on Terceira and São Miguel. Linen and woollen goods, lace and pottery are made at home or in small workshops, and – like the brandies which are distilled at a number of places in the islands – make popular souvenirs. Everything else, other than agricultural produce, has to be imported. For some years tourism has also been seen as a source of income but, with about 160,000 visitors a year, mostly from mainland Portugal, the Azores remains for the time being a destination for the individualist and nature-lovers.

From Lisbon there are regular flights to São Miguel, Faial and Terceira, from where there are domestic flights to the other islands. There is a regular ferry service only between the islands of the middle group (Faial, Pico, São Jorge, Terceira and Graciosa). The individual islands have bus services (not Corvo), and taxis or hire cars for reaching the more remote spots.

Transport

São Miguel/Ilha de São Miguel

São Miguel (St Michael) is in the east of the archipelago and the largest and most heavily populated of the islands (area 747sq.km/288sq. miles; 65km/40 miles long and up to 16km/10 miles wide; pop.133,000). It is the economic and cultural hub of the Azores, with more features of tourist interest and better facilities for visitors than any of the other islands, and its extraordinary fertility means it is also known as the "green island".

Situation and general

Most of its people live on the steep south coast and are engaged in agriculture, producing maize, figs, pineapples, oranges, wine and tea.

The highest points on the island are the Pico da Vara (1105m/3626ft) in the east and the Pico da Cruz (846m/2776ft) in the west; in the middle of the island, between these two peaks, are many basalt cones ranging in height

Topography

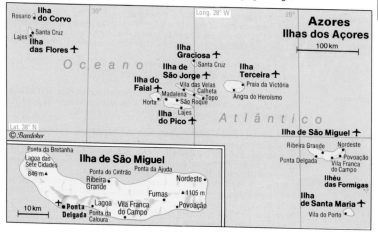

Ponta Delgada (São Miguel), the capital of the Azores

between 200m/650ft and 500m/1650ft. The volcanic character of this hilly island is reflected in the countless extinct craters, large and small, and the severe earthquakes and volcanic eruptions which have racked São Miguel since the 15th c. Some of the largest craters are now occupied by beautiful mountain lakes (Caldeira das Sete Cidades, Lagoa das Furnas, Lagoa do Fogo) which are now among the island's main tourist attractions. Warm and mineral springs are found, particularly in the valleys of Ribeira Grande near the north coast, and at Furnas near the south coast.

★Ponta Delgada

Situation and importance

Ponta Delgada, capital of the autonomous region of the Azores and the chief town and port of the whole archipelago, is at sea level, has a population of 29,000 and lies in a wide bay on the south coast of the island of São Miguel. West of the town is one of the two international airports in the Azores.

The pride of Ponta Delgada is its small university, opened in 1975 and boasting about a thousand graduates to date.

Townscape

The town is built on gently rising ground between green hills, and with its many churches, its trim white houses and the lush gardens on its outskirts presents an attractive spectacle to visitors arriving by sea.

Sights

The harbour, which mainly handles fruit and vegetables, is protected by a breakwater 1544m/1690yd long, from which there are fine views. At the landward end of the breakwater is Fort São Braz (1553), behind which stands a former Franciscan convent (now a hospital), with the beautifully decorated church of São José (15th–18th c.).

In the middle of town there are three linked squares. The first of these, as one comes from the harbour by way of the triple-arched Town Gate (1783), is the Praça de Gonçalo Velho, with a monument to Gonçalo Velho Cabral, discoverer and first governor of the Azores; then comes the Praça da República, with a statue of St Michael (São Miguel) in front of the Paço do

Hot springs at Furnas (São Miguel) . . .   *. . . Povoação, one of oldest settlements*

Concelho (Town Hall, 17th–18th c.); and finally the Largo da Matriz, with the church of São Sebastião (founded 1533, in the reign of Jõao III), mainly Baroque, with a tall tower which is a prominent landmark. The beautiful main doorway, on the west front, is in Manueline style. The church has a beautiful high altar of carved cedarwood (18th c.) and fine choir-stalls. The adjoining museum is devoted to religious art, especially 16th c. vestments. The former convent of Santo André (16th c.; chapel with azulejo decoration) now houses the interesting Museu Carlos Machado, with extensive collections illustrating the folk traditions, culture and natural history (birds, fishes) of the Azores. From here Rua Guilherme Poças leads to the Igreja do Colégio (1592), built for the Jesuits (who were expelled in 1759). The church has a sumptuous Baroque doorway and a magnificent Baroque altar.

On the outskirts of the town are a number of attractive gardens and parks, some of them privately owned (viewing by request), including the municipal park, formerly the Jardim António Borges (wild-life enclosure). Also worth a visit are the pineapple hothouses just outside the town.

There are superb panoramic views from the hills around the town: the Pico Salomão (3km/2 miles north), the Pico da Lima (6km/4 miles north-east) and the Pico do Fogo (10km/6 miles north-east).

Other sights on São Miguel
Views

About 17km/11 miles north-west of Ponta Delgada is the Caldeira des Sete Cidades ("Cauldron of the Seven Cities") in which, according to legend, seven towns founded by expelled Spanish bishops were sunk. This is a volcanic crater which collapsed during some mighty eruption in prehistoric times and was given its present form with a diameter of some 7km/4½ miles and a circumference of 17km/10½ miles, by another violent eruption in 1445. The caldera is occupied by three small and two large crater lakes, the latter two – the Lagoa Grande or Lagoa Verde, with clear green water, and the Lagoa Azul, with deep blue water – being separated only by a

★Caldeira das Sete Cidades

narrow strip of land. The walls of the crater, falling steeply down for some 300m/1000ft, are surrounded by a fringe of woods, ferns and laurels.

Ribeira Grande

18km/11 miles noth-east of Ponta Delgada, on a lava plateau above the north coast of São Miguel, is the town of Ribeira Grande (pop. 9000), with a town hall of the 16th–18th c. and a 17th c. parish church.

★ Lagoa do Fogo

From Ribeira Grande a road climbs to the south-east via Caldeira da Ribeira (6km/4 miles), a small spa with hot mineral springs containing carbonic acid and hydrogen sulphide, and Lombadas (11km/7 miles), which produces a mineral water esteemed throughout Portugal, to the Lagoa do Fogo ("Lake of Fire"), a crater lake 2km/1¼ miles long by 1km/¾ mile wide, surrounded by high hills, which was formed during an eruption in 1563.

It is worth climbing the Pico da Barrosa (949m/3114ft) to enjoy the panoramic view it affords over the whole island.

Vila Franca do Campo

About 25km/15 miles east of Ponta Delgada, on the south coast, is the former capital of the Azores, Vila Franca do Campo, birthplace of the navigator Bento de Góis, which was completely destroyed by an earthquake in 1522 (several 16th c. churches; potteries).

★ Furnas

From Vila Franca do Campo a road runs inland, passing the Lagoa das Furnas, a crater lake 2km/1¼ miles long, to Furnas, a popular summer resort (fine gardens, villas, golf course) in a beautiful forest-fringed valley basin (alt. 200–275m/650–900ft). Here after a violent volcanic eruption in 1630 there emerged a whole series of springs of various kinds (hot springs, mud springs, sulphur and mineral springs), some of which are used for medicinal purposes, either internally or in baths. There is magnificent luxuriant vegetation.

Povoação

12km/7½ miles south-east of Furnas on a beautiful road is Povoação (pop. 4000), one of the oldest settlements in the Azores, situated in a wide bay on the south coast. Above the little town stands the Ermida de Santa Bárbara, the first church to be built in the archipelago.

Santa Maria/Ilha de Santa Maria

Situation and general

Santa Maria, the most southerly of the Azores, lies 85km/53 miles south of São Miguel in lat. 37° north and long. 25°5′ west.

This rocky but fertile island, 17km/11 miles long and up to 8km/5 miles wide, has an area of 97sq.km/37sq. miles and a population of about 6500, who live mainly by crop-farming, stock-rearing and fishing, with pottery often as a sideline. Santa Maria has a well-equipped airport which dates from the Second World War when it was used as an American base.

Topography

The island is hilly, becoming flatter towards the west, with steep coasts fringed by long stretches of cliffs. The highest point is the double summit of Pico Alto (590m/1836ft). There are no calderas on Santa Maria.

Some 35km/22 miles north-east of Santa Maria is the Formigas Bank, an undersea ridge which emerges from the water to a height of up to 11m/36ft in a series of bare cliffs known as the Rocas Formigas.

Vila do Porto

Vila do Porto (pop. 6000), the chief town on the island, is a small port in a wide, open bay on the south coast, surrounded by cliffs. The town, defended by two forts, is believed to have been the first settlement founded by Portuguese colonists in the 15th c. It has a number of 16th and 17th c. churches, including the church of Nossa Senhora da Assunção (15th c.; partly rebuilt in 1832), with a fine tower.

São Lourenço

From Vila do Porto an attractive excursion (12km/7½ miles south) can be made, passing below the Pico Alto, to São Lourenço, which enjoys a beautiful setting above a sheltered bay on the east coast.

Terceira/Ilha Terceira

Terceira, i.e. the "third" island, was the third to be discovered and is also the third largest in the Azores. The most important of the islands after São Miguel, it lies 157km/98 miles north-west of that island and 56km/35 miles east of the neighbouring island of São Jorge. Like São Miguel Terceira is relatively well developed for tourism. However, its 60,000 inhabitants, many of them descended from the first Flemish settlers in the 15th c., live by arable farming (thanks to the extraordinary fertility of its soil Terceira is the Azores' largest cereals producer) stock-rearing and seaweed-gathering. Some of them work on the Lajes airforce base in the north-east of the island. The island's airport, which has been greatly extended, also plays an important international role.

General

The island is 31km/19 miles long and up to 18km/11 miles wide, with an area of 397sq.km/153sq. miles. Its highest point is the Caldeira de Santa Bárbara (1067m/3501ft), in the western half of the island. The eastern half consists mainly of a great volcanic plateau surrounded by high mountains. The coasts are steep, with many stretches of cliff, protected here and there by forts.

Topography

Angra do Heroísmo, the fortified chief town of its district and of the island of Terceira and the see of the Bishop of the Azores, lies in an open bay 2km/1¼ miles wide on the south coast of the island. On the west side of the bay is a peninsula, with Monte Brazil (210m/689ft). The attractive little town, which has a good harbour, was founded in 1534 and owes the second part of its name to its heroic resistance to the Spanish conquerors in the late 16th c., falling into Spanish hands only in 1583. Until 1832, when it was displaced by Ponta Delgada on São Miguel, Angra do Heroísmo was the capital of the Azores, and it still ranks as the cultural heart of the archipelago.

★★**Angra do Heroísmo**

Situation and importance

The town layout was originally planned in the first half of the 16th c. and it still boasts some imposing 17th and 18th c. Baroque buildings, due in no small measure to the substantial restoration carried out after UNESCO gave it International Heritage status.

Townscape

From the harbour the busy Rua de Lisboa (or Rua Direita) leads past the church of the Misericórdia, an imposing twin-towered Renaissance church, to the Praça da Restauração, the hub of the town's life. On the east side of the square is the 19th c. Câmara Municipal (town hall). The Rua de Lisboa ends in the Largo Prior do Crato, to the north of the Praça da Restauração, in which stands the former Jesuit College; the church (1652) has a richly decorated Baroque interior.

Sights

To the east of the Praça da Restauração, in the Rua de João de Deus, can be found the church of São Francisco (15th c., rebuilt in 17th c.). The convent buildings of the former Franciscan friary now house the municipal museum (Museu Municipal: folk traditions, coins, militaria, ships and the sea, art). The Franciscan friary is believed to contain the remains of Paulo da Gama (d. 1499), brother of the great navigator Vasco da Gama, who fell ill during the return voyage from the West Indies and died on Terceira; his tomb has not been identified. South-west of the Praça da Restauração, in Rua da República, is the twin-towered cathedral (Sé), built in 1568 on the site of an earlier church. Partially destroyed by fire in 1983 it was subsequently rebuilt according to the old plans. North-east of the Praça da Restauração, higher up, is an obelisk commemorating Pedro IV; from here there are far-ranging views of the town.

To the east of the Praça da Restauração, at the end of Rua Rainha Dona Amélia, is the 17th c. church of the Conceição (Conception), with rich talha dourada decoration in the interior.

Fort São João Baptista, above the town to the north-west, at the foot of Monte Brazil, is worth a visit. It was built by the Spaniards in the 17th c. and affords a magnificent panoramic view of the town. From the fort it is an easy climb up Monte Brazil (210m/689ft), a crater formed in a submarine eruption. From the rim of the crater there are superb views.

Other sights on Terceira

Praia da Vitória

About 21km/13 miles north-east of the town, in a wide bay on the east coast of Terceira, lies the old fortified port of Praia da Vitória (pop. 9000), named in honour of the Liberals' victory over the Royalists on August 11th 1829. The town has several times suffered earthquake destruction (1641, 1841; severe damage in 1980) and only two old buildings survive: the church (15th c.) in the upper part of the town, which has a rich Manueline doorway, and the 16th c. town hall. There is a fine long sandy beach.

Lajes

The busy little town of Lajes (pop. 6500) about 25km/16 miles north-west of Praia da Vitória depends almost entirely on the nearby airbase for its subsistence.

Caldeira de Santa Bárbara

An attractive trip can be made to the volcanic western part of Terceira and the Caldeira de Santa Bárbara (1022m/3353ft; view), the highest point on the island, a volcano with a number of explosion vents and collapsed craters. North-east and east of the volcanic plateau, between Pico Alto, Pico da Bagacina and Furnas do Enxofre, are several crater lakes and fumaroles.

Biscoitos

On a broad lava flow in the north of Terceira is the little wine-making town of Biscoitos.

Graciosa/Ilha Graciosa

General

Graciosa (the "lovely"), the most northerly island in the central Azores group, lies some 70km/45 miles north-west of Terceira and 55km/35 miles north of São Jorge in lat. 39°3′ north and long. 28° west. It owes its name to the abundance of its flowers. The island's 5500 inhabitants live by arable and fruit farming, and by raising livestock.

Topography

The island is 13km/8 miles long and up to 7km/4½ miles wide, with an area of 62sq.km/24sq. miles. Unlike the other islands in the Azores, it is not particularly hilly but, like them, it has steep and rocky coasts. Its highest point is the rim of the Caldeira do Enxofre (411m/1348ft).

Santa Cruz

Santa Cruz (pop. 2000), chief place on the island and its principal port, lies in a small plain on the north-east coast. The little town was founded in 1485. The parish church (1701) is worth seeing and has a fine altar.

★ Caldeira do Enxofre

About 5km/3 miles south-east of Santa Cruz is the little port of Praia da Graciosa, from which it is a 1½ hour climb to the Caldeira do Enxofre, 4km/2½ miles south. This crater, from which there are extensive views, is 1200m/1300yd long, 600m/650yd across and some 300m/1000ft deep, with a crater lake and several eruption vents. On the floor of the crater is the Furna do Enxofre, a cavern some 150m/165yd long, 100m/110yd wide and over 20m/65ft high formed by the collapse of a layer of solidified lava after the outflow of the molten lava below. In the cavern are a small warm lake and several fumaroles of carbonic acid.

Termas do Carapacho

At the foot of the Caldeira, in the extreme south of the island, is the little spa of Termas do Carapacho, with subterranean healing springs for rheumatic ailments.

São Jorge/Ilha de São Jorge

General

Roughly in the middle of the central group of the Azores is the long narrow island of São Jorge (St George), 55km/35 miles west of Terceira and separated from the islands of Pico to the south-west and Faial to the west by the 18km/11 mile wide Canal de São Jorge.

The 11,000 inhabitants live by livestock rearing and crop husbandry, fishing and exporting timber.

São Jorge has an area of 238sq.km/92sq. miles and consists of one long narrow ridge of forest-covered volcanic hills, 45km/28 miles from end to end, which reaches its highest point in the Pico da Esperança (1066m/3498ft) and falls down to the sea in steep and rugged cliffs. | Topography

The chief settlement on the island is the little port of Vila das Velas (pop. 2000) lying in a sheltered bay on the south-west coast. | Vila das Velas

About 22km/14 miles south-east of Vila das Velas is Calheta (pop. 1500; canning plant), a modest coastal village with a small harbour, from which the Pico da Esperança (1066m/3498ft) can be climbed. This is a now dormant volcano which last erupted in 1808; from the top there is a superb view of the whole archipelago. | Calheta/Pico da Esperança

At the eastern tip of the island is Topo, which is noted for its brighly coloured woollen blankets and cloth. | Topo

Faial/Ilha do Faial

Faial, the most westerly island in the central group of the Azores, gets its name from a beech-like shrub, myrica faya, which grows all over the island. Faial is separated from the neighbouring island of Pico to the south-east by the 7km/4¼ mile wide Canal de São Jorge. | General

The 16,000 inhabitants live by arable and livestock farming; Faial's centuries old whaling industry has ceased to be profitable.

In the early years of this century the island was important as a station for several transatlantic cables but this has ceased with the advent of satellites. Faial has frequently been devastated by earthquakes, as in 1759/60, 1862, 1926, 1958 and most recently on New Year's Day 1980.

Agriculture and cattle-rearing are the chief occupations of the inhabitants of Faial (Azores)

Azores

The Nuremberg cosmographer Martin Behaim (1459–1507), who made major contributions to nautical and geographical knowledge in the age of the great discoveries, lived on Faial from 1486 to 1490.

★ Topography

This hilly island, with a greatest length of 22km/14 miles and a greatest width of 15km/9 miles, has an area of 172sq.km/66sq. miles. Its highest point is the Pico Gordo (1043m/3422ft), a volcano which has been dormant since 1672.

The island has a soil of remarkable fertility and is covered with a luxuriant growth of vegetation. It is famous for its mass of hydrangeas which flower in June and July, and line the island's roads and tracks. The best way to get an idea of the beauty of the scenery is to go on a round-trip of the island.

★ **Horta**

Situation and Importance

Horta, the fortified main town of Faial, lies facing the imposing cone of Pico in a wide bay on the south-east coast of the island, with a beach of black volcanic sand. The town is attractively situated on gently rising ground, surrounded by handsome villas and beautiful gardens. The inhabitants, many of them of Flemish descent, live by trade and the sale of fine embroidery and basketwork.

The town is probably named after Josse van Hutere, who settled Flemish colonists here at the behest of the Infante Dom Henrique. A less likely theory is that Horta is derived from the island's hydrangeas (*hydrangea hortensia*) although the plant is actually East Asian in origin. The Parliament of the Azores usually meets in Horta. The town with its well-protected harbour is the most frequent port of call in the North Atlantic for transatlantic sailors of every nation.

Sights

The harbour, one of the best in the Azores, is protected by a breakwater 750m/820yd long (note the "painting wall", on which the seamen immortalise themselves). The bay is closed on the south by the Guia peninsula (148m/486ft), formed by a submarine crater, which is linked to the island by a narrow isthmus. There is an attractive walk or boat trip from the harbour around the peninsula to the water-filled Caldeira do Inferno on the south side, continuing to the former whaling station of Porto Pim on the seaward side of the isthmus.

Other sights on Faial

★ Caldeira do Pico Gordo

A road 18km/11 miles north-west ascends to the rim of the Caldeira do Pico Gordo, in the middle of the island. On the floor of the crater, which is 2km/1¼ mile in diameter and some 400m/1300ft deep, is a small lake.

There is an attractive walk with magnificent views around the rim.

Volcão dos Capelinhos

The western tip of Faial is formed by the Volcão dos Capelinhos, a submarine volcano which emerged from the sea in 1957, burying under its ash the fishing village of Comprido and partly covering the old lighthouse. When the volcano subsided in 1958 the island was larger than before.

There is a small museum containing relics of the eruption and explanations of the formation of the volcano.

Pico/Ilha do Pico

General

Pico, the most southerly island in the central group of the Azores, lies east of Faial and south-west of São Jorge, from which it is separated by the 18km/11 mile wide Canal de São Jorge.

The volcanic soil, of recent formation and spread over large areas without any covering of humus, affords little scope for agriculture, and the 15,500 or so inhabitants have to import much of their food from the neighbouring islands. The only extensive areas of cultivation are the vineyards which have been created with much labour on the slopes of the Pico Alto. The once considerable whaling industry died out in 1985.

The rugged and mountainous island of Pico, 48km/30 miles long and up to 15km/9 miles wide, with an area of 433sq.km/167sq. miles, rises at its western end to the prominent Pico Alto (2351m/7714ft), the highest peak not only in the Azores but in the whole of Portugal. The highest point in the eastern half of the island is the Pico Topo (1633m/5358ft). — Topography

The chief town of the island and its oldest settlement is the whaling port of Lajes (pop. 2500) on the south coast, with a town hall and parish church built of black lava. The whaling museum in Lajes graphically demonstrates just how perilous whaling has been even in our high-tech age. Two other little ports are Cais do Pico (or São Roque, fish-canning plant) on the north coast, and Madalena (regular boat services to Horta on Faial) on the north-west coast. The three places are linked by a road encircling the island which also gives access to a number of stalactitic caves, some only recently discovered, of which the Furna de Frei Matias at the north-west foot of the Pico Alto is the best known. — Lajes/Cais do Pico/Madalena

The main tourist attraction on the island is the Pico Alto (2351m/7714ft), a still active volcano with an unusually steepsided summit which is frequently shrouded in cloud. The most violent recorded eruptions took place in 1562 and 1718. The ascent of the volcano (guide advisable) should be undertaken only in clear weather. The best starting-point is Madalena. From the summit there is a superb view of the whole of the central group of the Azores. In the caldera, some 300m/330yd in diameter and 30m/100ft deep, are numerous hot fumaroles (temperatures up to 74°C/165°F) and the Pico Pequreno, a bare eruption cone 70m/230ft high (difficult but rewarding climb on south-east side). — ★ Pico Alto

Fishing is almost the only occupation on Pico (Azores)

Flores/Ilha das Flores

General
information

Flores, the "island of flowers", the most westerly of the Azores, lies 230km/145 miles north-west of Faial and 20km/12½ miles south of the neighbouring island of Corvo in lat. 39°25' north and long. 31°15' west. The 4500 inhabitants live by arable and livestock farming, producing abundant yields for domestic consumption and for export.

★Topography

The island owes its name to its masses of flowers – including, like Faial, the many hydrangeas – which make it one of the most beautiful of the Azores. 17km/11 miles long and up to 14km/9 miles wide, Flores has an area of 142sq.km/55sq. miles. Its highest point, the Morro Grande (942m/3091ft), is in the northern part of the island. The whole of the central and southern parts is made up of volcanic heights, with numerous crater lakes, waterfalls and hot springs.

Sights on Flores

The main town on the island is the port of Santa Cruz das Flores (pop. 2000) halfway along the east coast, which has several small 18th c. Baroque churches. Another little port is Lajes (pop. 800) in a bay on the south-east coast. It is well worthwhile taking a trip into the lush interior of the island with its numerous crater lakes (Funda, Lomba, Rasa, etc.) and their carp which are used as bait for deep-sea fishing.

Corvo/Ilha do Corvo

General
information

Corvo ("crow island"), the most northerly and the smallest (17.5sq.km/ 6¾sq. miles) of the Azores, lies 15km/9 miles north-east of Flores in lat. 39°42' north which is in roughly the same latitude as Palma de Mallorca in the Balearics and Corfu in the Ionian Islands.

The 400 or so inhabitants of the island gain a modest subsistence from fishing and rearing livestock. The women weave excellent woollen cloth for domestic consumption. In recent years the gathering of seaweed for the production of agar-agar (gelatine) has made an increasing contribution to the economy.

Virtually untouched by tourism, Corvo is the only island in the Azores not to have an airport.

Topography

The island, 7km/4½ miles long and up to 4.5km/3 miles wide, is made up of a single extinct volcano, Monte Gordo (777m/2549ft), the crater of which, over 1.5km/1 mile wide, contains a lake with nine small rocky islets.

Sights

With its rugged and cliff-fringed coasts, which are particularly steep on the west side of the island, Corvo has no proper harbour. Boats put in at Rosário on the south coast, the island's only settlement, with a radio station and meteorological observatory on the hill above the village.

Barcelos   B 3

Historical province: Minho
District: Braga
Altitude: 40m/130ft
Population: 10,000

Situation and
Importance

The very picturesque old town of Barcelos, once capital of the first County established in Portugal (1298), lies on the right bank of the Rio Cávado 18km/11 miles west of Braga. It is famous for the brightly coloured pottery cockerels which have become a ubiquitous symbol of Portugal. The best day to visit Barcelos is Thursday, when Portugal's largest weekly market is held here.

In the Market of Barcelos : the cockerel . . .   . . . and many ceramic articles

The story goes that a pilgrim travelling to Santiago de Compostela who had been wrongly accused of theft and condemned to death was saved from the gallows when he appealed to St James to make the hangman's roast cockerel crow in proof of his innocence. The grateful pilgrim then offered a pottery cockerel to St James in token of thanksgiving.

Barcelos Cockerel

Sights

The life of the town revolves around the spacious Campo da República, one of the largest squares in Portugal. Visitors flock to its Thursday market, which is much bigger than those held on the rest of the week, and where the goods on sale range from fruit, vegetables, meat and wine, to handicrafts and carved furniture.

★Campo da República

Next to the square is the flower-filled park of the Passeio dos Assentos.

On the north side of the square is the church of Nossa Senhora do Terço, belonging to a Benedictine house founded in 1705. It has a fine coffered ceiling with many painted panels and azulejo-clad walls (18th c.).

Nossa Senhora do Terço

The handsome Baroque church of the Bom Jesús da Cruz (16th–17th c.), an octagonal structure on a centralised plan with an imposing granite dome and a richly decorated interior, shows clear Italian influence.

Bom Jesús da Cruz

Near the church is the Torre de Menagem or Porta Nova, a relic of the town's 16th c. fortifications which today houses the tourist information centre and an exhibition of local arts and crafts.
   Opposite stands the former Capuchin convent of the Misericórdia (1649), now a hospital.

Torre de Menagem

131

Batalha

★Paço dos Duques de Bragança

The central point of the old town, uphill from the Torre de Menagem, are the ruins of the Paço dos Duques de Bragança, seat of the Counts of Barcelos and later of the Dukes of Bragança (15th–16th c.). With its wide terrace the palace is the setting for the Archaeological Museum (Museu Arqueológico), an open-air lapidarium with inscribed stones and sculpture from the Roman period to the Middle Ages. A particularly notable item is the Cruzeiro do Senhor do Galo, a 14th c. wayside cross relating to the legend of the crowing cockerel.

Igreja Matriz

Next to the palace stands the Romanesque and Gothic parish church (Igreja Matriz) dating from the 13th–14th c. and remodelled in the 18th c. It has a Romanesque doorway with an impressive rose window and fine azulejo decoration in the interior.

Solar dos Pinairos

Opposite the Paço dos Duques de Bragança is the Gothic Solar dos Pinairos (1448), a granite-built mansion with two towers and a beautiful arcaded courtyard.

In the middle of a grassed open space between the former duke's palace and the Solar dos Pinairos stands a 15th c. Gothic pelourinho, a pillory column, symbolising the jurisdiction of the municipal authorities.

Stone bridge

Below the former palace a five-arched stone bridge crosses the Rio Cávado. Originally built in the 14th c. it was rebuilt in the 16th c. and fully restored in the 19th c.

From the gardens on the other side of the bridge there is a fine view over Barcelos old town.

Surroundings of Barcelos

Abade de Neiva

About 5km/3 miles north-west of Barcelos is the Romanesque and Gothic Abade de Neiva, with a well-preserved church and a free-standing fortified belfry.

Esposende

The seaside resort of Esposende (pop. 2200) lies where the Cávado meets the Atlantic, about 14km/9 miles west of Barcelos. Its beach of fine sand has in recent years helped to put this rather unassuming little place on the tourist map, but despite a number of new hotels and a bungalow complex on its edge the town still tends to attract visitors who favour peace and quiet rather than wanting all kinds of leisure activities.

Ofir

South of the estuary of the Cávado is the newly developed resort of Ofir, which until quite recently was a small fishing village.

Monte Franqueira

Situated on the summit of Monte Franqueira (298m/978ft) about 6km/4 miles south-west of Barcelos is the pilgrimage church of Nossa Senhora da Franqueira. Built in the 12th c. and much altered in subsequent centuries it offers fine views over the surrounding countryside.

Near the summit are the ruins of the Castelo da Faria (1373) and remains of a pre-Roman settlement.

Areias de Vilar

At Areias de Vilar about 8km/5 miles east of Barcelos is the Benedictine abbey of Vilar de Frades, now a home for the mentally handicapped. Here, too, is the Manueline church of São Lóios, with 18th c. azulejo pictures in two side chapels and a 15th c. Gothic copper cross in the sacristy.

Manhetes

On a hill above the Cávado at Manhetes, 6km/4 miles north-east of Barcelos, stands a fine 12th c. Romanesque church.

Batalha   B 5

Historical province: Beira Litoral. District: Leiria
Altitude: 70m/230ft. Population: 3500

The unpretentious little town of Batalha, in a fertile basin of the Lena valley between Lisbon and Coimbra, would probably attract scarcely a visitor were it not for its internationally famous Dominican abbey.

Nowadays Batalha is well equipped to cater for its visitors. Close to the abbey, around the newly built pousada, there can be found a small shopping centre and various cafés, with a permanent market on the square behind the abbey.

Apart from the abbey Batalha also boasts a number of 17th/18th c. houses and the parish church of Santa Cruz (1512), which has a superb doorway.

★★Mosteiro de Santa Maria da Vitória

The abbey at Batalha, one of the largest and most important in Portugal, is protected by UNESCO as a world cultural heritage building. Open: daily 9am–5pm, to 7pm in summer.

Batalha Abbey, the Mosteiro de Santa Maria da Vitória, on the north side of town, was founded in 1388 by King Jão I in fulfilment of a vow he had made on August 14th 1385, at the beginning of the battle of Aljubarrota (see Batalha, Surroundings), in which he defeated King Juan I of Castile and re-established Portuguese independence. Hence the name "Battle Abbey", or Mosteiro da Batalha as it is usually called.

The Abbey's first architect, who was responsible for the overall plan, was Afonso Domingues who by the time of his death in 1402 had completed the church choir and nave, the Claustro Real and some of the other monastery buildings. His successor was David Houet (or Huguet or Huet) under whose direction until 1438 the church was finished and the Capella do Fundador

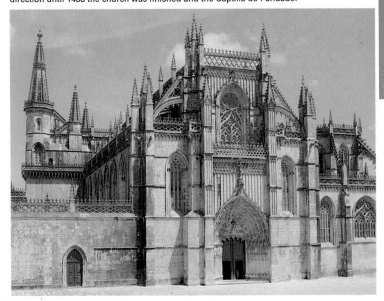

Batalha Abbey

Manueline –
an art style or simply decoration?

In 1760 Joseph Baretti, in his book "Journey from London to Genoa through England, Portugal, Spain and France", wrote as follows after he had visited the Hieronymite convent at Bélem: "It (the church) betrayed in general a Gothic flavour, and yet for the most part the convent is not Gothic". Felix Prince of Lichnovsky attempted to provide a more exact stylistic classification in his "Memories of the Year 1842": "The convent is built in half Moorish-Byzantine, half Normano-Gothic style; a confused mixture from which here and there, triumphing over all its alien neighbours, an example of one or other of the said styles stands out clearly in all its original purity". A few years later (1846) the German writer Karl August Varnhagen von Ense (1785–1858) devised the term still used today for the architectural style of the Hieronymite convent at Bélem and other contemporary edifices – *arte manuelina* (Manueline style). It is named after King Manuel I, whose reign from 1495 to 1521 was a period of cultural and architectural flowering.

Nearly every Portugal travel guide speaks of Manueline as a distinctively Portuguese style, but some experts now regard this idea with scepticism. Many art historians hold the view that the Emmanuel style (as it also known) is not in fact something unique but merely a form of decoration which marked the transition in Portugal from the Gothic to the Renaissance. This argument certainly cannot be completely dismissed out of hand; the simple and monumental basic structure of Manueline buildings is similar to other Late Gothic buildings which were to be found at the time in many places elsewhere in Europe, and the arcades, balconies, balda-

Hieronymite Convent in Belém (Lisbon)

chins, small towers and columns betray Mudéjar-style as well as Oriental and Indian influences. However, in Manueline buildings the constructional features take a back seat, so to speak – it is the ornamentation which holds centre stage. Doors and windows, steps and columns, interior and exterior walls, balconies and baldachins all so extravagantly decorated that the building design itself often completely "disappeared" was a novelty in European architecture.

And until this time Western art knew nothing of exotic and oceanic decorative subjects chiselled in stone with a great passion for detail – marine animals such as octopuses, starfish, coral and shells; nautical instruments including the Armillar sphere and the compass; marine equipment comprising anchors, nets, knotted ropes and hawsers; tropical flowers, leaves and plants, the cross of the Knights of Christ (symbol of the Portuguese explorers), the crown and "M" for Manuel, as well as fabulous creatures and terrifying sea-monsters – all of which tell of Portugal's greatest era, of the discoveries and conquests abroad which granted the country a brief period of economic and cultural ascendancy.

King Manuel the Fortunate, as he was known, was an inveterate spendthrift. The wealth he obtained from overseas conquests allowed him, his whole court and the upper strata of society to live in luxury while the rest of the people were close to starvation. The king displayed a degree of opulence in excess of anything known elsewhere in Europe – not least when he rode in procession, escorted by elephants, hippotamuses and other exotic animals gifted to him by Indian and African potentates. However, Manuel was also a connoisseur of the arts, and he devoted a large part of the state wealth to his passion for building churches, convents, castles and palaces. He was aided in this in a

Royal Cloister at Batalha

certain way by seafarers who discovered foreign lands and described their experiences, fantasies and fears. Their tales and descriptions seized the imagination of architects, builders and sculptors who skilfully translated into stone these innovative African, American or East Asian decorative forms and mingled them with the more familiar Gothic and now-dawning Renaissance styles. Examples include the Torre de Bélem at the mouth of the Tagus, the flat domes and fine loggias of which produce an Arabo-Moorish effect, the uncompleted chapel of the convent at Batalha, the west window of the Knights of Christ church in Tomar, in the Claustro do Silêncio (Silent Cloister) of the Convento de Santa Cruz in Coimbra, in the Paço Real (Royal Palace) in Sintra, on countless portals and window and door frames of the houses of noblemen and merchants, as well as on the *pelourinhos* (pillories) scattered throughout the country, on fonts and grave monuments, even on the cathedral in Funchal, capital of the island of Madeira, and on the church of São Sebastião in the Azores.

Only rarely can such buildings be said to be constructed wholly in the Manueline style; it is more frequently discernible only in individual details. The heyday of Manueline lasted but a few decades, between 1490 and 1540. The major architects of this period included Diogo de Boytaca, Diogo de Arruda, Francisco de Arruda and João de Castilho. During the reign of João III, who succeeded King Manuel, the Manueline style gave way to that of the Renaissance.

Whether or not Manueline is now described by experts as a unique Portuguese style, it was certainly one thing – a new attitude of mind hewn in stone of a nation which succeeded briefly between 1495 and 1521 in becoming the most powerful country in the Western world and which, spurred on by success and optimism, set out to discover and conquer more and more new worlds and derived pleasure from the unknown, the strange and the beautiful, in fact from everywhere it decided to colonise; in short, a country which in its naïve innocence thought the world equated with Portugal and Portugal represented the whole world.

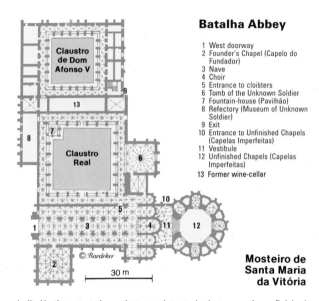

Batalha Abbey

1 West doorway
2 Founder's Chapel (Capelo do Fundador)
3 Nave
4 Choir
5 Entrance to cloisters
6 Tomb of the Unknown Soldier
7 Fountain-house (Pavilhão)
8 Refectory (Museum of Unknown Soldier)
9 Exit
10 Entrance to Unfinished Chapels (Capelas Imperfeitas)
11 Vestibule
12 Unfinished Chapels (Capelas Imperfeitas)
13 Former wine-cellar

Claustro de Dom Afonso V

Claustro Real

© Baedeker

30 m

Mosteiro de Santa Maria da Vitória

built. He then started on what were later to be known as the unfinished chapels, the Capelas Imperfeitas. The work on these and the second cloister was continued by Martin Vásquez (d. before 1448) and Fernão de Évora (d. 1477). After a pause in activity building was resumed, with the vestibule between the choir and the unfinished chapels, under King Manuel I by Mateus Fernandes the Elder (d. 1515) and Mateus Fernandes the Younger (d. 1528). This period also saw the sculptor Diogo Boytaca (d. *c.* 1525) carry out much of the magnificent decoration that graces the abbey buildings. The last of the major architects to be involved in building Batalha Abbey was João de Castilho, creator of the the Hieronymite convent at Belém (see Lisbon). 1533 saw the last of the works carried out on the building.

Batalha Abbey suffered to some extent in the 1755 earthquake, but was far more badly damaged by French troops in 1810. The Dominican monastery was dissolved in 1834 and in 1840 it was declared a national monument. Subsequently carefully restored this great memorial to the liberation of the Portuguese people is in excellent condition today.

Abbey church

The church, built during the reign of João I, is a finely conceived example of the noblest Gothic style. Particularly notable are the west front with its rich sculptural decoration (partly restored) and the lively articulation of the south side.

The interior (80m/260ft long, 32.5m/107ft high) is very impressive, with its high stained-glass windows (some of them very old, particularly in the choir) and its massive piers. Set in the floor immediately inside the main entrance is the flat tombstone of Mateus Fernandes the Elder.

From the south aisle a magnificent doorway leads into the Founder's Chapel (Capela do Fundador), almost 20m/65ft square, with many fine tombs. In the middle is the sarcophagus, supported on eight lions, of João I (d. 1433) and his English wife Philippa of Lancaster (d. 1416). In recesses on the south side of the chapel are the tombs of four of the royal couple's children: at the left-hand end the tomb of the Infante Dom Fernando, the "steadfast prince" of Calderon's tragedy, who died in Moroccan captivity in 1443; next to this the double tomb of the Infante João (d. 1442) and his wife

Isabella; and the tombs of the Infante Dom Henrique (1394–1460; see Famous People), known to history as Henry the Navigator, although he himself never took part in any voyages of discovery, and the Infante Dom Pedro (1392–1449). On the west wall of the chapel are the tombs of King Afonso V (d. 1481) and his wife, and King João II (d. 1495) and his son Afonso.

On the north side of the church is the Royal Cloister, the Claustro Real, a masterpiece of Portuguese Gothic with its richly decorated arcades overlooking a garden-like courtyard. Here can be seen the whole range of Gothic in Portugal, from the simplest and plainest forms to the fantastic profusion of ornament of later periods. The stone tracery is mostly modern. From the cloister there is a fine view of the richly decorated north side of the church.

Claustro Real

In the north-west corner of the cloister is the chapel-like fountain-house (Pavilhão), from which, too, there are attractive glimpses of the abbey.

The Chapterhouse (Sala do Capitulo), on the east side of the cloister, has an imposing doorway and fine stained glass depicting the Passion of Christ. The tomb of two unknown soldiers from the First World War has a permanent guard of honour.

The former Refectory, on the west side of the cloister beyond the fountain-house, now houses the Museum of the Unknown Soldier, and in the monks' former wine cellar various architectural items are on display together with an exhibition of Portuguese history.

A doorway at the north-west corner of the Claustro Real gives access to the Claustro de Dom Afonso V, with simple double windows and a plain pillared gallery (15th c.) on the upper floor.

Claustro de Dom Afonso V

To the east of this cloister is the Claustro de João III, destroyed by fire in 1811.

The Unfinished Chapels, the Capelas Imperfeitas, were built on to the east end of the church in the reigns of Duarte and Manuel I in the richest Manueline style. Surrounding a central octagon are seven large chapels, one of which contains the tomb of King Duarte (Eduard, son of João I) and his wife Eleanor of Aragon. The massive buttresses around the inside of the octagon were designed to support the dome, which was left unfinished. On the west side is a large vestibule, with a magnificent doorway almost 15m/50ft high and above this a gallery opening on to the octagon.

Capelas Imperfeitas

The equestrian statue placed before the southern façade of the church in 1961 is of Nuno Alvares Pereira, João I's commander at the battle of Aljubarrota.

Equestrian statue

Surroundings of Batalha

About 5km/3 miles south-west, on the edge of the battlefield of Aljubarrota, the little chapel of São Jorge was built on the spot from which Nuno Alvares Pereira directed the conflict. At the entrance to the chapel there still stands a jug of fresh water, originally set there for the thirsty warriors.

São Jorge

On the slopes of an isolated hill above the Rio Lena, 9km/5½ miles south of Batalha Abbey, is Porto de Mós, dominated by a massive castle, the origins of which go back to the 9th c. After recovering the castle from the Moors King Sancho I had it restored, but much of it was again destroyed in the 1755 earthquake. Since then it has been restored on a number of occasions, most recently in 1956. From the castle there are magnificent panoramic views.

Porto de Mós

About 10km/6 miles south-east of Porto de Mós lie the Grutas de Alvados (open: daily 9.30am–6pm, in summer to 9pm). These caves with curiously

★Stalactitic caves

The many impressive dripstone caves to be seen in the Batalha area are often effectively lit as shown here in the Grutas da Moeda

shaped dripstones and subterranean lakes were discovered in 1964. Somewhat similar are the Grutas de Santo Antonio, about 1km/¾ mile away (open: daily 9.30am–6pm, in summer to 9pm). This cave system stretches over an area of 6000sq.m/1½ acres; the largest single cave measures 80 by 50m/260 by 160ft and is 43m/140ft high. Near Mira de Aire a flight of steps leads down into a further underground system, the Grutas de Mira or Grutas dos Moinhos Velhos; the return is by elevator.

Finally there are the Grutas da Moeda, near São Mamede, 15km/9½ miles south-east of Batalha (via the N356). In these caves (open: daily 9am–6pm, in summer to 8pm), which were discovered by two hunters in 1971, visitors can enter for a distance of 350m/385yd.

Alcobaça	See entry
Fátima	See entry
Leiria	See entry
Nazaré	See entry
Tomar	See entry

Beira   B–D 3–5

Historical provinces: Beira Alta, Beira Baixa and Beira Litoral
Districts: Viseu, Guarda, Catelo Branco, Aveiro and Coimbra
Area: 27,398sq.km/10,578sq. miles. Population: 1,923,000
Principal towns: Guarda, Castelo Branco and Coimbra

The region of Beira in northern Portugal is a great tract of land between the Douro in the north and the Tagus in the south, consisting mostly of rugged mountain country and bleak plateaux. In this frontier territory, long disputed between Christians and Moors, the towns were always stoutly fortified.

Beira is made up of three old provinces of very different characters.

Beira Alta (Upper Beira) takes in the wooded highlands, geologically the continuation of the cordilleras of central Spain, which extend from the highest peaks on the Portuguese mainland, the Serra da Estrêla (see entry; 1991m/6532ft), to the valleys of the Douro (see entry) and Mondego.

The climate is hot and dry in summer and cold in winter, with a great deal of snow at the higher altitudes.

This is a region of extensive agriculture and pastoral farming (sheep). Excellent wine is produced, particularly in the Dão and Mondego valleys.

The population is sparse, reflecting the low fertility of the soil and the limited area of land suitable for cultivation. The main town of Beira Alta is Guarda (see entry) with a population of only 18,000, and its largest town is Viseu (see entry), with a population of 24,000.

Beira Baixa (Lower Beira), with Castelo Branco (see entry) as its capital, extends over an infertile plain between the southern foothills of the Serra da Estrêla and the Tagus.

The economy is similar to that of Alentejo; the predominant type of farming is monoculture (single-crop farming, in this case grain) on large estates, with mixed farming of Mediterranean type (grain, vegetables, fruit, including citrus fruits, olives) in the river valleys. In the extreme western part of the region the fragmentation of land holdings makes it difficult to achieve efficient and profitable working of the land.

Beira Litoral (coastal Beira) occupies a swathe of land extending along the coast from Ovar to Monte Real, relatively narrow in the north but becoming broader about the latitude of the chief town Coimbra (see entry). It is bounded on the east by the heights of the Serra do Caramulo, the Serra da Estrêla and the Serra de Lousã. This is a landscape of dunes with pinewoods planted to consolidate them, marshy river estuaries (Vouga, Mondego) and salt-pans (Ria de Aveiro). Only in the inland parts of the region are grain and vegetables grown.

Beja   C 6

Historical province: Baixo Alentejo. District: Beja
Altitude: 282m/925ft. Population: 20,000

The old town of Beja, the Roman Pax Julia (of which some remains survive: foundations of walls on the north side of the town and a gate on the south side), is commandingly perched on a hill in the fertile plain of Baixo Alentejo. It is the largest town in Alentejo after Évora and is chief town of the district and an important commercial centre, especially for agricultural produce.

In recent years a number of modern and purpose-built hotels have been built around the Old Town. More stylish accommodation is available at the pousada opened in 1994 in the Convento de São Francisco; this is one of the most beautiful state-run hotels in Portugal.

Although the little town of Beja has no very remarkable sights to boast of its many fine old buildings and winding alleys lined with gleaming white houses, some of them with charming iron grilles, windows, doorways and covered arcades, make its old town well worth a visit on any tour of

Beja: Convent of the Conception

Portugal. The best place to rest after a sightseeing walk is the pretty little park or on the lawned area with a simple café on the Praça Diogo Fernandes. There are car parking facilities in the centre on the Largo dos Duques de Beja under tall trees near the convent.

Sights

★Convento N.S.
da Conceição

The starting point for a tour of Beja's old town is possibly the Praça da Concaição, embellished with a modern statue (1958) of Queen Eleanor (1458–1525). In this square is the surviving part of the Convent of the Conception (Nossa Senhora da Conceição), a small house of Poor Clares founded by the Infante Dom Fernando and his wife Dona Brites and built between 1459 and 1506. It shows clear Manueline features and currently houses the regional museum.

In this convent lived the nun, Mariana Alcoforado (1640–1723; see Famous People) who, in 1665, from her window first saw the Chevalier de Chamilly. After getting to know him through her brother she embarked on an affair that ended with Chamilly's return to France in 1667. She is supposed to have sent her lover five passionate letters that were first published in 1667. These love letters which are enshrined in international literature as the "Lettres Portugaises" (letters of a Portuguese Nun) were probably, in fact, written not by the nun but by the Frenchman Gabriel-Joseph Guillerague (1636–1715).

The former convent church, richly decorated with talha, and the cloister with its beautiful 16th c. azulejo decoration, form part of the Museu Regional (open: Tues.–Sun. 10am–12.30pm and 2–5pm). Its collections, which are well worth seeing, include archaeological exhibits, paintings, one of Portugal's finest private collections of azulejos, coins, folk art, costumes and furniture.

Diagonally opposite the convent is the church of Santa Maria (13th c.). Its main façade is decorated with four small towers linked by Gothic arches.

Santa Maria

Opposite the entrance to the cloisters an alley leads through the old town to the Praça da República, the focus of life in Beja and the site of a fine Manueline pelourinho (pillory column).

Praça da República

At the north-west end of the square stands the church of the Misericórdia, which was originally built by the Infante Dom Luís in 1550 as a market hall and was later converted, by the addition of a chapel, into a church with a very spacious portico. The original function of the building, with its nine bays of vaulting which are borne on columns, can still be recognised.

Igreja da Misericórdia

Past the church and above the town to the north is the massive Castle, built by King Dinis I about 1300 on the remains of a Roman fortress; it has a handsome crenellated tower, built partly of marble, from which there is a fine view; it is 40m/131ft tall, making it the highest castle tower in Portugal. In the inner courtyard is the Military Museum of Lower Alentejo (Museu Militar do Baixo Alentejo) (open: Tues.–Sun. 10am–1pm and 2–6pm). On the lower floors of the castle are a small chapel and a large room with magnificent stellar vaulting.

Castelo

Near the castle, beyond the Roman Évora Gate, stands the early Romanesque church of Santo Amaro. This oldest church in the town now houses a Visigothic Museum.

Capela de Santo Amaro

Below the castle, to the east, is the former Cathedral, in Renaissance style (1590; restored 1940).

Sé

South-west of the town centre, on the main road to Lisbon, is the Ermida de Santo André, founded in 1162 in thanksgiving for the recovery of the town from the Moors.

Ermida de Santo André

Surroundings of Beja

About 8km/5 miles south-west of Beja on the N 18 to Aljustrel and taking the right fork at Penedo Gordo are the excavated remains of a Roman settlement at Pisões (baths, with mosaics, atrium, etc.).

Pisões

25km/15 miles west lies the little town of Ferreira do Alentejo (alt. 141m/462ft; pop. 6000) with a 16th c. parish church and the church of the Misericórdia with a 16th c. retable.

Ferreira do Alentejo

30km/19 miles south-east is the quaint little walled town of Serpa (alt. 230m/755ft; pop. 8000), still known by the name it bore in Roman times. Above the town are the ruins of a 13th c. castle which affords a superb view of the town and surrounding countryside. The narrow lanes of the old town are lined with white houses, many of them faced with azulejos. Other features of interest are the Gothic church of Santa Maria (13th c.; polychrome azulejo decoration, 17th c., in the interior), the former convents of São Paulo and São António (15th–16th c.; cloister) and the remains of an ancient aqueduct at the Porta de Beja.

★ Serpa

Belmonte   C 4

Historical province: Beira Baixa. District: Castelo Branco
Altitude: 610m/2000ft. Population: 2000

The charming little hill town of Belmonte, on a commanding eminence at the foot of the Serra da Estrêla and about halfway between Covilhã and

Situation and Importance

Belmonte: the Castle

Guarda, was the birthplace of the navigator Pedro Álvares Cabral (1467–1520), who discovered Brazil in 1500.

★ Townscape

Skilfully restored mansions grouped around the square in the centre of Belmonte bear witness to its past prosperity and status.

In the main street stands a monument to the town's great son which was erected in 1963 on the 500th anniversary of Pedro Álvares Cabral's birth.

Sights

Castelo

Above the town are the remains of the massive castle, built at the beginning of the 13th c., in the reign of King Dinis (restored 1940), from where there are extensive views of the Beira hills. The gate still bears the arms of the Cabral family.

Chapel of Santiago

Near the castle gate, is the little Romanesque and Gothic chapel of Santiago (restored 1971). The interior of the church is notable for its simplicity. It contains the tomb of Cabral's mother, the remains of old frescos in the choir and the tombs of Fernão and Henrique Francisco Cabral (17th c.). It also preserves the Gothic image of Nossa Senhora da Esperança (Our Lady of Hope) which Cabral took with him on his voyage to Brazil and later bequeathed to a Franciscan friary he founded near Belmonte. On the dissolution of the friary the image was transferred to the church of Santiago.

Surroundings of Belmonte

★ Centum Cellas

To get to Centum Cellas, a well-preserved Roman tower, follow the main road from Belmonte towards Guarda. About 1.5km/1 mile north of the centre of the village a signposted road bears off to the right and in about 200m/220yd comes to the remains of the tower which stands in the middle of fields. Centum Cellas was built square in plan, with two storeys and a crenellated roof and may have been just a watch-tower, or have served in the 2nd c. A.D. as a place of banishment for the Roman Bishop Cornelius.

Sabugal, 30km/19 miles north-east of Belmonte, is becoming increasingly dominated by modern buildings. The castle with its five towers dating from the 13th/14th c. is well preserved. The pentagonal Torre de Menagem reaches a height of 28m/92ft.

Sabugal

A journey through the Serra da Estrela (see entry) lying to the west of Belmonte is one of the highlights of a tour of Portugal.

Serra da Estrela

Berlenga Islands/Ilhas Berlengas   A 5

Historical province: Estremadura. District: Leiria
Altitude: 0–88m/0–289ft. Population: 50

The Ilhas Berlengas, 12km/7½ miles north-west of the rugged and imposing Cabo Carvoeiro (see Peniche), rear out of the shimmering green sea as bleak and bizarrely shaped masses of granite apparently cast asunder from the mainland.

Situation and Importance

This little archipelago consists of the main Ilha da Berlenga (4.5km/ 3 miles long and up to 800m/½ mile wide), the neighbouring islands of Estelas, Forcadeas and Farilhes, and numerous reefs and isolated rocks, offering magnificent opportunities for scuba divers. The main island can be reached by boat from Peniche in about an hour (regular services in summer).

On the highest point of the main island stands a prominent lighthouse, and below this, on a crag above the sheltered bay on the south-east side of the island, is a castle (Forte de São João Baptista) built in the reign of João IV, now containing an inn (the only accommodation on the island apart from the campsite).

Sights

From here a waymarked footpath (1½ hours) runs round the island, giving access to picturesque caves and tunnels, deep gorges and rocky coves lashed by the sea. Particularly fine is the Blue Grotto below the castle, which can stand comparison with the better known Blue Grotto on Capri. To the south of the castle is the Furado Grande, a natural tunnel 70m/75yd long which leads to the Cova do Sonho, a tiny rocky cove.

A boat trip around the island (enquire at the harbour or the inn) is highly recommended for the many fine views.

Braga   B 3

Historical province: Minho. District: Braga
Altitude: 185m/607ft. Population: 86,000

The old-world town of Braga in northern Portugal and situated in an extensive depression between the rivers Cávado and Este, is one of the largest towns in the country and the seat of the Primate of Portugal. It has long been an important religious centre and its many churches have earned it the flattering title of the "Portuguese Rome".

Situation and Importance

Braga is also a busy industrial town producing motor vehicles, electrical goods, leather goods and textiles.

The site seems to have been inhabited in prehistoric times. Later it was the Roman Bracara Augusta, chief town and military headquarters of the territory of the Callaeci Bracarii, linked by five military highways with other military posts in Lusitania. During the Great Migrations Braga became capital of the Suevic kingdom. In 716 it was occupied and devastated by the Moors. In 1040 Fernão I, the Great, recaptured the town for Castile and

History

Braga

200 m

Monção, Caldelas

Ponte de Lima
Capela de São Frutuoso

Bus station

Mercado

Praça
Conde de
Agrolongo

Igreja do
Pópulo

Câmara
Municipal

Antigo Paço
Episcopal

Palácio
dos
Biscainhos

Arco da
Porta Nova

Miseri-
córdia

Sé

Rua Andrade Corvo

Campo das
Hortas

Railway station

Rua do Caires

Rua da Cruz de Pedra

R. d Afonso Henriques

São Sebastião

Campo de
São Tiago

Barcelos, Porto

Guimarães   Oporto

R. de Castro

R. de S. Vicente

Rua de Camões

Praça
Mousinho
e Albuquerque

R. São André

Avenida dos Combatentes

Praça da
República

Largo
A.Branca

Torre de
Menagem

São João
de Souto

Capela da
Conceição

Santa
Cruz

Palácio
do Raio

Citânia de Briteiros
Bom Jesus do Monte

Rua de S. Margarida

Av. de João XXI

Chaves

© Baedeker

Christendom and at the beginning of the 12th c. it became the residence of the Portuguese kings. This was the beginning of an age of splendour, to which many buildings of the period still bear witness. When, after the great voyages of discovery, attention was increasingly focused on the coastal ports and the sea, the power and prosperity of the town began to decline and it sank back into the role of a provincial town.

Besides the notable number of churches, everywhere in the old town visitors will encounter fine old burghers' houses and noble mansions built of granite in an imposing style characteristic of Braga.

★ Townscape

Sights

The sturdy Torre de Menagem (1378) is a relic of the medieval fortifications.

Torre de
Menagem

About 150m/164yd along the Rua de Souto stands the former Archbishop's Palace, the Antigo Paço Episcopal, fronting a little square with a pretty fountain (1723).
   The Palace is made up of three ranges of buildings dating from the 14th–17th c.; these now house the District Archives and one of the finest old libraries in Portugal, with more than 300,000 volumes and over 10,000 valuable manuscripts, the earliest dating from the 9th c.

★ Antigo Paço
Episcopal

The west façade of the Paço Episcopal faces the Praça do Municipio, relatively recently the site of the 18th c. pelican fountain, with the Baroque Town Hall, the Câmara Municipal, at the western end of the square; a collection of azulejos from the town's old buildings is housed on the first floor.

Câmara Municipal

The Igreja do Pópulo, north of the square, was built in the 16th c. but its fine Baroque façade is 18th c.

Igreja do Pópulo

No walk through the town centre should miss the Palácio dos Biscainhos, west of the Town Hall. This Palace, which dates from the 16th c. but was subsequently much altered, today contains a small ethnographic museum.

Palácio dos
Biscainhos

◄ Braga: the pilgrimage church of Bom Jesús do Monte

145

Braga

Arco da Porta Nova

Just a few yards further south is the Arco da Porta Nova, the 18th c. gateway that for centuries served as Braga's main point of entry.

★★Sé

Returning through the pedestrian precinct, this time a few yards to the east and then through the Rua do Cabido, we can see the main façade of the Cathedral, the Sé or Catedral. This jewel in Braga's crown was built in the 11th c. on the site of an earlier Romanesque church, enlarged in later centuries and remodelled in Manueline style in the early 16th c.

Its most striking external features are the west porch, with three bays of groined vaulting and a beautiful iron grille, and a charming figure of Nossa Senhora do Leite (Our Lady of Milk), probably by the French sculptor Nicolas Chanteren, on the rear wall of the choir. Inside, above the richly ornamented Manueline font, is a magnificently carved organ-case. In the Coro Alto (high choir) are fine 15th c. choir-stalls. On the high altar is a 14th c. figure of the Virgin. Among the many monuments in the church is the very fine tomb in a side chapel of the Infante Dom Afonso, João I's natural son (15th c.).

An exit on the north side of the nave leads to the cloister built to replace a Gothic vestibule in the 18th c. From here a flight of steps leads up to the Treasury, richly stocked with precious objects, and a small Museum of Religious Art (fine talha dourada and azulejo decoration of the 17th–18th c., etc.).

From the cloister it is also possible to gain access to three chapels adjoining the cathedral. In the Capela dos Reis, built directly onto the nave, are the 16th c. tombs of Henry of Burgundy (d. 1112) and his wife Dona Teresa, and, behind glass, the mummified body of Archbishop Lourenço Vicente Coutinho (14th c.).

The Capela de São Geraldo has azulejos depicting scenes from the life of St Gerald, the first Archbishop of Braga (1096–1108). The next chapel, the Capela da Glória, decorated with azulejos and heraldic frescos, contains the tomb of Archbishop Gonçalo Pereira (1336), commander of the Minho forces in the battle of Rio Salado against the Moroccans.

Igreja da Misericórdia

Behind the Cathedral is the Renaissance church of the Misericórdia (1562).

Other Sights

Braga has about 30 churches and also worth seeing are the church of São João do Souto (18th c.), just south of the Rua do Suoto, with the adjoining Capela da Conceição or Capela dos Coimbra, founded by João Coimbra in 1525 (fine statues), and the church of Santa Cruz, with its 17th c. Rococo façade.

West of the church of Santa Cruz, on the Campo de São Tiago, is the Arco de São Tiago; a nearby building houses the Museu Pio XII with displays of archaeology and religious art.

The 18th c. Palácio do Raio, or Casa do Mexicano, in the south-eastern part of the centre, has a tiled Rococo façade, and the nearby Fonte do Idolo is worth seeing. This sculpture-bedecked fountain on the edge of a garden ranks as a "national monument".

Surroundings of Braga

★Capela de São Frutuoso

In the suburb of São Jerónimo Real, 3km/2 miles north-west of the town, is one of the oldest Christian buildings in Portugal, the Capela de São Frutuoso, founded by and named after an early bishop of Braga, Frutuoso de Dume (second half of 7th c.). The central part of the chapel and the east end date from the late 7th c. and show Byzantine influence – an unusual feature in Portugal. Other parts of the chapel were rebuilt or added after its destruction by the Moors in the 11th c. The simple interior shows a variety of styles (Visigothic, Romanesque, Lombard). Against the rear wall of the chapel is the sarcophagus of São Frutuoso.

The saint's remains are now in the adjoining Baroque church of the former Franciscan convent, in which the chapel, which has a fine carved pulpit, was incorporated in the 18th c.

East of Braga are three well-known places of pilgrimage. The one most worth seeing is the church of Bom Jesús do Monte (alt. 401m/1316ft), 6km/4 miles east of Braga in a park on the western slopes of Monte Espinho (564m/1850ft). The beautiful gardens, little boating lake and pretty walks make it a favourite spot for picnics and excursions. There is a road up to Bom Jesús do Monte but the actual church is reached by a funicular or on foot up a Way of the Cross leading to a terrace from which a monumental Baroque staircase ascends to the church (originally 15th c.; rebuilt in 18th and 19th c.). The effort of the climb is rewarded by a panoramic view.

★ Bom Jesús do Monte

About 3km/2 miles farther south, on Monte Sameiro (582m/1910ft), is another pilgrimage church (20th c.). This is Portugal's second most visited pilgrimage site after Fátima (see entry). It is reached by an enormous modern flight of steps, with a statue of Pope Pius IX (1954) at the foot.

Sameiro

Another 3km/2 miles beyond this is the Baroque chapel of Maria Madalena (mid 18th c.) with a pleasing granite façade.

Santa Maria Madalena

It is worth combining a visit to the pilgrimage churches with a trip just a few miles to the east to the Ice Age settlement of Citânia de Briteiros (see entry).

Citânia de Briteiros

See entry

Barcelos

See entry

Guimarães

Bragança   D 3

Historical province: Trás-os-Montes. District: Bragança
Altitude: 670m/2198ft. Population: 15,000

The attractive old town of Bragança, the Roman Iuliobriga, lies in a pleasantly cool setting on a hill above the valley of the Rio Sabor, in the extreme north-east corner of Portugal.
   The town is the original seat of the House of Bragança, which ruled in Portugal from 1640 to 1910 (for the last part of the period in the female line of Saxe-Coburg-Bragança) and in Brazil (as Emperors) from 1822 to 1889.
   As capital of the district of Bragança (area 6608sq.km/2550sq. miles; pop. 185,000) it is the cultural and economic heart of the surrounding countryside, which is mainly given over to farming, although in the town the traditional local craft of silk-weaving still flourishes.

Situation and Importance

The medieval upper town is encircled by fortified walls about 2m/6½ft thick, while the newer lower town boasts many fine burghers' houses and noble mansions of the Renaissance period, with handsome granite façades.

★ Townscape

Sights

In the middle of the newer part of the town, in the long Largo da Sé, stands the Cathedral, the Sé de São João Baptista, originally a Jesuit church, a plain and sturdy Renaissance building with the air of a secular building rather than a church. The aisleless interior is partly clad with azulejos. The choir has reticulated vaulting with bosses bearing coats of arms. The sacristy has a coffered ceiling and painted panels with scenes from the life of St Ignatius Loyola on the walls.

Sé de São João Baptista

Outside the main entrance to the Cathedral is a pelourinho (pillory column) of 1689, the symbol of municipal authority.

Pelourinho

From the Cathedral Rua do Conselheiro Abilio Beça leads to the former Bishop's Palace, now occupied by the interesting Museu do Abade de Baçal (archaeology, fine art, folk traditions, handicrafts).
   Nearby is the church of the Misericórdia.

Museu do Abade de Baçal

★ Fortaleza

Above the town stands the massive Castle (Fortaleza), an imposing strong-hold, long regarded as impregnable, which was built by King Sancho I in 1187 and later strengthened by João I. Originally the castle enclosed within its double circuit of walls and eighteen towers the whole of the medieval town. Contemporary views, however, show that by the 15th c. the town had expanded well beyond the castle walls.

In front of the castle gateway is a modern statue of Dom Fernando, Duke of Bragança and governor of Ceuta, erected to commemorate the 500th anniversary of the ceremonial granting of a charter to the town in 1464.

Within the walls are the remains of the Ducal Castle (12th c.), seat of the Dukes of Bragança. The 34m/112ft high keep, the Torre de Menagem, with two fine Gothic twin windows on the south and east sides, was built in the 15th c. Nearby is a 6m/20ft high pelourinho (pillory column), its Gothic shaft resting on the back of a wild boar carved from granite, probably dating from the late Iron Age. Also within the precincts of the castle is the church of Santa Maria do Castelo (16th c.), with a fine Renaissance doorway.

The most interesting building within the castle walls is the Romanesque Domus Municipalis (Town Hall), a severe granite structure of the 12th c., built over a Roman cistern. In form an irregular pentagon, it has a dwarf gallery under the roof ridge (recently restored). This is one of the few secular buildings of the Romanesque period in Portugal.

Surroundings of Bragança

Capela de São Bartolomeu

The Capela de São Bartolomeu, 5km/3 miles south of the town, offers an unusually fine panoramic view over the town and castle.

Parque Natural de Montezinho

The Montezinho Natural Park extends north of Bragança to the Spanish border. It covers an area of 75,000ha/187,000 acres and is still relatively unspoilt and well away from major roads. There are 91 villages in the park, many of them now deserted except for the new houses. Most of the young people have moved away to the towns, and the province of Ttás-os-Montes (see entry) ranks as one of the poorest regions in Portugal. The park derives its name from the hamlet of Montezinho, which lies a good 20km/12½ miles north of Bragança; its population today is only 50.

The nature park contains hills with stony plains, forests of oak, fir and chestnut, as well areas of boulders and gentle slopes covered in heath and gorse. The farmers use the narrow valleys to grow corn, potatoes, vegetables and vines. Almost all of them also own sheep and goats, and the demand for fresh pasture is one of the main problems faced by the park administrators. Fires are constantly being deliberately lit to provide fresh pasture land; the pine trees burn like tinder, destroying plant life with the result that the roots of bushes can no longer prevent erosion of the soil.

The park administrators own three simple shelters (*casas abrigos*) in the region, and these can be hired by walkers by prior arrangement (details can be obtained from the tourist information office in Bragança).

Castro de Avelãs

6km/4 miles north-east, in the village of Castro de Avelãs, are the remains of a 12th c. Benedictine abbey. Parts of the abbey church, the only brick-built church in Portugal, have been incorporated in the present parish church.

Buçaco National Park (Parque Nacional do Buçaco)   **B 4**

Historical province: Beira Litoral. District: Aveiro
Altitude: 220–541m/722–1775ft. Area: 105 hectares/260 acres

Situation and General

Buçaco National Park, which lies 25km/15½ miles north-east of Coimbra on the northern slopes of the Serra do Buçaco, is virtually unrivalled in its scenic beauty and richness of vegetation. The older spelling, Busaco, is

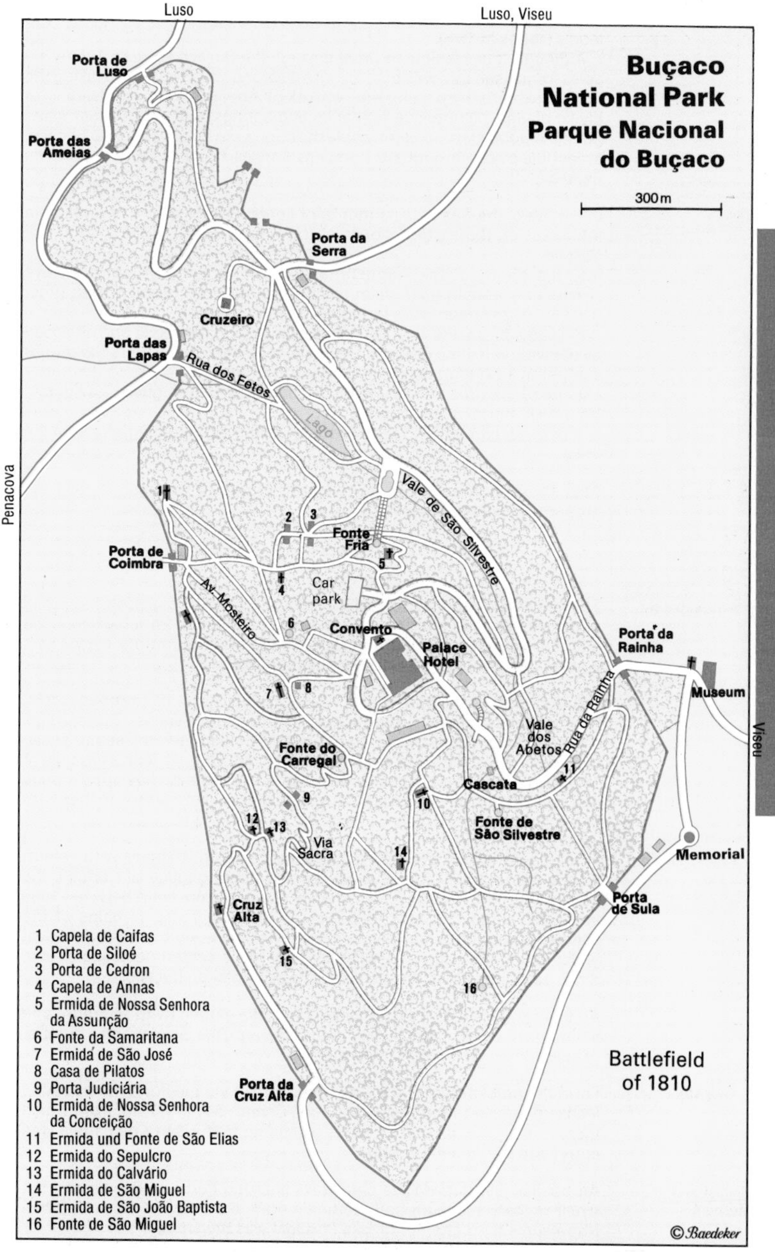

Luso

Luso, Viseu

Buçaco
National Park
Parque Nacional
do Buçaco

300 m

Porta de Luso

Porta das Amelas

Porta da Serra

Cruzeiro

Porta das Lapas

Rua dos Fetos

Lago

Penacova

1

2 3

Fonte Fria

Vale de São Silvestre

Porta de Coimbra

Av. Mosteiro

4

Car park

5

6

Convento

Palace Hotel

Porta da Rainha

Museum

7   8

Vale dos Abetos

Rua da Rainha

Viseu

Fonte do Carregal

9

Cascata

Fonte de São Silvestre

10

12
13

Via Sacra

14

Memorial

Cruz Alta

Porta de Sula

15

16

Porta da Cruz Alta

Battlefield
of 1810

© Baedeker

1 Capela de Caifas
2 Porta de Siloé
3 Porta de Cedron
4 Capela de Annas
5 Ermida de Nossa Senhora
   da Assunção
6 Fonte da Samaritana
7 Ermida de São José
8 Casa de Pilatos
9 Porta Judiciária
10 Ermida de Nossa Senhora
    da Conceição
11 Ermida und Fonte de São Elias
12 Ermida do Sepulcro
13 Ermida do Calvário
14 Ermida de São Miguel
15 Ermida de São João Baptista
16 Fonte de São Miguel

familiar in British history as the scene of Wellington's victory over Napoleon's troops in 1810.

Although it is possible to drive through the Buçaco Forest's 105ha/260 acres – enclosed by a wall over 5km/3 miles long – it is well worth taking the time to explore them using the network of attractive footpaths leading to idyllic glades, picturesque fountains and springs, and magnificent viewpoints. A good starting point inside the park is the Palace Hotel do Buçaco, accessible by car through the Porta das Ameias, Porta da Serra or Porta da Rainha.

History

In the 6th c. the Benedictine monks of Lorvão established a hermitage in the forest on the eastern slopes of the Cruz Alta hill. In the 11th c. this passed

into the hands of the Augustinian canons of Coimbra, who always strenuously upheld their claim to the area and maintained it with great care. In 1622 women were forbidden to enter the area.

In 1628 a Carmelite convent was established in the forest and enclosed by the wall, with nine gates, which is still to be seen today. Here the monks planted an arboretum which quickly became famous and was continuously enriched by exotic species brought back by the Portuguese navigators from their worldwide voyaging.

A papal decree of 1643 prohibited the felling or damaging of any of the trees.

After the secularisation of all religious houses in Portugal in 1834 the property passed to the crown.

Sights

★★ Topography

The forest now contains some 400 native and 300 exotic species. Its special pride is its array of enormous cedars of Lebanon, and from Mexico, India and Africa; other outstanding specimens include mighty cypresses, ancient ginkgo trees, sequoias, araucarias and palms.

Besides its trees the park is also well worth a visit for its grottoes, pools, fountainheads, chapels, hermitages, oratories and walks. The springs, carefully constructed by the monks, are particularly worth seeing. These include, north of the hotel, the Fonte Fria ("cold spring"), with a cascade of 144 steps descending to a basin surrounded by beautiful flowering shrubs and conifers, and the Fonte do Carregal, flowing out of a grotto, to the south of the hotel.

★ Palace Hotel do Buçaco

In the centre of the park, surrounded by flowerbeds ablaze with colour, stands the former summer residence and hunting lodge of Carlos I, the palace which he had the Italian architect Luigi Manini build between 1888 and 1907 alongside what had become the dilapidated remains of the convent. This sumptuous palace in Neo-Manueline style, with a great deal of sculpture and azulejo decoration, now has a certain nostalgic charm. Since 1909 it has been the luxurious Palace Hotel do Buçaco.

Convento

All that remains of the old convent is the little church (with sculpture and paintings illustrating the history of the convent), the cloister and a number of cells (small Wellington memorial).

★ Cruz Alta

From the hotel a Way of the Cross (and a road via the Porta da Cruz Alta) leads up the hill to the Cruz Alta ("High Cross", 541m/1775ft), from which there are superb panoramic views extending to the Serra da Estrela (see entry) and the Atlantic Ocean.

Obelisk and Museum

An obelisk just outside the park walls near the Porta da Rainha and the small military museum both commemorate the battle of Buçaco, when Napoleon's third attempt to take Portugal was thwarted.

Buçaco National Park: Palace Hotel

Surroundings of Buçaco National Park

On the north-western edge of the park, in a picturesque setting at the foot of the Cruz Alta, are the attractively located spa hotels of Luso (alt. 380m/1247ft), where the chalybeate and radioactive mineral springs are used in the treatment of rheumatic and bronchial disorders.
    Luso's bottled mineral water is Portugal's most popular brand.

Luso

Curia (pop. 3000, alt. 40m/130ft), about 10km/6 miles north-west of the park, is another well-known spa. Its hot springs containing calcium sulphate are favoured for ailments of the joints and metabolism. Curia has modern treatment facilities a variety of sport and recreational amenities and an attractive spa park.

Curia

Caldas da Rainha
A 5

Historical province: Estremadura. District: Leiria
Altitude: 50m/165ft. Population: 20,000

About 100km/62 miles north of Lisbon and only about 10km/6 miles from the Atlantic, Caldas da Rainha is one of Portugal's leading spas, with hot sulphur springs (34.5°C/94.1°F) which are particularly recommended for the treatment of rheumatism.
    Visitors flock from far and near to its Monday market in the central square. There are always some stalls selling the local majolica ware. This bright and often rather crudely coloured ware, which is also obtainable throughout the town, is very different from that found in the north.

Situation and Importance

The story to which the town owes its name – "the Queen's hot baths" – is that the virtues of the mineral springs were discovered by Queen Leonor,

History

Caminha: clocktower and . . .

. . . parish church

wife of João II, who observed the local peasants bathing in the water to cure pains in their joints. She then sold her jewels and used the money to found a hospital (1484), to which she herself often came to take the cure.

Sights

Hospital Termal

This bath-house in the old town centre was founded by Queen Leonor and rebuilt in the mid-18th c. under King João IV, who also frequented the spa.

Igreja Nossa Senhora do Pópulo

Adjoining the bath-house, to the east, is the Igreja Nossa Senhora do Pópulo. This too was founded by Queen Leonor, and built in 1500 by the famous architect Boytaca. It has a separate tower, the lower part of which is square and the upper part octagonal. Notable features of the interior are a fine triptych and a Manueline chancel arch. The little baptistery and the font are richly decorated with azulejos.

Parque Dom Carlos I

The origins of the spa park, the Parque Dom Carlos I, also go back to Queen Leonor. Nowadays it has beautiful gardens, fine old trees, and a small lake in the centre.

Museu de José Malhôa

The pavilion in the park houses the Museu de José Malhôa containing modern Portuguese sculpture and paintings, including works by Malhôa who was born in Caldas da Rainha in 1855.

Museu de Cerâmica

The Ceramic Museum is housed in an attractive villa on the edge of the park. Exhibits include works by Rafael Bordalo Pinheiro (1847–1905), who ran a ceramic workshop in Caldas da Rainha for a while.

Other museums

In modern buildings opposite the Ceramic Museum are two further museums dedicated to famous sons of the town. They are the workshop-museum of the portrait and decorative sculptor António Duarte, born here in 1912, and also that of sculptor João Fragoso (b. 1913).

A visit to Caldas da Rainha can be combined with a stay in Óbidos (see entry), 7km/4½ miles to the south. An excursion to the Atlantic coast (see Costa da Prata and Peniche) is also worthwhile.

Places to visit in the area

Caminha   B 3

Historical province: Minho. District: Viana do Castelo
Altitude: 30m/100ft. Population: 2000

The frontier town of Caminha, once strongly fortified, is charmingly set on a tongue of land between the rivers Coura and Minho, just above the mouth of the Minho.
  Once a bulwark in the defence of northern Portugal against Galicia, strategically situated south-west of the Spanish stronghold of Santa Tecla, Caminha is now a modest little fishing town, with handicrafts and lace-making as flourishing subsidiary activities.

Situation and Importance

Sights in Caminha

In the main square, the Praça do Conselheiro Silva Torres, stands the town hall (Paços do Concelho, 15th c.), with a beautiful coffered ceiling in the council chamber. The adjoining 15th c. clock-tower is a relic of the town's medieval fortifications. On the south side of the square can be seen the Gothic Palácio dos Pitas (1490), and in the middle of the square, opposite the town hall, is a Renaissance granite fountain (16th c.).

Praça do Conselheiro Silva Torres

The town's most notable building, located about 150m/164yd beyond the arch in the clock-tower, is the three-aisled Collegiate Church, the Igreja Matriz, built between 1488 and 1565 and combining Gothic with early Renaissance elements. It has a Renaissance façade with an imposing main doorway and a beautiful rose window. Inside there is a wood ceiling carved in Mudéjar style by a Spanish master, while the apse and the charming octagonal font are Manueline.

★ Igreja Matriz

Surroundings

Along the Atlantic coast south-west of Caminha lie several adjoining beaches; near the small resort of Moledo do Minho is the Praia de Moledo, to its south are the Praia do Pirata and the beach of Vila Praia de Âncora. All have fine, clean sand and rich dunes and are lined with pine-woods.

Beaches

2km/1¼ miles inland from Vila Praia de Âncora can be found one of Portugal's best preserved megalithic monuments the Barrosa Dolmen, a large stone tomb from the Neolithic Age.

Dólmen da Barrosa

Cascais   A 6

Historical province: Estremadura. District: Lisboa
Altitude: 0–20m/0–65ft. Population: 30,000

Situated 25km/15½ miles west of Lisbon on the Costa do Sol, Cascais is one of Portugal's most popular seaside resorts, with a correspondingly wide range of sporting and recreational facilities. Partly owing to the shelter from north winds afforded by the Serra de Sintra this former quiet fishing

Situation and importance

port swiftly expanded to become an elegant, almost cosmopolitan, coastal resort but little of this elegance remains today. Although prosperous folk from Lisbon still live here Cascais is thronged in the summer months by an endless stream of sunseekers.

Cascais

(map)

200 m

Sintra

Malveira

Avenida do 25 de Abril

Costa Pinto

Market

Av.

Avenida de Sintra

Estrada Marginal

Estoril, Lisboa

Railway station

Avenida do Ultramar

Rua Visconde

da Luz

Avenida Valbom

Rua Frederico Arouca

Praia da Rainha

Rua Dr. A Dias Pinheiro

Rua Etelias Reis

N.S. dos Navegantes

Largo do 5 de Outubro

Town Hall

Praia da Ribeira

AV. Vasco da Gama

AV. Emídio Navarro

N.S. da Assunção

Praia do Guincho

Avenida da República

Sport-palast

Racecourse

Rua do Parque Municipal

Parque do Marechal Carmona

Avenida

N.S. da Nazaré

Yacht Club

Citadel

Museu Condes de Castro Guimarães

Oceano Atlântico

Boca do Inferno

Estrada da Boca do Inferno

Farol de Santa Marta

© *Baedeker*

History
There was a settlement here in Roman times. Cascais was granted a charter in the 14th c., but it was devastated by the 1755 earthquake which destroyed most of its old buildings.

As the summer residence of the kings of Portugal (from 1870) and the President of the Republic, the turn of the century saw Cascais becoming a meeting-place for high society.

Townscape
In recent years Cascais has grown at a furious rate and has now almost joined up with Estoril (see entry). Around the outskirts of the town high-rise apartments predominate, together with some exclusive residential areas inhabited by rich Portuguese and many British, French and Germans. The old town centre is the only place where there are still a few narrow alleys lined by pretty white houses, while the "smart" area of the town centre is now a mass of restaurants, cafés and stalls catering for the tourist trade.

Sights

Above the south-west side of the bay stands the 17th c. citadel, now the President's summer residence (no admittance).

Just north of the citadel is the Manueline church of Nossa Senhora da Assunção, with 18th c. azulejos, and, somewhat further up the road, the Baroque-style church of Nossa Senhora dos Navegantes, which has a remarkable portal and fine azulejos in the interior.

Parque do Marechal Carmona	To the west of the citadel extends the Parque do Marechal Carmona, and on the south-east side of the park is the Palace of the Condes de Castro Guimarães, dating from the beginning of the century, which the family conveyed to the State in 1927. It houses a small museum containing family portraits and other paintings, as well as furniture, china, silver and gold objects and local prehistoric finds.
Museu do Mar	The history of Cascais is closely linked to the sea. The Maritime Museum north of the Parque do Marechal Carmona provides background information.

At the western exit from Cascais is the viewpoint above the Boca do Inferno, the "mouth of Hell", a cliff 15–20m/50–65ft high in which the sea has hollowed out a number of caves in which the pounding of the waves gives an impressive demonstration of the power of the Atlantic.

★Boca do Inferno

From the north side of the citadel the Avenida de Dom Carlos I promenade winds north-east above the Praia da Ribeira (sandy beach) as far as Estoril, affording beautiful views of Cascais Bay. Beyond this are the little beach of Praia da Rainha, picturesquely framed by rocks, and, still farther north-east in the direction of Estoril (see entry), the beach of Praia da Duquesa, with fine sand and good facilities for bathers. In the summer all these beaches are overcrowded.

Beaches

On the coast north-west of Cascais there are some larger beaches and pretty, small resorts. Also worth a visit is the Cabo da Roca – the westernmost point of the European mainland (see Costa do Sol).

Castelo Branco
C 5

Historical province: Beira Baixa. District: Castelo Branco
Altitude: 375m/1230ft. Population: 30,000

Castelo Branco, in central Portugal near the Spanish frontier, is the former capital of the old province of Beira Baixa and now chief town of the district which bears its name.

Situation and Importance

It has been celebrated since the 17th c. for the brightly coloured embroidered bedspreads known as colchas. Other local products much esteemed in Portugal are goat's milk cheese and olive oil.

Lying so near the Spanish frontier, the town was of great military and strategic importance. Of the medieval Templar castle, the "castelo branco" or white castle, probably built in the reign of King Dinis, only scanty remains survive. In spite of its defensive walls Castelo Branco suffered throughout its history from enemy assaults and raids, most recently in 1807, when Napoleon's troops did much damage.

History

Jardim Episcopal

155

Castelo Branco

Townscape

Apart from the lovely Jardim Episcopal Castelo Branco has no particularly notable sights or unusual townscape features. Today's Castelo Branco is centred around the broad Alameda da Liberdade and the adjacent square, with gardens and the tourist information centre. West of this newer part of town are the 16th c. town hall and some 16th–18th c. townhouses, grouped around the Praça Luís de Camões.

Sights

★ Jardim Episcopal

The town's principal attraction is the Jardim Episcopal, formerly the Bishop's gardens and certainly one of the loveliest Baroque gardens in Portugal. The terraced gardens, laid out in the early 18th c. for Dom João de Mendoça, are a showpiece of Baroque extravagance and fantasy, with carefully clipped trees and shrubs, elaborately patterned flowerbeds and a profusion of basins and fountains. There is also a lavish display of Baroque sculpture – archangels, evangelists, apostles, allegorical figures, animals and, flanking a flight of steps, the complete series of Portuguese kings with the Spanish Hapsburg kings (1580–1640) rather pointedly represented by much smaller figures.

Antigo Paço Episcopal

The old Bishop's Palace, on the northern edge of the park, which was originally Gothic and remodelled as Baroque in 1726, houses the Museu de Francisco Tavares Proença Júnior, with prehistoric and Roman material from the Castelo Branco area, pictures by Portuguese artists of the 16th, 18th and 19th c., tapestries, coins, furniture, armour, etc. The museum's chief treasures are the colchas mentioned above.

Other sights

The church of the Misericórdia (1519), opposite the Bishop's Palace, has a Manueline doorway, while the main attractions of the church of Nossa Senhora da Piedade are the azulejos, and of the church of Santa Isabel, the paintings.

The picturesque Monsanto – one of the villages in which time seems to stand still

Above the town are the ruins of the 12th c. Templar castle and the little church of Santa Maria do Castelo. From here a flight of steps leads up to the Miradouro de São Gens, a viewpoint from which there is a far-ranging prospect of the town and surrounding area.

Surroundings of Castelo Branco

About 5km/3 miles east is the Gothic pilgrimage church of Nossa Senhora de Mércoles (15th c.).

Nossa Senhora de Mércoles

The little village of Idanha-a-Velha some 50km/31 miles north-east of Castelo Branco boasts an illustrious past. Founded by the Romans it was the episcopal see under the Visigoths in the 6th c. before sinking back into obscurity following the Moorish invasion in the 8th c. It still has parts of a Roman street, bridge and gateway and remains of a basilica and an episcopal palace are from the Gothic period.

Idanha-a-Velha

About 10km/6 miles north-east of Idanha-a-Velha, below the summit of a rocky hill, is the picturesque little town of Monsanto da Beira (alt. 758m/2487ft), dominated by the ruins of a castle (fine view). With its trim white houses, sometimes hewn out of the rock, its steep and narrow lanes and its Celtic remains it is one of the most visited and most characteristic places in Beira Baixa – and in fact emerged from a competition in 1940 as "the most Portuguese village", although now only 250 people still live here.

★ Monsanto

About 30km/19 miles south-west of Castelo Branco the Tagus has carved out a magnificent rocky gorge, 45m/150ft wide, the Portas de Ródão. The best view of the gorge is from the bridge over the Tagus at Vila Velha de Ródão to the east.

Portas de Ródão

Castelo Branco is a good base for excursions in the Serra de Gardunha, a range of hills north of the town which in places take on an almost Alpine character, with bizarrely shaped rock formations bearing such names as the Cabeça de Frade ("monk's head") and Pedra Sobreposta ("rockpile").
   The pleasant little hill-town of Alpedrinha (alt. 555m/1855ft), about 30km/19 miles along the Castelo Branco road to Covilhã (see entry), is a good starting point for walks in the Serra da Gardunha. There is a lovely walk from here to the Penha da Senhora da Serra (hermitage), with beautiful panoramic views, and then on to the Pirâmide (1223m/4013ft), the highest point in this range of hills.
   The Pirâmide can also be climbed from the picturesque hill village of Castelo Novo (700m/2300ft), below the hermitage and boasting an 18th c. town hall and a Manueline pelourinho both of which are worth seeing.

★ Serra da Gardunha

The chief place in the Serra da Gardunha is the little town of Fundão (alt. 496m/1627ft; pop. 6000), 45km/28 miles north of Castelo Branco in a fertile fruit-growing region on the northern slopes of the hills, with an old-established textile industry. It has two attractive churches, the parish church of the Misericórdia (18th c.) and the chapel of São Francisco.

Fundão

Castelo de Vide   C5

Historical province: Alto Alentejo. District: Portalegre
Altitude: 460–628m/1509–2060ft. Population: 2600

On the north-west side of the bleak Serra de São Mameda, clustering in steps and stairs around the hilltop on which stands its castle, Castelo de Vide is 20km/12½ miles north of Portalegre, near the Spanish frontier. Although one of Portugal's most picturesque places, tourism is still within

Situation and Importance

reasonable bounds, and the townsfolk mostly still earn their living from agriculture and handicrafts, as well as from visitors to the cold mineral springs containing Glauber's salt and taken for the treatment of diabetes and skin and liver ailments.

★★Townscape

Castelo de Vide has managed to preserve its medieval townscape virtually intact, with its picturesque maze of narrow streets and trim whitewashed houses with their characteristic chimneys, and many charming little squares and nooks and corners. Flowers are everywhere and just about every house in the old town centre is resplendent with window boxes and rows of flowerpots.

Sights

Praça de Dom Pedro V

The centre of Castelo de Vide, and the best starting point for a walk round the town, is the Praça de Dom Pedro V, a well-proportioned square bounded by Baroque palaces, churches and the town hall with a statue of Dom Pedro V in the middle. Dominating the square is the Baroque church of Santa Maria with its squat pyramidal central tower.

Castelo

From the Praça de Dom Pedro V signs point the way along picturesque lanes up to the Castelo do São Roque, built in 1327 on the remains of a Moorish castle, from which an ingenious ventilation system still survives. Its massive keep was damaged by an explosion in 1705 but can still be climbed to obtain superb views over the town and countryside.

Within the castle perimeter stands the church of Nossa Senhora da Alegria, completely covered with 17th c. azulejos.

Judiaria

Just left of the exit from the castle is the old Jewish quarter, the Judiaria, where time seems to have stood still. The narrow steep alleyways are

The streets in the old town decorated with flowers and the limewashed houses contribute to the charm of Castelo de Vide

pedestrian only. Many of the little houses have fine Gothic and Manueline windows and doors. Easily viewable, the 14th c. synagogue on the main street is barely distinguishable from the other houses.

The main street ends in an attractive square with the covered Renaissance town fountain, the Fonte da Vile.

South of the Praça de Dom Pedro, in the opposite direction to the castle at the other end of town, and reached via gardens and the "Fonte do Montorinho" fountain, is the former Franciscan convent, the Convento de São Francisco, now a home for the visually handicapped.

Convento de São Francisco

Surroundings of Castelo de Vide

4km/2½ miles south-west is the Monte da Penha (700m/2300ft; chapel), from which there is a charming view of the town.

Monte da Penha

The little town of Nisa, 25km/15 miles north-west of Castelo de Vide, has a 13th c. ruined castle, the remains of its walls, with two 14th c. towers, and a fine Baroque parish church.

Nisa

To the west of Nisa flows the Ribeira de Nisa, a tributary of the Tagus, which is dammed about 10km/6 miles south-east of the town to form the Barragem da Póvoa (water sports).

Ribeira de Nisa

Within easy reach of Castelo de Vide and definitely worth a visit are Marvão, with its castle (12km/7½ miles south-east – see entry), and Portalegre (20km/12½ miles south – see entry).

Marvão, Portalegre

Castro Verde

B 7

Historical province: Baixo Alentejo. District: Beja
Altitude: 245m/804ft. Population: 6000

The modest little market town of Castro Verde (green castle) lies about 60km/37 miles south-west of the chief town of the district, Beja, and is surrounded by pastureland and forests of cork-oak.

Situation and Importance

Sights

The aisleless church of Nossa Senhora da Conceiáão has an interior completely clad with early 18th c. azulejos depicting scenes from the battle of Ourique (see Surroundings).

Igreja da Conceição

Also of interest is the church of the Chagas do Salvador, decorated with azulejos in a style typical of the region, which was built by Philip II of Spain in the 16th c. on the site of an earlier church.

Igreja das Chagas do Salvador

Surroundings of Castro Verde

Tradition has it that the battle of Ourique, when Afonso I Henriques won a decisive victory over the Moors in 1139, took place near the modest little village of Ourique, about 15km/9 miles south-west of Castro Verde. The actual site of the battle is supposed to be Campo de Ourique, between Castro Verde and the village, although historians cast doubt on whether the battle actually happened so far south.

Ourique

About 6km/4 miles south of Aldeia dos Palheiros a little road branches off (4km/2½ miles) to the remains of a settlement of the early historical period, the Castro de Cola (known in Roman times as Ossonoba). Roughly rectangular in shape, it is surrounded by a rampart 5m/16ft high.

Castro de Cola

Almôdôvar	Almôdôvar (alt. 289m/948ft; pop. 2500), 21km/13 miles south of Castro Verde, has a 17th c. Franciscan convent with a beautiful cloister, and a Gothic and Manueline parish church which are worth seeing.
Aljustrel	23km/14 miles north of Castro Verde lies the busy little town of Aljustrel (alt. 200m/655ft; pop. 10,000), with copper-mines, some of which have been worked since ancient times.

Chaves   C 3

Historical province: Trás-os-Montes.
District: Vila Real
Altitude: 324m/1063ft.
Population: 14,000

Situation and Importance	The old-world little town of Chaves, the Roman Aquae Flaviae, lies on a plateau in northern Portugal near the Spanish frontier, in an area watered by the Rio Tâmega which has been intensively cultivated since ancient times. As far back as the Romans there has been recourse to the town's hot springs (73°C/163°F) for the treatment of rheumatism and internal ailments, and the modern thermal baths below the castle are well used today.
History	The town has a history dating back to pre-Roman times. With a substantial stone bridge over the Rio Tâmega built in the reign of Trajan (98–117), it became an important staging point on the road between Asturica Augusta (Astorga) and Bracara Augusta (Braga). During the Middle Ages it was a stronghold defending Portuguese territory against Spain in the north.
Townscape	The town still presents a sturdy defensive face to the world, its powerful castle rearing above the white houses with their balconies and arcades.

Sights

Ponte Romana	The Rio Tâmega is spanned by a well-preserved Roman bridge of twelve arches, 140m/155yd long, dating from the 2nd c. A.D. The two Roman milestones, with inscriptions, in the middle of the bridge are copies of the originals which are in the town museum.
São João de Deus	Near the bridge, on the left bank of the river, stands the Baroque church of São João de Deus, an octagonal structure made particularly impressive by its fine granite façade.
Igreja Matriz	The life of the town revolves around the Praça da República, with a Manueline pelourinho (pillory column) and the parish church, the Igreja Matriz. Originally Romanesque, this was rebuilt in the 16th c., only the tower and part of the doorway surviving from the earlier church.
Igreja da Misericórdia	Behind the parish church the Baroque church of the Misericórdia (17th c.) has azulejo pictures (Biblical scenes) covering the interior walls and fine 18th c. ceiling paintings.
Museu Municipal	The nearby municipal museum in the 17th c. palace of the Dukes of Bragança contains archaeological material found locally, coins, azulejos and folk art.
Castelo	The massive castle above the town was built on the site of a Roman fortress. It was strengthened after the Moorish conquest, badly damaged during the Reconquista and rebuilt by King Dinis in the 13th/14th c. The medieval castle was the residence of the first Duke of Bragança, a natural son of King João I. In the 17th c. Vauban-style bastions were built on to the

castle, but these were later destroyed. The imposing keep, the Torre de Menagem, houses a small military museum.

Surroundings of Chaves

In Outeiro Seco, about 4km/2½ miles north of Chaves stands the church of Nossa Senhora da Azinheira, an aisleless Romanesque building with unusual figural decoration on the façade, and medieval frescos (much altered) in the interior.

Outeiro Seco
Nossa Senhora da Azinheira

The interesting feature of Santo Estêvão, 3km/2 miles east of Chaves, is its 13th c. castle ruins.

Santo Estêvão

About 15km/9 miles south-west of Chaves, Vidago (alt. 350m/1148ft) has hot springs used to treat internal ailments. Some sanatoria and hotels have been forced to close, however, but the Art Nouveau Palace Hotel is worth a visit.

Vidago

The name of Pedras Salgados (12km/7½ miles south of Vidago) is well-known as the name of a popular bottled mineral water.

Pedras Salgados

Carvalhelhos, about 30km/19 miles west of Chaves, is also a little spa. Nearby are the remains of an Iron Age settlement.

Carvalhelhos

Citânia de Briteiros

B 3

Historical province: Minho. District: Braga
Altitude: 336m/1102ft

About 12km/7½ miles east of Braga on Monte São Romão, surrounded by the pleasant hills of the Serra Falperra, are the remains of the Citânia de Briteiros, an Iron Age settlement. Together with Castro de Sabroso it is Portugal's oldest known settlement to date. Fragments of pottery (much of it painted), carved stones, weapons, implements and jewellery recovered during the excavations are now in the Museu de Martins Sarmento in Guimarães (see entry).

It is well worth taking the time to look round Citânia de Briteiros, climbing slowly up from the entrance located below the main excavation area to the two reconstructed round huts and then on to the small chapel of São Romão on top of the hill where there is an excellent general view over the site.

Situation and General

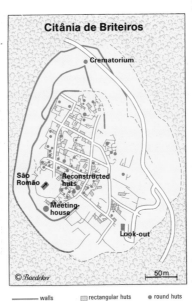

Citânia de Briteiros

● Crematorium

São Romão ◆

Reconstructed huts ●

Meeting-house ●

Look-out ■

© Baedeker

50 m

———— walls   ▨ rectangular huts   ● round huts

Citânia de Briteiros

History

The Celtic-Iberian settlement, discovered in 1874 and excavated from 1875 onwards under the direction of Franciso Martins Sarmento (1833–99), was probably established about 500 B.C.; its most flourishing period was in the 4th c. B.C. and, as the excavations have shown, it continued to be occupied into late Roman times.

★★Site

The ancient town was enclosed within three rings of ramparts and contained some 150 single-roomed dwellings, round, oval or rectangular in plan, and built from stone cut to fit so snugly and firmly that no mortar was needed. The water conduits can still be seen, as well as traces of the streets, already paved with stone slabs.

Two of the round huts were reconstructed on the theory that the circular dwelling with a conical roof was the basic type of human habitation. There remains considerable doubt, however, about the authenticity of the reconstructions.

A much bigger house (about 11m/36ft in diameter) is believed to have been used for meetings, and an isolated building outside the perimeter, near the Guimarães–Braga road, was probably a cremation site.

Castro de Sabroso

Also on a hill (278m/912ft), a short distance from Citânia de Briteiros, are the remains (less well preserved) of another prehistoric settlement, the Castro de Sabroso, which gets its name from the massive surrounding wall of dressed stone.

Sabroso, which was also excavated by Francisco Martins Sarmento, is older and smaller than Briteiros.

There are remains of numerous circular huts on this site, too, some of them with a block of stone in the middle which may have supported the roof.

Reconstructed houses of the Citânia de Briteiros

Places to visit in the vicinity of Citânia de Briteiros are described under Braga and Guimarães (see entries).   **Surroundings**

Coimbra   B 4

Historical province: Beira Litoral. District: Coimbra
Altitude: 75–100m/250–330ft. Population: 90,000

Rich in tradition, the old University town of Coimbra, principal town of its own district and the see of a bishop, lies halfway between Lisbon and Oporto in the hilly country of Beira Litoral. It is built on the right bank of the Rio Mondego, here skirting the chalk hills of the Serra de Lorvão.   Situation and Importance

The 18,000 or so Coimbra University students are very much a feature of life in the town. Bareheaded, they wear a long black robe (batina) under a black cape (capa), with facings of different colours for the various faculties. On the occasion of the Queima das Fitas, the examination celebrations held in the middle of May, these facings are ceremonially burned as part of a giant spectacle.

With its fine old buildings, many of them dating from the time of Manuel I, and many other art treasures Coimbra should be included in any visit to Portugal.

Archaeological material found on the site carries the history of the town back to prehistoric times. It was known to the Romans as Aeminium, but later, having become the see of a bishop, it took the name of the nearby Roman town of Conimbriga (see Surroundings), which was destroyed by the Suevi in 468. The area fell into the hands of the Moors in the 8th c., but the town was temporarily won back in 872 and finally recovered by Fernando the Great of Castile in 1064. In the 12th c. Coimbra became capital   History

Coimbra: panorama of the old university city

of the new Portuguese kingdom. It lost this status to Lisbon in 1260, but was compensated by the foundation (1307–08) of the University which, with interruptions, was until 1911 the only university in Portugal and which became a major element in the town's cultural and intellectual life.

★★ Townscape

From the more modern Lower Town on the right bank of the Mondego steep lanes climb to the Upper Town, with the extensive buildings of the University, on a hill 100m/330ft above the river. On the left bank is the district of Santa Clara with two former convents and a miniature village.

A good starting point for a tour of the town is the Largo da Portagem, which is also where the tourist information centre is located. The broad Avenida Emidio Navarro is resplendent with greenery. After enjoying the fine view of the town from the bridge opposite, the Ponte de Santa Clara over the Mondego, the best route is to stroll along the Rua Ferreira Borges/ Rua Visconde da Luz, Coimbra's main shopping street.

Sights

★ Praça do Comércio

To the west of the Rua Visconde da Luz lies the Praça do Comércio, the town's old market place. Nowadays one of the most impressive squares in Portugal, it is well worth lingering in a street café and looking at the façades of the nearby houses which have long been home to artisans and craftworkers.

São Tiago

At the northern end of the square stands the Romanesque church of São Tiago, founded by Fernando the Great in the 11th c. in thanksgiving for the

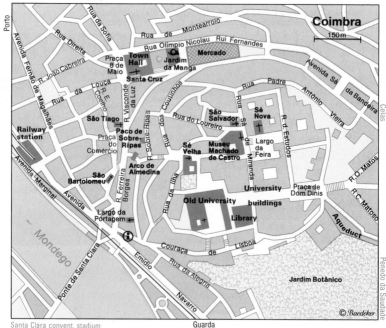

Santa Clara convent, stadium
Condeixa (Conimbriga), Lisboa

Guarda

164

The University square is to be found through the Porta Férrea, this elegant clocktower is not only a symbol of the University but of the whole town

reconquest of the town from the Moors. The church has a plain timber ceiling.

The Rua Eduardo Coelho, on the north side of the Praça do Comércio, leads eventually to the Praça 8 de Maio, focal point of life in the town. On the east side of the square is the Convento de Santa Cruz. This former Augustinian monastery was founded in 1131 and much altered and enlarged in later centuries. Fundamental innovation work was carried out in the 15th/16th c. in the reign of Manuel I by his celebrated architect Boytaca, and after his death by Nicolas de Chantarène.

★ Convento de Santa Cruz

The whole of the north wing is now occupied by the town hall, the Câmara Municipal.

The south wing contains the aisleless convent church (1131–32), which has a Manueline façade with rich sculptural decoration, and a vaulted interior with side chapels. On the north wall is a magnificent pulpit (1522), a relic of the rich furnishings which are referred to in historical documents. In the Gallery are fine 16th c. stalls, the only ones of that period in Portugal, carved with representations of Vasco da Gama's voyages and scenes from Camões' "Lusiads".

In the Sacristy, entered from the right-hand side of the church and a Renaissance structure of 1622 with coffered barrel vaulting and polychrome azulejo decoration on the walls, are a number of notable pictures by Portuguese artists ("Pentecost" by Cristóvão de Figueiredo; "Calvary" by São Bento).

In the Choir, reached through the Sacristy, are the tombs (mainly in late Gothic style) of the first Portuguese kings; they were commissioned by Manuel I from Nicolas de Chanterène: on the left the recumbent figure of Afonso I Henriques (1139–85), on the right Sancho I (1185–1211), each surrounded by seven saints.

Love Beyond the Grave

Coimbra, January 7th 1355. She knew there was no escape and that she could not hope for mercy. The men had only one aim – to carry out their orders. She was forced to kneel. One of the men approached and raised his sword. The cold steel swished through the air and struck her white neck a mighty blow . . .

Lisbon, July 1340. King Alfonso IV (1325–57) beamed with satisfaction. His son, the 20 year-old Infant Dom Pedro, and Constanza, the considerably older ideal candidate for his hand, had become betrothed. Yet the king still nursed doubts – and not without reason, as will be seen. In the royal retinue was a Galician maiden of exceptional beauty, Inês de Castro, with whom the heir to the throne soon fell passionately in love. While Pedro did follow his father's wishes and marry Constanza, his only true love was the lady-in-waiting from Galicia. Theirs was a secret and furtive affair; the two young lovers could meet only in the small hours. However, the king soon learned of the liaison; to avoid a scandal he ordered Inês to leave the country, which she did. However, when Constanza died shortly after while giving birth to Crown Prince Fernando, Pedro – strictly against the express wishes of his father – invited Inês back to court. For four happy years they lived together in Coimbra, during which time she bore him four children. Alfonso IV viewed this liaison with increasing concern, fearing that through the Galician woman Pedro would fall under the influence of Castile. Paternal resistance, however, merely brought Dom Pedro even closer to the beautiful Inês. Not only did he openly display his love for her in public, he also made a point of spending much time with her brothers and other Castilian nobles, while concerning himself but little with affairs of state. He also paid little attention to the legitimate son whom Constanza had borne him. Alfonso feared more and more that as a result of his love for Inês his son would gamble away Portugal's hard won independence to its more powerful neighbour, Castile. Early in January 1355 he called a meeting of the crown council to find a way of getting the beautiful Inês out of the way. Their solution was – condemn her to death. On January 7th 1355, a cheerless, dull day, three hired assassins forced their way into the country house where she lived (and which was later named "Quinta das Lágrimas", or House of Tears). The thugs had chosen their moment well, as Pedro was out hunting with some friends. On his return he made a gruesome discovery; Inês had been beheaded. Pedro lost all reason and could think of only one thing – revenge! With his faithful supporters he unleashed a bloody civil war against his father, but his troops were no match for the king's forces. After his mother had intervened Pedro finally surrendered and swore not to take further revenge for what had happened. However, those responsible for the death of his beloved feared he might not keep his word and quickly fled to Castile.

Alfonso IV died in 1357, and people feared the worst. But the new king, Pedro I (1357–67), appeared to have kept his promise and to be no longer plotting revenge. Perhaps, people conjectured, his new lover, who had borne him another son, João – the future Grand Master of the House of Avis and founder of the second royal dynasty – would help him to get over the shameful murder of Inês. But appearances were deceptive. Pedro established close ties with neighbouring Castile and obtained the extradition of two of his father's three advisors who had hatched the murder of his beloved Inês; the third had fled in time to England. Pedro's revenge on the "ex-advisors" was terrible indeed. First they were most cruelly tortured. Then he had their hearts cut out as he watched. Then he is said to have ordered that the body of his dead lover be removed from her grave in the convent of Santa Clara and taken to Coimbra cathedral where she was ceremonially crowned. According to legend, two thrones were set up in the cathedral; the skeleton was placed on one and Pedro took his place on the other. The corpse was dressed in coronation robes decorated with jewels and on its head it wore a crown. And then, it is said, the whole court had to pay homage to it and kiss its hand. To underline the correctness of this macabre "coronation" the Bishop of Braga stated that he had at one time married Pedro and Inês in secret. When night fell Inês' body was taken in a ghostly torch-light procession to the cathedral in Alcobaça and interred there . . .

Although there is no historical evidence to support this, the facts are that Pedro did maintain that he had at one time secretly married Inês and had buried his former lover in a chapel in Alcobaça cathedral. He had had made for himself and Inês two magnificent sarcophagi, each adorned with a figure of the deceased. In accordance with the king's wishes the coffins stand one opposite the other "so that on the Day of Judgment the gaze of each will fall upon their beloved".

Pedro died ten years later. During his reign he made himself a reputation above all as a fanatical supporter of justice. Because of the cruel revenge he wreaked on the murderers of his beloved Inês, however, and also as a result of his often merciless and brutal behaviour in court proceedings (he personally whipped offenders until the blood ran) he was named "the Cruel One". However, the Portuguese people revered him because all his subjects were regarded as equal and

Sacophagus of Inês de Castro in the Cathedral of Alcobaça

because his jurisprudence did not differentiate between rich and poor or between those of high and low birth. Therefore he was also recognised by the people as "the Just One".

The touching and at the same time cruel story of the love of Pedro and Inês does, of course, provide gripping material for stage, screen and the fine arts. Most of all, however, it is the *fado* songs sung in Coimbra and Alcoboça which tug at the heart-strings. They tell how on certain nights of the year flickering torches bathe the great church of Alcobaça in a sombre light. Then one can see King Pedro step out of his tomb, go to fetch his dead queen from hers and seat her next to him on the throne, dress her in coronation robes and then watch as their courtiers approach hesitantly and pay homage to the murdered queen and kiss her hand with trembling lips as pale shafts of light shoot forth from her eye sockets.

Also reached from the Sacristy, via the Chapterhouse, is the picturesque Claustro do Silêncio (16th c.), a two-storey Manueline cloister with three magnificent reliefs (scenes from the Passion) in the south-west and north-east corners and on the south side, and in the centre a beautiful Renaissance fountain.

Jardim da Manga

Adjoining the monastery complex to the east is the Jardim da Manga, all that is left of a second, later cloister built by João III according to a design drawn on his sleeve, hence the name "Manga". The domed building in the centre is surrounded by water and four small round chapels, to which access used to be by drawbridge only. Once these were raised there was nothing to disturb the monks' meditation.

Arco de Almedina

The Upper Town is reached on foot by turning south down the Rua Visconde da Luz and then turning left, beside number 75, through the Arco de Almedina. The arch is a relic of the Moorish town walls. The Gothic two-storey tower built over it in the 15th c. was occupied by a municipal court in the 16th c. and now houses a Museum of Ethnography.

Paco de Sobre-Ripas

North of the Arco de Almedina in the Rua de Sobre-Ripas is the 16th c. palace of the same name which has a fine Manueline portal.

★Sé Velha

A stepped lane leads up to Sé Velha, the old cathedral, a fortress-like structure built in the reign of Afonso I Henriques (12th c.), with a plain exterior, crenellated walls and a massive Romanesque west doorway. Only the Porta Especiosa, a richly decorated early Renaissance doorway on the north side of the church, relieves the sombre effect of the exterior.

The Romanesque interior, with three aisles, is strikingly impressive. The most notable features are a number of fine tombs, including that of Bishop Almeida (16th c.); the large Late Gothic high altar, with representations of the Assumption by two Flemish masters, Oliver of Ghent and John of Ypres; and the Renaissance font (16th c.). From the south aisle a flight of steps leads up to the Early Gothic cloister (13th c.).

In the square in front of the Old Cathedral Dom João was proclaimed King of Portugal in 1385.

Sé Nova

From the north side of the Old Cathedral the steep Rua do Cabido goes up to the Largo da Feira, which has been considerably enlarged in recent years. On the north side of the square stands the Sé Nova, the new cathedral. Originally constructed for the Jesuits, building was begun in the late 16th c. but work continued well into the 17th c. and, with the banishment of the Jesuits, it was raised to cathedral status in 1772. It has a handsome Early Baroque façade and, inside, barrel vaulting, Baroque altars and a 17th c. organ.

★Museu Nacional de Machado de Castro

On the west side of the Largo da Feira, in the former Bishop's Palace (rebuilt in the late 16th c.) and in the church of São João, is the Museu Nacional de Machado de Castro, named after the Coimbra-born sculptor Machado de Castro (1736–1828) and containing Roman material from excavations,

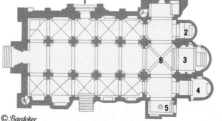

© Baedeker

Coimbra

Old Cathedral
Sé Velha

1 Porta Especiosa
2 North apse (tomb of Bishop Almeida)
3 Choir
4 South apse
5 Font
6 Crossing

medieval sarcophaguses, Romanesque and Gothic sculpture in stone and wood, goldsmiths' work, furniture, tapestries, porcelain, paintings of the 16th–18th c. (including some notable Flemish pictures), a special section devoted to work by modern Portuguese painters and a department of religious art..

From the double loggia in the beautiful courtyard there is a very fine view of the town.

To the south of the Largo da Feira, within the area once occupied by the castle, are the imposing modern buildings of the University; to the east the Faculty of Medicine, adjoining it on the right the Faculty of Arts, with a small archaeological museum, and the library (Biblioteca Geral).

Universidade

To the west, on the highest point of the upper town, where the royal palace (now represented only by a Manueline doorway) once stood, is the Old University, partly rebuilt in the 17th and 18th c., with the earlier Porta Férrea ("iron gate", 1634) leading into the fine courtyard. Enclosed on three sides by buildings, it has a terrace on the south side from which there is a magnificent view.

★★Universidade Velha

On the north side is the actual Old University building, the Colégio, with the Chancellery and the Law Faculty, and, up flights of steps, the "Via Latina" colonnade where once only Latin was allowed to be spoken. On the east side of the courtyard is the observatory (Observatório) and on the west the University Church, built in 1517–52 as the palace chapel, with a 33m/110ft high tower (1733) and an adjacent small museum of sacred art.

Adjoining the church is the sumptuous Old Library, built 1716–23 on the model of the Court Library in Vienna (João V's queen, Ana Maria, being Austrian). It has ceiling and wall paintings by António Simões Ribeiro and valuable furniture with intarsia decoration. Its 300,000 books and 3000 medieval manuscripts come from all parts of Portugal and since 1910 can only be viewed with a special permit. Certain parts of the university (library, church and the Sala dos Capelos) are open to the public each day 9.30am–12.30pm and 2–5pm. Admission tickets can be obtained near the stairs up to the principal's room.

Go back through the Porta Férrea and straight on to the Praça de Dom Dinis then down the steps and under the 16th c. aqueduct to arrive at the entrance to the Jardim Botânico, the botanic gardens, commissioned by Marquês de Pombal (see Famous People) and laid out in terraces on the slopes of a side valley of the Mondego, with large numbers of subtropical plants. Unfortunately the gardens are only partly open to the public since they also form part of the University.

★Jardim Botânico

North-east of the botanic gardens is Penedo da Saudade, traditionally a meeting place for the students but above all a superb viewpoint.

Penedo da Saudade

On the left bank of the Mondego, to the left of the Lisbon road, are the partly sunken ruins of the Gothic Convent of Santa Clara-a-Velha, founded in 1286, which has gradually been destroyed by the flooding of the river. Here the saintly Queen Isabel (1271–1336) spent the last ten years of her life and here she was buried, as was the murdered Inês de Castro (see Alcobaça), Pedro I's secret bride. Their remains were moved elsewhere after the destruction of the convent.

★Convento de Santa Clara-a-Velha

About 1km/½ mile east of the old convent along the Rua António Augusto Gonçalves is Quinta das Lágrimas, the "villa of tears", where Inês de Castro is said to have been murdered in 1355.

Quinta das Lágrimas

The Fonte dos Amores, the "lovers' fountain", in the park recalls her tragic love story.

Opposite the old Santa Clara Convent can be found Portugal dos Pequenitos, a miniature village established in 1940, with reproductions of the country's most important buildings and of typical homes and buildings

★Portugal dos Pequenitos Parque

Miniature buildings in the Pequenitos Parque

from the former colonies. The garden setting makes a visit here enjoyable for adults as well as children.

Convento de Santa Clara-a-Nova

Since the old Convent of Santa Clara was almost completely destroyed in the 17th c. a new convent, the Convento de Santa-Clara-a-Nova, was built between 1649 and 1696 to the right on the Monte da Esperança. It is possible to visit the convent church, cloister and the rooms containing a small military museum. The other buildings now serve as a barracks. The Renaissance convent church is dedicated to St Isabel, wife of King Dinis and Coimbra's patron saint, and contains her silver shrine (1614) which was originally in the old convent and was transferred here to its current position in the choir by Pedro II at the end of the 17th c. St Isabel's empty stone sarcophagus is also worth seeing. Dating from the early 14th c. it is borne on six crouching lions, with the recumbent figure of the queen dressed in the simple habit of the Poor Clares but wearing a crown to show her rank.

Surroundings of Coimbra

Celas

About 1.5km/1 mile east of Coimbra, in the suburb of Celas, is the former Benedictine abbey of Celas, founded in the 13th c. by Dona Sancha, daughter of King Sancho I, and much altered in the 16th c. It has a fine late 13th c. cloister which is worth seeing.

Santo António dos Olivais

Farther east is the church of the former Franciscan convent of Santo António dos Olivais, which was burned down in the middle of the 19th c. St Antony is said to have lived in the convent (founded at the beginning of the 13th c.) in about 1220.

Condeixa

Condeixa, 15km/9 miles south-west of Coimbra, has some fine palaces, including the 17th c. Palácio dos Lemos.

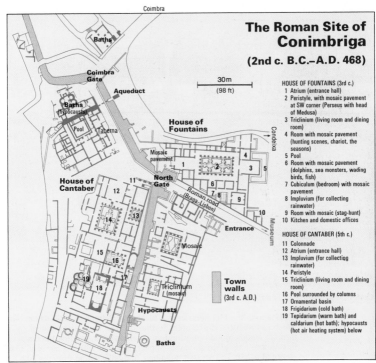

The Roman Site of Conimbriga
(2nd c. B.C.–A.D. 468)

HOUSE OF FOUNTAINS (3rd c.)
1 Atrium (entrance hall)
2 Peristyle, with mosaic pavement at SW corner (Perseus with head of Medusa)
3 Triclinium (living room and dining room)
4 Room with mosaic pavement (hunting scenes, chariot, the seasons)
5 Pool
6 Room with mosaic pavement (dolphins, sea monsters, wading birds, fish)
7 Cubiculum (bedroom) with mosaic pavement
8 Impluvium (for collecting rainwater)
9 Room with mosaic (stag-hunt)
10 Kitchen and domestic offices

HOUSE OF CANTABER (5th c.)
11 Colonnade
12 Atrium (entrance hall)
13 Impluvium (for collecting rainwater)
14 Peristyle
15 Triclinium (living room and dining room)
16 Pool surrounded by columns
17 Ornamental basin
18 Frigidarium (cold bath)
19 Tepidarium (warm bath) and caldarium (hot bath); hypocausts (hot air heating system) below

Town walls (3rd c. A.D.)

Only 2km/1¼ miles south-east of Condeixa lies the extensive site of the Roman town of Conimbriga (open in summer: daily 9am–1pm and 2–8pm; in winter: Tue.–Sun. 9am–1pm and 2–6pm), founded in the 2nd c. B.C. and destroyed by the Suevi in A.D. 468. Although still being excavated, it is already clear that this settlement, to which present-day Coimbra owes its name, constitutes the largest Roman site in Portugal.

★★Conimbriga

The town was secured by a wall about 2km/1¼ miles long, and some of it, dating from the 3rd c. A.D., still remains. The many ruins of houses, baths and fountains, and their mosaics, some of which are quite well preserved, are testimony to the wealth and good taste of Conimbriga's inhabitants. The 3rd c. "House of Fountains" is especially well worth seeing. The mosaics depict hunting scenes, dolphins and Perseus with the head of Medusa.

In the Museu Monográfico adjoining the site is displayed material recovered by the excavators (mosaics, pottery, marble busts, a colossal head of Augustus, etc.).

About 15km/9 miles south-east of Condeixa, picturesquely situated on a spur of high ground, is Penela, with a massive castle (11th/12th c.).

Penela

About 15km/9 miles west of Coimbra can be found the convent church (1510) of St Mark, containing some notable 15th and 16th c. sculpture, and all that is left of the Hieronymite Convento de São Marcos which was destroyed by fire in 1860.

Convento de São Marcos

In this case it is almost better to travel than to arrive, since the journey from Coimbra towards Penacova passes through the beautiful, virtually unspoilt

★Lorvão

Conimbriga: House of Fountains

landscape of the Mondego valley, turning at Rebodosa towards Lorvão, which lies about 25km/15 miles further on. The last part of the route is through woods (good opportunities for walks) then the first buildings in this remote little place suddenly appear, together with the convent, first recorded in 878. The present buildings, originally dating from the 10th c., were remodelled at the Renaissance. Only the church and cloister can be visited since the rest of the complex is a mental health institution. The imposing church (late 16th c.) has interesting choir-stalls and 18th c. silver shrines, with elaborate intarsia decorations, containing the remains of Sancho I's daughters Sancha and Teresa (13th c.). The cloister is enclosed by an intricately wrought grille.

This trip can easily be combined with a visit to the Bucaço National Park (see entry) which lies north of Lorvão.

Lourosa

Lourosa, a little place about 75km/47 miles east of Coimbra, has a pre-Romanesque, early 10th c. church. The belfry has been relocated because it was found to be on top of a very old burial site.

Costa de Lisboa   A/B 6

Historical province: Estremadura. District: Setúbal

Location and General

The Costa de Lisboa, or "Lisbon coast", is the name given to the coast of the peninsula formed by the Serra da Arrábida and its northern outliers between the estuaries of the Tagus and the Rio Sado. Although still largely untouched by international tourism the area is very popular in summer with the people of Lisbon and is especially attractive because of its beautiful scenery and fine beaches. The southern section in particular still has appealing and relatively unspoilt places and empty beaches, although accommodation is limited.

Sights

Once a small fishing village, Costa da Caparica, 15km/9 miles south-west of Lisbon, has developed in recent years into a none too attractive resort, complete with concrete apartment blocks and fast-food outlets.

Costa da Caparica

The Convento dos Capuchos above the town was fully restored in 1960 enabling concerts to be staged in the former Capuchin convent in the summer.

The Praia do Sol, a broad beach fringed by dunes, with wooded hills lying just inland, runs south from Costa da Caparica for some 22km/14 miles. Access to the remoter beaches is by a narrow-gauge beach railway that runs as far as Fonte da Telha.

★ Praia do Sol

Cabo Espichel is the western tip of the peninsula, formed by a westerly outlier of the Serra da Arrábida. This bleak landscape affords impressive views of the coastal scenery, the cliffs falling sheer into the sea. Just north of the lighthouse warning seafarers of the dangers is the Baroque pilgrimage chapel of Nossa Senhora do Cabo, flanked by long two-storey buildings to accommodate the pilgrims.

Cabo de Espichel

The fishing town of Sesimbra (see entry) is about 13km/8 miles east of the cape, and the port of Setúbal a further 25km/16 miles east.

Sesimbra, Setúbal

A tiny fishing village, now attracting increasing numbers of foreign visitors, Portinho da Arrábida is idyllically situated in a small sandy cove below the south side of the Serra da Arrábida, which here falls steeply down to the sea. There is excellent scuba diving to be had in the many little rocky coves, such as Praia de Galápos and Praia da Figuerinha, along this section of coast.

Portinho da Arrábida

Tucked away above Portinho da Arrábida on the southern slopes of the Serra da Arrábida is the Franciscan convent, the Convento Novo da Arrábida, founded in 1542, surrounded by a wall and now in private hands.

About 500m/¼ mile west of Portinho da Arrábida in the little grotto of Lapa de Santa Margarida are early traces of man's existence (access by steps).

There are pleasant excursions into the solitude of the hills in the beautiful Serra da Arrábida, now a national park, where the luxuriant vegetation includes many rare species. These include the wild olive tree, the strawberry tree, the mastic tree, holm oak, heather, lemon trees, woodbine and myrtle.

★ Serra da Arrábida

The highest point is the Alto do Formosinho (501m/1643ft), and there are fantastic views from the N 379.1 which winds through the hills.

Tróia holiday village, its high-rise buildings making it visible from afar, is at the northern tip of the Peninsula de Tróia, a spit of land extending into the lagoon at the mouth of the Rio Sado, south-west of Setúbal (ferry and fast motor-launch services).

Tróia

About 6km/4 miles south-east are the remains of the Roman town of Cetobriga, destroyed by a tidal wave in A.D. 412 (open: Mon., Tues., Fri.–Sun. 9am–1pm and 3–6pm).

The peninsula, which boasts the longest sandy beach in Portugal (30km/19 miles), great stretches of dunes and areas of woodland but few roads, is ideal for walking.

Costa de Prata

A/B 3–6

Historical provinces: Beira Litoral and Estremadura
Districts: Aveiro, Coimbra, Leiria and Lisboa

The Costa de Prata, the "silver coast", the central stretch of the Portuguese Atlantic coast between the Cabo da Roca and the mouth of the Douro, has long been favoured for summer holidays by the people of Portugal.

Location and General

Fishing boats on the Costa da Prata

The attractive landscape is one of broad beaches, fringed by dunes or edged by cliffs, of pinewoods and olive-groves, with its working windmills adding a touch of the picturesque.

Its cold sea temperatures and bracing, if not windy, climate make the Costa de Prata less than ideal for anyone wanting a holiday spent solely on the beach.

Sights on the Costa de Prata

Azenhas do Mar

Azenhas do Mar, some 35km/22 miles north-west of Lisbon, is an idyllic village beautifully situated on a cliff-slope, making it one of the most charming resorts in the region. It attracted many artists in the early years of this century.

Ericeira

Picturesquely located above the steep and rocky coast, full of clefts and caves, Ericeira (pop. 4500), which has a long tradition as a little port and fishing village, is 50km/31 miles north-west of Lisbon. Nowadays the fishing is mostly for crayfish and its decline as a port earlier this century has meant Ericeira has come increasingly to rely on earnings from tourism generated by the nearby beaches.

Praia de Santa Cruz, Praia do Porto Novo

Around Praia de Santa Cruz and Praia do Porto Novo are extensive beaches of fine sand, bordered by rocks and green hills.

Vimeiro

About 4km/2½ miles inland is the spa of Vimeiro, with a golf-course.

Peniche, Nazaré

Further north are Peniche (see entry) and the famous seaside resort of Nazaré (see entry).

São Pedro de Muel

The pretty beach resort of São Pedro de Muel is set in pinewoods some 20km/12 miles north of Nazaré.

Aveiro (see entry) is still full of character, and Figueira da Foz (see entry) is another popular resort.

Figueira da Foz, Aveiro

A seaside resort 15km/9 miles south of Oporto, Espinho is dominated by foreign tourists, and has a broad beach of coarse sand and a fine seafront promenade. It has a wide range of recreation facilities, including an 18-hole golf-course, a landing-field for light aircraft, and a casino.

Espinho

Costa do Algarve

See Algarve

Costa do Sol   A 6

Historical province: Estremadura. District: Lisboa (Lisbon)

The Costa do Sol, the "sunshine coast", the coastal stretch west of Lisbon and known with some justification as the Portuguese Riviera, is undoubtedly one of the loveliest sections of Portugal's west coast. The attractive scenery, good beaches and pleasant climate, with correspondingly lush vegetation, mean that the towns and resorts on the Costa do Sol attract large number of visitors, especially from among the Portuguese, but this also means that at the height of the season the beaches are overcrowded and traffic on the coast road is extremely heavy.

Location and General

Sights

The route west out of Lisbon, through the suburbs of Belém, Algés and Dafundo (see Lisbon), ends after 10km/6 miles in the centre of Caxias. The

Caxias

Cabo da Roca on the Costa do Sol, Europe's most westerly point

fortress high above this little place housed political prisoners until 1974. Another fort, the Forte de São Bruno, is a youth hostel.

Oeiras

Oeiras (pop. 14,000), 4km/2½ miles west of Caxias, is a popular resort with the summer residence of the Marquês de Pombal (see Famous People), a handsome 18th c. villa set in beautiful gardens (statues, fountains and cascades). The building now belongs to the Gulbenkian Foundation (see Lisbon).

Forte São Julião da Barra

About 2km/1¼ mile beyond Oeiras, on the left of the road, is the Fort São Julião de Barra, a 17th c. fortification complete with tower and bastions.

Estoril, Cascais

The well-built dual carriageway ends just before the much expanded resorts of Estoril and Cascais (see entries).

The road out of Cascais passes the viewpoint over the Boca do Inferno (see Cascais).

In summer both sides of the road, beyond the Boca do Inferno are lined with the stalls of vendors selling goods to tourists.

Cabo Raso

Cabo Raso, with its lighthouse, is about 5km/3 miles beyond Cascais, and there is a superb view from here of the Cabo da Roca.

Praia do Guincho

Praia do Guincho is a magnificent dune-fringed beach sheltered by pine-woods, about 3km/2 miles from Cabo Raso. It gets very crowded in the high season and its general appearance is marred by a new hotel complex.

★ Cabo da Roca

About 7km/4¼ miles beyond Praia do Guincho a left-hand turn from the main road leads down a little road to Cabo da Roca, the most westerly point in Europe, rising to a height of 144m/472ft above the Atlantic (a visitor's certificate is offered).

The headland, known to the Romans as Promontorium Magnum, is a granite outlier of the Serra de Sintra (see Sintra). The view from the lighthouse is not to be missed.

Colares

Back on the main road and going north just before Colares, famous for its wine (see Sintra), there is a road off to the right to Convento dos Capuchos (see Sintra).

Costa Dourada   B 6/7

Historical province: Baixo Alentejo. Districts: Sétubal and Beja

Location and General

Portugal's "golden coast", the Costa Dourada, extends along the open Atlantic between the Ponta da Arrifana in the south of the country and the mouth of the Rio Sado. Although very scenic, with its cliffs and seemingly endless beaches, it is still virtually undeveloped in terms of tourism. This is because of its fairly raw climate and the wind blowing constantly off the sea, so that only a few sheltered coves are suitable for swimming.

Sights

Aljezur

Aljezur (pop. 4000), 30km/19 miles north of Lagos, is dominated by the ruins of a Moorish castle. Narrow side-roads run down from the little town to the beaches of Praia de Arrifana (south-west) and Praia de Monte Clérigo (north-west).

Vila Nova de Milfontes

About 50km/31 miles north of Aljezur, Vila Nova de Milfontes is a fishing village and developing seaside resort, picturesquely situated above the mouth of the Rio Mira. Its 17th c. castle was built under King João IV. South of the river there are some fine beaches. A few new pensions and holiday

Vila Nova de Milfontes

apartments have sprung up, but for ten months of the year it remains quiet and peaceful. In July and August, however, the beaches are full of mostly young Portuguese holidaymakers. In summer a shuttle ferry service operates across the river.

The little fishing port of Porto Covo, 20km/12½ miles further north, is surrounded by fine beaches but with formidable breakers. It is gradually developing into a tourist resort – a promenade has been built, together with holiday apartments and rows of houses.

Porto Covo

See entry

Sines

Costa Verde

B 3

Historical provinces: Douro Litoral and Minho
Districts: Porto (Oporto), Braga and Viana do Castelo

The Costa Verde, the "green coast" and the stretch of the northern Portuguese Atlantic coast between the mouths of the Douro and the Minho, has long been a favourite holiday area for the Portuguese, together with the adjoining Costa de Prata (see entry) to the south. Its long beaches of fine sand are fringed by dunes or sheltered by cliffs. With its relatively cold water and its frequent high winds off the sea this is not the place for simply swimming and sunbathing but it is a good base for enjoyable trips inland to such destinations as Braga, Guimarães and Peneda-Gerês National Park (see entries).

Location and General

The route north from Oporto (see entry) passes through a number of neighbouring resorts – first Vila do Conde and Póvoa de Varzim (see

Resorts

177

entries), with a good deal of industry inland, followed by the quieter Ofir and Esposende (see Barcelos) and, finally, the attractive little town of Viana do Castelo (see entry). Seemingly endless beaches then extend northwards to the Spanish frontier, and the only tourist bases in this area are the little resorts of Vila Praia de Âncora and Moledo do Minho (see Caminha).

Covilhã   C 4

Historical province: Beira Baixa. District: Castelo Branco
Altitude: 700m/2300ft. Population: 30,000

Situation and Importance

Picturesquely situated on the south-east slopes of the Serra da Estrela, the hill town of Covilhã is a popular base with the Portuguese for exploring the Serra da Estrela. The look of the town is marred somewhat by the surrounding industrial development, since Covilhã is the focus of the Portuguese textile industry, producing woollen goods under British licence for the international market.

Townscape

Covilhã presents a charming picture, with its steep and winding little streets. The town's life is focused on the flower-bedecked Praça do Município with the Câmara Municipal (town hall, and location of the tourist information centre) and, above the square, the 15th c. church of Santa Maria, its façade decorated with azulejos depicting scenes from the life of the Virgin. Also of interest are the Romanesque chapel of São Martinho and the 16th c. chapel of Santa Cruz, with pictures and woodcarvings. Within the walls that once enclosed a Franciscan convent is the Municipal Park, and there are fine views from the Monumento de Nossa Senhora da Conceição.

Nearby destinations

As already mentioned, Covilhã is a good base for drives and walks in the Serra da Estrela (see entry). To the south of the town, between the Serra da Estrela and Serra da Gardunha (see Castelo Branco), is the Cova da Beira, the wide and fertile valley of the Zêzere. The evident prosperity of this area stems from its woods, cornfields, orchards, vineyards and, above all, its wool.

Douro Valley   B–D 3

Course of the river

The Douro (Spanish Duero), known to the Romans as the Durius, one of the great waterways of the Iberian peninsula, rises on the Pico de Urbión (2252m/7389ft) in the Spanish province of Soria and flows into the Atlantic after a total course of 925km/575 miles through Spain and Portugal. In its upper reaches it traverses the plateau of Old Castile and León; it then forms the frontier between Spain and Portugal for a distance of 122km/76 miles, flowing through a gorge up to 400m/1300ft deep; and finally cuts through the Portuguese highlands between Trás-os-Montes and Beira in a wild and scenic valley, to reach the Atlantic at Oporto.

Dams

Along the stretch of the river between Spain and Portugal there is a series of impressive dams providing hydro-electric power, built under an agreement between the two countries. The Portuguese also generate hydro-electricity in the Duoro's lower reaches, with the dams beyond Pinhão turning it into a slow, broad river.

Navigation

Hitherto the extreme seasonal variations in water level (highest in autumn and spring, lowest usually in summer) have meant that the stretch around the mouth of the river, below Oporto, was the only one navigable by regular shipping. Above Oporto the only vessels were the rabelos, skiffs with a shallow draught used for shipping port (although this is now conveyed to Oporto by road tanker). However, an ambitious project has been

Valley of the Douro near Oporto

under way for some time to make this section of the river navigable as well, and since the late 1980s the last 210km/130 miles of the Douro as far as its mouth have been opened up. The "Douro Azul" company runs regular excursion trips on the Douro at weekends between March and November. For example, they offer a day trip along the stretch of the river between Oporto and Régua and back, or a half-day trip between Régua and Pinhão (departures from Ribeira Quay in Oporto; for information tel. 02/2 08 34 04, Rua de S. João 68, 4050 Porto.

The steep valley of the Douro, plus those of a few tributaries, is the world's oldest legally defined wine-producing region (see Practical Information, Wine), starting 100km/61 miles east of Oporto and covering 120km/75 miles in the direction of the Spanish frontier. Port wine may only be produced in this region, the "Pais do Vinho" – "wine country". ★★Wine
production

The steep slopes of the Douro Valley have been terraced to make vineyards as narrow as 2m/6½ft, where mechanisation is very limited indeed. Hopefully this landscape, which it has taken centuries of cultivation to create, will not be put at risk by the quest for greater agricultural efficiency.

Elvas C 6

Historical province: Alto Alentejo. District: Portalegre
Altitude: 300m/985ft. Population: 14,000

Approximately in the same latitude as Lisbon, Elvas is an old fortress town near the Spanish frontier and set amid rich fruit orchards and olive groves. To counter its Spanish opposite number, Badajoz, the town was ever more strongly fortified from the late medieval period onwards, and in the 17th and 18th c. was still further reinforced by powerful forts, which are among the best preserved and most impressive of their period in Portugal. Situation and
Importance

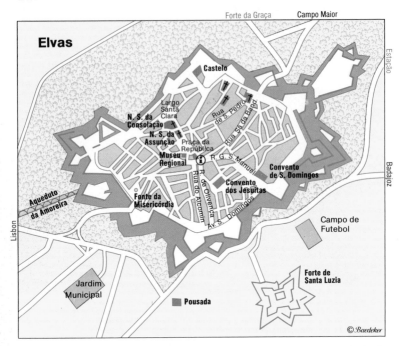

Nowadays the centre for marketing the agricultural produce of the fertile surrounding area, Elvas is also popular with tourists and has several fairly large hotels in the middle of town, set in pleasant gardens.

While in Elvas it is worth trying the local delicacy of candied plums.

★ Townscape

Within its massive walls Elvas has retained much of its original Moorish character, and in and around the alleys of the old town there are still houses with elegant iron window grilles, fine archways and many picturesque squares.

The town revolves around the Praça da República; on its south side stands the old 16th c. town hall with a small regional museum and the tourist information centre.

Sights

Igreja de Nossa Senhora da Assunção

On the north side of the Praça da República is the church of Nossa Senhora da Assunção which served as a cathedral from 1570 to 1882 when Elvas was the episcopal see.

Originally Late Gothic, the church was rebuilt in the 16th c. in Manueline style. The main façade, with its classic portico, stems from the 17th/18th c. It has a beautiful three-aisled interior with polychrome azulejo decoration.

Igreja de Nossa Senhora da Consolação

Uphill from the former cathedral is the church of Nossa Senhora da Consolação. Its unusual octagonal central building is part of a Dominican monastery founded in the mid 16th c. The church was substantially altered in the mid 17th c. The dome, borne on columns, is entirely covered with azulejos.

Elvas: Igrela de Nossa Senhora da Assunção

Adjoining the Dominican church is the picturesque Largo Santa Clara, surrounded by handsome houses with elegant iron window grilles. In the middle of the square is a fine 16th c. pelourinho (pillory column).

Largo Santa Clara

Just north-east of the Largo Santa Clara stands the castle built by the Moors in the 13th c. on the site of an earlier Roman fortress and enlarged in the 15th c., with a massive keep. There are fine views from the bastions.

Castelo

South of the Praça da Repúblic, in the former Jesuit convent, the Convento dos Jesuitas, is the town library and its museum, the Museu de António Tomás Pires, containing a collection of religious art, archaeology (Roman mosaics), coins, pictures and sculpture of the 13th–16th c. and folk art. The library's 55,000 volumes include some very rare editions (e.g. a 16th c. bible).

Convento dos Jesuitas

To the east of the Jesuit convent is the former Dominican convent (Convento de S. Domingos), founded in 1267 and frequently modified in the 15th, 16th and 17th c. The convent church, which is open to the public, has impressive stellar vaulting in the chancel.

Convento de S. Domingos

To the north of the town rises the 18th c. fort of Nossa Senhora da Graça, also known as Forte de Lippe after Count Wilhelm von Schaumburg-Lippe, who commanded the Portuguese army in 1762–64.

Forte de Nossa Senhora da Graça

To the south of the town is the Santa Luzia fort, an excellent and well-preserved example of 17th c. Portuguese military engineering.

Forte de S. Luzia

The road into Elvas from Estremoz or Lisbon enters the town alongside the Aqueduto da Amoreira, an aqueduct more than 7km/4½ miles long, built between 1498 and 1622 on the foundations of a Roman aqueduct, which still supplies water to the 17th c. Misericórdia fountain on the western edge

★Aqueduto da Amoreira

A place full of atmosphere – Largo Santa Clara in Elvas

of the town centre. The aqueduct's 843 arches – about half of them still from the original construction – are in up to four tiers, reaching a maximum height of 31m/100ft.

Surroundings of Elvas

Campo Maior

About 20km/12½ miles north-east of Elvas is the picturesque little town of Campo Maior (alt. 277m/909ft, pop. 9000), still enclosed within a complete circuit of walls (17th/18th c.), with a 14th c. castle built by King Dinis and a Gothic parish church (charnel-house).

Estoril	A 6

Historical province: Estremadura. District: Lisboa
Altitude: sea level. Population: 25,000

Situation and Importance

Once a modest fishing village on the Costa do Sol, Estoril (pronounced shturíu) has expanded to merge with nearby Cascais (see entry). Thanks to its equable climate and beautiful subtropical gardens, it had by the end of the 19th c. become an elegant resort and winter spa, frequented by the rich and famous of the international set, and in fact its residents still include some illustrious figures. In the peak holiday season its exclusivity is very much a thing of the past, as it is swamped by day-trippers from nearby Lisbon. Its radioactive hot springs (33°C/91°F), containing carbonic acid, are recommended for the treatment of rheumatism and diseases of the joints.

Each summer the Portuguese Formula 1 Grand Prix motor race is held on the race track north of Estoril (on the road to Sintra). The race is over 61 laps of the 4.35km/2¾ mile course.

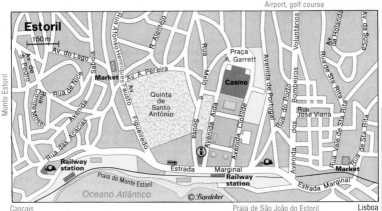

Estoril itself has no particularly outstanding features of interest; it is visited primarily for its atmosphere of international elegance, its fine villas, its palm-lined promenades and the magnificent park, full of tropical and exotic plants, around the spa and the casino.

    About 1.5km/1 mile west of the park is Monte Estoril (109m/358ft) which has become the new smart residential district. There are fine beaches nearby, but these are usually crowded.
Townscape

There are plenty of trips that can be made from Estoril (e.g. to Lisbon, Sintra, or along the Costa do Sol – see entries).
Surroundings

Estremadura   A/B 5/6

Historical province: Estremadura. Districts: Leiria, Lisboa and Setúbal
Area: 11,430sq.km/4413sq. miles
Population: 3,000,000. Chief town: Lisbon (Lisboa)

The historical Portuguese province and region of Estremadura (from the Latin "extrema durii" – "farthest land on the Douro"), consists of the districts of Lisboa (Lisbon), Leiria and Setúbal, together with the national capital Lisbon, comprising in its centre the estuary area of the Tagus as far as the basin of the Ribatejo. It extends to the north by way of the Serra de Sintra and the south-western outliers of the Serra da Estrela, dropping steeply to the sea just south of Coimbra. To the south it includes the Setúbal peninsula (Serra da Arrábida) as far as the mouth of the Rio Sado.
General

    Because of its fertility and diversity of landscape within a relatively small area, Estremadura, together with Ribatejo (see entry) adjoining it on the east has since Roman times been central to the development of Lusitanian and later Portuguese culture. This area contains Lisbon, the intellectual focal point, as well as the religious centres of Alcobaça and Batalha, and the former royal seats of Queluz, Mafra and Sintra (see entries).

    Another thing that Estremadura has in common with Ribatejo is the fact that between them they contain the largest single wine-producing area in Portugal.

The intricate geological and landscape makeup of this region, affected in many places by tectonic action, is reflected in a degree of economic and cultural diversity scarcely to be found in any other province of Portugal.
Landscapes

183

The northern uplands, part of a massif of Mesozoic limestones, show typical karst landscape features, with poljes and swallowholes, sparse undergrowth in the depressions and mainly the herding of sheep and goats.

To the west of this area is a chain of hills of fertile clay and sandstone, the agricultural heartland of the province where, around Alcobaça, there is mostly mixed Mediterranean-type farming (wheat, maize, citrus fruits, vegetables, olives, wine).

To the south of this rises the Serra de Sintra, a range of volcanic hills where the fertile soils and mild, damp maritime climate have resulted in a beautiful park-type landscape which, with the many thermal springs (Caldas da Rainha, Estoril, etc.; see entries), has helped this to become one of Portugal's leading holiday regions.

The narrow coastal strip in the north and the areas around the mouths of the Tagus, the Sado, the Mondego and the Vouga, with areas of marshland, lagoons and long sandspits, are chiefly orientated towards the sea. Here are the old-established fishing ports which are used by the deep-sea fishermen sailing to distant waters, especially Newfoundland, with their fish-canning and drying establishments and their extensive saltpans. The marshy land in the river basins is also good for rice-growing.

Estremoz   C6

Historical province: Alto Alentejo. District: Évora
Altitude: 430m/1410ft. Population: 8000

Situation and Importance

The little old-world town of Estremoz lies 50km/31 miles north-east of Évora, in the undulating landscape of the Alto Alentejo, and is particularly notable for the number of buildings made from the locally quarried white marble, which was already widely renowned in the Middle Ages.

Estremoz is also important as a centre for pottery, wood-carving and leatherwork, although agriculture continues to be the main occupation.

Townscape

The older part of Estremoz is the upper town, with its picturesque narrow lanes clustered on the hill around the castle. The lower town, which goes back to the 16th c., is centred on the "Rossio", the Praça do Marquês de Pombal, the enormous square where the principal weekly market is held on Saturdays, although there are usually a few stalls here throughout the week, selling the characteristic red Estremoz pottery.

Sights

Lower town

At the southern end of the Rossio is the town hall, the Câmara Municipal, originally built (1698) as a convent, and containing fine azulejo depictions of scenes from the life of St Philippus. The folk-art museum on the east side of the Rossio is worth a visit.

Adjoining the Rossio on the north is the Largo do General Graça with the 17th c. Tocha Palace (azulejo pictures) and the former Franciscan convent, originally 13th c., in which King Pedro I died in 1367. Although this is now used as a barracks the Gothic convent church can be visited.

★Upper town

The upper town, enclosed within 17th c. Vauban-style fortifications with several massive towers, still has a rather Moorish aspect, and its white-washed houses, with their small window-openings, are designed to afford protection against the fierce heat of the summer.

Castelo

The highest point of the town is the castle, the Castelo, built in the first half of the 13th c. All that remains of the original building is the massive keep, 27m/89ft high, and topped by splendid battlements. The royal palace was built onto this keep in the early 14th c. and, with the castle, served as the

Estremoz: the castle keep . . .   *. . . and a pousada in the Upper Town*

residence of King Dinis I and his wife, St Isabel, who died here in 1336 and is commemorated by a monument in the castle square. The palace was restored in the 18th c. and is now a luxurious pousada.

Opposite the palace is the three-aisled church of Santa Maria do Castelo which was built on the site of a Gothic predecessor in 1559 and contains two paintings of the Virgin by El Greco. Adjoining the church is the Manueline, but originally Gothic, royal audience chamber.

Igreja de Santa Maria do Castelo

The castle square is also bordered to the south by the municipal museum (furniture, pottery, etc.; open: Tues.–Sun. 9–11.45am and 2–5.45pm).

Museo Municipal

Surroundings of Estremoz

25km/16 miles south of Estremoz on a road which runs through the Serra de Ossa (653m/2142ft), passing the Convento da Berra, lies Redondo (alt. 305m/1000ft; pop. 7000), a pleasant little town with the ruins of a 14th c. castle built in the reign of King Dinis I and, higher up, the church of the Misericórdia, which has a Manueline choir.

Redondo

Sousel (pop. 2000), 18km/11 miles north-west of Estremoz, founded by Nuno Álvares Pereira (see Batalha) in 1387, has a 16th c. parish church and another 16th c. church, the Misericórdia, with 18th c. azulejo decoration. The pousada in Sousel can be recommended for those seeking peace and quiet. It lies completely alone, surrounded by olive-groves.

Sousel

13km/8 miles north of Sousel lies Fronteira (pop. 2500), with several fine 17th/18th c. residences and a late 16th c. parish church. In the main square stands a 17th c. marble pillory. A fine view of the town can be obtained from the tower of the Town Hall.
    Above the town stands the church of Nossa Senhora da Vila Velha, which is completely clad with 17th c. azulejos.

Fronteira

Avis

Avis, 24km/15 miles west of Fronteira, is now an unprepossessing little country town, but it has a famous history. It first became important in 1211, when Afonso II moved here the military order known as the "Freires de Évora" (also the first order of knights in Europe) which had been formed by Afonso Henriques in 1147 as a defence against the Moors. The splendour and influence of the order of "São Bento de Aviz" lasted until the late 18th c. As a result of the crowning of the Grand Master of Avis as King Jão I of Portugal in 1385 Avis became the cradle of a royal dynasty which controlled the country's fortunes until 1580 and under its victorious rule, especially during the reigns of João II and Manuel I, brought Portugal to its peak and made it the world's major sea-faring nation. Of the simple wall built in 1214 around the knights' castle only one gateway, the keep (restored in the 15th c.) and two further towers now remain. In the church of the order (restored in the 17th c.) there are several 15th c. tombs as well as a valuable gilded reliquary.

Barragem de Montargil

By the Barragem de Montargil, a 20km/12½ miles long artificial lake about 40km/25 miles west of Avis, there is a holiday centre built with the aid of German capital which offers extensive sporting facilities.

Veiros

The village of Veiros, 15km/9¼ miles north-east of Estremoz, prides itself on having produced the Bragança line since it is the birthplace of Afonso, illegitimate son of King João I and later Duke of Bragança. Very little remains of the old castle.

Other destinations

Other places worth visiting from Estremoz include Evoramonte (see Évora), Borba and Vila Viçosa (see entries).

Évora   C6

Historical province: Alto Alentejo. District: Évora
Altitude: 300m/985ft. Population: 38,000

Situation and Importance

Évora, built on a low hill surrounded by rolling plains, was the old capital of the upland region of Alentejo and is now the chief town of its own district, the see of an archbishop and, since 1979, a University once more. In economic terms, it is the trading centre for the agricultural produce of Alentejo (wool, cloth, cork) and has its own important electrical goods industry.

In 1986 UNESCO declared Évora a world cultural inheritance site – there is no question that the chief town of the Alentejo, with its many important buildings in the old town centre, is well worth a visit. To see it properly will take at least two days or more to include the places of interest in the countryside around. In the last few years some sizeable modern hotels have sprung up around the old town; the pousada in the town centre is particularly stylish.

History

Évora is one of the oldest trading posts on the Iberian peninsula. In Roman times it was a very important town, first called Ebora, under the praetorship of Sertorius, then renamed Liberalitas Iulia under Julius Caesar.

In 715 the town fell into the hands of the Moors and became known as Yebora. It was reconquered by Giraldo Sempavor (Gerald the Fearless) in 1165 and reunited with the kingdom of Afonso Henriques. From the 14th to the 16th c. it was intermittently the residence of the Portuguese kings and hence the focus of political and cultural life; however, with the permanent transfer of the seat of government to Lisbon and the eventual closing of its university, Évora's splendour and influence declined. and it is only in recent decades that this has partially been recovered, owing to some extent to its importance as a tourist centre.

Ermida de São Bras, Railway station

With its walls of the Roman, Moorish and later periods, still largely pre-served, and its narrow lanes, sometimes lined with arcades, Évora's town-scape still has a Moorish and medieval appearance, hence its entitlement to the term "cidade museu" – museum city.

★★ Townscape

A good starting point for a tour of the town is the square by the cathedral. In the central area of the town there is only short-term parking available for non-residents. The best thing is to leave the car on one of the large car parks on the ring road which runs along the town wall. From there it is only a few minutes' walk to the centre.

Sights

The Cathedral – Catedral or Sé – is a severe and fortress-like structure in Early Gothic style which was begun in 1186 and completed in the 13th and 14th c. The façade is dominated by the two asymmetrical towers flanking the massive doorway. Above the crossing is an octagonal belfry with a helm roof of scale-like tiles. The twelve figures of apostles on the doorway are masterpieces of Portuguese Gothic sculpture.

★★ Catedral

The interior, notable for its regular masonry with white mortar joints, is of impressive simplicity and harmony. The gently sweeping lines of Baroque are only apparent in the raised Choir, entered by a flight of steps in the south aisle. This was remodelled in the 18th c. by Johann Friedrich

Évora: view from the Roman temple over the Cathedral

Ludwig, architect of the convent of Mafra (see entry), and lavishly decorated with marble. The fine carved choir-stalls date from 1562.

Also in the south aisle is the entrance to the Gothic cloister, with statues of the evangelists. Several dark narrow corridors lead from the cloister up to the roof terrace (intermittent access), affording a close look at the tower helm roof, as well as fine views over the town and surrounding countryside.

The Cathedral Treasury, which used to be kept in the Sacristy, is now housed in the Museu de Arte Sacra in the cathedral's south tower. Its precious items include a 13th c. ivory triptych of the Virgin and Child, as well as many outstanding examples of 16th and 17th c. gold and silver and enamel work (open: Tues.–Sun. 9am–noon and 2–5pm).

Museu de Évora

The former Archbishop's Palace (open: Tues.–Sun. 10am–12.30pm and 2–5pm), on the north side of the Cathedral, now houses the well-stocked Museu de Évora, the regional museum, displaying Roman archaeological finds, Romanesque and Gothic architectural fragments, Portuguese and Flemish pictures of the 16th–18th c., applied and decorative art, and two cenotaphs by Nicolas Chanterène for Dom Álvares de Costa (1535) and Dom Afonso de Portugal (1537).

★Templo Romano

Opposite the museum entrance is what has become the symbol of Évora, its Roman temple (Templo Romano). Dating from the 2nd or 3rd century A.D., it is one of the best preserved Roman structures in Portugal and is popularly known as the Temple of Diana, although it is not clear to which deity it was actually dedicated. On the 3m/10ft high base, which is almost completely preserved, there still stand 14 of the original 18 Corinthian columns, with part of the architrave. During the Middle Ages the temple was converted into a fortress, and later served for many years as a slaughterhouse, a use which ultimately saved it from demolition.

Since 1986 fresh archaeological digs and investigations have been undertaken, and these have concentrated mainly on the position of the temple inside the Roman town centre. It was discovered that the open square in front of the temple was covered with large slabs of marble (they lie about one metre below the present ground level) and in 1992 the south border and the west entrance gate of what is presumed to have been the forum came to light.

The gardens behind the temple overlook a terrace with good views over the northern part of Évora.

Opposite the temple, to the east, is the church of the Convent dos Lóios, which was built between 1485 and 1491 and much altered in the following centuries. The Manueline porch was part of the original building, and bears the arms of the de Melos who founded the church and chose to be buried there.

Convento dos Lóios

Parts of the former convent have been converted into a pousada, and the beautiful cloister now serves as a charming garden for its guests, with the restaurant located in the galleries. The former chapterhouse, through the cloister, has Manueline stellar vaulting.

The Biblioteca Pública, the public library, is in another part of the building and contains about 2000 incunabula and manuscripts.

There used to be direct access from the north front of the convent church to the Paço dos Duques de Cadaval, the palace that King João I presented to the de Melos, ancestors of the Cadavals, at the end of the 14th c. Because of its pentagonal north tower – originally part of the medieval town fortifications – it is also known as the pentagonal palace, the "Palácio das Cinco Quinas". The interior houses the Museu da Casa dos Duques de Cadaval. Exhibits include 15th c. sculpture, paintings and manuscripts, together with items from the Cadavals.

Paço dos Duques de Cadaval

The Paço dos Condes de Basto is several hundred yards to the right beyond the Paço dos Duques de Cadaval. This Gothic-Manueline palace of the Counts of Basto which was intermittently the residence of various kings contains part of the Romanesque cum Visigothic town walls.

Paço dos Condes de Basto

On the other side of the street is the extensive University complex. The Universidade, in Italian Renaissance style, was founded in 1551 as a Jesuit college, raised to the status of a university in 1558 and closed in 1759, after the dissolution of the Jesuit order in Portugal. After Évora acquired its university status again in 1979 lecture rooms were reinstated around the cloister, many of them embellished with azulejos and marble.

Universidade

The university church (Nossa Senhora da Conceição) was consecrated in 1574, and also boasts marble and talha in its single-nave interior.

A route down the alleys leading southward from the university then westward along the Rua de Machede brings the visitor to the Largo das Portas de Moura, which owes much of its picturesque, quaint character to the Renaissance fountain (1556) in its centre, with a globe looming over its marble basin as the symbol of the dawn of a new age.

★Largo das Portas de Moura

On the south side of the square stands the Casa Cordovil, an elegant 16th c. palace in Moorish and Manueline style, catching the eye with its loggia and four graceful pillars.

Opposite the Casa Cordovil a double flight of steps leads down into the forecourt of the early 17th c. church of the former Carmo convent and bearing over its portal the bold motto of the Dukes of Bragança "depois de vós – nós", after You (i.e. the King), us!

The Igreja da Graça, west of the Largo das Portas de Moura, was founded by João I in the 16th c, and its façade is reminiscent of the Italian Renaissance. The interior is extemely plain and likewise in Renaissance style.

Igreja da Graça

Quite close by stands the church of São Francisco, a former convent church dating from the second half of the 15th c. and perhaps the finest example of Manueline architecture in southern Portugal. The severe

Igreja Real de São Francisco

Largo das Portas de Moura with Renaissance fountain

white interior, with the same white mortar joints as in the Cathedral, creates an effect of greater spaciousness than the latter.

★Casa dos Ossos

Adjoining the south aisle is the Casa dos Ossos, a 17th c. charnel-house (open: Mon.–Fri. 8.30am–1pm and 2.30–6pm). Those of a more sensitive disposition should think twice before venturing inside, since the walls are formed by carefully arranged layers of human bones. The macabre effect is heightened by the skeletons of a man and a child hanging from this gruesome wall, and to top it all the motto over the door reads "our bones that lie within are waiting for yours to join them".

Museu de Artesanato Regional

Opposite the side of the Igreja Real de São Francisco is what purports to be a regional handicrafts museum, the Museu de Artesanato Regional, but is in fact more of a sales outlet.

Jardim Público

Farther south lies the town park, the Jardim Público, with its inviting shady walks and lovely flowers. The Galeria das Damas inside the park was part of the 15th/16th c. royal palace and its Moorish arcades today serve as exhibition areas. Together with the rest of the now demolished palace buildings it once enjoyed the glittering life of Manuel I's court, and was where the King received Vasco da Gama.

Ermida de São Brás

Further south along the Rua da República there is a monument, topped by an angel, commemorating the soldiers of Évora who fell in the First World War. This is within sight of the Ermida de São Bras, the hermitage of St Blaise, a fortress-like building in a Late Gothic style showing Moorish influence which was erected in 1485 in thanksgiving for survival from the plague. The flat roof is crenellated and flanked by six conical pinnacles along each side, and the interior is unusually plain.

Igreja das Mercês

The tour of the town continues by returning to the walls around the Jardim Público, built in the 17th c. according to the Vauban system, then turning west along the fortifications as far as the Rua do Raimundo, and the Igreja das Mercês, the church of the Mercês, built 1669.

A couple of hundred yards to the north-east, in the centre of the town, is the elongated Praça do Giraldo, the picturesque square that was once a place of execution where many victims of the Inquisition went to the stake. Its street cafés provide a good opportunity to appreciate the scenic effect of the beautiful houses and arcades surrounding the square. The Renaissance fountain in Estremoz marble (by Afonso Avares, 1581) stands on the site of a Roman triumphal arch demolished in 1570. On the north side of the square is the collegiate church of Santo Antão, built in 1557 by the archbishop who later became King Henrique II; it has a clearly defined Renaissance façade.

★Praça do Giraldo

The Rua 5 de Outubro, full of souvenir shops and the favourite precinct for promenading, soon brings the walk round the city back to its starting point.

The other sights worth visiting, if staying longer in Évora, include the former convent of Santa Clara, west of the Praça do Giraldo. Founded in 1452, it was substantially altered in the 16th c. and its church, with its elegant belfry, is worth seeing. Another interesting convent, further north, is the Convento do Calvário, its church and 16th c. cloister open to the public. North-east, nearby, are the remains of an aqueduct, built in the 16th c. probably to replace a Roman equivalent.

Other sights

Surroundings of Évora

The countryside around Évora is rich in examples of megalithic culture. Particularly impressive is the stone circle of Almendres (Cromeleque dos Almendres), on the N 114 from Évora. In the town of São Matias (about 8km/5 miles west of Évora) turn off towards Guadalupe. The Cromeleque dos Almendres consists of 92 upright stones forming an oval 60m/200ft long and 30m/100ft across. The stones are coloured red and are marked with symbolic signs. Assumed to have been used for cult purposes, the site is dated somewhere between 4000 and 2000 B.C.

★Cromeleque do Almendres

A few miles south of the Cromeleque dos Almendres, near the town of Valverde, can be found the "Anta do Zambujeiro", a setting of stones with dolmens over 6m/20ft high. A stone covered each dolmen, and over this earth was originally heaped. Most of the grave-goods found in these tombs are now on display in the Évora Museum.

Anta do Zambujeiro

The Convento d'Espinheiro, 3km/2 miles north-west of Évora, has a beautiful cloister dating from the 15th/16th c.

Convento d'Espinheiro

The Convento de São Bento de Castris, 4km/2½ miles north-west of Évora on the N114-4 to Arraiolos, stands at the foot of Mt São Bento (367m/1203ft, fine views). The convent was founded in 1274 and has a 14th/15th c. church containing 18th c. azulejo decoration; there is also a fine 16th c. cloister.

Convento de São Bento de Castris

Évoramonte, about 35km/22 miles north-east of Évora, is worth a visit. Prominently situated above the newer town on a hill (474m/1555ft), the old town centre, with its winding alleys and little white houses, is still surrounded by its walls. At its highest point stands Évoramonte Castle, built in the 14th c. on the ruins of a Moorish predecessor and rebuilt after an earthquake in 1531. The recently restored, yellow-painted fort can be visited. A plaque on the wall of a house on the left side of the main street, past the walls, commemorates the fact that the Treaty of Évoramonte concluding the "Miguelist" wars (see History) was signed here on May 26th 1834.

Évoramonte

Monsaraz

★ Monsaraz

Monsaraz, 50km/31 miles east of Évora, near the Spanish border, still has a very medieval look, and is worth a visit. Its fortifying walls date from the 16th c., and a walk round the sleepy little town should take in the Gothic parish church, the 17th c. pelourinho, the Gothic palace of justice and, above all, the castle, built in the early 14th c. during the reign of King Dinis.

Cromeleque do Xerez

The narrow road leading south from Monsaraz to Mourão soon passes the Cromeleque do Xerez (signposted). The collection of menhirs here is, however, not quite as impressive as that at Almendres (see above).

Mourão

A short way past this latter circle of stones the road meets the N 256; 5km/ 3 miles further on in a southerly direction lies the town of Mourão, protected by a medieval castle. Characteristic of the town are the cylindrical chimneys with hemispherical cowls.

Portel

About 40km/24 miles south-east of Évora lies the small country town of Portel. Its 13th c. Bragança castle was largely rebuilt under Manuel I (fine view). The little chapel of Santo António is lavishly decorated with polychrome azulejos.

Viana de Alentejo

Viana de Alentejo, 30km/19 miles south of Évora, has a 15th c. castle and a 16th c. parish church with a magnificent Manueline doorway and azulejo decoration inside.

Alvito

The little country town of Alvito, 10km/6 miles south of Viana de Alentejo, boasts a parish church with magnificent 17th c. azulejo decoration and a fine fortified castle (15th c.) built by the Marquês de Alvito. The castle has recently been converted into a pousada.

Agua de Peixes

A little road north-east out of Alvito leads to Agua de Peixes, where the Dukes of Cadaval, who also owned a magnificent urban palace in Évora, sited their fine 16th c. Hispano-Mauresque country mansion.

18km/11 miles north-west of Viana do Alentejo, at the foot of the Serra de São João, lies Alcáçovas, with a handsome 15th c. palace of the Counts of Alcáçovas and a notable 16th c. parish church.

Some 3km/2 miles west above the town lies the chapel of Nossa Senhora da Esperança (16th c.), the remains of a Dominican monastery; from here there are fine views.

Other places to visit include Arraiolos (see entry), north of Évora, famous for its townscape and its rugs, and Montemore-o-Novo (see Arraiolos), 25km/15½ miles to the west. Estremoz (see entry), about 45km/28 miles north-east of Évora, is definitely worth a visit, while Redondo (see Estremoz) offers yet another castle.

Alcáçovas

Other destinations around Évora

Faro   C7

Historical province: Algarve. District: Faro
Altitude: sea level. Population: 30,000

The busy industrial town and port of Faro, chief town of its district in the south of Portugal, lies at the north end of a lagoon dotted with saltpans and

Situation and Importance

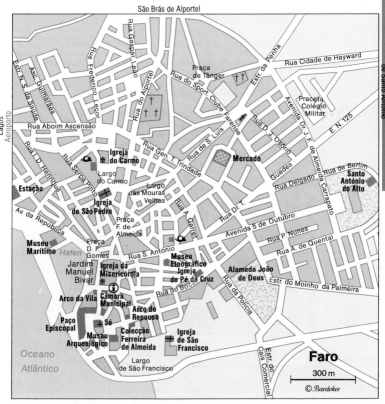

islands. Wine, fruit, cork and fish are shipped out through its small, sheltered harbour. Its airport (7km/4½ miles south-west) has made it the focal point of the whole of the Algarve's tourist trade, especially since a new, three million passenger capacity terminal was opened. Despite the nearby beaches Faro is no holiday resort as such, and its immediate vicinity is lacking in comfortable hotels with adequate grounds. A devastating earthquake in 1755 robbed this originally Moorish city of many of its major buildings but the centre is quite inviting, with many 18th and 19th c. houses.

The main attraction of any stay in Faro is its good shopping. Some of the smaller streets in the centre around the Rua de Santo António, east of the Praça de Dom Francisco Gomes, have been made pedestrian precincts and offer plenty of restaurants and cafés to relax in.

Sights

Praça de Dom Francisco Gomes

The Praça de Dom Francisco Gomes to the north-east of the harbour is a good starting point for a tour of Faro. The obelisk erected in 1910 commemorates the diplomat Ferreira d'Almeida, who was born in Faro and who, during his period of office as minister of naval affairs, founded a naval college and promoted the fishing industry.

Jardim Manuel Bivar

Peace and quiet can be enjoyed in the Jardim Manuel Bivar, to the south of the square. This garden with its attractive flower-beds, tall palms and jacaranda trees is a favourite haunt of the elder citizens of Faro who sit here and watch the world go by.

On the east side of the park stands the Igreja da Misericórdia, a 14th c. church that was restored after the 1755 earthquake.

One can reach the historic centre through the Arco da Vila – a symbol of Faro

At the south end of the park stands the Arco da Vila, an arched gateway built by the architect Francisco Xavier Fabri, surmounted by a bell-tower and a statue of Faro's patron saint, St Thomas Aquinus. Through the gateway lies the very attractive historical centre of Faro, part of which is still surrounded by a 13th c. wall.

Arco da Vila

The centre of the Old Town is dominated by the Cathedral. Large parts of the originally Gothic church were destroyed in the 1755 earthquake and rebuilt later; of the original building only the tower and a south window remain. Overall, the cathedral presents elements of Gothic, Renaissance and Baroque. The pleasing interior is light and almost basilica-like. The nave has three aisles separated almost imperceptibly from one another by three slender pillars. Above the choir is a coffered barrel-vaulted ceiling. The Capela de Santo Lenho to the right of the chancel contains the tomb of António Pereira da Silva, Bishop of the Algarve from 1704 to 1715.

Sé

In the square in front of the cathedral, the Largo Sé, stand the town hall (Câmara Municipal) and the Bishop's Palace (Paço Episcopal). The long west wing was added to the original building in the 18th c.

A few hundred metres south of the Cathedral, on the Praça Afonso III, stands the Archaeological Museum (open: Mon.–Fri. 9am-noon and 2–5pm), housed in the former convent of Nossa Senhora da Assunção, a house of St Clare founded in 1518. In addition to the exhibits (especially finds from Milreu, see Surroundings), the two-storey cloister is particularly worthy of attention.

Museu Arqueológico

Other rooms grouped around the cloister house the private collection of the diplomat and art-lover Ferreira d'Almeida, including mainly 19th c. paintings but also portraits, silver and glass.

The church of St Francis, on the spacious Largo de São Francisco, is reached through the Arco de Repouso. The 17th c. church once formed part of a Franciscan convent, now occupied by the military.

Igreja de São Francisco

The Museum of Regional Ethnography (open: Mon.–Fri. 9.30am–12.30pm, and 2–5.30pm), just north of the Franciscan church, affords an insight into the way of life and folk art of the local people.

Museu Etnográfico

The harbour commander's office in the north of the harbour houses a Maritime Museum (open: Mon.-Fri. 2–5pm). The exhibits provide a background to seafaring and fishing in the Algarve.

Museu Maritimo

To the north-east of the museum the church of St Peter stands on the São Pedro (St Peter's) Square. It dated originally from the 16th c.

Igreja da São Pedro

To the north St Peter's Square lies the wide Largo do Carmo, dominated by the twin-towered Baroque church. Through the sacristy is a cemetery and the Capela dos Ossos (Chapel of Bones), which was dedicated in 1816 (open: Mon.–Fri. 10am–1pm and 3–5pm, Sat. 10am–1pm). The vaulted ceiling and the walls are made of human skeletons.

Igreja do Carmo Capela dos Ossos

There are plenty of cafés and restaurants in the centre of Faro where visitors can refresh themselves after a tour of the town. The most traditional of these is the Café Aliança on the Praça Francisco Gomes (corner of Rua 1° de Maio), which opened in 1908.

Café Aliança

Surroundings of Faro

North-west of the town, beyond the airport, on an offshore island connected to the mainland by a bridge, stretches the extensive sandy beach of Praia de Faro.

Praia de Faro

Estói, a town typical of the Algarve hinterland, lies 12km/7½ miles north of Faro. It is known mainly for the Palácio de Estói, a palace built in the late 18th c.

★Estói

Visitors are not allowed inside. It is surrounded by an attractive small park (open: Mon.–Sat. 9am-noon and 2–5pm). The gardens, which were laid out in the 18th and 19th c., are on several levels and lavishly decorated with azulejos and busts. Tiled steps lead down to the lower part of the gardens, with a grotto which is completely covered in mosaics from nearby Milreu.

Milreu

At the western end of Estói, by the road leading to Santa Bárbara de Nexe, near the village of Milreu, lie the remains of a Roman town (open: Tues.–Sun. 9.30am–12.30pm and 2–5pm). Archaeological digs were undertaken here as early as 1877. In Roman times Milreu was a "summer residence" for well-to-do families from Faro, then known as Ossonoba (Milreu is also sometimes called by this name). The remains of a Roman villa and thermal baths decorated with mosaics have been unearthed; they probably date from the first century A.D. The walls of an early Christian church are relatively well preserved.

Olhão

See entry

Algarve

Other places worth seeing around Faro can be found under the entry for the Algarve.

Fátima   B 5

Historical province: Ribatejo. District: Santarém
Altitude: 800m/2625ft. Population: 7300

Situation and Importance

Fátima, internationally famous as a place of pilgrimage, is in central Portugal a good 20km/12 miles south-east of Leiria and on what was once the barren plateau of Cova da Iria. Every year it attracts thousands of believers from far and wide to beseech forgiveness for their sins or pray for a cure. Fátima also figures in every organised excursion or coach tour of this part of Portugal. On the eve of the chief annual pilgrimages (May 13th and October 13th) there are large torch-light processions.

"Miracle of Fátima"

On May 13th 1917, and again on the 13th of each subsequent month until October in that year, the "Virgin of the Rosary" is said to have appeared to the three peasant children, Lúcia de Jesús and Francisco and Jacinta Marto. At first sceptical about these visions, on the last appearance, October 13th 1917, the Church saw over 70,000 people making the pilgrimage to Fátima where they are supposed to have witnessed not only the appearance of the Virgin but also an amazing natural phenomenon – in pouring rain the sun suddenly began to revolve on its axis and throw out multicoloured rays of light. There were also a number of miraculous cures in the days that followed. The Church authorities investigated the incidents for several years before finally giving the Fátima cult of the Madonna the official seal of approval in 1930.

Speculation continues to this day about the three "revelations" that the children – who were seven, nine and ten at the time – said had been vouchsafed them by the Virgin on July 13th 1917. The first two are public knowledge, the first being a description of "Hell", and the second prophesying a speedy end to the First World War, but also foretelling a dreadful war if the world did not cease offending God.

The third prophesy was confided in writing to the Vatican in 1941 by Lúcia, who had entered a convent in 1928, but she also stipulated it should not be made public before 1960 and to date no Pope has unveiled the secret.

Miniature Railway

A miniature railway runs through Fátima; information about the pilgrimage town is given in five languages.

Sights

Esplanade

The esplanade that serves as the rallying point for the kneeling pilgrims is of huge proportions (150,000 sq.m/37 acres). It is dominated by the

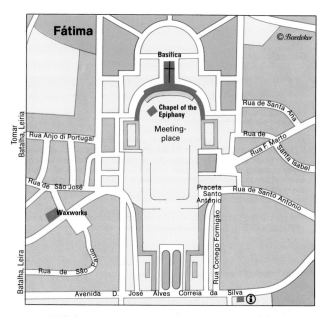

Fátima

© Baedeker

Basilica

Chapel of the Epiphany

Meeting-place

Rua de Santa Ana

Rua de

Rua F. Marto

Santa Isabel

Tomar Batalha, Leiria

Rua Anjo di Portugal

Rua de São José

Praceta Santo António

Rua de Santo António

Waxworks

Rua Conego Formigão

Batalha, Leira

Rua de São

Avenida D. José Álves Correia da Silva ℹ️

Neo-Baroque Basilica, with its 65m/215ft high central tower. Building was begun on May 13th 1928 and it is flanked by colonnades linking it with the extensive conventual and hospital buildings. Inside the Basilica are the tombs of Francisco and Jacinta Marto, who died in 1919 and 1920 respectively. The place where the Virgin Mary is supposed to have appeared to the children in the branches of an oak in 1917 is marked by the little chapel of the apparitions, the Capela das Aparições, in front of the Cathedral. The first chapel built here in 1918 was later destroyed by an explosion.

West of the esplanade is a wax museum, the Museu de Cera de Fátima, opened in 1984 and depicting the miraculous events at Fátima in a series of 29 scenes.

Wax museum

A short distance east of the esplanade stands the Museum of Sacred Art and Ethnology. It tells the story of the Redemption by means of pictures, crucifixes, cribs and other exhibits. The ethnological department concerns itself with those cultures which influenced the Gospels.

Museu de Arte Sacra e Etnologia

Surroundings of Fátima

About 10km/6 miles north-east of Fátima, on an isolated hill rising out of the valley, is the little medieval walled town of Ourém, a huddle of narrow lanes and picturesque nooks and corners in the shadow of the 15th c. castle of the Margraves of Ourém.

Ourém

In the crypt of the collegiate church, originally Gothic but rebuilt in the 18th c., is the magnificent tomb of Dom Afonso de Ourém, a descendant of João I, who rebuilt and enlarged the original Moorish castle. Ourém also has a beautiful Gothic fountain and a pelourinho, both of the 15th c.

Many of the inhabitants of Ourém have moved to Vila Nova de Ourém, 2km/1¼ miles to the east.

See entry

Alcobaça

Batalha	See entry
Leiria	See entry
Tomar	See entry

Figueira da Foz   B 4

Historical province: Beira Litoral. District: Coimbra
Altitude: sea level. Population: 26,000

Situation and Importance

At the mouth of the Mondego, the regularly laid out little port town of Figueira da Foz, the "fig-tree on the estuary", is one of the principal bases of the cod fisheries off the Portuguese Atlantic coast – the fish market is held every morning on the south bank of the Mondego. Because of its broad beach of fine sand, stretching for 3km/2 miles, Figueira da Foz is also one of the most popular resorts on Portugal's west coast, with a range of sport and leisure facilities to match, including a marina and casino.

Townscape

The park on the coast road divides the new hotel district from the old town of Figueira da Foz, near the harbour and mostly 19th c.

Sights

Forte Santa Catarina

At the mouth of the river stands the old Santa Catarina fort, dating from the 17th c.

Casa do Paço

Another 17th c. building is the Casa do Paço in the old town, near the main post office, much of it decorated with Delft tiles showing biblical themes, landscapes and riding scenes.

Museu Municipal do Dr Santos Rocha

The municipal museum, together with its library, is housed in a building surrounded by a park, and has displays of prehistoric finds as well as Roman exhibits, applied and decorative art, pottery, furniture, religious art, ethnography of the Portuguese overseas territories, etc.

Santo António

Just east of the museum is the Franciscan convent of Santo António, founded in 1527 and much altered in the 18th c., its walls decorated with scenes from the life of St Antony.

Figuaira da Foz: the beach, shared by fishermen and visitors

Surroundings of Figueira da Foz

The fishing village of Buarcos to the north-west, now almost a suburb of Figueira da Foz, is partly surrounded by a wall, and has two 16th c. Manueline pelourinhos.

Buarcos

About 3km/2 miles farther on is Cabo Mondego, a rocky headland falling sheer down to the Atlantic in a mighty cliff. Adjoining the lighthouse is an observatory and nearby there are abandoned lignite mines and limestone quarries.

Cabo Mondego

The Serra de Boa Viagem (up to 258m/846ft), a few miles north of Figueira da Foz, is an area of scattered woodland which offers some very good walks.

From the summit of the Alto da Vela (209m/686ft) there are superb panoramic views.

Pinhel

Guarda

C 4

Historical province: Beira Alta. District: Guarda
Altitude: 1057m/3468ft. Population: 18,000

The old district capital of Guarda, the see of a bishop and once an important stronghold in the province of Beira Alta, lies on a plateau in the north-east of the Serra da Estrela. As Portugal's highest town, with a healthy and very pleasant climate, it has become a popular health resort.

Situation and Importance

There was already a stongly fortified town on this strategically important site in Roman times. In 80 B.C. it sided with Quintus Sertorius in his attempt to break away from Rome, and thereafter withstood many years of assaults

History

and sieges by Caesar's forces. After the town was devastated by the Moors its inhabitants fled and the remaining buildings became derelict. Much later, in the 12th and 13th c., Guarda was rebuilt by Sancho I and Dinis I and strongly fortified against attack by the Moors and Castilians.

Coimbra, Lisboa

Townscape

At first sight the town, built largely of granite, has a rather grey appearance, but a closer look reveals finely decorated old patrican houses, particularly in the Cathedral Square and the Rua de Dom Luis I.

Of the town's 12th and 13th c. fortifications there remain the keep, three town gates and parts of the town walls.

Sights

★ Catedral

The Catedral (cathedral), which is in the middle of the town, is a granite building of fortress-like appearance, with crenellated walls. It was begun in Gothic style in 1390 and completed in the 16th c., although the portal on the northern transept still looks Gothic. The Manueline additions, notably the west front and doorway, were built by Manuel I's great architect, Boytaca, on the model of Batalha Abbey (see Batalha).

The magnificent three-aisled interior achieves its effect by its harmonious proportions and simplicity of line. The stone retable (1550), on which over 100 figures enact scenes from the life of Christ, was the work of John of Rouen (João de Ruão); the gilding was added in the 18th c. It is well worth climbing up to the roof terrace to see the method of construction of the roof, spanned by flying buttresses, and to enjoy the superb view over the town to the Serra da Estrela.

Praça de Luís de Camões/Praça da Sé

In front of the northern façade of the cathedral is the Praça de Luís de Camões, or Praça da Sé, containing a modern monument to Sancho I, to whom the town owed its economic and cultural advancement in the Middle Ages. The tourist information centre is in the 16th c. Manueline town hall, the Câmara Municipal.

Museu Regional

The former Bishop's Palace (15th/16th c.) now houses the Regional Museum, where the exhibits range from archaeological finds and pictorial archives to paintings and sculpture.

Churches

Also worth seeing are two Baroque churches, the 17th c. Misericórdia and 18th c. São Vicente. Though perhaps somewhat provincial in style, they are no less attractive for that.

About 1km/¾ mile from the town centre is the Romanesque Ermida de Nossa Senhora da Póvoa de Mileu, with finely carved capitals. It is believed to have been founded by the wife of Alfonso Henriques.

Guarda Cathedral

Surroundings of Guarda

Celorico da Beira (alt. 550m/1804ft), 28km/17 miles north-west of Guarda, is a little town with a ruined castle (view), destroyed by French troops in the early 19th c., and several old houses with some Manueline windows.

Celorico da Beira

Trancoso, which is at an altitude of 880m/2886ft about 20km/12 miles north of Celorico da Beira, is encircled by walls that were still being extended in the 16th c., signifying its former importance as a fortress. Trancoso castle, now a ruin, was where King Dinis I married his Queen, later Saint, Isabel in 1282. Also worth seeing are several houses of the nobility, complete with coats of arms, a Manueline pelourinho, and the 13th c. church of Santa Luzia.

Trancoso

Another excursion leads north-east from Guarda along the N 221. 30km/ 19 miles along the road lies Pinhel, a little town surrounded by defensive walls with six towers. Inside the decayed castle, built by King Dinis I, stands the 14th c. church of Santa Maria de Castelo with a fourteen-part picture cycle portraying the life of Mary (17th c.). As well as some typical old houses, the town boasts a monolithic pillory and, outside the walls, the remains of the Romanesque Igreja de Trinidade (church) are of interest.

Pinhel

17km/10½ miles further along the road, on a hill on the right, lies the old defensive town of Castelo Rodrigo which, though now in ruins, was a place of some importance in medieval times. Remains of the 15th c. castle with its defensive tower, the palace and a well can still be seen; also of interest are a small Gothic church and a Manueline pelourinho (pillory). Most beautiful of all, however, is undoubtedly the view from the castle.

Castelo Rodrigo

Since the 19th c. the inhabitants of Castelo have enjoyed taking walks to Figueira de Castelo Rodrigo 3km/2 miles away on a plateau used for fruit-growing. The town has made a real effort to preserve its medieval

Figueira de Castelo Rodrigo

Town gate of Almeida – two of the three town entrances remain

appearance. Inside the 18th c. Baroque church are several gilded and carved altars.

Santa Maria de Aguiar

6km/4 miles south-east of Figueira de Castelo Rodrigo lies the former 13th c. Cistercian convent of Santa Maria de Aguiar (privately owned), with a triple-aisled church and a beautiful columned hall. The loggia is supported on pillars from Tuscany.

Freixada do Torrão

In the village of Freixada do Torrão, just over 6km/4 miles west of Figueira de Castelo Rodrigo, there is an old castle and a church with a Romanesque doorway. The wines of the district are highly prized.

Freixo de Espada á Cinta

20km/12½ miles north of Figueira de Castelo Rodrigo the N 221 crosses the Douro, follows the course of the river for a while and after 45km/28 miles (measured from Figueira de Castelo Rodrigo) it comes to Freixo de Espada á Cinta. This is the birthplace of the seafarer Jorge Álvares and of the poet Guerra Junqueiro (1850–1923), to whom a small museum is dedicated. The 16th c. parish church has some rich interior decoration.

★Almeida

In the middle of some very precipitious countryside and some 45km/28 miles north-east of Guarda lies the town of Almeida. It is surrounded by some well-preserved Vauban defensive works laid out in the form of a twelve-pointed star. Until the 19th c. Almeida remained impregnable until the French succeeded in entering it in 1810.

Serra da Estrela

Trips from Guarda through the Serra da Estrela (see entry) to the west and to the little mountain town of Belmonte (see entry) are extremely charming.

Guimarães — B 3

Historical province: Minho. District: Braga
Altitude: 200m/655ft. Population: 55,000

Guimarães, in the north of Portugal at the foot of the Serra de Santa Catarina, is reverentially known as the "cradle of the nation", the berco da nação, owing to the fact that it was the first capital of the newly established kingdom of Portugal, as well as being the birthplace of its first king, Afonso Henriques, not to mention the celebrated poet and dramatist Gil Vicente. Its well-preserved old town and profusion of historic monuments and art treasures make it a worthwhile destination for the visitor.

Situation and Importance

There is a welcoming feel about Guimarães, with so much greenery everywhere. Town life revolves around the Praça Toural, lined with shops, houses and banks and the beginning of the town's main shopping street, the Rua de S. António, but tourists tend to be drawn more towards the picturesque old town, with its imposing granite houses. Many have wrought-iron balconies, smothered with flowers, and the finest are to be found in the Rua de Santa Maria, around the Largo da Oliveira and to the west of it.

★Townscape

Sights

Above the town rears the grey bulk of the 10th c. castle (Castelo), with its high, slender battlements, one of the most complete and best preserved medieval strongholds in Portugal. As the birthplace on June 24th 1110 of the first Portuguese king, Afonso Henriques, it is also something of a national shrine.

★Castelo

In the middle of the oval courtyard rises the tall and massive keep, the Torre de Menagem, which could hold out on its own if need be. This is believed to have housed in the 11th c. a Benedictine convent founded by the Galician Countess Mumadona.

The curtain walls of the castle, with their eight towers, afford magnificent views, including those of the battlefield of Mamede (open: daily 9am–5pm).

Below the castle entrance stands the small chapel of São Miguel (1105), built of massive courses of dressed stone, in which Afonso Henriques was baptised.

Capela de São Miguel do Castelo

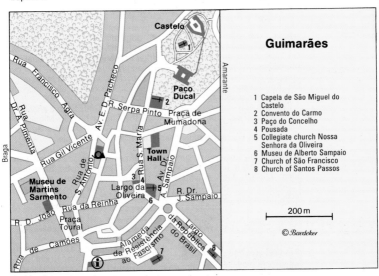

Guimarães

1 Capela de São Miguel do Castelo
2 Convento do Carmo
3 Paço do Concelho
4 Pousada
5 Collegiate church Nossa Senhora da Oliveira
6 Museu de Alberto Sampaio
7 Church of São Francisco
8 Church of Santos Passos

200 m

© Baedeker

Mass is celebrated here annually on the king's birthday to commemorate the event.

★ Paço Ducal

At the foot of the castle hill, surrounded by greensward, is the large Paço Ducal, the Palace of the Dukes of Bragança, a magnificent Gothic residence originally built by Afonso, first Duke of Bragança, in the French style fashionable in his day (completed 1442). After the seat of the Bragança family was transferred in the early 16th c. to Vila Viçosa (see entry) the palace lost its earlier importance, and over the centuries fell into ruin. It was extensively restored and rebuilt in 1933 under Salazar and became the official residence of the president in northern Portugal.

Its fine interior contains 16th–18th c. furniture, Flemish tapestries and valuable porcelain (open: in summer daily 9am–7.30pm, in winter 10am–5.30pm).

Convento do Carmo

The route back to the old town passes below the ducal palace through the Praça de Mumadona, with a modern monument to the Duchess and, somewhat further west, the former Carmelite convent, the Convento do Carmo, its little church in an unpretentious local version of Baroque.

★★ Largo da Oliveira

The impressive Largo da Oliveira, in the heart of the old town, has been particularly successful in managing to retain its medieval aspect

The story goes that the square, and the church, Nossa Senhora da Oliveira, owe their name – "Oliveira" means olive-tree – to Wamba the Visigoth. Called on to be King, Wamba refused to accept unless a dry olive twig stuck in the sand put forth green shoots again. No sooner was the twig in the ground, presumably where the Gothic/Manueline canopy now stands, than it began to turn green.

The old town hall, the Paço do Concelho, on the north side of the square contains the town archives. With its Gothic arcades, it was begun in the 14th c., during the reign of João I, and radically altered in the 17th c. The adjoining building contains a luxurious pousada.

In the centre of the square is the Gothic/Manueline alpendre (a canopy sheltering a crucifix) erected to commemorate victory in the battle on the Rio Salado in 1340, when the allied Portuguese and Spanish forces defeated the troops of the Sultan of Morocco.

★ Nossa Senhora da Oliveira

The Largo da Oliveira is dominated by the collegiate church of Nossa Senhora da Oliveira. The church, originally founded by Afonso Henriques in the 12th c., in thanksgiving for his victory in the battle of Ourique, stands on the site of an earlier convent founded by Countess Mumadona in the 10th c. It was considerably enlarged in 1387–1400 by João I to commemorate the battle of Aljubarrota, when most of the original Romanesque cloister was demolished. The church as it appears today is largely 16th c.; the Manueline tower was added in 1505.

Features of the interior of the church include a Gothic stone altar and the Romanesque baptismal font from the Capela de São Miguel do Castelo, where Afonso I Henriques is said to have been christened. The silver altar in the sacramental chapel is particularly valuable.

★ Museu de Alberto Sampaio

The adjoining cloister and part of the former Dominican convent now house the very impressive Museu de Alberto Sampaio (open: Tues.–Sun. 10am–12.30pm and 2–5.30pm), with pictures and sculpture, mainly by Portuguese artists of the 14th–16th c., goldsmiths' work and a valuable collection of historical costume and furniture. Outstanding among the exhibits are the splendid sarcophagus of Constança de Noronhas, first Duchess of Bragança (in the cloister), a superb silver processional cross (16th c.) and the cloak which João I wore over his armour at the battle of Aljubarrota.

Santos Passos

From the collegiate church the long Largo da República do Brasil leads to the twin-towered Baroque church of the Santos Passos (18th c.), richly decorated with azulejos and sculpture showing Italian influence on the façade.

To the west stands the church of São Francisco, founded by João I about 1400 and remodelled in Baroque. The spacious interior is entirely faced with azulejos. The sacristy has a massive coffered ceiling.

São Francisco

In the west of the town centre it is worth visiting the Museu de Martins Sarmento (open: Tues.–Sun. 9.30am–12.30pm), an archaeological museum in a former Dominican convent (13th c.) containing finds from the prehistoric settlements of Citânia de Briteiros (see entry) and Castro de Sabroso.

Museu de Martins Sarmento

Surroundings of Guimarães

About 5km/3 miles south-east above the town, reached by a lovely mountain road, is the Penha or Serra de Santa Catarina (617m/2024ft), a rocky height with a pilgrimage church (1898) and a statue of Pope Pius IX. There are superb views from the summit south-east to the Serra de Marão (see Amarante) and, on a clear day, north to the Serra do Gerês (see Peneda-Gerês National Park) and west to the Atlantic.

Penha de Santa Catarina

10km/6 miles south-west of Guimarães, attractively situated on both banks of the Rio Vizela, is the spa of Caldas de Vizela (pop. 3000), with sulphurous springs which were already being frequented in Roman times. There are altogether 55 springs with an abundant flow of water at temperatures ranging from 16°C/61°F to 65.6°C/150°F, used for the treatment of bronchial and skin ailments, rheumatism, and conditions of the joints. There is an attractive park on the banks of the river (swimming, rowing) where a week of events is staged annually at the end of August, including folk-dancing, various sporting competitions, clay-pigeon shooting, etc.

Caldas de Vizela

Within easy reach of Caldas de Vizela are the late 17th c. pilgrimage chapel of São Bento (4km/2½ miles) and the 12th c. Romanesque church of São Miguel de Vilarinho (3km/2 miles), with a 12th c. Gothic cloister adjoining the church.

Another spa, Caldas das Taipas, about 7km/4½ miles north-west of Guimarães, was also known to the Romans. It too has hot sulphurous springs (30°C/86°F), used for treating bronchial and digestive system ailments, as well as rheumatism, etc. Here, too, there is an attractive park, this time on the banks of the Rio Ave.

Caldas das Taipas

Lagos

Historical province: Algarve. District: Faro
Altitude: sea level. Population: 11,000

Once capital of the old province of the Algarve, Lagos lies on the west side of a bay of the Rio Alvor, here fully 2km/1¼ miles wide, which is sheltered on the east by the Ponta dos Três Irmãos and on the west by the Ponta da Piedade (see below) and the broad estuary of Ribeira de Bensafrim. The excellent beaches nearby have led to a great deal of recent hotel development around the town, together with apartment buildings and camp sites. Restaurants and cafés abound in the town, but the people of Lagos continue to make part of their living from fishing (tuna, sardines). An ultra-modern yacht marina near the fishing harbour came into operation in 1995.

Situation and Importance

"Lacóbriga" to the Romans, Lagos became "Zawaya" under the Moors, who built the walls that originally fortified the town. These eventually succumbed to the Portuguese kings and Sancho II was able to take the town in the mid-13th c. In the centuries that followed it developed into an important ship-building town and port, thanks partly to Henry the

History

Lagos

Navigator. It was also from here that Gil Eanes, who was born in Lagos, set sail in 1434 to become the first seafarer to round Cape Bojador in West Africa. The voyages of discovery brought Lagos fame and fortune. Trade flourished, and the slave-trade with it – the first slaves from Africa were auctioned in 1443 in a building on the present Praça da República. Lagos became the capital of the historical province of Algarve in 1577 and remained so until 1756, the year following the destruction of much of the town by an earthquake. Its subsequent decline in importance was only halted in the late 20th c. when tourism has brought new prosperity.

★ Townscape

The outer districts of Lagos, with their tower-blocks and large apartment buildings, are really rather ugly. The town centre is much more attractive. Although it has developed into a typical tourist centre it still has the feel of a pleasant compact town which has retained its own character. Parts of the old town are still surrounded by the medieval wall. A small area in the centre around the Praça Gil Eanes and the Praça da República is now a pedestrian precinct. There are many small shops and a plethora of restaurants and cafés with tables outside.

Sights

Praça Gil Eanes

The Praça Gil Eanes is one of the two main squares in the centre of Lagos. In the middle stands a famous statue (1973) of the "longed-for" King Sebastião, who set out from Lagos on a voyage to conquer North Africa and never returned. The statue is by the well-known Portuguese sculptor João Cutileiro. On the east side of the square stands the town hall (câmara municipal; 1798).

Igreja de São Sebastião

From the Praça Gil Eanes a street curves round to the little Praça Luis de Camões and thence further north to the Igreja de São Sebastião. Steps lead up to the attractive church square. A start was made on building the church in the 15th c., but considerable changes were made later. A chapter-house adjoins the church.

Praça da República

We Saw

A second central square, the Praça da República, lies at the southern end of the pedestrian zone and opens on to the Avenida dos Desacombrimentos and the seafront promenade. In the square stands a statue of Henry the Navigator (see Famous People), looking out to sea; it was erected in 1960 to mark the 500th anniversary of his death.

Igreja de Santa Maria

We saw

On the south side of the square stands the Igreja de Santa Maria, a church which can trace its origins back to the 14th c., but was rebuilt following the 1755 earthquake. Henry the Navigator was buried in the old church in 1460; later his remains were transferred to the Capela do Fundador in Batalha Abbey (see entry).

Palácio dos Governadores

Behind the church stands the former Governor's Palace, part of which is formed by the old town wall. Until 1756 the Algarve province was administered from here.

Delegação da Alfândega

We Saw

The north side of the Praça da República is dominated by the narrow building of the Delegação da Alfândega (customs authority). Black African slaves were auctioned here in 1444; they were shackled to the iron posts while potential buyers examined them.

Forte da Ponta da Bandeira

The Avenida dos Descobrimentos (Avenue of Discoveries), opened in 1961, runs along the bank of the harbour channel as far as the Ponta da Bandeira. The Forte da Ponta da Bandeira, with its four round towers at the corners, was built in the 17th c. to guard the harbour. The narrow drawbridge leads to the Museu Marítimo inside the fort (open to visitors).

Santo António

The Baroque Chapel of Santo António just to the west of the Praça da República was built in 1769 in place of an earlier church. It boasts a

206 The 'Golden Chapel' of St. Anthony Decorated waist high with 18th Cent. AZULEJOS & above lined with

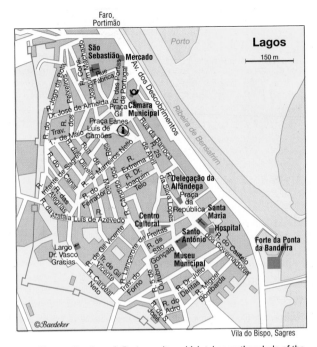

Faro, Portimão

Porto

Lagos

150 m

São Sebastião · Mercado

Av. dos Descobrimentos

Câmara Municipal

Praça Gil

Praça Eanes · Luís de Camões

Ribeira de Bensafrim

Delegação da Alfândega

Praça da República · Santa Maria

Centro Cultural

Santo António · Hospital

Museu Municipal

Forte da Ponta da Bandeira

Largo Dr. Vasco Gracias

©Baedeker

Vila do Bispo, Sagres

magnificent *talha dourada* Baroque altar which takes up the whole of the wall of the choir.

The collections of the Museu Municipal de Lagos (open: Tues.–Sun. 9.30am–12.30pm and 2–5pm) have been housed in the building adjoining the church since 1934. As well as an azulejo collection and some religious exhibits there is a small archaeological section.

Museu Municipal de Lagos

Those interested in modern art should visit the Culture Centre opened in 1992 (open: daily 10am–midnight, to 8pm in winter). As well as exhibitions by contemporary artists there are theatrical and dancing performances and concerts.

Centro Cultural

Surroundings of Lagos

The beaches of Lagos are scenically extremely attractive but get very crowded in the high season. To the north-east of the town the Meia Praia curves gently around the Baia de Lagos for several miles. Here there are all kinds of water sports facilities. The beach can be reached by bus, by small boat from Lagos, or on foot past the Lagos railway station.

To the south of the town lie the small Praia do Camilo and the well-known Praia de Dona Ana with rocky islets lying offshore. The latter is the most beautiful of the bays around Lagos, but is usually very crowded in the high season.

Praia do Camilo, ★Praia de Dona Ana

From the Praia de Dona Ana it is possible to drive or go on foot – there is a path which in places leads along the very edge of the cliffs – to the Ponta da

★★Ponta da Piedade

207

Praia Dona Ana, near Lagos

Piedade 2km/1¼ miles to the south. Here are undoubtedly the most beautiful rock formations to be found anywhere along the Algarve coast. They can be seen from the land, but the best view is from the water. Boats sail from Lagos to the Ponta da Piedade; from Lagos, too, there are boat trips to the various caves in the vicinity. The Ponta da Piedade is an imposing foothill which falls away into the sea from the southern end of the Baia de Lagos. At their highest point the rocks are 20m/66ft tall. There are rock overhangs, crags and pillars, natural arches and gateways behind and next to one another, producing a bizarrely beautiful fantasy landscape. A lighthouse marks the entrance and exit to the Bay of Lagos.

Odiáxere

The village of Odiáxere, 6km/3¾ miles north of Lagos, has suffered considerably from the busy N 125 road which runs through it. There is a pretty village church in Odiáxere which was rebuilt after the 1755 earthquake; the Manueline doorway of the old church survives.

Barragem da Bravura

In Odiáxere a road branches north off the N 125 to Barragem da Bravura or Barragem de Odiáxere. A 10km/6 mile drive through some magnificent countryside ends at the artificial lake (viewing point and small restaurant).

Lamego   C 3

Historical province: Beira Alta. District: Viseu
Altitude: 490m/1610ft. Population: 10,000

Situation and Importance

The little episcopal town of Lamego, charmingly situated amid vineyards and fields on the slopes of Monte Penude about 100km/62 miles east of Oporto, has been since medieval times an important market for the agricultural produce from the fertile countryside around it. It was here that the

Portuguese Estates met for the first time in 1143 to proclaim Afonso Henriques king of the newly established state. Lamego is also famous for its sparkling wine (Caves da Raposeira can be visited).

Lamego is a relatively undistinguished little town but does have some fine 16th–18th c. townhouses.

Townscape

Sights

In the centre of town rises the massive Gothic Cathedral (Sé), founded by Afonso Henriques in 1129 and much altered in the 16th and 17th c. Of the original building there survives only the sturdy square tower. The interior was completely remodelled in the 18th c. The adjoining Renaissance cloister has several fine chapels.

Sé

The Regional Museum (Museu de Lamego) is housed in the former Bishop's Palace (18th c.), on the Largo de Camões diagonally opposite the Cathedral. Its interesting collection includes 16th c. Flemish tapestries that once furnished the palace itself, Portuguese painting of the 16th–18th c., sculpture of the 13th–17th c., and religious and folk art.

Museu de Lamego

Another interesting feature of the town is the Capela do Desterro (1640) south of the cathedral on the main road to Guarda. Richly decorated with 17th c. azulejos and talha dourada, it has a Renaissance portal and a fine painted coffered ceiling.

Capela do Desterro

On a hill above the town is the 11th–13th c. castle, originally Moorish, with only its 13th c. keep and some of the walls still standing.

Castelo

Just below the castle, to the west, is the Romanesque Igreja de Almacave with fine carved capitals and a 16th Renaissance pulpit.

Igreja de Almacave

The main sight of Lamego is undoubtedly the pilgrimage church of Nossa Senhora dos Remédios. From the town a magnificent Baroque staircase with 14 Stations of the Cross leads up to the sumptuous 18th c. twin-towered church on the Monte de Santo Estêvão. (It is also accessible by car, forking right at the entrance to Lamego coming from Viseu.) Thousands of pilgrims gather here at the beginning of September every year to seek healing and consolation.
   The terrace below the church holds statues of kings and biblical figures, with an obelisk in the centre, and affords an impressive view over Lamego and the surrounding fertile countryside.

★Santuário Nossa Senhora dos Remédios

Surroundings of Lamego

About 3km/2 miles north-east of Lamego (right fork just before reaching Lamego on the Guarda road), in the valley of the Rio Balsemão, stands the Visigothic church of São Pedro de Balsemão, which is believed to be the oldest church in Portugal (7th c.). The church was restored in 1643 and given a coffered ceiling. It contains the sarcophagus of Afonso Pires, a 14th c. bishop of Oporto.

São Pedro de Balsemão

Barrô, 16km/10 miles north-west of Lamego on the N222, is delightfully situated above the Douro valley (see entry) and has a 12th c. Romanesque church.

Barrô

5km/3 miles further along the N222, as it winds its way along the Douro valley, São Martinho de Mouros has a Romanesque church (9th–11th c.) at the end of the village and is notable for its richly carved capitals and a picture of St Martin ascribed to Vasco Fernandes.

São Martinho de Mouros

Resende	Resende is a further 8km/5 miles along the road to the west. It is a trim little town, with above it the Romanesque church of São Salvador (view).
Santa Maria de Cárquere	A side-road at Anreade (2km/1 mile further west) leads, after 8km/5 miles, to the Manueline church Santa Maria de Cárquere, which belonged to a convent founded in the 11th c.
Caldas de Aregos	The little spa of Caldas de Aregos, 5km/3 miles west of Anreade, is beautifully situated on a wooded hill above the Douro valley. It has hot sulphur springs (50–61°C/122–142°F) used to treat ailments of the joints and bronchial diseases. It has a lovely park and there are fine views from the Penedo de São João, a crag above the town.
Cinfães	Famed for its vinho verde, Cinfães is 15km/9 miles further west and has an 18th c. mansion, the Quinta da Fervança.
Tarouquela	Tarouquela, 15km/9 miles west of Cinfães, has a well-preserved hilltop Romanesque church, Santa Maria Maior, which belonged to a 12th c. Benedictine convent. Close by is the Romanesque/Gothic chapel of São João Baptista.
Castelo de Paiva	10km/6 miles further along the road Castelo de Paiva, or Sobrado de Paiva as it is also known, is a little town surrounded by hills and famous for its wine. A good centre from which to explore the surrounding area, it boasts an attraction of its own in the Quinta da Boa Vista, an 18th c. country house.
Peso da Régua	13km/8 miles north of Lamego on the N2, Peso da Régua (pop. 6000; alt. 380m/1246ft), Régua for short, is a pretty little town situated at the point where the little rivers Corgo (right bank) and Baroso (left bank) flow into the Douro. It is the focal point of the "País do Vinho" (the wine country – see Douro valley), and the busy centre of the port wine district. The town is particularly lively during the vintage (end of September to end of October) when helpers arrive from far and near. Two wine-producers, Martinez and Sandeman, welcome visitors.
Tarouca	Off the road to Guarda, 10km/6 miles south of Lamego, is the pretty village of Tarouca, in a beautiful setting at the head of a valley flanked by rugged walls of rock. In the church of the former Cistercian convent of São João de Tarouca, probably founded by Afonso I in 1171, is the imposing tomb of Conde Pedro de Barcelos (d. 1354), illegitimate son of King Dinis I and author of the "Livro das Linhagens", a register of the nobility. The sarcophagus of his wife, formerly in the church, is now in the museum in Lamego.
Sernancelhe	Sernancelhe, about 50km/31 miles south-east of Lamego, has a Romanesque parish church with a separate belfry and a 16th c. pelourinho.

Leiria   B 5

	Historical province: Beira Litoral. District: Leiria Altitude: 30–113m/100–370ft. Population: 30,000
Situation and Importance	Leiria is a busy district capital and market town in central Portugal, 10km/6 miles north of Batalha (see entry). The Rio Liz flows through its centre. Called Collipo by the Romans, the little town was a royal residence for a time under King Dinis I and since 1545 has been the see of a bishop. The fertile farming area around Leiria and its rural population still practice many old crafts and customs (basketwork, pottery, woven blankets; glass-blowing; traditional costumes).
Townscape	In the old town centre there are still some attractive 16th and 17th c. urban residences and noble mansions. The heart of the town is the Praça de

Rodrigues Lobo and the bordering Jardim Público (with the tourist information centre). In the middle of the square stands a memorial to Rodrigues Lobo (1579–1621) who, like many a later writer, waxed lyrical about the idyllic little town.

Sights

High above Leiria towers its castle, built originally by Afonso Henriques in 1135 on the remains of a Moorish castle, which itself had succeeded an earlier Roman fortress. When Portugal's frontier shifted further south in 1147 the castle lost its strategic importance. Its dilapidation was halted, however, in the early 14th c. when King Dinis had it rebuilt and extended to make a palace that would serve as a residence for himself and his queen, St Isabel. The keep (1324), from which there is a magnificent view, and part of the castle walls are well preserved. The rest of the royal castle has been restored, and from the loggia with its Gothic columns there are also good views over the town. The early Gothic church of Nossa Senhora da Pena (1314) remains a ruin.

★ Castelo

Below the castle is the 12th c. church of São Pedro, originally Romanesque but much altered in later centuries.

São Pedro

The Cathedral (Sé) is a plain Renaissance building in the old part of Leiria (16th c.; restored in 18th c.).
  The small adjoining museum contains pictures, furniture, pottery and glass.

Sé

Opposite the castle mound, on another hill, is the Santuário de Nossa Senhora da Encarnação (1588), reached by an 18th c. staircase, with panoramic views from the top.

Santuário de Nossa Senhora da Encarnação

Leiria: the Castelo

Surroundings of Leiria

Milagres

About 7km/4½ miles north of Leiria is the little town of Milagres with pretty houses and a popular 18th c. pilgrimage church.

Monte Real

The little spa of Monte Real, 15km/9 miles north of Leiria, is used for treatment of liver and stomach ailments (park).

Pombal

About 27km/17 miles north-east of Leiria, in the valley of the Rio Soura, is the busy town of Pombal (pop. 11,000; alt. 221m/725ft). It owes its fame to José I's powerful minister Sebastião José de Carvalho e Mello, Marquês de Pombal (see Famous People), who died here in exile in 1752. A monument to the Marquês de Pombal stands in the main square near the church of São Martinho (founded 1323, rebuilt 1520). There is a castle (renovated in the 16th c.) above the town together with the 12th c. church of Santa Maria do Castelo.

Rio Caranguejeira

About 8km/5 miles east of Leiria is an impressive gorge on the Rio Caranguejeira, with rock faces fully 100m/330ft high.

Marinha Grande/
Pinhal de Leiria

Marinha Grande is about 12km/7½ miles west of Leiria amidst the Pinhal de Leiria, or Pinhal Real, the pinewoods which were planted by King Dinis I using maritime pines from the south of France to provide protection against the drifting sand. Nowadays the trees yield resin and turpentine. Marinha Grande developed in the mid-18th c. when the glass-works, now one of the most important in the country, were set up here.

Lisbon (Lisboa)   A 6

Historical province: Estremadura. District: Lisboa (Lisbon)
Altitude: 23–112m/75–365ft
Population: 850,000 (Greater Lisbon: 2.1 million)

Situation and
Importance

Lisbon, in Portuguese Lisbóa (pronounced "Lishbóa"), capital of Portugal and its principal port and business centre, the see of an archbishop, and a university city, lies some 17km/10½ miles from the Atlantic on the north bank of the Tagus, which here opens out into the Mar de Palha ("sea of straw"), 7km/4½ miles wide. To the west of the city the estuary narrows again to 2–3km/1–2 miles across, forming a fine sheltered natural harbour.

Thanks to its wonderful setting Lisbon, the "white city", is rightly numbered among the world's most beautiful cities. The many treasures of art and architecture still testify to its glorious past and, together with the charm of the old town and its steep narrow streets, make a stay here a memorable experience for any visitor.

History

The Phoenicians were the first to take advantage of this excellent harbourage at the mouth of the Tagus, establishing a settlement which they called Alis Ubbo. Later the Lusitanian port of Olisipo, it was taken over by the Romans, surrounded by walls and, as Felicitas Iulia, became the administrative capital of the Roman province of Lusitania, the second most important town (after Mérida) in the Iberian peninsula.

In A.D. 407 the town was taken by the Alani; from 585 to 715 it was under Visigothic rule; and after the battle of Jerez it fell into the hands of the Moors, who called it Al Oshbuna or Lishbuna. Under the Moors (until 1147) it enjoyed economic prosperity and a great flowering of culture.

Lisbon became of major importance again in 1260, when King Afonso III made it his capital. The great discoveries of the late 15th c. and the conquest of the East Indies principally benefited the capital, which rapidly developed into one of the wealthiest cities in Europe.

On November 1st 1755 most of the town was laid in ruins by a devastating earthquake, but rebuilding soon began under the direction of the Marquês de Pombal. The new city was laid out on a magnificent scale,

EXPO'98®

Under the motto "The Ocean, the Heritage for the Future", the Lisbon Expo, the last World Exhibition of the 20th century, was held between May 22nd and September 30th 1998. The theme was well chosen. More than any other European people, the Portuguese are closely linked to the sea through the country's geographical location and through its history. Some 160 countries and organisations accepted Portugal's invitation to exhibit.

Expo 98 was held on a 70ha/175 acre site to the north-east of the city centre, on the banks of the Tagus where the river widens to form the Mar de Palha (Lake of Straw). A harbour basin (the Doca de Olivais) in the centre, and a refinery tower converted into a viewing platform, are evidence that the area was once a petroleum refinery.

The main attraction on the Expo site is the Pavilhão dos Oceanos; designed by the American Peter Chermayeff, it is the largest aquarium in Europe. It has remained in existence since Expo 98 came to an end and it is hoped that it will attract between one and two million visitors a year. Behind curved glass the fascinated visitor can watch more than 15,000 fishes, including swarms of sardines, rays and sharks. At the northern end of the Doca de Olivais stands the Pavilhão da Utopia, easy to recognise because of its dome-like roof. It was designed as a multi-purpose hall to be used after the exhibition; it can house 15,000 visitors, making it the largest function hall in Lisbon.

The final weeks of Expo 98 seemed to indicate that, like its predecessors, it would fail by quite a margin to meet the financial expectations of its organisers. However, the Portuguese have given a lot of thought to the future use of the site. Some 80 percent of the buildings are to be used as museums, sports stadia and exhibition halls. A giant exhibition complex will house Lisbon's International Fair, while blocks of apartments will be built on another part of the site. Above all, however, the organisers are planning a completely new city district to be known as "Expo-Urbe", where some 25,000 people will be living and working by the year 2010. This new quarter will boast an excellent infrastructure, with schools, youth centres, leisure and sports facilities, a hospital and car parks, as well as 450,000sq.m/4,840,000sq.ft of office space and 153,000sq.m/1,650,000sq.ft of shops.

This district of the city already enjoys excellent transport facilities. The new Estação Oriente (East Station) near the Expo Site, a well-lit, filigree-like construction by the Spaniard Santiago Calatravas, is expected to be Lisbon's main traffic centre providing a link-up between the railway station and the public transport system. The Ponte Vasco da Gama, which was completed in time for the opening of Expo 98, has brought welcome relief to motor traffic. This bridge over the Tagus has six lanes and is 17km/10½ miles long, making it the longest in Europe.

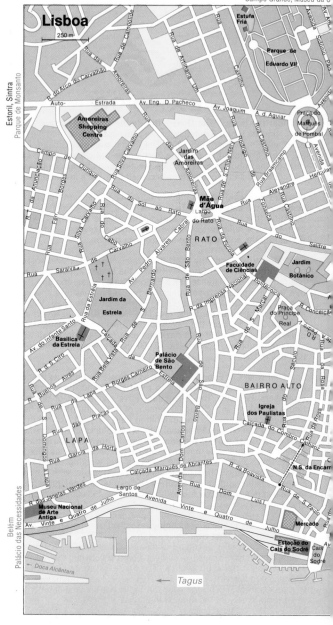

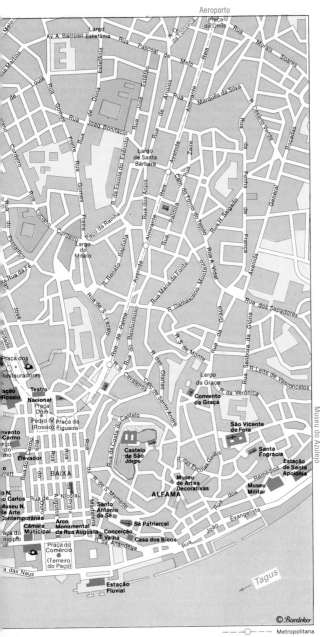

which is still visible today, to the plans of Manuel da Maira, incorporating such of the older Gothic and Manueline buildings as had survived.

The transfer of the capital to Rio de Janeiro from the French invasion (1807–08) until 1821, followed by the loss of Brazil as a colony, were considerable setbacks to Lisbon, from which it only gradually recovered in the second half of the 19th c. The twentieth century has seen Lisbon develop into a modern and enlightened city whilst generally retaining its individuality, despite the impact on its history by the fire that destroyed 7500sq.m/8970sq.yd of the centre in August 1988. Since then many of the old buildings have been rebuilt, retaining their original façades. In 1992 the contract for the construction of Expo 98 was awarded. Once the former large industrial area in east Lisbon had been decontaminated, then the building of the exhibition complex on the banks of the Tagus and the adjoining town quarter "Expo Urbe" began. A new station (Estação Oriente) and a huge bridge over the Tagus (Ponte Vasco da Gama) were opened to the public in time for the start of Expo 98.

★★Cityscape

Lisbon's sea of whitish-grey houses extends over seven hills on the southern slopes of the Estremadura plateau, with considerable variations in height, the different parts of the city being linked by steep streets and a number of lifts and funiculars.

At the heart of the city is the Baixa, the lower town, completely rebuilt in a depression just above the level of the Tagus after the quarter had been destroyed by the 1755 earthquake. It is full of gardens and broad promenades, along with narrow streets lined by great business houses. East of the Baixa, on the slopes of the castle mound, are Lisbon's oldest quarters, the Alfama and Mouraria, with their mass of secretive, medieval-seeming alleys that survived the earthquake virtually unscathed. The same was true of the other old part of town, the Bairro Alto, the upper town west of the Baixo. This is bordered on the west by Lapa, one of Lisbon's smartest residential suburbs and also the diplomatic quarter, where many countries have their embassies and the homes of their diplomats, while the suburb of Belém, farther west, has its own impressive buildings that serve as reminders of Portugal's past greatness.

The most radical changes to the face of Lisbon in recent decades have been in the north and east with the building of enormous housing estates such as Alvalade, in the north, designed to accommodate 50,000, while modern office and retailing complexes such as the Amoreiras shopping centre have also made their mark on the city's skyline.

A city's problems

In the "bairros da lata" in the northern and eastern outskirts of Lisbon the poorest of the community live in shanties, often without electricity or running water. Many of these deprived people have come from the former Portuguese colonies or from other parts of Portugal, or are simply unable to afford higher rents. The housing shortage in the inner city is another pressing problem, and most people who work in the capital have to commute daily. In its turn this has led to chaotic traffic conditions, especially in the rush-hours. Attempts are now being made to alleviate the housing shortage and to control rents, but it will be some time before the effects of these measures can be assessed.

Anyone who can only manage a brief stay in Lisbon should at least spend a little time on the Rossio, go for a walk around the Alfama and get out to the suburb of Belém.

Lisboa Card

With a "Lisboa Card" all forms of public transport (bus, tram, metro, elevators) can be used free of charge; in addition, the card allows free admission to almost 30 museums. There are "Lisboa Cards" which are valid for one, two or three days (price for one day is approximately the equivalent of £5.50, three days £12). Cards obtainable at the Posto Central (Rua Jardim do Regedor 50), the Museu Nacionale de Arte Antiga or at the Hieronymite convent in Belém.

An ideal way to see Alfama is to wander aimlessly through the labyrinth of winding streets, little archways and steps ▶

Lower Town (Cidade Baixa)

Praça dos Restauradores

The best place to start a walk around the Lower Town is the Praça dos Restauradores, where the tourist information centre is situated. This busy square contains the Monumento dos Restauradores de Portugal, an obelisk almost 30m/100ft high erected in 1882 to commemorate the rising on December 1st 1640 which ended sixty years of Spanish rule.

Estação do Rossio

At the south-west corner of the square is the Rossio Station, the Estação do Rossio, looking more like a theatre or a monumental building than a station. It is in fact the local station for trains to Sintra and Leiria, which leave the city via a tunnel 2600m/2850yd long.

Teatro Nacional de Dona Maria II

Diagonally opposite the station is the side of the national theatre, the Teatro Nacional de Dona Maria II, which has its frontage on the Rossio. The Classical building, completed in 1846, was burnt down in 1964 and not reopened, after modernisation, until 1978.

★Rossio

The Rossio, or the Praça de Dom Pedro IV, as it's officially known, is the real centre of Lisbon, where it is worth taking the time to relax in one of the street cafés and watch the passers-by, streetsellers, shoe-shine boys, etc. In the middle of the square stands a marble column, 23m/75ft high, put up in 1870 and topped by a bronze statue of King Pedro IV. It also boasts two lovely fountains, some fine mosaic pavements (see above) and is surrounded by elegant 18th c. houses. South of the square, leaving by the Rua do Ouro or Aurea, the right of the street is in the shadow of the iron Elevador de Santa Justa (see upper town).

Quarter between Rossio and Praça do Comércio

The grid of streets between Rossio and Praça do Comércio was laid out like a chessboard on Marquês de Pombal's orders after the 1755 earthquake. The streets were arranged to accommodate certain guilds, hence the Rua da Prata (silver street for the silversmiths), Rua Aurea, or Rua do Ouro (goldsmiths) and the Rua Augusta for the cloth merchants. Although this system is no longer discernible today this is still Lisbon's trading and shopping quarter.

Praça do Comércio

At the far end of these streets, looking out onto the Tagus, is the Praça do Comércio, also known as the Terreiro do Paço after the royal palace (da Ribeira), which was destroyed in the 1755 earthquake. Its traditional English name is Black Horse Square, after the bronze equestrian statue of King José I (erected 1775) in the middle of the square. The square is surrounded by arcades and by various public buildings (mainly government departments), most of which were built by Santos de Carvalho after the earthquake. On the north side of the square towers a huge triumphal arch completed in 1873, the Arco Monumental da Rua Augusta, with statues of famous Portuguese figures.

The centre of the square is no longer used as a car park so the title "one of the finest squares in Europe" is again justified.

Boats for Cacilhas (see Surroundings of Lisbon) on the opposite bank of the Tagus regularly leave from the embankment at the south end of the square; the boat trip provides a superb view of the gently rising terraces of houses that make up Portugal's capital.

Old town

Igreja da Conceição Velha

A short distance along Rua da Alfândega from the north-east corner of the Praça do Comércio is the church of Nossa Senhora da Conceição Velha, rebuilt after the earthquake but preserving a richly decorated Manueline façade from an earlier church.

Casa dos Bicos

A little further east, and worth looking at, is the Casa dos Bicos, "the house of points", which owes its name to the diamond-shaped ashlar blocks that clad its striking façade. The ground floor of the 16th c. palace was all that survived the earthquake, but the upper storeys have since been rebuilt according to the old plans but with modern materials. Nowadays the building is used for exhibitions.

To the north-west, after a relatively short walk up through the narrow lanes of the old town, we reach the Cathedral, the Sé Patriarcal, the oldest church in the city. The greater part of it dates from 1344 onwards, when it replaced an earlier church which is believed to have been converted from a mosque in 1150. The fortress-like west front with its two towers was built in 1380.

★ Sé Patriarcal

Although the interior of the Cathedral appears predominantly Romanesque, the choir and ambulatory are Gothic. The font immediately left of the entrance is where St Antony is supposed to have been baptised in 1195. In the first chapel on the left is a beautiful terracotta Nativity group by Joaquin Machado de Castro. The choir contains the tombs of King Afonso IV and his queen, Brites. St Vincent's Chapel, at the near end of the ambulatory, used to hold the reliquary of St Vincent. Another chapel off the ambulatory contains the interesting sarcophagi of Lopo Fernandes Pacheco, a supporter of King Afonso IV, and his wife. The valuable treasures in the Sacristy include the silver reliquary of St Vincent.

A visit to the church should include the fine two-storey 14th c. cloister, with a superb Romanesque wrought-iron screen. Nearby in the cloister, excavations have revealed remains of walls from the Phoenician and Roman eras.

On the west side of the square opposite the cathedral is the church of Santo António da Sé, rebuilt between 1757 and 1812 following the earthquake, and said to mark the site of the house in which St Antony of Padua was born. The saint, who is supposed to have cured the lame and raised the dead, is commemorated by a monument and small museum nearby.

Igreja de Santo António da Sé

The slopes east and north-east of the Cathedral are taken up by the Alfama, Lisbon's highly picturesque old quarter. Its stepped lanes and romantic squares attract lots of visitors, particularly in the evening when locals and tourists alike come to hear the fados sung in some of the cafés and restaurants.

★ Alfama

The name Alfama comes from the Arabic "al-Hama", meaning hot springs. In the Middle Ages this quarter was home to Lisbon's nobility and prosperous bourgeoisie. Later came the craftspeople, fisherfolk and seafarers and in the 18th c. the Alfama was also the red-light district. Nowadays Lisbon's old town is where those at the bottom of the income ladder live, and it is questionable whether life has the quaint charms for them that appeal to the tourist.

The best course is to wander aimlessly through the maze of narrow lanes, steep steps and hidden backyards. Despite the obvious poverty the place has a lively feel, with canaries trilling in each alley and plants trailing from every façade. The busiest street is the Rua de São Pedro, with its little shops, *tabernas* and street vendors.

Lisbon

Cathedral
Sé Patriarcal

1 Font
2 Crib (Nativity group)
3 Sacristy
4 High altar
5 Patriarchal throne
6 Tomb of Lopo Fernandes Pacheco
7 Entrances to cloister
9 St Vincent's Chapel
9 Chapel of the Sacrament

219

View of the Tagus and central Lisbon from Castelo de São Jorge

Miradouro de Santa Luzia

On the north-west edge of the quarter, by the Rua do Limoeiro, the Miradouro de Santa Luzia (Belvedere) offers a superb view from its terrace of the jumble of houses.

Museu de Artes Decorativas

Opposite the terrace, in the former palace of the Visconde de Azurara (17th c.), on the Largo das Portas do Sol, is the Museum of Decorative Arts, with a school and workshops as well as a fine collection of 18th and 19th c. furniture, silver, carpets and ceramics (open: Mon., Wed.–Sun. 10am–5pm).

★Castelo de São Jorge

X SAW ABOVE CITY

On top of the hill, once the middle of the Moorish town, is the Castelo de São Jorge. The oldest parts of the castle date from the 6th c. In the 12th c. the Moorish fortress was converted into a royal palace and until the 16th c. it served as a royal residence, then was used as an armoury and prison. It was severely damaged in the 1755 earthquake and what was left of the castle walls was restored in 1938–40, when the courtyard was made into gardens. From the tree-planted terrace on the south side of the castle and from the wall-walks and towers there are fine views of the city and the Tagus Mar de Palha (orientation table). (Open: daily 9am–7pm, in summer to 9pm.)

Museu de Marionetas

Immediately east of the castle mound, on the Largo Rodrigues de Freitas, there is a small marionette museum sponsored by the Gulbenkian Foundation.

Convento da Graça

There are good views of the castle from the Convento da Graça, a former convent now used as a barracks, to its north-east. The church of this former convent, Nossa Senhora da Graça, dates from 1556 and was rebuilt after 1755. Its south transept contains an image of Christ, Nosso Senhor dos Passos, that is revered as miraculous.

Ermida Nossa Senhora do Monte

On a ridge some 300m/328yd north is the Ermida de Nossa Senhora do Monte (alt. 100m/330ft), built in 1243. Its terrace (orientation table) also has a panoramic view of Lisbon.

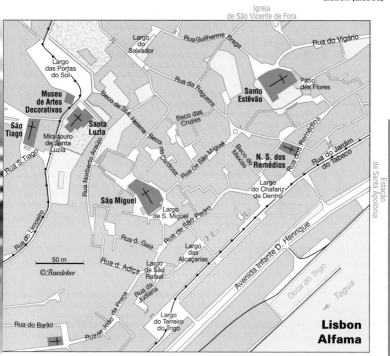

Igreja
de São Vicente de Fora

Lisbon
Alfama

About 500m/550yd east of the castle mound is the imposing church of São Vicente de Fora by the Italian architect Filippo Terzi; it was built between 1582 and 1627 and has a rather severe twin-towered façade which contrasts markedly with the rich Baroque of the interior.

São Vicente de Fora

In the adjoining convent, a former Augustinian house, the entrance and cloisters boast a profusion of 18th c. azulejos. In the former refectory is the Panteão Real (Royal Pantheon), installed here in 1855, with the tombs of members of the House of Bragança from João IV (d. 1656) to Queen Amalia (d. 1951).

Below São Vicente is the church of Santa Engrácia, or the Panteão Nacional, which has an unusual history. An earlier church was demolished in 1630 after theft of the host caused its deconsecration, only for the new building to collapse in 1681. Building of the present church was begun in 1682 but had taken almost three centuries to complete when it was finished with the dome in 1966.

Santa Engrácia

Its interior is on the plan of a Greek cross, and serves as a pantheon for such famous Portuguese as Vasco da Gama and Henry the Navigator.

The Military Museum on the banks of the Tagus is in the former Army Arsenal (Arsenal do Exército), which was producing armaments up until the early 20th c. Nowadays the public can visit its large collection of arms and trophies which include 14th c. cannon and Vasco da Gama's sword. Some of the rooms have rich Baroque decoration (open: Tues.–Sat. 10am–4pm; Sun. 11am–5pm).

Museu Militar

Lisbon (Lisboa)

Estação de Santa
Apolónia

The Santa Apolónia Station east of the Military Museum is the terminus for trains to Oporto and France.

Museu da Agua
Manuel da Maia

About halfway between the Apolónia Station and the azulejo museum, at Rua da Alviela 12, is the civic waterworks museum, the Museu da Agua Manuel da Maia, opened in 1987. Displays in the former pumping station tell the story of Lisbon's water supply (open: Tues.–Sat. 10am–12.30pm; 2–5pm).

★ Madre de
Deus/Museu do
Azulejo

About 500m/550yd east of the Apolónia Station is the Museu do Azulejo which is housed in part of the Madre de Deus, the former convent of the Poor Clares, founded in 1509.

This building was also largely destroyed in 1755 and rebuilt in the second half of the 18th c. The ornate main portal of the church was reconstructed in 1872 in its original Manueline style.

Although most of the interior of the church is post-1755, the two cloisters survived the earthquake almost unscathed, with the larger being Renaissance in appearance and the smaller ranking as Manueline in style. These cloisters and other convent buildings contain the azulejo museum. This has a very extensive collection of Portuguese and foreign ceramic tiles, and includes an enormous azulejo portrait of Lisbon before the 1755 earthquake with the royal palace and the Casa dos Bicos easily recognisable (open: Tues. 2–6pm, Wed.–Sun. 10am–6pm).

Upper Town (Bairro Alto)

Elevador de Santa
Justa

The Lower Town (see above) and the Upper Town (Bairro Alto) adjoining it on the west are rather bizarrely linked by the Santa Justa Elevator, near the Rossio. This wrought-iron structure is often ascribed to Gustave Eiffel but was in fact built between 1898 and 1901 according to the designs of Mesnier de Ponsard, a Portuguese of French descent.

On alighting from the Elevador de Santa Justa in the Upper Town there is a superb view of the Rossio and the chessboard street-layout of Baixa.

★ Chiado

Chiado is the quarter lying on the slope to the west of Baixa and linking the Upper Town to the Lower Town. Often the name is also given to the elegant shopping street Rua Garrett in the centre of the quarter. It derives its name from the writer and actor António Ribeiro (*c.* 1520–91), who was commonly known in Lisbon as "Chiado".

For a long time the Chiado quarter was Lisbon's most elegant shopping district. Since then, however, people have preferred to shop in streets such as Avenida de Roma and Rua Braancamp and, especially, in the Amoreiras Shopping Centre and in Baixa. Nevertheless, there are still some exclusive fashion boutiques to be found in Chiado.

Around the turn of the century and in the early 20th century Chiado was the meeting-place of writers and artists, and many a political and cultural discussion could be heard in the local cafés.

Chiado hit the headlines when a part of the quarter was destroyed by fire in 1988. Although "only" 2ha/5 acres were burned down (the main buildings ravaged were in Rua do Carmo), the very heart of Chiado was affected. During lengthy discussions about rebuilding the main alternatives put forward were either to rebuild the damaged parts of the town as truly to the original as possible, incorporating the original façades, or to redesign it completely and erect modern buildings. Finally Siza Vieira, an architect from Oporto, was asked to submit designs. The decision was taken to rebuild while retaining the original character. It was planned to complete the reconstruction of Chiado within five years. However, because of various legal and administrative problems, this could not be achieved. In the meantime, Rua do Carmo has regained something of its old splendour.

★ Convento do
Carmo

Near the upper exit from the Santa Justa Elevator is the former Convento do Carmo. Built between 1389 and 1423, most of it was destroyed in 1755, and never rebuilt. However, even the ruins of what was once Lisbon's largest church are still impressive as a Gothic monument. The open nave of the church now houses an Archaeological Museum (Museu Arqueologico), showing classical and medieval tombs and architectural fragments as well as arms and coins (open: from Apr. 1st to Sept. 30th: Mon.–Sat. 10am–6pm; from Oct. 1st to Mar. 31st: Mon.–Sat. 10am–1pm and 2–5pm).

In front of the ruins of the church, in the middle of the Largo do Carmo, stands the Chafanz do Carmo, a lavishly designed fountain decorated with figures of four dolphins.

North-west of the Convento do Carmo is the Igreja São Roque. Its sumptuous Baroque interior makes it Lisbon's most magnificent church. Built for the Jesuits with the assistance of Filippo Terzi it dates from the second half of the 16th c. The sober façade is in stark contrast to the azulejos, paintings, marble and talhas douradas (gilded wooden carving) that adorn the interior. This embellishment reaches its apotheosis in the fourth side chapel on the left, the Capela de São João Baptista, built in Rome in 1742 for King João V from the most precious of materials – marble, alabaster, semi-precious stones, gold and silver – and brought to Lisbon by sea in 1747.

Igreja São Roque

Near the church in the former Misericórdia almshouses and orphanage is the Museu de São Roque, the museum of sacred art, with exhibits that include outstanding work by Italian goldsmiths (open: Tues.–Sun. 10am–5pm).

Museu de São Roque

The Rua de S. Pedro de Alcântara leads northwards to a terrace with a fine view over the city and the Tagus (orientation table).

From here the Calçada da Gloria funicular descends to the Avenida da Liberdade (see Northern Districts) and the Praça dos Restauradores (see Lower Town). Further north-west, along the Rua de Dom Pedro V, is the highest point of the new town, the Praça do Principe Real; there is another excellent view of the city from the western corner of the square.

Praça do Principe Real

Even finer gardens than the Praça do Principe Real can be found in the Jardim Botânico opposite, dating from 1873 and richly stocked with tropical and subtropical plants. The botanical gardens are part of the Faculdade das Ciêncas, the science faculty of the university, which is located in the Classical building on the west side of the park.

Jardim Botânico

The centre of the Upper Town is the Largo do Chiado, where the Rua Garrett ends. It owes its second name, "Largo das duas Igrejas", to the two churches on it, Nossa Senhora da Encarnação (1784) in the south and the Loreto church (1517) in the north.

Largo do Chiado

Fortunately the historic Café Á Brasileira, rich in tradition, in the Rua do Carmo survived the fire unscathed. Its rooms have been declared a national monument of the architecture of the turn of the century. One of its regulars was Fernando Pessoa (see Famous People), whose statue was placed in front of the Café in 1988 on the centenary of his birth.

Café Á Brasileira

The Largo do Chiado opens into the tree-lined Praça de Camões, with a monument erected in 1867 to the famous Portuguese poet Luis de Camões (see Famous People).

Praça de Camões

From the Praça de Camões a walk north-west through a succession of streets beginning with the Rua do Loreto ends at the Igreja dos Paulistas, or Santa Catarina. The church was built in the mid-17th c. and its woodcarvings are particularly worth seeing.

Igreja dos Paulistas

Still further west is the Parliament building (Palácio de São Bento; Assembleia da República), converted from a 17th c. convent in 1834 and subsequently much altered. It also contains the National Archives, dating back to 1375.

Palácio de São Bento

Central to modern Lisbon is the Pombal Square – to the north are views of the Parque Eduardo VII and from its terrace the bustle of the Portuguese capital can be seen

Lisbon (Lisboa)

Basílica da Estrela

On the north-west edge of the inner city stands the Basílica da Estrela. The "star basilica" was built between 1779 and 1790 and its imposing twin-towered façade and high dome over the crossing make it a prominent cityscape feature. There is a good view from the dome over the city.

Queen Maria I, who died in Brazil in 1816, is interred in the church. She commissioned the building after the birth of the heir to the throne but he died before it was complete.

Jardim da Estrela

Opposite the church is the Jardim da Estrela, attractive gardens with a profusion of flowers, ponds, fountains and grottoes.

Casa Fernando Pessoa

Just to the north-west of the Jardim da Estrela, in the quarter known as Campo de Ourique (Rua Coleha da Rocha 16/18), the last house occupied by the writer Fernando Pessoa (see Famous People) is open to visitors. The house in which Pessoa lived from 1920 until his death in 1935 was restored in 1995 and made into a library.

Lapa

The district of Lapa, south-west of the Jardim da Estrela, is the hub of diplomatic life and one of Lisbon's smartest residential areas.

Teatro Nacional de São Carlos

In the south of the Upper Town is Lisbon's famous opera-house, the Teatro Nacional de São Carlos, built in Classical style between 1792 and 1795 and recently restored.

Museu do Chiado

After a complete overhaul the Museu de Arte Contemporânea was re-opened in 1994 under the name of Museu do Chiado. It displays works by Portuguese artists from 1850 to 1950 (later works are exhibited in the Centro de Arte Moderna of the Gulbenkian Institute). The collection includes pictures by Tomás da Anunciação, Marquês de Oliveira, Silva Porto, José Malhoa ("Outono"), Alfredo Keil, Columbano Bordale Pinheiro, Carlos Reis, Eduardo Viana ("A Viola"), Francisco Smith and Carlos Botelho, as well as sculpture by Soares dos Reis, Teixeira Lopes and Diogo de Macedo. There is also a small international collection which includes drawings by Rodin and French sculpture from about 1900 (open: Tues. 2–6pm, Wed.–Sun. 10am–6pm).

Northern Districts

Avenida da Liberdade

Lisbon's main traffic artery is the Avenida da Liberdade, the broad (90m/100yd) avenue, with its ten rows of trees and its gardens, and lined with shops, hotels, banks and government buildings, that runs for 1.5km/1 mile through the city from the Praça dos Restauradores (see Lower Town) to the Praça do Marquês de Pombal.

Praça do Marquês de Pombal

At the northern end of the Avenida da Liberdade, the Praça do Marquês de Pombal is an important traffic intersection with a huge monument to the Marquês de Pombal (see Famous People) at its centre.

Parque de Eduardo VII

The circular Praça merges to the north into the Edward VII Park, so named in honour of the King Edward VII's visit to Lisbon in 1903. In the upper part of the park is the Estufa Fria (cool house), an open-roofed greenhouse with slats, for sub-tropical trees and cacti. There is also a smaller hot house for tropical plants. Pools, grottoes, rocks, waterfalls and streams abound in the park and from the terrace higher up there are extensive views of the city and the Tagus estuary.

★★ Museu Calouste Gulbenkian

About 1km/¾ mile north of the Parque de Eduardo VII is the 17 acre-park of the Gulbenkian Foundation, the Fundação Calouste Gulbenkian, an institute of culture with a theatre, concert and conference halls, a library of some 400,000 volumes and the Gulbenkian Museum, one of the world's greatest private collections. The museum was opened on the centenary of

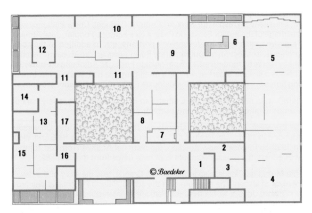

Museu Calouste Gulbenkian

1 Egyptian art
2 Greco-Roman art
3 Mesopotamian art
4 Oriental-Islamic art
5 Armenian art
6 Art from the Far East
7 Work in ivory; illuminated manuscripts
8 15th, 16th and 17th c. painting and sculpture:
  Germany, Holland, Flanders, Italy
9 Renaissance art

PERMANENT EXHIBITIONS

10 18th c. decorative art: France
11 18th c. painting and sculpture:
   France
12 18th and 19th c. silverwork: France
13 18th and 19th c. painting: England
14 18th c. painting: Italy
15 19th c. painting and sculpture:
   France

the birth of its founder, the Armenian oil magnate Calouste Sarkis Gulbenkian, who lived in Lisbon from 1942 until his death in 1955.

The modern open-plan buildings of the Gulbenkian Museum, covering an area of 25,000sq.m/30,000sq.yd, were built between 1964 and 1969 and the architects were Alberto Passoal, Pedro Cid and Ruy Athouguia. The museum highlights include the extensive and outstanding collections of Oriental art, especially from Egypt, Mesopotamia, Islam and the Far East (China and Japan), an unusually rich collection of ceramics, and important Greek and Roman antiquities, particularly a fine collection of coins.

The picture gallery has works by German artists, including a "Presentation in the Temple" (1445) by Stefan Lochner, artists from the Low Countries, such as Rubens ("Portrait of Hélène Fourment"), Thierry Bouts ("Annunciation"), Van Dyck ("Portrait of a Man"), Gossaert, Frans Hals and Rembrandt ("Pallas Athene"), the French artists Fragonard, Corot, Manet, Monet, Renoir and Degas (self-portrait), the English painters Hoppner, Gainsborough, Romney, Lawrence and Edward Burne-Jones ("Mirror of Venus"), the Venetian Carpaccio ("Virgin and Child with Donor"), and the Florentines Ghirlandaio and Guardi (ten pictures on Venetian themes).

There is also sculpture by Houdon (Diana) and Rodin (Burghers of Calais, in the inner courtyard), textiles, 18th c. French furniture and more modern jewellery (Art Nouveau by Lalique). In the tropical park around the buildings of the foundation there is a 3m/10ft high seated bronze of Calouste Gulbenkian (by L. de Almeida) in front of a stone Horus falcon. The Calouste Gulbenkian Museum is open from June to September Tues., Thur., Fri. and Sun. 10am-5pm, Mon. and Sat. 2–7.30pm; October to May Tues.–Sun. 10am–5pm.

Parque Gulbenkian

The Centro de Arte Moderna in the south-west corner of the Gulbenkian Foundation site dates from 1984 and is a lively cultural centre with a Museum of Modern Art which completes the original Gulbenkian collection which ended with Impressionism. Artists represented include Jaime Azinheira,

Centro de Arte Moderna

with his sculpture "The Kiss", Jorge Pinheiro, with "The Bishop", 1981 and an unusually disrespectful work for Catholic Portugal, Costa Pinheiro, with an image of the author Fernando Pessoa (see Famous People), José Almada Negreiros, with three interesting self-portraits, etc. In addition to the comprehensive collection of contemporary Portuguese art the Museum also has many works by modern artists from outside Portugal. Adjoining the museum there is a sculpture park as well as a multi-purpose hall, studios, etc. (opening times are the same as for the Calouste Gulbenkian Museum: see above).

Campo Grande 1km/¾ mile north-east of the Gulbenkian Foundation is the lovely park of Campo Grande with boats and outdoor cafés.

Cidade Universitária To the west of the Campo Grande lie the buildings of the University, founded in 1911. "University City" developed here between 1955 and 1960. In 1990 an imposing new building, the National Archive (Torre do Tombo) was added; the oldest document kept here dates from the year 882.

Museu da Cidade The Museu da Cidade, also in the Campo Grande, tells the story of the development of Lisbon. The museum is in the 18th c. Palácio Pimenta, at one time a gift from João V to his mistress. Particularly interesting is the scale model of Lisbon before the 1755 earthquake (open: Tues.–Sun. 10am–1pm, 2–6pm).

Museu Rafael Bordalo Pinheiro Opposite the Museu da Cidade is the Museu Rafael Bordalo Pinheiro, the museum dedicated to the artist Rafael Bordalo Pinheiro (1846–1905) who was particularly famous for his ceramics (open: Tues.–Sun. 10am–1pm, 2pm–6pm).

Museu Nacional de Trajo The National Costume museum, north of the Campo Grande in the Lumiar district (Museu Nacional de Trajo, 12 Estrada do Lumiar) is worth a visit. It is in the Palácio do Monteiro-Mor, surrounded by a large park, and features costumes throughout the ages in appropriate settings (open: Tues.–Sun. 10am–6pm).

Museu Nacional do Teatro The Theatre Museum (Museu Nacional do Teatro) is also in the Parque de Monteiro-Mor at Estrada do Lumiar 10. Displays include theatrical costumes, sets, tickets, etc., and give an overall view of theatrical history (open: Tues. 2–6pm, Wed.–Sun. 10am–6pm).

★Amoreiras Shopping Center The Amoreiras Shopping Center on the Sintra/Estoril road in the northwest of the city has, since its advent in the early Eighties, added a whole new dimension to the Lisbon scene. For its architect, Tomás Taveira, the Amoreiras (mulberry trees) is his most important, and most controversial, work to date, reflecting his "neomodern" approach and, with its interplay of colours and shapes, the idea that there is more to architecture than pure utilitarianism. Behind the bright tower block façades there are houses, offices and, of course, shopping arcades (open: daily 10am–midnight).

Centro Colombo Competition developed with the Amoreiras Shopping Centre in 1997 with the opening, near the Colégio Militar metro station, of the Centro Colombo complex. Here, spread over three floors are 420 shops – a gigantic "playcenter", not only for children and young people (open: daily 10am to midnight).

Jardin Zoológico About halfway between the Amoreiras Shopping Centre and the Centro Colombo lie the Zoological Gardens (Jardim Zoológico) (open: daily summer 9am–8pm; winter 9am–6pm). The gardens were first opened in 1884 but moved twice before opening its doors here in 1905.

Western Districts

Praça do Municipio To the west of the Praça do Comércio is the Praça do Municipio, City Hall Square, which, because of the 18th c. pelourinho with a twisted shaft in the middle, is also known as Largo do Pelourinho.

The City Hall (Câmara Municipal) on the west side of the square was built between 1865 and 1880.

Amoreiras Shopping Centre: despite the city centre, this very popular modern shopping centre is home to almost 15% of the city's retail trade

A short distance west of the Praça do Município is the Estação do Cais do Sodré, the station for trains to Cascais, and the quay for the Tagus ferries. From here, passing the market (Mercado) on the right, it is 2km/1¼ miles along the Avenida Vinte e Quatro de Julho, via the Tagus quays, to the Museu Nacional de Arte Antiga, Portugal's National Gallery.

Popularly known as the "Casa das Janelas Verdas" – house of the green windows – the National Museum of Ancient Art occupies a palace that belonged to the Marquês de Pombal and its modern extension (open: Tues. 2–6pm, Wed., Fri. and Sun. 10am–6pm, Thur. and Sat. 10am–7pm).

★★Museu Nacional de Arte Antiga (See plan page 231)

The museum owns a collection of Egyptian, Greek and Roman sculpture, ceramics and porcelain, as well as some superb silver and goldsmiths' work, ornaments, Portuguese furniture, carpets, tapestries, Indo-Portuguese craftwork and Namban art.

Numerous masterpieces are included in the collection of European paintings of the 14th–19th c. These include works by Hans Memling ("Virgin and Child"), Piero della Francesca ("St Augustine"), Dürer ("St Jerome"), Cranach ("Salome"), Holbein the Elder ("Virgin and Child with Saints"), Bassano ("Virgin with Child"), Pieter Brueghel the Younger ("The Young Man"), Velázquez, van Dyck, Reynolds, Hoppner and Romney. Hieronymus Bosch's triptych "Temptation of St Anthony" is one of the museum's most valuable treasures; thanks to the sensitive way in which it is displayed the visitor can also see the black-and-white Golgotha scenes on the reverse.

The most important of the Portuguese paintings is undoubtedly the polyptych on the Altar of St Vincent, which was found in the São Vicente de Fora convent and was restored in 1910. Doubts still exist as to the origin of the "Veneration of St Vincent" (Veneração a São Vicente); neither the exact date nor the artist have yet been definitely established, but it is generally accepted that this six-part altarpiece was painted by Nuno Gonçalves, who was court painter to Afonso V from 1450 to 1467. The work is regarded as

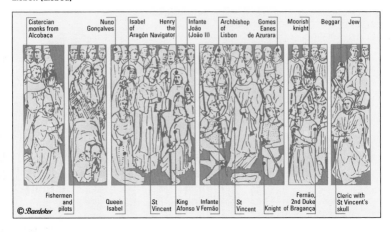

Cistercian monks from Alcobaca | Nuno Gonçalves | Isabel of Aragón | Henry the Navigator | Infante João (João III) | Archbishop of Lisbon | Gomes Eanes de Azurara | Moorish knight | Beggar | Jew

Fishermen and pilots | Queen Isabel | St Vincent | King Afonso V | Infante Fernão | St Vincent | Knight | Fernão, 2nd Duke of Bragança | Cleric with St Vincent's skull

© *Baedeker*

an important historical document, as it portrays some prominent 15th c. personalities, although art-historians also find themselves unable to agree on the identities of the persons concerned.

Palácio das Necessidades

About 1km/¾ mile north-west of the Museu Nacional de Arte Antiga is the Palácio das Necessidades, built in 1743–50 on the site of the Ermida Nossa Senhora da Necessidades. It was a royal palace until 1910 and is now occupied by the Ministry of Foreign Affairs. The adjoining park, the Tapada das Necessidades, is not usually open to the public.

★Ponte 25 de Abril

The road westward along the river bank soon comes to the Ponte 25 de Abril, or Ponte Suspensa, as the bridge is also known. The 945m/1034yd long approach-road to this toll-bridge over the Tagus rests on massive pillars. The actual suspension bridge, one of the longest in the world, was opened in 1966. It is 2277m/2471yd long, with a span of 1013m/1108yd between the piers which are 190.5m/625ft high; the carriageway is 70m/230ft above the water. It became evident some time ago that the bridge could no longer cope with the ever-increasing volume of traffic, and discussions were held over a period of years in an attempt to seek a solution to the traffic problem. Now it is hoped that with the opening of the Ponte Vasco da Gama over the Tagus (built 1995–98) to the east of the city centre, the traffic situation will be eased. (See Baedeker Special p. 213).

Museu da Electricade

The most recent museum to be opened in Lisbon is the Electricity Museum on the banks of the Tagus (on the edge of the suburb of Belém). It is housed in the red and white-painted headquarters of the "Central Tejo" electricity company (open: Tues.–Sun. 10am–12.30pm and 2–5.30pm).

Belém

Belém, short for Bethlehem, the south-western suburb of Lisbon, is on the right bank of the Tagus at the point where the river begins to open out again as it enters the sea. Its fine old buildings and fascinating museums probably warrant a whole day there (map on p. 235).

Praça do Império

It is suggested that a tour of Belém might commence from the Praça do Império, in front of the Mosteiro dos Jerónimos (from here a miniature railway goes to the most important tourist sights of Belém). This square

Museu Nacional de Arte Antiga of Lisbon

Casa das Janelas Verdes

National Museum of Art Lisbon

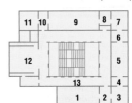

SECOND FLOOR

FIRST FLOOR

©Baedeker

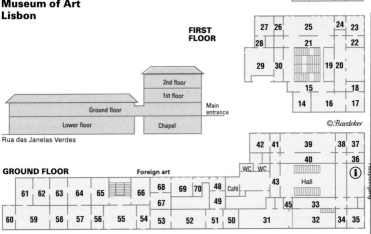

Rua das Janelas Verdes

GROUND FLOOR Foreign art

1 Portraits (15th–19th c.)	20/21 Chinese porcelain (12th–19th c.)	31 St Albert's convent chapel
2–9 Portuguese painting (16th/17th c.)	22 Portuguese porcelain (19th c.)	33–35 Textiles
10/11 Portuguese painting (17th–19th c.)	23–25 Portuguese ceramics (17th–19th c.)	36–43 Furniture (15th–19th c.)
12/13 Sculptures (16th–19th c.)	26–30 Gold and silversmiths' work (12th–19th c.)	45 Gulbenkian Room
14–19 Oriental art		48–65 European painting (14th–19th c.)
		66–70 Applied art (17th–19th c.)

was laid out on the occasion of the World Exhibition of 1940. It consists mainly of a small park with hedges cut in the shape of the various municipal coats of arms of Portugal. The large fountain in the centre is also decorated with coats of arms and is illuminated on special occasions.

Adjoining the Praça do Império to the west is the Centro Cultural, opened in 1993. It consists of a conference centre and two concert halls

Centro Cultural

Works of Art – underfoot

"... and the floor is mosaic-like, of small black and white stones laid in wavy strips snaking their way across the width of the square, while a multi-patterned black and white background produces a colourful and cheerful wavy effect overall. On the two shorter sides of the square these black and white backgrounds are marked with a series of numbers. Exactly what their purpose is I cannot say; perhaps they are an aid to easier identification of damaged sections if they should require replacement ..." these were the words of Heinrich Karl Brandes when describing the Rossio in his "Journey to Portugal in the Summer of 1863".

Following the 1755 earthquake the people of Lisbon conceived the idea of making small paving-stones from the marble debris with which to cover pavements and squares in a lasting and artistic manner. A happy idea! Thus, in many parts of Lisbon – and in many other Portuguese towns and villages – one finds mosaic surfaces with black and white stones (the black ones are volcanic basalt) with a great variety of subjects and patterns. They can be seen on city squares (near the Rossio on the Praça do Império with the signs of the zodiac), on streets such as the Avenida da Liberdade, in pedestrian zones and on pavements. Sometimes they incorporate simple geometric patterns, sometimes animals or inscriptions, or house numbers and coats of arms (especially the Lisbon municipal arms).

This artistic and laborious work is carried out by the *calceteiros*. If you are lucky you may be able to watch them at work – as they sit on the sidewalk with a mosaic stone in their hand and chip away at it with a hammer until it attains the required shape and will fit a wooden mould laid on the carefully levelled ground. These moulds are carefully preserved old wooden templates. So that the joins

between the stones are as small as possible each mosaic must be cut very accurately. It is doubtful whether one will be able to enjoy watching the stone-masons at work for much longer, as it is a dying trade. The work is too costly, toilsome and extremely badly paid – asphalt is much cheaper. Whereas there were some 400 *calceteiros* at work in Lisbon in the early years of this century, now there are fewer than 30. They will in future be employed only to carry out repairs and maintenance.

Plaster mosaic of discovery in Belém

with seats for 400 and 1500 respectively. There are also large rooms reserved for exhibitions.

On the north side of the spacious Praça do Império, with its large illuminated fountain (Fonte Luminos) surrounded by formal gardens, is the crowning glory of Belém, the world-famous Hieronymite monastery, the Mosteiro dos Jerónimos de Belém. This is the supreme achievement of Manueline architecture and the most impressive symbol of Portugal's power and wealth in the age of the great colonial conquests (open: Tues.–Sun. 10am–noon and 2–5pm).

★★Mosteiro dos Jerónimos de Belém

The origins of the monastery go back to a chapel for seamen built here by Henry the Navigator, within easy reach of the harbour at Restelo from where the voyages of discovery set out, and served by the Knights of Christ. Tradition has it that Vasco da Gama spent the nights before sailing for India in 1497 praying in this chapel; and here, too, he was received by the king on his triumphant return. To commemorate and give thanks for the voyage Manuel I built on the site of the little chapel one of the most splendid buildings in Portugal, and indeed the whole of Christendom. The building of the monastery began in 1502 to the plans of Boytaca, who was also concerned in the construction of Batalha Abbey (see entry). The detailed work was carried out in 1517–22 under the direction of João de Castilho, who also built the cloister. After the dissolution of the monastery in 1834 it was occupied by the Casa Pia orphanage.

At the south-east corner of the complex is the three-aisled church of Santa Maria, with a magnificent south front. The south doorway (by João de Castilho) and the west doorway (by Nicolas Chanterène) are particularly fine. The choir, in High Renaissance style, was added in 1571–72.

In the spacious interior (92m/302ft long, 22.6m/74ft wide and 25m/82ft high) the octagonal piers are richly decorated with reliefs. In the magnificent transepts and apse are the tombs, borne on elephants, of Manuel I and his successors and relatives – a total of five kings, seven queens and nineteen princes and princesses of the House of Avis. Under the organ-loft are the sarcophaguses of Vasco da Gama and Luís de Camões (who died of the plague in 1580). In the Coro Alto (access from cloister) are fine Renaissance choir-stalls (1560).

On the north side of the church is the splendid two-storey Cloister (Claustro) around a square courtyard, each side 55m/180ft long and the masterpiece of João de Castilho. In the north-west corner is a Lion Fountain, which once stood in a basin in the middle of the cloister. Here, too, is the entrance to the former Refectory which has beautiful reticulated vaulting and rich azulejo decoration (17th c.) on the walls. At the north-east corner of the cloister is the former Chapterhouse, which contains the tombs of the writer and politican João Baptista da Silva Leitão

Mosteiro dos Jerónimos de Belém (Lisboa)

Hieronymite Monastery of Belém (Lisbon)

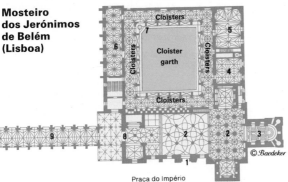

© Baedeker

Praça do Império

1 South door
2 Church of Santa Maria de Belém
3 Choir
4 Sacristy
5 Chapterhouse
6 Refectorium
7 Fountain of Lions
8 West door
9 National Museum of Archaeology in former Dormitorium (Dorter)

233

The Praça do Império with the façade of the Mosteiro dos Jerónimos

de Almeida Garrett (1799–1854), the historian Alexander Herculano (1810–77) and Oscar António de Fragosa Carmona (1869–1951), President of Portugal from 1928 until his death.

Museu Nacional de Arqueologia

In the unfinished south wing of the cloister is the Dorter (dormitory), which now houses the National Museum of Archaeology (Museu Nacional de Arqueologia; open: Tues. 2–6pm, Wed.–Sun. 10am–6pm). In temporary exhibitions the earliest evidence of metalworking, agriculture and fishing will be given. A film shows the places where the archaeological exhibits were found. Of special interest is a display of pieces of jewellery and a collection of Egyptian artefacts.

Museu da Marinha

The west wing of the monastery is the interesting Naval Museum (Museu da Marinha). Here and in the modern extension to the west a series of models of ships tell the story of Portuguese navigation. The two 18th c. ceremonial barges are particularly worth seeing (open: Tues.–Sun. 10am–5pm, in summer to 6pm).

Planetário Calouste Gulbenkian

Between the two parts of the Naval Museum is the Calouste Gulbenkian Planetarium (1965; performances: Wed., Thur. 11am, 3pm, 4.15pm, Sat., Sun. 5pm).

Praça de Afonso de Albuquerque

Nearby, to the east of the Convento dos Jerónimos, is the Praça de Afonso de Albuquerque, with a monument in the middle to Afonso de Albuquerque (c. 1450–1515), the second Portuguese Viceroy of the East Indies.

Palácio de Belém/Museu dos Coches

On the north side of the square stands the former royal palace, the Palácio de Belém, built by the Conde de Aveiro in 1700, which is now the residence of the President of Portugal.

On the ground floor of the east wing the former Riding School (built 1726) now houses the National Coach Museum (Museu Nacional dos Coches), one of the largest and most valuable collections of its kind, with

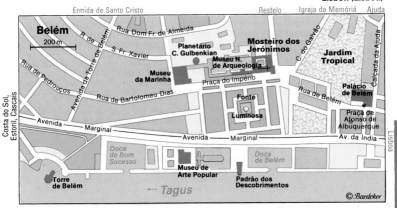

Ermida de Santo Cristo   Restelo   Igreja da Memóriá   Ajuda

Belém
200 m

Rua Dom Fr. de Almeida
R. de Belém
S. Fr. Xavier
Avenida da Torre de Belém
Rua de Pedrouços
Rua de Bartolomeu Dias

Planetário C. Gulbenkian

Mosteiro dos Jerónimos

C. do Galvão

Museu N. de Arqueologia

Museu da Marinha

Praça do Império

Jardim Tropical

Rua de Belém

Palácio de Belém

Calçada da Ajuda

Fonte Luminosa

Praça de Afonso de Albuquerque

Costa do Sol, Estoril, Cascais

Avenida — Marginal

Avenida — Marginal

Av. da Índia

Lisboa

Doca de Bom Sucesso

Doca de Belém

Museu de Arte Popular

Torre de Belém

← *Tagus*

Padrão dos Descobrimentos

© *Baedeker*

some 60 state and ceremonial coaches and carriages from the 17th to the 19th c. (open: Tues.–Sun. 10am–6pm).

Padrão dos Descobrimentos

To the south of the Praça do Império, on the banks of the Tagus, towers the 54m/175ft high Monument of the Discoveries (Padrão dos Descobrimentos), in the form of a ship's prow, erected in 1960, the 500th anniversary of the death of Prince Henry the Navigator. It commemorates the Portuguese seamen who set out from here in the 15th c. on their voyages of discovery. At the head of the row of people on the prow stands Henry the Navigator, a model ship in his hands. Inside there is a lecture

Cloister of the Hieronymite convent

235

theatre and several smaller rooms with displays, including one of photographs relating to the discovery period. A lift takes visitors up to the observation platform on top of the monument. The mosaic in the square in front of the monument is of a compass with a map of the world.

Museu de Arte Popular

To the west of the Monument of the Discoveries the Museu de Arte Popular is a museum of folk art with a large collection of Portuguese costumes, tools, furniture, domestic utensils, pottery, etc. arranged according to provinces (open: Tues.–Sun. 10am–12.30pm, 2–5pm).

★★Torre de Belém

✗

Some 500m/550yd farther west, on the Tagus, is the Belém Tower, the Torre de Belém, in the purest Manueline style, built in 1512–21 to protect the harbour of Restelo at the entrance to the Tagus. The tower was long used as a state prison. After the capture of Lisbon in 1807 French troops destroyed the top two storeys of the tower but these were restored to their original splendour in 1845. Facing the Tagus the tower has a bastion with embrasures and, below the waterline, powder and storage chambers.

The tower itself (open: Tues.–Sun. 10am–5pm, in summer to 6.30pm) contains the "King's Chamber" taking up the whole width of the main façade, and the Governor's room. The furnishings are not the originals.

There are fine views from the tower platform over Belém and the Tagus.

Palácio Nacional da Ajuda

To the east of the Paço de Belém the Calçada da Ajuda leads 1km/¾ mile upstream to the Palácio Nacional da Ajuda. This former royal palace was begun in 1802 but never completed. Finely situated above Belém, it now contains the Monument Protection Office. On the way there the road passes the Adjuda Botanic Garden (on left: view), with a dragon tree planted in 1598.

Museu de Etnologia

About 600m/656yd west of the Palácio Nacional da Ajuda, in the Avenida Ilha da Madeira, is the ethnological museum, the Museu de Etnologia. Although the museum was only opened in 1985 there is room for no more than the most important exhibits to be put on display, so there are changing exhibitions on various themes (open: Tues. 2–6pm, Wed., Fri. and Sun. 10am–6pm, Thur. and Sat. 10am–7pm).

Parque Florestal de Monsanto

North of the Ajuda district is the extensive Monsanto Forest Park (Parque Florestal de Monsanto, campsites) which is traversed by the western motorway. In the northern half is an old fort, the Forte de Monsanto.

Aqueduto das Águas Livres

Along the north-west edge of the park runs the Aqueduto das Águas Livres (1728–48), an aqueduct 18km/11 miles long which supplies Lisbon with its drinking water.

Benfica

Benfica, once an elegant suburb on the north-west edge of Lisbon, has undergone rapid expansion in recent decades and today its townscape is predominantly one of highrise and shopping centres.

Estádio do Benfica

The suburb is known far beyond the frontiers of Portugal as the home of Benfica, Lisbon's famous football club, whose large stadium, the Estádio do Benfica (completed in 1944) on the Avenida do Marechal Carmona, holds 60,000 spectators.

Igreja São Domingos

In the Largo de São Domingos stands the church of São Domingos, belonging to a Dominican convent which was founded in 1399 and rebuilt after the 1755 earthquake.

It contains azulejo pictures by António de Oliveira. The marbles in the Capela de São Gonçalo are also worth seeing.

Casa dos Marqueses de Fronteira

Near the church is the Casa dos Marqueses de Fronteira, a palatial 17th c. mansion. In the beautiful gardens is a pool surrounded by blind arcades decorated with azulejo pictures. The palace is privately owned but is open to the public, as are the gardens (guided tours daily 10.45am: however, this time changes frequently; it is best to enquire from the tourist information office in Lisbon on tel. 7782023).

Surroundings of Lisbon

Visible from Lisbon centre, the Christ the King Monument (Monumento Cristo Rei) stands on the south bank of the Tagus. Erected in 1959, it consists of a base 82m/270ft high (containing a chapel) topped by a 28m/90ft high reinforced concrete figure of Christ.
   A lift takes you up to a platform from which there is a sweeping view of Lisbon.

Monumento Cristo Rei

The little port of Cacilhas is on a promontory below the town of Almada and can be reached by ferry from Lisbon. Its good fish restaurants make it very popular with visitors and there is also a fine view from here of the terraces of houses on the north bank of the Tagus.

Cacilhas

From Cacilhas a road runs along the Tagus and then a little way inland to the west coast and the resort of Costa da Caparica (see Costa de Lisboa).

Costa da Caparica

12km/7½ miles north of Lisbon, at Odivelas, is the Cistercian Convento de São Dinis e São Bernardo (1295–1305), which was partly destroyed in the 1755 earthquake and rebuilt in Baroque style from 1757 onwards. In the church is the tomb of King Dinis, founder of this convent.

Odivelas

15km/9 miles north of Lisbon, on the Rio Trancão, is the little town of Loures, where the wooden carving in the 17th c. parish church (Igreja Matriz) is worth seeing. The nearby Quinta do Correio-Mór, a palace with a Baroque main block and two wings, contains azulejos, stucco decoration and paintings by José da Costa Negreiro; the kitchen (18th c.) has azulejo pictures.

Loures

In Lousa, 10km/6 miles farther north-east, the church of São Pedro has a fine Manueline doorway and azulejo decoration; in front of the church is a large fountain.
   Near the church of São Miguel is the Manueline doorway of a demolished church, now incorporated in a house.

Lousa

From Lousa it is about 15km/9 miles to Mafra (see entry) with its enormous convent palace.

Mafra

The Vasco da Gama aquarium in the suburb of Algés holds the oceanographic collection of King Carlos I, as well as all kinds of fish from Portugal's coastal waters and the former overseas territories (open daily: 10am–6pm).

Aquário Vasco da Gama

It makes a pleasant trip to travel westward along the Costa do Sol, with the popular resorts of Estoril and Cascais (see entries).

Costa do Sol, Estoril, Cascais

It would also be a pity to leave this part of Portugal without visiting picturesque Sintra (see entry), with its two palaces, and the castle of Queluz (see entry).

Sintra, Queluz

Loulé   B 7

Historical province: Algarve. District: Faro
Altitude: 170m/560ft. Population: 9000

Loulé

Set in fertile countryside Loulé, just 15km/9½ miles north-west of Faro,
chief town of the district, is an important market centre; its big Saturday
market attracts many local and foreign visitors. Handicrafts are also an
important part of its economy and the narrow alleys of the old town are
full of potters, saddlers and coppersmiths.

The town's main claim to fame, however, is its carnival that takes
place every year on the four days before Ash Wednesday, and the
almond blossom festival.

Townscape

A detour to Loulé is worthwhile for the many beautifully decorated chimneys on the white-washed houses. No two are alike, and most house-
holders have given their imagination free rein to produce minor works
of art.

Sights

Castelo

Part of the walls are all that remain of the old castle complex which
probably dates back to Moorish times. Near the tourist information
office a flight of stone steps leads up to the castle walls.

Convento do
Espírito Santo/
Museu Municipal

Close by, in a wing of the tastefully restored Convento do Espirito Santo,
is the Municipal Museum (open: Mon.–Fri. 9am–12.30pm and 2–5pm).
The convent, founded in the late 17th c., was partially destroyed by the
1755 earthquake and dissolved in 1836.

Ermida de Nossa
Senhora da
Conceição

Opposite the convent can be seen the simple façade of the Ermida de
Nossa Senhora da Conceição. The chapel was built in the mid-17th c. in
gratitude for Portugal having regained its independence from Spain.

Igreja Matriz de
São Clemente

The chief church in Loulé lies in the old town between Largo da Silva and
Largo da Matriz. Its origins date back to the second half of the 13th c.

The village of Salir in the Algarve hinterland region

Surroundings of Loulé

2km/1¼ miles west of Loulé along the road to Boliqueime stands the 16th c. Capela de Nossa Senhora da Piedade. A pilgrims' way leads up the hill. From the square in front of the church there is a magnificent view of the hilly countryside to the north and the sea to the south.

Capela de Nossa Senhora da Piedade

Alte is an extremely pretty village 25km/15½ miles north-west of Loulé, in the midst of some relatively unspoiled and hilly countryside. In recent years, however, increasing numbers of tourists have been attracted here, and it is to be hoped that its appearance will not change too rapidly as a result. As well as its rural setting, the village itself is most attractive, with its white-washed Algarve houses, narrow streets, gardens filled with flowers and hanging baskets.

★Alte

Almost as attractive as Alte is the considerably quieter village of Salir, resting on two hills 15km/9½ miles to the east. On the hill to the west there are some scattered remains of a Moorish castle. The Castelo quarter, with its tiny white houses and many flowers, is particularly idyllic.

Salir

Madeira/Archipélago da Madeira

Autonomous Region of Madeira (Região Autónoma da Madeira)
Area of islands: 791sq.km/305sq. miles. Population: 300,000

The archipelago of Madeira lies in the Atlantic some 535 nautical miles south-west of Lisbon and 240 miles north of Tenerife in the Canaries, between latitude 33°7' and 30°1' north and between longitude 15°51' and 17°15' west.
   The group consists of the main island of Madeira, rising from a depth of 4000–5000m/13,000–16,500ft below sea level to an average height of something over 800m/2600ft, with an area of 741sq.km/286sq. miles (length 57km/35 miles, width 22km/14 miles), together with the island of Porto Santo (highest point 507m/1663ft), 23 miles north-east, and the three almost uninhabited islets of Ilhéu Chão, Deserta Grande and Ilhéu do Bugio, 11 nautical miles south-west. Also belonging to the group are the five uninhabited Ilhas Selvagens ("Wild Islands"; area 4sq.km/1½sq. miles) which lie some 170 miles south on the northern fringe of the Canaries.

Location and General

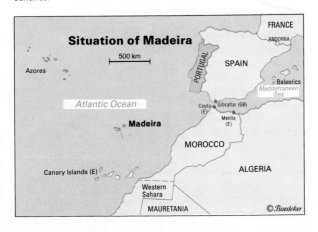

Funchal, Madeira's capital lies picturesquely on the south coast surrounded by lush subtropical vegetation. With a population of approx. 120,000 Funchal is home to almost half of the archipelago's population

Madeira/Archipélago da Madeira

★★ Topography
All the islands in the archipelago are hilly and, like the Spanish Canaries, of volcanic origin. The oldest diabase formations have thus been overlaid since the Miocene period by many volcanic craters, now extinct (lagoas). The later upthrust of the underlying rocks to some 400m/1300ft above their original level also parallels that of the Canaries.

The backbone of Madeira is a range of mountains with jagged ridges reminiscent of the Dolomites which runs in an east–west direction, reaching its highest point in the Pico Ruivo (Red Peak) de Santana (1861m/6106ft). In the west of the island is the Paúl de Serra plateau, in the east the smaller plateau of Santo António da Serra.

On the southern and northern slopes of the range are the magnificent rugged valleys, enclosed within high cliffs, known as *currais* (singular *curral*), which make their way down to the sea in deep eroded gorges, patterned with alternating layers of volcanic ash and lava. The gorges on the north coast are particularly impressive.

The coasts of Madeira are steep and rocky, with narrow strips of coastal plain only here and there as the lava flows reach the sea.

Climate
Madeira owes its mild and equable climate to its southern latitude and its location in the open Atlantic. The daily and annual ranges of temperature on the sunny and sheltered south coast are lower than in any Mediterranean resort. The average January temperature in Funchal is 16.2°C/61.2°F, the average for July 29.8°C/85.6°F. The average annual rainfall is 590mm/23in., with five times as much rain in the north as in the south. Most of the rain falls between October and January or March in the form of cloudbursts. The number of hours of sunshine for the year averages 2124 (minimum of 97 hours in January, maximum of 251 hours in August). In spite of the nearness of the sea the relative humidity of the air is low (68%).

Water temperature averages 17.4°C/63.6°F in February, 22.4°C/72.3°F in September. From time to time there is a hot east wind, the *leste*, that blows from Africa carrying dust with it. Here it remains within tolerable limits, driving away the banks of cloud which regularly form in the middle of the day at a height of 1200–1500m/4000–5000ft.

Vegetation
Madeira's vegetation – the *flor do oceano*, flower of the ocean – is of almost tropical luxuriance, thanks to the mildness of the climate, the abundant winter rains and the system of irrigation which carries water from the hills to the fields and gardens along the coast through countless canals (*levadas*) and underground tunnels (*furados*). The trees which grow here include not only pines and European deciduous species but also a great range of evergreen trees and shrubs of subtropical and tropical origin: palms, araucarias, hickory, cork-oaks, camphor trees, fig-trees, yuccas, medlars, mimosa, eucalyptus, bamboos, papyrus, tree ferns, agaves, etc. There are also small numbers of dragon trees, wild laurels and Oreodaphne foetens (Portuguese tíl), a handsome tree of the laurel family which is found only on Madeira. These relics of the primeval forest which once covered the island and gave it its name are now found only in the gorges on the north coast and are protected by law.

The gardens of Funchal, usually surrounded by high walls, are filled in winter and particularly spring with a glorious profusion of flowers of every hue: roses, camellias, rhododendrons, azaleas, pelargoniums, begonias, bignonias (including *jacaranda cuspidifolia*), daturas, bougainvillea, wisteria and many more.

Population
The population, originally purely Portuguese and still exclusively Portuguese-speaking, has in the course of the centuries received an admixture of Moorish, Jewish, Italian and African blood, particularly on the south coast. The high population density (320 to the sq.km, or 829 to the sq. mile) and the predominance of large landholdings have long been reflected in a high emigration rate, particularly to South America (Brazil). Since Portugal joined the European Union a number of these emigrants have returned.

History
According to legend Madeira was part of the lost kingdom of Atlantis. The islands were known to the Phoenicians, and in the time of King Juba II of

242

Mauretania (1st c. B.C.) they were called the Insulae Purpuriae, after the purple dye produced there. When they were rediscovered by the Portuguese navigator João Gonçalves Zarco in 1419 they were uninhabited and covered with dense forest, hence the name Ilha da Madeira – island of timber.

After the Portuguese colonisation Madeira prospered by the growing of sugar-cane and later also by the production of wine. Together with mainland Portugal and the Azores it was under Spanish rule from 1580 to 1640. Between 1807 and 1814 it was occupied by Britain. The influx of tourists (at first mainly British) began in the middle of the 19th c. and has grown steadily since then.

Only about a third of the island's area can be cultivated. Soon after Madeira's rediscovery in the 16th c. deforestation by burning was begun, leading to the almost total destruction of the natural forest. Thereafter centuries of effort went into building up thousands of terraces (*poios*) on the hillsides which now constitute the major part of the cultivable land and give the island its characteristic appearance from the sea.

Economy

Since 1452 sugar-cane was one of Madeira's most important products. In the 20th c., however it declined considerably in importance, and the few remaining sugar plantations supply small distilleries with sugar which is used in providing "aguardente de cana". Today the main crops include bananas, sweet potatoes, grain and early vegetables of all kinds. Much fruit is also grown, including, in addition to melons and grapefruit, such less usual species as the sugar apple or sweet-sop (anona), passion fruit (maracuja) and loquat. Wine production was introduced to Madeira soon after the discovery of the island and developed on a flourishing scale from the 17th c. onwards, only to suffer subsequent setbacks as a result of a grape disease (*oïdium tuckeri*, from 1852) and phylloxera (1878–88) and also from competition from the port produced on the mainland. The main wine-producing area lies west of Funchal, around Câmara de Lobos, Estreito and Campanário.

The intensive use of even the smallest cultivable area is only possible because of the irrigation system that has been in place for centuries whereby countless canals (*levadas*) carry the water from the north of the island, where rain is plentiful, to the south which is drier but where the farming is more intense.

Further contributions to the economy are made by cattle-farming, and the dairy produce associated with it, and, along the coasts, fishing for tuna, mackerel, etc.

Needlework has been an additional source of income since the mid 19th c. when the craft was introduced by an Englishwoman named Miss Phelps. Nowadays Madeira's internationally famous embroidery employs some 30,000 women, most of them working at home. Baskets made in the workshops at Camacha are mostly for export (mainly to South America and South Africa).

Tourism nowadays is another more substantial factor in the economy. The first prosperous English visitors came to Madeira in the mid 19th c., and they still come in large numbers today, but the island is also a popular winter destination for Scandinavians and Germans. Madeira has around 20,000 hotel bedspaces altogether, many of them in the de luxe category. About 350,000 holidaymakers overnight here in a year, plus a further 60,000 or so cruise passengers.

Tourism

The attraction for most visitors to Madeira is the pleasant climate and the luxuriant vegetation, but many also come for the unique opportunities for walking that exist on the island because of the narrow paths installed for the repair of the levadas. These paths now function as a network of walks, many of them easy to use and lined with flowers, others only a foot's width and difficult for even the most experienced walker. As Madeira cannot boast much in the way of beaches it is not really a suitable holiday destination for families with children or for those who love to spend much of their to spend much of their time on the beach. The only good beaches are to be found on the neighbouring island of Porto Santo.

Funchal

Situation and Importance

Funchal (from *funcho*, i.e. fennel), capital of the archipelago, a seat of a university, a hotel college and the see of a Roman Catholic bishop, is picturesquely situated amid rich subtropical vegetation on the south coast of Madeira. It has a population of about 120,000 and as the only port of any size on the island, though often exposed to heavy surf, it is an important port of call for cruise ships. The town's steep streets, like most streets in the hilly parts of the island, are paved with smooth round basalt cobbles which make stout footwear very desirable. The *carros de cesta*, which now serve more as a tourist attraction than a means of transport, are toboggans with a basketwork frame that depend for their motive power on the force of gravity and are controlled by ropes held by two men running alongside. The ox-drawn *carros de bois*, the other sleds that used to transport goods and people around Funchal, have become museum pieces.

There is plenty to do of an evening in the island capital, with theatres, cinemas, casino and nightclubs, and folk-dancing displays almost every night in one or other of the large hotels. A traditional firework display greets the New Year. The most popular souvenirs are wickerwork, embroidery and, of course, Madeira wine.

★★Townscape

Funchal is ranged amphitheatre-like on hillslopes climbing up to 1200m/3936ft, with some of its outskirts as high as 550m/1804ft above sea level, making it a spectacular sight, particularly seen from the sea. Hotels have come increasingly to dominate the townscape; almost all Madeira's 12,000 hotel beds are in Funchal, and not all of these establishments share the venerable appearance of Reid's Hotel which dates from 1891. However, around nearly every hotel, and private villa as well, there are superb parks and gardens – Funchal has trees and flowers wherever you look.

West town centre

Near the seafront promenade, the Avenida das Comunidades Madeirenses, is the Palácio de São Lourenço (16th c.; much altered in later

1 Quinta Vigia
  (Quinta Angustias)
2 Theatre

3 Palácio de São Lourenço
4 Antiga Alfândega
  (Old Customs House)

5 Vicentes Photographic
  Museum
6 Museum of Sacred Art

7 Convent church of Santa
  Clara
8 Quinta das Cruzes

periods), the first fort built on Madeira and now the Governor's Palace (not open to the public). In front of the Governor's Palace, reaching out into the sea, is the Cais (landing stage) and alongside it the new marina.

Over from the Governor's Palace, to the north-west, is the start of the Jardim de São Francisco, a park luxuriantly planted with palms and other tropical species. On the south side of the park is the theatre, the teatro, built at the turn of the century.

Just east of the park, and worth a visit, is Vicente's photography museum, containing the original photographer's studio founded in 1865, and hence Portugal's first, by Vicente Gomes da Silva, where many historical pictures of Madeira are also on display.

Back on the Avenida do Dr Manuel de Arriaga, this runs westward into the Praça do Infante, and above this square, to the south-west, is the little chapel of Santa Catarina (15th c.), one of the oldest churches on the island, with beyond it the Parque de Santa Catarina, on the site of an old cemetery, the Cemitério das Augustas. The pink building on the west side of the park is the Quinta Vigia, also known as Quinta das Angústias, where Madeira's government is based. The original Quinta Vigia, once home to the Austrian Empress Elisabeth (Sissi), had to give way to the Casino Hotel. Next to it is the round casino building, with a fine view of the town from its terrace.

From the west end of the Avenida das Comunidades Madeirenses the Rua da Pontinha continues south-west along the seafront, passing below the Parque de Santa Catarina to the old Molhe da Pontinha, a breakwater begun in the 18th c. and several times extended, below the Fort of Nossa Senhora da Conceição. From the end of the breakwater there is a fine general view of the town.

The harbour promenade east of the new marina has been given a recent facelift, and the floating cafés include the "Beatles Boat" which actually belonged to the Beatles at one time.

East town centre

The old Customs House, the Antiga Alfândega, is on the other side of the Avenida das Comunidades Madeirenses. Little is left of the 16th c. original, and there was considerable rebuilding in the 18th c.

Just north of the Customs House the relatively new pedestrian precinct leads to the cathedral, the Sé, which is Manueline and was built between 1485 and 1514 – the first Portuguese cathedral overseas. The interior has an interesting ceiling of juniper-wood with ivory inlay.

To the east of the cathedral is the market, the Mercado, with fine tiling decorating the main entrance. It is at its busiest on Fridays and Saturdays when farmers bring in their produce from the surrounding villages. Beyond the Campo Dom Carlos I, the former drill ground, to the east of the beach is the Forte de São Tiago, built in 1614 and named after St James the Less, patron saint of Funchal. Close by is the church of Nossa Senhora do Socorro (or Santa Maria Maior), where a great procession is held on May 1st every year commemorating the plague of 1538.

The Câmara Municipal (town hall), begun in 1758, is on the east side of the Praça do Municipio, which is flanked on the north-west by the 17th c. collegiate church of São João Evangelista. On the south side of the square (entrance at 21 Rue do Bispo) is the former Bishop's Palace containing a Museum of Sacred Art, with an important collection of Flemish paintings (expected to close soon for renovations).

North town centre

A stroll westward from the Praça do Municipio passes through the Rua C. Pestana and then on up to the church of São Pedro, its interior clad entirely with tiles, and the Municipal Museum of Natural History opposite, which has its own library and small aquarium. The steep Calçada de Santa Clara leads up to the former convent church of the same name (the oldest convent on the island: it is now a kindergarten), containing the tomb of the navigator João Gonçalves Zarco, who rediscovered Madeira in 1419. North-west of the church is the Quinta das Cruzes, set in beautiful gardens and said to have been where the Zarcos lived. The manor house (1745) is now a museum of the island's cultural history (furniture made from sugar-crates, azulejos, silver from the Gulbenkian Foundation, and parts of a sunken Dutch sailing ship). The park contains carvings in stone ranging from the 15th to the 19th c. including the original town pillory (pelourinho). Continuing north-west up the Calçada do Pico and turning left along Rua do Castelo we come to the Forte de São João do Pico (1632), famed for its view. Below it lies the English Protestant Cemetery (1765).

★★Botanic Garden

About 4km/2½ miles north-east of Funchal centre, on the old estate of Quinta do Bom Sucesso, is the very fine Botanic Garden (Jardim Botánico), with a rich and varied collection of plants and flowers. From the terraces there are delightful views.

Excursions on Madeira

Madeira's roads are good, albeit often narrow and winding. Some byroads are paved rather than asphalted, making it advisable to keep average speeds down to about 30kmph/20mph.

Funchal to Faial via Monte (about 35km/22 miles)

★Monte

From Funchal a good road winds its way up between handsome villas and beautiful gardens to the little town of Monte (alt. 550m/1804ft; pop. 8000), 8km/5 miles north. Set amid magnificent plane and oak-forests, this was once a popular health resort.

On a spur of hill near the old cableway station is the pilgrimage church of Nossa Senhora do Monte (founded 1470, completely rebuilt in the 18th

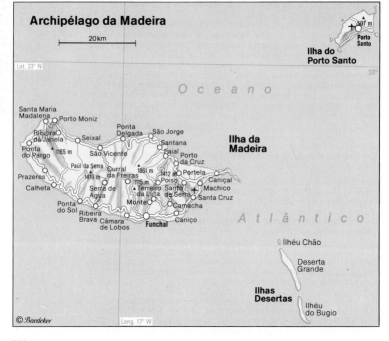

c.), with the tomb of Karl of Habsburg, the last Austrian Emperor, who died in the nearby Quinta do Monte in 1922. From the terrace in front of the church (68 steps) there is a superb view of Funchal and the sea, extending south-west as far as Cabo Girão. At the foot of the flight of steps is the Neo-Baroque chapel of Nossa Senhora da Conceição (1906).

From here it is possible either to return direct to Funchal – perhaps in one of the local wickerwork toboggans – or to walk down by a longer route (3 hours) on beautiful footpaths.

An attractive alternative is to continue 3km/2 miles north (either by road or on footpaths) to Terreiro da Luta (876m/2874ft), with a statue of Nossa Senhora da Paz (Our Lady of Peace, 1918, commemorating the end of the First World War) and even more extensive views than from the church at Monte. | Terreiro da Luta

From Terreira da Luta the road continues up through the hills and reaches in another 6km/4 miles the pass on Pico Poiso (1412m/4633ft). | Pico Poiso

From here a good road (7km/4¼ miles) goes off left to viewpoints on the Pico de Juncal (1800m/5941ft) and Pico do Arieiro (1810m/5940ft), the second highest summit on the island. From both of these viewpoints there are magnificent panoramas of Madeira's central mountain range. Close to the car park is the Pico de Juncal viewing terrace (1800m/5908ft). | ★★Pico do Arieiro

From the Poiso pass it is another 20km/12½ miles through wild mountain scenery to the little town of Faial. | Faial

Funchal to Curral das Freiras (14km/9 miles)

The road runs north-west from Funchal, at first through hilly country, well wooded and bright with flowers. After 6km/4 miles it reaches Pico dos Barcelos (355m/1165ft). From the viewpoint terrace, with its profusion of flowers, there is a magnificent prospect of the south coast of Madeira. | Pico dos Barcelos

The road continues uphill, with many bends, through a forest of euca-lyptus trees and passing a number of superb viewpoints, to Eira do Serrado (1026m/3366ft), the "Serrado saddle" on the north-east edge of the Pico Serrado. From the saddle itself, and particularly from the nearby summit of the Pico Serrado (literally, sawn-off peak, 1115m/3658ft), there is perhaps the very best view of Madeira's central mountain range, extending from the Pico Ruivo (1861m/6106ft) and Pico Arieiro (1810m/5939ft) in the east to the Pico Grande (1607m/5273ft) and Pico do Jorge (1692m/5515ft) in the west. | Pico Serrado

From the saddle it is possible either to drive down on the modern road or to walk down the old bridle-path, endlessly twisting and turning, into the Curral das Freiras (nuns' valley) or Gran Curral, the crater of an extinct volcano, enclosed within high rock walls. | ★Curral das Freiras

Far below, above the rock-strewn bed of the Ribeira dos Socorridos, can be seen the village of Curral das Freiras (690m/2265ft), an oasis in a waste of stone. The village was founded in the middle of the 16th c. by nuns from the convent of Santa Clara in Funchal who sought safety from pirate raids in the seclusion of the mountains and in later centuries pastured their cattle here. From Curral das Freiras a very attractive footpath descends through the valley of the Ribeira dos Socorridos to the north coast of the island.

Funchal to São Vicente via Câmara de Lobos (55km/34 miles)

Travel west from Funchal either on the motorway or on the coast road from where there are magnificent views.

9km/6 miles further on is the little fishing port of Câmara de Lobos (wolves' gorge), picturesquely situated under the east side of Cabo Girão (589m/1933ft), a rugged headland falling almost vertically down to | Câmara de Lobos/★Cabo Girão

Today, the picturesque Camara da Lobos on Madeira's south coast is still the fishing centre of the island

the sea and said to be the highest cliff of its kind in Europe. The village has long been a favourite with painters, among them Sir Winston Churchill. The village owes its name to the wolf-fish which were once found here in large numbers. The grapes grown on the terraces around the village provide some of the finest wine on the island.

Beyond Câmara de Lobos the road climbs away from the coast, with numerous turns, to make its way around the north side of Cabo Girão.

Next comes Estreito de Câmara de Lobos (alt. 500m/1640ft), a village renowned for its wine.

From here a minor road runs 4km/2½ miles north to the Jardim da Serra (750m/2460ft), from which there are beautiful views. About 4km/2-½ miles beyond Estreito de Câmara de Lobos a road forks left to the viewpoint over Cabo Girão.

Estreito de Câmara de Lobos

Campanário (alt. 300m/985ft) is a village perched attractively on the hillside, with a 17th c. church.

Campanário

It is a further 6km/4 miles from Campanário to Ribeira Brava (pop. 7500), a little fishing town beautifully situated at the mouth of the stream of the same name, which is beginning to be modernised. In the main square, which is paved with pebble mosaic, is a charming 16th c. church. Standing above the stream is a small 17th c. fort. The picturesque Festas de São Pedro, with a procession and various folk events, take place here at the end of June every year.

Ribeira Brava

The São Vicente road running north from Ribeira Brava climbs inland, mostly on the west side of the river, through magnificent scenery.

◀ *The "Eagle Rock", near Faial*

Madeira/Archipélago da Madeira

Pousada dos Vinháticos	12km/7½ miles further on the road passes the Pousada dos Vinháticos (alt. 660m/2165ft), a good climbing base (Pico Grande, Pico do Jorge, Pico Ruivo, etc.) in a beautiful setting.
Boca da Encumeada	2km/1¼ miles beyond this the road reaches the pass, the Boca da Encumeada (1007m/3304ft), with superb views of the Serra de Água (1405m/4610ft) to the left and the Pico Grande to the right. From the pass a path runs west to the Paúl da Serra plateau and the Rabaçal mountain hut.
São Vicente	Once through the pass, the road descends via Rosário to the coast and São Vicente (pop. 5000). This is a straggling settlement in wild mountain scenery on the north coast of the island. It was partly buried by a land-slide in 1928. São Vicente is a good base for climbing the Pico dos Tanquinhos (1524m/5000ft) and the Pico Ruivo do Paúl (1642m/5387ft), both offering magnificent views of mountain scenery, as well as opportunities for exploring the beautiful Paúl da Serra area.

From Ribeira Brava to São Vicente via Calheta (92km/57 miles)

Ponta do Sol	Ponta do Sol (pop. 6000) is on the coast road north-west out of Ribeira Brava. It is a picturesque little place built on both sides of the river of the same name. The church of Nossa Senhora da Luz (15th c.) has a painted wooden ceiling and some fine examples of silversmith's work. About 2km/1¼ miles north-east of Ponta do Sol, surrounded by banana plantations, is the Capela do Santo Espírito, rebuilt in the 18th c. but founded in the 16th by João Esmeraldo, one of Columbus's companions, who owned big sugar-cane plantations in this area.
Paúl da Serra	About 5km/3 miles beyond Ponta do Sol a road forks right to the plateau 12km/7½ miles north of Paúl da Serra (1419m/4656ft). Often shrouded in

Ponta do Sol, on the south coast of Madeira

mist, this is sheep country, and a good starting point for treks in the mountains.

5km/3 miles further on is the chapel of Nossa Senhora de Loreto, in Mozarabic and Manueline style.

Nossa Senhora de Loreto

Calheta (pop. 4000) is a little port below the coast road set amid banana plantations and vineyards. The choir of the parish church (1639) has a carved wooden ceiling in Mudéjar style.

Calheta

From Calheta a minor road runs 10km/6 miles north to the Rabaçal hut (1143m/3750ft). From the "Balcão" (balcony), a short distance northeast, there are superb views of the Risco Falls and the green gorge known as Vinte e Cinco Fontes (twenty-five springs).

★Risco Falls

Beyond the Calheta turning the coast road continues to climb, with many bends, to Estreito da Calheta, off to the left (339m/1112ft). The 16th c. Capela dos Reis Magos (chapel of the Magi) has fine painted woodwork, a carved wooden ceiling and a triptych depicting the Three Kings.

Estreito da Calheta

From here a side road runs down to Jardim do Mar, in a beautiful setting.

Prazeres (621m/2038ft), further along the main road, is finely situated on a wooded plateau, and also has magnificent views.

Prazeres

6km/4 miles farther on a road forks left to the village of Fajã da Ovelha, which lies in a forest setting at the foot of a massive crag, and to the little fishing settlement of Paúl do Mar (canning factory).

Ponta do Pargo (473m/1552ft), near the western tip of the island (lighthouse), is a little country town in an area that has preserved many old traditions and customs. The beautiful old local costumes are still worn on highdays and holidays.

Ponta do Pargo

From the village a footpath leads down to the Praia do Pesqueiro (fisherman's beach), enclosed by cliffs.

Santa Maria Madalena (500m/1640ft; pop. 800), with an unusual church, is reached via Achadas da Cruz (673m/2208ft).

Santa Maria Madalena

The road now drops down to the coast, with lots of hairpin bends, to Porto Moniz (pop. 2500), a little fishing town at the north-west corner of the island. Protected by a rocky headland and the offshore islet of Ilhéu More with its fishermen's houses, this is the most sheltered harbour and the principal port on the north coast of Madeira. There are many natural swimming pools on the rugged coast about 2km/1¼ miles south-east of the village.

Porto Moniz

Ribeira da Janela lies at the mouth of the river of the same name. Just off the rivermouth are three rock-stacks, one of which, the Ilhéu da Ribeira da Janela, has the natural rock window (janela = window) from which the village gets its name.

Ribeira da Janela

The coast road next passes Seixal (pop. 900) which is beautifully situated amid vineyards on the slopes of a projecting spur of hill.

Seixal

Beyond Seixal begins the most impressive section of the road along the north coast and one of the finest stretches of scenery in the whole of Madeira.

The magnificently engineered road, hewn out of the almost vertical cliffs, with numerous tunnels and projecting sections, runs high above the thundering sea and under the shadow of mighty rockfaces, as if suspended between sea and sky.

About 2km/1¼ miles beyond Seixal is a viewpoint with a famous view of the gorge at the mouth of the Ribeira do Inferno. The road then continues through tunnels and under waterfalls to São Vicente.

Ribeira do Inferno

São Vicente

251

From São Vicente to Funchal via Machico (90km/56 miles)

Ponta Delgada

The coast road continues east from São Vicente along the steep rock-face. The next place is Ponta Delgada (pop. 2000), delightfully perched on a promontory amid orange-groves and sugar-cane plantations, with a simple little white church and a sea-water swimming pool.

Ponta Delgada has a "romaria" festival on the first Sunday in September.

Boaventura

The road now leaves the coast and describes a wide bend inland before returning to the coast. After 2km/1¼ mile it reaches Boaventura (pop. 3000), set in fruit orchards and willow plantations (raw material for the local wickerwork), and popular with tourists as a starting point for walks, especially to the Curral das Freiras.

Arco de São Jorge

Beyond Arco de São Jorge is a viewpoint with a famous prospect of the north coast.

São Jorge

São Jorge (pop. 3000) has a 17th c. Baroque church (fine altarpieces). From the nearby Ponta de São Jorge there are extensive views of the north coast, extending to Porto Moniz in the west and Porto da Cruz in the east.

★ Santana

Santana (420m/1380ft; pop. 4500) is chief town of the Comarca de Santana, the most fertile district on Madeira, and one of the most picturesque places on the island, with its thatched houses set amid a profusion of flowers.

From Santana it is a pleasant excursion to the mountain hut of Casa das Queimadas (883m/2896ft), continuing south on foot to the Parque das Queimadas on the slopes of the Pico Ruivo (1861m/6102ft), which can be climbed from here. From the summit, on clear days (which are rare), there is a magnificent panoramic view of the mountains of Madeira.

Faial

7km/4½ miles beyond Santana, the road, now running close to the sea again and affording constantly changing views, reaches Faial (150m/490ft; pop. 1500), a modest little village surrounded by terraced vineyards, sugar-cane plantations and vegetable patches. There is a good view from the church terrace.

Penha de Aguia

Towering over the landscape is the mighty crag of the "Eagle Rock", the Penha de Aguia.

Porto da Cruz

The port of Porto da Cruz (pop. 4000) at the foot of massive rockfaces, has a little volcanic beach.

Portela pass

Beyond Porto da Cruz the road turns away from the sea southward and climbs up into the mountains, reaching 662m/2172ft at the Portela pass, with a view of Porto da Cruz and Machico Bay.

Shortcut to Funchal via Santo da Serra

It is 30km/19 miles from the pass on the EN 102 straight back to Funchal, passing through beautiful forest scenery, via the health resort of Santo (António) da Serra (671m/2200ft; pop. 2000; golf-course), on a plateau of grazing land and with the Quinta Jardim da Serra, which is worth seeing, and Camacha (715m/2345ft; pop. 6500), a little town notable for its folklore and its thriving wickerwork industry.

Quinta do Palheiro Ferreiro

About 8km/5 miles before Funchal, to the left of the road, is the Quinta do Palheiro Ferreiro, a beautiful private park to which the public are admitted and which harmoniously combines French and English gardening skills.

Machico

Beyond the Portela pass the main road descends the Machico valley to the coast and Machico itself (pop. 13,000), an important fishing port (boatyard) at the mouth of the Rio Machico, with a government school for Madeira embroidery. This was the landing place of the first settlers.

The town is said to be named after an Englishman called Machin who was shipwrecked here about 1344 while eloping with his bride and who has been claimed as the discoverer of Madeira. The Capela dos Milagres (1420; rebuilt in the 19th c.) is said to have been erected over the graves of the two lovers. The late 15th c. parish church (originally Manueline but later much altered) has a painted wooden ceiling. In the Capela de São Roque there are fine azulejo paintings. Above the northern entrance to the bay stands a small 17th c. fort. The feast of the Senhor dos Milagres is celebrated every year on the evenings of October 8th and 9th by the lighting of bonfires on the surrounding hills.

From Machico the EN 101-3 runs east via the little whaling station of Caniçal (8km/5 miles) to the bathing beach of Prainha, on the south side of the narrow peninsula of Ponta de São Lourenço, the most easterly tip of Madeira, and a place where many fossils have been found. The road ends above the Baia de Abra (several excellent viewing-points).

Detour to the peninsula of Ponta de São Lourenço

The coast road continues south-east from Machico, running close to the sea. About 1km/¾ mile beyond Machico a road off to the right leads to the Miradouro Francisco Álvares Nóbrega (another 1km/¾ mile), with a beautiful view of Machico Bay and the São Lourenço peninsula.
   Beyond the turning the main road continues along the coast, passing the Água de Pena tourist village and the Santa Catarina airport.

Miradouro Francisco Álvares Nóbrega

Below the coast road is Santa Cruz, with a 16th c. church and town hall. The locals catch ornamental fish.

Santa Cruz

Caniço, at the mouth of the river of the same name, has an 18th c. parish church and the Manueline chapel of the Madre de Deus (16th c.). There is a pleasant walk from here to Cabo Garajau (underwater national park).

Caniço

There is a last, lovely view from the Miradouro do Pináculo before the final 5km/2½ miles to Funchal.

Miradouro do Pináculo

Other islands in the Madeira archipelago

Porto Santo

Some 23 nautical miles north-east of Madeira (by boat, several times weekly, 3 hours; by air, several times daily, 20 minutes) is the table-shaped island of Porto Santo (pop. 3000; highest point Pico do Facho, 517m/1696ft), surrounded by five small rocky islets. Porto Santo, 12km/7½ miles long by 6km/4 miles wide, covering 42sq.km/16sq. miles, is very different in character from the main island of Madeira. Its sandy uplands and aridity make farming very difficult for its inhabitants. Tourists seem little interested in the barren island, and there are only a few holiday bungalows and flats.

Location and General

In the little port of Porto Santo, or Vila Baleira, on the south-east coast, the chief settlement on the island, is the house where Columbus, whose father-in-law was the first governor, lived in about 1479.

Sights

Porto Santo has the only long beach of fine sand in the whole of the Madeira archipelago. It extends right along the south coast, but the tourist facilities are still limited.

★Beach

Ilhas Desertas

About 11 miles south-east of Madeira are the Ilhas Desertas, the "deserted" islands, three waterless and uninhabited rocky islets: Deserta Grande (491m/1611ft), Ilhéu do Bugio (411m/1348ft) and the flat Ilhéu Chão (104m/341ft). They are the home of the great wolf spider (*geolycosa ingens*), one of Europe's biggest spiders; seals live in the caves of Deserta Grande. The islands are a nature reserve and are not open to tourists.

Location and General

Porto Santo and its seemingly endless sands

Mafra   A 6

Historical province: Estremadura. District: Lisbon
Altitude: 237m/778ft. Population: 13,500

Situation and Importance

The modest little town of Mafra, about 50km/30 miles north-west of Lisbon, is widely famed for its enormous monastery-palace, the largest complex of the kind in the Iberian peninsula.

It is where King João V founded the "Mafra school", a major school for instruction in the art of sculpture by teachers that included such leading artists as José Almeida and Joaquim Machado de Castro.

Townscape

Mafra is an unassuming little town, its centre dominated by the enormous monastery-palace. The carefully restored 13th/14th c. Gothic church of Santo André, containing the tombs of Dom Diogo de Sousa and his wife, is also worth a visit.

★★ Palácio Nacional de Mafra (Plan page 256)

History

The Palácio Nacional de Mafra was founded in 1717 by João V and his queen, Maria Ana of Austria, in fulfilment of a vow made in 1711 and in thanksgiving for the birth of an heir (later José I). It was built by a force of as many as 50,000 workmen under the direction of the Italian-trained German architect Johann Friedrich Ludwig and his son Johann Peter Ludwig and consecrated in 1730, although it was 1750 before the whole complex was finally complete.

The monastery buildings were originally occupied by Franciscans but in the late 18th c. were transferred to the Augustinians. When the monastery was closed following the dissolution of all religious orders in 1834 parts of it were allocated to the army.

Mafra: the gigantic Palace-Monastery

The former royal apartments were hardly ever occupied. King João V and his Queen spent only a few days here, and it wasn't until the early 19th c. that the palace enjoyed its brief heyday when João VI resided here in 1806–07. With the approach of French troops the royal family made a hurried departure from the palace, en route for Lisbon and subsequently Brazil, taking most of the valuable furnishings and works of art with them. Nor did later Portuguese rulers spend much time in Mafra, usually only stopping here in order to hunt nearby.

Layout

The huge building consists of the monastery church, the monastery accommodation containing the cells and the communal rooms used by the monks, and a further section to serve the royal family as their accommodation. Built on an almost square plan and designed with the strictest regard for symmetry, the building as a whole is 251m/825ft long by 221m/725ft wide and covers a total area of 40,000sq.m/48,000sq.yd. It has 900 rooms, with 4500 windows and doors. It bears comparison with the Escorial, Philip II's monastery-palace near Madrid, but was intended by its founder to surpass even the Escorial in size and splendour. It is the supreme exemplification in Portugal of cool Baroque magnificence, lavish extravagance and absolute royal power. It was financed by gold from the Brazilian mines. The church is open to the public (Mon., Wed.–Sun. 10am–1pm and 2–5pm), as are the former royal apartments (guided tours), but parts of the monastery cannot be visited since they are occupied by a military academy, etc.

Basilica

The basilica is in the middle of the main front, which is precisely articulated and almost without decoration and was later used as a model for the building of the Basilica da Estrela. It is flanked by twin towers 68m/223ft high which are smoothly integrated into the front of the palace. The carillon of 114 bells was made by an Antwerp bell-founder named Lavache.

Through the vestibule of the church, with 14 statues of saints in Carrara marble by the Italian sculptor Alexandre Giusti, lies the aisleless interior

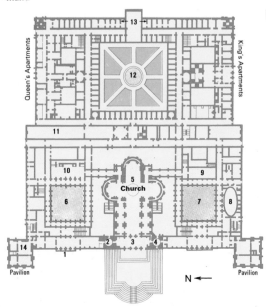

Palácio Nacional de Mafra

1 Entrance

2 Tower

3 Vestibule (statues of saints)

4 Tower

5 Dome

6 Cloister

7 Cloister

8 Chapterhouse

9 Sacristy

10 Campo Santo Chapel

11 Refectory

12 Cloister garth (gardens)

13 Library (upper floor)

14 Museum of Sculpture

N ←

faced with limestone. The ground plan of the church is in the shape of a Roman cross. It is 58.5m/192ft long and 43m/141ft wide at the crossing. It took two years to construct the crossing dome (65m/213ft high, 13m/43ft across) and its 2m/6½ft wide lantern. The interior has a coffered barrel-vaulted ceiling and 62 fluted pillars. Various types of marble – pink, white, black, grey, blue and yellow – were combined in a geometric pattern. The influences of German Baroque and Italian Classicism are evident; the architect Johann Friedrich Ludwig is thought to have derived inspiration from St Peter's Church in the Vatican and the Jesus Church in Rome.

Also striking are the six organs constructed for João V between 1792 and 1807 in accordance with plans drawn up by the organ-builders Joaquim António Peres Fontanes and António Xavier Machado.

The church has eleven chapels. Until well into the 18th c. oil paintings by Portuguese and Italian masters hung here. However, they were damaged by the high humidity to the extent that they had to be replaced by the bas-reliefs in Carrara marble that we see today. The altar-pieces in the large chapels in the crossing are the combined work of Alexandre Giusti and his famous pupil Machado de Castro. The marble statues in the side-chapels are of various saints; they were completed in Italy and then brought to Mafra. Together with the statues on the exterior façade and in the vestibule they represent the most important collection of works by Italian sculptors to be found anywhere in Portugal.

Other monastery buildings

Guided tours of the palace also take in the pharmacy, the infirmary, with the original 18th c. fittings, the kitchen, faced with blue azulejos, the oval chapterhouse, some of the communal rooms and the monks' cells.

Royal apartments

The former royal apartments are in the east section of the palace, with those of the king in the south and the queen in the north.

Although much of the valuable furnishings was removed in the early 19th c. what remains is still considerable. All the rooms are furnished with 18th and 19th c. furniture and objets d'art. The throne-room is most impressive, with its early 19th c. murals. Other rooms included in the tour include several bedrooms, the Room of Discoveries, the music room and a comically furnished hunting hall. One room contains various kinds of lutes, while in the games room are two old billiard tables and some forerunners of present-day gaming machines. In the vestibule is a bust of the founder of the palace, João V, with a laurel wreath on his head.

Of particular interest is the Library, 88m/290ft long, with 40,000 volumes, including many incunabula and manuscripts, first editions of Camões' "Lusiads", and the plays of Gil Vicente, a trilingual Bible of 1514 and the earliest edition of Homer in Greek.

Library

In the left-hand corner pavilion on the main front is the Museum of Comparative Sculpture (Museu de Escultura Comparada), with casts of famous works by Portuguese, Italian and French sculptors of the 12th to 16th c.

Museu de Escultura Comparada

To the rear of the palace extends the Tapada de Mafra, the royal deer-park enclosed by a wall 20km/12½ miles long, in which the royal family still hunted at the beginning of the 20th c.

Tapada de Mafra

Marvão

C 5

Historical province: Alto Alentejo. District: Portalegre
Altitude: 862m/2828ft. Population: 500

The little market town of Marvão, the Roman Herminio Minor, lies near the Spanish frontier on a steep-sided hill in the Serra de São Mamede. Its great attractions are its unspoiled medieval atmosphere and its castle, with a commanding view from above the town.
  This strategically situated little town was strongly fortified by King Dinis in the 13th c. In 1833, during the Miguelist wars, it played an important part as stronghold of the Liberals.

Situation and Importance

The town is still completely surrounded by its medieval walls. The steep and narrow streets are paved with stone slabs, spanned by flying buttresses and lined with flower-decked houses, many of them with fine 17th c. wrought-iron window grille, including one that has been turned into a pousada. It is advisable to leave cars outside the walls and to walk up through the maze of alleyways to the castle.

★★Townscape

Sights

Above the town stands the castle (Castelo), built in the 13th c. and enlarged in the 15th and 17th c.
  From the keep, enclosed within several rings of walls, there are panoramic views, extending northward to Castelo Branco and the Serra da Estrela, southward and westward to the Serra de São Mamede and eastward to Spain.

Castelo

Outside the town is the former Convento de Nossa Senhora da Estrela (originally 15th c.), now a hospital. The church has a fine Gothic door-way.

Convento de Nossa Senhora da Estrela

Surroundings of Marvão

A visit to Marvão can easily be combined with one to the equally interesting Castelo de Vide (see entry), 12km/7½ miles north-west, and Portalegre (see entry), 12km/7½ miles south-west.

Castelo de Vide, Portalegre

Marvão: the castle fort offers views across the area and beyond as far as Spain

Mértola   C 7

Historical province: Baixo Alentejo. District: Beja
Altitude: 85m/280ft. Population: 7000

Situation and
Importance

Mértola is picturesquely set on the slopes above the left bank of the Guadana, joined here by its tributary the Oreias, about 70km/43 miles north-west of the coastal border town of Vila Real de Santo António.

In Roman times the site was occupied by the town of Mirtilis, mentioned by the Alexandrian geographer Ptolemy (2nd c. A.D.), which later had to give way to a Moorish stronghold.

★ Townscape

With its narrow and twisting alleys Mértola is still rather Moorish in appearance. From the main square its narrow streets, lined with little white houses, lead uphill to the parish church and then on up to the castle.

Sights in Mértola

Igreja Matriz

The fortified Romanesque parish church, Igreja Matriz, with crenellated walls and a handsome Renaissance doorway, was converted in the 16th c. from an earlier mosque – an origin revealed by the square ground-plan, the arrangement of the clustered columns, the mihrab, or Islamic prayer niche, behind the high altar, and the horseshoe arch above the sacristy door.

Castelo dos
Mouros

It is a short distance from the parish church up to the old Moorish castle, the Castelo dos Mouros, which was considerably enlarged in the late 13th c. From the keep there is a magnificent view of the town and the River Guadiana, which is navigable below this point.

Mértola: Igreja Matriz

Since 1980 archaeologists have been systematically digging near the castle and church, exposing Roman foundations and mosaic, and unearthing Islamic ceramics. The oldest pieces date from the 10th c. and are from Andalusia. These finds, together with other exhibits, are on display in four small museums in Mértola. The Roman finds can be seen in the basement of the town hall (Museu Romano). A few yards away are the Islamic Museum and the Museum of Religious Art. In the newer part of the town will be found the Museu Paleocristão, with the remains of an early Christian basilica.

Archaeological digs and museums

Minho

B/C 2/3

Historical province: Minho. Districts: Braga and Viana do Castelo
Area: 4928sq.km/1902sq. miles
Population: 966,000. Chief town: Braga

The ancient province of Minho in the extreme north-west of Portugal – formerly known, more accurately, as Entre Douro e Minho, the land between the Douro and Minho rivers – lies to the south of the river of the same name. It is bounded on the south by the province of Douro Litoral and on the east by Spain and the province of Trás-os-Montes; on the west it lies open to the Atlantic on the Costa Verde (see entry), an almost northern-seeming stretch of coast.

Location and General

Formerly part of Castile the Minho region has, ethnically and culturally, a unity with Galicia, an affinity which is reflected also in certain linguistic features which the two provinces have in common.

The Minho region is occupied by an ancient mountain massif of granites, gneisses, argillaceous schists and quartzes which increases in height towards the east, reaching almost 2000m/6560ft in the Serra do

Topography

Gerês, and is traversed from north-east to south-west by the three wide parallel valleys of the Minho, the Lima and the Cávado. These valleys allow moisture-bearing winds from the Atlantic to penetrate far inland, making this the rainiest part of the whole Iberian peninsula (1000–3000mm/40–120in. a year). Numerous recent fault lines allow the water to sink deep underground, where it is heated and re-emerges in many places as thermal springs.

The Minho landscape is more reminiscent of northern Europe than of the south. The easy availability of granite has resulted in a very individualistic form of architecture in stone, giving a grey appearance to the towns and villages.

Population

The people of Minho, the Minhotes, are particularly attached to tradition and to the Catholic faith, and the many church festivals and romarias are celebrated enthusiastically with music and dancing.

Its very fertile soil has meant that the Minho region has always been densely populated. However, the very limited area of the smallholdings which form the farms, and the consequently unviable working that this entails, has meant there has never been adequate subsistence for its population so that many of the Minhotes, particularly the ablebodied younger men, have had to find jobs elsewhere.

Economy

Minho's economy is predominantly based on agriculture. The fertile, well-watered basins and valleys yield two harvests a year, wheat followed by maize, providing food for human consumption and feed for the flourishing livestock sector. Another major source of revenue is the production of wine. The vines, trained in the ancient Roman fashion on young trees (mainly eucalyptus) or on trellises, produce the much esteemed vinho verde (or vinho não murado), a wine that because of the early autumn has an early vintage, and is characterised by youthful freshness, a slightly sharp taste and a natural effervescence (see Practical Information, Wine).

The uplands, deforested in ancient times, now provide pasturage for sheep.

In addition to agriculture the region has old-established small-scale industries: textiles (originally linen-weaving, now also cotton), the manufacture of cutting instruments and blades, leather-working, pottery and crafts such as embroidery and lace-making. There is no heavy industry. In recent years hydro-electric power stations have been established on the rivers in the mountains.

Throughout the countryside can be seen what amounts to the symbol of the region, the little grainstores that the Portuguese call *espigueiros*. Their walls are made of tablets of stone with slits in them that are designed, with an aperture of only 5mm, to let the wind in but keep the birds and larger insects out. The espigueiros have stone supports to render them dampproof by raising them off the ground, and the flat stone discs at the top of these supports serve to stop mice getting in, since they can't negotiate the smooth undersurface. Nowadays the grain they used to hold has largely been replaced by maize cobs.

Espigueiros

Miranda do Douro   D 3

Historical province: Trás-os-Montes. District: Bragança
Altitude: 690m/2264ft. Population: 2000

The old episcopal city of Miranda do Douro in the north-east of Portugal lies on a rocky hill above the deep valley of the Douro (Spanish Duero and dammed at this point), which here marks the frontier with Spain (no frontier crossing). The remoteness of the region, one of the most thinly populated parts of Portugal, has acted as a brake on its cultural and linguistic development, so that it has preserved not only many old customs and traditions but also a local dialect close to Vulgar Latin, the *lingua charra* or *mirandês*.

Situation and Importance

Traditional crafts such as weaving and pottery are still widely practised. Every year on the third Sunday in August (the feast of St Barbara) the dance of the *pauliteiros* (wooden staves) takes place, a folk dance for men that harks back to the Roman sword-dances.

Rather a sombre little town, around its marketplace Miranda do Douro has a number of handsome old burghers' houses with coats-of-arms and Manueline ornamentation.

Townscape

Sights in Miranda do Douro

The 12th c. castle which once dominated the town was destroyed by an explosion in 1760, leaving only a watch-tower.

Castelo

On a projecting spur of rock above the Douro stands the Cathedral (Sé), a 16th c. building with a wide west front flanked by towers. The spacious interior gets its effect from the massive piers. The high altar depicts scenes from the life of the Virgin and the Crucifixion. A quaint feature is the "Infant Jesus in a Top Hat", a naive ex-voto of the mid 19th c.

Sé

From the terrace in front of the Cathedral there is an impressive view of the grey rocky valley of the Douro.

Near the Cathedral is the Baroque arcaded courtyard which is all that remains of the Archbishop's Palace, burned down in 1706.

Paço Episcopal

The small regional museum contains curios and many popular everyday items.

Museu Municipal

Surroundings of Miranda do Douro

About 3km/2 miles east of Miranda do Douro is the Barragem de Miranda do Douro, the first of a series of five dams on the Douro built

Dams on the Douro

and operated jointly by Spain and Portugal. Some 25km/15 miles downstream the Barragem do Picote is followed by the Barragem da Bemposta, the Barragem de Aldeiadávila and the Barragem de Saucelle.

Caçarelhos

About 17km/11 miles north-west of the town, at the village of Caçarelhos, are large marble and alabaster quarries and beautiful stalactitic caves.

Vimioso

The village of Vimioso, 10km/6 miles farther west, has the ruins of a castle of King Dinis which was destroyed in the 18th c. An attractive church, Roman bridges and the idyllic village square are also of interest.

Mirandela C 3

Historical province: Trás-os-Montes. District: Bragança
Altitude: 250m/820ft. Population: 8000

Situation

The attractive little town of Mirandela lies on the left bank of the Rio Tua about 70km/44 miles south-west of Bragança in one of the most isolated areas of the Portuguese mainland. It has a small, medieval centre, but this is being increasingly invaded by new buildings.

Sights

Paço dos Távoras

On an eminence in the heart of the town stands the 18th c. Paço dos Távoras, with a granite Baroque façade, now the Town Hall.

Museu de Arte Moderna

A Museum of Modern Art has recently been housed in the new Culture Centre. Some 400 paintings are on display.

Bridges

There was a crossing of the Rio Tua here in Roman times, and the position of the Roman bridge is now occupied by a medieval bridge of 18 arches, 232m/254yd long. Beside it is a modern bridge.

Surroundings of Mirandela

★Murça

Murça, 33km/20 miles south-west of Mirandela, was granted a municipal charter by King Sancho II in 1224. It is famous for the granite figure of a wild boar (on the main street), the subject of many legends, and originally thought to be Iron Age but now considered more likely to be 7th c.

Other features of interest are the 17th c. church of the Misericórdia, the parish church (Igreja Matriz) with a Classical granite façade in the pretty market square, and a Manueline pelourinho (pillory column), the symbol of municipal authority.

Vila Flor

About 28km/17 miles south of Mirandela is the little country town of Vila Flor (alt. 565m/1855ft; pop. 2000), with a handsome 18th c. palace, a Gothic town hall, an azulejo-clad parish church and remains of the town walls. A small museum exhibits household items from the first half of the 20th c.

Carrazeda de Ansiães

It is also worth making a detour to Carrazeda de Ansiães (18km/11 miles south-west of Vila Flor). On a hill 4km/2½ miles south of the town lie the ruins of an 11th c. castle which played an important role in the *Reconquista*. A few remains with the castle walls indicate that there was a settlement here in the Bronze Age. The Romanesque Igreja de São Salvador near the entrance to the castle has a splendidlly decorated west door.

Monção B 2

Historical province: Minho. District: Viana do Castelo
Altitude: 98m/322ft. Population: 2700

The old fortified frontier town of Monção, situated on the left bank of the River Minho (Spanish Miño) opposite the Spanish town of Salvatierra de Miño, is now a spa, with hot springs used for the treatment of rheumatism, skin and bronchial ailments.

Situation and Importance

The local delicacies are salmon trout and *lampretes* (lampreys).

The centrepoint of the town, still surrounded by its 17th c. walls, is the flower-bedecked Praça Deu-la-Deu. The square is named after the local hero, Deu-la-Deu Martins, who distinguished himself in 1368 in the battle against the Castilians and whose monument graces the square. Around the square and the adjoining Largo do Loreto there are many attractive balconied houses. The northern end of the Largo do Loreta has a broad view over the river landscape of the Rio Minho.

Townscape

Above the town are the ruins of a medieval castle.

Sights

The original Romanesque parish church of Santa Maria dos Anjos (Holy Mary of the Angels), remodelled in the 16th c., has a fine Manueline main doorway. Inside is the tomb of Deu-la-Deu Martins among others, as well as rich talha dourada decoration, and azulejos in the choir. A Manueline side-chapel dating from 1521 is also worth seeing.

Igreja Matriz

Surroundings of Monção

About 3km/2 miles south of the little town, on the road from Braga, is the imposing early 19th c. Brejoeira Palace (not open to the public), set in beautiful gardens.

Palácio de Brejoeira

About 24km/15 miles east of Monção is the health resort of Peso de Melgaço (alt. 180m/590ft), with mineral springs used in treating digestive and metabolic ailments.

Peso de Melgaço

Rural idyll near Monção

The neighbouring village of Melgaço has a 12th c. Romanesque parish church, and, above the village, a 12th c. castle.

Valença do Minho   See entry

Montemor-o-Velho   B 4

Historical province: Beira Litoral. District: Coimbra
Altitude: 51m/167ft. Population: 2400

Situation and
Importance

The little town of Montemor-o-Velho, about halfway between Figueira da Foz and Coimbra, on a hill above the right bank of the Mondego, was of importance during the Middle Ages as an outpost defending the approach to Coimbra against the Moors advancing from Estremadura. The local economy is mainly given over to agriculture, with rice the main crop.

Montemor-o-Velho is the birthplace of the navigator Cavaleiro Diogo de Azambuja (1432–1518), the writer and world traveller Fernão Mendes Pinto (*c.* 1510–83), and the poet Jorge de Montemor (1520–61).

Sights

★ Castelo

Above the town are the forbidding ruins of its massive castle (Castelo), at one time amongst Portugal's strategically most important fortresses. Nothing remains of the original castle, first mentioned in 716 when occupied by the Moors. The existing ruins date from the 11th and 12th c. and are enclosed within a double circuit of walls, oval in plan, with imposing towers and battlements. From the top of the towers, some of which can be

*Surrounded by attractive parkland: the Santa Maria Alcacova church
inside the castle walls of Montemor-o-Velho*

Pregnant Madonna in the Santa Maria de Alcacova church

climbed, there is a superb view over the surrounding countryside. Within the walls is the Manueline church of Santa Maria de Alcáçova (16th c.) by the famous architect Boytaca, with a beautiful wooden ceiling, azulejo decoration in 16th c. Moorish style and a double font.

In the romantic little town itself is the noteworthy Manueline church of Nossa Senhora dos Anjos (Our Lady of the Angels), originally a monastic church. The real treasure lies in the spacious interior which holds Renaissance sculpture of the Coimbra school, including the magnificent sarcophagus of Diogo de Azambuja, carved during his lifetime by Diogo Pires-o-Moço.

Nossa Senhora
dos Anjos

Surroundings of Montemor-o-Velho

About 10km/6 miles north-east is the little town of Tentúgal, with the church of Nossa Senhora do Mourão, belonging to the former Carmelite convent (15th c.), the church of the Misericórdia (16th c.) and a number of handsome patrician houses. Some 3km/2 miles farther north-east the church of the Hieronymite convent of São Marcos (burned down in 1860) was a dependency of the convent at Belém (see Lisbon); it was founded in 1452 by Dona Brites de Meneses, later Afonso V's wife, and subsequently became the burial place of the Silva Meneses family. The decoration of the church, with its clearly articulated structure, betrays the hand of the architect of the convents of Belém and of Santa Cruz in Coimbra.

Tentúgal

From Tentúgal it is a further 15km/9 miles to Coimbra (see entry), famous for its university and rich in tradition.

Coimbra

Figueira da Foz (see entry), the seaside resort 16km/10 miles west of Montemor-o-Velho, is a popular destination in the summer months.

Figueira da Foz

Moura   C 6

Historical province: Baixo Alentejo. District: Beja
Altitude: 180m/1062ft. Population: 8500

Situation and Importance

The little spa of Moura, some 60km/37 miles north-east of Beja on the left bank of the Guadiana, has alkaline mineral springs in its park that are particularly called upon in the treatment of rheumatism. Known by the Romans as Nova Civitas Arruccitana, the town owes its present name (Moura = Moorish girl), and its coat of arms – a dead girl below the castle-walls – to a young Moorish maiden called Salúquia. She was the daughter of the town's leading citizen and is supposed to have plunged from the castle battlements after her betrothed and his followers had been ambushed and slain by the Christians on the eve of the wedding. The Christians had then donned the clothing of their ambushed enemies to trick their way past the guards to capture the castle.

Sights

Praça de Sacadura Cabral

The Praça de Sacadura Cabral is the town's central square on which stands the Church of John the Baptist, the Gothic-Manueline Igreja de São João Baptista. In the right-hand side chapel are azulejo versions of the Cardinal Virtues.

The town hall on the opposite side of the square houses a small regional museum with displays of archaeological finds.

In front of it is the Três Bicas fountain (with three jets). The Arabic inscription recalls Almotadide, Emir of Seville, who wrote much of his poetry in Moura.

Moura: Igreja de São João Baptista

Also on the square is the entrance to Moura's little spa park, full of flowers and with an inviting café and a view from the terrace at the end of the gardens.

The Convento de Nossa Senhora do Carmo in Moura is the oldest Carmelite convent in Portugal, founded about 1250. Its elegant cloister dates from the 16th/17th c., and the convent church has an interesting choir fresco.

Convento de Nossa Senhora do Carmo

The old quarter of Mouraria, near the main square, betrays Moura's Moorish past. Many of its low white houses are embellished with azulejos and the characteristic chimneys, and one of them, on the Largo da Mouraria, has been reconstructed in the Eastern style, complete with courtyard.

Mouraria

Above the town centre are the ruins of the Castle, originally Moorish but rebuilt by King Dinis at the end of the 13th c. Within the walls stands the church of Nossa Senhora da Assunção with the Capela dos Rolins, the last resting place of the conquerors Álvaro and Pedro Rodrigues.

Castelo

Surroundings of Moura

About 3km/2 miles south-east are the mineral springs of Pisões-Moura, the source of "Aguas de Castelo", a popular Portuguese mineral water.

Pisões-Moura

Nazaré   A 5

Historical province: Estremadura. District: Leiria
Altitude: 0–110m/0–360ft. Population: 13,000

The particularly picturesque little fishing town of Nazaré has drawn increasing numbers of visitors in recent years because of its good beaches and the still genuinely colourful life and activity of its fisherfolk. It is now one of the most popular seaside towns on this part of Portugal's Atlantic coast, or the Costa de Prata as it is known.

Situation and Importance

Nazaré is believed to have been founded by the Phoenicians. It is on what used to be a bay, but which is now silted up, sheltered on the north by Monte Sítio. The harbour has been reconstructed relatively recently, doing away with the need to push the brightly painted local boats, with their high pointed prows, into the water from the beach by hand, and then, on their return, using oxen to haul them up on shore again to be unloaded by the waiting women and the fishermen. Another fishing method was *arte xávega*, whereby nets

267

Nazaré

Nazaré

were laid offshore then hauled in from the beach. Since this no longer pays its way, tourists have to content themselves with the traditional fish auctions that take place daily on the return of the fishermen.

Costume

For special occasions and for the folk-dance displays laid on by the tourist information centre the people of Nazaré still wear their characteristic traditional costumes. The fishermen have check shirts, trousers in a different check, and black stocking caps, used like a purse for money, etc. The women's costume is covered in lace and has wide bouffant skirts with up to seven petticoats.

Townscape

Nazaré has no historic buildings, and what makes a visit a lasting experience is solely the lively, colourful activity of its people and the singular sense of being in a little town imbued with tradition.

Although the building of the harbour has meant the fishing activity is more in the southern part of town, tourists still share the sizeable beach with fishermen drying their catch on wire racks.

It is quite crowded at the weekends when day-trippers flock here from Lisbon, Coimbra and Oporto.

View

In the Pederneira district in the lower part of the town the square in front of the 16th c. church of the Misericórdia has a fine view over the beach towards Monte Sítio.

Sítio

★ View

A much better view is to be had from the district of Sítio (110m/360ft) on the small promontory of Monte Sítio, reached by car, by funicular, or by walking up the steps of the Ladeira de Sítio.

According to legend the Capela da Memória was founded by a local digni-
tary named Dom Fuas Roupinho who was out hunting here in 1182 when
the stag he was chasing leapt off the cliff at this point. His horse was about
to follow when the Virgin heard the Dom's fast and fervent prayer and,
dazzling the beast with her appearance, halted the horse on the brink of the
precipice. In thanksgiving for this miraculous aid Dom Fuas Roupinho
forthwith had the Capela da Memória built at this point.

Capela da
Memória

Near the chapel there is a pillar with an inscription which commemorates
Vasco da Gama's visit here, after his voyage to India, to give thanks to
Nossa Senhora de Nazaré for his safe return.

Opposite the Capela da Memória is the 17th c. pilgrimage chapel of Nossa
Senhora de Nazaré, containing an image of the Virgin which is revered as
miraculous.

Nossa Senhora de
Nazaré

The annual pilgrimages here on August 15th and in the second week of
September attract visitors from near and far.

Some 500m/550yd west is the old Fort of São Miguel, now a lighthouse.

São Miguel

Surroundings of Nazaré

About 12km/7½ miles south of Nazaré, on the north-east side of a narrow
sheltered bay, rather like a lake and known as "concha" (conch shell),
because of its unusual shape, is the little seaside resort of São Martinho do
Porto, much favoured by families with small children.

São Martinho do
Porto

See entry

Costa de Prata

Óbidos

A 5

Historical province: Estremadura. District: Leiria
Altitude: 70m/230ft. Population: 1000

Óbidos is probably included in every tour of western central Portugal.
Because of its prettiness and general attractiveness the whole town has
been declared a national monument. This also means that in order to
preserve the original townscape there are no big hotels in Óbidos, although
there are several small, de luxe establishments inside the old walls. The
number of beds is therefore extremely limited, and it is almost impossible
to get a room here in the summer months without early reservation.

Situation and
Importance

In earlier centuries the Lagoa de Óbidos, a big lagoon with a narrow
opening into the sea and now more than 10km/6 miles north-west of
Óbidos, reached almost to the little town. This Atlantic dimension made
Óbidos strategically important and it was therefore strongly fortified in
Moorish times. Already a place of great attraction in the Middle Ages,
Óbidos was frequently chosen as the queen's dowry, and it was a favourite
residence of St Isabel and other queens and kings of Portugal. Queen
Leonor lived here for several years, mourning her only son who had been
killed in a riding accident.

The old town centre is surrounded by walls 13m/45ft high, battlemented
and reinforced by towers, and laid out on the lines of an acute-angled
triangle. Within the walls is the picturesque old town full of interesting
corners and alleys with handsome patrician Renaissance and Baroque
houses, most of them covered in flowers. Nowadays Óbidos is obviously a
place for tourists and artists, so that there is a correspondingly large
number of antique shops and selling points for arts and crafts, including
locally woven carpets, together with commercial art galleries.

★★Townscape

Sights

The main street, the Rua Direita, leads from the town gate, the Porta da Vila
(decorated inside with 18th c. azulejos), to the main square, the Praça de

Pelourinho

Santa Maria, which has a beautiful fountain and a 15th c. pelourinho bearing the emblem of Queen Leonor, a fisherman's net. The Queen chose this emblem when her dying son was brought to her by fishermen who had wrapped his body in a net from the Tagus.

The town museum is in the old town hall on the Praça de Santa Maria. Exhibits range from archaeological finds to 15th–17th c. sculpture and paintings.

Museu de Óbidos

Also on the Praça de Santa Maria is the parish church of Santa Maria (originally Gothic but later remodelled in Renaissance style), its interior entirely faced with 17th c. azulejos. The church also contains the tomb of João de Noronha, the castle governor who died in 1575, by Jean de Rouen, and the painting the "Mystic Marriage of St Catherine" by Josefa de Ayala Figueira (17th c.).

Igreja de Santa Maria

Close by the parish church is the Igreja da Misericórdia with a fine Baroque doorway.

Igreja da Misericórdia

There was a castle on the town's highest point in Moorish times. This was rebuilt and reinforced by Afonso I Henriques after the capture of Óbidos in 1148. The former palace within the castle walls has been converted into a pousada. From the keep there are fine views of the town and surrounding area.

Castelo

Outside the town walls, on the road to Caldas da Rainha, is the church of Senhor Jesus da Pedra, a Baroque church built on a hexagonal plan between 1740 and 1747. The cross on its altar is probably 2nd or 3rd c.

Senhor Jesus da Pedra

Surroundings of Óbidos

To the south of the town is the Amoreira aqueduct, built at the behest of Catherine of Austria in 1575.

Aqueduct

About 7km/4½ miles west of Óbidos is Serra d'El Rei (141m/463ft) where there is a magnificent view of Peniche (see entry). The place's only other interesting feature is the ruined 14th c. castle built by King Pedro I.

Serra d'El Rei

See entry

Caldas da Rainha

See entry

Peniche

Olhão   C 7

Historical province: Algarve. District: Faro
Altitude: sea level. Population: 25,000

Relatively unaffected by tourism, Olhão is the second largest town on the Algarve, a few miles east of its chief town, Faro. The town's main industry is its sardine and tuna fisheries, the catches being processed straightaway in the local cannery. The port has the second largest turnover in the Faro district (after Portimão).

Situation and Importance

The townscape and atmosphere of Olhão are different from those found in all other towns in the Algarve. It is often described as the most North African of Algarve towns, and it certainly has a very Moorish air about it. This is mainly because of its characteristic white flat-roofed houses. The fishing quarter in particular consists of labyrinths of two or three-storey

Townscape

◄ *Old streets with whitewashed houses and rampant greenery contribute to the appeal of Óbidos*

square houses of this kind; they are all similar but no two are exactly the same. They are all topped with terraces (açoteias), on which is a small look-out used, so it is said, by the wives of fishermen to watch for their menfolk sailing home. The North African influence on the architecture is mainly the result of trade links between Olhão and towns on the coast of North Africa. This style of building was, however, also adopted here as being particulary suited to the climatic conditions. Large areas of the town were built in the 19th c., with new buildings being found further inland on the N 125.

Olhão has no particularly outstanding sights, but the harbour has plenty of atmosphere. Those wishing to see buildings would do well to follow the Avenida da República towards the sea. It passes by the parish church erected by fishermen in 1681–89 (fine view from the tower); opposite is the chapel of Nossa Senhora where the wives prayed for the safe return of their menfolk. The pedestrian zone leads to the two covered fish markets and the promenade.

Surroundings of Olhão

★ Quinta de Marim/
Parque Natural da Ria Formosa

Places of interest around Olhão include the Quinta de Marim (open: 9am–12.30pm and 2–5pm), 1km/1200yd east of Olhão harbour, near the camp site. The Quinta de Marim Environmental and Nature Conservation Centre forms part of the Parque Natural da Ria Formosa. In a small information kiosk visitors can obtain details of the Ria Formosa lagoon region, its flora and fauna and also general information on matters concerning the environment and nature conservation. There are temporary exhibitions, an auditorium and library and a pleasant cafeteria.

When walking around the area visitors can inspect various agricultural and fishing techniques which are rarely seen elsewhere, including, for instance, an old tuna fishing boat (barca de atum). The tidal mill (moinho de maré) is especially interesting; it is the last mill of its kind to be used since the Middle Ages. In the east of the area the remains of Roman salination plants have been unearthed.

★ Farol, Culatra, Armona

These three lagoon islands are accessible by boat from Olhão several times a day between June and September, three times a day in winter. One boat goes to Farol and Culatra the smallest island in the west, and another to Armona in the east. The landing stages are on Avenida 5 de Outubro near the harbour.

All three islands are of flat dunes with very good beaches. Hardly any houses are to be found, but there are a few simple restaurants and cafés.

The Serra de Monte Figo, which reaches a height of 410m/1346ft by São Miguel, lies beyond the town of Moncarapacho, 8km/5 miles north-east of Olhão. A very narrow little road leads up the mountain; when visibilty is good there is a fine view of the coastal strip from the top.

Algarve

Places particularly worth visiting around Olhão include Faro and Tavira (see entries), while those further afield are described under the entry for Algarve.

Oporto/Porto   B 3

Historical province: Douro Litoral. District: Porto
Altitude: 0–140m/0–460ft. Population: 310,000

Situation and Importance

The lively port, industrial and commercial city of Oporto (known in Portugal as Porto: the traditional English name preserves the older form, from "o porto" – the harbour), a university town and the see of a bishop, is Portugal's second largest town but also its least typical, with a matter-of-fact and

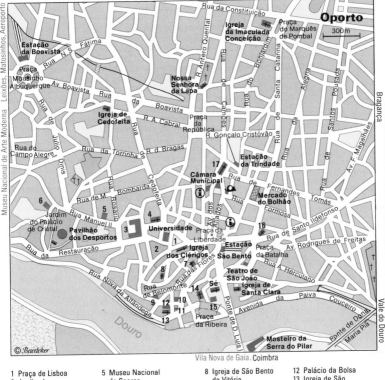

Map showing Oporto with numbered locations.

1 Praça de Lisboa
2 Jardim de João Chagas
3 Hospital de Santo António
4 Igreja do Carmo Igreja das Carmelitas
5 Museu Nacional de Soares dos Reis
6 Museu Romântico/ Solar do Vinho do Porto
7 Igreja da Misericórdia
8 Igreja de São Bento da Vitória
9 Igreja dos Grilos
10 Mercado de Ferreira Borges
11 Praça do Infante Dom Henrique
12 Palácio da Bolsa
13 Igreja de São Francisco
14 Casa do Infante
15 Casa Guerra Junqueiro
16 Centro Regional de Artes Tradicionais

business like approach to life which perhaps owes something to its British connections; a much-quoted proverb says that money is earned in Oporto and spent in Lisbon. Its enchanting location alone makes it one of the most beautiful towns in the Iberian peninsula.

Here, barely 6km/4 miles above its mouth, the River Douro cuts a narrow passage through granite rocks, with Oporto on the north side and the suburb of Vila Nova de Gaia on the south side. Farther west the banks of the river become lower, finally ending at the cliffs of São João da Foz.

Oporto is the economic hub of the best cultivated and most thickly populated northern part of Portugal. Trade in and out is mainly handled by its port and by the outer harbour at Leixões (see Matosinhos), while international air travel passes through Oporto's airport Francisco de Sá Carneiro, 13km/8 miles to the north.

The city is internationally famed for its port, made from the wine of the upper Douro valley (see entry) by a process which is practised here and nowhere else (see Baedeker Special, pp. 282–83 and Practical Information, Wine). The wine is stored in the wine lodges of the southern suburb of Vila Nova, and no visit to Oporto would be complete without a visit to one of these establishments.

History

In the Hellenistic period there was a trading post here, in Roman times the settlement of Portus Cale. Later the Suevi had a stronghold on this site, followed by the Visigoths. The town became the see of a bishop, but was taken by the Arabs in 716 and destroyed in 825. After the Christian reconquest in the 10th c. the territory between the rivers Minho and Douro, with the rebuilt town of Oporto as its capital, became the County of Portucalia, the nucleus of the later kingdom of Portugal.

Oporto was and still is a traditionally cosmopolitan and liberal city. It is the birthplace of Henry the Navigator, who opened up the way to Portugal's conquest of the world. Over the centuries the people of Oporto repeatedly opposed arbitrary and dictatorial rule in bloody uprisings, as in 1628, 1661, 1757 and 1927. Here in 1808 French troops under Junot suffered their first defeat. The Liberals' fight against absolutism also began in Oporto, and as a result the town was besieged and partly destroyed by Dom Miguel's forces in 1832/33.

★★ Cityscape

The houses are packed close together against the steep rockfaces, forming highly picturesque terraces. Oporto is like Lisbon in having the old town on a hill to the east and the newer districts on another hill to the west. Large-scale replanning in recent years has given the heart of the city attractive new streets and squares, with parks and gardens mingling northern and southern flora.

Oporto's main shopping street is the Rua de Santa Catarina, which, like its side-streets, is full of shops, cafés and restaurants. The nearby Mercado do Bolhão is the best place to buy fruit and vegetables. The city's main sights can easily be seen on a day's walkabout, starting from the busy traffic intersection of the Praça da Liberdade. However, those wishing to do justice to the major museums will need to stay longer.

Oporto: View over the town

Sights

The spacious Praça da Liberdade is graced by a statue, on horseback, of King Pedro IV (d. 1834), who was also Emperor Pedro I of Brazil from 1822 to 1831. Off the north side of the square opens the Avenida dos Aliados, a broad avenue laid out in 1923–29 after the demolition of an old residential quarter and now lined by banks and imposing office blocks, leading up to the City Hall. With its high central tower this early 20th c. granite building is reminiscent of its Dutch and Belgian counterparts.

★Praça da Liberdade

From the south-west corner of the Praça da Liberdade the busy Rua dos Clérigos runs up to the Igreja dos Clérigos, built by the Italian architect Nicoló Nasoni in 1732–48, a Baroque church with an oval interior.

Igreja dos Clérigos

Linked to the church is the Torre dos Clérigos, 75m/245ft high and built in 1755–63 at the expense of the Oporto clergy. It has come to be the symbol of Oporto and there is a panoramic view from the top (open every day except Wed.) over the city and the Douro Valley to the Atlantic coast.

★Torre dos Clérigos

North and west of the Clérigos church is the broad Campo dos Mártires da Pátria. A part of it is taken up by the Praça de Lisboa, with its market stalls, while another part holds the beautiful Jardim de João Chagas (Jardim da Cordoaria). On the south side stands the old prison (18th c.), and at the north-west corner the Hospital de Santo António (begun 1769). On the north side of the Campo is the University (founded in 1911; previously a technical college), which also has a small Natural History Museum.

Campo dos Mártires da Pátria

To the north-west, opposite the University, on the Praça de Gomes Teixeira, are two adjoining churches. To the right is the Igreja do Carmo (1756), its east end covered with 19th c. blue azulejos, and to the left the Igreja das Carmelitas (1619–28), both of them containing richly gilded altars.

Igreja do Carmo, Igreja das Carmelitas

Some 500m/550yd north-west of the Campo dos Mártires, in Rua de Dom Manuel II, the Palácio dos Carrancas, built in 1795 as a royal palace, now houses the Soares dos Reis National Museum (Museu Nacional de Soares dos Reis, closed Mon. and public holidays). The museum's collections are of prehistoric and Roman antiquities, medieval and modern sculpture, pictures, pottery and porcelain, goldsmith's work, furniture and textiles.

★Museu Nacional de Soares dos Reis

The art collection deserves special mention, including as it does work by the Oporto sculptor Soares dos Reis (1847–99; "O Desterrado", "Inglesa", "Flor Agreste"), and by Teixeira Lopes ("Infância de Caim") and Diogo de Macedo. In the field of painting the 16th c. Portuguese school is represented by Vasco Fernandes and Frei Carlos, the 19th and 20th c. by Henrique Pousão (collection of his principal works), Columbano Bordalo Pinheiro, António Carneiro, António Carvalho da Silva Porto, Marques de Oliveira, Aurélia de Sousa ("Self-portrait"), Eduardo Viana and Dordio Gomes ("Casas de Malakoff"). Works by non-Portuguese artists include pictures by Frenchmen Jean Clouet and Jean-Baptiste Pillement.

A little way south-west of the Soares dos Reis Museum is the flower-filled Jardim do Palácio de Cristal, the setting for the Pavilhão dos Desportos, the sports arena, with seating for 10,000 spectators and also a venue for concerts, exhibitions, etc., which in 1952 replaced the former "Crystal Palace".

Jardim do Palácio de Cristal

From the south side of the park, where a chapel commemorating King Charles Albert of Sardinia was built in 1851 (see Museu Romântico), there is a superb view over the city, the river and the sea.

Hidden away to the west of the Jardim do Palácio de Cristal is the Romantic Museum (Museu Romântico, closed Mon. and Sun.), fully furnished as a Portuguese house of the 19th c., with also on view the room in which King Charles Albert of Sardinia (b. 1798) died in 1849.

Museu Romântico/ Solar do Vinho do Porto

Next to the museum is the Solar do Vinho do Porto, the port wine institute where there are tastings of some 200 varieties of port from various producers every day except Sunday.

Praça de Mousinho de Albuquerque

North of the Jardim do Palácio de Cristal, outside the actual city centre – and therefore probably not for inclusion on a first trip round Oporto – is the Praça de Mousinho de Albuquerque (or Rotunda da Boavista), in the middle of which stands a massive monument 45m/148ft tall (erected 1923–29) commemorating the war with France of 1808/09.

Igreja de Cedofeita

Just east of the square is the little Romanesque Igreja de Cedofeita (12th c.), the city's oldest church whose name – cedo feita = soon finished – indicates the speed with which it was built.

Fundação de Serralves

A visit to the Serralves Foundation (closed Mon.) in the western outskirts of Oporto, is also best left out of a first day's exploration of the city. The museum is in the impressive Casa de Serralves (Rua Serralves 977), formerly a textile factory, which stands in a French-style park. Here a variety of modern art is displayed in temporary exhibitions.

Igreja de São Bento da Vitória

Continuing with the tour of the city, the route goes back from the Jardim do Palácio de Cristal to the Jardim de João Chagas and then takes a turn to the right through one of the alleys to the twin-towered church of São Bento da Vitória. Its simple and rather shabby exterior, dating from the early 17th c., belies the magnificent furnishings and gilt carving of the interior.

Rua das Flores

From the terrace in front of the church steps lead down east to the Largo de São Domingos, on the north side of which is the end of the Rua das Flores. This former street of goldsmiths and cloth-merchants still has many jewellers' shops in it today.

Igreja da Misericórdia

The Igreja da Misericórdia, in the Rua das Flores, is a church built in the first half of the 18th c. by Nasoni, who was also responsible for the Clérigos church.

Praça do Infante Dom Henrique

From the Largo de São Domingos Rue Ferreira Borges runs southward into the Praça do Infante Dom Henrique, with a monument to Henry the Navigator. The Mercado de Ferreira Borges on the north side of the square provides an exhibition venue in the covered market built in 1883.

On the west side of the square is Portugal's most important authority for the supervision of its wine trade, the Instituto do Vinho de Portugal.

Palácio da Bolsa

Also on the west side of the Praça do Infante Dom Henrique, occupying the site of a Franciscan convent which was destroyed by fire, is the Stock Exchange, the Palácio da Bolsa, built in 1842 and headquarters of Oporto's Chamber of Commerce. A modern glass building also stands where the convent cloisters once stood. The interior of the building can be visited on weekdays (guide compulsory), and the Moorish Hall, used for official receptions, is particularly worth seeing.

Igreja de São Francisco

South of the Palácio da Bolsa is the former church of the Franciscan convent, the Igreja de São Francisco (closed Sun. and Mon.). Originally Gothic but remodelled in Baroque style, it has a large rose window. The interior has sumptuous *talha dourada* decoration (17th/18th c.); also of interest is the elegant Renaissance tomb of the merchant Francisco Brandão Pereira (d. 1528) decorated with gilded vines, birds and angels. Adjoining the church is a small museum of sacred art. Above the museum there is access to the catacombs which were used in the 17th and 18th c. as tombs for members of the Franciscan order.

Caso do Infante

Until a few years ago it was considered very doubtful whether the Casa do Infante, or its predecessor (in the Rua Alfândega Velha, below the Praça do

View over Porto's sea of houses to the twin-towered Cathedral

Infante Dom Henrique) actually is the site of the house where Henry the Navigator was born. During investigations made in 1992 traces of 15th c. works were discovered together with some from the Roman era, under the foundations. Today it houses the city archives.

The Rua de São João continues down to the banks of the Douro. Although the only boats that moor in the former harbour quarter of Ribeira are those taking people for trips on the river, this part of Oporto still retains much of its former charm. Life centres on the Praça da Ribeira. Here and in the alleys around about, the "travessas", there is a maze of colourful houses which are a picturesque attraction for the tourists, albeit less attractive for the people who live here as the quarter is in urgent need of investment. Only some of the houses along the bank of the Douro were renovated and refurbished. Today they are art galleries, boutiques and high-class restaurants.

★★Ribeira

This centre lies in Rua Reboleira, to the west of Praça da Ribeira. Here visitors can see handicraft items from the north of Portugal; there is also the opportunity to purchase some nice gifts (closed Mon.).

Centro Regional de Artes Tradicionais

Walking east, passing by innumerable stalls, shops and simple restaurants, the visitor arrives at the lower tier of the Dom Luis I Bridge.

Ponte de D. Luis

From here it is possible either to walk over the bridge, enjoying the view of Oporto's sea of houses, and ending up by looking around one of the port wine lodges in Vila Nova de Gaia (see entry), or carrying on with the tour to the north and the Cathedral.

The twin-towered Cathedral (Sé) was originally a Romanesque church built in the 12th c. but later altered in Gothic style and almost completely rebuilt in the 17th and 18th c. while retaining much of its fortified character. The rosette over the portal on the west façade is still Romanesque, and the

★Sé

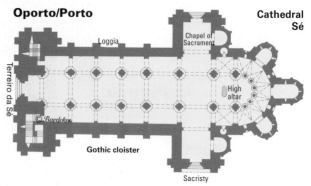

loggia on the north façade was by Nasoni in 1736. The interior is predominantly Romanesque and there are several richly decorated altars, including
the carved and gilded wooden main altar below the choir from the early
18th c., and, even more magnificent, the silver Altar of the Sacrament to the
left of the high altar, in the Capela-mór, and the work of several Portuguese
artists between 1632 and 1732. In the left-hand aisle can be seen the statue
of Nossa Senhora de Vendoma, patron saint of Oporto. In the south aisle is
an entrance, through the sacristy, into the Gothic cloister (1385); the azulejos date from the early 18th c. Adjoining this are the remains of the Romanesque cloister.

The terraces on the north and west sides of the cathedral afford views far
out over Oporto's maze of streets and houses. The Manueline pelourinho
on the Cathedral's west façade dates from the late 19th c.

Paço Episcopal

To the south of the cathedral is the former Bishop's Palace (begun 1771), an
imposing building with an elegant staircase and now occupied by civic
offices.

Igreja dos Grilos

The terrace on the west façade of the Cathedral faces the Igreja dos Grilos
which was built in 1614 by Baltazar Alvarés as a Jesuit seminary church. It
derives its name from the barefoot Augustinian monks to whom the church
passed in 1780. Because of their brown habits they were known as *grillos*
(crickets).

Casa Guerra
Junqueiro

To the east of the cathedral is an 18th c. Baroque building, at 32 Rua D.
Hugo, which is also ascribed to Nasoni. It was the abode of Abílio Manuel
de Guerra Junqueiro (1850–1923), the poet and political activist whose
verses vehemently championed the Republican cause.

Igreja de Santa
Clara

Further east the other side of the road onto the Ponte de D. Luis I, is the
church of Santa Clara, originally Gothic but much altered at the time of the
Renaissance and with an interior full of talha dourada.

Praça da Batalha

The Rua Augusto Rosa leads north-east from the Santa Clara church to the
traffic-thronged Praça da Batalha. Here the most impressive buildings are
the Igreja de Santo Ildefonso, with blue and white azulejos on its Baroque
façade, and the Teatro de São João (1920).

Rua de Santa
Catarinha

Igreja da
Immaculada

Oporto's main shopping street, the Rua de Santa Catarina, now partly
pedestrianised, runs from the north end of the square to the Praça do
Marquês de Pombal, where the church of the Immaculate Conception, the
Igreja da Imaculada Conceição, built between 1939 and 1947, is a good
example of more modern Portuguese church architecture. Those seeking

Street scene in Oporto

refreshment should visit the Café Majestic. This Art Nouveau style establishment has a unique atmosphere and stays open until 2am.

For another magnificent view, take the Rua de Alexandre Herculano from the southern end of the Praça da Batalha to the Alameda das Fontainhas, a lovely promenade high above the Douro.

To return to the start of the city-walk go west from the Praça da Batalha along Rua 31 de Janeiro to the main railway station, Estação de São Bento.

This station was built in the early 20th c., and the walls of its concourse are covered in azulejos depicting historical themes and the story of various means of transport.

Opposite the station stands the Igreja dos Congregados, built around 1700 and flanked by shops and flats, with azulejos over much of its façade.

It is just a few hundred yards from here to the Praça da Liberdade, thus completing this walk round the city.

Café Majestic

Estação de São Bento

Igreja dos Congregados

Vila Nova de Gaia

The port-wine trade, and its lodges, to which Oporto owes much of its fame, is concentrated in the suburb of Vila Nova de Gaia on the south bank of the Douro. "Gaia" is a version of the Latin "cale", i.e. lovely, as in "Portus Cale" (i.e. Portugal). Five bridges link Vila Nova de Gaia with Oporto:

Situation and General

Ponte de Dona Maria Pia, east of the centre, is a railway bridge, operational since 1877 and designed by Alexandre Gustave Eiffel. Its iron structure is 344m/1128ft long and about 60m/197ft above the river. To cope with the increasing volume a new railway bridge has been built close by.

Ponte de Dona Maria Pia

The bridge further west, outside the centre, is the Ponte da Arrábida which was opened in 1963 and carries the motorway. There is now a new motorway bridge to the east beyond the city centre.

Ponte da Arrábida

Oporto

★ Ponte de Dom Luis I

The bridge of Louis I, the Ponte de Dom Luis I, leads directly from the centre of Oporto to Vila Nova de Gaia. An iron bridge, it was built between 1881 and 1885 by the Belgian Willebroeck Company and spans the Douro in a single arch 172m/565ft wide. There are two roads, the lower one 10m/33ft, the upper one 68m/223ft above the water. From the upper road, which is also open to pedestrians, and from the south end in particular, there are magnificent views of the city and the river within its steeply sloping banks.

Mosteiro da Serra do Pilar

On a hill east of the Ponte de Dom Luis is the former Augustinian monastery of Serra do Pilar (17th c.). Adjoining the round church with its splendid dome is a cloister, also circular, its barrel-vaulting borne on 36 Ionic columns (only the church is open to visitors).

From the terrace there is what is probably the very best view over Oporto and the Douro Valley with its bridges.

★ Port lodges

West of the Ponte de Dom Luis are the long, low *armázens*, or lodges, often sunk deep in the granite, of Oporto's wine merchants, many of them British in origin.

Almost all the port producers offer tours daily (except Sun.) of their lodges. These include tastings and an opportunity to buy. (The section Wine, in Practical Information, includes some of the vocabulary used for port wine.)

Surroundings of Oporto

Foz do Douro

About 5km/3 miles downstream from Oporto, on a road which runs immediately above the steep bank of the Douro, with fine views back over the city, lies São João da Foz (or Foz do Douro), a suburb of Oporto, and a very popular bathing resort, beautifully situated at the mouth (foz, from Latin *fauces*) of the Douro. The Douro Litoral beach is fringed by palms, and from the breakwater with the harbour light there is an impressive view of the coast and the mouth of the river, commanded by the Castelo da Foz (1570).

Further north-west, on the road to Matosinhos, is the 17th c. Castelo do Queijo, built to protect the coast against pirates from North Africa.

Matosinhos

Matosinhos, 10km/6½ miles north of Oporto, at the mouth of the Leça river, is an industrial town and port. Fish canning factories make an important contribution to its economy. Ignoring the "industrial background", many Portuguese visit the town to enjoy the good bathing beaches.

The church of Bom Jesus de Bouças (originally 16th c., extended in the 18th c.), is of historical interest. The choir has ormolu carvings and there is a

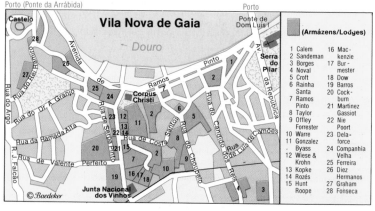

Porto (Ponte da Arrábida)   Porto

Vila Nova de Gaia

Castelo

~ Douro

Ponte de Dom Luis I

Serra do Pilar

Corpus Christi

Junta Nacional dos Vinhos

© Baedeker

(Armázens/Lodges)

1 Calem	16 Mac-
2 Sandeman	kenzie
3 Borges	17 Bur-
4 Noval	mester
5 Croft	18 Dow
6 Rainha	19 Barros
Santa	20 Cock-
7 Ramos	burn
Pinto	21 Martinez
8 Taylor	Gassiot
9 Offley	22 Nie
Forrester	Poort
10 Warre	23 Dela-
11 Gonzalez	force
Byass	24 Companhia
12 Wiese &	Velha
Krohn	25 Ferreira
13 Kopke	26 Diez
14 Rozés	Hermanos
15 Hunt	27 Graham
Roope	28 Fonseca

Barcos rabelos: the boats in which port was once transported from the Duoro Valley to Vila Nova de Gaia now only serve a decorative purpose

beautiful coffered ceiling and a very old crucifix much revered by the many pilgrims who come here. The Quinta da Conceição municipal park is very attractive. It was laid out on the site of a former convent, of which the 18th c. Capela de São Francisco and the 15th c. cloister are preserved.

At the mouth of the Leça river lies the modern port of Porto de Leixões. It has a harbour basin, protected by two pincer-like breakwaters (1597m/1750yd and 1145m/1256yd long respectively), which serves the city of Oporto as an outer harbour. It was built in 1884, constantly extended during the 20th c., and is today one of the largest harbours on the Iberian Peninsula.

Porto de Leixões

Leça do Bailio, a few miles north of Oporto, has a fortified Romanesque/Gothic church (1336) from what was a monastery of the Hospitallers of John of Jerusalem. It contains richly sculpted capitals, 16th c. tombs and a fine 16th c. Manueline font. The Manueline calvary next to the church dates from 1514.

Leça do Bailio

About 14km/9 miles south of Oporto is the village of Grijó, with a monastery founded in the 12th c. and comprehensively remodelled in the 16th c. The cloister has beautiful azulejo decoration and contains the tomb of Rodrigo Sancho (d. 1245), son of Sancho I. The church has a fine altar with talha dourada decoration.

Grijó

35km/22 miles east of Oporto on the hill between the valleys of Rio Sousa and Rio Tâmega is the long straggling little town of Penafiel (alt. 500m/1640ft; pop. 6000) which was known until the late 18th c. as Arrifana de Sousa. It has a 14th c. castle and the Renaissance-style church of the Misericórdia (16th c.), originally the church of a Franciscan convent.

Penafiel

Some 10km/6 miles south-west of Penafiel is the important Romanesque monastic church of Paço de Sousa (12th c.). Comprehensively restored

Paço de Sousa

Do you know Dr Wright of Norwich?

Tawny, Red, Ruby, Late Bottle Vintage, White Port – no wonder that with such names many people believe port wine to be a British product, and everyone knows how much the British value this noble drink. It is indeed correct that without Britain Portugal's most famous export from the upper and lower reaches of the Douro would probably never have materialised.

Back in Roman times grapes from which wine was produced were grown on the steep slopes of the upper reaches of the Douro river. However, this wine, sold in the Oporto region, was known as *vinho de cale*, not port. In the course of time it became more popularly known as *vinho para nobres* (wine for the nobility). This juice of the grape, an ordinary red wine, was also exported. As early as the Middle Ages the British are thought to have developed a taste for the "Portugal red", as it was originally called. During the Wars of the Roses the Duke of Clarence was taken prisoner by his brother King Richard III and supposedly drowned by him in a barrel of wine – a Malvasier from Oporto. The export of wine from the Oporto region to Britain is believed to have expanded considerably after King Charles II (1630–85) and the Portuguese Princess Catarina of the House of Bragança became betrothed. In 1666 a "factory house" was founded in Oporto, a type of guild of British merchants which has survived to this day as the British Association. Shortly afterwards some of the families whose names still appear on bottles of port established businesses in the area – the Warres and Crofts from Britain, the Kopkes and, somewhat later, the Zellers from the Netherlands and the Burmesters from Germany. The Britishers formed by far the largest group. In 1680 port wine, the *vinho de Porto* as it is now known, was born. In that year British merchants began to mix up to 25% of spirit with the red wine from the Douro valley in order to help it to keep better during the sea voyage to Britain. In the early 19th century the ferment, 76% proof, was also prized as a special wine – the softer, sweeter nectar, 20% proof, which we know today was developed from this former crude "rotgut".

Port wine led to a particularly close economic liaison between Oporto and Britain, and to Portugal's economic independence. On December 17th 1703 Portugal and Britain signed a trade agreement, known as the Methuen Treaty, named after the British envoy in Lisbon, John Methuen, whose father and father-in-law owned textile mills. This agreement governed the interchange of British textiles and Portuguese wine. Since 1684 the importation of British wool and cloth into Portugal had been prohibited, but now Britain obtained relief on its exports of wool while Portugal could export its wine to Britain at favourable terms and fill a profitable gap which had arisen after the British crown, in protest against the protective customs duties and taxes levied by Louis XIV, had prohibited the import of French wines.

Although the agreement was intended as an indirect attack on the French economy it was in fact Portugal who suffered most. In spite of the boom in port wine which now ensued there were devastating effects on the Portuguese economy. For one thing, the country was flooded with British woollen goods, resulting in the devastation of the local woollen industry, and for another many farmers and landowners changed their production – instead of corn and vegetables they grew only wine grapes in anticipation of greater profit. The wine which was now produced in great quantities naturally became cheaper and cheaper; on the other hand, there was an increasing shortage of corn which had to be met by increased imports from Britain. Clearly the British were rubbing their hands, while the enormous imports of corn and textiles had to be paid for with two-thirds of the gold which the Portuguese throne received from its colonies.

In 1757 the royal minister the Marquês de Pombal set up a Portuguese monopoly company for trading in port wine, known as the Companhia Geral da Agricultura dos Vinhos do Alto Douro, and later as the Old Wine Company and the Royal Oporto Wine Company; under the latter name it is still today one of the largest port wine firms in Portugal. However, the only people to profit from the lucrative port wine trade were the land-owning nobility, not the small dealers and wine-growers, many of whom lost everything they owned. In that same year the wine-growers formed a resistance group against the hated trading company. They forced their way into its offices and cellars in Oporto and burned them down. Pombal reacted promptly. Of the several thousand who took part in the revolt 442 were taken to court; 26 were sentenced to death, with 17 actually going to the gallows. Pombal's aim of undermining the predominant position of the British met with only limited success, however. The large British firms remained in existence and developed to become the most respected producers of port wine, as can be seen from such household names as Sandeman, Delaforce, Croft, etc.

For centuries the British were the largest consumers of port. In the 18th and 19th centuries it was regarded as *the* drink for British gentlemen; in the opinion of many patriots it was port which held the British Empire together, and woe betide anybody who criticised or defiled it! Even Lord Nelson has never been forgiven for reportedly sketching plans for his sea battles on his plate with old port wine. For a time this wine seemed to be better known in Britain that in its country of origin; at least, many Englishmen travelling to Lisbon in the 18th century are said to have sadly missed the port wine they had become used to at home!

Port wine cellar in Vila Nova de Gaia

The British national drink also resulted in drinking habits some of which appear strange, and in countless entries in books of etiquette and good manners. One custom is to "pass the port" from guest to guest. If one guest fails to do this he is gently reminded with the traditional question "Do you know Dr Wright of Norwich?". The reference is to a gentleman from the 1850s who was renowned for talking too much and consequently failing to remember to "pass the port".

after a fire in 1927, the church belonged at one time to a Benedictine monastery, and a part of its cloister has been retained.

The church has also maintained its Romanesque strength in the interior; the column bases are hewn from millstones. At the far end of the church is the sarcophagus (12th c.) of Egaz Moniz (1050–1140), tutor and confidant of Afonso Henriques, who played a major part in the history of his time. He is particularly remembered for an occasion in 1130 when, after Afonso Henriques I had broken his word to Afonso VII of León, he made his way to the Spanish king's court with a rope around his neck, accompanied by his wife and children, in order to do penance on behalf of his master. Impressed by his honesty and nobility, the Spaniard forgave the offence and allowed Moniz to return to Portugal. The very affecting reliefs on the sarcophagus, supported by lions, show scenes from the life of the dead man.

Palmela   B 6

Historical province: Estremadura. District: Setúbal
Altitude: 238m/781ft. Population: 18,000

Situation and Importance	The little hill town of Palmela, in the Serra de São Luís, an eastern outlier of the Serra da Arrábida, is famous for the local wine, and the vintage in September and October is accompanied by several festivals.

The town owes its name to the Roman praetor of Lusitania province, Aulio Cornelio Palma. In 1995 Volkswagen and Ford opened a joint factory near Palmela to manufacture stretch limousines. At present it employs 3000 workers.

Townscape — Palmela is a simple hill-town with no particular sights other than its castle. However, a walk round the town should take in the 18th c. church of São Pedro on the Largo do Município, below the castle, with fine azulejo pictures of scenes from the life of St Peter. The hall in the 17th c. town hall diagonally opposite is adorned with portraits of Portuguese kings.

★ Castelo

History — During the Moorish period Palmela had the most formidable fortress in southern Portugal. This was captured by King Afonso Henriques first in 1147 and then finally, after the Moors had retaken it, in 1166 when he had it further enlarged and gave it to the knightly Order of Santiago, who made it their headquarters in the 15th c. In the 18th c. the castle was again strengthened to protection it against attack from artillery as well.

Torre de Menagem — From the late 14th c. keep, the Torre de Menagem, there is a good view over the whole castle complex and on a clear day you can see as far as Lisbon and the Tagus estuary. In 1484 the bishop of Évora, Garcia de Meneses, was incarcerated in the cistern of the keep, with other prisoners, for his involvement in a conspiracy, and presumed to have been poisoned there.

Igreja de Santa Maria do Castelo — Within the castle precincts are the ruins of the Igreja de Santa Maria do Castelo, a Renaissance church built on the site of an earlier Moorish mosque and which collapsed in the 1755 earthquake.

São Tiago — The western end of the castle precinct is occupied by the former Convent of Santiago, built in the 15th c. but subsequently much altered. Nowadays part of it is a pousada. The convent church, in a style transitional between Romanesque and Gothic, has beautiful azulejo decoration (17th and 18th c.) in the interior, and contains the tomb of Jorge de Lencastre (1481–1550), a natural son of King João II.

Surroundings of Palmela

Quinta do Anjo — At Quinta do Anjo, 3km/2 miles west of Palmela, there are tombs which were carved out of the rock about 5000 years ago, and which served as burial chambers until the Middle Ages. These are reached by turning left in the centre of Quinta do Anjo, coming from Palmela, and turning left again at the end of the houses into a track across the fields.

See entry

Setúbal

See Costa de Lisboa

Serra da Arrábida

Peneda-Gerês National Park/Parque Nacional da Peneda-Gerês B/C 2/3

Historical provinces: Minho and Trás-os-Montes
Districts: Viana do Castelo, Braga and Vila Real
Area: 50,000 hectares/193sq. miles. Altitude: up to 1545m/5070ft

The Peneda-Gerês National Park extends along the Spanish frontier from the Castro Laboreiro plateau by way of the Peneda, Soajo, Amarela and Gerês mountains to the Mourela plateau in the south. Large areas within the park boundaries, which were officially defined in 1971, are protected nature reserves. The park can be explored by car, and also has several good walks. Accommodation is limited: there are a few pensions in the spa town of Gerês. Detailed information about the national park can be obtained from the visitors centres in Arcos de Valdevez, Gerês and Montalegre.

The park includes expanses of completely unspoilt country with magnificent forest and mountain scenery and beautiful artificial lakes. The highest peaks are in the Serra do Gerês, which rises within Portuguese territory to 1545m/5069ft in the Nevosa and 1538m/5046ft in the Altar de Cabroês.

★★ Topography

The very varied pattern of relief gives rise to widely different microclimates, and in consequence the plant life of the park shows unusual variety. Moreover, the remoteness of this region has protected many endemic species from destruction by man, so that plants are found here which have disappeared from the rest of Europe. In addition to great tracts of coniferous forest there are stands of centuries-old oaks (particularly at Pincães and São Lourenço), cork-oaks (at Ermida), eucalyptus, and expanses of rocky country covered with heather.

Vegetation

The wildlife includes deer, wild boar, hares, partridges, wild horses, lizards, snakes and even wolves and golden eagles.

Fauna

The many archaeological sites show that the Peneda-Gerês National Park area was one of ancient human settlement. The dolmens (megalithic chamber tombs) of Mezio, Paradela, Cambezes, Pitões and Tourém date from the 3rd millennium B.C. Pre-Roman, presumably Celtic, castros (camps) have been excavated at Pitões, Tourém and Cidadelhe, and there are believed to be still more prehistoric settlements as yet undiscovered. Today some 15,000 people inhabit over 100 villages in the park.

Human settlement

Touring by car

The names in the margin refer to the park entrances.
Although not all the park roads are surfaced with tarmac most of them are quite good to drive on. The signing is minimal, and it's not unusual to find that what seems at first a reliable way ahead suddenly comes to a dead end. Since all the roads are full of bends it is wise to allow plenty of time for the tours.
It should be borne in mind that the Spanish frontier crossing-points are only open in the summer. Further information can be had from the tourist information centre in Braga (see Practical Information, Information).

The Lamas de Mouro entrance is at the north end of the park, about 10km/ 6 miles south-east of Melgaço. Castro Laboreiro is about 8km/5 miles

Lamas de Mouro

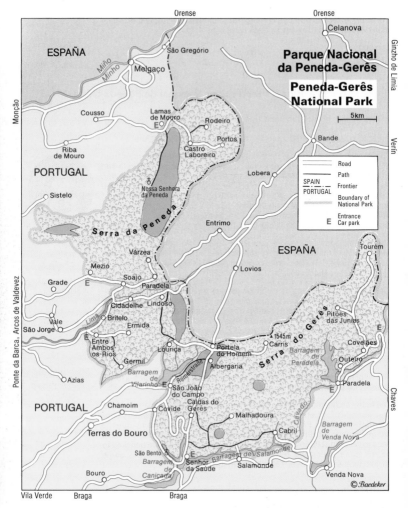

south-east of the entrance. Its nearby castle was probably originally a Roman fortress, and was then rebuilt by Afonso Henriques and extended by King Dinis. It was, however, almost completely destroyed by an explosion when the powder tower was struck by lightning. From Castro Laboreiro visitors can enter Spain by way of Ameijoeira (and if desired, return to the national park through another entrance).

It is also possible to drive south from Lamas de Mouro to the pilgrimage church of Nossa Senhora da Peneda (pilgrimages in first week in September) and then further south to the Mezio park entrance.

In the Peneda-Gerês National Park ▶

Mezio

The Mezio entrance is 18km/11 miles north-east of Arcos de Valdevez. Five km/3 miles south-east on a tarmacked road is the mountain eyrie of Soajo, its houses built of undressed granite blocks without the use of mortar. Its 10th c. pelourinho is the oldest stone column in Portugal. On the roadside there are a number of espigueiros, the small stone grainstores that are characteristic of this region (see Minho). A road runs south from here through the valley of the Rio Lima, past electric power-stations, to Cidadelhe, where the route described in the next paragraph can be joined.

Entre-Ambos-os-
Rios

The Entre-Ambos-os-Rios entrance, 13km/8 miles north-east of Ponte da Barca, is also often used for through traffic to Spain. The route runs east along what used to be the very scenic valley of the Rio Lima. The road passes the rather gloomy-looking mountain villages of Britelo and Cidadelhe, with their sombre granite houses, ascending to Lindoso (alt. 468m/1536ft; pop. 1000), just before the Spanish frontier. Looming over it is a castle built under King Dinis in 1287, and here you can see more of Minho's typical espigueiros (see Minho). Lindoso is the jumping-off point for a number of good walks – to the artificial lake of Viarinho das Furnas; to the Miradouro Leira do Canto, with a beautiful view of the Lima valley; to the pass of Portela do Homem (822m/2697ft) on the Spanish frontier, affording a magnificent prospect of the rocky valley of the Rio Homem; and south to the Cabril Forest.

São João do
Campo

From the São João do Campo entrance, 17km/10 miles north-east of Terras do Bouro, you can either drive south-east along the narrow, winding little road to Caldas do Gerês, or take the old Roman road. This was built between 79 and 353 A.D., and runs along the south-east side of the Vilarinho reservoir up to the Portela do Homem on the Spanish frontier. It has the largest number of original Roman milestones on the Iberian peninsula.

Senhor da Saúde

Probably the most frequented road in the National Park runs from the Senhor da Saúde entrance, 32km/20 miles north-east of Braga, near the Barragem de Caniçada. It is also the main road to the little spa of Caldas do Gerês (alt. 400m/1312ft), scenically located in a narrow valley. Also known simply as Gerês, the spa specialises in complaints connected with the gall-bladder and the liver, and is a good base for walking and clmbing in the Serra do Gerês. From here a good road runs north to Portela do Homem, on the frontier. The route then takes you east, on foot in places, to Carris at the foot of the Altar de Cabrões, which has a fine lookout point.

Paradela/Covelães

The easternmost section of the park has two entrances, Paradela (65km/ 40 miles north-east of Braga, on the Barragem de Paradela reservoir), and Covelães (75km/47 miles north-east of Braga, 13km/8 miles north-west of Montalegre), providing access to narrow, little-used tracks leading to the prehistoric sites of Pitões and Tourém.

Peniche   A 5

Historical province: Estremadura. District: Leiria
Altitude: 0–15m/0–50ft. Population: 15,500

Situation and
Importance

The busy little fishing town of Peniche is one of Portugal's most important places for crayfish, sardine and tuna fisheries (cannery). It lies on a rocky peninsula on the Portuguese Atlantic coast, almost 3km/2 miles long and just over 2km/1¼ miles wide, edged by rugged cliffs and linked to the mainland by a narrow sandspit. Peniche's tourism has remained within reasonable bounds. There are few hotels of any size in the town itself, and seaside pursuits tend to be enjoyed on the long sandy beaches on both sides of the isthmus (istmo).
   Peniche has a State school of pillow-lace making, which is a traditional local craft.

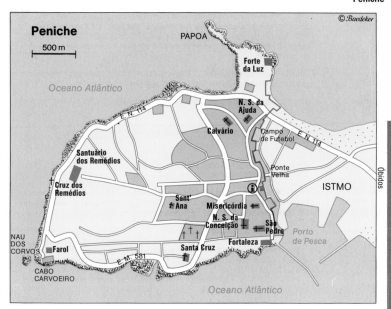

Fortifying walls and a moat, securing the town to landward, run from the fortress in the south of the town to the northernmost point of the peninsula. The harbour, protected by two breakwaters, is the scene of lively activity. In the summer a regular boat service runs from here to the Berlenga Islands (see entry), and there is also the spectacle of the arrival of the fishing boats to be speedily unloaded. Their perishable cargoes are then auctioned on a conveyor belt in a large hangar.

Townscape

Sights

The town, and indeed the whole peninsula, is dominated by the well-preserved fort (fortaleza) near the harbour, built by Filippo Terzi in the 16th c. and considerably enlarged in the 17th c., with Vauban-style fortifications. It achieved notoriety under Salazar's dictatorship when he used it to incarcerate political prisoners. Part of the former prison – cells, visitors' room and other communal facilities – is open to the public, and there are also displays designed to give an idea of the repression and the resistance during the Salazar regime. Also in the fortress is the regional museum, with exhibits particularly related to the fishing industry.

★ Fortaleza

In the centre of the town, near the ramparts, is the Baroque church of the Misericórdia, with scenes from the New Testament on its wooden ceiling. A few yards further south is another Baroque church, the 17th c. church of São Pedro, with 18th c. talha dourada in the choir, while right in the north of the town, near the football field, is the Igreja Ajuda, with rich azulejo decoration and ceiling paintings in the choir.

Other sights

Surroundings of Peniche

Several roads lead to Cabo Carvoeiro, and its lighthouse (farol), 2km/ 1¼ miles west of the town, on a rocky headland which has been eroded

★ Cabo Carvoeiro

into bizarrely shaped pinnacles and sea-caves and has excellent fishing and crayfish grounds. There are views of the Nau dos Corvos ("raven's ship") rock offshore, and beyond to the Berlenga Islands (see entry). There are also fine views from the fish restaurant that has been opened on this exposed spot.

Santuário dos Remédios
Several hundred yards north of the cape stands the chapel dos Remédios, a place of pilgrimage entirely clad with azulejos.

Óbidos
The picturesque town of Óbidos (see entry) is 25km/15½ miles east of Peniche.

Ponte da Barca   B 3

Historical province: Minho. District: Viana do Castelo
Altitude: 178m/584ft. Population: 1500

Situation and Importance
Ponte de Barca is a quiet little market town 30km/19 miles north of Braga on the left bank of the Rio Lima. It is also a popular base for excursions around the Peneda-Gerês National Park (see entry).

Townscape
There is a fine view of the town from the old 15th/16th c. bridge over the Rio Lima.
The main building in the town centre is the handsome 15th c. parish church, which has a beautiful coffered ceiling and a silver crucifix presented by King Manuel I.
The pelourinho in the market place in the lower part of town dates from the 16th c.

Surroundings of Ponte da Barca

★Bravães
About 5km/3 miles west of Ponte da Barca, on the outskirts of Bravães, is the 12th c. little Romanesque church of São Salvador which owes its fame to its elaborately sculpted portals, where animal and plant motifs vie with geometric patterns and human faces. The interior also has rich relief decoration and carved friezes, as well as what is left of 14th c. frescos, the best of these being on display in the Soares dos Reis Museum in Oporto (see Oporto).

Ponte de Lima
The old-world little town of Ponte de Lima lies a further 15km/9 miles west of Bravães, where the river Lima is spanned by a medieval bridge of 24 arches. The town also has several impressive 16th c. town-houses, an interesting Manueline portal on the former convent church Santo António dos Frades, and, in the Torre de São Paulo, a remnant of the medieval ramparts.

★Arcos de Valdevez
Five km/3 miles north of Ponte da Barca, straddling the Rio Vez, is the extremely picturesque little market town of Arcos de Valdevez (pop. 3000), with a 14th c. parish church (remodelled in the 17th c.). In front of the church is a remarkably fine Manueline pelourinho; behind it, in the Praça do Terreiro, stands the 16th c. Casa do Terreiro. Also worth looking at are the Baroque façade of the church of Nossa Senhora da Lapa and a monolithic column in front of the Espírito Santo church in the upper town, commemorating the town's support of Afonso Henriques in his conflict with the Spaniards.

Portalegre   C 5

Historical province: Alto Alentejo. District: Portalegre
Altitude: 477m/1565ft. Population: 16,000

Ponta da Barca: an old bridge over the Rio Lima

The district capital of Portalegre (happy gate), the Roman Amoea, lies near the Spanish frontier at the foot of the Serra de Portalegre, a westerly outlier of the Serra de São Mamede. With its white houses reaching up the steep slopes of the hill and its numerous handsome old palaces it is the great showcase of Portuguese Baroque architecture. The old episcopal city rose to prosperity in the 16th c. through its woollen industry, in particular the production of tapestries, but its real heyday came in the late 17th c. with the rise of the silk-weaving industry. Today Portalegre is still important for its woollens, but also for woodworking and cork-processing.

Since its nearby industry makes Portalegre a rather noisy and hectic place tourists usually only pause briefly on their way through to the two pleasant resorts further north, Castelo de Vide and Marvão (see entries).

Situation and Importance

The old town centre of Portalegre is surrounded by medieval walls, with the ruins of the massive medieval castle (1290) at the highest point. The town's most notable buildings, many of them no longer at their best, are grouped around the Praça do Município. North of it is Portalegre's modern centre, the traffic swirling round the Rossio, in its splendid garden setting. Around the busy square are handsome mansions, government buildings, the Misericórdia hospital, with an 18th c. façade and a beautiful patio, and the tourist information centre.

Townscape

Sights

The Cathedral, or Sé, forms the west side of the Praça do Município. Built in the 16th c. it was considerably altered in the 18th c. when the main façade, flanked by two towers, was also added. The three-aisled Renaissance interior has been preserved in its 16th c. form. In the second chapel on the right can be seen an altarpiece with scenes from the life of the Virgin, while the sacristy has an azulejo version of the Flight into Egypt. The cloister is 18th c.

Sé

Portalegre

Museu Municipal	Opposite the Cathedral, to the north-east, is the little Municipal Museum, which has a collection of Chinese porcelain, ivory, woodcarvings and religious art.
Câmara Municipal	The 18th c. town hall, the Câmara Municipal, on the same square is also of interest.
Palácio Amarelo	Take the alley between the Cathedral and the Museum, then keep right to reach the Palácio Amarelo (yellow palace, after its colour), or Palácio dos Albrançalhas, to give it its proper name. Nowadays used as a house, and not in the best state of repair, the 17th c. ironwork on its balconies and windows is among the finest in Portugal.
Convento de Santa Clara	South-east of the Praça do Município in the Rua Santa Clara is the 14th c. Convent of Poor Clares, with a noteworthy cloister. It is at present being converted into a library.
Praça da República	From the Praça do Município the Rua do 19 de Junho, lined by fine 17th and 18th c. patrician houses, leads south-east to the Praça da República. Here too there are handsome mansions, some of them faced with azulejos, including the Palácio dos Condes de Avilés (now occupied by the Civil Governor) and the Palácio dos Fonseca Acciolo (now a school). Also on the Praça da República is a former Franciscan convent, founded in the 13th c. and largely rebuilt in the 18th c.
Casa de José Régio	Lovers of religious sculpture would be well advised to visit the Casa de José Régio Museum, once the home of the poet José Régio (1901–69), in the Rua de José Régio, just south of the Praça da República. Its contents include the Portuguese poet's unusual private collection of figures of Christ and other religious statuettes.
Manufactura de Tapeçarias	The Manufactura de Tapeçarias, north-east of the old town by the Parque do M. Bombarda, can be traced back to silk-weaving and tapestry workshops founded by Marquês de Pombal in 1772. It is based in a former 17th c. Jesuit convent.
Convento de São Bernardo	The former convent of São Bernardo is a short distance north of the Parque do M. Bombarda. Now a barracks, it can be visited on request. It was founded in 1518 and later remodelled in Baroque style. It contains the splendid marble tomb of the bishop of Guarda, Dom Jorge de Melo, founder of the convent, which is ascribed to the 16th c. French sculptor Nicolas de Chanterène. The convent also has two fine cloisters, one Manueline and the other Renaissance; in the larger of the two can be seen a beautiful marble fountain. The chapterhouse has fine groined vaulting.

Surroundings of Portalegre

Viewpoints	The scenery around Portalegre is exceptionally attractive. There are superb views from Penha de São Tomé, a rocky outcrop 2km/1¼ miles north-west of the town, and from Pico São Mamede (1025m/3363ft), 13km/8 miles to the east and the highest point in the Serra de São Mamede.
Castelo de Vide	See entry
Marvão	See entry
Medóbriga	About 12km/7½ miles north of Portalegre, near the village of Aramenha, are the remains of the Roman settlement of Medóbriga. Discoveries from the site can be seen in the National Museum of Archaeology and Ethnology in Belém (see Lisbon).

Crato is about 20km/12 miles west of Portalegre and was the headquarters of the Maltese Order. Little is left of the great convent complex which was destroyed by Spanish troops in 1662.

Crato

The former Maltese convent in Flor da Rosa, 2km/1¼ mile north of Crato, is much better preserved, and parts of the complex, which was built around 1350 and extended in the 16th c., now contain a pousada. The convent church is impressive, and the Late Gothic cloister boasts sleek marble columns.

Flor da Rosa

Alter do Chão, 30km/19 miles south-west of Portalegre, is famous for having the National Stud which dates back to 1748 when the "Coudelaria Real", or royal stud, was founded. In addition to some 18th c. mansions the interesting little town has a 14th c. castle, complete with battlements, a lovely Renaissance fountain (1556), and the Vasconcelos family castle (1732).

Alter do Chão

Portimão

B 7

Historical province: Algarve. District: Faro
Altitude: 0–35m/0–115ft. Population: 30,000

Together with Faro and Olhão, Portimão is one of the largest towns in the Algarve. For a number of years it was the centre of the heavily subsided Portuguese sardine fishing and canning industries. By the mid-1970s more than 70 trawlers regularly went out to catch the fish which were then processed in 61 factories. After the end of the Salazar regime the subsidies were drasticaly reduced. Today there is only one fish canning works in Portimão, six trawlers operate and the bank of the river is lined with sardine

Situation and importance

Ferragudo, often featured on postcards, is one of the most scenic areas in the Algarve

293

factories which have closed down. There are some wharves in the north of the town.

Economically speaking, tourism plays but a minor role; visitors to Portimão are mainly those coming just for the day from nearby tourist resorts. The town offers good opportunities for shopping – in the centre, to the north-west of Praça Manuel Teixeira Gomes, there is a large selection of shops. In the north of Portimão an iron bridge and an old vehicle bridge cross the Rio Arade, and leads to the town centre. For many years the latter bridge was the only one over the Arade and therefore proved a permanent bottleneck. Finally a new bridge was built further north, and today the N 125 expressway passes over it.

| Townscape | Portimão is a very lively town. A degree of port atmosphere pervades the area near the approach to the old bridge. Here there are numerous simple eating-places, small family businesses, where one can enjoy excellent fresh fish, especially sardines, of course. Further south lies an attractively laid out river-bank zone with spacious squares, where both tourists and locals while away the time in cafés. |

Sights

| Praça Visconde de Bívar | The Praça Visconde de Bívar on the bank of the river is attractively laid out as a park. From here there is a fine view across the Rio Arade to the opposite bank and the town of Ferragudo (see Surroundings). |

| Largo 1° de Dezembro | The main attractions in the homely Largo 1° de Dezembro are the ten banks which display azulejo pictures portraying important events in Portuguese history. |

| Igreja Matriz | On a hill to the north of Largo 1° de Dezembro stands the Igreja Matriz. A 14th c. church stood here before the 1755 earthquake; only the Gothic portal remains. Note the small, weathered capitals showing various heads. The interior has three aisles and contains statues of saints saved from the old church. |

Surroundings of Portimão

| Praia da Rocha | The tourist resort of Praia da Rocha (see entry) lies to the south. |

| ★ Ferragudo | On the opposite bank of the Rio Arade lies the attractive fishing village of Ferragudo, with its narrow streets lined with fishermen's houses, a few pensions and restaurants. Above the village stands a very pretty church, as well as the Fortaleza de São João, built in 1622 to protect the river entrance. It is now in private ownership.

South of Ferragudo stretches the Praia Grande, a long beach. A breakwater ensures safe bathing, and it is also very popular with surfers. Restaurants offer refreshments. |

| Silves | Silves (see entry), about 15km/9 miles north-east of Portimão, still has an old-world air about it. |

| Algarve | Other destinations worth visiting around Portimão are described in the entry on the Algarve. |

Póvoa de Varzim   B 3

Historical province: Douro Litoral. District: Porto
Altitude: sea level. Population: 24,000

| Situation and Importance | The little fishing town of Póvoa de Varzim straggles along the Atlantic coast 20km/12 miles north of Oporto, almost merging with neighbouring Vila do |

Conde (see entry). Because of its 2km/1¼ miles long, broad beach it is a popular seaside resort, particularly with the Portuguese themselves.

Póvoa de Varzim is the birthplace of the great Portuguese novelist Eça de Queirós (1845–1900), who is commemorated by a monument outside the Town Hall.

The local speciality is a fish stew – caldeirada à Póvoa.

Póvoa de Varzim's skyline is dominated by innumerable imposing apart- **Townscape** ment buildings, and the businesses that have sprung up around the centre have also made Póvoa de Varzim look less like a seaside resort.

The Municipal Museum, the Museu Municipal de Etnografia e História, contains interesting material on local history and folk traditions.

Praia da Rocha B 7

Historical province: Algarve. District: Faro
Altitude: 20m/65ft. Population: 2000

The popular seaside resort of Praia da Rocha, or "rocky beach", boasts an **Situation and** unusually mild climate and beautiful golden-yellow sandy beaches edged **Importance** by rugged cliffs. Administratively part of the town of Portimão (see entry) 3km/2 miles to the north, it is in one of the most beautiful parts of the Algarve. Originally a favourite residential area with well-to-do citizens of Portimão, who built their elegant villas here, around the turn of the 19th c. Praia da Rocha started becoming increasingly attractive to visitors from other parts of Portugal and abroad, especially Britain. Today it offers ample sports and entertainment facilities, as well as numerous restaurants, cafés and bars.

Along the clifftop above the chief beach, almost 2km/1¼ miles long and **Townscape** 100m/110yd wide, runs the Avenida Tomás, the town's promenade and

Beautiful wide sandy beaches at Praia da Rocha

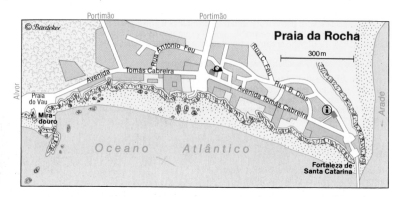

main thoroughfare, lined with hotels, restaurants, cafés, shops and boutiques. At its eastern end the 16th c. Fortaleza de Santa Catarina, nowadays a restaurant with a view of Ferragudo (see Portimão), overlooks the mouth of the Rio Arade.

The western end of the Avenue provides a particularly good view of Praia da Rocha's rocky scenery.

★ Beaches

Praia da Rocha's main beach is very picturesque, and consequently very popular. To the west extends a series of idyllic sandy bays separated from one another by projecting crags and reefs, although since a number of large holiday colonies are located around here, particularly near Alvor (see Algarve), it is not easy to find a secluded little spot. Recent developments have led to increasing numbers of highrise blocks, giving rise to overcrowding and commercialisation. There is an extremely pleasant boat trip from Praia da Rocha past rugged seacliffs, with their bizarre rock formations, to Praia dos Três Irmãos, the "beach of the three brothers".

Queluz   A 6

Historical province: Estremadura
District: Lisboa
Altitude: 125m/410ft
Population 48,000

Situation and Importance

This town, 15km/9 miles north-west of Lisbon, owes its importance and its fame to the charming Rococo palace of Queluz ("what light!"), once a summer residence of the Bragança kings, and still used today for official government receptions.

Townscape

Apart from the palace Queluz has no sights to recommend it, but since it is on a direct commuting line to Lisbon it now has additional housing for about 30,000 people.

★ Palácio Nacional de Queluz

The palace and gardens are normally open Mon., Wed.–Sun. 10am–1pm and 2–5pm, but since they are used for official receptions it pays to check with the tourist information centre in Lisbon whether the palace complex will be open.

The Palace of Queluz, surrounded by beautiful gardens

The palace was built between 1747 and 1794 for Pedro III and his wife, later Queen Maria I, originally to the design of the Portuguese architect Mateus Vicente de Oliveira (1706–85), a pupil of the German architect Johann Friedrich Ludwig who built the Convent-Palace of Mafra (see entry). The central block was complete by 1758, then in 1760 the west wing of the palace was built by the French architect, Jean-Baptiste Robillon, who also designed the gardens and many of the rooms. He completed the work in 1794.

History of the building

In front of the palace is the spacious Largo do Palácio, with a statue of Queen Maria I. The Palace Chapel, in the purest Rococo style and containing the military music school and accommodation for the royal guard (one wing was opened as a pousada in 1995), is separated from the rest of the palace buildings by a road.

Castle square

The Palácio Nacional de Queluz – consisting of a central block and two wings – gives the impression of a warm and friendly building and is therefore sometimes compared, not unreasonably, with Frederick the Great's palace of Sanssouci near Berlin. The rich interior decoration is notable for the high quality of the craftsmanship and the sure taste with which the details are contrived and related to one another. Outstanding among the many rooms in the palace are the Throne Room, the Queen's Wardrobe (beautiful azulejo pictures) and the Hunting Room (ceiling paintings of hunting scenes). The Kitchens, also decorated with azulejos, are now occupied by a luxury restaurant, the Cozinha Velha.

Palace of Queluz

Behind the palace are Jean-Baptiste Robillon's Rococo gardens, with fountains, grottoes and sculpture, some of them in lead cast in England. In the lower part of the gardens is the 115m/126yd long Ribeira de Jamor basin, beautifully faced with azulejos.

Gardens

Ribatejo

Historical province: Ribatejo
District: Santarém
Area: 6600sq.km/250sq. miles
Population: 460,000
Chief town: Santarém

Location and Topography

Taken in the narrowest sense, the Ribatejo ("bank of the Tagus") region, roughly corresponding to the present district of Santarém, comprises only the alluvial basin of the lower Tagus valley, in the east of the province of Estremadura. This is a highly fertile area of some 600sq.km/230sq. miles which is still sinking as a result of tectonic movements.

The historical province of Ribatejo, however, with its capital at Santarém, also includes the fertile upland regions to the north and south and the plateau to the east – all relics of the Tertiary and Quaternary tableland through which the Tagus has carved its course.

Population and Agriculture

The drier upland region to the north is densely populated and intensively farmed, mainly by smallholdings practising mixed farming (wheat, olives, wine, citrus fruits, figs). The area to the south, on the other hand, is sparsely populated. Here the large estates and the increasing custom of single-crop farming (wheat, olives, cork-oaks) show the same agricultural structure as in the Alentejo region (see Alentejo) to the south.

The water meadows, which form a strip some 50km/30 miles wide along the Tagus and which are flooded every spring (January–April), provide ideal conditions for growing grain and rice.

Here, too, is the grazing land, often rather acidic, for the traditional horse and cattle rearing. Most of Portugal's fighting bulls come fron Ribatejo, especially from around Vila Franca de Xira (see Alenquer).

The fertile Tagus valley near Santarém

Sagres B 8

Historical province: Algarve. District: Faro
Altitude: 35m/115ft. Population: 2000

Situation and importance

Sagres, lying 5km/3 miles from Cabo de São Vicente and the most south-westerly point of Portugal and indeed of Europe, is for the Portuguese – and indeed for others too – a magical place. It is here that Henry the Navigator is said to have founded his school of seamanship, where in the 15th c. the country's major geographers, cartographers and astronomers are supposed to have assembled. However, current thinking suggests this was simply a temporary meeting of these various experts, without any real purpose in mind (see Baedeker Special, pp. 300/302). However, that does not alter the fact that the whole region around Sagres still benefits from its legendary historical importance, be it real or not.

Both Sagres and Cabo de São Vicente lie on a rocky plateau which terminates abruptly at the coast to form steep cliffs of up to 150m/500ft in height. The countryside around Sagres is as raw as the climate, and the plateau is bare apart from a few clumps of semi-shrubs and the like. Tourism has not yet taken a hold, and although there are a few hotels and private guest houses in and around Sagres the tourist infrastructure is not comparable with that in the holiday resorts further east in the Algarve.

Townscape

The modest little houses of the port and fishing harbour lie widely dispersed over the rocky and windswept plateau. Sagres possesses no town centre as such; the main street ends at the busy harbour.

Beaches

The beaches around Sagres are not ideally suited to bathing and sunbathing. The best section, protected from the wind, is probably the 4km/2½ mile Praia do Martinhal to the north, but it is not popular with surfers.

Fortaleza at Sagres

In Search of New Worlds

This time the Portuguese appeared with a fleet of 19 ships and crews numbering 1400. Dom Alfonso de Albuquerque, commander of this armed force and the King of Portugal's governor in the East Indies, was determined to revenge the ignominious flight forced upon his countryman Admiral Diego Lopes de Sequeira. On September 1st 1509 the latter had arrived with a few ships at the south-east Asian town of Malacca (on the peninsula of the same name, opposite Sumatra). Never before had a European succeeded in sailing so far east. However, he failed in his aim of establishing trading relations with the port. Resident traders, concerned for their own livelihood, had prevailed upon the ruler of Malacca to take up arms against these unwelcome "competitors". Being militarily much inferior, Sequeiro had no choice but to set sail and return to Portugal. Nineteen of his crew had been taken prisoner by the Malays and he was obliged to leave them behind. Two years later (1511) Albuquerque was now to seek atonement for this humiliation. When the Malays met his request to release his imprisoned countrymen immediately but refused to reimburse Sequeiro's trading losses and to allow Portugal to set up a base there he replied with force. The Malays had no chance against the superiority of the Portuguese. Many of the inhabitants of Malacca were slaughtered; even women and children were shown no mercy. The conquerors laid claim to Malacca and built a fort there – with stones from mosques and old royal tombs which were demolished out of hand for the purpose.

The taking of Malacca in 1511 is typical of the Portuguese voyages of discovery. If towns, countries or people they discovered on their way to the Indies were not prepared to trade with Portugal they felt the full impact of the superior Portuguese military fist – "new trading partners" became colonial underlings.

The Portuguese had undertaken their first voyage of discovery and conquest a hundred years before the taking of Malacca – with the conquest in 1415 of the North African town of Ceuta (which today belongs to Spain). What was it that drove Portuguese mariners to venture out into the open sea in search of unknown coasts and ports which they seized in the name of their king? One reason was the imbalance between the growing population and the country's dwindling resources, especially corn and gold. As a result Portugal was obliged to seek other sources of income. Since it was in constant conflict with its powerful neighbour Castile, and already boasted a strong seafaring tradition, Portugal's best course clearly lay in the wide, open sea. But in which direction should the Portuguese fleet sail? At the time there was only one possibility – Africa! The Mediterranean was ruled by Genoese, Florentines and Venetians, and to the east of the Mediterranean the Turks prevented any links between Europe and the rich wonderlands of India and China. By sailing around the African coast it would perhaps be possible, the Portuguese thought, to form trading links with the gold and slave markets of East Africa and, if they could find a sea route to India, to break the lucrative spice monopoly held by the Islamic merchants and the trading centres of northern Italy. Religion also played a decisive role. The medieval crusading spirit had by no means disappeared from the Iberian peninsula (no wonder, as the people effectively still lived cheek by jowl with the world of Islam – the neighbouring Moorish kingdom of Granada would last until 1492) and so sailing around Africa served to combat Islam, for then they would at last find the Christian priest-king John who was believed to be living in Abysinnia and with his help they would conquer the Holy Land and finally crush Islam.

However, if the age of discovery had not emerged until later there is certainly one man that would not have been there – Henry the Navigator. In remembering his deeds he has been called "the Navigator", but in fact Henry went to sea only once, in 1485 when Ceuta was seized. As the third son of King João I of Portugal Henry clearly had little chance of succeeding to the throne, and perhaps for that reason he devoted his life entirely to other matters and developed an enthusiasm for scientific subjects. In Sagres, in the province of the Algarve in the extreme south-west of Portugal, after his father had introduced him to the governor, he built a centre named "Vila do Infante", consisting of a few houses. There was in fact no school of seafaring here, although it is often described as such; rather was it a kind of scientific centre, bringing together under one roof all contemporary knowledge in the fields of astronomy, geography, cartography, mathematics and nautical science. It was probably here that plans were drawn up for the caravel, a vessel faster and more manoevrable than conventional sailing ships. Although it had a smaller cargo capacity its square sails on the two foremasts and the triangular sail – the "latin" sail – at the stern or, alternatively, three large "latin" sails, it was well suited for transatlantic voyages, especially because it could tack against the wind.

The fact that ships could now at last dare to leave coastal waters was due largely to new technical discoveries such as the astrolab, a device to measure the position of the stars and by means of which distances at sea could be calculated with reasonable accuracy, other astronomical sighting equipment such as Jacob's staff, the Armillarsphere and the quadrant (the forerunner of the sextant), together with the compass. Instructed in the latest knowledge about the stars and the sea, equipped with the latest technical aids and financed by the wealthy Order of Christ (of which Henry was the Grand Master) and by businessmen from among the now much stronger middle classes who were prepared to take risks, as well as by members of the aristocratic circles and by foreign investors, Portuguese seafarers now sailed forth and reconnoitred the west coast of Africa. Their findings were then evaluated and used for further expeditions.

But still there existed a small obstacle – Cape Bojador (now in the western Sahara, 1500km/930 miles south of Gibraltar). For here began the *mare tenebrosum*, where cruel sea-monsters lay in wait for unsuspecting sailors, where magnets pulled nails out of deck-planks or where ships simply disappeared into a void. Henry held no brief for these horror stories, and so when a certain Captain Gil Eanes turned back after reaching Cape Bojador he received a thorough dressing-down from his master on his return to Sagres. He then sailed forth once more, as ordered by Henry, and in 1434 sailed round the "Cape of Grey". As a result the sea lost its irrational terror and now the race to discover new lands and to conquer distant worlds across the sea began in earnest (see History, p.29).

★Fortaleza de Sagres

History

The Fortaleza de Sagres lies on the Ponta de Sagres, 2km/1¼ miles south of Sagres. This narrow promontory reaching out into the sea was called Promontorium Sacrum (sacred promontory) by the Romans, who thought this remote area was a home of the gods.

The fortress still forms a focal point in the story of Portuguese discovery and conquest in the 15th and 16th c., even though, as mentioned above, it seems improbable that an international centre ever existed here. Henry the Navigator is said to have preferred his house in Lagos to that on the cliffs at Sagres and to have come here only very occasionally. Sagres harbour remained unimportant, as the expeditions that Henry financed and organised set out from Lagos.

Fortifications

Little remains of the original fort built in Henry the Navigator's time. This was largely destroyed in an attack by Sir Francis Drake and by the 1755 earthquake, but the fortifications were rebuilt in the 18th c.; hence the date of 1793 above the entrance to what are among the earliest defensive walls to be restored using concrete. Inside the walls there are very few remains from Henry's time.

Wind-rose

After passing through the gate of the fort the large Rosa dos Ventos (wind-rose) can be seen to the left. It consists of a stone circle, 43m/140ft in diameter. For centuries is was overgrown with grass and it was between 1918 and 1959 when it was finally uncovered. It probably dates from the 15th c., but its exact function is unclear. Usually wind roses have only 32 segments, but that at Sagres has 48 lines runing from the centre of the circle to its circumference.

Igreja de Nossa Senhora da Graça

On the other side can be seen the little Church of Our Lady of Grace, dating from the 16th c. It is believed that there was previously an earlier church dedicated to Mary on this same site. The commemorative column nearby was erected in 1960 for the 500th anniversary of Henry's death.

Visitor centre

In the former stables, at the edge of the fortifications a small museum has been opened (history of the fortifications, the Voyages of Discovery, geological facts of the Cape; temporary exhibitions). There is also a souvenir shop and a cafeteria.

Surroundings

For destinations around Sagres see Algarve.

Santarém   B 5

Historical province: Ribatejo. District: Santarém
Altitude: 108m/354ft. Population: 29,000

Situation and Importance

Santarém, capital of the old province of Ribatejo, is a town of low whitewashed houses built on a hill above the right bank of the Tagus, occupying a position of great strategic importance.

The town is worth visiting for its interesting churches and the splendid views from here over the Tagus. Santarém is the centre of an important agricultural region growing mainly corn, fruit and vegetables. An important agricultural fair (Feira Nacional de Agricultura) is held here in early June each year. It interests tourists because of the accompanying folk-lore programme and the bull-fights.

History

In Roman times, as Iulianum Scalabitanum, the town ranked with Braga and Beja as one of the main trading posts in Lusitania. During the Moorish period (8th–12th c.) it was fortified by a castle. After its recapture by Afonso Henriques in 1147 Santarém became the residence of several kings. Here in 1319 King Dinis received the papal bull recognising the order of the Knights of Christ which he had founded.

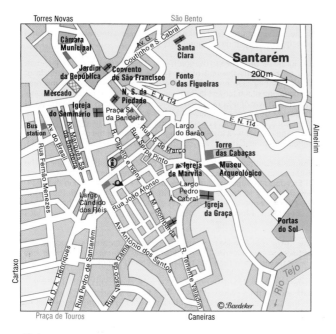

Sights

The Jardim da República, the fine park in the north of the town, is a good starting point for a walk round Santarém.

Jardim da República

On the east side of the park is the Convento de São Francisco, founded as a Franciscan convent in the mid-13th c., now a barracks but still with its original cloister.

North of the Jardim da República is the 18th c. town hall, while the covered market on the west has a façade with azulejo pictures of the local sights and rural motifs.

North-east of the Jardim da República, just outside the old town, stands the Gothic church of Santa Clara (13th c.), belonging to a convent founded by Queen Leonor. The queen's mortal remains were brought here in 1634 and rest in a tomb decorated with her coat-of-arms. A sarcophagus from the first half of the 14th c. which was intended for the queen remains empty.

Igreja de Santa Clara

The Gothic fountain, the Fonte das Figueiras, is just south of the Igreja de Santa Clara, while the São Bento viewpoint is about 500yd to the east.

The main sights of Santarém are south of the Jardim da República. The Praça de Sá da Bandeira was the scene of the gruesome execution in 1357 of Álvaro Gonçales and Pedro Coelho, the murderers of Inês de Castro. The Igreja do Seminário, the seminary church of the former Jesuit convent, is on the west side of the square. It has a Baroque façade (1676) by Baltasar Álvares, and, inside, an impressive high altar, painted wooden ceiling and 17th c. azulejo pictures.

★ Igreja do Seminário

The Capela de Nossa Senhora da Piedade is opposite the Igreja do Seminário. It was founded by Afonso VI in 1665 in thanksgiving for his victory over Juan de Austria, commander of the Spanish army.

Capela de Nossa Senhora da Piedade

303

Igreja de Marvila | From the Praça de Sá da Bandeira the Rua Serpa Pinto runs south-east to the Marvila church which has a fine Manueline doorway (16th c.) and polychrome azulejo decoration (17th c.).

★Igreja da Graça | The Igreja da Graça lies to the south-east. This late Gothic convent church was built towards the end of the 14th c. possibly by the architects of Batalha Abbey (see entry). The chief feature of the façade is the rose window, one of the largest in Portugal, made from a single block of stone. The church was the burial-place of the Meneses family. The founders of the family, João Afonso Teles de Meneses and his wife Dona Guimar de Vila Lobos, lie under grave-slabs in the choir which bear their coats-of-arms, their daughter's tomb adjoining. To the right of the choir is the tomb of Pedro Álvares Cabral (1467/68–1526), discoverer of Brazil, and his wife.

Museu Arqueológico de São João de Alporão | The walk continues back to the Igreja de Marvila and then right to the Archaeological Museum, housed in the Romanesque and Gothic church of São João de Alporão. Apart from the fine stellar vaulting in the choir, and the many sculptures, ceramics and azulejos, it is worth looking at the Gothic cenotaph of Duarte, son of Pedro I, who fell in the battle of Alcácer-Kibir (Morocco) in 1458. One of his teeth was all that was brought back to Portugal!

Torre das Cabaças | The Torre das Cabaças, Santarém's great landmark, is opposite the archaeological museum. Probably originally a minaret, the tower has sound-boxes around the bell to heighten the resonance.

★Portas do Sol | Several hundred yards farther south-east is the Portas do Sol, where a park and a terrace were laid out on the site of a Moorish castle at the end of the 19th c., affording magnificent views over the Tagus valley, spanned at this point by the Ponte Dom Luís, built between 1876 and 1881 and 1200m/1312yd long.

Surroundings of Santarém

Almeirim | Almeirim, where the Infante Afonso, son of João II and Queen Leonor, was killed while out riding in 1491, lies about 6km/4 miles south-east of Santarém.

Alpiarça | Alpiarça, 7km/4¼ miles north-east of Almeirim, has a museum well worth a visit in the Casa dos Patudos, the country house that belonged to the Portuguese statesman and art lover José Relvas (1858–1929). The collection contains notable works by many European painters, tapestries (17th–19th c.), porcelain and faience.

Golegã | Golegã is 25km/15½ miles further on. The highpoint of its year is the horse show in the second week of November. The parish church, built about 1500, has a Manueline portal, ascribed to Diogo Boytaca.

Almoster | Almoster, 10km/6 miles west of Santarém, has a church from a late 13th c. convent containing 17th c. azulejos.

Santiago do Cacém   B 6

Historical province: Baixo Alentejo. District: Setúbal
Altitude: 210–254m/689–833ft. Population: 18,000

Situation and Importance | The little country town of Santiago do Cacém occupies a commanding spot on a hill crowned by a castle in the southern part of the Serra de Grândola, 20km/12½ miles north-west of the port of Sines. With its two pousadas it is a convenient place to stop over from the Algarve to Lisbon when driving.

Sights

The town is dominated by its Castelo, the old Templar castle, which can be reached by road. There is a pleasant walk round the outside of the walls, with views as far afield as Cabo de Sines. The parish church cemetery is within the walls, shaded by lovely cypresses.

Castelo

The parish church, the Igreja Matriz, alongside the castle, is originally 13th c. with later alterations including the façade, which is 18th c. while the side portal is still Romanesque-Gothic. The church contains a 14th c. relief of St Tiago, who was killed during a Moorish attack on the town.

Igreja Matriz

The municipal museum on the lawned Praça do Municipio contains local archaeological discoveries from Miróbriga and an interesting collection of old coins.

Museu Municipal

Surroundings of Santiago do Cacém

The remains of the Roman settlement of Miróbriga, with temple ruins and a stretch of Roman road, are rather more than 1km/¾ miles east of the town, near the road to Beja (closed Mon.).

Miróbriga

See Alcácer do Sal

Grândola

A pleasant excursion is to the seaside lagoon of Lagoa de Santo André, passing through the dunes (waterbirds) to the quiet beaches on this section of the Atlantic coast, known here as the Costa Dourada (see entry).

Lagoa de S. André

Santo Tirso   B 3

Historical province: Douro Litoral. District: Porto
Altitude: 75m/245ft. Population: 12,000

The little town of Santo Tirso, situated in pleasant wooded country on the left bank of the Rio Ave about 25km/15½ miles north-east of Oporto, attracts many visitors who come to explore the surrounding area. The town's main source of income is the textile industry, supplemented by various handicrafts, including pottery.

Situation and Importance

The town's most important building is the Convent of São Bento (photograph above), now containing an agricultural college. The Benedictines founded a convent here in the 10th c. The present building, with its impressive Baroque façade, dates from the 14th to 18th c. The church is richly decorated with talha dourada and sculpture. There is also a beautiful two-storey cloister (14th–17th c.), with fine capitals.
  The adjoining little Abade Pedrosa museum has prehistoric and medieval archaeological displays.
  A reddish granite calvary stands in front of the church.

Convento de São Bento

Surroundings of Santo Tirso

In Roriz, about 10km/6 miles east of the little town, is the interesting 12th c. Romanesque church of the former Benedictine convent, its main portal embellished by an early Gothic rose window.

Roriz

The village of Paços de Ferreira lies 14km/9 miles east. It has an unusual Romanesque church with a separate tower.

Paços de Ferreira

About 10km/6 miles north of Santo Tirso, Vila Nova de Famalicão is a centre for Portuguese watchmaking. The place is dominated by the former convent church of São Tiago de Antas (13th c.). The choir was decorated with azulejos in the 17th c.

Vila Nova de Famalicão

São Pedro do Sul   B 4

Historical province: Beira Alta. District: Viseu
Altitude: 168m/551ft. Population: 3500

Situation and
Importance

The attractive little town of São Pedro do Sul in the northern foothills of the
Serra do Caramulo at the junction of the Rio Vouga and the Rio Sul, is a
popular base for exploring the beautiful wooded hills in the immediate
surroundings, particularly the Serra da Gralheira and the Serra do Caramulo (see Viseu).

Surroundings of São Pedro do Sul

Termas de São
Pedro do Sul

The little spa of Termas de São Pedro do Sul 3km/2 miles south has hot
sulphur and sodium springs (68°C/154°F) which were already being frequented in Roman times (remains of Roman baths) and are still used.
   King Afonso Henriques spent some time here receiving treatment for a
broken leg after the battle of Badajoz in 1169.

Vouzela

Another 3km/2 miles south-west is the ancient little town of Vouzela (pop.
1500), dominated by a 12th c. Romanesque and Gothic parish church which
is decorated with remarkable sculpture. It has an unusual belfry which is
basically just a narrow wall fronting one of the façades.
   The 18th c. Rococo chapel of São Gil in the market square is also worth
seeing.
   The do Castelo church, on a hill with a view 3km/2 miles south of Vouzela,
receives pilgrimages on the Sunday after August 5th.

Cambra

The village of Cambra is 6km/4 miles south-west of Vouzela and is overshadowed by castle ruins. Nearby to the south is the Celtiberian site of
Cova de Lobishomem, or "cave of the werewolf".

Serra da Estrela   C 4

Historical province: Beira Alta
Districts: Viseu, Guarda, Coimbra and Castelo Branco

Location

Famous for its scenery as the "star mountains", the Serra da Estrela is a
mighty granite ridge which extends for some 100km/60 miles, with a
breadth of 30km/20 miles, from Guarda to south of Coimbra. It is Portugal's
main watershed range, formerly the southern frontier of the country and
historically the dividing line between its north and south.

★★ Topography

With its bizarrely shaped crags and gorges, mountain streams and lakes,
beautiful forests and magnificent views, the Serra da Estrela ranks among
Portugal's outstanding scenic attractions. The range contains the country's
highest peak, the Torre or Malhão da Estrela (1991m/6532ft).
   The bare hills provide grazing for sheep and goats, and the valleys have a
centuries old woollen industry.

Walks

Walking is the only way to obtain a true impression of the raw beauty of this
mountain ridge. In recent years the administrators of this nature park have
laid out a comprehensive network of paths. Details about these can be
obtained from the information centres in Covilhã, Manteigas or Gouveia.
Between November and April walkers must expect snowstorms and mists,
and it is advisable not to undertake long treks during this period. The
Pousada de São Lourenço (14km/8¾ miles north-west of Manteigas) is a
good base for treks in the mountains.

In Serra da Estrela

Tour

The following route covering about 140km/87 miles takes in the scenic highlights and main places of interest in the Serra da Estrela, starting at Covilhã (see entry) and finishing at Belmonte (see entry).

To extend the tour, instead of first going to Penhas de Saúde leave Covilhã on the N 230 travelling south to Unhais da Serra, beautifully situated in the Rio Alfora valley, and possessing sulphur springs. The route then winds its way uphill, with fine views, and leaves the N 230 20km/12 miles beyond Unhais da Serra turning north on the N 231 to Loriga (740m/2430ft). Beyond Loriga the road climbs steeply then descends in hairpin bends to Valezim, crossing the Rio Alva with lovely views from the Ponte da Jugais, to reach São Romão (590m/1935ft). From here there is a road running 12km/7½ miles south-east to the Senhora do Desterro hermitage (790m/2590ft), built in 1650, although the nearby power station detracts somewhat from the scenic effect.

Extension

The tour described below can be joined at Seia, 4km/2½ miles north.

Leave Covilhã on the N 339 going north-west – the road, which is not well signposted, goes uphill to the right out of the centre of Covilhã by the town hall. Passing through dense woods it gradually climbs up to the mountain and winter sports resort of Penhas de Saúde (10km/6 miles; 1453m/4767ft). With February temperatures of as low as −10°C/14°F the conditions here are very good for winter sports.

Penhas da Saúde

Past a reservoir, 10km/6 miles beyond Penhas da Saúde, is the Torre or Malhão da Estrela (1991m/6532ft), Portugal's highest peak, topped by a granite monument.

Torre

Seia (532m/1745ft) farther north-west, and a total of 52km/32 miles from Covilhã, has a parish church on a hill with a view, overlooking the township.

Seia

About 2km/1¼ miles beyond Seia the route joins the N 17 which comes in from the left from Coimbra, and carries on north-east to the right along this main road.

Gouveia

After 13km/8 miles turn right off the main road on the N 232 for 5km/3 miles to Gouveia (alt. 650m/2135ft), a little town on the Rio Mondego and a popular base for exploring the Serra da Estrela. The façade of the parish church is covered in blue and white azulejos, as is the Misericórdia church, which is part of what was an 18th c. Jesuit abbey.

Penhas Douradas

Beyond Gouveia the road winds its way up the rocky hillside, with ever more extensive views of the beautiful mountain scenery. After about 20km/12 miles there is a sign to Penhas Douradas (formerly Poio Negro, 1496m/4908ft), a group of houses and holiday villas (viewpoint), a good walking and climbing base for the mighty rock faces, such as the "golden rocks" from which the place takes its name.

Manteigas

Beyond Penhas Douradas the road descends through the forest to the Pousada de São Lourenço (1450m/4755ft), with a superb view of Manteigas and the Zêzere valley, which the road eventually reaches via many a hairpin bend. Since earnings from textiles have dwindled to next to nothing Manteigas (720m/2360ft, pop. 4000) has fallen back increasingly on tourism.

The spa of Caldas de Manteigas, with hot carbonic acid and sulphur springs (43°C/109°F), is in the upper Zêzere valley about 2km/1¼ miles south.

Poço do Inferno

The Poço do Inferno, the springs of Hell, where a waterfall hurtles down into a cavern, lies 3km/2 miles farther up the valley.

From Manteigas the route descends the Zêzere valley, past wooded slopes and cultivated fields and gardens, crossing the river on a narrow bridge just beyond Valhelhas. 23km/114 miles from Manteigas it joins the N 18 from Covilhã, turning left for 3km/2 miles before the appearance of the houses of Belmonte (see entry).

Serra da Lousã   B 4

Historical province: Beira Litoral
Districts: Coimbra, Leiria, Castelo Branco and Santarém

Location and General

The Serra de Lousã, a quartz and schist massif eroded into picturesque rock formations, extends south-west of the mighty granite ridge of the Serra da Estrela south-east of Coimbra. Reaching a height of 1204m/3950ft in the Alto do Trevim, it falls sharply down to the Lousã basin in the north and is bounded on the south by the Zêzere valley. The main crop is the maize grown on terraces in the often narrow river valleys, and there is also grazing of sheep and goats.

Sights

Lousã

The best base from which to explore the Serra de Lousã is the little town of Lousã (alt. 172m/564ft, pop. 7500), at the northern foot of the range, which has some handsome 18th c. patrician houses and the Igreja da Misericórdia, which is worth seeing – built around 1550 with a beautiful Renaissance door.

High above the town (3km/2 miles south on the road to Castanheira de Pêra) is the Miradouro de Nossa Senhora da Piedade, from which there are panoramic views. A nearby castle has a massive 14th c. keep.

A pleasant walk from Lousã is along the narrow valley of the Rio Aronce, past many little white chapels, up to the Penhasco dos Eremitas, where there is a fine view.

Figueiró dos Vinhos (pop. 5000), about 50km/32miles south of Lousã, is famous for its pretty pottery. It has a church with 18th c. azulejos lining the choir.

Figueiró dos Vinhos

Serra de Monchique

B 7

Historical province: Algarve. District: Faro

The Serra de Monchique extends from east to west along the north side of the coastal plateau of the western Algarve, forming a protective barrier against cold air from the Atlantic and thus helping to give this area its almost North African climate. Geologically the range is a much broken-up mass of volcanic rock overlying the basement schists of the region, divided up into a western and an eastern half by the Ribeira de Odelouca. Because of the impermeability of the ground the abundant rainfall is channelled into innumerable rivers and streams (some of them dammed to form lakes), running down to the coastal plain, thus rendering it well watered and suitable even for rice. The volcanic nature of the region is also reflected in the presence of a number of hot springs.

Location and Geology

The pleasant upland landscape of the Serra de Monchique reaches its highest point in the peaks of Fóia and Picota, 902m/2959ft and 774m/2538ft respectively. The varied and lush vegetation is somewhat unusual. The lower slopes are clothed with extensive forests of eucalyptus, cork-oaks, spruce and mimosa, while higher up are shrubs and rhododendrons. In the foothills to the south will be found some lovely fruit gardens in which lemons, figs, almonds and olives flourish.

★★Topography

Sights

The chief place in the Serra de Monchique is the little hill town of Monchique (458km/1503ft, pop. 8000). Steep streets and alleys bisect the town centre, and there are fine views of the surrounding mountains. There are cafés on Largo 5 de Outubre, and the square is adorned by a modern fountain representing a "nora", which was a part of the irrigation system introduced into the Algarve by the Moors. From the square narrow streets lead up to the Convento de Nossa Senhora do Desterro (15 minute climb). The ruins of the convent are surrounded by cork-oaks, and there is a wonderful view of Monchique.

Monchique

The Monchique region is known for the production of "medronho", a brandy derived from the fruit of the arbutus or strawberry tree.

From Monchique a picturesque little road winds its way for 6km/4 miles up to the highest peak of the Serra de Monchique, the Fóia (902m/295ft), passing decorated houses and several cafés on the way. Gradually the vegetation becomes more sparse, and after taking a bend the visitor suddenly finds himself looking north into Alentejo. On arriving at the peak the scenery will be found to be inhospitable; Portuguese Telecom have installed a forest of masts here. There is a café and a souvenir shop.

Fóia

Monchique owes its fame to the Caldas de Monchique (warm springs), 6km/4 miles further south. They are recommended for the treatment of rheumatism, liver and bladder complaints and problems of the digestive system. Bottles of its waters are on sale all over Portugal. Caldas de Monchique is one of the most idyllic places in the Algarve hinterland, with a turn-of-the-century charm which seems unbelievable a few miles further along the coast. The tiny little spa lies in a narrow valley under tall, shady trees, and a quiet square invites the visitor to linger awhile.

★Caldas de Monchique

Sesimbra   A 6

Historical province: Estremadura. District: Setúbal
Altitude: 0–249m/0–817ft. Population: 14,500

Situation and Importance

The pleasant little fishing town of Sesimbra, below rugged red cliffs on the southern slopes of the Serra da Arrábida, is also a popular seaside resort.

Townscape

The promenade along the shore is lined with simple white houses and a few smaller hotels, with the larger hotel complexes outside the centre. Fishing still dominates the scene, however, together with tourism. Visitors can watch the fishermen mending their nets on the beach, or see them unloading their catch in the harbour at the western end of the town. The spectacle is particularly lively when the fish are auctioned, and the freshly landed fish and other seafood can be sampled in the relaxed atmosphere of one of the town's restaurants.

Sights

Fortaleza de Santiago, Museu Municipal

In the town centre, right on the beach, stands the Fortaleza de Santiago, a little 17th c. fort, at times a prison, with a lighthouse. The town museum, containing archaeological finds, a collection of coins and sacred objects, is a few hundred yards north.

Castelo

High above the town stands the Castelo, the castle originally built during the 12th and 13th c. but almost totally rebuilt early in the 17th c. by Cosmander, the Flemish Jesuit architect, for King João IV.

Surroundings of Sesimbra

Sesimbra is a good base for exploring the Costa de Lisboa (see entry) and the Serra da Arrábida (see Costa de Lisboa).

Setúbal   B 6

Historical province: Estremadura. District: Setúbal
Altitude: sea level. Population: 90,000

Situation and Importance

The industrial city and district capital of Setúbal, situated on the wide estuary of the Rio Sado, is Portugal's fourth largest city and third largest port, with important fish canneries, a car assembly plant, shipyards and salt-pans. The Roman town which occupied this site was founded in the 5th c. to replace the Celtic settlement of Cetobriga on the Tróia peninsula to the south-east, which was destroyed by a tidal wave.

A royal residence for a time in the 15th c., Setúbal is also the birthplace of the poet and satirical writer Manuel Maria de Barbosa du Bocage (1765–1805; small museum in the house where he was born in the Rua do São Domingo).

Townscape

Setúbal is quite attractive for an industrial city. On the Rio Sado waterfront are the docks, the marina and the fishing harbour, where brisk auctions take place every morning when the fishermen have unloaded the day's catch. North of the waterfront runs one of the city's main throughfares, the Avenida de Luisa Todi, named after the celebrated opera-singer (1754–1833), who was born in Setúbal. The crowded and picturesque old town, centred around the Praça do Bocage with its statue of the poet, is on the other side of this avenue, and contains the few sights of the city spared by the 1755 earthquake.

Sights

Igreja de Jesús

The Igreja de Jesús is in the west of the old town. It was Portugal's first Manueline church, begun in 1490/91 under the direction of Diogo de

The attractive landscape of the Serra de Monchique ▶

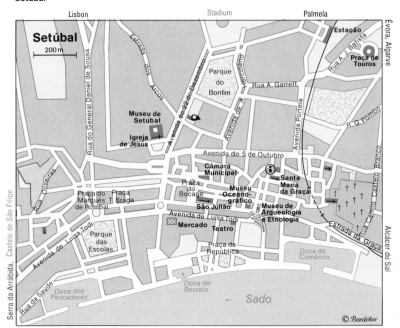

Boytaca, who went on to be architect of the convents at Batalha (see entry) and Belém (see Lisbon). Inside the relatively unadorned exterior can be seen impressive stellar vaulting in the choir and azulejo scenes from the life of the Virgin.

Museu de Setúbal	The adjoining monastic buildings and 17th c. Arrábida marble cloister of the Convento de Jesús now house the city's museum, with pictures by Portuguese, Flemish and Catalan artists and local archaeological discoveries.
Igreja de São Julião	The church of Saõ Julião just south-east of the Praça do Bocage is worth seeing. Originally 16th c., it was almost completely rebuilt after the 1755 earthquake.
Igreja de Santa Maria da Graça	The church of Santa Maria da Graça at the east end of the old town dates back to a 13th c. building which was almost completely reconstructed in the 16th c. Its carved and gilded altars date from the 16th and 17th c., and the azulejos are 18th c.
Museu de Arqueologia e Etnologia	The Archaeology and Folklore Museum next door has displays of tools and implements used in farming and fishing around Setúbal, and also model ships.
Castelo de São Filipe	Above the city, to the west, is the Castelo de São Filipe, built in the late 16th c. by the Italian military engineer Filippo Terzi. Part of it is now a pousada and there is a good view from here over the city and its surroundings."

Setúbal Harbour

Surroundings of Setúbal

Some 15km/9 miles west of Setúbal is the village of Vila Fresca de Azeitão, with the church of São Simão, with 17th c. azulejo decoration, and the Quinta das Torres, now a hotel surrounded by lovely gardens.

Vila Fresca de Azeitão

The nearby Palácio da Bacalhoa (privately owned), on the road to Setúbal, is a late 15th c. three-part building with Moorish domed towers, which was substantially altered in the 16th c. In the middle of its magnificent park stands the Casa de Prazer, a pleasure seat with an early tile version of Susanna and the Elders (mid 16th c.).

Vila Nogueira de Azeitão, 2km/1¼ miles west of Vila Fresca de Azeitão, is famous for its wine cellars, which can be visited. It also has the palace of the Dukes of Aveiro, built by Jorge de Lencastre between 1520 and 1523.

Vila Nogueira de Azeitão

There are very worthwhile trips from Setúbal into the Serra da Arrábida and to the Tróia peninsula, which can be reached by ferry from Setúbal (see Costa de Lisboa for both).

Costa de Lisboa

Silves

B 7

Historical province: Algarve. District: Faro
Altitude: 85m/280ft. Population: 12,000

The little country town of Silves, situated on the Rio Arade (Rio de Silves) 11 miles north-east of Portimão and surrounded by forests of cork-oak, was once the Moorish city of Xelb, capital of the Al-Gharb (see Algarve), and as such, with its 40,000 population at that time, was an intellectual and cultural centre that rivalled Granada in splendour and influence. Silves no longer presents itself as the large town it once was, however, now it is just a sleepy

Situation and Importance

View of Silves

little place, although with some historically significant buildings which attract large numbers of day visitors. However, restaurants and cafés are rather few and far between.

History

The town is believed to have been founded by the Phoenicians, and was ruled by the Moors from the first half of the 8th c. until its recapture from the Moors by Afonso III in 1242. It became the see of a bishop, but after the transfer of the see in 1580 to the new capital, Faro, and the destruction caused by the 1755 earthquake it sank into obscurity and insignificance.

Townscape

Silves is still an attractive old-world little town, presenting a charming picture with some venerable and handsome burghers' houses.

Sights

★Castelo dos Mouros

Above the town rears the massive Moorish castle, the Castelo dos Mouros, with its imposing battlemented walls of red sandstone, restored in 1940, and the ventilation systems and cisterns, up to 60m/197ft deep, put in by the Moors. A walk along the top of the walls provides views far out over the surrounding countryside, and in the summer there are son et lumière performances in the castle courtyard, full of ancient trees. (Open daily: 8am–6pm.)

Sé

Diagonally opposite the entrance to the castle stands the Gothic Cathedral, or Sé, built over a mosque in the 13th c. and subsequently much altered, containing the tombs of a number of crusaders.

Igreja da Misericórdia

The Igreja da Misericórdia opposite the cathedral has fine Manueline windows.

Museu Municipal de Arqueologia

A few hundred yards south of the cathedral the Archaeological Museum in the Rua das Portes de Loulé was opened in 1990. Most of the exhibits are from Silves and its surroundings. A Moorish well was integrated into the museum building.

The 16th c. Cruz de Portugal at the eastern exit from the town is an example of Manueline stone-masonry, rare in this region. It is a white limestone wayside cross, 3m/10ft high, with Christ on the Cross on the front, and a Piéta on the back.

Cruz de Portugal

Surroundings of Silves

Silves is a good base for some interesting excursions into the Serra de Monchique (see entry).

Serra de Monchique

The busy little city of Portimão (see entry) is about 15km/9 miles south-west of Silves.

Portimão

Other sights around Silves can be found under the entry on the Algarve.

Algarve

Sines

B 7

Historical province: Baixo Alentejo. District: Setúbal
Altitude: sea level. Population: 10,000

Once an unassuming little fishing town in a rocky bay on a dune-fringed stretch of Portugal's southern coast, Sines has grown since the early 1970s to become one of the country's biggest ports and industrial centres (industry park, with oil refinery), although it has only been possible to achieve part of the ambitious plans for the town and it can quite happily be omitted from a tour of Portugal.

Sines is the birthplace of Vasco da Gama (1469–1524), discoverer of the sea-route to India in 1497/98.

The house where Vasco da Gama was born has been reconstructed as a museum.

Situation and Importance

Sights

Above the port is the fishermen's chapel of Nossa Senhora das Salas. The original chapel, built in 1335, was completely renovated by Vasco da Gama after his discovery of the passage to India. It has a magnificent Manueline doorway, with a terrace with a view in front of it.

There is another fine view from the recently restored 13th c. castle, which contains a small museum.

In the parish church (Igreja Matriz) are the relics of St Torpes, said to have been found on an abandoned ship which ran aground here in A.D. 45.

Statue of Vasco da Gama

The Cabo de Sines, a 56m/184ft high headland, with a lighthouse, extends into the Atlantic west of the town.

Cabo de Sines

Santiago do Cacém (see entry), perched on its hilltop, is about 17km/10½ miles north-east of Sines.

Surroundings

Sintra

A 6

Historical province: Estremadura. District: Leiria
Altitude: 225m/740ft. Population: 21,000

The small city of Sintra (perhaps better known in English in the older spelling of Cintra) lies between Lisbon and the Atlantic on a promontory of

Situation and Importance

315

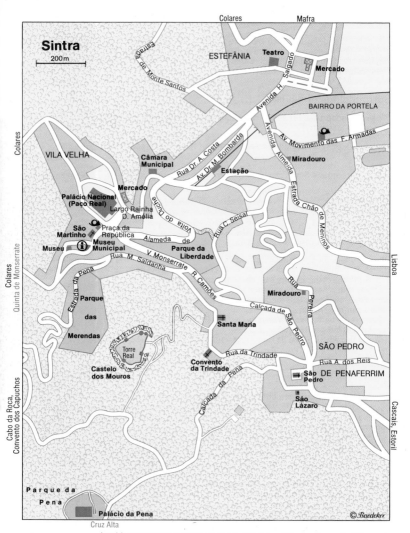

land between two gorges on the north side of the well-wooded Serra de Sintra. With its beautiful setting and equable climate it was an early choice as the summer seat of the Portuguese royal family. The beauty of the scenery, combined with the magnificent subtropical vegetation and the nearness of the sea, is almost beyond compare, making Sintra one of the loveliest spots in the Iberian peninsula, wholly justifying Lord Byron's description of it as "glorious Eden".

Early in 1996 UNESCO included Sintra in its list of world cultural heritage sites. During the next few years increased efforts will be made to restore the town's unique architectural character and to ban private cars from the centre in summer if possible.

Sintra is centred on the Largo Raínha D. Amélia with the imposing Palácio Nacional de Sintra on its northern side. In front of the Palácio stands a Late Gothic pelourinho which has been made into a fountain.

Cityscape

In the Praça da República, on the south-west corner of the Largo Raínha D. Amélia, are the Igreja de São Martinho, originally a 12th c. church and subsequently much altered, and the Museu Municipal, the municipal museum, which holds the tourist information centre as well.

Past Parque Liberdade, or Liberty Park, the Igreja de Santa Maria (another much altered 12th c. church) and the Convento da Trindade, lies the São Pedro part of town, with the parish church, and the location of a big market which is held every second and fourth Sunday in the month.

Immediately above the town, on its steep rocky mount, stands the Moorish castle which Afonso Henriques captured from the Arabs in 1147, and then, higher up, the Pena topped by its palace.

During June and July there is a very popular series of piano recitals of works by the Romantic composers in the palaces in and around Sintra.

Sintra festivals

A good way of covering the relatively long distance between the centre of Sintra and the Palácio da Pena is to take one of the horse-drawn carriages. These can be found plying for trade in front of the Palácio Nacional de Sintra.

Horse-drawn carriages

Sights

The Palácio Nacional de Sintra, or Paço Real (open: daily except Wed., 10am–1pm and 2–5pm), is the ancestral seat of the House of Avis. It

★★ Palácio Nacional de Sintra

Sintra: Palácio Nacional

Palácio Nacional de Sintra

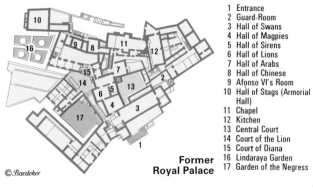

1 Entrance
2 Guard-Room
3 Hall of Swans
4 Hall of Magpies
5 Hall of Sirens
6 Hall of Lions
7 Hall of Arabs
8 Hall of Chinese
9 Afonso VI's Room
10 Hall of Stags (Armorial Hall)
11 Chapel
12 Kitchen
13 Central Court
14 Court of the Lion
15 Court of Diana
16 Lindaraya Garden
17 Garden of the Negress

Former Royal Palace

© Baedeker

appears that there was definitely a Moorish castle on this site in the 10th c., and its walls served as the foundations for the summer palace built there by King João I (1385 to 1433). This was extended and altered during the reign of Manuel I (1495–1521). Its most characteristic, and prominent, features are the two tall conical chimneys added in the 18th c. Completely restored and refurnished under Maria II, the palace was then chosen by Luís I as his favourite residence, and it became the dower house of his widow Maria Pia.

The Palace is not a single, uniform building, but consists of different, linked individual components. Through its history it has brought together Moorish, Gothic and Manueline architectural elements, together with Renaissance features. The palace frontage on the Largo Rainha D. Amélia, with its gently sloped flight of steps and the five Joanine double windows, was part of the first phase of the building and Manuel I then added the many Manueline-style windows and doorways.

The interior of the former royal palace offers an overview of Portuguese art and architecture of many different periods, with its shady patios and their refreshing fountains, its carpeted halls, its coffered ceilings and its many rooms faced with 15th and 16th c. azulejos.

The tour of the building usually begins in the Guardroom, then passes through the enormous kitchen into the Hall of the Arabs, furnished like an old Moorish palace. Next comes the Hall of the Stags, or Armorial Hall, which has an octagonal wooden domed ceiling embellished with the coats-of-arms and heraldic devices of 72 Portuguese noble families; that of King Manuel, who had the room built, is in the centre of the dome, and those of his eight children are grouped around it. The walls of the room are covered with azulejo murals of hunting scenes.

The Hall of the Magpies owes its name to the 136 magpies painted on the ceiling, each one holding in its beak the motto of King João I, "por bem", i.e. for the best. The story goes that João I's Queen caught him kissing a lady in waiting, and his cool response was "Foi por bem", i.e. "I did it for the best". Since the ladies in waiting delighted in repeating this ever afterwards on every possible occasion, their chatter goaded João I into commissioning the ceiling. The 16th c. Carrara marble fireplace is by Nicolas Chanterène.

Through a courtyard is the Hall of Swans, the largest room in the palace, its doors and windows embellished in the 16th c. in a sumptuous Moorish-Manueline style. This former banqueting hall is still used today on festive occasions.

Another of the palace rooms was where Afonso VI was imprisoned for nine years until his death in 1683, following his exclusion from affairs of state by his brother, Pedro II, who had him declared insane.

A few hundred yards to the west is the Toy Museum (open: Tues.–Sun. 10am–6pm), with over 20,000 exhibits.

Museu do Brinquendo

On the northern outskirts, housed in a magnificent 1920s building, is the Museum of Modern Art with the Berado Collection (open: Tues. 2–6pm, Wed.–Sun. 10am–6pm). It provides a good insight into European and American art since the Second World War. Artists such as Andy Warhol, Gerhard Richter, Tom Wesselmann and Dan Flavin are represented.

Museu de Arte Moderna

From the south side of the town a road forks right and snakes uphill, with many hairpin bends, first through magnificent gardens and then park-like woodland. After about 3km/2 miles a side-road branches off to the left to the Moorish castle, the Castelo dos Mouros (alt. 429m/1408ft; open: 10am–5pm). Ramparts and towers are still standing from the castle, which was originally built in the 8th or 9th c., recaptured in 1147 by Afonso Henriques and subsequently much altered. There is a splendid view of Sintra from the Torre Real. The inner courtyard has trees planted in the mid-19th c. for Ferdinand von Coburg-Koháry, consort of Queen Maria II.

Castelo dos Mouros

Following the road uphill from the Castelo dos Mouros, after about 1km/¾ mile we reach the entrance into the park of the Palácio Nacional da Pena, or Castelo da Pena, perched on its rocky crag (alt. 528m/1732ft; open: Tues.–Sun. 10am–5pm).

★★Palácio da Pena

This palace was also a royal summer residence and was built, as a medieval-style castle, for Ferdinand von Coburg-Koháry, Queen Maria II's consort (Fernando II), by Colonel von Eschwege 1840–50, who was instructed to incorporate elements of a 16th c. convent, and otherwise mix various building styles. Gothic, Manueline, Renaissance, Rococo, Moorish and Far Eastern features are all detectable, and Eschwege also incorporated Portuguese examples, such as modelling the principal tower on the Tower of Belém (see Lisbon). Probably the finest views of the Serra de Sintra are to be had from the walk along the top of the walls, the Galeria, and from the dome (external staircase).

The rooms of the "fairytale castle", which likewise lack any stylistic uniformity, are packed full of furniture, china, weapons, etc. The palace has also retained parts of the old 16th c. convent, namely, the two-storey Manueline cloister, with azulejo-lined walls, and the chapel, which has a Renaissance altar (1532) by Nicolas Chanterène and 19th c. German stained-glass windows.

Ferdinand von Coburg-Koháry was also responsible for the extensive Parque da Pena around the castle. (The park is closed at night; cars are admitted for a fee, but there is no charge for admission to the castle car park.) The estate, which covers about 200ha/494 acres, contains over 400 species of trees and shrubs, including tree ferns; it is especially beautiful in spring when the camellias, rhododendrons and azaleas are in bloom.

★Parque da Pena

Cars can be driven up to the Cruz Alta (540m/1771ft), a stone cross (1522) on the highest point in the Serra de Sintra, where there is a good view of the Palácio da Pena and of the whole mountain range and plain as far away as Lisbon.

Surroundings of Sintra

The Palácio de Seteais, or Palace of the Seven Sighs, is on the N 375 westward to Colares, just outside Sintra. It gets its name from the fact that the Treaty of Sintra – the surrender declaration of the French forces – was signed here in 1808. The palace was built in the last quarter of the 18th c. and extended early in the 19th. The triumphal arch (1802) commemorates a visit by João VI. The magnificent building is now a luxury hotel, with a gourmet restaurant.

Palácio de Seteais

Pena Palace near Sintra

★Quinta de Monserrate

A few miles past the Palácio de Seteais, on the same road, is the entrance to the Quinta de Monserrate, a Moorish-looking villa built in the 19th c. Originally owned by an Englishman, Sir Francis Cook, it is now the property of the State. It is worth a visit if only to look round its lovely hilly park, where there is an abundance of tall tree ferns along with many other species of subtropical plants.

Colares

Further along the road is Colares, famous for its wine, where a growing number of prosperous Lisbon citizens have their holiday homes.

About 1km/¾ mile beyond Colares the coast road that runs along the Costa do Sol (see entry) goes off to the left, but the right hand fork brings the visitor, after 3 and 4km/2 and 2½ miles respectively, to the little resorts of Praia das Maçãs and Azenhas do Mar, where the pounding of the waves has eaten deep into the rugged coastline.

★Convento dos Capuchos

The Convento dos Capuchos is 10km/6 miles along the road to the Palácio da Pena south-west out of Sintra. The Capuchin monastery, in its woodland setting, was founded in 1560. On entering this remote monastery (open: daily 10am–5pm, to 6pm in summer) the visitor steps into another world. Some of the tiny monks' cells – in which it was impossible to stand upright or to sleep fully stretched out – are hewn out of the solid rock and were insulated against cold and damp with layers of cork.

Monte Peninha

A little road goes from here to Monte Peninha (489m/1604ft), with good views over the Serra de Sintra and the sea. The small chapel perched up here was built in 1711 and is decorated with azulejos.

Other nearby destinations

A few miles south of Sintra are the popular coastal resorts of Cascais and Estoril (see entries), while Mafra (see entry), with its enormous convent-palace, is 20km/12 miles to the north.

The trip to Lisbon (see entry), the Portuguese capital, can be broken at Queluz (see entry) to see its palace and fine parks and gardens.

Quinta de Monserrate, near Sintra

Tavira

Historical province: Algarve
District: Faro
Altitude: sea level
Population: 10,000

The little town of Tavira, straddling the mouth of the Rio Gilão, or Rio Séqua, in the "sandy Algarve" part of the Algarve (see entry), has a Moorish look about it. Compared with other places on the Algarve it still has a certain restfulness, with tourism kept within reasonable bounds.

Tavira is the centre of the Algarve's tuna-fisheries, and has extensive salt-pans in the river estuary.

Situation and Importance

Tavira is one of the prettiest little towns in the Algarve. As it had to be rebuilt following the 1755 earthquake few of the buildings are more than 250 years old. Nevertheless it still presents a very harmonious picture; typical are the many old hip-roofed houses, a feature which has also been introduced into the more modern buildings.

★Townscape

Sights

The centre of Tavira is the Praça da República, on the right bank of the river. To the east it is bordered by the municipal park and at its south-east end stands the town's covered market, with street cafés nearby.

Praça da República

In recent years several bridges have been built across the Rio Gilão, and this has changed the character of the town centre. Previously, for hundreds of years, the only bridge was the seven-arched one north of the Praça da

Ponte

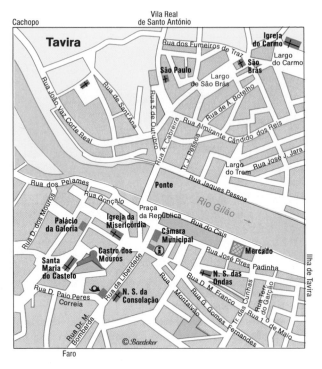

República; it was of Roman origin and over it passed the Roman road which linked Faro with Mértola. The present bridge is a 17th c. reconstruction. In the winter of 1989/90 it was badly damaged by floods and had to be blocked off. Since then it has been open to pedestrian traffic only.

Igreja da Misericórdia

Branching off the Rua da Liberdade, the narrow Rua da Galeria leads to the Igreja da Misericórdia. In spite of the rebuilding done after the 1755 earthquake the church, originally built in 1541, is one of the best examples of Renaissance religious architecture in the Algarve. The azulejos in the interior date from the 18th c.

★ Castro dos Mouros

Above the town, the Travessa da Fonte leads to the former castle (open: daily 9.30am–5.30pm). Only a few sections of the defensive wall remain of the original Roman, later Moorish castle, which was rebuilt after the town was captured by the Portuguese under Dom Dinis I. Today, in a part of the wall, a pretty garden has been laid out; it is privately owned, but can usually be visited. From the garden and from the top of the walls and tower there is a fine view of Tavira and the Rio Gilão.

Igreja Santa Maria do Castelo

Close by the castle ruins, the Santa Maria do Castelo church is Gothic, having been converted from a mosque. It too had to be completely rebuilt following the earthquake. The church choir holds the tombs of seven knights killed by the Moors in 1242 even though a ceasefire had been agreed.

Igreja do Carmo

The Igreja do Carmo, lying on the other side of the river in the north of the town, dates from the 18th c. and boasts splendid choir-stalls and fine talha dourada decoration.

Evening in Tavira

Surroundings of Tavira

The Ilha de Tavira lies offshore from Tavira and can be reached by boat from the town, the ferry landing stage being at the end of the road which runs along the right bank of the Rio Gilão behind the covered market. There is also a pedestrian bridge to the island further west near Santa Lucia. The Ilha de Tavira has a beach several miles long and flat dunes.

★Ilha de Tavira

See entry

Algarve

Tomar

B 5

Historical province: Ribatejo. District: Santarém
Altitude: 122m/400ft. Population: 15,000

Tomar is charmingly situated just north of the lower Tagus on its tributary, the Nabão, in the fertile Ribatejo landscape of central Portugal, and is very popular with tourists on account of its mighty convent-castle of the Knights of Christ.

Situation and Importance

The little Rio Nabão divides this attractive small town into a west end and an east end, with the old centre around the Praça da República west of the river and a lovely park on a sandbank in the river.
   A winding road leads past the chapel of Nossa Senhora da Conceição up to the castle of the Knights of Christ, above the west of the town.

Townscape

★★Convento da Ordem de Cristo de Tomar

The Order of the Knights of Christ (Ordem de cavalharia de Nosso Senhor Jesús Cristo) was founded by King Dinis in 1317 for the purpose of

History of the Order

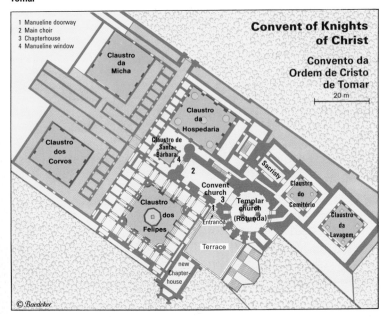

1 Manueline doorway
2 Main choir
3 Chapterhouse
4 Manueline window

Convent of Knights of Christ

Convento da Ordem de Cristo de Tomar

20 m

Claustro da Micha

Claustro dos Corvos

Claustro da Hospedaria

Claustro de Santa Bárbara

Claustro dos Felipes

Convent church

Templar church (Rotunda)

Sacristy

Entrance

Terrace

Claustro do Cemitério

Claustro da Lavagem

new Chapter-house

© Baedeker

"defending the faith, fighting the Moors and enlarging the Portuguese monarchy", following the dissolution in 1314 of the order of Knights Templar which had been established at Tomar since 1159. The new order flourished, particularly under its famous Grand Master Henry the Navigator (see Famous People).

The Order financed voyages of discovery to the west coast of Africa and thus began the process of colonial acquisition by the European nations. In the reign of King Manuel I (Grand Master from 1484) its possessions in Africa and the East Indies made it the wealthiest order in Christendom. The knightly order became a monastic order in 1523, was secularised in 1789 and dissolved in 1910.

History of the building

In the 12th c., in order to defend the line of the Tagus, the Knights Templar built a castle high above the right bank of the Nabão, and some of this castle's walls, its keep and the round Templar church are still part of the complex.

The Order of the Knights of Christ was first based in Castro Marim (see Vila Real de Santo António), when it was founded in 1317, then moved to Tomar in 1356. As Grand Master, Henry the Navigator was responsible for the building around the Templar castle in the early 15th c. of the Claustro da Lavagem and Claustro do Cemitério. The Order's next flowering was under Manuel I, who around 1500 had the Church of the Knights of Christ added on to the Templar church, and had the Claustro de Santa Bárbara and the new Chapterhouse built. Although the Order waned in political significance in the 16th and 17th c. there was further building during this period in the convent precincts, and four more cloisters were added, the Claustro dos Felipes, Claustro dos Corvos, Claustro da Micha and Claustro da Hospedaria. The buildings were restored by the Counts of Tomar in the mid-19th c., and the green setting for the convent-castle was first landscaped in the 1930s.

The entrance to the great complex of 12th to 17th c. buildings that go to make up the convent-castle of the Knights of Christ (open: daily 9.30am–12.30pm and 2–5pm, to 6pm in summer), high above Tomar, is through two gates of the old Templar castle. Passing through gardens to reach the terrace of the Templar Church, access to the interior of the convent is through the southern door of the Church of the Knights of Christ on the western end of the Templar building.

Tour of the complex

The crenellated Templar Church, or Rotunda, was begun in 1162 and modelled on the Church of the Holy Sepulchre in Jerusalem as a 16-sided polygon. This is supported by massive wall-pillars, one of which was later converted into a belfry, around a central octagon, or Charola, which was to hold the high altar. With the construction of the church of the Knights of Christ in the 16th c. the Charola became the choir of the new church.

All the extravagant embellishment of the interior – talha dourada, frescos and statues – dates from the 16th c.

Templar Church

Manueline window in the Knights of the Cross church

The church of the Knights of Christ on the west end of the Templar church is one of Portugal's finest Manueline monuments. The work of João do Castilho, it was begun in 1515. Its exterior is sumptuously decorated. Statues of the prophets surround the portal on the southern façade, with the Virgin and Child under a baldachin in the centre. The west front is no less impressive, where the splendour of the ornate window of the Old Chapterhouse shows the Manueline style at its most accomplished (best view from the terrace of the Claustro de Santa Bárbara, see below).

Almost three-quarters of the church interior is taken up by the Coro Alto (the choirstalls are 19th c.), once reserved for the monks at prayer. The rest was originally intended to be the vestry but later became the chapterhouse, while the Templar Church served as the choir for the Knights of Christ Church.

Knights of Christ Church

The Gothic Claustro do Cemitério, or cemetery cloister, on the north-east of the Templar church, is the oldest of the convent cloisters, and has Mudejar azulejos. This is the resting place of Vasco da Gama's brother, Diogo da Gama, as well as other important members of the Order.

Claustro do Cemitério

East of the Claustro do Cemitério is the two-storey Claustro da Lavagem, the "ablutions" cloister, which, like its neighbour, dates from the time of Henry the Navigator.

Claustro da Lavagem

From the church of the Knights of Christ a richly ornamented doorway leads into the upper gallery of the Claustro dos Felipes, or Claustro de João III, a beautiful Late Renaissance building (1557–62). The terrace on the top of the cloister's two storeys affords a view over the whole of the convent. While the ground level gallery has Tuscan columns, the upper storey has Ionic pillars. The well-proportioned fountain in the courtyard dates from the 17th c.

A doorway on the east side of the Claustro dos Felipes leads into the so-called "New" Chapterhouse which remained unfinished and was destroyed by the collapse of the vaulting.

Claustro dos Felipes

The little early Renaissance cloister of Santa Bárbara is next to the Claustro dos Felipes and from it can be seen the detail of the magnificent Manueline window on the west façade of the Knights of Christ Church. The window is set between two convoluted masts around which twine coral, ropes, seaweed, anchor chains, cables and other stonework motifs associated with the sea. It is crowned with the Portuguese coat-of-arms and, above it all, the cross of the Order of Christ.

Claustro de Santa Bárbara

To the north and west are three other cloisters. One of these, the Claustro da Hospedaria, or hostelry cloister, was, as its name suggests, for lodging noble guests visiting the convent. The Claustro da Micha, or bread cloister – where bread was handed out to the poor – contains a mission seminary and military hospital, and is not normally open to the public. The same applies to the Claustro dos Corvos, the cloister of the ravens, which used to hold the convent kitchen, storerooms and monks' cells.

Other convent buildings

The convent originally drew its water from springs and cisterns but from the late 16th c., with the building of an aqueduct, the Aqueduto dos Pegões, it was brought here from outlying springs in the north-east.

Aqueduto dos Pegões

Other sights in Tomar

The church of St John the Baptist stands in the centre of Tomar on the Praça da República, where there is a statue of Gualdim Pais, the Templar Grand Master who founded Tomar in 1162. The church, which was built about 1490, has an elegant Manueline doorway and contains six pictures from the 16th c. Portuguese school.

Igreja de São João Baptista

The 15th c. synagogue a few hundred yards south of the Praça da Républic contains a small Jewish museum (open: Mon., Tues.–Sun. 9.30am–noon and 2–5pm).

Synagogue

In the former Convento de São Francisco (in the south of the old town, near the railway station), is the Matchbox Museum. Some 43,000 matchboxes from more than 100 countries are on display (open: Mon.–Fri. and Sun. 2–5pm).

Museu dos Fosforos

Eastward across the old bridge, the Ponte Velha, on the other side of the Rio Nabão, is the Capela de Santa Iria, with a fine Renaissance doorway (1536).

Capela de Santa Iria

The Rue de Santa Iria leads south from here to the Igreja de Santa Maria do Olival on the edge of town. This was long the seat of the Grand Chapter of the Templars and later the Knights of Christ, the mother church of all the Order's churches in the colonies. All that is left of the first church building (*c.* 1160) is the porch and doorway. The interior of the former Templar church is overwhelmingly Renaissance, and contains the tombs of many of the Order's Knights and Masters.

Igreja de Santa Maria do Olival

In the north-east part of town, near the path up to the Knights of Christ Castle, is the 16th c. chapel of Nossa Senhora da Conceição, a lovely Renaissance building with delicately carved Corinthian capitals.

Nossa Senhora da Conceição

The pilgrimage chapel of Nossa Senhora da Piedade is farther north, on a hill above the town. It can be reached on foot up a flight of 286 steps, flanked by gardens. Built in 1613, it has azuelejo decoration in the interior. On the way up we pass São Gregório, an octagonal chapel with a shingle-roofed gallery all round it. Originally Manueline, it was later remodelled as Baroque.

Nossa Senhora da Piedade

Surroundings of Tomar

Castelo de Bode (see Abrantes) stands in attractive surroundings 13km/ 8 miles south-east of Tomar.

Castelo de Bode

◀ *Tomar: Castle of the Knights of Christ – the Templar Church*

Rock Drawings in the Côa Valley

Only a strong police cordon prevented the four government ministers from actually being attacked by the inhabitants of Vila Nova de Foz Côa. The people of this small town on the River Côa, a tributary of the Douro in northern Portugal, failed completely to comprehend the decision made in October 1995 by the new Socialist government to discontinue building the second largest artificial reservoir in Portugal, construction of which was already under way. The alternative proposals put forward by the government representatives failed to appease the populace of Vila Nova de Foz Côa. Their fury was understandable. The decision not to continue building the hydro-electric power station would immediately put 300 workers out of work, and the little community – already seriously affected by unemployment and certainly anything but prosperous – could not expect any financial support from the electricity company, the sponsors of the project. But their protests fell on deaf ears; the newly-elected government stood by their decision not to build the reservoir – and instead to preserve the rock paintings.

In the rugged gorges of the little Côa river a sensational discovery had been made soon after work was started on building the power station – hundreds of prehistoric rock drawings which had remained hidden from sight for thousands of years. More and more of these works of art carved in the rock face were found almost every day. The workers even found a tool which had been used to make the carvings – an extremely carefully made quartz scraper. Almost every time a stone was turned the Côa valley revealed one of its wonderful secrets.

Nobody knows how many drawings remain to be discovered, as so far only two-thirds of the reservoir site has been explored. It is estimated that it will take at least a further ten years to comb the area thoroughly.

Initial examinations suggest that the bulk of the illustrations carved in the slate date from the Paleolithic or Old Stone Age, the epoch which began after the Ice Age and covered the period 50,000 to 10,000 B.C. Experts believe that most of the drawings in the Côa valley were done 20,000 years ago. They portray animals which are always shown sideways on. Many of the engravings suggest a degree of movement, some are even in perspective. The animals are either those that would be hunted for food or else domesticated breeds. Two animals with S-shaped horns reminiscent of goats were carved in an astonishingly true-to-life way in a block of slate with a surface area of only just over a half a square metre/five and a half square feet. Of the two heads of the goats one is partly covered, so as to convey an idea of movement. The rear part of the drawing provides the most spectacular detail. The hoof and rump of one of the animals are almost identical to those in drawings found in the caves of Altamira. On another rock can be seen two horses which appear to be kissing. This very expressive carving is one of the oldest so far found in the valley. Next to it are a large number of drawings using very fine lines, so fine that at first sight they are hard to distinguish. One drawing of this kind is viewed by archaeologists as the Stone Age jewel of the Côa valley – it is a tiny portrayal, almost invisible to the naked eye, and even with a magnifying glass one has to look closely to make it out.

Why did primitive man, who had to struggle each day to survive in such a wild and dangerous environment, go to so much trouble to leave behind on the rock walls graphic evidence of his existence? Was he fascinated by the beauty of the animals he hunted? By researching primitive tribes, especially in Australia, scientists are convinced that over 20,000 years ago man produced drawings of animals for magical or religious reasons. To portray an animal, even in the form of a rock drawing, meant that man had conquered it and subjected it to his rule. However, there are also other possible explanations based on the legend that animals come forth out of the earth or are re-born there. Figures of animals appearing to be coming from out of the rock, therefore, could be a kind of invitation to Mother Nature to give birth to more prey to be hunted. The men of the Old Stone Age who completed these works of art possessed a degree of skill in line-drawing which leads one to conclude that their visual senses were already finely honed and educated.

The area around the Côa river is the only large open air site for Paleolithic finds so far discovered in Europe. The Côa, which enters the Douro from the south, is one of the few rivers in the Iberian Peninsula which flows from south to north. The heartland of rock drawings in the Côa valley could have been in a region where there are no caves. Whatever the answer is, the number of rock drawings to be found along the river have served to intensify still further the mystery surrounding the Paleolithic art of rock painting. Were this river and this valley holy in any way? Or was the Douro the main backbone of civilisation and the Côa, its remote tributary which was more difficult to get to, the only place where the rock drawings have managed to survive 20,000 years of human existence? An answer to these questions may be possible only when the valleys of the tributaries of the Douro have been thoroughly explored and researched.

The discovery of these rock drawings resulted in arguments as to whether prehistoric works of art should be preserved or a modern reservoir constructed; discussions raged throughout Portugal on whether portrayals from the past are more important than water and electricity for the future. At first the Portuguese state electricity company carried on building regardless. As a result a number of paintings from the Côa valley are now under water. They were swallowed up by the river twelve years ago, when the reservoir near Pocinho was constructed, and were not discovered until the electricity company lowered the water-level of the reservoir by 10m/33ft in 1993. Archaeologists had already suspected that some of the rock drawings might be under water; they therefore gave the symbolic name "Iceberg" to the peak of a rock which stood straight up out of the water.

When the new government placed a ban on further building early in October 1995 a giant 80m/260ft deep hole remained and there, where Portugal's second largest reservoir had been planned, the region suffered a financial loss of nearly £100 million/US$150 million. At the end of 1995 the Portuguese Minister of Culture stated that the rock paintings could act as a kind of engine to generate the development of the region. Perhaps. But how can such a cultural heritage thousands of years old be preserved and safeguarded? Apart from the Altamira Cave can the several square miles of rock drawings in northern Portugal be adequately protected from souvenir hunters?

Torres Novas | Torres Novas is an industrial town 25km/15½ miles south-west of Tomar. The ruins of its 14th c. castle, and its Misericórdia church, with a fine Renaissance doorway, are worth seeing.

Torre de Moncorvo   C 3

Historical province: Trás-os-Montes
District: Bragança
Altitude: 390m/1279ft. Population: 2500

Situation and Importance | The ancient little town of Torre de Moncorvo, or Moncorvo for short, is situated in a vast dry landscape dotted with fruit groves and vegetable plots in the north of the Serra do Roboredo (800m/2625ft; iron-mining), roughly halfway between Bragança and Guarda. Its "cobertas", or sugared almonds, are a local delicacy.

Townscape | The town has a number of handsome old houses bearing coats-of-arms. The 19th c. town hall stands on the site of one of King Dinis's castles.

Sights

Igreja Matriz | The parish church is a 16th c. three-aisled Renaissance building.
Inside there are beautiful talha dourada and a fine Gothic triptych of carved wood with scenes from the life of the Virgin's parents, St Anne and St Joachim. The choir has a coffered ceiling.

Igreja da Misericórdia | Also worth seeing is the Igreja da Misericódia, near the Largo do Castelo, which has an exceptionally fine Gothic granite pulpit.

Surroundings of Torre de Moncorvo

Vila Nova de Foz Côa | The village of Vila Nova de Foz Côa (alt. 439m/1440ft; pop. 2500) is about 16km/10 miles south-west of Torre de Moncorvo and has a Manueline church (remodelled in the 18th c.) and a fine pelourinho.

★Parque Arqueológico do Vale do Côa | In 1996 this area was declared the Parque Arqueológico do Vale do Côa. The park stretches for a length of 17km/10 miles and embraces three areas (Vila Nova de Foz Côa, Muxagata and Castelo Melhor) with more than 10,000 rock drawings. Accompanied by a guide the prehistoric pictures can be seen. Information from the headquarters of the open-air park in Vila Nova de Foz Côa (appointments for a guided tour: tel. 079/764317, fax 079/765257). There is another visitor centre in Muxagata, and in 1999 in Canada do Inferno a museum is to be opened in which didactic prehistoric evidence will be presented.
The town hit the headlines when some unique prehistoric drawings came to light in the course of a giant project to build an artificial reservoir (see Baedeker Special, pp. 328/329).

Freixo de Numão | About 18km/11 miles farther west there is a Romanesque church and some interesting castle ruins in the village of Freixo de Numão.

Torres Vedras   A 5

Historical province: Estremadura
District: Lisboa
Altitude: 66m/217ft. Population: 13,000

Situation and Importance | The ancient town of Torres Vedras, on the left bank of the Rio Sizandro, is about 60km/37 miles north of Lisbon, in a region famous for its wine.
It has a place in British military history as the base for Wellington's Torres Vedras Lines, fortified to defend Lisbon during the Peninsular War. Otherwise its rather unassuming townscape means that most tourists only pause briefly on their way through.

Sights | Features of interest in the town are the 16th c. churches of São Pedro and São Gonçalvo, a conventual church. Above the town are the ruins of an old

Moorish castle, the Castelo dos Mouros, from which there is a good view. King Manuel added a handsome battlemented gateway after the reconquest of the town.

The little spa of Termas dos Cucos, which specialises in rheumatic ailments, is about 2km/1¼ miles east of the town.

Termas dos Cucos

Trás-os-Montes

C/D 3

Historical province: Trás-os-Montes
Districts: Bragança, Vila Real, Viseu and Guarda
Area: 11,000sq.km/4246sq. miles
Population: 500,000. Chief town: Bragança

The rugged mountain province of Trás-os-Montes, or "beyond the mountains", lies in the extreme north-east corner of Portugal, bounded on the north and east by Spain, on the west and south-west by Minho and Douro Litoral, and on the south by Beira Alta.

Location and General

Because of its remoteness Trás-os-Montes has kept many of the old customs and traditions. The famous "romarias", which take place at many locations and which are very popular with visitors, are accompanied by processions in colourful national costume.

Geologically the province is part of the Spanish Meseta, which here reaches heights of between 1300m/4250ft and 1500m/4900ft (Serra do Mogadouro), and is fissured by broad tectonic collapse zones.

Geology

Its relative distance from the Atlantic reduces the moderating oceanic influence on the climate. This is a region of raw winds and widely fluctuating temperatures, marked by precipitation (often as snow in winter) that decreases towards the east.

Climate

The host of archaeological evidence shows that Trás-os-Montes, like Minho province, is an area of prehistoric settlement. Now as in the past population is clustered in the fertile valleys (especially the upper Douro valley, see entry), where the soil is good for growing grapes and fruit. The bare, dry arid plateaux provide grazing for sheep and goats. In addition to agriculture the region has a long tradition of handicrafts such as weaving, lace and pottery.

Population and Economy

Valença do Minho

B 2

Historical province: Minho. District: Viana do Castelo
Altitude: 72m/236ft. Population: 3000

The ancient little town of Valença do Minho lies on commanding heights above the left bank of the River Minho, Miño in Spanish, which here forms the frontier between Spain and Portugal (frontier crossing). Nowadays there is hardly any sense of the past rivalry between the two states and there is a lively cross-border traffic between Valença do Minho and Tui on the other side of the river. The Spaniards come to Valença do Minho chiefly to purchase cloth goods, especially terry towelling. Valença is busy on market day (Wed.); Thursday is market day in Tui.

Situation and Importance

The old core of Valença do Minho is enclosed by the ramparts of its massive walls. Although the town was always strongly fortified, the present Fortaleza, or fort, is 17th c., in the Vauban style. From various points on the walls there are superb views over the "new" town, some way below, the Minho valley and the mountains of Galicia.

★ Townscape

331

Valença do Minho

1 Capela de São Sebastião

2 Baluarte do Faro (bastion)

3 Igreja Matriz (main church)

4 Church of Santa Maria dos Anjos (St Mary of the Angels)

5 Pousada (hotel)

Valença do Minho

Narrow alleys between whitewashed house criss-cross the old town, and this is where the textile shops can be found. Buildings worth seeing are the Capela de São Sebastião, the late 13th c. Igreja de Santa Maria dos Anjos, and the Igreja Matriz, which was founded as a collegiate church by João I in about 1400.

Surroundings of Valença do Minho

Monte do Faro	The Monte do Faro (566m/1857ft; chapel) is about 7km/4½ miles south-east of the town, on the left bank of the Minho. From the top there are views far into the Minho valley, as well as eastward to the Peneda-Gerês National Park (see entry) and westward to the Atlantic.
Vila Nova de Cerveira	15km/9½ miles along the Minho in a south-westerly direction lies Vila Nova de Cerveira, from where there is a ferry link to Spain. The pousada, in the castle built by Dinis I in 1321, offers stylish accommodation.
Monção	See entry
Caminha	See entry

Viana do Castelo   B 3

Historical province: Minho. District: Viana do Castelo
Altitude: 20m/65ft. Population: 14,000

Situation and Importance

The district capital of Viana do Castelo, charmingly situated at the mouth of the Rio Lima below Monte de Santa Luzia, is an important harbour on this part of the Portuguese Atlantic coast, here called the Costa Verde. Although it has some industry – textiles, timber, fish-processing and shipbuilding – its attractive townscape and good beaches also make it popular with tourists.

History

Originally a Greek trading post, and still a modest little port in the Middle Ages, Viana achieved prosperity and importance at the time of the great voyages of discovery in the reign of Manuel I, especially on account of the then very profitable cod fisheries off the coast of Newfoundland.

In the 19th c., during the conflict between the Liberals and the monarchy, it sided with the Royalists and thus earned its charter from Queen Maria II and was henceforth known as Viana do Castelo, having previously been called Viana da Foz do Lima.

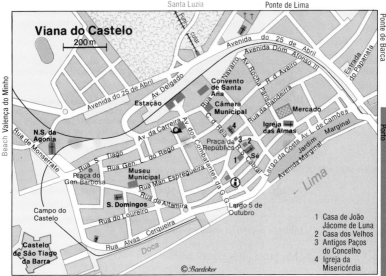

Its many handsome Manueline and Renaissance mansions and palaces, with their ornate granite façades, recall the splendours of the town's past. ★Townscape

Largo 5 de Outubro (car parking), on the Rio Lima, makes a good starting point for a walk round Viana do Castelo. Walk a short way upstream, then turn north, along the Rua S. Cabral, to the cathedral.

Sights

The cathedral was built in the first half of the 15th c. and substantially altered in the 19th c. The two crenellated towers flanking the façade are Romanesque. The interior has fine polychrome wood carving, mainly 17th c. The Casa dos Velhos, north of the cathedral, is a 15th c. building with a distinct Galician look. Opposite the cathedral stands the Casa de João Jácome de Luna, mid 16th c. and with sculpture probably from a previous building on the south façade. Sé

Just north of here is the Praça da República, one of Portugal's most picturesque squares, with the broad basins of its Renaissance fountain dating from 1559 in the centre. ★Praça da República

The old town hall, the Antigos Paços do Concelho on the east side of the square, is an early 16th c. granite building, now used for exhibitions, where bread used to be sold in its arcades at street level.

The Igreja da Misericórdia, rebuilt in the 18th c., is on the north side of the square and has fine talha dourada and 17th c. ajulejos in the interior. Adjoining the church is the Misericord Hospice, a Flemish Renaissance-style building begun in 1589.

North along the Rua C. dos Reis is the present town hall, the Câmara Municipal, a mansion begun in the 16th c. and completely remodelled in the 18th c. Next comes the Convento de Santa Ana, now the Hospital da Caridade, a former Benedictine convent dating, with its Manueline tower, from the 16th c. Its church has rich talha dourada decoration. Convento de Santa Ana

333

Viana do Castelo

Nossa Senhora da Agonia	The walk round the town continues westward through the Avenida da Carreira and the Rua S. Tiago to Nossa Senhora da Agonia, the chapel of Our Lady in Sorrow, a place of pilgrimage approached by a Baroque flight of steps. Begun in the mid 18th c., the chapel did not have a belfry until the late 19th c.
Castelo de São Tiago da Barra	In the south corner of the broad Campo do Castelo, south of the chapel, is the Castelo de São Tiago da Barra, built in the 16th c. to defend the harbour. The two towers were added in the 18th c.
Igreja de São Domingos	Back at the square below Nossa Senhora da Agonia and then past the well-shaded Praça do Gen. Barbosa the walk continues to the Igreja de São Domingos which was built in Renaissance style between 1566 and 1575 as the church of a Dominican abbey. According to the local guidebook the talha dourada altar in the Nossa Senhora do Rósario side-chapel is the finest in Europe.
Museu Municipal	The municipal museum diagonally opposite is housed in the 18th c. mansion of the Barbarosa Macieis family, and has displays of furniture from Portuguese India (17th c.) and Moorish Spain, as well as an important collection of 18th c. Portuguese glazed earthenware.
Rua de Altamira	The Rua de Altamira leading down to the river soon brings this walk round the town back to its starting point.

Surroundings of Viana do Castelo

Igreja de Santa Luzia	The Monte de Santa Luzia (250m/820ft) is about 5km/3 miles north-east of the town, topped by its 19th c. Neo-Byzantine church of Santa Luzia, a place

Near to Viana do Castelo where the pilgrimage church rises out of the Monte de Santa Luzia the views are magnificent!

of pilgrimage. It can be reached by car and by a funicular which leaves from near the station. It is worth making the trip if only for the magnificent view.

There are traces of a Celtic-Iberian settlement just north of the church which was inhabited until the 4th c. A.D.

Vila do Conde   B 3

Historical province: Douro Litoral. District: Porto
Altitude: sea level. Population: 22,000

Vila do Conde, "town of the Counts", is about 20km/12 miles north of Oporto on the left bank of the mouth of the Rio Ave. Its people get their living from shipbuilding, cotton manufacture and, traditionally, pillow-lace making, while many other businesses have established themselves around the little town, which is also a seaside resort. Its old town centre makes it a favourite excursion for tourists from Póvoa de Varzim (see entry), a few miles to the north, which it now almost adjoins.

Situation and Importance

Sights

The imposing bulk of the Monastery, or Mosteiro, of Santa Clara looms over the town. All that remains of the original monastery, founded in 1318, is the Gothic fortress church, still virtually unchanged. The monastery building, on the other hand, which looks more like a palace, dates from the end of the 18th c. and now houses a school.

Mosteiro de Santa Clara

The west face of the Gothic church has a beautiful rose window, while the interior, in the form of a single aisle, has the magnificent 16th c. Renaissance tombs of the founders of the monastery, Dom Afonso Sanches, illegitimate son of King Dinis I, and Dona Tareja Martins, and their children. The carved coffered ceiling and the choir screen are also worth looking at.

The convent gets its water supply from an 18th c. aqueduct (7km/4½ miles long, with 999 arches) which runs from Póvoa de Varzim.

Aqueduto

The fortified parish church, the Igreja Matriz, is in the old part of town and was built in the 16th c. to a cruciform groundplan. It has a Manueline doorway and 17th c. belfry. Its gilded wood pulpit dating from the 17th and 18th c. is well worth seeing. The pelourinho in the little church square is 16th c., and the sword stands for justice.

Igreja Matriz

The 16th c. town hall, bearing Manuel I's coat-of-arms, is on the north of the square.

The Centro de Artesanato, the arts and crafts centre a few hundred yards east of the parish church, displays the products of Vila do Conde's traditional pillow-lace making.

Centro de Artesanato

The 17th c. Forte de São João Bapatista, with its five bastions, is outside the centre of town at the mouth of the Rio Ave.

Forte de São João Baptista

Surroundings of Vila do Conde

The little fishing port of Azurara is just 2km/1¼ miles south of Vila do Conde on the right bank of the river. It has an interesting 16th c. Manueline fortified church, which also has a pelourinho in its square.

Azurara

The remains of the Celtic settlement of Cividade de Bagunte, where there have been some beautiful stone and bronze finds, are about 6km/4 miles east of Vila do Conde, not far from where the Rio Este joins the Rio Ave.

Cividade de Bagunte

Rio Mau is barely 10km/6 miles north-east of Vila do Conde. Its Romanesque church of São Cristóvão, built for a convent founded in 1151, has interesting sculptural decoration.

Rio Mau

Rates

Rates, 4km/2½ miles north-east of Rio Mau, is worth a detour for its important Romanesque church of São Pedro. It was built by French architects for Henry of Burgundy at the beginning of the 12th c., replacing an earlier church on the spot where St Pedro of Rates is believed to have been martyred by Roman soldiers in the 1st c. A.D. Subsequently altered in parts, the church still has rich 12th c. sculptural decoration.

Vila Real   C 3

Historical province: Trás-os-Montes. District: Vila Real
Altitude: 422m/1385ft. Population: 14,000

Situation and Importance

Vila Real is an attractive old episcopal city and district capital, amid orchards and vineyards, 100km/62 miles east of Oporto and on the north side of the Serra de Marão, where the Rio Corgo joins with the Rio Cabril. It still has many fine 15th to 18th c. patrician houses. The black pottery from the locality, especially Biselhães, is famous.

Also produced nearby, and well-known throughout Europe, is the wine called Mateus rosé, in its characteristically shaped bottles.

Sights

The town's main shopping street and thoroughfare is the Avenida de Carvalho Aráujo, where Vila Real's main sights are also to be found. The birthplace of the navigator Diogo Cão, who discovered the mouth of the Congo, is at number 17, an Italian Renaissance building. The town hall is early 19th c.

The 14th c. Gothic Cathedral, or Sé, was originally the church of a Dominican convent, and still has Romanesque capitals from the first church on the site.

Solar de Mateus – well known for its wine far beyond the Portuguese borders. Here the vineyards start from which the famous rosé wines are pressed

The 16th c. church of São Pedro is richly decorated with 17th c. polychrome azulejos and has a gilded coffered ceiling in the choir.

There are fine views from the hill above the town, once occupied by a castle, and from the Calvário (460m/1509ft), with the 16th c. church of Santo António.

View

Surroundings of Vila Real

Mateus is a village about 4km/2½ miles east of Vila Real, and owes its fame to its rosé wine and the manor of the Counts of Vila Real, the Solar de Mateus, considered to be a perfect example of Portuguese Baroque. Although the Mangualde family still live there, parts of it are open to the public. Inside the palace there are magnificent wood ceilings as well as valuable furniture, carpets, paintings and silverware, and an interesting porcelain collection. The small private museum contains correspondence between members of the Mangualde family and royalty and other famous people, as well as engravings for Camões' Lusiades.

★Mateus

However, the beauty of the gardens actually surpasses that of the Solar de Mateus, and the ancient tunnel formed by topiaried thuya is a minor work of art; the trees allow scarcely any light to enter.

3km/2 miles beyond Mateus a road branches off to the Celto-Iberian cult-site of Panóias. Six granite rocks bear Greek and Latin inscriptions. One of the rocks must have served as a sacrificial stone; the channels down which the blood of the slaughtered animals ran, can still be seen.

Panóias

Termas de Pedras Salgadas is a spa 35km/22 miles north of Vila Real on the Chaves road which is much visited for its radioactive springs and pleasant park.

Termas de Pedras Salgadas

The village of Vila Marim about 4km/2¼ miles west of Vila Real has an interesting 14th c. granite tower, the Torre de Quintela.

Vila Marim

There is a beautiful drive of 50km/30 miles westward from Vila Real through the wild and romantic Serra do Marão to Amarante (see entry).

Serra do Marão

Peso da Régua (see Lamego) is a wine-producing and trading centre about 25km/15½ miles south of Vila Real.

Peso da Régua

Vila Real de Santo António

C 7

Historical province: Algarve. District: Faro
Altitude: sea level. Population: 14,000

The little frontier town of Vila Real de Santo António lies on the right bank of the Guadiana which is navigable as far as Mértola. There are regular ferries to Ayamonte, the Spanish port on the other side, although these have been used less since a motorway bridge was built across the river a few miles to the north. However, river excursions from Vila Real de Santo António are most enjoyable.

Situation and Importance

The many visitors to the town come for the day to take advantage of the bargains in the shops. Until the 1960s there were a number of fish canning factories here, especially for tuna and sardines, but now there are only two.

The town was founded in 1774 by the Marquês de Pombal on the site of Santo António da Avenilha which had been destroyed by a tidal wave at the beginning of the 17th c. He had it laid out like a chessboard, and settled it with fisherfolk from Aveiro (see entry).

Townscape

The town centre is the Praça do Marquês de Pombal, paved with a black and white mosaic radiating from the obelisk (1775) that is a monument to José I, and lined with inviting street cafés.

Surroundings of Vila Real de Santo António

Algarve

There are very enjoyable drives along the Algarve coast to Cape St Vincent (see Algarve).

★ Castro Marim

Castro Marim, which overlooks the Guadiana plain about 4km/2½ miles north-west of Vila Real de Santo António, gets its name from the closeness of its castle to the sea. It was the seat of the Order of the Knights of Christ, founded in 1319, until this was transferred to Tomar (see entry) in 1356.

The castle ruins, which tower over the village to the north, date from this brief and glorious period in its history. The castle was probably originally late 13th c. and then extended by the Knights of Christ in 1319. From its towers and ramparts there is a lovely view of the village and Castelo Novo, a 17th c. fortification. The Igreja da Misericórdia inside the castle walls has an attractive Renaissance door.

Another building in the castle complex houses the information office of the Sapal Nature Park (Reserva Natural do Sapal de Castro Marimi). The park stretches from south of Castro Marim to Vila Real de Santo António. Many species of birds breed here; guided tours are available at times.

★ Alcoutim

Alcoutim, 40km/25 miles north of Vila Real de Santo António, is also on the Guadiana. It is a charmingly modest little town, with relatively few visitors during the week although sometimes coach parties arrive at weekends. When river conditions are suitable excursion ships from Vila Real de Santo António call here.

Its situation made Alcoutim strategically important at one time. The present castle forms part of a Moorish fort of the 11th c.; Dinis I ordered that the castle walls should be rebuilt in 1304. Inside the restored walls is an exhibition of archaeological finds.

Alcoutim by the Guadiana

Vila Viçosa C 6

Historical province: Alto Alentejo. District: Évora
Altitude: 422m/1385ft. Population: 4000

Vila Viçosa is about 55km/34 miles north-east of Évora, on the slopes of hills covered with orchards. It was at one time the seat of the Dukes of Bragança, and several kings from the same house, but with the abolition of the monarchy in 1910 it declined into provincial obscurity. The economy of the region depends on marble quarrying. | Situation and Importance

Sights

The main attraction, on the way into the town from Borba, is the Paço Ducal, the palace of the Dukes of Bragança. Built in the 16th and 17th c. on the remains of Moorish, possibly even Roman buildings, for centuries it hosted a brilliant court and was a hub of intellectual life. In 1640 João IV was the first of the Dukes of Bragança to ascend the Portuguese throne. Although Lisbon then became the seat of the monarchy João IV and his successors continued making frequent visits to Vila Viçosa. | ★ Paço Ducal

There are guided tours round the palace, which is full of objets d'art from the 16th to the 19th c., although the most valuable were taken to the new quarters in Lisbon in the mid-17th. What remains is quite grand enough – painted ceilings and family portraits, 17th c. azulejos, tapestries, porcelain, a well-stocked armoury and a collection of coaches. The chapel, which has a 16th c. triptych, is particularly worth seeing. The inner courtyard appears to have been modelled on a cloister.

The spacious Terreiro do Paço, or palace square, in front of the palace has an equestrian statue of King João IV in the centre, and before the palace was built served at times as a bullring. | Terreiro do Paço

Vila Viçosa: Paço Ducal

339

On the east side of the square, opposite the palace, is the church of the former Augustinian convent (17th/18th c.), with a richly decorated interior. It contains the tombs of the Dukes of Bragança; their spouses were interred in the Antigo Convento das Chagas, built in the 16th c. and restored in the 18th, which is on the south side of the square. Today the building is a Pousada.

Porta dos Nós

The Porta dos Nós is the eyecatching "knot gate" north of the palace on the Borba road. It was part of the old 16th c. wall round the town and is the entrance to the 5,000-acre Tapada, once the royal deer-park, where the Portuguese royal family hunted until early this century.

Igreja de Santa Cruz

Adjoining the 16th c. Igreja de Santa Cruz in the town centre is a small museum of sacred art.

Castelo

The massive battlemented castle, or *castelo*, that looms over the town, was built by King Dinis in the 13th c. and reinforced with bastions in the 17th. Visitors can walk around the ramparts surrounding the old town. Within the ramparts can be found the Renaissance da Conceição church and a hunting museum.

Pelourinho

There is a 16th c. pelourinho on the main road near the castle.

Surroundings of Vila Viçosa

Borba

The attractive old-world little town of Borba (6km/4 miles north of Vila Viçosa) is renowned for the white marble quarried nearby and for its wine. The life of the town revolves around the Praça do Cinco de Outubro with the town hall (1797) and parish church. Also worth a visit is the church of São Bartolomeu, a 16th c. Renaissance building with a beautiful door, brightly painted stone vaulting and rich azulejo cladding. In the Convento das Servas note the two-storey cloister with an azulejo-clad fountain in the middle.

Near the town centre, at the junction with the road to Vila Viçosa (see entry), stands the Fonte das Bicas (1781), a magnificent marble fountain in its own little park.

Alandroal

The village of Alandroal, with the ruins of one of King Dinis's 13th c. castles, is about 10km/6 miles south of Vila Viçosa. There is an impressive fountain in the market square.

Terena

Above Terena, 10km/6 miles farther south, are the ruins of another medieval castle, with panoramic views.

Borba

See entry

Estremoz

See entry

Redondo

See Estremoz

Viseu   C 4

Historical province: Beira Alta. District: Viseu
Altitude: 540m/1770ft. Population: 24,000

Situation and Importance

The old district capital of Viseu is on the left bank of the Rio Pavia, set in woodland in the famous wine-producing Dão region. It is an important centre for agriculture (grain, fruit, livestock) and crafts (lace, carpets, black pottery).

In the 16th c. Viseu had one of Portugal's most important schools of painting, foremost among them being the landscape painter Gaspar Vaz

Misericórdia

Viseu: Igreja da

(d. *c.* 1568) and Vasco Fernandes, known as Grão-Vasco (d. *c.* 1542), who was born here.

Its handsome Renaissance and Baroque mansions and palaces, narrow alleys paved with granite sets, flights of steps and intriguing corners lend Viseu a particular charm.

★Townscape

Sights

The Praça da República, in the centre with the town hall on its west side, is a good place to start a walk round the town.

Praça da República

The Baroque church of São Francisco, on the south side of the square, has rich azulejo and talha dourada decoration.

Igreja de São Francisco

The works of art, pictures, ceramics, porcelain, furniture, etc., collected by the connoisseur Almeida Moreira are on show in the Almeida Moreira museum north of the Praça da República.

Museu de Almeida Moreira

North from here, through the Porta do Soar, built in the town wall in the 15th c., is the old town, and at its heart, the Praça da Sé, where it is thought that in prehistoric times there was already a Celtic-Iberian fort.

Praça da Sé

A broad flight of steps leads up from the square to the church of the Misericórdia, a building of pure Baroque, its granite pilasters standing out against whitewashed walls.

Igreja da Misericórdia

The Romanesque and Gothic Cathedral, or Sé, opposite the Misericord Church, was first built in the 12th c., remodelled in the 16th and extended in

★Sé

Viseu: the Cathedral

the 18th. In the central niche above the door is a statue of St Theotonius, the town's patron saint.

The interior was transformed into a hall church in the 16th c. by the reconstruction of the vaulting, which is Manueline but supported by Gothic pillars. Above the monumental Baroque high altar is a 14th c. figure of the Virgin. The chapterhouse contains a remarkable treasury of sacred art.

The ground floor of the cloister is Renaissance, the gallery in the upper storey having been added in the 17th c.

★ Museu de Grão Vasco

The Grão Vasco, or "great Vasco" Museum is in the Paço dos Três Escalões, the Renaissance palace, remodelled in the 18th c., which adjoins the Cathedral. The museum has some 13th to 16th c. sculpture but primarily shows the work of the Viseu School of painting, including "St Peter" and "Crucifixion" by Vasco Fernandes, etc.

There are also works by more modern Portuguese artists (19th and 20th c.), as well as by Spanish, French, Flemish and Dutch masters, together with ceramics (16th–18th c.), carpets and furniture (17th and 18th c.).

Rua Direita

From behind the Cathedral little streets lead down to Viseu's main street, now largely pedestrianised, the Rua Direita with particularly lovely 16th to 18th c. houses, some of them with wrought-iron grilles.

To get back to this little walk's starting point go south down the Rua Direita then right into the Rua Formosa, ending up back at the Praça da República.

Cava de Viriato

The Cava de Viriato, outside the town centre and in the northern part of Viseu, is a big pentagonal-shaped park where there was once a Lusitanian-Roman camp. There is a monument to the Lusitanian leader Viriathus who was supposed to have made his heroic stand against the Romans here in the 2nd c. B.C.

Surroundings of Viseu

A very attractive trip is the 40km/25 miles south-west through the scenic   ★Caramulo
rugged hills of the Serra do Caramulo (up to 1071m/3514ft) to the charmingly situated hillside health resort of Caramulo (800m/2625ft). Its main
attraction is the Museu do Caramulo, with exhibits ranging from
medieval art, furniture, tapestries, porcelain and ceramics, to a remarkable collection of works by Portuguese and other European artists, particularly of the 19th and 20th c., including works by such famous
painters as Picasso, Dalí, Miró, Chagall, Léger, Dufy and Vlaminck. The
exhibition on the ground floor traces the development of the car since
1902 (about 50 veteran and vintage vehicles). One of the most valuable
vintage cars is a 1937 Mercedes Pullman. The valuable treasures and old
cars were collected by Abel de Lacerda; since his death his brother has
continued this unique museum.

The little town of Mangualde about 13km/8 miles south-east of Viseu has   Mangualde
a 17th c. palace of the Counts of Anadia in the middle of a rather wild
park. The pilgrimage church of Nossa Senhora do Castelo (628m/2060ft)
stands on a hill with a view about 1.5km/1 mile to the north.

**Practical
Information
from A to Z**

Accommodation

See Camping, Hotels, Pousadas, Youth Hostels

Airlines

Lisbon

Air Portugal (TAP)
Praça Marquês de Pombal 3A; tel. 01/3179100
Lisbon airport: tel. 01/8416990

British Airways
Avenida da Liberdade 36; tel. 01/3217900

Portugália Airlines (PGA)
Rua C. Edifício 70; tel. 01/8425500
Lisbon Airport: tel. 01/8464232 (weekday), 01/8471306 (weekend)

Faro

Air Portugal (TAP)
Rua D. Francisco Gomes 8; tel. 089/800200
Faro airport: tel. 089/800800

British Airways, c/o TAP

Portugália Airlines (PGA)
Faro Airport: tel. 089/800852 ext. 2852

Oporto

Air Portugal (TAP)
Praça Mouzinho de Albuquerque 105; tel. 02/6080227
Oporto airport: tel. 02/94822141

British Airways
Avenida do Aeroporto, Francisco Sá Carneiro; tel: 02/9449989
freephone 0800/212125

Portugália Airlines (PGA)
Avenida da Boavista 1361; tel. 02/6004766
Oporto Airport: tel. 02/9412075 or 9411663

Madeira

Air Portugal (TAP)
Avenida Dr António José de Almeida 17, Funchal; tel. 091/239243
Funchal airport: tel. 091/524864

Azores

Air Portugal (TAP)
Rua Rio da Sé, Angra do Heroísmo, Terceira; tel. 095/26489

Air Portugal (TAP)
Avenida Infante D. Henrique 55, Ponta Delgada, São Miguel;
tel. 096/205210

Air Portugal (TAP) outside Portugal

Canada

1801 McGill College, Suite 1410
Montreal, P.Q.; tel. (514) 8494217

151 Bloor Street West, Suite 450
Toronto, Ontario; tel. (416) 9640783

◄ *Festa dos Tabuleiros in Tomar: held in even numbered years in July*

Air Services

Air routes ——

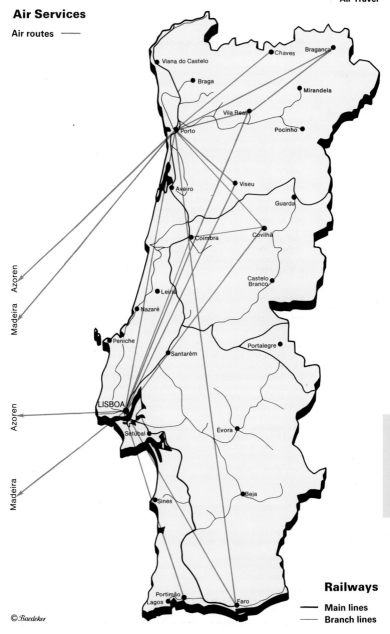

Viana do Castelo

Braga

Chaves

Bragança

Mirandela

Vila Real

Porto

Pocinho

Aveiro

Viseu

Guarda

Coimbra

Covilhã

Castelo Branco

Leiria

Nazaré

Peniche

Portalegre

Santarém

LISBOA

Setúbal

Évora

Sines

Beja

Azoren

Madeira

Azoren

Madeira

Portimão

Lagos

Faro

© Baedeker

Railways

—— Main lines
—— Branch lines

Air Travel

United Kingdom	19 Regent Street London SW1Y 4LR; tel. (0171) 8391031/2
	Room 25, Level 7, International Airport Manchester; tel. (0161) 4992161
United States	521 Fifth Avenue New York, N.Y. 10175; tel. (212) 6610035

Air Travel

Portuguese Mainland	Air Portugal (TAP) operates a number of Portuguese mainland domestic flights daily between Lisbon and Oporto and Lisbon and Faro. Portugália Airlines (PGA) provide mainland domestic flights among Lisbon, Oporto and Faro, plus major European destinations.
Mainland/Madeira	There are several flights a day between Lisbon and Funchal (Madeira), and several a week between Oporto and Funchal. Once a week in summer there is a direct flight from Faro to Funchal. There are also several services a day from Funchal to the little island of Porto Santo.
Mainland/Azores	TAP has several flights a day from Lisbon to Ponta Delgada (São Miguel), and a number of flights a week to Terceira and Horta (Faial). The local airline SATA operates light planes on inter-island flights in the Azores.
Madeira/Azores	There are usually two flights a week between Funchal and Ponta Delgada, three during summer.

Beaches

| Beach signs | The sign for a beach that is supervised is a green arrow and the words "Area Concessionada", while a red rectangular sign with a double arrow and the words "Praia Não Vigiada" means the beach is unsupervised. Coastal areas where swimming can be dangerous have a round red sign with a red arrow and the word "Danger".
    Supervised beaches use flags to show when it is safe to go swimming. A red flag means it is forbidden to enter the sea, even close to the coast for paddling; a yellow flag means no swimming; and a green flag indicates that paddling and swimming are safe. A blue/white chequered flag means the beach is temporarily unsupervised. |

The following list gives the major beaches on the Portuguese mainland, numbered as on the map on page 349.

Costa Verde

1 Moledo do Minho
Fine sand, dunes (on this part of the coast the climate is rather raw); restaurants.

2 Vila Praia de Ancora
Fine sand, dunes; restaurants.

3 Viana do Castelo
South of the Rio Lima beaches of fine sand – probably the best on the Costa Verde – shallow, dunes; restaurants.

4 Esposende
Lagoon, sandbanks, the long sandy beach is often better for walks than for swimming and sunbathing because of the wind; swimming can be more sheltered in the Rio Cávado estuary.

Bathing Beaches in Portugal

(Mainland)

- 🔵 **Costa Verde**
- 🔘 **Costa de Prata**
- ⚪ **Costa do Sol**
- ⚪ **Costa do Lisboa**
- ⚪ **Costa Dourada**
- ⚪ **Costa do Algarve**

Atlantic Ocean

Atlantic Ocean

National Parks

© Baedeker

5 Ofir
Fine sand, shallow, woods; restaurant, growing tourist centre.

6 Póvoa de Varzim
Sandy beach, dirty in parts; several restaurants; outlook industrial rather than scenic.

7 Vila do Conde
Sandy beach, some cliffs, on the whole more attractive than Póvoa de Varzim beach; restaurants.

8 Miramar
Sandy beach, shallow, rather like the North Sea; several restaurants.

9 Espinho
Flat sandy beach, high surf sometimes; several restaurants.

Costa de Prata 10 Praia de São Jacinto
Fine sand, dunes, woods.

11 Palheiros de Mira
Sandy beach, dirty in parts.

12 Figueira da Foz
Flat sandy beach on the main road, very crowded in the high season, high surf sometimes – Figueira da Foz, with Nazaré, is the largest resort on this coast; several restaurants.

13 Pedrógão
Flat sandy beach, some rocks, good surf; fishing harbour.

14 Praia da Vieira
Fine sand, surf; several restaurants.

15 São Pedro de Muel
Fine sand, shallow, rocks, one of the most pleasant places for bathing on this coast; several restaurants.

16 Nazaré
Sandy beach, lying beside the main road; it is necessary to book a place early in the high season, water can be polluted; several restaurants.

17 São Martinho do Porto
Deep bay with calm water, dunes separate the bay from the open sea; scuba diving; several restaurants.

18 Peniche
Nearby sandy beach, shallow, rocks; scuba diving; several restaurants; fishing harbour.

19 Praia de Santa Cruz
Fine sand, good surf, dunes, cliffs and coves; restaurant.

20 Ericeira
Flat sandy beaches, rocks, cliffs, pleasant swimming and sunbathing but very crowded at weekends; several restaurants; fishing harbour.

Costa do Sol 21 Praia Grande
Flat sandy beach, cliffs; very busy at weekend; several restaurants.

22 Praia do Guincho
Fine sandy bay near road, pinewoods in background, but very overcrowded in high season; restaurants.

23 Cascais/Estoril
Small bays with flat beaches of fine sand extend out from these two resorts, which have merged to become one, rocks; very crowded in fine weather; water sports; pigeon shooting; restaurants.

Portugal's finest coast: The rocky Algarve at Praia da Rocha ▶

Fine beach at Vila Nova de Milfontes on the Costa Dourada

Costa de Lisboa   24 Costa da Caparica
A long expanse of dunes stretches southward from here, with particularly fine beaches at the southern end; restaurants.

25 Sesimbra
Small sandy beach extending directly from the resort, very busy at weekends; scuba diving; fishing boats; several restaurants.

26 Portinho da Arrábida
Beaches in sheltered scenic coves, rocks, quiet beaches at the foot of Serra do Arróbida; several restaurants; fishing harbour.

27 Tróia
Wooded peninsula, broad beaches of fine sand (the best are well apart from the hotels); scuba diving; several restaurants; ferry to Setúbal.

Costa Dourada   28 Porto Covo
Flat sandy beach, rocks, heavy surf; several restaurants; fishing harbour.

29 Vila Nova de Milfontes
Attractive long sandy beach, dunes; several restaurants.

Although there are no more big resorts on the rest of the Costa Dourada there are plenty of pretty little coves with a beach, such as Zambujeira do Mar and Praia de Odeceixe; some stretches of beach acquire impromptu bars in summer.

Algarve   30 Aljezur
Flat sandy beach, rocks, dunes, good surf; restaurant.

31 Sagres
Flat beaches of fine sand, as yet uncrowded, but quite windy; good scuba diving; restaurants; submarine caves.
   There is good surfing at Beliche beach, 5km/3 miles north-west of Sagres, with a path leading down to a half-mile long stretch of beach;

Praia do Martinhal, 2km/1¼ miles east of Sagres is another quite good beach: half a mile of white beach with dunes, protected by the harbour. It is also possible to swim at Zavial, further east, where there is a flat beach of fine sand with no rocks.

32 Salema/Burgau
Salema has a flat sandy beach about half a mile long where there are usually some fishing boats as well, cliffs; several restaurants; good surfing possible.

A mile or so further east there is a sandy beach at Burgau; fishing harbour; restaurants; surfing for beginners.

33 Praia da Luz
Broad sandy beach, rocks; scuba diving and various other water sports; several restaurants – beach also very good for children.

34 Lagos
Long sandy beach in Lagos, many others close by (e.g. Praia da Dona Ana, west of Lagos at the Hotel Golfinho), rocks; scuba diving; several restaurants; fishing harbour.

Meia Praia, east of Lagos, has one of the Algarve's longest beaches; good surfing.

35 Alvor
Flat sandy beach, rocks; tourist complex; several restaurants; water sports also at Três Irmãos beach, just to the east (surfing suitable for beginners).

36 Praia da Rocha
Closely packed beach in the high season, picturesque rocks (road runs along top of cliff); scuba diving; several restaurants.

37 Carvoeiro
Sandy little cove, crowded in high season; a few fishing boats, rocks; several restaurants.

38 Armação de Pêra
Very long beach of fine sand, and relatively uncrowded compared with other Algarve resorts, dunes; scuba diving; restaurants.

Bathing is also possible farther west at Senhora da Rocha where there are also caves to be explored.

39 Albufeira
Beaches of fine sand, rocks, cliffs; scuba diving, several restaurants; fishing harbour. The beach in Albufeira is very overcrowded in the high season but there is more chance of finding some space further east at, for instance, the Praia da Oura.

40 Olhos de Agua (Praia da Falesia)
Flat beach of fine sand, rocks, cliffs; good surfing; restaurants.

41 Vilamoura
Sandy beach, some cliffs; several restaurants, big tourist complex with many facilities for sports, excellent surfing conditions, ideal for children.

42 Quarteira
Sandy beach, big tourist centre with various sports facilities; several restaurants; safe swimming for children.

43 Vale do Lobo
Fine sand, flat in parts, rocks, cliffs; several restaurants; plenty of sports facilities, usually good surfing conditions.

44 Quinta do Lago
Sandy beach, dunes, lagoon; good surfing conditions; speed boats.

45 Faro
Long flat beach of fine sand, lagoon; several restaurants (access by road and by boat).

46 Olhão
In the high season boats ply every hour and a half between Olhão and the offshore islands of Culatra and Armona which have fine long sandy beaches and dunes.

47 Tavira
From Tavira you can go by boat to the wooded Tavira Island with a flat sandy beach and dunes. It is still relatively undisturbed here since there is no mass tourism facility in the vicinity; restaurants.

48 Cabanas/Cacela
Still one of the Algarve's loveliest beaches: you cross by fishing boat to the little island with a flat beach of fine sand.

49 Monte Gordo
Flat beach of fine sand, dunes; several restaurants.

Naturist beaches   There are specially designated beaches and holiday complexes where "naturism" can officially be practised, but nude sunbathing and swimming is also usually tolerated on more remote beaches. There is also plenty of topless sunbathing on the more popular beaches.

Banks

See Opening Times and Currency

Bullfighting

Bullfighting in Portugal (see Arts and Culture, Folklore) is far less gory than the Spanish variety, especially since the bull gets out of the arena alive, although it is tormented and later killed.

There is bullfighting between April and October, primarily in Lisbon and the Ribatejo, but in the summer many tourist centres, such as Lagos, Quarteira and Albufeira, also stage bullfights once a week, usually on Saturdays.

Business Hours

See Opening Times

Camping

Unofficial camping   As a general rule Portugal does not allow overnight camping at the roadside, in lay-bys, parks or open country.

Camping permit   In addition to a passport, some camp sites require a camping permit which must have been issued by an officially recognised national or international organisation.

Camp sites   Portugal currently has about 140 public and private camp sites, classified according to quality and ranging from one star to four stars.

Camping guide   The Direcção-Geral de Turismo in Lisbon issues a camping guide (Parques de Campismo, Guia Oficial) in several languages. The address is Direcção-Geral de Turismo, Av. António Augusto de Aguiar 86, 1050 Lisboa; tel. 01/575086, fax 01/3575220.

Detailed information about the amenities and situation of camp sites is also given in the yearly publication ADAC Camping Guide (part 1).

Car Rental

To hire a car in Portugal you must be 21 or over and have held a driving licence for at least one year.

Avenida Praia da Victória 12C; tel. 01/3561176 Hotel Ritz, Rua Rodrigo da Fonseca; tel. 01/3811451 Airport: tel. 01/8494836	**Avis** Lisbon
Rua Igreja Nova 13; tel. 089/512678	Albufeira
Estrada do Aeroporto; tel. 082/818625	Faro
Largo das Portas de Portugal 11; tel. 082/763691	Lagos
Rua Guedes Azevedo 125; tel. 02/2051235 Airport: tel. 02/949525	Oporto
Avenida António Augusto de Aguiar 24; tel. 01/3535115 Airport: tel. 01/801176	**Europcar** Lisbon
Rua Dr. Diogo Leote; tel. 089/512444	Albufeira
Avenida República 2; tel. 089/823778 Estrada do Aeroporto; tel. 089/818777	Faro
Rua de Santa Catarina 1158–1164; tel. 02/2057735 Airport: tel. 02/2057737	Oporto
Rua Castilho, 72 A/B/C; tel. 01/3812430/35 Airport: tel. 01/8492722	**Hertz** Lisbon
Hotel Apart. O Trópico, Areias de S. João; tel. 089/542920	Albufeira
Rua 1° de maio 9; tel. 089/21272 Airport; tel. 089/818248	Faro
Rossio de S. João, Edifício Panorama, Loja 3; tel. 082/769809	Lagos
Rua de Santa Catarina 899; tel. 02/2052393 Airport; tel. 02/9449400	Oporto
Rua do Castilho 167B; tel. 01/3860516 Airport: tel. 01/8491603	**Sixt/Budget** Lisbon
Páteo Aldeia, Areias de São João; tel. 089/587080	Albufeira
Airport; tel. 089/817907	Faro
Airport; tel. 02/9416534	Oporto

Casinos

French and American roulette, blackjack and baccarat are usually played in Portuguese casinos. There are also one-armed bandits, fruit machines, etc. Most of the casinos have their own restaurant where international shows are presented. You should take your passport if you are going to gamble. Casinos are usually open daily between 5pm and 4am.

Casino de Praia da Rocha Praia da Rocha	Algarve
Casino de Vilamoura, Vilamoura, near Quarteira	

Chemists

	Casino de Monte Gordo Monte Gordo, near Vila Real de Santo António
Northern Portugal	Casino Solverde, Rua 19, no. 85, Espinho
	Casino de Póvoa de Varzim Póvoa de Varzim, about 20km/12 miles north of Oporto
	Casino da Figueira, Figueira da Foz
Central Portugal	Casino do Estoril, Estoril, near Lisbon
Madeira	Casino da Madeira, Funchal

Chemists

Medication	Chemists (farmácias) sell both locally produced medicines and those imported from abroad. These are usually cheaper in Portugal than in their country of origin.
Opening times	See Opening Times
Chemists on call	There is a rota for chemists who are on call outside normal opening times, which is displayed in all chemist's shops, printed in the local newspaper or obtainable by telephoning 118.

Currency

Currency	The Portuguese unit of currency is the escudo, pronounced "shkudoh", made up of 100 centavos, and its symbol – the dollar sign $ – is written between the escudos and the centavos. There are banknotes for 500, 1000, 2000, 5000 and 10,000 escudos, and coins in denominations of 1, 2½, 5, 10, 20, 50, 100 and 200 escudos. 1000 escudos is officially known as a conto.
Euro	On 1 January 1999 the euro became the official currency of Portugal, and the Portuguese escudo became a denomination of the euro. Portuguese escudo notes and coins continue to be legal tender during a transitional period. Euro bank notes and coins are likely to start to be introduced by 1 January 2002.
Currency import and export	There is no limit on how much foreign currency can be taken into Portugal but to avoid problems on the way out it is advisable to declare large sums.
Bancomaten	The easiest and quickest way of getting escudos is from bank automatic machines which display multilingual operating instructions. Money can be obtained with an EC card or various credit cards in conjunction with a PIN number.
Eurocheques	Eurocheques can be issued up to an amount of 40,000 escudos. With a Eurocheque Card (and usually with most credit cards) up to the same amount can be withdrawn from bank machines. If a Eurocheque card is lost it should be reported immediately by telephone to the relevant number in the country of issue, so that it is cancelled immediately.
Credit Cards	Banks, the larger hotels, top restaurants, car hire firms and many shops accept the major international credit cards. If credit card(s) are lost the relevant organisation in the country of issue should be notified immediately.

Foreign currency, eurocheques, travellers' cheques, etc. can be changed or cashed at banks, and money changing is exclusive to banks. These are open Monday to Friday from 8.30 to 3.00pm. Banks stay open during lunch times. Only in small rural towns may they shut for lunch.

Outside these times money can be changed at Lisbon airport and central station (Santa Apolónia), at Oporto airport, and at the airport in Faro, but here only up until 8pm. On the Algarve you can change money at banks outside the regular business hours all year round. Some places also have money-changing cash dispensers which accept various foreign currencies.

Banks, Changing Money

Customs Regulations

In theory there are no limits to the amounts of goods imported from one EU country to another, *provided they have been purchased tax paid in an EU country, are for personal use and are not intended for resale.* However the customs authorities have issued a list of maximum amounts considered reasonable for persons over 17 years of age of alcoholic drinks and tobacco goods. These are: spirits or strong liqueurs over 22% volume – 10 litres; fortified wines (port, sherry, etc.) – 20 litres; table wine – 90 litres (of which not more than 60 litres may be sparkling wine); beer – 110 litres; cigarettes – 800 or cigarillos 400 or cigars 200 or pipe tobacco 1 kg. There is no limit on perfume, toilet water, coffee, tea or other goods. Personal use includes gifts, but if a passenger is receiving any payment in return for buying alcohol and tobacco (such as help with travelling expenses) the transaction will be dutiable and the duty must be paid to the Customs authorities.

Customs allowances in European Union countries

For those coming direct from a country outside the EU or who have arrived from another EU country without having passed through customs control with all their baggage, the allowances for goods obtained anywhere outside the EU are (for persons over 17 years of age): spirits – 1 litre or fortified wine – 2 litres or table wine – 3 litres plus a further 2 litres of table wine. Perfume – 60 cc; toilet water – 250 cc, 200 cigarettes or 100 cigarillos or 50 cigars or 250 g of tobacco; (for those over 15 years of age) coffee – 500 g, coffee extract – 200 g, tea – 100 g, tea extract – 40 g.

Entry from non-EU countries

"Duty-free" goods are still available at major airports, on aircraft and ferries; amounts are the same as those above and are controlled by the carriers concerned. The duty-free allowances are scheduled to be phased out by January 1st 1999.

Duty-free goods

Video equipment must be declared to customs. Six hunting guns and 400 cartridges may be brought in for 60 days, but must be declared, and 1000 escudos deposit is required for each gun.

Caravanners must have an inventory (in Portuguese, English or French) of the contents of their caravan for presentation to the Portuguese customs officials. There are no special requirements for the temporary import of boats, provided the usual international papers are available.

"Citizens' band" radios may only be operated with an official Portuguese permit. Further information can be obtained from motoring organisations or the Portuguese tourist offices; applications should be sent to Direcção dos Serviços Rádio-Eléctricos, Rua do Conde de Redondo 70, P-1100 Lisbon tel. 01/3538772.

Diplomatic Representation

Embassy/Consulate
Rua de São Bernardo 33
1200 Lisbon.
Tel. 01/3924000, 01/3961191

United Kingdom

Consulate (Hon)
Avenida Do Zarco 2–4°, Funchal, Madeira. Tel. 091/221221

Consulate
Avenida da Boa Vista 3072, Oporto. Tel. 02/6184789

Consulate
Rua Almas 23, Pico Pedra.
Tel. 096/489313

Consulate
Largo Francisco A Maurício 7, 1°, Portimâo. Tel. 082/417800

United States of
America

Embassy
Avenida das Forças Armadas, Lisbon. Tel. 01/7273300

Consulate
Avenida da Boavista 3523, Edifício Avis 5° Andar, 4150 Oporto.
Tel. 02/6186607

Consulate
Avenida Dom Henrique 209, Ponta Delgada
Azores. Tel. 096/282216

Canada

Embassy
Avenida da Liberdade 144–4°, 1250 Lisbon. Tel. 01/3474892

Electricity

The usual voltage on the Portuguese mainland, Madeira and Azores is
AC 220 with continental two pin plugs. In the large hotels most standard
European plugs can be used, but American flat pin plugs should be used
with a transformer for 220 volts and an adaptor.

Emergency

Police,
Ambulance

The emergency number for police, fire, ambulance, etc. throughout
Portugal is 112. The call is free of charge.

Emergency
phones

For motorway accidents there are orange-coloured phones on the hard
shoulder.

Breakdown service

See Motoring

Events

Almost every place in Portugal has its own saints and its quite special ceremonies for honouring them at the "romarias". Although originally
purely pilgrimages these romarias have become popular festivals that last
for days, with praying and penance, but also singing, dancing, drinking
and courting. The following calendar of events lists the most impressive
of these romarias, as well providing a selection of other events.

January

Northern Portugal

Vila Nova de Gaia (Oporto): Festa de São Gonçalo e São Christóvão.
Vila de Feira (Aveiro): Festa de São Sebastião with processions.

February

Ovar (Aveiro): carnival.	Northern Portugal
Nazaré: carnival.	Central Portugal
Évora: Festa da Senhora das Candeias with fair and religious ceremonies in the São-Brás Chapel.	Southern Portugal

Loulé and Portimão (Algarve): carnival.
Carnival week, preceding Shrove Tuesday, takes place all over the country.

March

Aveiro: Feira de Março, this region's biggest industrial and trade fair with   Northern Portugal
various forms of entertainment (until April).
Braga, Póvoa de Varzim and Ovar: see April for ceremonies during Holy
Week.
Ovar (Aveiro): Procissão dos Terceiros; procession.

Lisbon: Procissão do Senhor dos Passos da Graça; procession.   Central Portugal

Loulé (Faro): Romaria da Senhora da Piedade; romaria.   Southern Portugal

April

Braga, Póvoa de Varzim (Oporto) and Ovar (Aveiro): Festas da Semana   Northern Portugal
Santa; Holy Week is celebrated in these places on a particularly grand
scale with many processions. The streets of Braga are decorated with
lights and flowers, and Ovar has a romaria and fireworks.
Fão and Esposende (Braga): Romaria do bom Jesús de Fão; romaria in
honour of Lord Jesús de Fão, processions, fireworks.
Barcelos and Guimarães (sometimes in early May): Festas das Cruzes;
big popular festival, processions, fair, fireworks.

Idanha-a-Nova (Castelo Branco): Romaria à Senhora do Almurtão; the fore-   Central Portugal
most romaria in Beira Baixa, with folk events and religious ceremonies.
Monsanto (Castelo Branco: sometimes in early May); Festa das Cruzes
or Festa do Castelo; religious ceremonies, popular festival, folk events.

May

Viana do Castelo: Festa da Senhora das Rosas; festival honouring the   Northern Portugal
Madonna of the Roses, with processions and popular festivals.
Alvarães (Viana do Castelo): Festa da Santa Cruz or Festa dos Andores
Floridos; procession with flower-bedecked statues of saints.
Barcelos: Festas das Cruzes; flower carpeted procession of sixteen
crosses, culminating in dancing and fireworks.

Vila Franca de Xira: Agrinxira; industrial and agricultural show.   Central Portugal
Leira: Feira de Maio; May Fair with exhibition of regional products,
including handicrafts.
Fátima: Primeira Peregrinação Anual a Fátima; the season of pilgrimages
to Fátima opens on the eve of May 13th (although there are pilgrimages
on the eve of the 13th of each of the following months until October, the
first and last of these pilgrimages attract the most pilgrims).

Alte (Faro): Festa da Fonte Grande or Festa do Primeiro de Maio; popu-   Southern Portugal
lar festival, folk events, and lots of flowers.
Sesimbra (Setúbal): Festa do Senhor das Chagas; fishermen's festival,
procession on May 4th.

359

Events

Azores   Ponta Delgada (São Miguel): Festas do Senhor Santo Cristo dos Milagres; big festival on the island, when those who still live there and those who have left celebrate together; religious celebrations, sporting contests, lengthy festival programme.

June

Northern Portugal   Amarante: Romaria de São Gonçalo; romaria, folk events, bullfights, fireworks.
Matosinhos (Oporto): Festas do Senhor de Matosinhos; folk dancing, bull-running, fireworks, fair.
Quintela (Viseu): Romaria da Senhora da Lapa; romaria, processions.
Vila Praia de Ancora (Viana do Castelo): folk festival.
Amares and Vila Verde (both near Braga): Festas de Santo António; processions, folk events, in Vila Verde, also regional produce and livestock show.
Penafiel (Oporto) and Monção: Festa do Corpo de Deus; Corpus Christi is celebrated in Penafiel by processions in traditional costume, with flowers and, in Monção, by traditional folk events.
Braga, Barcelinhos, Oporto, Vila do Conde: Festas de São João; the traditional festival is celebrated every year in the various places from June 23rd to June 25th with processions, fireworks, regional folk events and, in Barcelinhos, a pottery fair.
Viseu: Cavalhadas de Vil de Moínhos; cavalcade of horsemen and festival church service, medieval games, folk song and dance.
Póvoa de Varzim (Oporto): Festas de São Pedro; popular festival, with folk dances and processions.
São Torcato (Braga): Romaria de São Torcato; romaria, processions, folk events.

Central Portugal   Santarém: Feira Nacional de Agricultura; National Agricultural Show.
Lisbon: Festas dos Santos Populares; popular festival, fairs, lengthy festival programme with the greatest displays on the 12th and 13th.
Figueira da Foz: Festas de São João; midnight procession in traditional costume, dancing in the casino, folk events.
Sintra: Feira Grande de São Pedro; big regional fair with agricultural produce, antiques, handicrafts, regional specialities.

Southern Portugal   Reguengos de Monsaraz (Évora): Festas de Santo António; festival in honour of the town's patron saint, bullfights, Alentejo male-voice choirs.
Évora: Feira de São João; one of the most important fairs in southern Portugal, exhibitions of handicrafts and folk displays.
Montijo (Setúbal): Festas de São Pedro; popular festival, bullfights, the fishermen hand out sardines to visitors.

Madeira   Ribeira Brava: Festas de São Pedro; religious ceremonies, processions, folk dancing.

Azores   Ribeira Grande (São Miguel): Cavalhadas de São Pedro; medieval horseback contests.

July

Northern Portugal   Maia (Oporto): Romaria da Senhora do Bom Despacho; romaria, pilgrimage, folk events, fireworks.
Santo Tirso (Oporto): Festas de São Bento; pottery exhibition, folk festival.
Paredes (Oporto): Festas do Divino Salvador; procession, animal contests, fireworks.
São Torcato (Braga): Festival Internacional de Folclore de São Torcato; International Folk Festival, contest of the top Portuguese and foreign folk groups.

Vila do Conde (Oporto): Feira de Artesanato; handicraft fair, exhibition of work from all over Portugal.
Lousada (Oporto): Festas do Senhor dos Aflitos; processions, folk events.
Gulpilhares (Oporto): Festival Internacional de Folclore de Gulpilhares.

Vale da Maceira (Coimbra): Romaria da Senhora das Preces; romaria, with popular festival and market.   *Central Portugal*
Vila Franca de Xira: Festas do Colete Encarnado; contests, folk events, bullfights.
Estoril: Feira de Artesanato do Estoril; exhibition of handicrafts, folk events, specialities.
Ançã (Coimbra): Romaria de São Tomé e São Tiago; romaria of the patron saints, folk dances, etc., horseback games.
Sintra: Jornadas Musicais de Sintra; concerts in castles and palaces in and around Sintra (in the summer months)
Tomar: Festa dos Tabuleiros (even-numbered years only): festival with processions of girls bearing tabuleiros, or platters, on their heads, piled very high with loaves, etc.

Faro: Feira da Senhora do Carmo: fair of regional handicrafts, folk displays.   *Southern Portugal*
Setúbal: Feira de São Tiago; regional agricultural, industrial and crafts fair, folk displays, bullfights (usually until August).

August

Meadela (Viana do Castelo): Festas da Meadela, em Honra de Santa Cristina; traditional costumes, folk events, processions.   *Northern Portugal*
Terras de Bouro (Braga): Festas de São Brás; processions, parades, bull-running.
Mirandela (Bragança): Festas da Senhora do Amparo e Feira de Santiago; religious ceremonies, popular festival, cultural and sporting events.
Viana do Castelo: Festas da Senhora da Agonia; one of Portugal's most distinctive festivals and pilgrimages, festival of regional dancing and singing and procession in regional costumes, bull-running, carnival parade, fireworks.
Neves (Viana do Castelo): Festa da Senhora das Neves; religious ceremonies, popular festival, fireworks, folk festival, handicrafts exhibition, and one particular custom, the "marriage market", where the girls stroll down one side of the street and the boys down the other, and through eye contact try to find the right partner.
Guimarães (Braga): Festas Gualterianas; popular festival, with many regional specialities and wines, fireworks, folk events.
Caminha (Viana do Castelo): Festas de Santa Rita de Cássia; processions in traditional costumes, water sports contests, fireworks.
Portuzelo (Viana do Castelo): Festas de Santa Marta de Portuzelo; fairs, folk festivals with Portuguese and foreign groups.
Baião (Oporto) and Ponte da Barca: Festas de São Bartolomeu; religious ceremonies, old dances and songs, traditional riding contests, bullfights, and, in Ponte da Barca, processions.
Monção: Festa da Virgem das Dores; processions, show of handicrafts, popular festival, fireworks.
Oporto: Festa de São Bartolomeu e Cortejo de Papel; religious ceremonies, popular festival, procession with paper figures satirising important people.
Viseu: Feira de São Mateus; agricultural, wine, livestock and handicraft fair, folk festival, bullfights.
Arga de São João (Viana do Castelo): Romaria de São João de Arga; romaria, magnificent processions, old dances and songs.
Ria Caldo (Braga): Romaria de São Bento da Porta Aberta; romaria.
Torno (Oporto): Romaria à Senhora Aparecida; romaria, processions.
Castelões (Aveiro): Romaria da Senhora da Saúde da Serra; pilgrimage, romaria, mainly religious.

Póvoa de Varzim (Oporto): Festas da Senhora da Assunção; traditional fisher-festival, procession of decorated boats on the sea, bullfights, folk festival, fireworks.

Esposende (Braga): Festa da Senhora da Saúde e Soledade; traditional fisher-festival, water sport contests on the Rio Cávado, folk events, processions.

Vila Boas (Bragança): Romaria à Senhora da Assunáa o; romaria, large festival programme.

Caldas de Vizela (Braga): Festas de Vizela; varied festival programme, processions, traditional costumes, folk festival.

Miranda do Douro: Festas de Santa Bárbara; popular festival with male traditional dances.

Mar (Braga): Romaria de São Bartolomeu do Mar; religious celebrations, popular festival.

Central Portugal
Peniche: Festas da Senhora da Boa Viagem; traditional fisher-festival in honour of their patron saints, seaborne procession, folk events, fireworks, popular festival.

Batalha: Festas da Senhora da Vitória; popular festival, folk events.

Coruche (Santarém): Festas da Senhora do Castelo; folk events, bullfights and bull-running.

Alcobaça (Leiria): Feira de São Bernardo; industrial and agricultural show, with folk events and handicrafts.

Gouveia (Guarda): Festas do Senhor de Calvário; procession, sheep fair and sheepdog competition, folk song and dance festival.

Southern Portugal
Beja: Feira de Agosto or Feira de São Lourenço e Santa Maria; big fair with handicrafts show, festival programme, bullfights.

Alcochete (Setúbal): Festas do Barrete Verde e das Salinas; very local festival, with blessing of the saltpans, bullfights, popular festival.

Azores
Ponta Delgada (São Miguel): Festas do Divino Espírito Santo; island festivities with tradition.

Madeira
Monte: Festa da Senhora do Monte; processions, traditional costumes, dances and songs.

September

Northern Portugal
Guimarães: Peregrinação à Senhora da Penha; pilgrimage.

Monte Farinha (Vila Real): Romaria da Senhora da Graça; romaria.

Gavieira (Viana do Castelo): Romaria da Sehora da Peneda; romaria, traditional costumes.

Lamego: Romaria da Senhora dos Remédios; pilgrimage, folk festival, processions, sporting events.

Vila Praia de Ancora (Viana do Castelo): Festas da Senhora da Bonança; fisher-festival in honour of their patron saints, processions and blessing of the boats, popular festival, folk events, fireworks.

Praia da Torreira (Aveiro): Romaria de São Paio da Torreira; traditional "holy bathe", waterborne processions, blessing of the boats, popular festival, fireworks.

Póvoa (Bragança): Romaria à Senhora do Nazo; pilgrimage, big fair.

Póvoa de Varzim (Oporto): Festas da Senhora das Dores; religious ceremonies, festival events.

Ponte de Lima: Feiras Novas e Festas da Senhora das Dores; fairs, processions, folk festival, procession in traditional costumes, fireworks on the Rio Lima.

Cabeceiras de Basto (Braga): Feira e Festas de São Miguel; popular festival, religious ceremonies, ancient contests.

Buçaco (Aveiro): Festa da Senhora da Vitórem em Comemoração da Batalha do Buçaco; festival commemorating the battle of Buçaco, processions in uniforms of the period, popular festival.

Vila Nova de Famalição (Braga): Feira Grande de São Miguel; agricultural show, handicrafts, folk events.
Arouca (Aveiro): Feira das Colheitas; fair for regional handicrafts, folk events.

Rio Maior (Santarém): Frimor; annual industrial and agricultural show, regional handicrafts, folk events, bull-running. — Central Portugal
Arganil (Coimbra): Feira de Montalto; fair, with lengthy festival programme.
Nazaré: Romaria da Senhora de Nazaré; romaria, with impressive processions, traditional costumes, folk events, fair, fireworks, bullfights.
Castelejo (Castelo Branco): Romaria de Santa Luzia e Santa Eufémia; romaria with folk events.
Elvas: Festas do Senhor Jesus da Piedade e Feira de São Mateus; among the most typical of Alentejo's festivals, processions, popular festival, bullfights.
Reguengo de Fétal (Leira): Festas da Senhora do Fétal or Festas dos Caracóis; popular festival, processions.

Palmela (Setúbal): Festa das Vindimas; popular festival, bullfights, fireworks. — Southern Portugal
Many places in the Algarve: Festival de Folclore do Algarve; folk festival, with groups from the mainland and the islands, processions in traditional costume and fireworks.
Moita (Setúbal): Festas da Senhora da Boa Viagem; impressive procession, with blessing of the boats, popular festival, funfairs, bullfights, big firework displays.
Viana do Alentejo (Évora): Romaria da Senhora de Aires; romaria, bullfights.

October

Vieira do Minho (Braga): Feira da Ladra; festival fair, with regional agricultural and livestock show, lengthy festival programme. — Northern Portugal
Gondomar (Oporto): Romaria da Senhora do Rosário e Feira das Nozes; festival procession, funfair and folk dance evening, Walnut Fair.
Chaves: Feira dos Santos; fair.

Vila Franca de Xira: Feira de Outubro; October fair. — Central Portugal
Fátima: last of the big pilgrimages to Fátima on the eve of October 13th.

Moura (Beja): Festa da Senhora do Monte do Carmo; processions, regional folk events. — Southern Portugal
Faro: Feira de Santa Iria; a wide variety of entertainments take place at the same time as the industrial fair.
Castro Verde (Beja): Feira de Outubro; October Fair.
Algarve: Algarve Car Rally (sometimes early in November).

November

Cerdal (Viana do Castelo): Feira dos Santos; traditional fair. — Northern Portugal
Penafiel (Oporto): Feira de São Martinho; fair, regional specialities.
Cartaxo (Santarém): Feira dos Santos; fair with bullfights.
Golegã (Santarém): Feira de Sa o Martinho – Feira Nacional do Cavalo; national horse fair, riding competitions, bullfights.

December

Freamunde (Oporto): Romaria de Santa Luzia e Feira dos Capões; romaria and fair. — Northern Portugal

Funchal: Festas de São Silvestre or Festas do Fim do Ano; internationally famous New Year's Eve celebration, with magnificent fireworks. — Madeira

Portuguese Song of Destiny

Lisbon. Alfama. A small restaurant. Outside, facing the street, people are seated at the tables and eating their evening meal. There is the clicking of knives and forks, the diners are chattering to one another, nodding, joking, laughing. Tourists. Only here and there does one of them look up and listen to the man standing on the terrace and singing Portuguese melodies. A street musician, guitar under his arm, who goes from restaurant to restaurant, sings his songs and then pushes a tin can under the noses of his audience hoping to be rewarded for his musical efforts with a few escudos. Do these tourists understand what he is singing? And even if they did – would they also comprehend the message in his songs? Two elderly Portuguese with flat caps on their heads have approached the restaurant. They stop, listen – spellbound, almost reverent, their eyes shining. The two men seem as though they have been transported far away into the distance. One of them purses his lips, lowers his head and nods – as if to say "Yes, that's just how it was, that's just how it happened to me". What? Unrequited love, like that which the street-singer is describing? The *fado*, this song which for the non-Portuguese is mysterious, so difficult to understand, indeed scarcely comprehensible at all, is frequently heard in Lisbon and Coimbra, the old university town.

Only these two towns are the true home of the fado. In the same way that one does not see the flamenco danced in all regions and towns of Spain, so one rarely hears the fado outside its strongholds of Lisbon and Coimbra (the kind of fado heard in the Algarve is not really typical as it is put on solely for tourists). Although the fado can be described as a form of music for the people it is not folk-music as such relevant to the whole of Portugal. Furthermore, the Coimbra fado is very different from the Lisbon version.

The Lisbon fado is always sung by a solo *fadista*, who may be female or male. The female singers always wear a black stole around their shoulders, and the male singers also appear dressed in black. They are accompanied by two guitarists, one playing the melody on the silvery-toned twelve-stringed *guitarra*, the other supplying the rhythm on the six-stringed *viola* or Spanish guitar. The guitarra, the special fado guitar, evolved from two instruments – the zither, which was introduced into Portugal from Italy and Flanders in the 16th century, and the English guitar, which reached the Portuguese kingdom by way of Oporto in the 18th century. The Lisbon fado has both its supporters and its opponents among the Portuguese. Some condemn it as sentimental and affected, nostalgic and melancholy, even fatalistically stultifying (Lopes Graça, who has written Portuguese folk-songs, dismisses it as commercial and artificially crass); others, on the other hand, value it as an expression of Portuguese popular sensitivity and regard it as Portugal's most important cultural asset. Fatalistic it certainly is. Even the name underlines that fact, as it comes from the Latin *fatum*, meaning fate. So most of the songs deal with the inevitability of destiny – of amorous disappointments, unrequited love and sad partings, of social deprivation, homesickness and wanderlust, of mourning, of Lisbon's lost glories, of Portugal's former greatness; in brief they tell of longing, wistfulness, melancholy, and of *saudade* (from the Latin *solitudo*, loneliness), as it is known in

Portuguese, the prevailing mood of the Portuguese soul. From time to time the songs tell of city life or recite superficial or perhaps amusing and lively anecdotes. Anyone can find in the words of the fado *his* own failing, *his* unfulfilled love, *his* own longings. Here at last he can find the bitter-sweet expression of his dreams, his wishes and his hopes. And he is not alone. The fado joins all lonely people together into one

Fado performance in Lisbon

society and invites them to participate in a collective ritual. As soon as a fado strikes up, with all its plaintive half-tones and nuances and its pronounced juxtaposition of the major and the minor keys it produces in a flash a momentary silence among the chattering guests. Faces become impassive, eyes – often moist with tears – gaze vaguely into the distance. Regardless of their social standing, those listening feel themselves for a short time to be joined together as one, no longer just isolated strangers – united with a mutual feeling of resignation. The dictator Salazar hated the fado for this reason; for him it was simply "pathologically fatalistic" and, fearing its allegedly negative effect on public feeling, tried to ban it, but without success. The fado is not to be abolished that easily.

And not in Coimbra either, even though here the fado differs from that heard in Lisbon. Much more recent in origin, the Coimbra fado evolved among the students of the old university. It is less melancholy than the Lisbon variety, being more amusing and full of humour, predominantly lyrical with echoes of the ballad, taking its themes from student life. It is sung solely by male students (in black capes – and with trained voices), accompanied by the guitarra de Coimbra and often going from tavern to tavern. Occasionally the Coimbra fado contains political undertones. Before 1910 fado singers from Coimbra mocked the king and even demanded the dissolution of the monarchy.

Even musical experts cannot agree on the the true origin of the fado. Some maintain it is a legacy of 500 years of Moorish rule in Portugal; they believe that Portuguese troubadours adopted the melancholy love lyric of the Moors and carried it on, and so the plaintive modulation and elaborate cadences of the present-day fado are reminiscent of the Arabic form of singing, and that 12th century troubadour songs are related in form and content with the fado singing of today. According to another theory, however, the fado developed from an African dance (the *lundum*), brought by slaves to Brazil and thence to Portugal, where the major musical elements were translated into song. Because of the often melancholy and wistful character of the music and words the view is also held that the fado evolved from Portuguese seafarers who sang of home during their long absences afloat. In the early 19th century, however, the fado spread to the less reputable city quarters of Alfama, Mouraria and Bairro Alto and for a long time was regarded as somewhat indecent and shady, the music of sailors, pimps, prostitutes, vagrants, common labourers, the poor, the criminal element and unfortunate lovers. The fact that it then gradually became acceptable in society and the drawing-room was due mainly to aristocratic idlers who frequented the more disreputable taverns and made the fado the "latest fashion". Some of them tried their hand at singing or composing fado songs themselves. Others hit the headlines after falling in love with fado singers, for example, the young Count Vimioso, who in 1840 fell in love with the incredibly pretty and vivacious fado singer Maria Severa, which led to a scandal. (Maria Severa was the best-known and and most admired *fadista* of the 19th century; when she died at the age of only 26 the whole of Lisbon went into mourning and many writers later dedicated novels and plays to her.)

In the 20th century the fado has also become known far beyond the frontiers of Portugal, thanks mainly to a magnificent fadista, the Lisbon-born Amália Rodrigues, who in her 50-year career as a singer brought the fado to the world-wide stage (see Famous People).

Obviously the fado can be heard in what are known as *casas do fado* for the benefit of tourists. But in these eating places, which are not exactly cheap and are found mostly in the night-life quarter of Bairro Alto, the atmosphere is not quite right, as the patrons are mainly tourists who cannot really experience a genuine feeling for and affinity with the music. The original Lisbon fado can be experienced more cheaply in Alfama, best of all in the back-street fado cafés where the patrons usually stand up and join in the singing. Or else take a seat in a small restaurant in the Old Town and wait until a wandering street musician, a *fadista*, arrives on the scene.

Fado

The Portuguese fado (see Baedeker Special, pp. 364–65), with its sad, soulful songs, usually about the forces of destiny, is based on Lisbon. Students in Coimbra also have their own special version, and the odd fado venue can be found in Oporto as well. The kind of fado put on in the Algarve is not really to be recommended since this is solely for tourists.
   Although as a rule there is no admission charge to listen to fado customers are expected to buy something to eat or drink. Plenty of time is needed as the best fado singers mostly do not appear until midnight or later. It is advisable to book a table at the following fado venues.

Lisbon

Senhor Vinho
Rua do Meio à Lapa 18. Tel. 01/3977456
Open: Mon.–Sat. 8.30pm–3.30am.
Very good singers and guitar players, but considerably more expensive than other fado venues.

Adega Machado
Rua do Norte 91. Tel. 01/3224640
A pleasant and cosy room, with walls covered with pictures.

O Forcado
Rua da Rosa 221. Tel. 01/3468579
A typical fado venue in Bairro Alto; mainly foreign clientele.

Adega do Ribatejo
Rua Diário de Noticas 23. Tel. 01/3468343
Simple and very typical venue, with guests joining in the singing.

Forte Dom Rodrigo   Cascais
Estrada de Birre.
Tel. 01/4871373
Closed Mon.

A Ponte Restaurante
Bairro S. José
Fado performances Fridays and Saturdays.

Food and Drink

Eating habits

Breakfast in Portugal, as in other southern countries, is a rather frugal   Meals
affair, and only the larger tourist hotels, particularly in the Algarve, serve
meat, cheese and eggs as well as bread, butter, jam and coffee.
   Midday and evening meals are, however, taken very seriously.
Meetings of any kind are always associated with a meal, and the
Portuguese normally have two hot meals a day, even when there is no
special excuse. There are often three courses at both the midday and the
evening meal, with a light soup frequently served as the starter, although
in the north of Portugal soup is traditionally not dished up until after the
main course. Generally speaking the main course is accompanied by rice
or potatoes, and only rarely by vegetables, although in the summer
months an appetising salad is offered. Bread is always on the table.

Lunch is earlier than in other southern countries. It can be as early as   Mealtimes
noon, and is seldom later than 1 o'clock. The evening meal is generally
after 8 o'clock but seldom later than 9.

Portuguese cooking is solid and nourishing, its mainstays being olive oil   Cuisine
and such herbs as thyme, bay, rosemary, etc. Expectations should not be
too high so far as typical Portuguese cuisine is concerned since even in
the best restaurants the choice and quality of the dishes is simple. This
should come as no surprise given the fact that in the past Portugal was
a relatively poor country and that in the south at least there were severe
limitations on what local agriculture could produce. Like other examples
of peasant cuisine this one does, however, have the advantage of being
genuine, because pains are taken to make the most of the local produce.
It therefore pays to try the simple fish and meat dishes, which are
usually freshly prepared, and to avoid sauces, etc. with fancy names.

See Language   Vocabulary

Dishes

The Portuguese national dish is "cozido à portuguesa", a tasty thick   Soup
stew of vegetables with various kinds of meat. "Caldo verde" is a finely
shredded kale soup found in the Minho; though originating in the north,
it is served throughout the country. A favourite of southern Portugal is
"gaspacho", a cold, spicy vegetable soup. "Caldeirada", a nourishing
fish soup, is found everywhere along the coastline.

One of Portugal's national dishes: grilled sardines

Fish

Naturally Portugal has a particularly wide variety of fish dishes, but other sorts of seafood, shrimp and crayfish, crab and lobster, are almost always available relatively cheaply and fresh; they can actually be seen crawling around in many restaurant windows!

One of Portugal's national dishes is "bacalhau" (dried, salted cod). Anyone who can not afford bacalhau for a special occasion has to be very poor indeed. There are very many different ways of preparing it – "bacalhau com todos" is dried cod with a selection of vegetables, "bacalhau à brás" is with onions, potatoes and olives, and "bacalhau dourada" is with tomatoes, parsley, garlic and wine.

Throughout Portugal people can be seen at midday and in the evenings grilling their "sardinas assadas" (grilled sardines) in front of their houses.

Anyone who orders "arroz de lampreia" will get the Minho speciality of lampreys on rice. "Bife de atum", tuna steaks, and "amàijoas na cataplana", clams and sausage spiced with herbs steamed in a copper pan, often appear on menus in the Algarve. Visitors to Peniche should sample "lagosta suada" (casseroled crayfish).

Meat

One of the really famous creations of Portuguese cuisine is "carne de porco à alentejana", the Alentejo dish of pork garnished with clams. Sucking pig, or "leitão assado", is another excellent Portuguese speciality.

Not to everyone's taste, but typical of Oporto, "tripas à moda do Porto", tripe with haricot beans, is a dish that has quite a history. When Henry the Navigator, who was born in Oporto, sent a vessel to conquer Ceuta the people of Oporto slaughtered all their livestock to provision the crew. They just kept the intestines, and hence have been popularly known as "tripeiros", or tripe-eaters, ever since.

Oporto is also the source of "linguiças", smoked tongue sausages. "Presunto", smoked ham, is generally excellent, especially if it comes from Chaves. "Espeta da Madeira", meat roasted on a spit, is a speciality from Madeira, and "alcatra dos Açores", a form of beef roast, comes from the Azores.

Beans are a favourite vegetable in Portuguese cooking. "Feijâo guisado" are haricot beans braised with bacon and served with a tomato sauce, while "feijâo verde à poviciana" are French beans braised with onions, garlic and small sausages, served up with a poached egg. "Grâo com tomates" consists of chick-peas in a purée of garlic, olive oil and tomatoes.

Portugal has some good cheeses. "Queijo da serra" is a sheep's cheese from the Serra da Estrela, "Cabreiro", which is widely available, is a salty goat's cheese, and "Rabaçal", which is a speciality from around Pombal, is another goat's cheese. "Queijo da ilha" is a strong-flavoured hard cheese produced in the Azores but also obtainable on the mainland. "Queijinhos" are small white cheeses that are a speciality from the Tomar area.

The Portuguese are fond of very sweet confections, not only after meals but also between them, so there are plenty of cake shops selling delicious little pastries.

"Doces de ovos" is a sweet egg speciality of central Portugal. The Algarve has excellent marzipan cakes, "bolo de ovos e amêndoa", and on Madeira you get "bolo de mel" which are honey cakes. Popular desserts found on most menus are "arroz doce", which is rice pudding sprinkled with cinnamon, and "pudim flan", a kind of individual egg custard à la crème caramel.

See entry

Drink

Agua Mineral, mineral water, can be obtained still or carbonated (com/sem gás), and even the carbonated variety is only mildly fizzy. Portugal has long been proud of its mineral waters. The Romans were familiar with their therapeutic qualities, and in the 19th c. Portugal had the most elegant spas in Europe (see Spas), with luxury hotels, casinos, bathing establishments and, of course, pump-rooms. This tradition continues, though only relatively few spas bottle their water – there are only ten firms bottling a total of fifteen brands of mineral water. At least 75% of the mineral water market is taken up by the still mineral water. The most popular brand is "Luso", which is still, and has a low mineral content. There are also "Vimeiro" and "Castelo de Vide", both either still or carbonated, and with a moderate mineral content, and "Pedras Salgadas", which has a high mineral content, and is naturally slightly fizzy.

In addition to the internationally marketed soft drinks there are local variants, and frequently fresh-pressed fruit juice can be obtained.

Lunch and dinner are often rounded off with strong black coffee (café or bica), although many Portuguese prefer their coffee with milk (galâo).

Portugal's most popular form of beer (cerveza) is "Sagres", a kind of pale ale, while the same brewery, which is based at Vialonga, near Lisbon, also brews "Presta", which is more of a stout. There are also "Cristal" and "Cergal", which are both of the lager type. Beer consumption in Portugal has tripled since 1970, but wine continues to be the traditional drink with meals.

See entry

Coffee after a meal is often accompanied by a marc (bagaáo) or a brandy (aguardente or brandy). Fruit brandies include "medronho" from the arbutus berry, "cana" from sugar cane, and "ginjinha", which is a cherry brandy. Imported spirits – whisky is popular – are relatively expensive.

Getting to Portugal

By air　　　　There are scheduled services from London (Gatwick) to Lisbon and Oporto (British Airways); from London (Heathrow) to Lisbon, Oporto, Faro, Madeira and the Azores (TAP from London (Heathrow) to Lisbon, Oporto, Faro, Madeira (British Airways). Seats are also available on many charter services.

There are direct services to Lisbon from the major cities in the United States and Canada.

By road　　　　There is a wide choice of cross-channel car ferry services between Britain and France. From the French Channel ports it is approximately 1200 miles to Lisbon, 1100 miles to Oporto and 1400 miles to Faro.

The most direct road route is to cross the frontier between France and Spain at Hendaye/Irún, then, via San Sebastián, cross from Spain to Portugal between Ciudad Rodrigo and Guarda. The longer way round, which allows you to see something of Spain en route, is to travel south through France down the Rhône valley, via Nîmes, Montpellier and Perpignan, to cross the Spanish frontier at Le Perthus/La Junquera, then follow the coast from Barcelona to Tarragona before turning inland and driving via Monreal to Madrid, when the route turns south-west, via Trujillo, to the Portuguese frontier at Badajoz.

There are regular coach services between London and Lisbon, Oporto, Coimbra, Lagos and Faro.

Frontier crossings　　All frontier crossings with Spain are now open 24 hours a day.

By sea　　　　An alternative route is by the car ferry from Plymouth to Santander in northern Spain. From Santander it is some 600 miles to Lisbon, 500 miles to Oporto and 800 miles to Faro. Information from Brittany Ferries, Millbay Docks, Plymouth PL1 3EW; tel. (0990) 360360.

Another, more infrequent, sea-route is the service run three or four times a year from Antwerp, Le Havre and Bordeaux to Lisbon by Compagnie Maritime Zairoise.

By rail　　　　There is a service from London (Waterloo) to Lisbon via Paris. For passenger information contact Rail Europe c/o French Tourist Office, 178 Piccadilly, London W1V 0AL; tel. (0990) 848848, or your travel agent. The journey from Paris to Lisbon takes about 25 hours.

Travel documents　　See entry

Golf

Golf has been played in Portugal since 1890 when the Oporto Golf Club was founded. Portugal now has over 70 courses, varying widely in their degree of difficulty, and new ones are constantly being opened.

Northern Portugal　　Estela (18 holes)
Rio Alto, Estela, 4490 Póvoa de Varzim
Tel. 052601814, fax 052/612701
Right on the Atlantic coast, very demanding.

Miramar (9 holes)
Avenida Sacadura Cabral, Miramar, 4405 Valadares
Tel. 02/7622067, fax 02/7627859
A flat course, ideal for beginners.

Oporto Golf Club (18 holes)
Lugar do Sisto, Paramos, 4500 Espinho
Tel. 027342008, fax 027346895
Easily walked; Portugal's oldest golf course.

Vidago (9 holes)
Pavilhão do Golfe, 5425 Vidago
Tel. 076907356, fax 076909662
In beautiful countryside. For all degrees of difficulty.

Vimeiro (9 holes)
Termas do Vimeiro, Praia do Porto Novo, 2560 Torres Vedras
Tel. 061/984157, fax 061/984621
Small, well-kept course on both sides of a little river.

Aroeira (18 holes)   Around Lisbon
Herdade da Aroeira, Fonte da Telha, 2825 Monte de Caparica
Tel. 01/2971314, fax 01/2971238
Located in a pine forest; very easy to walk.

Estoril (18 holes and 9 holes)
Avenida da Républica, 2765 Estoril
Tel. 01/4680176, fax 01/4682796
Relatively short but interesting course.

Estoril-Sol Golf (9 holes)
Estrada da Lagos Azul, Linhó, 2710 Sintra
Tel. 01/9232461, fax 01/9232461
One of the most beautiful 9-hole courses in Europe. Ideal for experienced golfers.

Lisbon Sports Club (18 holes)
Casal da Carregueira, Belas, 2745 Queluz
Tel. 01/4310077, fax 01/4312482
Easily walked; wonderful view.

Montado (18 holes)
Algeruz, 2950 Palmela
Tel. 065/706648, fax 065/706775
Located on a plain. With old cork-oaks, a rivulet and lakes.

Penha Longa (18 holes)
Quinta da Penha Longa, Linhó, 2710 Sintra
Tel. 01/9240014, fax 01/9249024
A demanding course in a hilly and wooded region; from some parts there are superb views of the Atlantic.

Quinta da Beloura (18 holes)
Estrada da Albarraque, 2710 Sintra
Tel. 01/9106350, fax 01/9106359
A flattish course, heavily wooded. Beautiful view over the Serra de Sintra.

Quinta da Marinha (18 holes)
Quinta da Marinha, 2750 Cascais
Tel. 01/4869881, fax 01/4869032
Very uneven and hilly course.

Quinta do Perú (18 holes)
Quinta do Perú, 2830 Quinta do Conde
Tel. 01/2134320, fax 01/2134321
Suitable for amateur golfers.

Golf

Tróia Golf (18 holes)
Complexo Turístico de Tróia
Tel. 065/494112, fax 065/494315
Easily walked fairways, attractive location on the Atlantic coast.

Algarve

Alto do Vale (18 holes)
Caixa Postal 1, Alvor, 8500 Portimão
Tel. 082/416913, fax 082/401046
Demanding, with very narrow and winding fairways.

Palmares (18 holes)
Apartado 74, 8600 Lagos
Tel. 082/762961, fax 082/762534
Not too easy, hilly and very variable fairways.

Floresta Parque (18 holes)
Vale do Poço, Budens, 8650 Vila do Bispo
Tel. 082/695333, fax 082/695338
A very varied course with many hilly and demanding fairways; one of
Europe's most impressive golf courses.

Penina Golf Hotel (18 holes and 2×9 holes)
P.O. Box 146, Penina, 8502 Portimão Codex
Tel. 082/415415, fax 082/415000
One of Portugal's most difficult courses.

Pine Cliffs (9 holes)
Pinhal do Concelho, 8200 Albufeira
Tel. 089/501884, fax 089/501795
On the Atlantic coast, near impressive rocky bays.

Pinheiros Altos (18 holes)
Quinta do Lago, 8135 Almansil
Tel. 089/394340, fax 089/394392
Easily walked, with many water-filled bunkers.

Quinta do Gramacho (9 holes)
Quinta do Gramacho, 8400 Lagoa
Tel. 082/342927, fax 082/340901
Hilly fairways, with beautiful, lush vegetation.

Quinta do Lago (4×9 holes)
Quinta do Lago, 8135 Almansil
Tel. 089/390700, fax 089/394013
The four separate 9-hole courses can be combined with one another.
Easy to walk. Ranks as the finest golf course in the Algarve.

São Lourenço (18 holes)
Hotel Dona Filipa, Vale do Lobo, 8135 Almansil
Tel. 089/396534, fax 089/396908
A very varied course making heavy demands on the players.

Salgados (18 holes)
Apartado 2266, Vale do Rabelho, 8200 Albufeira
Tel. 089/591111, fax 089/591112
Located by the sea. Many water-filled bunkers. Demanding.

Vale do Lobo (3×9 holes)
Vale do Lobo, 8135 Almancil
Tel. 089/394444, fax 089/394713
Hilly site, delightful courses.

Vale do Milho (9 holes)
Algar Seco, Carvoeiro, 8400 Lagoa
Tel. 082/358502, fax 082/358497
Very short and easily walked, particularly ideal for less proficient golfers.

Vale da Pinta (18 holes)
Quinta do Gramacho, 8400 Lagoa
Tel. 082/342927, fax 082/340901
In a small old wood of olive trees. Championship course.

Vilamoura The Old Course (18 holes)
Vilamoura, 8125 Quarteira
Tel. 089/310341, fax 089/310321
The Portugal open was held here in 1979.

Vilamoura Pinhal (18 holes)
Vilamoura, 8125 Quarteira
Tel. 089/310390, fax 089/310393
Small greens, with a beautiful sea view.

Vilamoura Laguna (3×9 holes)
Vilamoura, 8125 Quarteira
Tel. 089/310180, fax 089/310183
Long fairways.

Vila Sol (18 holes)
Alto do Semino, Vilamoura, 8125 Quarteira
Tel. 089/300505, fax 089/300592
Demanding course with hilly fairways, some of them narrow.

Madeira (18 holes)   Madeira
Casala Próximos, Santo António da Serra, 9200 Machico
Tel. 091/552356, fax 091/552367
Located in some wonderful countryside, with a magnificent view of the
sea. The course is not very long.

Palheiro (18 holes)
Sítio do Balancal, São Gonçalo, 9050 Funchal, Madeira
Tel. 091/792116, fax 091/792456
Hilly. Fantastic view of Funchal Bay.

Ilha Terceira (18 holes)   Azores
Caixa Postal 15, 9760 Praia da Vitória
Tel. 095/902444, fax 095/902445
Slightly hilly fairways, with many small lakes and ditches forming
natural bunkers.

Verdegolf Country Club (18 holes)
Rua do Bom Jesus, Aflitos, 9545 Fenais da Luz
Tel. 096/498559, fax 096/498284
Beautifully situated.

Hotels

Hotels in Portugal are classified according to the quality of the accom-   Hotels, motels
modation, ranging from five star de luxe to simple one star, and with a   and aparthotels
considerable quality range within the individual categories.
   For motels and aparthotels the categories, in terms of price and comfort, are approximately the same as for hotels.

Pousadas are state-owned hotels in important tourism sites. They are   Pousadas
listed, with a map, in their own separate section.

Hotels

<table>
<tr><td>Estalagens</td><td>Estalagens (estalagem in the singular) are similar to pousadas but are privately owned. They are often in old restored buildings.</td></tr>
<tr><td>Turismo de habitação</td><td>A particular form of accommodation in Portugal is known as "turismo de habitação". Owners of stately houses or small palaces offer holiday-makers the chance to stay in very spacious rooms. Most of the houses are tastefully appointed with antique furniture and offer leisure facilities in the surrounding countryside; they are registered with the central tourist board and must bear a sign at the entrance. In addition to "turismo de habitação" there is also "turismo rural" offering overnight stays in country houses or on wine-estates, and "agroturismo", with accommodation in farmhouses, barns or other farm buildings.</td></tr>
</table>

Further information can be obtained from the TURIHAB-Associação de Turismo de Habitação (Praça da República, 4990 Ponte de Lima; tel. 058/741672, fax 058/741444), or from travel agents.

<table>
<tr><td>Pensões, residencials, albergarias</td><td>Portugal has a great many pensions (pensões, singular pensão), or guest houses. They fall into four categories (although there are some that are unclassified) and, although in terms of comfort they often do not differ from the hotels in the categories given below, they do tend to be less expensive than hotels with the same number of stars. Proprietors are permitted to add up to 20% to the price of the room if the guest does not have a main meal in-house. "Residencials" are comparable with pensions so far as price and comfort are concerned, while "albergarias" correspond to top category pensions.</td></tr>
</table>

Hotel prices vary considerably according to the season. The following table gives the rates for a double (hotel) room with bath. A single room costs 30% less than a double. A double room in the pensions on the following list will cost between 3000 and 15,000 escudos.

category	double room	meals
★★★★★	35,000–55,000 esc.	2500–6000 esc.
★★★★	20,000–35,000 esc.	1800–4000 esc.
★★★	15,000–25,000 esc.	1000–3500 esc.
★★	9000–16,000 esc.	800–3000 esc.
★	6000–12,000 esc.	600–2500 esc.

The hotels that follow are listed with their official category, address and number of rooms (r.). SP stands for swimming pool, and T for tennis court. In the high season, at least, it is advisable to reserve a room well in advance.

<table>
<tr><td>Albufeira</td><td>★★★★★Alfa Mar (263 r., SP, T)
Praiada Falesia, 8200 Albufeira, tel. 089/501351, fax 089501069
This hotel is getting on in years. Mainly German guests. Beach 1km/¾ mile long. Also a riding stable.</td></tr>
</table>

★★★★Hotel Boavista (100 r., SP)
Rua Samora Barros 6, 8200 Albufeira; tel. 089/589176, fax 089/589180
Two plus points – the magnificent view and the attractive decor of pale wood and azulejos.

★★★★Hotel Sol e Mar (74 r., SP)
Rua José Bernardino de Sousa, 8200 Albufeira; tel. 089/586721, fax 089/587036
It was with this hotel that tourism first took hold in Albufeira in the 1960s. Beautifully situated between cliffs on the top of the beach.

<table>
<tr><td>Alcobaça</td><td>★★Hotel Santa Maria (31 r.)
Rua Dr. Francisco Zagalo, 2460 Alcobaça
Tel. 062/597395, fax 062/590161
This hotel lies diagonally opposite the convent, and its rooms are very spacious and modern. The relatively quiet location is very pleasant. No restaurant.</td></tr>
</table>

★★Hotel Vale da Telha (52 r., SP, T)
Vale da Telha – Apartado 101, 8670 Aljezur
Tel. 082/998180, fax 082/998176
Outside the town with superb and isolated beaches nearby. A beautiful terrace adds to the amenities.

★★★★★Hotel Quinta do Lago (149 r., SP, T)
Quinta do Lago, 8135 Almansil; tel. 089/396666, fax 089/396393
A golfing hotel which blends beautifully into the landscape. Also for the non-golfer this is a charming place to stay with every conceivable comfort. An Austrian chef is responsible for the excellent cuisine.

★Albergaria Dona Margaritta (22 r.)
Rua Cândido dos Reis; tel. 055432110, fax 055/437977
The location alone makes this the finest hotel in the town. There is a superb view from the rooms facing the river; on the side facing the street, however, it can be very noisy.

★★★★★Hotel Vila Vita Parc (180 r., SP, T)
Alporchinhos, 8365 Armação de Pêra; tel. 082/310200, fax 082/315333
De luxe class holiday accommodation in the centre of an extensive park. A member of the "Leading Hotels of the World". With all sports facilities.

★★★★Hotel Garbe (109 r., SP, T)
Avenida Marginal, 8365 Armação de Pêra; tel. 082/315187, fax 082/315087
A pleasant hotel immediately adjoining a long beach.

★★Hotel Arcade (49 r.)
Rua Viana do Castelo 4, 3800 Aveiro; tel. 034/23001, fax 034/21886
An old Art Nouveau style building by the canal. The rooms are beautifully appointed and very clean; spacious bathrooms.

★★★★Hotel de São Pedro (26 r.)
Largo Almirante Dunn, 9500 Ponta Delgada (São Miguel)
Tel. 096/282223, fax 096/629319
This hotel on the harbour promenade dates from 1812 and is furnished with many antiques of that period.

★★★★Hotel Fayal (83 r., SP, T)
Rua Consul Dabney, 9900 Horta (Faial); tel. 092/292181, fax. 092/292189
A hotel complex comprising six houses in parkland. Situated above the town with a fine view of the harbour. The rooms are modern but give a very cool impression.

★★★Hotel de Angra (82 r.)
Praça da Restauração, 9700 Angra do Heroismo (Terceira)
Tel. 095/217041, fax 095/217049
Right in the town centre, which is not exactly quiet. But apart from the rooms facing the street the others in this modern hotel which face the municipal park are relatively quiet.

★★★Hotel Terra Nostra (81 r., SP, T)
Rua Padre José J. Botelho, 9675 Furnas (São Miguel)
Tel. 096/584133, fax 096/584304
Old, but roomy and very well kept, with floors of Brazilian hardwood. Very quiet location. Most of the rooms have a small balcony looking out on to the park.

★★★★Pensão Conde de Barcelos (30 r.)
Avenida Alcaide de Faria, 4750 Barcelos: tel. 053/811061
This modern hotel with ten floors lies between the old town and the railway station, only a few minutes from the town centre. The rooms are very spacious; those facing the street have large balconies.

Hotels

Batalha

★★Pensão Batalha (22 r.)
Largo da Igreja, 2440 Batalha; tel. 044/767500, fax 044/767467
A pleasant hotel in the centre of Batalha. No restaurant.

Beja

★★★★Pensão Cristina (32 r.)
Rua de Mértola 71, 7800 Beja; tel. 084/323035, fax 084/320460
Central, clean, modern – one of Beja's best hotels.

★★★Pensão Bejense (21 r.)
Rua Capitão João F. de Sousa 57, 7800 Beja; tel. 084/325001, fax 084/325002
Central location. Simple and cheap. However, it must be admitted that some rooms are somewhat dark – a homely atmosphere, nevertheless.

Braga

★★★★Hotel do Elevador (22 r.)
Bom Jesus do Monte, 4700 Braga; tel. 053/603400, fax 053/603409
Located 5km/3 miles outside Braga near the famous pilgrimage church. It was built for pilgrims in the late 1960s. The spacious rooms, most of them with a balcony, provide fine panoramic views.

Bragança

★★★★Albergaria Santa Isabel (14 r.)
Rua A. Herculano 67, 5300 Bragança; tel. 073/331427, fax 073/326937
Guests can enjoy friendly service, a cosy atmosphere and first-class comfort.

**Buçaco
National Park**

★★★★★Palace Hotel do Buçaco (62 r., T)
In the National Park, 3050 Mealhada; tel. 031/930101, fax 031/930509
The Palace Hotel was built in magnificent neo-Manueline style shortly before the turn of the century. The parkland surrounding this de luxe hotel is unsurpassable.

Entrance hall of the Palace Hotel do Buçaco

★★★Hotel Cristal Caldas (113 r.; SP)
Rua António Sérgio 31, 2500 Caldas da Rainha
Tel. 062/840260, fax 062/842621
The town's best hotel. There is no need to be bored during your stay in this building of several floors; as well as the swimming pool there is a sauna, disco, bar, etc.

★★★★★Albatroz (40 r., SP)
Rua Frederico Arouca 100, 2750 Cascais
Tel. 01/4832821, fax 01/4844827
In a stylish palace on a cliff by the beach. A beautiful terrace with a view of the sea. Friendly, perfect service.

★★★★Albergaria Valbom (40 r.)
Avenida Valbom 14, 2750 Cascais; tel. 01/4865801, fax 01/4865805
Centrally located and not entirely quiet, but the rooms of this three-storey hotel are clean and spacious.

★★★Pensão Arraiana (31 r.)
Av. 1 de Maio 18, 6000 Castelo Branco; tel. 072/341634, fax 072/331884
All the rooms are sumptuously appointed with antique furniture and bath. This well-run pension also has its own restaurant.

★★★Pensão Casa do Parque (26 r.)
Avenida de Aramenha 37, 7320 Castelo de Vide; tel. 045/91250
This pension is located at the entrance to the town, hidden behind the park. The rooms are large and the hotel has its own restaurant.

★★Pensão Jaime (64 r.)
Rua Joaquim José Delgado, 5400 Chaves; tel. 076/321273
This pension is rather old and offers little in the way of comfort; nevertheless, it is very well kept. Most rooms do not have a bath.

★★★★Tivoli Coimbra (90 r., SP)
Rua João Machado 4, 3000 Coimbra; tel. 039/826934, fax 039/826827
The first hotel on the square. Modern comfort. Conference facilities available.

★★★Hotel Astória (64 r.)
Avenida Emidio Navarro 21, 3000 Coimbra; tel. 039/822055, fax 039/822057
A centrally located middle-class hotel dating from the 19th c. Because of the street noise its rooms are not particularly quiet and some of them are very shabby. However, a number of rooms have a magnificent view of the Rio Mondego. There is a restaurant in the former ballroom where guests can still sense the sparkle and splendour of days gone by.

★★★Hotel Bragança (83 r.)
Largo das Ameias 10, 3000 Coimbra; tel. 039/822171, fax 039/836135
A building of several floors located near the railway station. The rooms are modern and air-conditioned. Own restaurant.

★★★★Costa da Caparica (353 r., SP)
Avenida General Humberto Delgado 47, 2825 Costa da Caparica
Tel. 01/2910310, fax 01/2910687
New and modern hotel close to the church, in the Lisbon catchment area. Seven rooms are specially equipped for wheel-chair users.

★★★★Estalagem D. Sancho II (26 r.)
Praça da República 20, 7350 Elvas; tel. 068/622686, fax 068/624717
Central location. As far as the furnishings and decor are concerned, the hotel has style and flair. Very helpful and accommodating staff.

Hotels

Ericeira

★★★Hotel de Turismo da Ericeira (154 r., SP)
Rua Porto Revez, 2655 Ericeira; tel. 061/860200, fax 061/863146
Large hotel complex by the Praia do Sul. From the swimming pool there is a magnificent view of the sea.

Esposende

★★★★Hotel Sopete Ofir (190 r., SP, T)
Avenida Raul de Sousa Martins, 4740 Esposende
Tel. 053/981383, fax 053/981871
A 400-bed hotel. Those who are not keen on swimming or tennis can hire a "bone-shaker" bicycle and enjoy the surrounding countryside.

Estoril

★★★★★Hotel Palácio (200 r., SP)
Parque do Estoril, 2765 Estoril; tel. 01/4680400, fax 01/4684867
Over 50 years old, this is the town's best hotel. The swimming pool in the garden is filled from a mineral spring. The hotel restaurant is also first class.

Faro

★★★Hotel Eva (150 r.)
Avenida da República 1, 8000 Faro; tel. 089/803354, fax 089/802304
A solid hotel centrally located near the marina with attractive rooms. Very good road links.

★★Pensão Marim (27 r.)
Praça Silva Porto 25, 8000 Faro; tel. 089/824063
Quiet location, only a few minutes from the town centre. Rooms are small but very clean, and all are en suite (shower) and with a balcony.

Fátima

★★★Hotel São José (80 r.)
Av. Dom José Coreia da Silva, 2495 Fátima
Tel. 049/532215, fax 049/533217
100m/110yd from the pilgrimage church. The rooms are neatly furnished. Own restaurant.

Figueira da Foz

★★★Hotel Costa de Prata 2 (108 r.)
Rua M. Bombarda 59, 3080 Figueira da Foz
Tel. 033/422082, fax 033/426610
From outside the hotel appears very dull and cold-looking; the rooms are plain and functional. The large picture-windows provide a beautiful sea-view. Quiet location.

Guarda

★★★Hotel Turismo da Guarda (102 r., SP)
Avenida Coronel Orlindo de Carvalho, 6300 Guarda
Tel. 071/223366, fax 071/223399
An elegantly appointed hotel in an impressive old building. Luxuriously fitted bathrooms. As well as a swimming pool there is also a sauna, a night club and parking facilities nearby.

Guimarães

★★★★Hotel de Guimarães (72 r., SP)
Rua Eduardo de Almeida, 4800 Guimarães
Tel. 053/515888, fax 053/516234
Together with the pousada, this is one of the town's best hotels.

★★★Pensão São Mamede (27 r.)
Rua de São Gonçalo 1–4, 4800 Guimarães; tel. 053/513092
A not particulary attractive concrete block, but very popular with guests and frequently fully booked.

Lagos

★★★★Hotel de Lagos (287 r., SP, T)
Rua Nova da Aldeia, 8600 Lagos; tel. 082/769967, fax 082/769920
Built in the Moorish style, located in the Old Town. Being on a slope, almost every room has a fine view. There is a shuttle service to the hotel's own beach 500m/550yd away. Those who prefer to swim in fresh water can enjoy the pool situated in the middle of a subtropical garden.

Pensão Lagosmar (45 r.)
Rua Dr. Faria e Silva 13, 8600 Lagos; tel. 082/763523, fax 082/767324
The rooms are small but modern and quiet. With roof terrace.

★★★★★Hotel Lapa (94 r.)
Rua Pau de Bandera 4, 1200 Lisboa; tel. 01/3950005, fax 01/3950665
A member of the "Leading Hotels of the World". All rooms are fitted
with Arraiolos carpets. Perfect service. Quiet location.

★★★★★Tivoli Lisboa (298 r., SP, T)
Avenida da Liberdade 185, 1200 Lisboa; tel. 01/3530181, fax 01/579461
A luxury hotel, as reflected in the lounges, restaurants and lobby, but the
guests' rooms, on the other hand, (or some of them at least) are not all
that luxuriously appointed. The pool in the hotel's small garden is very
pleasant.

★★★★Hotel Lisboa Plaza (106 r.)
Travessa do Salitre 7, 1250 Lisboa; tel. 01/3463922, fax 01/3471630
In a quiet side street off the Avenida da Liberdade, i.e. centrally located.
An elegantly appointed hotel. Very stylish.

★★★★Hotel Sofitel (168 r.)
Av. da Liberdade 125, 1250 Lisboa; tel. 01/3429202, fax 01/3429222
Well-equipped and friendly rooms, pleasant restaurant. A municipal
hotel which is also popular with business people.

★★★Hotel Veneza Lisboa Resid (38 r.)
Av. da Liberdade 189, 1250 Lisboa; tel. 01/3522618, fax 01/3526678
Located on Lisbon's magnificent main boulevard. Middle price category.

★★★★Pensão Residencia York House (48 r.)
Rua das Janelas Verdes 32, 1200 Lisboa
Tel. 01/3962435, fax 01/3972793
This exclusive pension, housed in an old 16th c. convent, is located
some way away from the city centre, in the direction of Belém. Attractive
rooms. Beautiful convent garden with a fountain.

★Pensão Portuense (18 r.)
Rua Portas de Santo Antão 153, 1100 Lisboa; tel. 01/3464197, fax
01/3424239
In a street running parallel to the Avenida da Liberdade, in the middle of
the "restaurant quarter". Friendly service and very clean. At night the
street noise can be somewhat disturbing.

★★★Loulé Jardim (52 r., SP)
Praça Manuel d'Arriaga, 8100 Loulé; tel. 089/413094, fax 089/463177
A town mansion with modern decor. Owned by a Norwegian couple.

★★★★★Reid's Hotel (168 r., SP, T)
Estrada Monumental 139, 9000 Funchal; tel. 091/763001, fax 091/717177
Reid's – a luxury hotel opened in 1891 by the Scotsman William Reid –
is without doubt the best known establishment on Madeira. Many
famous people, including well-known actors, have stayed here. Even if
you prefer cheaper accommodation, the lounges and terrace cafés make
the detour here worthwhile (particularly for the traditional afternoon tea
at five o'clock).

★★★★Hotel Vila Ramos (108 r., SP, T)
Azinhaga da Casa Branca 7, 9000 Funchal
Tel. 091/764181, fax 091/764156
A quietly located middle class hotel about 2km/1¼ miles from the town
centre. From the roof there is a magnificent view of the sea and the harbour.

Hotels

★★★Pensão Santa Clara (14 r., SP)
Calçada do Pico 16 B, 9000 Funchal; tel. 091/742194, fax 091/743280
In a grand house but with simple albeit cosy rooms. A superb view from the breakfast room and from the terrace. Friendly landlady.

Mirandela ★★Hotel Mira Tua (37 r.)
Rua da República 42, 5370 Mirandela; tel. 078/2680140, fax 078/2680143
Best hotel in town. Central location.

Monchique ★★★★Estalagem Abrigo da Montanha (8 r.)
Corte Pereira Fóia, 8550 Monchique; tel. 082/92131, fax 082/93660
A little way outside the town. Small but cosy rooms with a wonderful view towards the coast; some rooms have a balcony.

Nazaré ★★★Hotel da Nazaré (52 r.)
Largo Afonso Zuquete, 2450 Nazaré; tel. 062/561311, fax 062/561238
Small and relatively simply furnished rooms. Sunbathing on the roof terrace. From the dining room there is a fine view of Nazaré.

Óbidos ★★★★Albergaria Santa Isabel (20 r.)
Rua Direita, 2510 Óbidos; tel. 062/959323, fax 062/959115
This hotel firm has been in existence since 1985. The rooms are comfortable, with telephone and TV. Four rooms have a balcony. Lift available.

Olhão ★★Pensão Bela Vista (10 r.)
Rua Téofilo Braga 65, 8700 Olhão; tel. 089/702538
In Olhão there is only one hotel but a number of pensions of the middle and lower categories. The Pensão Bela Vista is a nice, attractive house full of interesting nooks and crannies.

Oporto See Porto

Portalegre ★★★Estalagem Quinta da Saúde (12 r.)
Quinta da Saúde, 7300 Portalegre; tel. 045/22324
Near a camping site. The rooms offer a view across the plain. The hotel restaurant is good.

Portimão ★★★Hotel Globo (71 r.)
Rua 5 de Outubro 26, 8500 Portimao; tel. 082/416350, fax 082/83142
A hotel of several floors with comfortably appointed rooms. The best view over the roof-tops of the town is from the upper floors.

Porto ★★★★★Sheraton Porto (253 r, SP)
Avenida da Boavista 1269, 4150 Porto; tel. 02/6068822, fax 02/6091467
Luxury class hotel with comfort and service to match.

★★★Grande Hotel do Porto (100 r.)
Rua de S. Catarina 197, 4000 Porto; tel. 02/2008176, fax 02/2051061
An old, well-run hotel of three storeys. Quiet location. Comfortable rooms. However, "olde worlde" charm will be found only in the drawing rooms. Many business people number among the guests.

★★★★Pensão Escondidinho (23 r.)
Rua Passos Manuel 135, 4000 Porto; tel. 02/2004079
Central location. The rooms are spacious with wooden floors, but the furniture is somewhat sad and worn.

Praia da Rocha ★★★★★Hotel Algarve (209 r., SP, T)
Avenida Tomás Cabreira, 8500 Portimão; tel. 082/415001, fax 082/411315
One of the best hotels in the Algarve. Almost all the rooms have a balcony and a sea view. Children's paddling pool and playground with crèche.

★★★Hotel Bela Vista (14 r.)
Avenida Tomás Cabreira, 8500 Portimão; tel. 082/424055, fax 082/415369
In a former palace; with a well-tended and wide beach. From the breakfast room there is a fine view of the sea. In summer concerts are held in
the palm court.

★★★Hotel Baleeira (118 r., SP, T)   **Sagres**
8650 Vila do Bispo (Sagres); tel. 082/624212, fax 081/64425
The rooms are furnished in rustic fashion; with a superb view of Sagres
Bay. The swimming pool is filled with water from the sea.

★★Pensão Abidis (28 r.)   **Santarém**
Rua Guilherme de Azvedo 4, 2000 Santarém; tel. 043/22017
Pleasant hotel in the middle of a shopping centre.

★★★Pensão Esperança (76 r.)   **Setúbal**
Avenida Luisa Todi 220, 2900 Setúbal; tel. 065/525151
Apart from the Pousada de São Filipe this is the town's most expensive
hotel. There is a fine view of the Rio Sado from the restaurant on the 5th
floor.

★★★Pensão Búzio (38 r.)   **Sines**
Rua Américo Nunes 17, 7520 Sines; tel. 069/862558
There are not that many places to stay in Sines. In this pension there is
a 30% discount during the low season.

★★★★★ Palácio de Seteais (18 r., SP, T)   **Sintra**
Rua Barbosa du Bocage 10, 2710 Sintra (Seteais)
Tel. 01/9233200, fax 01/9234277
This 18th c. palace is now an exquisite hotel.

★★★★Hotel Tivoli Sintra (75 r.)
Praça da República, 2710 Sintra; tel. 01/9233505, fax 01/9231572
Located in the town centre. Comfortable, with a fine view over the Serra
de Sintra. Attentive service.

★★★Pensão Nova Sintra (12 r.)
Tel. 01/9230202
A pension in an old mansion. Huge rooms with double doors. Garden,
pool and peace and quiet. Advance bookings advisable.

★★★Eurotel Tavira (80 r., SP, T)   **Tavira**
Quinta das Oliveiras, 8800 Tavira; tel. 081/325041, fax 081/325571
Outside the town, on the road to Vila Real. Not a beach location, but this
is compensated for by a large garden with a pool. The rooms are relatively large and well appointed.

★★★★Hotel dos Templários (84 r., SP, T)   **Tomar**
Largo Cândido dos Reis 1, 2300 Tomar; tel. 049/321730, 049/322191
Located by Mouchão Park. The town's most luxurious – and most
expensive – hotel.

★★★★Hotel Grão Vasco (86 r., SP)   **Tomar**
Rua G. Barreiros, 3500 Viseu; tel. 032/423511, fax 032/227047
Spacious rooms, almost all with balcony. A well-tended garden sur-
rounds the hotel.

Information

Portuguese National Tourist Offices outside Portugal

United Kingdom	22–25A Sackville Street London W1X 2LY. Tel. (0171) 4941441
U.S.A. New York	590 Fifth Avenue New York, NY 10036 – 4785. Tel. (212) 3544403
San Francisco	88 Kearny Street, Suite 1770 San Francisco, CA 94108. Tel. (415) 3917080
Washington	1900 L Street NW, Suite 310 Washington, DC 20036
Canada Montreal	2075 University, Suite 1206 Montreal, Quebec H3A 2L1. Tel. (514) 2821264
Toronto	60 Bloor Street, West Suite 1005 Toronto, Ontario M4W 3B8. Tel. (416) 9217376

Tourist Information Centres in Portugal

Information in
Portugal

In all the larger towns and cities, and in many of the smaller ones also, there are tourist information offices (*turismo*) which can provide information about the place in question and its region, and will also help in obtaining accommodation. Opening times are not all the same, but most are open Mon.–Fri. 10am–1pm and 3–5pm. In popular tourist centres they are often open longer and for a few hours at weekends.

Abrantes	Largo 1° de Maio; tel. 041/22555, fax 041/371661
Albufeira	Rua 5 de Outubro; tel. 089/585279
Alcobaça	Praça 25 de Abril; tel. 062/582377
Algarve	See individual places
Amarante	Rua Cândido dos Reis; tel. 055/432980
Armação de Pàra	Avenida Marginal; tel. 082/312145
Arraiolos	Praça Lima e Brito; tel. 066/499105
Aveiro	Rua João Mendonça; tel. 034/23680, fax 034/28326
Azores	See Ponta Delgada
Barcelos	Largo da Porta Nova; tel. 053/811882, fax 053/8822188
Batalha	Praça Mouzinho de Albuquerque; tel. 044/765180
Beira	See Castelo Branco, Coimbra and Guarda
Beja	Rua Capitão Francisco de Sousa 25; tel 084/323693
Braga	Avenida da Liberdade 1; tel. 053/262550
Bragança	Avenida Ciudade de Zamora; tel. 073/381273

Rua E. Duarte Pacheco; tel. 062/831003	**Caldas da Rainha**
Rua Ricardo Joaquim de Sousa; tel. and fax 058/921952	**Caminha**
Rua Visconde da Luz; tel. 01/4868204	**Cascais**
Alameda da Liberdade; tel. 072/341002	**Castelo Branco**
Rua Bartolomeu Alvares da Santa 81; tel. 045/901361, fax 045/901827	**Castelo de Vide**
Terreiro da Cavalaria; tel. 076/333029	**Chaves**
Largo da Portagem; tel. 039/833019, fax 039/825576	**Coimbra**
See Lisbon, Sesimbra and Setúbal	**Costa de Lisboa**
See Aveiro, Ericeira, Espinho, Figueira da Foz, Nazaré, Oporto, Peniche and Torres Vedras	**Costa de Prata**
See Cascais and Estoril	**Costa do Sol**
See Setúbal	**Costa Dourada**
See Barcelos, Caminha, Oporto, Póvoa de Varzim, Viana do Castelo and Vila do Conde	**Costa Verde**
Praça do Municipio; tel. 075/322170	**Covilhã**
Praça Dr Luis Navega (3780 Anadia); tel. 031/512248, fax 031/512966	**Curia**
Praça da República; tel. 068/622236, fax 068/629060	**Elvas**
Rua Dr Eduardo Burnay 46; tel. 061/863122, fax 061/865909	**Ericeira**
Câmara Municipal; tel. 02/7340911, fax 02/7311053	**Espinho**
Avenida Marginal; tel. 053/961354	**Esposende**
Arcadas do Parque; tel. 01/4664414, fax 01/4672280	**Estoril**
See Lisbon	**Estremadura**
Largo da República, 26; tel. 068/333541	**Estremoz**
Praça do Giraldo; tel. 066/22671, fax 066/22955	**Évora**
Airport; tel. 089/818582, fax 089/817787 Rua da Misericórdia 8–12; tel. 089/803604	**Faro**
Avenida D. José Alves Correira da Silva; tel. 049/531139	**Fátima**
Avenida 25 de Abril; tel. 033/402820, fax 033/402828	**Figueira da Foz**
Avenida Arriaga 18; tel. 091/229057, fax 091/232151	**Funchal**
Avenida Manuel Francisco da Costa (Terras do Boura); tel. 053/391133, fax 053/391282	**Gerês**
Largo do Municipio; tel. 071/221817	**Guarda**
Largo Valentim Moureira da Sá; tel. 053/412450	**Guimarães**

Information

Lagos	Largo Marquês de Pombal; tel. 082/763031
Lamego	Avenida Visconde Guedes Teixeira; tel. 054/62005
Leiria	Jardim de Luís de Carmões; tel. 044/823773, fax 044/833533
Lisbon	Praça dos Restauradores (Palácio Foz); tel. 01/3466307, fax 01/3468772 Airport; tel. 01/8494323, fax 01/8485974
Madeira	See Funchal
Mafra	Avenida do 25 de Abril; tel. 061/812023, fax 061/815104
Marvão	Rua do Dr. Matos Magalhães; tel. 045/93104, fax 045/93526
Minho	See Braga
Monção	Praça Deu-la-Deu; tel. 051/652757
Monte Gordo	Avenida Marginal; tel. 081/544495
Nazaré	Avenida da República; tel. 062/561194, fax 062/5501019
Óbidos	Rua Direita; tel. 062/959231, fax 062/959770
Olhão	Largo Sebastião Martins Mestre 6A; tel. 089/713936
Oporto	Rua do Clube dos Fenianos 25; tel. 02/3393470, fax 02/3323303 Airport; tel. 02/9412534
Palmela	Castelo de Palmela; tel. 01/2332122
Peneda-Geràs National Park	See Gerês
Peniche	Rua de Alexandre Herculano; tel. 062/789571
Pombal	Largo do Cardal; tel. 036/213230
Ponta Delgada	Avenida do Infante Dom Henrique; tel. 096/285743, fax 096/282211
Portalegre	Palácio Povas; tel. 045/331359
Portimão	Largo 1 de Dezembro; tel. 082/419131
Póvoa de Varzim	Avenida Mouzinho de Albuquerque 166; tel. 052/298120
Praia da Rocha	Avenida Tomás Cabreira; tel. 082/419132
Quarteira	Avenida Infante Sagres; tel. 089/389209
Ribatejo	See Santarém
Sagres	Rua Comandante Matoso; tel. 082/624873
Santarém	Rua Capelo Ivens 63; tel. 043/391512, fax 043/333643
Santo Tirso	Praça 25 de Abril; tel. 052/830411
São Pedro do Sul	Largo dos Correios, Termas; tel. 032/711320

Largo D. Jorge de Melo 2/3; tel 084/53727	**Serpa**
See Covilhã	**Serra da Estrela**
See Coimbra	**Serra da Lousã**
Largo de Marinha; tel. 01/2235743	**Sesimbra**
Tv. Frei Gaspar 10; tel. 065/539120	**Setúbal**
Rua 25 de Abril; tel. 082/442255	**Silves**
Jardim das Descobertas; tel. 069/634472	**Sines**
Praça da República; tel. 01/9231157, fax 01/9235176	**Sintra**
Rua da Galeria 9; tel. 081/322511	**Tavira**
Avenida Dr Cândido Madureira; tel. 049/322427	**Tomar**
Rua Manuel Seixas; tel. 079/252289	**Torre de Moncorvo**
Rua do 9 de Abril; tel. 061/314094	**Torres Vedras**
See Bragança	**Trás-os-Montes**
Avenida de Espanha; tel. and fax 051/23374	**Valença do Minho**
Praça da Erva; tel. 058/822620, fax 058/827873	**Viana do Castelo**
Centro de Artesanato – Rua 5 de Outubro; tel. 052/642700	**Vila do Conde**
See Quarteira	**Vilamoura**
Avenida Diogo Leite 242; tel. 02/3751902	**Vila Nova de Gaia**
Avenida Carvalho Araújo; tel. 059/322819	**Vila Real**
See Monte Gordo	**Vila Real de Santo António**
Avenida de Calouste Gulbenkian; tel. 032/422014, fax 032/421864	**Viseu**

Insurance

Visitors are strongly advised to ensure that they have adequate holiday insurance including loss or damage to luggage, loss of currency and jewellery.

General

British citizens, like nationals of other European Union countries, are entitled to obtain medical care under the Portuguese health services on the same basis as Portuguese people. This means that they must pay the cost of treatment and medicine but are reimbursed 70–80% of the cost through the local sickness insurance office. The level and nature of the payments depend on the Portuguese rules and regulations, but it is necessary to have obtained an E111 form from the local DSS office before leaving home, which certifies entitlement to insurance cover. In the event of treatment being necessary (apart from casualty-type emergencies) a set of vouchers for medical treatment must be obtained from the relevant regional health authority, the Administração Regional de Saúde; a list of these can be obtained from health insurance agencies.

Health

Language

Additional Private
Insurance

It is nevertheless advisable, even for EU nationals, to take out some form of short-term health insurance providing complete cover and possibly avoiding delays. Nationals of non-EU countries should certainly have insurance cover.

Vehicles

Visitors travelling by car should ensure that their insurance is comprehensive and covers use of the vehicle in Europe.

See also Travel Documents.

Language

Knowledge of
foreign languages

The foreign languages most commonly spoken in Portugal are Spanish, English and French, and there are now also numbers of returned "guest workers" who have learnt some German while working in Germany. In any event, however, it is well worth having at least a smattering of Portuguese.

Portuguese

On first hearing Portuguese spoken a visitor may not quite know what to make of it because it can sound rather like a Slav language (e.g. Polish). The written form of the language, however, can at once be recognised as a Romance language, and some knowledge of Latin or Spanish will be a great help in understanding it.

Grammar

Portuguese grammer is notable for the rich tense system of the verbs, in particular for the preservation of the Latin pluperfect (e.g. fora, "I had been"). A further peculiarity is the inflected personal infinitive: "entramos na loja para comprarmos pão" = "we go into the shop to buy bread".

The plural is formed by the addition of "s", in some cases with the modification of the preceding vowel or consonant:

Singular	Plural
o animal	os animais
o hotel	os hotéis
a região	as regiões

The definite article is "o" (masculine) or "a" (feminine) in the singular, "os" or "as" in the plural. The declension of nouns and adjectives is simple. The nominative and accusative are the same; the genitive is indicated by "de" (of), the dative by "a" (to). The prepositions "de" and "a" combine with the definite article as follows:

de + o = do	de + a = da
de + os = dos	de + as = das
a + o = ao	a + os = aos
a + a = à	a + as = às

The Portuguese spoken in Portugal seems lacking in resonance, but is soft and melodious, without the hard accumulations of consonants and the rough gutturals of Castilian Spanish. It is notable for its frequent sibilants and for the nasalisation of vowels, diphthongs and triphthongs. Unstressed vowels and intervocalic consonants are much attenuated or disappear altogether. The stressed syllable of a word so dominates the rest that the vowels of the other syllables are radically altered in tone quality and not infrequently are reduced to a mere whisper. In the spoken language the boundaries between words are so blurred (in the phenomenon know as "sandhi") that the individual word within a group largely loses its independence: thus the phrase "os outros amigos" ("the other friends") is run together into a single phonetic unit and pronounced something like "usótrushamígush".

The nine vocalic phonemes used in Portuguese are represented by the five vowels a, e, i, o and u together with three diacritic signs or accents (ˆˊˋ), two of which (ˊ and ˆ) also indicate the stress. Nasalisation is indicated by the tilde (Portuguese "o til": ˜) or by the consonant "m" or "n".

The stress is normally on the penultimate syllable of a word ending in a vowel or in "m" or "s" and on the last syllable of a word ending in a consonant other than "m" or "s". Exceptions to this rule are marked by the use of an accent. It should be noted that "ia", "io" and "iu" are not treated as diphthongs as in Spanish but as combinations of separate vowels.Thus the word "agrário", for example, with the stress on the second "a", requires an accent to indicate this in Portuguese but not in Spanish where it is "agrario" without an accent.

a	unstressed, like a whispered e	Some peculiarities of Portuguese pronunciation
à	long "ah"	
c	k before a, o and u; s before e and i	
ç	s	
ch	sh	
e	unstressed, like a whispered i; in initial position before s, practically disappears ("escudo" pronounced "shkúdo"; Estoril pronounced "Shturíl")	
ê	closed e	
é	open e	
g	hard g (as in "go") before a, o and u; zh (like s in "pleasure") before e and i	
gu	hard g	
h	mute	
i	nasalised after u ("muito" pronounced "muínto")	
j	zh	
l	in final position as in English or, in Brazil, like a weak u ("animal" pronounced "animáu")	
lh ly	(with consonantal y): cf. Spanish ll	
m, n	in final position nasalise the preceding vowel	
nh ny	(with consonantal y): cf. Spanish ñ	
o	unstressed, like u	
ô	closed o	
ó	open o	
qu	k	
r	trilled	
rr	strongly rolled	
s	s before vowels; z between vowels; sh before hard consonants and in final position; zh before soft consonants	
v	v	
x	sh	
z	in final position sh; otherwise z	

The Brazilian pronunciation of Portuguese is markedly different from the Portuguese mainland. In particular final "s" and "z" are pronounced "s" and not "sh", and initial "r" sounds almost like "h".

Numbers

0	zero	Cardinals
1	um, uma	
2	dois, duas	
3	três	
4	quatro	
5	cinco	
6	seis	
7	sete	

8	oito
9	nove
10	dez
11	onze
12	doze
13	treze
14	catorze
15	quinze
16	dezasseis
17	dezassete
18	dezoito
19	dezanove
20	vinte
21	vinte-e-um
22	vinte-e-dois (duas)
30	trinta
31	trinta-e-em (uma)
40	quarenta
50	cinquenta
60	sessenta
70	setenta
80	oitenta
90	noventa
100	cem, cento
101	cento-e-um (uma)
200	duzentos, -as
300	trezentos, -as
400	quatrocentos, -as
500	quinhentos, -as
600	seiscentos, -as
700	setecentos, -as
800	oitocentos, -as
900	novecentos, -as
1000	mil
2000	dois (duas) mil
1 million	um milhão de

Ordinals		
	1st	primeiro, -a
	2nd	segundo, -a
	3rd	terceiro, -a
	4th	quarto, -a
	5th	quinto, -a
	6th	sexto, -a
	7th	sétimo, -a
	8th	oitavo, -a
	9th	nono, -a
	10th	décimo, -a
	11th	undécimo, -a; décimo primeiro
	12th	duodécimo, -a; décimo segundo
	13th	décimo terceiro
	20th	vigésimo, -a
	21st	vigésimo primeiro, -a
	30th	trigésimo, -a
	40th	quadragésimo, -a
	50th	quinquagésimo, -a
	60th	sexuagésimo, -a
	100th	centésimo, -a

Fractions   ½ meio, meia
⅓ um terço, uma terça parte
¼ um quarto
¾ três quartos, três quartas partes

Idioms and Vocabulary

Men are usually addressed as "Senhor", women as "minha Senhora". If you know a man's name you should address him by his name with the prefix "Senhor"; ladies are addressed by "Senhora Dona" and their Christian name, if this is known. "You" in direct address is "o Senhor", "a Senhora" or "Você", in the plural "os Senhores", "as Senhoras" or "Vocês".

In Portuguese names, which are frequently very long, the maternal surname usually comes first.

Good morning, good day	Bom dia	Idioms
Good afternoon	Boa tarde	
Good evening, good night	Boa noite	
Goodbye	Adeus, Até à vista	
Yes, no (Sir)	Sim, não (Senhor)	
Excuse me (apologising)	Desculpe, Perdão	
Excuse me (e.g. when passing in front of someone)	Com licença	
After you (e.g. offering something)	A vontade!	
Please (asking for something)	Faz favor	
Thank you (very much)	(Muito) obrigado	
Not at all (You're welcome)	De nada, Não tem de què	
Do you speak English?	O senhor fala inglês?	
A little, not much	Um pouco, não muito	
I do not understand	Não compreendo (nada)	
What is the Portuguese for ...?	Como se diz em português ...?	
What is the name of this church?	Como chama-se esta igreja?	
Have you any rooms?	Tem um quarto livre?	
I should like ...	Queria ...	
A room with private bath	Um quarto com banho	
With full board	Com pensão completa	
What does it cost?	Quanto custa?	
Everything included	Tudo incluído	
That is very dear	É muito caro	
Bill, please!	Faz favor, a conta!	
Where is ... Street?	Onde fica a rua ...?	
the road to?	a estrada para ...?	
a doctor?	um médico?	
a dentist?	um dentista?	
Right, left	À direita, esquerda	
Straight ahead	Sempre a direito	
Above, below	Em cima, em baixo	
When is it open?	A que horas está aberto?	
How far?	Que distância?	
Wake me at six	Chamé-me às seis	

Alfândega	Customs	Road signs
Alto!	Stop	
Atenção!	Caution	
Auto-estrada	Highway	
Bifurcação	Road fork	
Cuidado!	Caution	
Curva perigosa	Dangerous curve	
Dê passagem!	Give way/yield	
Desvio	Diversion	
Devagar!	Slow	
Direcção única; Sentido único	One-way street	
Estacionamento proibido	Parking prohibited	
Ir a passo!	Dead slow	
Ir pela direita, esquerda	Keep right, left	
Nevoeiro	Mist, fog	
Obras na estrada	Road works	

Language

Parque de estacionamento	Car park, parking place
Passagem proibida	No entry
Peões	Pedestrians
Perigo!	Danger!
Portagem	Toll
Praia	Beach
Proibido ultrapassar	No overtaking
Rebanhos	Beware of livestock
Serviço de reboque	Towing service

Vehicle terms		
	accelerator	o acelerador
	automobile	o auto, o carro
	axle	o eixo
	battery	a bateria
	bearing	a chumaceira
	bolt	o parafuso
	bonnet/hood	o capot
	brake	o travão
	breakdown	a avaria
	bulb	a lâmpada eléctrica
	bumper	o pára-choque
	bus	a camioneta (de passageiros)
	car	o auto, o carro
	carburettor/carburetor	o carburador
	change (oil, tyre/tire, etc.)	mudar
	charge (battery)	carregar
	check	verificar
	clutch	a embraiagem
	contact	o contacto
	cylinder	o cilindro
	damaged	avariado, avariada
	diesel engine	o motor Diesel
	direction indicator	o indicador de direcção
	distributor	o distribuidor
	driver	o motorista, o condutor
	driving licence	a carta de condutor
	dynamo	o dínamo
	engine	o motor
	exhaust	o escape
	fan belt	a correia da ventoinha
	fault	a avaria
	float	o flutuador
	fuse	o fusível
	garage	a garage, a garagem
	gas/petrol	a gasolina
	gas/petrol pump	a bomba de gasolina
	gas/petrol station	o posto de gasolina
	gas/petrol tank	o depósito de gasolina
	gasket	o empanque
	gear	a velocidade, a mudança
	gearbox	o câmbio de velocidades
	grease (verb)	lubrificar
	headlamp	o farol
	hood/bonnet	o capot
	horn	a buzina
	ignition	a ignição
	inflate	dar à bomba
	inner tube	a câmara-de-ar
	jack	o macaco
	jet	o gicleur
	lorry/truck	o camião
	magneto	o magneto

make (of car)	a marca
map	o mapa das estradas
maximum speed	a velocidade máxima
mixture	a mistura
motorcycle	a motocicleta
number-plate	a placa, a matrícula
nut	a porca
oil	o óleo
oil-pump	a bomba de óleo
park (verb)	estacionar
parking place, car park	o estacionamento
petrol/gas	a gasolina
petrol/gas pump	a bomba de gasolina
petrol/gas station	o posto de gasolina
petrol/gas tank	o depósito de gasolina
piston	o postão
piston ring	o segmento de pistão
pump	a bomba
radiator	o radiador
rear light	a luz traseira
repair	reparar
repair garage	a oficina de reparação
road map	o mapa das estradas
scooter	o scooter
shock absorber	o amortecedor
snow chain	a cadeia antideslizante
spanner	a chave inglesa
spare part	a peça de sobresselente
sparking plug	a vela
speedometer	o velocimetro
spring	a mola
starter	o arranque
steering	a direcção
steering wheel	o volante
tow away	levar a reboque
transmission	a condução
truck/lorry	o camião
two-stroke engine	o motor do dois tempos
tyre/tire	o pneu
tyre/tire pressure	a pressão dos pneus
valve	a válvula
wash	lavar
water-pump	a bomba de água
wheel	a roda
windscreen/windshield	o párabrisas
windscreen/windshield wiper	o limpa-pára-brisas
wing	o guarda-lama

aircraft	aeroplano, avião	Travelling
airport	aeroporto	
all aboard!	partida!	
all change!	mudar!	
arrival	chegada	
baggage	bagagem	
baggage check	guia, senha	
bus	autocarro, camioneta	
conductor (ticket-collector)	revisor	
couchette car	furgoneta	
departure	partida	
fare	preço	
flight	vôo	
information	informação	

Language

line (railway)	via férrea
luggage	bagagem
luggage ticket	guia, senha
no smoking (carriage)	não fumadores
platform	plataforma, gare
porter	moço de fretes
restaurant car	carruagem restaurante
railway station	estação
sleeping car	carruagem-cama
smoking (carriage)	fumadores
steward	comissário de bordo
stewardess	hospedeira (do ar)
stop	paragem
ticket	bilhete
ticket-collector (conductor)	revisor
ticket office	bilheteria, guichet
timetable	horário
toilet	lavatório
train	combóio
waiting room	sala de espera

Months	January	janeiro
	February	fevereiro
	March	março
	April	abril
	May	maio
	June	junho
	July	julho
	August	agosto
	September	setembro
	October	outubro
	November	novembro
	December	dezembro
	month	mês
	year	ano

Days of the week	Monday	segunda-feira
	Tuesday	terça-feira
	Wednesday	quarta-feira
	Thursday	quinta-feira
	Friday	sexta-feira
	Saturday	sábado
	Sunday	domingo
	day	dia
	holiday, feast-day	dia de festa, dia feriado

Holidays and Religious Festivals	New Year's Day	Ano-Novo
	Easter	Páscoa
	Ascension	Ascensão
	Whitsun	Espírito Santo, Pentecostes
	Corpus Christi	Festa do Corpo de Deus
	All Saints	Todos os Santos
	Christmas	Natal
	New Year's Eve	Véspera do Ano-Novo, Noite de São Silvestre

At the post office	address	endereço
	air mail	correio aéreo
	by airmail	por avião
	express letter	carta urgente
	letter	carta

letter-box, post-box	marco postal
packet	embrulho
parcel	pacote
postage	porte
postcard	bilhete postal
poste restante	poste-restante
postman	carteiro
post office	correio
registered letter	carta registrada
stamp	selo, estampilha
telegram	telegrama
telephone	telephone
telex	telex

abadia	abbey	Glossary
água	water	
aldeia	small village, hamlet	
altura	hill, eminence	
ancoradouro	anchorage	
anfiteatro	amphitheatre	
aqueduto	aqueduct	
arquipélago	archipelago	
avenida	avenue	
azulejos	glazed tiles	
baía	bay	
bairro	district of town	
balneário	bath(s)	
barco	boat	
barragem	dam, reservoir	
bolsa	purse	
cabo	cape	
caldas	hot springs, spa	
calvário	calvary	
câmara municipal	town hall	
caminho	path, track road	
caminho de ferro	railway	
campo	field, countryside	
capela	chapel	
capela-mór	main chapel with high altar	
casa	house	
casal	farm, hamlet	
cascata	waterfall	
castelo	castle	
cemitério	cemetery, churchyard	
cidade	town, city	
ciências naturais	natural history	
circulação	round trip	
citânia	prehistoric fortified settlement	
claustro	cloister	
colina	hill	
convento	convent (in the general sense of religious house)	
coro	choir	
costa	coast	
cova	cave, pit	
cumeada	mountain ridge	
cúpula	dome	
desfiladeiro	pass, defile	
doca	dock	
encruzamento de ruas	street intersection	
ermida	pilgrimage chapel, hermitage	
estabelecimento balnear	spa establishment	

estrada	road
estreito	straight
farol	lighthouse
floresta	forest
fonte	spring, fountain
fortaleza	fortress, castle
foz	mouth of river
fronteira	frontier
funicular	funicular
garganta	gorge
hospital	hospital
hotel	hotel
igreja	church
ilha	island
janela	window
jardim	garden
lago	lake
lagoa	small lake, lagoon
landa	heath, moor
leste	east
mar	sea
mirador	viewpoint
montanha	mountain (range)
monte	hill
muralha	(town) wall
museu	museum
norte	north
oeste	west
paço	palace
paço de concelho	town hall
padrão	monument
palácio	palace
pântano	marsh, bog
parque	park
parque nacional	national park
pátio	courtyard
pelhourinho	pillory column
península	peninsula
pensão	pension; guest house
pico	peak
pintura	painting
planalto	plateau
planície	plain
poço	well, spring
ponte	bridge
portão	gateway
porto	harbour, port
pousada	(State-run) hotel, inn
povoação	village
praça	square
praça de touros	bullring
praia	beach
quinta	country house
retábulo	retable, reredos
rio	river
roca, rocha	rock, crag
rua	street
sala	hall, room
sé	cathedral
serra	mountain range, range of hills
sul	south
tapeçaria	tapestry

termas	hot springs, spa	
tesouro	treasure	
torre	tower	
vale	valley	
a conta	the bill	Portuguese menu
açorda	garlic and bread soup	
água	water	
água mineral	mineral water	
aguardente, brandy	brandy	
alho	garlic	
almoço	lunch	
amêndoa	almond	
antepastos	starter, hors d'oeuvre	
arroz	rice	
assado	grilled	
aves	poultry	
azeite	olive oil	
azeitonas	olives	
batatas	potatoes	
batatas fritas	fried potatoes	
bebidas	drinks	
bife	steak	
bolo	cake	
cabrito	kid (goat)	
caça	game	
café	coffee	
café com leite	coffee with milk	
carne	meat	
carneiro	mutton	
carta (or lista, ementa)	menu	
cebolas	onions	
ceia	late-night snack, supper	
cerveja	beer	
chá	tea	
chávena	cup	
chocolate	chocolate	
coelho	rabbit	
colher	spoon	
colher de chá	teaspoon	
copo	glass	
corço	venison	
cordeiro	lamb	
couve	cabbage	
couve-flor	cauliflower	
cozido	cooked	
doces	sweets	
ervilhas	peas	
espargos	asparagus	
espinafre	spinach	
faca	knife	
feijões	beans	
frango	chicken	
fruta	fruit	
garfo	fork	
gelado	ice cream	
guardanapo	napkin	
jantar	dinner, evening meal	
javalí	boar	
laranja	orange	
lebre	hare	
leitão	sucking pig	

leite	milk
legumes (hortaliça)	vegetables
maçã	apple
manteiga	butter
massa(s)	pasta
molho	sauce
mostarda	mustard
óleo	oil
ovo (ovos estrelados)	egg (fried)
pão	bread
pãozinho	roll
pato	duck
peixe	fish
pepinos	cucumber
pequeno almoço	breakfast
pera	pear
perdiz	partridge
peru	turkey
pimenta	pepper
pimento	paprika, green pepper
porco	pork
prato	plate
prato do dia	dish of the day
presunto	ham
queijo	cheese
repolho	white cabbage
sal	salt
salada	salad
salame	salami
sobremesas	dessert
sopa	soup
sumo de fruta	fruit juice
talher	cutlery
tomates	tomatoes
uvas	grapes
vaca	beef
vinagre	vinegar
vinho	wine
vitela	veal

Language courses

Various institutes in Lisbon, Oporto, Coimbra and the Algarve provide courses in the Portuguese language, both at advanced level and for beginners, usually lasting from two to four weeks. A number of courses include "learn while on holiday" programmes, whilst others are aimed at the business community. Some tour operators also offer special language-learning holidays.

Cambridge School
Avenida da Liberdade 173; tel. 01/3527474, fax 01/3534729

CIAAL – Centro de Línguas
Avenida da República 41; tel. 01/3533733, fax 01/7960783

Cambridge School
Rua Duque da Terceira 381; tel. 02/560380, fax 02/5012652

Oporto

Faculdade de Letras da Universidade do Porto
Rua do Campo Alegre 1055; tel. 02/698441, fax 02/6005833

Faculdade de Letras da Universidade de Coimbra
Praça Porta Férrea; tel. 039/4109991, fax 039/34613

Coimbra

Instituto Línguas de Faro
Avenida 5 de Outubro 40, Faro; tel. 0 89/824556

Algarve

Interlínguas
Largo 1° Dezembro 28, Portimão; tel. 082/416030, fax 082/27690

A full list of all the language schools in Portugal that offer courses in
Portuguese as a foreign language is available from the Portuguese
National Tourist Offices (see Information).

Markets

Portugal's major towns and cities have covered markets which are open
in the mornings from Monday to Saturday, selling a great variety of
produce.

Covered markets

Mercado do Bolhao in Porto: the place to go for fresh fruit and vegetables

Medical Assistance

Weekly markets	Almost every smaller place has a weekly market, as well as some stalls selling fruit and vegetables during the rest of the week.
Markets in Lisbon	Mercado da Ribeira Nova, Avenida 24 de Julho Big covered market; Mon.–Sat. 6am–2pm
	Rua de São Pedro in the Alfama Fish market in the open; Mon.–Sat. mornings
	Feira da Lada, Campo de Santa Clara (near the church of São Vicente de Fora) Tuesdays and Saturdays, 9am–6pm. This famous flea-market is where all kinds of curios, antiques, junk and jumble change hands.
	Almost every part of Lisbon also has its own fruit and vegetable market.

Medical Assistance

Medical Care	Adequate medical care is available in Portugal, with rural areas the only places where it may prove difficult to consult a specialist. There are also many English-speaking doctors in Portugal and a British Hospital at 49 Rua Saraiva de Carvalho, Lisbon; tel. 01/3955067, fax 01/3974066. In a real emergency you should contact the casualty department (urgência) of the nearest hospital. UK visitors requiring emergency treatment can, on production of their British passport, receive free hospital treatment (outpatient only) under the medical/social agreement between the UK and Portugal.
Medical Insurance	See Insurance
Emergency Services	See Emergency

National Holidays

	See Public Holidays

Motoring

Automobile Service and Assistance	The Portuguese Automobile Club (ACP) represents all the motoring organisations which belong to FIA and AIT.
Automobile Club Head Office	Automóvel Club de Portugal (ACP) Rua Rosa Araújo 24–26, P-1200 Lisbon. Tel. 01/3522469, fax 01/3540903
	ACP has other branches in Aveiro, Braga, Coimbra, Évora, Faro, Figueira da Foz, Funchal, Leiria, Setúbal, Vila Real and Viseu.
Breakdown service	The ACP's breakdown service can be reached on the following numbers:
	Tel. 01/9425095 (ACP Lisbon) for breakdowns between Pombal and the Algarve Tel. 02/8301127 (ACP Oporto) for breakdowns north of Pombal.
Emergency phones	Motorways have orange-coloured emergency phones on the hard shoulder.

See Emergency	Emergency services

See entry

As in the rest of continental Europe, the rule of the road in Portugal is drive on the right, with overtaking on the left. (As a general rule, hoot when overtaking on very narrow roads.) Road signs and markings conform with the international standards.

Traffic on the main road – which is indicated by a yellow rectangular sign edged with black and white – has priority, but at junctions or intersections of roads of equal importance traffic coming from the right has priority. However, motorised vehicles always have priority over non-motorised traffic.

For cars and motorcycles the speed limits are 50kmph/31 mph in built-up areas, and 90kmph/56mph on roads outside built-up areas other than expressways (max. 100kmph/62mph) and motorways (max. 120kmph/74mph).
For lorries, coaches and cars with trailers speed limits are lower at 70kmph/43mph outside built-up areas, and 80kmph/50mph on motorways. The minimum speed on motorways is 40kmph/25mph.

Seat-belts must be worn at all times.

The legal alcohol limit for drivers is 0.5 grammes per litre.

Portugal has quite a good network of filling stations on the main roads. The only time when it can prove difficult to fill up is at night.

Petrol and diesel prices are considerably higher than in other parts of Europe.

Lead-free petrol (gasolina sem chumbo) is now available at all filling stations throughout the country.

Portugal has developed a good road network but there are still many little villages in the more remote parts of the country that can only be reached by unadopted roads.
There is at present no complete motorway link between the Algarve and the north of Portugal (tolls are payable on some sections) but work is going ahead to achieve this. Only in the underdeveloped regions in the extreme north-east are there still some small villages with no made-up roads.
The national highways between the larger towns and cities are well surfaced and provided with stopping places. Emergency lanes and laybys are, however, few and far between. In the thinly populated south of the country a good speed can be maintained on the trunk roads, but in the more mountainous northern regions a maximum speed of only about 40kmph/ 25mph is possible. The roads have many bends and there are few places for overtaking.
Secondary roads to important tourist points are often being improved but are pleasant alternatives to main roads, even though road markings are sometimes missing. If using side roads to explore the country it is advisable to have a good road map since road signs in the smaller places can be totally inadequate; the Portuguese Automobile Club (see above) publishes a revised map every two years.

In the north of the country and around Lisbon in particular the main roads can get very congested, with travel reduced to a snail's pace in the rushhours. In the Algarve also there are traffic jams to contend with in the summer although a new motorway has improved the situation considerably.

Warning   The standard of driving is not particularly high and motorists should beware of drivers overtaking, etc., dangerously.

Newspapers and Periodicals

In major Portuguese towns and cities and in holiday areas British and American newspapers and magazines are usually obtainable on the day of publication.

Opening Times

Shops   Most shops are open Mon.–Fri. from 9am to 1pm, and from 3 to 7pm, and Sat. 9am to 1pm. In the winter months, in particular, many open on Saturday afternoons as well. Tobacconists and food stores are often open until late in the evening, some of them also on Sundays.

Shopping Centres   The large shopping centres of Lisbon are open until midnight, even at the weekends.

Chemists   Chemists (farmácias) are open Mon.–Fri. 9am to 1pm and 3 to 7pm, Saturdays 9am to 1pm. They display notices showing which chemists are open outside these hours. Lists can also be found in local newspapers.

Banks   Banks are open Mon.–Fri. 8.30–3pm. They stay open longer at airports and some tourist centres in the Algarve.

Post Offices   Post Offices are generally open Mon.–Fri. 9am–12.30pm and 2.30–6pm, although there can be regional variations. In large towns and cities they remain open at lunchtimes.

Filling Stations   Filling stations providing a 24-hour service can be found in tourist centres and the larger towns and cities.

Museums   Museums are generally open Tues.–Sun. from 10am to 5pm, though most close for one or two hours at midday.

Restaurants   Restaurants are usually open in the middle of the day from noon, and in the evening from 7pm.

Post

Postal Services   Stamps (selos) are sold in post offices (correios) and in shops displaying the sign "CTT Selos". Post to the United Kingdom normally takes between 3 and 7 days. Express post (correio azul) is quicker but much dearer.

Postage   The postage rates for letters (cartas) and cards (postais) within Europe is 85 esc. (100 esc. outside the EU).

Letterboxes   Portuguese letterboxes are red, except those for "correio azul", which are blue.

Post Offices   See Opening Times

Poste Restante items should be sent to the appropriate post office marked "Posta restante". A passport or other form of personal identification is necessary when collecting mail.

Telegrams can be handed in at post offices and hotel reception desks or sent by telephone 183 (Portugal and Spain), 182 (other countries).

Pousadas

Pousadas – the Portuguese means something like "place of rest" – are state-run inns located in castles, palaces, and monasteries as well as modern buildings, and they are predominantly near places of interest or in areas of exceptional scenic beauty. Even the modern buildings are in the local traditional style, with furnishings of a very high standard, often including antiques. Meals in the pousadas are usually very good with an outstanding range of wines available.
   Generally speaking the maximum stay is five days.

Pousadas fall into four categories – CH, CSUP, C and B, with B standing for the simplest, and CH always for pousadas in historic buildings.

In the high season, from July to September, a double room with breakfast in the CH category is around £90 to £100, in the C category about £70 and in the B category £55. Single rooms cost about 15% less than doubles.

Since pousadas normally have a very limited number of rooms it is advisable to make a reservation well in advance. This can be done with the pousada direct, through a local travel agent or via the Portuguese national tourism agency, Enatura:

> ENATUR (Empresa Nacional de Turismo E.P.)
> Avenida Santa Joana Princesa 10A
> P-1749 Lisboa (Lisbon); tel. 01/8442001, fax 01/8442087

The following list gives the category of the pousada and the number of rooms; SP = swimming pool; T = tennis courts.

1 Pousada de São Teotónio (C SUP; 16 r.)
   P-4930 Valença do Minho; tel. 051/824020, fax 051/824397
   Inside Valença castle.

2 Pousada do Dom Dinis (C; 29 r.)
   P-4920 Vila Nova de Cerveira; tel. 051/795601, fax 051/795604
   Housed in the palace built on the orders of King Dinis in 1321. With an excellent restaurant, from which there is a fine view of the Minho. Fishing and water sports.

3 Pousada de São Bartolomeu (C; 28 r.)
   P-5300 Bragança; tel. 073/331493, fax 073/323453
   At the top of Mount Nogueira, with a magnificent panoramic view of the 17th c. castle which dominates the town. Walks and shooting.

4 Pousada de São Bento (C SUP; 29 r., SP, T)
   P-4850 Vieira do Minho (Caniçada); tel. 053/647190, fax 053/647867
   An old hunting-lodge on the edge of the Peneda-Gerês National Park. From most of the rooms there is a fine view of the wooded valleys and artificial lakes. Fishing, water sports and shooting.

5 Pousada de de Santa Catarina (B; 12 r.)
   P-5210 Miranda do Douro; tel. 073/431005, fax 073/431065
   Above the Miranda do Douro dams. Shooting.

Pousadas
in Portugal
(Festland)

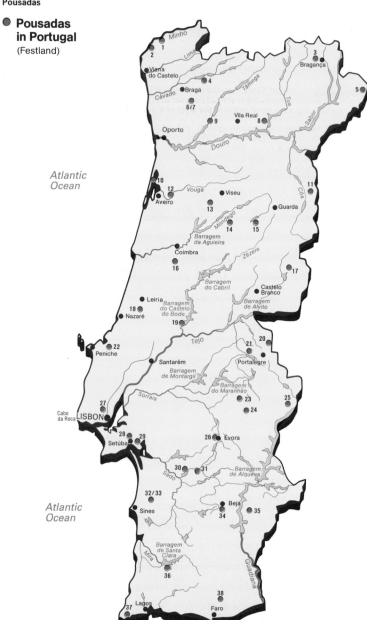

6 Pousada de Nossa Senhora de Oliveira (C SUP; 16 r.)
P-4801 Guimarães Codex; tel. 053/514157, fax 053/514204
In an old mansion in the town centre. The bedrooms and drawing
rooms are thickly carpeted and hung with modern pictures.

7 Pousada de Santa Marinha da Costa (CH, 51 r.)
P-4800 Guimarães; tel. 053/514453, fax 053/514459
In the old convent of Santa Marinha da Costa, which dates back to
the 12th c. Some rooms are in the old convent cells; the new sections
of the building were constructed in the style of the original.

8 Pousada de Barão Forrester (B; 11 r., SP, T)
P-5070 Alijó; tel. 059/959215, fax 059/959304
This pousada was named after the Englishman Baron James
Forrester 1809–62), who came to Portugal to work in his uncle's port
wine business, Offley, Forrester and Co. Fishing and shooting.

9 Pousada de São Gonçalo (B, 15 r.)
P-6400 Amarante; tel. 0 55/461113, fax 055/461353
Located in the Serra de Marão, this extremely peaceful pousada was
opened in 1942 and so is one of the oldest establishments of this
kind.

10 Pousada da Ria (C; 19 r., SP, T)
P-3870 Murtosa (Torreira); tel. 0 34/838332, fax 034/838333
On the Aveiro lagoon, not too far from the beach. Angling and water
sports. Ideal for relaxing or as a base for a sightseeing trip to Aveiro.

11 Pousada da Senhora das Neves (C; 21 r.)
P-6350 Almeida; tel. 071/574283, fax 071/574320
In an historical fortress.

12 Pousada de Santo António (B; 13 r., SP)
P-3570 Águeda (Serém); tel. 034/523230, fax 034/523192
One of the very first pousadas (opened in 1942). On the highest hill
overlooking the Vouga valley.

13 Pousada de São Jéronimo (B; 12 r., SP)
P-3475 Caramulo; tel. 032/861291, fax 032/861640
Attractive house with a large park.

14 Pousada de Santa Bárbara (C; 16 r., T)
P-3400 Oliveira do Hospital (Póvoa das Quartas); tel. 038/59551,
fax 038/59645
A mountain pousada, with a magnificent view over the Serra da
Estrela.
Very quiet location.

15 Pousada de São Lourenço (B; 20 r.)
P-6260 Manteigas; tel. 075/982450, fax 075/982453
From this pousada, housed in a 1948 granite building, there are
excursions into the Serra da Estrela.

16 Pousada de Santa Cristina (C; 45 r., SP, T)
P-3150 Condeixa-a-Nova; tel. 039/941286, fax 039/943097
Near the ruins of the Roman town of Conimbriga and not very far
from the famous university town of Coimbra.

17 Pousada de Monsanto (B; 10 r.)
P-6060 Monsanto IDN; tel. 077/314471, fax 077/314481
With its narrow streets and alleyways and granite-built houses
Monsanto has become known as "the Portuguese village".

18 Pousada do Mestre Afonso Domingues (C; 21 r.)
P-2440 Batalha; tel. 044/765260, fax 044/765247
Luxury hotel with a highly recommended restaurant.

19 Pousada de São Pedro (C; 24 r.)
P-2300 Tomar (Castelo do Bode); tel. 049/381175, fax 049/381176
Above the Rio Zêzere, on the Castel do Bode dam. Fishing and water
sports on one of Portugal's largest artificial lakes.

20 Pousada de Santa Maria (C SUP; 29 r.)
P-7330 Marvão; tel. 045/93201, fax 045/93202
In this pousada in the medieval atmosphere of Marvão it is easy to
imagine one has gone back in time.

21 Pousada de Flor-da-Rosa (CH; 24 r., SP)
P-7430 Crato; tel. 045/997210, fax 045/997212
A luxurious pousada in an old convent.

22 Pousada do Castelo (CH; 9 r.)
P-2510 Óbidos; tel. 062/959105, fax 062/959148
In the *castelo* at Óbidos, once the favourite summer residence of the
kings of Portugal. Ranks as one of the best pousadas.

23 Pousada de São Miguel (C; 32 r.)
P-7470 Sousel; tel. 068/551160, fax 068/551155
Opened in 1992. Anyone spending the night here should enjoy peace
and quiet.

24 Pousada da Rainha Santa Isabel (CH; 33 r., SP)
P-7101 Estremoz Codex; tel. 068/332075, fax 068/332079
In Estremoz castle. A most stylish pousada with valuable antique
furniture.

25 Pousada de Santa Luzia (C, 25 r., SP, T)
P-7350 Elvas; tel. 068/622194, fax 068/622127
The first pousada, opened on April 19th 1942. Very tastefully
appointed with antique furniture.

26 Pousada dos Lóios (CH; 32 r., SP)
P-7000 Évora; tel. 066/24051, fax 066/27248
In the centre of Évora, in an old convent dating from 1485, with traces
of Manueline decoration.

27 Pousada de Dona Maria I (CH; 26 r.)
P-2745 Queluz-Lisboa; tel. 01/4356158, fax 01/4356189
This pousada at the charming Rococo palace of Queluz was first
opened in 1995. As might be expected, everything is very stylish, and
the cuisine in the "Cozinha Velha" restaurant (in the old palace
kitchen) receives high praise.

28 Pousada de Palmela (CH; 28 r.)
P-2950 Palmela; tel. 01/2351226, fax 01/2330440
Accommodation within historic walls – far from any hurly-burly.
Superb view.

29 Pousada de São Filipe (CH; 14 r.)
P-2900 Setúbal; tel. 065/523844, fax 065/532538
Housed in the Castelo de São Filipe; with a magnificent view of the
funnel-shaped mouth of the Rio Sado, which flows around the town
of Setúbal and the Tróia promontory. Every comfort.

30 Pousada do Vale de Gaio (B; 13 r., SP)
    P-7595 Torrão; tel. 065/669610, fax 065/669545
    Above the dam in the Vale do Gaio, surrounded by magnificent
    countryside. Fishing, water sports and shooting.

31 Pousada de Castelo de Alvito (CH; 20 r., SP)
    P-7920 Alvito; tel. 084/485343, fax 084/485383
    In the 15th c. castle.

32 Pousada de São Tiago (B; 8 r., SP)
    P-7540 Santiago do Cacém; tel. 069/22459, fax 069/22459
    Friendly and cosy country house with a beautiful garden.

33 Pousada de Quinta da Ortiga (B; 21 r., SP)
    P-7540 Santiago do Cacém; tel. 069/22871, fax 069/22073
    Very suitable for an overnight stop on the journey between Lisbon
    and the Algarve. Also ideal for a longer and relaxing.stay.

34 Pousada de São Francisco (CH; 35 r., SP, T)
    P-7800 Beja; tel. 084/328441, fax 084/329143
    This pousada in the little town's old Franciscan monastery is one of
    the most beautiful in Portugal.

35 Pousada de São Gens (C; 18 r., SP, T)
    P-7830 Serpa; tel. 084/53724, fax 084/53337
    This pleasant house lies somewhat outside the small old town.

36 Pousada de Santa Clara (C; 19 r., SP)
    P-7665 Santa Clara-a-Velha; tel. 083/882250, fax 083/882402
    At the Santa Clara-a-Velha dam, in an old engineer's house. Not
    luxurious, but quiet and pleasant service. Fishing, water sports and
    shooting.

37 Pousada do Infante (C SUP; 39 r., SP, T)
    P-8650 Sagres; tel. 082/624220, fax 082/624225
    Named after Henry the Navigator, this seems like the end of the
    world. The surrounding countryside is bare and rocky and there are
    frequent strong winds – and yet the atmosphere near the Cabo de
    São Vicente is fantastic.

38 Pousada de São Brás (C; 24 r., SP, T)
    P-8150 São Brás de Alportel (please contact reservations for
    details)
    Located in the mountains; very quiet. Restaurant. Fishing and water
    sports

    Central reservations office:
    Tel. 091/765131 or 765658

Pousadas on
Madeira

39 Pousada dos Vinháticos (B; 15 r.)
    P-9350 Ribeira Brava; tel. 091/952344, fax 091/952540
    Built of dark basalt. 37km/23 miles from Funchal, high above the
    wide valley of the Serra d'Agua. With a beautiful panoramic
    restaurant. Long mountain walks are possible.

40 Pousada do Pico do Arieiro (C; 25 r.)
    P-9006 Funchal Codex; tel. 091/230110, fax 091/228611
    20km/12½ miles from Funchal, in one of Madeira's highest regions
    (1800m/5900ft). There is a superb view of the countryside from the
    large terrace. Spacious dining room which can be heated by three
    open fires.

41 Pousada Casa de Santo Antão (5 r.)
P-9240 São Vicente, Seixal; tel. 091/854210, fax 091/854212
On the north coast of the main island, in the fishing village of Seixal,
50km/31 miles north of Funchal. All the rooms have a view of the
rocky bay.

Public Holidays

January 1st	New Year's Day
February	Shrove Tuesday (often including the week before)
March/April	Good Friday
April 25th	Liberation Day (anniversary of the Carnation Revolution on April 25th 1974)
May 1st	Labour Day
May/June	Feast of Corpus Christi
June 10th	Camões Day (anniversary of the poet's death on June 10th 1580)
August 15th	Feast of the Assumption
October 5th	Republic Day (fall of the monarchy on October 5th 1910)
November 1st	All Saints Day
December 1st	Independence Day (anniversary of the restoration of the independent kingdom of Portugal on December 1st 1640 after expulsion of the Spaniards)
December 8th	Feast of the Immaculate Conception
December 25th	Christmas Day

Radio and Television

Portuguese Radio

In the summer Radiodifusão Portuguesa, the Portuguese radio service, RDF, broadcasts daily bulletins of news and information for visitors (in English at 8.15am, French at 8.30 and German at 8.45) on 1034 and 782 kHz (medium wave) and 94.3 MHz (VHF).

Broadcast messages for visitors

In cases of extreme emergency the Portuguese radio service will transmit messages for visitors to Portugal; details of this service can be obtained from the police and motoring organisations.

Television

Portuguese television transmits many English-language films in the original version with Portuguese sub-titles. Many of the larger hotels also have satellite TV.

Railways

Portuguese railways are run by a semi-State owned company, Companhia dos Caminhos de Ferro Portugueses, or CP. There are "comboios tranvias", local trains, "comboios regionais", regional trains, "comboios directos", intercity trains, and "comboios rápidos", express trains. Most trains have first and second class, and some of the coaches have old-style interiors. The frequency and punctuality of trains is very much on a par with the rest of Europe, although it has greatly improved recently; many services are very crowded on Friday and Sunday nights.

Apart from around Lisbon and Oporto the rail network is rather sparse (see map of Air Services and Railways on page 347). However, the routes run through some truly wonderful scenery, as on the Douro line for example.

Rail network

This journey starts from the São Bento station in Oporto; after 2½ hours the train reaches Régua station – the terminus for many trains. However, it is worthwhile going on from here to Pinhão and Tua, from where a narrow gauge line winds its way through some superb countryside to Mirandela.

Rail fares in Portugal are relatively low. At smaller stations the ticket office often only opens an hour before the train leaves. For local trains the journey has to be within two hours of having bought the ticket. One-way tickets are only valid for the date of purchase. Tickets can only be bought in advance at the stations in Lisbon and Oporto.

Rail fares

Children under four travel free and children between four and twelve travel half-price.

Tourist tickets, which are non-transferable, are available and permit the holder to travel anywhere in the country for one, two or three weeks. There are also reduced rates for families, groups, senior citizens, etc. Further details can be had from the Portuguese Tourist Office (see Information), from the information kiosks on railway stations or from the Companhia dos Caminhos de Ferro Portugueses, Edificio Principal, Santa Apolónia, 1100 Lisbon; tel. 01/8884025.

See Getting to Portugal

Motorail

Along the narrow gauge lines (some of which are no longer in use) some Railway Museums have been set up in recent years. Vintage locomotives and carriages can be seen in, for example, Arco de Baúlhe (1905 steam locomotive, dining cars, a simple passenger coach, luggage vans), Bragança, Chaves, Macinhata do Vough and Lousado.

Railway museums

Restaurants

A number of restaurants, especially the good-class ones, are closed on Sundays and public holidays. At the better class establishments it is usually advisable to book in advance. The food in simple eating places is often as good as in restaurants with more elaborate decor.

Tip

Many Portuguese restaurants open for lunch between noon and 2pm and then again in the evenings from 6 or 7pm. There is usually no problem in obtaining an evening meal up to 10pm.

Opening times

Those just seeking light refreshments can readily obtain toast, filled rolls or sandwiches or typical Portuguese snacks (see Food and Drink) in many cafés and bars.

Snacks

Bremen: Av. Sacadura Cabral 19; tel. 089/515659
As the name suggest, "mine host" is German, offering German and Portuguese specialities. From the terrace on the second floor there is a view of the beach and fishermen.

Albufeira

A Ruina: Cais Herculano; tel. 089/512094
Freshly caught fish and sea-food. Nice view of the "Fishermen's Beach" from the roof restaurant. Giant-sized starters!

Vila Joya: on the road to Praia da Galé; tel. 089/591795
This restaurant has a German chef and ranks among the best in Portugal.

Restaurants

Amarante

Casa do Zé de Calçada: Rua 31 de Janeiro 79; tel. 055/422023
Beautiful terrace by the river. Very well run, but not cheap.

Aveiro

A Conzinha do Rei: Rua Dr. Manuel das Neves 65; tel. 034/26802
Top restaurant, with prices to match. Fabulous choice of sea-food dishes. Very large dining-room.

Azores

Coliseu: Avenida Roberto Ivens, Ponta Delgada (São Miguel)
Generous portions, freshly prepared, good service – but somewhat lacking in comfort and rather noisy.

Beira Mar: Rua de São João, Angra do Heroismo (Terceira)
In an old urban palace. Excellent, good service, cheap.

Capitolio: Rua Cons. Medeiros 23, Horta (Faial)
Specialities include fish dishes. Ideal for the larger appetite.

Barcelos

Turismo: Rua Duques de Bragança; tel. 053/811479
With terrace, from which there is a fine view of the river. Regional dishes. Excellent.

Beja

Os Infantes: Rua dos Infantes 14; tel. 084/322789
In the historic quarter of Beja.

Inácio: Campo das Hortas; tel. 053/613225
A typical eating place, with an open fire burning on cold days. The old wooden ceiling and granite walls make it friendly and cosy.

Bragança

Restaurante Marisqueira; Avenida do Sabor; tel. 073/322494
A simple, cheap restaurant – the fishcakes are superb.

Caldas de Monchique

Paraiso da Montanha; tel. 082/912150
Specialities include home-cured ham and chicken with piripiri. Superb view.

Cascais

Porto de Santa Maria; Estrada do Guincho; tel. 01/4870240
This is "the" establishment for those who like sea-food. The wines are also of the finest, and the restaurant has without doubt the region's best cellar. A glance at the visitors' book will give an idea of the quality of its clientele – the likes of Mick Jagger, Plácido Domingo and Dustin Hoffman have patronised the restaurant.

O Batel: Travessa das Flores 4; tel. 01/4830215
A widely-known restaurant, friendly atmosphere, specialises in fish dishes.

Reijos: Rua Frederico Aroucha 35; tel. 01/4830311
Recommendable cuisine, moderate prices.

Chaves

Ponte Romana: Rua da Ponte; tel. 076/322712
From the terrace there is a fine view of the nearby river. Specialises in ham dishes.

Coimbra

Dom Pedro: Avenida Emidio Navarro 58; tel. 039/829108
Attractively appointed. Specialities include trout and cod dishes. Service could be better.

Real das Canas: Vila Mendes 7; tel. 039/814877
Traditional cooking, tastefully prepared. Beautiful view of the Old Town.

Elvas

Dom Quixote: Pedras Negras; tel. 068/622014
3km/2 miles outside the town, on the road to Lisbon. The best establishment in Elvas. Excellent cod.

Cabana do Pescador: Rua 5 de Outubro; tel. 061/863246   **Ericeira**
Ostentatious decor. Friendly establishment, regional dishes, large choice
     of fish, prices modest.

A Cabana: Rotunda da Praia da Seca; tel. 02/7341322   **Espinho**
Terrace, also snack bar.

A Choupana: in the São João district of Estoril, Avenida Marginal 5579.   **Estoril**
Tel. 01/4683099
A simple establishment, delectable fish dishes.

Dom Pepe: in the Parede district, Avenida Marginal; tel. 01/4570636
Beautiful view over Estoril/Cascais Bay.

English Bar: Estrada Marginal; tel. 01/4680413
International and Portuguese cuisine, rustic English decor.

Ze Varunca: Avenida Tomaz Alcaide   **Estremoz**
A new, modern building, good selection of meat and fish dishes.

Cozinha de Santo Humberto: Rua da Moeda 39; tel. 066/24251   **Évora**
An expensive restaurant which has won several prizes. Food is served in
     a beautifully converted vaulted cellar. Particularly delicious – pork with
     clams.

O Fialho: Travessa das Mascarenhas 16; tel. 066/23079
Alentejo cuisine prepared with great imagination. The two brothers who
     run the establishment are to date the only Portuguese restaurateurs to
     be awarded a gold medallion by the Ministry of Tourism for their ser-
     vices to the tourist industry.

Cidade Velha: Rua Domingos Guieiro 19; tel. 089/27145   **Faro**
In an 18th c. building with Biedermeier chairs. Not a wide choice of
     dishes, but exquisitely prepared. Not many tables, but extremely cosy
     and intimate; not cheap, but highly recommended.

Dois Irmãos: Largo Terneiro do Bispo 13; tel. 089/803912
Faro's oldest restaurant (opened 1925). Portuguese cuisine; very good
     value for money.

Monte do Casal: in the Estói district; tel. 089/91503
Pleasant atmosphere, pretty terrace.

Teimoso: in Buarcos, Estrada do Cabo Mondego; tel. 033/422785   **Figueira da Foz**
Popular with the local inhabitants. Good food at average prices.

Vira Bar: Largo Condessa do Juncal; tel. 053/414116   **Guimarães**
Good salads and pizzas at attractive prices. On the upper floor there is a
     restaurant of the higher price category.

Veneza: Avenida 25 de Abril 74; tel. 082/760183   **Lagos**
One of the town's most pleasant restaurants. Very good service, tasty
     food, average price category.

Dom Sebastião: Rua 25 de Abril 20; tel. 082/762795   **Leiria**
Stylish, rustic decor, and the food is a sight for sore eyes.

Tromba Rija: Rua Prof. Portelas 22 (Marrazes); tel. 044/855072
In the "Stiff Trunk" there is no printed menu. There is a large selection
     of *entradas* (hors d'öuvres) laid out in an inner courtyard. The superb
     main dishes are served in a pleasant and cosy restaurant.

Restaurants

Lisbon

Tágide: Largo da Academia das Belas Artes 18; tel. 01/3420720
Elegant interior with antique tile-pictures. A beautiful view of the city and river. Portuguese and international cuisine. Expensive.

Tavares: Rua da Misericórdia 37; tel. 01/3421112
Luxurious and prestigious and Lisbon's oldest restaurant, where the visitor feels transported back into the 19th c. On the upper floor is a self-service restaurant (separate entrance). Closed Saturday and Sunday lunch.

Cervejaria da Trindade: Rua Nova da Trindade 20; tel. 01/323506
In a former convent, with *azulejos* (tile-pictures) on the walls. The fish dishes are excellent. Good value for money.

Faz Figura: Rua do Paraiso 15; tel. 01/8868981
Terrace with view of the Tagus. Higher price category.

Sua Excelelencia: Rua do Conde 38; tel. 01/3903614
Exclusive atmosphere, interesting clientele, high prices, one of Lisbon's most attractive restaurants.

Loulé

Avenida: Avenida José da Costa Mealha 13; tel. 089/462106
Good Portuguese cooking, friendly service.

Madeira

Les Faunes: Monumental 139, Funchal; tel. 091/717171
The finest restaurant on the island. French cuisine.

Caravela: Avenida do mar 15, Funchal; tel. 091/228464
Close to the harbour. Popular with tourists both for its food and the viewing terrace on the 3rd floor. Fish dishes and international cuisine.

Cachalote: Porto Moniz; tel. 091/853180
Built into the lava rock face. Specialities are fish and sea-food.

Monchique

Paraiso da Montanha: tel. 082/912150
Ideal interim stop when making an excursion from the Algarve into the mountainous hinterland.

Óbidos

Dom João V: on the road to Caldas da Rainha; tel. 062/959134
Wide choice of food, large dining room, very busy at weekends.

Oporto/Porto

Portucale: Rua da Alegria 598; tel. 02/2007861
On the 13th floor of a multi-storied building, with a panoramic view over Oporto's roof-tops. The town's most prestigious restaurant. Luxury category.

O Escondidinho: Rua Passos Manuel 144; tel. 02/2001079
Another prestigious restaurant with local and French cuisine. Furnished in typical Portuguese style, it seats only 50, so reservations are recommended.

Tripeiro: Rua Passos Manuel 195; tel. 02/2005886
A typical, simple establishment. Centrally situated. As well as tripas (tripe and offal) there are also fish and meat dishes. Not always good value for money.

Ponte de Lima

Tulha: Rua Formosa; tel. 058/942879
Good, substantial country cooking. Popular with the local inhabitants. Good value for money.

Portalegre

Alpendre: Rua 31 de Janeiro 19; tel. 045/21611
Nothing out of the ordinary, but the only better-class restaurant in the town.

O Bicho: Largo Gil Eanes 12; tel. 082/22977
A rich selection of sea-food. Upper price category. Pleasant service.
Sometimes a bit noisy.

Portimão

A Casa de Jantar: Rua de Santa Isabel 14; tel. 082/422072
International cuisine.

Falésia: Avenida Tomás Cabreira; tel. 082/23524
With terrace. Average prices.

Praia da Rocha

Alphonso's: Centro Comercial Abertura Mar; tel. 089/314614
Prestigious, with prices to match.

Quarteira

Cozinha Velha: Largo do Palácio; tel. 01/4350232
Housed in the former palace kitchen. Exquisite cuisine. No need to ask if
prices are high!

Queluz

Fortaleza do Beliche: on the Cabo de São Vicente road; tel. 082/64124
High above the sea, in wonderful countryside. Sophisticated.

Sagres

O Rui: on the road to Algoz; tel. 082/443106
Good Portuguese cooking. Fine view of the river and mountain from the
terrace.

Solar de São Pedro: Praça D. Fernando II 12; tel. 01/9231860
A small, but very fine restaurant. Portuguese cuisine with the "French touch".

Sintra

Imperial: Rua José Padinha
Recommended cuisine. Very popular. The "chicken à la maison" is particularly delicious.

Tavira

Ponto de Encontro: Praça Dr. António Padinha 39; tel. 081/323730
Simple establishment with a friendly, cosy atmosphere. Fish specialities.

Bela Vista: Fonte do Choupo 6; tel. 049/312870
Attractive decor. Food is also served outside. Beautiful view; situated
near the bridge, on the river bank. Standard dishes on the menu.

Tomar

Chico Elias: Algarvias 70; tel. 049/311067
Best restaurant in town. Known far and wide for its cuisine.

São Gabriel: on the road between Vale do Lobo and Quinta do Lago. Tel.
089/394521
High class, sophisticated restaurant. With terrace.

Vale do Lobo

Os 3 Potes: Beco dos Fornos 7–9; tel. 058/829928
Rustic decor and good country food. Very pleasant service.

Viana da Castelo

Casa d'Armas: Largo 5 de Outubro 30; tel. 058/824999
The best restaurant in town. The prices are surprisingly moderate.

Costa Verde: Rua Monserrate 411–413; tel. 058/829240
Popular with the local inhabitants.

Edmundo: Avenida da República 55; tel. 081/544689
On the riverside road. A simple establishment.

**Vila Real de
Santo António**

Shopping and Souvenirs

In Portugal many folk-art products are still items of everyday use. This is
particularly true of pottery and ceramics which vary in form and style
according to where they are made, and which range from the blackish

Ceramics

ware for everyday use to brightly painted ornaments. The famous multi-hued clay Barcelos cockerel has come to be a symbol for Portugal as a whole.

Azulejos

Azulejos, the glazed, decorative, often blue-coloured tiles, are a form of ceramics dating back to Moorish times. Nowadays, however, the tendency is very much for those on sale to have been mass-produced. Older examples can often be found in antique shops.

Arraiolos carpets

The town of Arraiolos specialises in colourful embroidered woollen carpets. These are for sale and on display in Arraiolos town hall, but can also be bought throughout Alentejo, especially in Évora.

Other handicrafts

Beautiful lace is made all along the coast, while inland hand-woven blankets, cloth, etc. are produced. Filigree work in gold and silver wire, sometimes forming part of the traditional costume, is another popular souvenir.

Fine carvings, basket-work and wrought-iron objects are also on offer.

Port

Port is undoubtedly a favourite souvenir from Portugal. Although the best known makes are not much cheaper than they are in the UK, the range of different kinds and qualities of port is much greater. A tour of the port-wine lodges in Vila Nova de Gaia (see Wine) usually includes port-tasting.

Music

Fado tapes and CDs are certainly a good souvenir of Portugal. They can be bought cheaply at most of the weekly markets, but really good fado is for the most part obtainable only in specialist shops. Highly recommended are recordings by Alfredo Marceneiro or Carlos Ramos, with the best known Portuguese *fadista* Amália Rodrigues; some of her historic items are also now obtainable on CD. More recent fado compositions are by Carlos do Carmo, Rão Kyão (flute and saxophone), Carlos Paredos and Pedro Caldeira Cabral play purely instrumental fado. The Madredeus Group have become known world-wide; their work incorporates elements of Portuguese folk-music. Also very popular is the music of the legendary José Afonso. Dulce Pontes interprets traditional Fado and Portuguese folk music.

Spas

Towards the end of the 19th c. Portugal's spas were the most elegant in Europe, with stylish pump-rooms and casinos, and exclusive hotels and restaurants. It has continued to uphold this tradition and the Portuguese mainland and the Azores together have over 40 spas. In the summer, in particular, more than 150,000 people go to a spa for a one or two-week cure. Most of the spas have, however, become somewhat less grand than they were at the turn of the century.

Selection

A selection of these spas is listed below:

Caldas da Felgueira
Skin, respiratory passages, rheumatism.

Caldas da Rainha
Rheumatism, respiratory passages, gynaecological conditions

Caldas de Chaves
Stomach and intestines, liver, rheumatism, metabolic disorders

Ceramics are a popular souvenir from Portugal ▶

Sport

Caldas de Manteigas
Rheumatism

Caldas de Monchique
Stomach and intestines, liver, rheumatism, respiratory passages

Caldas de São Jorge
Rheumatism, skin, respiratory passages

Caldas de Vizela
Rheumatism, skin, respiratory passages, gynaecological disorders

Caldas do Gerês
Liver, diabetes

Caldelas
Stomach and intestines, skin

Curia
Kidneys and urinary tract, rheumatism, hypertension

Fonte Santa de Monfortinho
Liver, kidneys and urinary tract, skin

Luso
Kidneys and urinary tract, rheumatism, skin, circulation, hypertension

Melgaço
Diabetes

Monção
Rheumatism, respiratory passages, bronchitis

Pedras Salgadas
Stomach and intestines, liver, diabetes

Piedade
Stomach and intestines, liver, skin

Termas de Monte Real
Stomach and intestines, liver

Termas de São Pedro do Sul
Rheumatism, skin, respiratory passages, gynaecological disorders

Termas de São Vicente
Respiratory passages, rheumatism, hypertension

Vidago
Stomach and intestines, liver, metabolic disorders

Vimeiro
Stomach and intestines, liver, skin

Sport

Angling, sea fishing

Portugal is a land of opportunity for anglers. There is still very good fishing near the coast and inland, in the lakes and river, while deep sea fishing is to be had at Sagres, in the Algarve (including the chance to fish for shark), and off Madeira and the Azores.

The best bathing beaches are in and around those places listed in the entry for Beaches. Nearly all the big hotels also have their own swimming pools.

Swimming, bathing

See entry

Golf

Portugal (particularly the Algarve and the area around Lisbon) is ideal both for riding holidays and for those who just want to spend a few hours on horseback. Most riding stables also give tuition.

Horse riding

Portugal has over 20 clubs for clay pigeon or target shooting. Most are in the Algarve (Albufeira, Faro, Portimão, Praia da Falésia, Vale do Lobo and Vilamoura) or on the Costa Verde at Espinho, Ofir, Póvoa de Varzim and Viana do Castelo, as well as Estoril.

Shooting

The Azores have three shooting clubs.

Portugal also has some extensive hunting grounds (in the Alentejo, in the Beira provinces in central Portugal, in Trás-os-Montes). Animals which can be shot include partridge, snipe, quail, hare and red deer.

Many places have sailing clubs which hire out boats and offer courses both for beginners and more advanced sailors. Besides Vilamoura in the Algarve, probably the finest marina of them all, with the best facilities for boats and crew, there are lots of smaller harbours and anchorages all along the Portuguese coast. The best places to stay on a Portuguese sailing holiday are in the Algarve, at Albufeira, Armação de Pêra, Alvor, Lagos, Monte Gordo, Portimão, Praia da Falésia, Praia da Oura, Praia da Rocha, Quinta do Lago, Tavira, Vale do Lobo and, of course, Vilamoura, as well as Cascais and Estoril or Sesimbra, plus, on the Costa Verde, Póvoa de Varzim and Viana do Castelo.

Sailing

There is also good sailing to be had around Madeira and the Azores.

There are many places in the Algarve for learning how to surf and hiring surfboards. Surfing is becoming increasingly popular from the beaches on the Estoril coast; Carcavelos is ideal for beginners, while Guincho and Figueira da Foz are is a challenge to the more expert. There is surfing around Madeira as well.

Surfing

Scuba divers who take their own equipment with them will find scenic bays and still virtually untouched diving grounds in the south-west of the Algarve around Sagres, the Costa Verde and the Costa de Prata. To hire equipment and have one or two hours tuition the best place to go is the Algarve where there are new scuba diving centres in Albufeira, Alvor, Lagos, Monte Gordo, Praia da Falésia and Vilamoura. The most fascinating diving grounds are between 5 and 30m/16 and 98ft, so snorkellers can also share in the discovery of this wonderful undersea world.

Scuba diving

There are tennis courts at nearly all Portugal's big hotels, many of them with floodlighting (see the entries for Hotels and Pousadas). There are also public tennis courts as well as the special tennis centres run by professionals, the Roger Taylor Tennis Centre in Vale do Lobo in the Algarve being one of the best. The area around Cascais and Estoril is also particularly well endowed with tennis facilities. On Madeira and the Azores it is possible to play on the hotel courts.

Tennis

The island of Madeira is a veritable rambler's paradise. However, rambling is becoming increasingly popular on the Portuguese mainland as well, and a few tour operators are already offering organised walking holidays in the Algarve (Serra de Monchique). For solo travellers the Peneda-Gerês National Park is also a particularly attractive terrain.

Rambling

There are water ski centres where equipment can be hired and tuition is given in the major tourist centres of the Algarve, Cascais, Estoril and Sesimbra, and on the Costa Verde, in Ofir, Vila do Conde and Póvoa de Varzim, as well as Madeira and the Azores.

Water ski-ing

Taxis

Taxis in Portugal, which in towns and cities are cream colour (older ones are black and green), tend to be considerably cheaper than in some other parts of Europe. They are fitted with meters and it is wise to check that these are at zero before starting a journey. Outside built-up areas the fare is calculated by the kilometre, and even on one-way journeys the passenger has to pay for the return trip.

Extra is charged for baggage over 30kg/67lb (up to 50%) and for journeys at night.

It is customary to give a tip of 10 to 15% of the fare.

Telephone

It is possible to make international calls from public call boxes in Portugal, but these only take coins for 10, 20, 50 or 100 escudos. It is therefore necessary to have a good supply of these coins before making such calls. For longer calls it is more convenient to telephone from a post office or one of the public exchanges found in the major towns and tourist centres. Here it is possible to get enough change or to pay after making the call. Many telephones now take phone-cards; the latter can be bought at post offices, most newsagents or from the telephone companies. Phone-card telephones also take credit cards. Cheap rate overseas calls can be made between 8pm and 8am every day and at weekends.

Hotels add large surcharges to the normal phone-call rates.

International codes

From the United Kingdom to Portugal 00351
From the USA or Canada to Portugal 011351

From Portugal to the United Kingdom 0044
From Portugal to the USA or Canada 061

The initial "0" of the local area code should be omitted.

Time

Mainland and Madeira

Portugal is on Greenwich Mean Time, but 1 hour ahead of GMT from late March to late October.

Azores

The Azores are always one hour behind mainland Portugal.

Tipping

Service is included in the bill for hotels and restaurants. Tipping is optional, but a tip ("gorjeta") of 5 to 10% of the total bill is always acceptable. An appropriate tip is expected for special services, tour guides, hairdressers, room maids, porters and taxi drivers, etc.; attendants at tourist sites and ushers at the theatre, cinema, bullfights, etc. also expect a tip.

Traffic Regulations

See Motoring

AVEIRO																									
380	**BEJA**																								
120	500	**BRAGA**																							
320	560	230	**BRAGANÇA**																						
345	180	470	450	**CAIA**																					
216	254	330	310	150	**CASTELO BRANCO**																				
64	333	170	314	300	160	**COIMBRA**																			
306	78	425	484	100	175	255	**ÉVORA**																		
499	152	620	697	330	455	215		**FARO**																	
136	256	261	402	206	156	90	178	380	**FÁTIMA**																
315	207	421	400	93	91	251	130	340	160	**GALEGOS**															
180	360	260	203	255	106	169	282	495	259	199	**GUARDA**														
121	265	238	380	231	170	67	190	390	23	183	236	**LEIRIA**													
242	193	361	510	237	250	196	150	300	136	253	365	128	**LISBOA**												
310	181	410	390	68	80	240	104	317	150	24	188	170	228	**PORTALEGRE**											
68	450	53	255	415	277	118	370	575	208	366	220	185	314	360	**PORTO**										
355	600	260	30	487	339	343	510	727	433	430	233	410	539	419	284	**QUINTANILHA**									
185	195	310	450	204	169	138	118	300	61	160	281	70	79	145	254	479	**SANTARÉM**								
285	315	388	370	207	59	218	234	450	215	150	165	226	304	136	335	396	225	**SEGURA**							
290	139	417	560	190	270	246	108	250	240	218	372	180	50	192	362	590	121	324	**SETÚBAL**						
194	580	91	323	538	407	250	502	702	338	497	348	314	443	484	123	350	384	467	492	**VALENÇA DO MINHO**					
140	524	49	280	480	355	194	448	648	283	444	295	261	390	434	71	310	331	409	440	53	**VIANA DO CASTELO**				
185	512	107	138	413	264	207	440	661	300	355	160	271	403	344	117	168	340	320	450	198	155	**VILA REAL**			
506	125	625	685	306	378	451	203	52	381	330	485	387	317	306	580	714	318	436	267	707	650	640	**V. REAL DE SANTO ANTÓNIO**		
440	65	563	600	237	292	394	140	202	318	245	399	326	254	220	512	680	256	350	203	640	587	580	153	**VILA VERDE DE FICALHO**	
230	410	312	207	307	156	216	333	547	304	247	49	285	414	236	266	228	323	214	421	397	344	207	533	447	**VILAR FORMOSO**
95	450	187	238	340	190	96	370	580	187	283	85	164	293	270	131	267	233	250	343	263	210	111	570	483	135	**VISEU**

Distances on the Portuguese mainland
between important towns and frontier crossings
(in km)

Transport

There are bus services in the towns and cities. Lisbon and Oporto also have trams, and these provide an unusual but excellent way of exploring both Portuguese big cities. Lisbon has an Underground as well, the Metro, that consists of four lines serving 36 stations. Another special feature of the Portuguese capital is the "elevadores", the lift-cum-funicular that carries people from one to the other of Lisbon's widely differing levels.

Urban Public Transport

The fact that rail services are rather limited means that coaches provide the main form of public transport. The intercity coaches, the "expressos", cover long distances in a relatively short time.

Coaches

Regular boat trips operate from the tourist centres along the Algarve.

From Oporto there are boat trips on the Douro (see A to Z, Douro Valley). Regular ferries ply from several landing stages in Lisbon to and from the south bank of the Tagus.

A cargo boat leaves Lisbon from time to time for Funchal on Madeira. Information and bookings can be obtained from Empresa de Navegação Madeirense (Rua de São Julião 5,1°, P-1100 Lisbon; tel. 01/8870121). A scheduled service operates several times a day between Madeira and the neighbouring island of Porto Santo.

There is no regular shipping service between Lisbon and the Azores.

Shipping

See entry

Air Travel

See entry

Car Rental

Travel Documents

Passports and
Visas

UK, US and Canadian citizens (and nationals of many other countries) only need a passport to enter Portugal. They do not require visas for visits of up to 90 days. This period may be extended by applying, before the expiry of the initial period, to the Foreigners' Registration Service, Avenida António Augusto de Aguiar 20, Lisbon 1050; tel. 01/3143112, or one of its regional branches.

Visitors intending to take up employment in Portugal need a visa and a work permit.

Vehicle
Documents

Foreign registered cars may enter Portugal for any period up to 6 months on production of the registration documents and a "green card", the international insurance certificate that will be required in the event of an accident. A British driving licence is valid in Portugal for up to 6 months, and drivers should have their licences with them.

Drivers taking vehicles into Portugal which are not registered in their name must have a letter of authority from the owner which should be officially recognised by the Portuguese Consulate General.

Caravanners should have an inventory – in English, French or Portuguese – of the main contents of their caravan or trailer which they can show customs officials.

Pets

In view of the strict quarantine regulations imposed on their return to Great Britain, visitors are strongly advised not to take pets to Portugal. If animals such as cats and dogs are taken, however, they need an official veterinary health certificate which has been issued shortly before departure, and a rabies vaccination certificate, giving the date of vaccination and the type of vaccine used, that has been valid for at least 30 days but no more than 12 months. Pets may not be taken to the Azores.

Water Pleasure Parks

Aquaparks, with their giant slides, diving boards, fountains, white-water rapids, etc., are still a relatively new attraction in Portugal.

Aqualino
West of Monte Gordo at Altura, on the N 125

Slide & Splash
East of Portimão at Lagoa, on the N 125

The Big One
East of Portimão at Porches, on the N 125

Pinguim
Monte Gordo, near the camp site

Atlântico Park
Near Quartiera, on the N 125

Aqua Show
Near Quarteira, on the N 396

Zoomarine
Near Guia/Albufeira, on the N 125

When to go

The spring and autumn, about mid-March to early June and early September to early November, are the best times for touring Portugal, staying on the south coast or visiting the cultural sights of Lisbon. At these times of year the weather on the Algarve is pleasantly hot and quite consistent, although it is not unusual, particularly in the north of the country, for there to be several days of continuous rain.

Mainland Portugal

For a beach holiday on the west Atlantic coast the time to go is in high summer when the persistent strong winds ensure that the temperature does not become too hot. Rain is possible even in July and August, and in the north of Portugal the water temperature never exceeds 18°C/64°F. Even the Algarve is bearable in high summer, since the temperature seldom gets above 30°C/86°F, although the fact that summer is the height of the tourist season for Portugal means that there is some over-crowding in the Algarve and particularly in the resorts around Lisbon.

Portugal's south coast has a very mild winter climate, with the minimum temperatures only dropping briefly below 10°C/50°F, and in some shel-tered places it is possible to sit in the sun even in December and January.

Since Madeira has a mild climate all the year round many people choose to go there in winter and springtime. Even in the winter months the tem-perature in Funchal never drops below 12°C/53.6°F, with the highest day-time temperatures around 20°C/68°F. There is some rainfall, but usually only in the form of brief showers; in summer there is considerably less. The sea is rarely colder than 18°C/64°F. The highest average tempera-tures occur in August, about 23°C/73°F in Funchal.

Madeira

It makes little difference whether you visit the Azores in the height of summer or the depths of winter since the fact that the islands lie on the Gulf Stream means they have an equably mild climate all the year round. The coldest month is January, with averages temperatures about 14°C/57°F, and the hottest is August, 22°C/71.6°F. However, the weather is never consistently fine in the Azores since there is high rainfall all year round, plus a persistent wind.

Azores

For a more detailed account of climatic conditions see Facts and Figures.

Climate

Wine

The climate in central and northern Portugal, where almost all the country's vineyards are concentrated, is ideal for the production of wine. The summer is long and fine, but not too hot, with some rain. The table wine produced in Portugal is just as good as its average French or Italian counterpart, even if the top wines do not stand comparison with the best in France or Italy. The exception, of course, is port.

Portugal has been a regular exporter of wine since the 15th c. In the past its main customers were the British, but the French have since over-taken them, and nowadays 40% of the port produced is drunk in France.

The steep slopes of the upper reaches of the Douro are where the grapes are grown from which the famous port is produced. The boundaries of this, the world's oldest legally defined wine-producing region, were first established by Marquês de Pombal in 1756; nowadays the area of culti-vation is about twenty times what it was then. The slate in the soil con-tributes to the characteristic taste of the wine: whereas everywhere else slate is in horizontal beds, here in the upper Douro valley it is at an angle to the earth's core of 60–90°. By day the rock does not permit the burning rays of the sun to penetrate too deeply into the ground, thus allowing the

Port

The Barcos Rabelos, once used to transport port wine

bacteria to thrive in the damp soil, but at night it acts as a cushion of warmth for the vines. Port, which takes its name from the town of Oporto, is made from partly fermented red wine fortified with brandy (about 75% wine to 25% brandy). Fermentation is inhibited by the high alcohol content of the brandy, producing a mixture of considerable strength but also with a high sugar content. The wine is taken down to Vila Nova de Gaia at Oporto to be put in store; it used to come down the river Douro on the distinctive "barcos rabelos", but is now taken by road and by lorry.

The time the port spends in store in the cask in Vila Nova de Gaia can range from two to fifty years. Wine aged in the cask is generally made up from wines from different locations, years and types of grape, blended to produce a standard quality. When it is a particularly fine year for port this is declared a vintage port, and sold as such. Vintage port is bottled after two to three years and then needs on average another fifteen years to mature in the bottle. The best recent vintages were 1955, 1963, 1970, 1977, 1980 and 1983. As a rule vintage port is sweeter than the blended wines that have been matured in the cask because port stored in casks matures much faster and loses sugar content by doing so. White port has attracted increasing attention in recent years. Made from white grapes, the storage period is distinctly more limited than for red port. There are sweeter and drier variations, with the current trend being towards the dry and extra dry white port.

While the dry port is drunk mostly as an aperitif, sweet port is famous for being served at the end of the meal. The Instituto do Vinho do Porto contributes to port's reputation by carrying out regular quality checks, and ensuring that the strict port-wine legislation is observed.

Port Tastings

Visitors to northern Portugal should be sure to visit one of the port wine lodges in Oporto's Vila Nova de Gaia. These are nearly all open Monday to Saturday (Monday to Friday in the winter), morning and afternoon, for tours and free tastings.

Wine Producing Districts in Portugal

(mainland)

- Mainly red wine
- White and red wine
- Mainly white wine
- Port

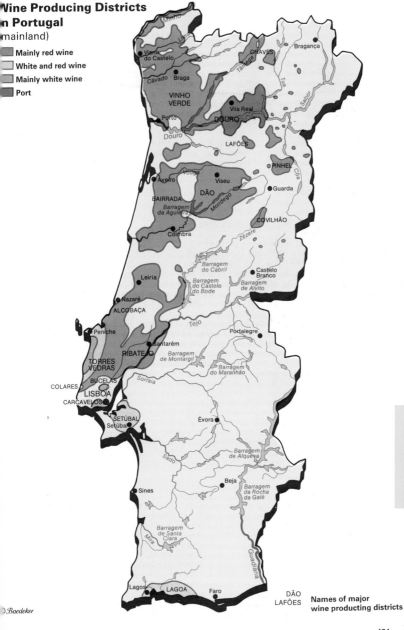

Minho

Lima

Viana do Castelo

CHAVES

Bragança

Cávado · Braga

Tâmega

VINHO VERDE

Vila Real

Porto

DOURO

Tua

Sabor

Douro

LAFÕES

PINHEL

Côa

Aveiro

Vouga

Viseu

Guarda

BAIRRADA

DÃO

Barragem da Aguieira

Mondego

COVILHÃO

Coimbra

Zêzere

Barragem do Cabril

Castelo Branco

Leiria

Barragem do Castelo do Bode

Barragem de Alvito

Nazaré

ALCOBAÇA

Tejo

Portalegre

Peniche

Santarém

RIBATEJO

Barragem de Montargil

TORRES VEDRAS

Barragem do Maranhão

COLARES

BUCELAS

Sorraia

LISBOA

CARCAVELOS

Évora

SETÚBAL

Setúbal

Sado

Sines

Barragem de Alqueva

Beja

Barragem da Rocha da Galé

Barragem de Santa Clara

Mira

Guadiana

Lagos

LAGOA

Faro

DÃO
LAFÕES Names of major
wine producing districts

©Baedeker

421

Wine

Port tastings are also held in Oporto itself in the the Solar do Vinho do Porto (Rua Entre Quintas 220; open: Mon.–Sat., 11am–11.45pm).

Vinho Verde

Vinho Verde, Portugal's best-known table wine, comes from the area north and east of Oporto. It is called "verde" (green) not because of the colour – there is red Vinho Verde as well – but from the way in which it is made. The grapes are gathered relatively early and fermented for only a short time, producing a light, rather sharp wine that carries on fermenting for a time in the bottle. The result is a fresh, often semi-sparkling wine which does not, however, keep for very long.

"Green" wines make up about 20% of Portugal's wine output. One particularly good Vinho Verde is the wine from the Alvarinho grape produced around Monção.

Bairrada

Many of the table wines from this district are the product of co-operatives. While the white wines are relatively light, with some of them further processed into sparkling wine, the red wines are dark in colour, full-bodied and more alcoholic.

Colares

Colares is a wine producing area on the coast north-west of Lisbon. The vines, some of them grown in the dunes, are protected from the wind by woven reed screens. Colares produces an excellent dark red wine, low in alcohol, and famous since the 13th c.

Dão

Both red and white grape varieties thrive equally well along the Dão River valley. The white wine is a good table wine which is best drunk young.

The red wine is dry and, when sufficiently matured, develops a heady bouquet which most closely resembles a Burgundy. The red must be aged for at least eighteen months before it is bottled, then it must rest for at least two months. Dão white wine has to be at least ten months old before it can be put on sale.

Madeira

Madeira's most famous product is the wine which takes its name from the island and which is prized as an aperitif and a dessert wine, as well as for its use in cooking. Like port, its distinctive flavour is achieved through blending. For four or five months it is submitted to a heat of 50°C/122°F, hence its special caramel savour. Madeira is made from four different grape varieties, of which Malmsey is frequently rated the best, followed by Bual, Verdelho and Sercial.

Other Wine Regions

To the east of Alcobaça, stretching south towards Lisbon, is the old province of Estremadura and its two best-known wine regions, Ribatejo and Torres Vedras, mainly producing red wine.

Wine production becomes less as you go farther south. Muscatel grapes, used mainly for dessert wines, grow well around Setúbal. In the extreme south, on the Algarve, there is another wine area producing mainly red wine with a relatively high alcohol content.

The Language of the Wine Label

vinha	vineyard
quinta	estate, "château"
adega	cellar (usually of a commercial winery)
colheita	year (vintage)
região demarcada	statutorily defined region
denominação de origem	"appellation controlée"
reserva	reserve (better quality wine)
garrafeira	"private cellar", i.e. best quality
vinho verde	"green" or young wine; regional designation for the very light red and white wines of the Minho province
vinho de mesa	table wine
vinho de consumo	*vin ordinaire*, ordinary drinking wine
maduro	old or matured

engarrafado na origem	estate/château bottled
branco	white
tinto	red
rosado	rosé
clarete	light-red or dark rosé
seco	dry
doce, adamado	sweet
espumante	sparkling
vintage	vintage port, bottled early to carry on fermenting in the bottle
late bottled vintage	port that has been in store in the cask for 6 years before bottling (see Port); lighter than "vintage"
red, ruby	relatively young port, deep red in colour, comparatively dry
tawny	honey-coloured, brownish gold port (gets its lighter colour from longer aging in the wood); lighter than Vintage

Youth Hostels

Youth hostels (pousadas de juventude) offer accommodation at reasonable prices. They are particularly suitable for young people, but Portuguese hostels have no upper age limit.

Because there are relatively few hostels it is necessary to book in advance, especially in July and August. This can be done via Movijovem, the central reservation office in Lisbon:

Movijovem
Avenida Duque d'Avila 137, P-1050 Lisbon
Tel. 01/3138820, fax 01/3528621

The address, etc. is followed by the number of beds (b.)

Youth hostels on the mainland

8970 Alcoutim; tel./fax 0 81/546004, 54 b. Canoe trips possible
Alcoutim

Praia da Areia Branca, 2530 Lourinhã; tel./fax 061/422127, 116 b.
A modern hostel situated on cliffs above a small sandy beach.
Areia Branca

Rua de Santa Margarida 6, 4700 Braga; tel./fax 053/616163, 62 b.
A quiet location near the town centre.
Braga

Rua Henrique Seco 12–14, 3000 Coimbra; tel./fax 039/822955, 85 b.
A little way out of town, very clean and very quiet.
Coimbra

Aparto 32, 4740 Esposende; tel./fax 053/981790, 85 b.
Canoe trips possible.
Foz do Cávado

Rua Lancerote Freitas 50, 8600 Lagos; tel./fax 082/761970, 62 b.
Newly furnished, in the old town.
Lagos

Largo Cândido dos Reis 7 D, 2400 Leiria; tel./fax 044/831868, 36 b.
Not far from the town centre
Leiria

Rua Andrade Corvo 46; tel./fax 01/3532696, 164 b.
A "Key Hostel", i.e. bookings can be made from other Key Hostels; built 1993.
Lisbon

Estrada Marginal (near the INATEL motel), 2780 Oeiras
Tel./fax 01/4430638, 102 b. Beach location, rustic furnishings.

Youth Hostels

Mira	Parque de Campismo Jovens, 3070 Mira; tel./fax 031/471275, 58 b.
Oporto	Rua Paulo de Gama 551, 4150 Porto; tel. 02/6177257, fax 02/6177247, 164 b. Newly built, modern youth hostel.
Penhas da Saúde	In the Serra da Estrela, Apartado 148, 6200 Covilha Tel./fax 075/335375, 160 b. In a brown wooden house, on a through road 1500m/4900ft above sea-level; cheap meals.
Portimão	Lugar do Coca Maravilhas, 8500 Portimão; tel./fax 082/491805, 180 b. About 2km/1¼ miles outside the town in the Monchique direction, 3km/ 2 miles to the beach; swimming pool.
São Martinho Alfeizerão	Near Alcobaça, Estrada Nacional 8, 2455 Alfeizerão Tel./fax 062/999506, 69 b. On the road to Alcobaça; buses run from the hostel to the beach.
Sintra	Santa Eufémia, 2710 Sintra; tel./fax 01/9241210, 56 b. In a former forester's lodge, 2km/1¼ miles above the São Pedro district of Sintra; from São Pedro it can only be reached on foot – 2km/1¼ miles uphill! – or by taxi; facilities for horse riding.
Vila Nova de Cerveira	Largo 16 de Fevreiro, 4920 Vila Nova de Cerveira Tel./fax 051/796113, 56 b.
Vila Real de S. António	Rua Dr. Sousa Martins, 8900 Vila Real de S. António Tel./fax 081/544565, 60 b. In the town centre.
Vilarinho dasFurnas	In Peneda-Gerês National Park, 4840 Terras de Bouro Tel./fax 053/351339, 122 b. Simply furnished, in wonderful surroundings; bicycles can be hired.

Index

Index

Index

Principal Sights of Tourist Interest

A map of the principal tourist sights can be found on page 430

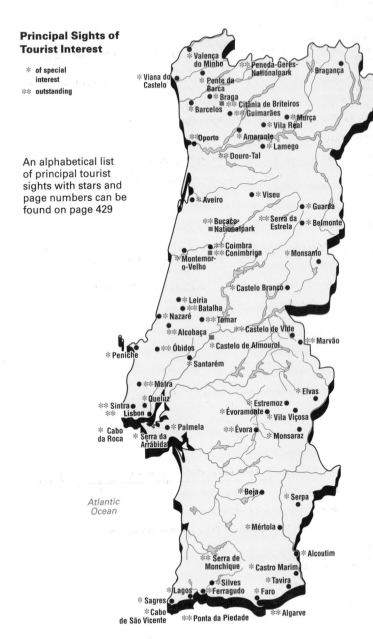

Principal Sights of Tourist Interest

* of special interest
** outstanding

An alphabetical list of principal tourist sights with stars and page numbers can be found on page 429

* Valença do Minho
** Peneda-Gerês-Nationalpark
* Bragança
* Viana do Castelo
* Ponte da Barca
* Braga
** Citânia de Briteiros
* Barcelos
** Guimarães
** Murça
* Vila Real
* Oporto
* Amarante
* Lamego
** Douro-Tal
* Aveiro
* Viseu
* Guarda
** Bучаco-Nationalpark
** Serra da Estrela
* Belmonte
** Coimbra
** Conimbriga
* Monsanto
* Montemor-o-Velho
* Castelo Branco
* Leiria
** Batalha
* Nazaré
* Tomar
* Castelo de Vide
** Alcobaça
* Castelo de Almourol
** Marvão
** Óbidos
* Peniche
* Santarém
** Mafra
* Elvas
** Sintra
* Queluz
** Lisbon
* Estremoz
* Évoramonte
* Vila Viçosa
* Cabo da Roca
* Serra da Arrábida
* Palmela
** Évora
* Monsaraz
* Beja
* Serpa
* Mértola
** Alcoutim
** Serra de Monchique
* Castro Marim
* Silves
* Tavira
* Lagos
* Ferragudo
* Faro
* Sagres
** Algarve
* Cabo de São Vicente
** Ponta da Piedade

Atlantic Ocean

©Baedeker

Imprint

153 colour photographs
32 town plans, 16 general maps, 10 ground plans, 7 special plans, 2 drawings, 1 large map of Portugal (at end of book)

Text: Rosemarie Arnold, Walter R. Arnold, Monika I. Baumgarten, Prof. D. H. Bloss, Birgit Borowski, Achim Bourmer, Werner Fauser, Prof. Dr Hans-Dieter Haas, Prof. Dr Wolfgang Hassenpflug, Dr Eva Missler, Christine Wesseley

Editorial work: Baedeker Stuttgart (Birgit Borowski)

English language edition: Alec Court

General direction: Dr Peter Baumgarten, Baedeker Stuttgart

Cartography: Franz Huber, Munich; Mairs Geographischer Verlag GmbH & Co., Ostfildern-Kemnat (large map of Portugal)

English translation: Babel Translations Norwich (Brenda Ferris) and James Hogarth

Updating and additional text: David Cocking, Margaret Court

Source of illustrations: Air Portugal, Baedeker-Archiv, Borowski, Brödel, Fauser, Fischer, Historia-Photo, Lade, Portuguese Tourist Office, Rau, Rudolf, Südbayerische Redaktionsgemeinschaft, ZEFA

Front cover: Tony Stone Images. Back cover: AA Photo Library (P. Wilson)

5th English edition 1999

© Baedeker Stuttgart
Original German edition 1998

© 1999 The Automobile Association
English language edition worldwide

Published by AA Publishing (a trading name of Automobile Association Developments Limited, whose registered office is Norfolk House, Priestley Road, Basingstoke, Hampshire RG24 9NY. Registered number 1878835).

Distributed in the United States and Canada by:
Fodor's Travel Publications, Inc.
201 East 50th Street
New York, NY 10022

A CIP catalogue record of this book is available from the British Library.

Licensed user:
Mairs Geographischer Verlag GmbH & Co.,
Ostfildern-Kemnat bei Stuttgart

Printed in Italy by G. Canale & C. S.p.A., Turin

ISBN 0 7495 1992 4

Good soup
Calde Verde (cabbage soup)
Sopa de Aguol (cream)
Caldeivada de p   (FISH)

Beef
Bifes de Cebeda.
Steak&onien slices   white
of smoked ham butter & wne

Lamb

Cordevo Assado
    Lamb with garlic

Dont have Sopa de peize
    Corn massa or
        garlic soup

English Speaking Doctors

Dr. Tony Woolfson, International
Health Centre, Bugonvillia Plaza,
Quinta do Lago. 8135 ALMANSIL
Tel (039) 396157 or at Albufeira
039 533923
Dr. Maria Alice Silva, Rua 25 de Abril nº 12,
Praia da Luz, 8600 Lagos.

(082) 788217
Dr Henri Godefroy, Edificio Riamar,
Bloco 'Pt. D., Largo Camoes.
8000 FARO. Tel (089) 81 34 83